Pro Java 9 Games Development

Leveraging the JavaFX APIs

Wallace Jackson

Apress®

Pro Java 9 Games Development: Leveraging the JavaFX APIs

Wallace Jackson
Lompoc, California, USA

ISBN-13 (pbk): 978-1-4842-0974-5
https://doi.org/10.1007/978-1-4842-0973-8

ISBN-13 (electronic): 978-1-4842-0973-8

Library of Congress Control Number: 2017959341

Cover image by Freepik (`www.freepik.com`)

Managing Director: Welmoed Spahr
Editorial Director: Todd Green
Acquisitions Editor: Steve Anglin
Development Editor: Matthew Moodie
Technical Reviewer: Jeff Friesen
Coordinating Editor: Mark Powers
Copy Editor: Kim Wimpsett

Distributed to the book trade worldwide by Springer Science+Business Media New York, 233 Spring Street, 6th Floor, New York, NY 10013. Phone 1-800-SPRINGER, fax (201) 348-4505, e-mail orders-ny@springer-sbm.com, or visit `www.springeronline.com`. Apress Media, LLC is a California LLC and the sole member (owner) is Springer Science + Business Media Finance Inc (SSBM Finance Inc). SSBM Finance Inc is a **Delaware** corporation.

For information on translations, please e-mail rights@apress.com, or visit http://www.apress.com/rights-permissions.

Apress titles may be purchased in bulk for academic, corporate, or promotional use. eBook versions and licenses are also available for most titles. For more information, reference our Print and eBook Bulk Sales web page at http://www.apress.com/bulk-sales.

Any source code or other supplementary material referenced by the author in this book is available to readers on GitHub via the book's product page, located at www.apress.com/9781484209745. For more detailed information, please visit http://www.apress.com/source-code.

Printed on acid-free paper

This Pro Java 9 Games Development book is dedicated to everyone in the open source community who is working diligently to make professional new media application development software, operating systems, and content development tools, freely available for all of us game application developers to utilize to achieve our iTV Set creative dreams and financial goals. Last but certainly not least, I dedicate this book to my father William Parker Jackson, my family, my life-long friends, and all of my ranching neighbors, for their constant help, assistance, and those starry late-night Red Oak BBQ parties.

Contents

About the Author

Wallace Jackson has been writing for leading multimedia publications about his work process for interactive new media content development since the advent of Multimedia Producer Magazine, nearly two decades ago, when he wrote about an advanced computer processor architecture for the issue centerfold (removable "mini-issue" insert) distributed at the SIGGRAPH trade show. Since then, Wallace has written across a significant number of popular publications about his work product in interactive 3D and new media advertising campaign design, including: 3D Artist Magazine, Desktop Publisher Journal, Cross Media Magazine, AV Video and Multimedia Producer Magazine, Digital Signage Magazine, and even Kiosk Magazine.

Wallace has authored more a dozen books for Apress including *Beginning Java 8 Games Development, Android Apps for Absolute Beginners, Pro Android Graphics, Pro Android UI, Pro Android SmartWatch, Learn Android Design, VFX Fundamentals, Digital Audio Editing, Digital Image Compositing Fundamentals, HTML Quick Markup Reference, Digital Illustration Fundamentals, Digital Painting Fundamentals, Android Studio 3 New Media Fundamentals, Digital Video Editing Fundamentals*, and many other titles.

He is currently the CEO of Mind Taffy Design the new media content production and digital campaign design and development agency, located in North Santa Barbara County, halfway between clientele in Silicon Valley to the north and in Hollywood, "The OC," and San Diego, to the south. Mind Taffy will also produce Interactive 3D content for major brands around the world, from their content production studio on Point Concepcion Peninsula in the California Central Coast area. Mind Taffy Design has created open source technology (HTML5, Java, and Android) and digital new media content deliverables for more than a quarter century (starting in 1991) for a large number of the top branded manufacturers in the world, including Sony, Samsung, IBM, Epson, Nokia, TEAC, Sun, SGI, Dell, Compaq, ViewSonic, Western Digital, Mitsubishi, KDS USA, CTX International, NEC, Micron, KFC, Tyco Electronics, and ADI Systems.

Wallace Jackson received his undergraduate degree in Business Economics from the University of California at Los Angeles (UCLA) and his graduate degree in MIS Design and Implementation from the University of Southern California. His post-graduate degree from USC is in Marketing Strategy. He also completed the USC Graduate Entrepreneurship Program at USC's popular Marshall School of Business MBA evening program. You can connect with Wallace at his business social media account at: https://www.linkedin.com/in/wallacejackson. His Twitter account is: **@wallacejackson**.

About the Technical Reviewer

Jeff Friesen is a freelance teacher and software developer with an emphasis on Java. In addition to authoring *Java I/O, NIO and NIO.2* (Apress) and *Java Threads and the Concurrency Utilities* (Apress), Jeff has written numerous articles on Java and other technologies (such as Android) for JavaWorld (`JavaWorld.com`), informIT (`InformIT.com`), Java.net, SitePoint (`SitePoint.com`), and other websites. Jeff can be contacted via his website at `JavaJeff.ca.` or via his LinkedIn profile (`www.linkedin.com/in/javajeff`).

Acknowledgments

I would like to acknowledge all my fantastic Editors, and their support staff at Apress, who worked those long hours and toiled so very hard on this book, to make it the ultimate *Pro Java 9 Games Development* application production book title.

Steve Anglin, for his work as the **Lead Editor** on the book, and for recruiting me to write Java, HTML5 and Android programming titles at Apress covering the most popular open source application development platforms available anywhere today.

Matthew Moodie, for his work as the **Development Editor** on the book, and for his experience and guidance during the process of making this book one of the great *Pro Java 9 Games Development* titles currently available in the market.

Mark Powers, for his work as the **Coordinating Editor** on the book, and for his constant diligence in making sure I either hit my Java 9 chapter delivery deadlines or surpassed them.

Jeff Freisen, for his work as the **Technical Reviewer** on the book, and for making sure that I did not make any Java 9 programming mistakes, because Java code with mistakes does not run properly, if at all, unless the Java code includes very lucky mistakes, which is quite rare in computer programming these days.

Introduction

The Java 9 Programming Language is currently the most popular object-oriented programming (OOP) language in the world today. Java runs on consumer electronic devices from SmartWatches to UHD Smartphones, to Touchscreen Tablets, to eBook Readers, to Game Consoles, to SmartGlasses, to Ultra-High Definition (UHD) 4K Interactive Television Sets (or iTV Sets), with even more types of consumer electronics devices, such as those found in the automotive, home appliances, healthcare, digital signage, security, home automation market, VR AR and so on, increasingly adopting this open source Java 9 platform for usage to drive i3D new media experiences within their hardware devices.

Since there are literally billions of Java 9 compatible consumer electronics devices, owned by the billions of users all over the world, it stands to reason that developing popular Pro Java 9 Games for all of these people could be an extremely lucrative undertaking, given that you have the right game concepts, artwork, new media assets, game design, and optimization processes, of course.

Java 9 (and its multimedia engine, JavaFX 9) code can run on just about every operating system out there, including Windows 7, 8.1 and 10, Linux distributions such as Ubuntu LTS 18 or Fedora, 32-bit Android 1-4 and 64-bit Android 5-8, Open Solaris, Macintosh OS/X, iOS, Symbian, and the Raspberry Pi, it's only a matter of time before any other popular OSes will add support for this popular open source programming language. Additionally, every popular Internet Browser has Java capability. Java provides the ultimate flexibility in installing software, as an application, or in the browser, as an applet. You can even drag a Java application right out of the browser, and have it install itself on a user's desktop. Java 9 is truly remarkable technology all the way around.

There are a plethora of embedded and desktop hardware support levels currently for Java 9 and for JavaFX 9, including the full Java SE 9, Java SE 9 Embedded, Java ME (Micro Edition) 9 and Java ME 9 Embedded, as well as Java EE 9 for Enterprise Application Development.

Talk about being able to "code once, then deliver everywhere!" This is the pipe-dream of every programmer, and Oracle (Java) and Apache (NetBeans 9) is making it a reality with the powerful JavaFX 9 multimedia programming platform. This book will go a long way towards helping you to learn exactly how to go about developing Java 9 games, using the Java programming language in conjunction with the JavaFX 9 multimedia engine. These Java 9 game applications will be able to run across a plethora of Java-compatible consumer electronics devices. Developing Java 9 game applications which play i3D smoothly across all of these different types of consumer electronics devices requires a very specific work process, including game asset design, game code design, UI design, and data footprint optimization, all of which I'll be covering during this Pro Java 9 book.

I wrote the Pro Java 9 Game Development title from scratch, using a real world Interactive 3D or i3D game project that I am actually working on, and will be delivering to the public sometime in 2017. I am targeting those readers who wish to become i3D Game Developers, and who haven't coded in Java 9 with JavaFX 9. The readers are technically savvy, but are not completely familiar with Java 9 object-oriented computer programming concepts and techniques, or with i3D game development. Since Java 9 has now been released to the public on September 22, 2107 the book will be more advanced than many of the other Java books out there. Java 9 has added some very advanced features, such as a more secure module system and the JavaFX 9 API. This gives Java 9 its own interactive 3D capable new media engine supporting SVG, 2D, 3D, audio or video media.

I designed this book to contain a comprehensive overview of optimal Java 9 games development work processes. Most professional Java 9 application development books only cover the language; however, if you really want to become that well known Java 9 game or IoT application developer that you seek to become, you will have to understand, as well as master, all of the areas of game design, including multimedia asset creation, user interface design, Java 9 Programming, JavaFX 9 class usage, and data footprint optimization, as well as memory and CPU usage optimization.

Once you've mastered these areas, hopefully, by the end of this book, you will be able to create the memorable user experience that will be required to create popular, best-selling Java 9 games. You can do it, I know you can!

Java 9 games are not only developed using a NetBeans 9 Integrated Development Environment (IDE) alone, but also in conjunction with the use of JavaFX 9 and several other different types of new media content development software packages (more than a dozen, at this point; all open source). For this reason, this book covers the installation and usage of a wide variety of other popular open source software packages, such as GIMP 2.9.7 and Audacity 2.1.3, for instance, in conjunction with developing Java 9 game applications using the NetBeans 9.0 IDE and the JavaFX 9 new media game engine, which brings the "wow factor" to the Java 9 programming language.

I am architecting this book in this fashion so that you can ascertain precisely how your usage of new media content development software will fit into the overall Pro Java 9 Game Development work process. A comprehensive approach will serve to set this unique book title distinctly apart from all of the other Java 9 game application development titles which are currently out on the market. The book startes out in Chapter One with downloading and installing the latest Java JDK as well as NetBeans 9 IDE, along with a dozen open source content development applications.

In Chapter Two you'll learn about new media concepts for the 2D and i2D capabilities in JavaFX 9, and in Chapter Three you will learn about more advanced 3D new media concepts for the 3D and i3D capabilities in JavaFX 9. In Chapter Four we will cover game design concepts for JavaFX.

In Chapter Five, you'll learn about the fundamentals of the Java 9 programming language, which you'll be implementing to create a Java 9 game during the remainder of the book. In Chapter Six, you will learn about NetBeans 9, and create your first JavaFX 9 game application, and take a look at useful NetBeans 9 features, such as code completion and code profiling.

In Chapter Seven, you will learn all about the JavaFX 9 new media engine (JavaFX API), and how its impressive features can take your Pro Java 9 Game Development and place it in the stratosphere. Thus, the first third of this book is "foundational" material, which you will need to understand in order to be able to understand how NetBeans 9.0, Java 9, JavaFX 9.0, and the various new media genres and asset types supported by the JavaFX 9 game engine function together as a platform.

In Chapter Eight, you will learn all about the JavaFX 9 Scene Graph and how to use its hierarchy to begin to design the first i2D parts of the Java 9 Game, the top-level splashscreen and its user interface design. This is where we start into coding Java 9 and JavaFX 9 APIs more aggressively.

In Chapter Nine, you will learn about user interface design, including using digital image assets and text assets. Major JavaFX classes we will cover include the Image class, the ImageView class, and the TextFlow class. We will be looking at digital image compositing pipelines in the creation of the SplashScreen as well as game information overlays such as game play instructions, legal disclaimers, content production credits, and starting the game play to remove the SplashScreen.

In Chapter Ten we will learn about the JavaFX event processing engine, which will process all of the different types of action, key, mouse, and drag events that you are likely to utilize in your Java 9 game development work process in the future when you create your own custom pro Java 9 games. We will implement event handling in Java 9 during this chapter which will make the user interface and SplashScreen created in the previous chapter interactive.

In Chapter Eleven we will start coding our primary i3D Game SceneGraph for the i3D Board Game. During the chapter you'll be learning about the different types of JavaFX 9 **Camera** and **LightBase** subclasses which are contained in the core **javafx.scene** package, which, in turn, is contained (as of Java 9) in the **javafx.graphics** module. We will cover **PerspectiveCamera**, since you will be using this for your basic

3D scene infrastructure, which we'll be creating during this chapter, as well as **ParallelCamera**, another Camera subclass which is better suited for 2D or 2.5D game development pipelines. We will also learn about the LightBase abstract superclass, and its two core lighting subclasses, **AmbientLight** and **PointLight**.

In Chapter Twelve you will learn about 3D modeling classes in the JavaFX API. You'll be learning about the different JavaFX 9 3D model classes, which are contained in your **javafx.scene.shape** package. You will cover **Sphere**, which can be used to create **a Sphere** primitive, and which you have used already to test your 3D Scene setup in Chapter Eleven. We will also look at the other two primitive classes, **Box** and **Cylinder**, which can also be used to create your **Plane** and **Disk** primitives. These primitives are based on the Shape3D superclass, which we will be looking at first. We will also look at the more advanced **TriangleMesh** class, which allows you to build a polygon-based Mesh object, and finally, at the **Mesh** and **MeshView** class hierarchy, which will allow you to render your 3D Mesh objects.

During Chapter Thirteen you'll be learning about the JavaFX 9 3D shader class hierarchy, which is contained in the **javafx.scene.paint** package. In Java 9 and Android 8 the **Paint** class applies pixel colors and attributes to the **Canvas**, and in this case, the surface of your JavaFX 9 i3D primitives. The paint package contains classes which are related to this "skinning," or "texture mapping" 3D object shading objective. You will cover **Material**, a superclass which holds the top level shader definition, and the **PhongMaterial** class, which can be used to create a texture map, or "skin," for the i3D primitives for your game which were covered in Chapter 12.

In Chapter Fourteen, you will create an advanced i3D object for your game using the JavaFX 9 SceneGraph hierarchy and JavaFX 3D primitives. During this chapter, you will be building your **gameBoard Group** branch of your SceneGraph, which is under the SceneGraph root, next to the SplashScreen (UI) branch, which we have already built in Chapter Nine. Under your gameBoard Group branch, we will segment your i3D game board into four quadrants, so the middle of the gameboard can have four larger 300x300 unit areas which we can use for gameplay. Each of the four game quadrants will have another 5 (of 20) perimeter game board squares as child objects.

In Chapter Fifteen, we'll be using i3D primitives in JavaFX, to create i3D UI elements for your i3D Scene, and will work through some of the 3D face rendering anomalies which we saw in Chapter 14. The i3D UI element we'll create will spin the gameboard, to select a quadrant topic for play.

In Chapter Sixteen, we'll take a detailed look at the JavaFX 9 (abstract) **Animation** and **Transition** superclasses, and all of the powerful property transition subclasses, which you can implement as different types of **Animation** objects in your i3D boardgame. Animation adds professionalism to any game because motion, especially in a 3D game, adds a ton of realism to the user experience.

In Chapter Seventeen, we'll take a close look at a public **PickResult** class and public **MouseEvent** class, and use these for our own game play design in a custom .createSceneProcessing() method which will be used to process i3D game elements (Box or Sphere objects) selection by the player (more event handling coding), so that our players can interact with their i3D game components.

During Chapter Eighteen, we will look at the work process for creating alternate texture maps, which will be changed during game play, by changing the Image object asset reference to add content to game board squares and quadrants, based on random spins and player mouse clicks (or screen touches). Although this particular chapter does not get into Java code too deeply, it is important to note that developing professional Java 9 games involves digital image artisans, as well as digital audio engineers, 3D modelers, 3D texture artists, animators, 2D illustrators, and VFX artists, so we will need to cover some non-Java-specific topics as well during this book.

During Chapter Nineteen, an i3D game AI chapter, we will create two new int (integer) variables; **spinDeg** for spin degrees, and an accumulator (total) of the sum of the rotational degrees which have been spun by the players, and quadrantLanding, for holding the latest result of a simple yet powerful calculation which will always tell us what quadrant the latest spin landed on.

During Chapter Twenty, we'll be creating over a dozen .setupQSgameplay() methods, which will contain the Java code that sets up the next level of gameplay for each gameboard square so that when a player clicks a gameboard square, a method will be called to set up the Q&A experience.

In Chapter Twenty-One, we will finish coding the .setupQSgameplay() methods, by adding the Q&A parts of the game play logic. We will also be looking at the JavaFX **AudioClip** class, which will allow us to add digital audio sound effects. This will further enhance the pro Java 9 game play experience using yet another new media component (digital audio) of the JavaFX 9 API.

During Chapter Twenty-Two, we'll be implementing a single player game play and scoring engine, to get your game scoring user interface in place, because a lot of game players will want to play the game against the content, as a learning experience. That said, there will still be a lot of code to write for each Button UI element, that looks at if the answer is the correct answer, and if it is, will increments the "Right:" score, and if it is not, will increment the "Wrong:" score.

During Chapter Twenty-Three, we'll finish populating the **setupQSgameplay()** methods with the text-based answer content that matches up with the questions. We'll also finish the createQAprocessing() method, which holds the answer scoring code that updates the Score UI panel. The players will use these to select the correct answer revealing what the visual for that square represents and scoring their answer. Once we finish coding the bulk of the game play "answer display, selection, and scoring" infrastructure, and test each square to make sure it is working, we can create the "error-proofing" portion of the Java code, to finish up a professional game, which makes sure the players use it properly. This involves using Boolean variables (called "flags") to hold "click" variables, where once a player clicks the spinner, game board square or answer Button element, the "elementClick" variable is set to "false" so your game player cannot click it again and "game" the game play code.

During Chapter Twenty-Four on Data and Memory Footprint Optimization, we will convert your digital image assets to use 8-bit (indexed) color, rather than the 24-bit truecolor depth, for your texture maps, and we'll run the NetBeans Profiler to see how much memory and CPU processing your Java 9 code is using to run your game.

This book attempts to be the most comprehensive Pro Java 9 Games application development programming title on the market, by covering most, if not all, of the major Java 9 and JavaFX 9 classes that will need to be used to create i3D Java 9 Game Applications.

If you're looking for the most comprehensive, up to date overview of the Java 9 programming language for games, including JavaFX 9.0 and NetBeans 9.0 IDE all seamlessly integrated with new media content development work processes, as well as a "soup to nuts" knowledge about how to optimally use these technologies in conjunction with the leading open source new media game content design and development tools, then this book will really be of significant interest to you.

It is the intention of this book to take you from being an Intermediate in Java 9 game application development to a solid professional knowledge level regarding Java 9, NetBeans 9, and JavaFX 9 game application development. Be advised, this book, even though it's ostensibly a professional title, contains a significant amount of new media technical knowledge. All of the work processes which are described during the book could take more than one or two read throughs in order to assimilate this knowledge into an application development knowledge base (into your quiver of technical knowledge). It will be well worth your time, however, rest assured, so read it more than once. There is also a *Beginning Java Games Development* book from Apress called *Beginning Java 8 Games Development* that covers i2D game development using different classes from the JavaFX API.

CHAPTER 1

■ ■ ■

The Different Faces of Java: Create a Java 9 Development Workstation

Welcome to the *Pro Java 9 Games Development* book. In this first chapter, I'm going to discuss the various versions of Java which are still being used today to develop software applications for open source platforms such as Android, as well as for open source browsers based on WebKit, such as Google Chrome, Mozilla Firefox, Apple Safari, and Opera. After going over which versions of Java, spanning from JDK 1.6, also known as Java 6, through JDK 1.9, which was recently released as Java 9, will need to be used to develop for various versions of these popular platforms. We'll also need to take a detailed look at how to create a professional Java 9 software development workstation for use during the rest of this book. This will include other software such as new media content production software packages which can be used with your Java software development packages to create games and IoT (Internet of Things) applications.

The core of your workstation will be either a **Java 8** SDK or **Software Development Kit** which is also referred to as the **JDK** or **Java Development Kit**, or the new **Java 9** JDK, which came out in 2017 and is more **modular** than Java 8, but which features the same classes and methods for creating games or IoT user experiences. This fact will allow us to safely focus on both Java 8, as well as Java 9, during the course of the book. This is because, for our purposes, these are fundamentally the same, allowing us to focus on the latest Java APIs, and not on what Java version you are using. In fact, since we are going to focus on Java's multimedia APIs, commonly known as JavaFX, what you learn during this book can also be coded in Java 7 as well! Android recently upgraded to Java 7 and Java 8 compatibility (from Java 6).

We will also set you up with a **NetBeans 9.0** IDE, or **Integrated Development Environment**, which will make coding Java 8 or 9 games so much easier. Expect to use NetBeans 9 once Java 9 comes out in Q4 of 2017, since NetBeans 9 IDE will have been upgraded significantly to accommodate the new modular nature of Java 9 and will allow you to mix functional **modules**, to create custom Java package collections (API versions) for any type of application development.

After your Java JDK and NetBeans IDE are configured, we will get you setup with the latest open source new media content creation software packages, including professional software packages such as GIMP for digital imaging, InkScape for digital illustration, DaVinci Resolve for digital video editing or special effects, Audacity for digital audio editing, Fusion for special effects and 3D, Open Office 4 Suite for Business and Project management, Blender for 3D modeling, texturing, animation, rendering, particle systems, fluid dynamics or special effects, and Terragen 4 for virtual planets.

At the end of this chapter, I might even suggest some other professional level software packages, which you should consider adding to this professional game development workstation that we will be creating during the course of this chapter. In this way, you will have an incredibly valuable production resource for your business, by the time we are finished with this first chapter. Hopefully, just this first chapter alone will be worth what you've paid for this entire book, as you can pay $500 for a powerful 64-bit workstation, and make it worth five figures in just a couple of hours!

© Wallace Jackson 2017
W. Jackson, *Pro Java 9 Games Development*, https://doi.org/10.1007/978-1-4842-0973-8_1

We will also be going over some hardware requirements and considerations for your new Java 9 content production workstation. Finally, note the Java code in this book will work just as well in a Java 8 IDE (or integrated development environment), so this book could just as easily be called the *Pro Java 8 Games Development* book!

Java Dichotomy: Versions Used in Various Platforms

There are a number of different versions of Java which are still widely used for development across a number of different popular platforms, including Java 6 for 32-bit Android (Versions 1.x, 2.x, 3.x and 4.x of Android are 32-bit), as well as Java 7 for early 64-bit Android versions (5.0, 5.1, and 6.0), Java 8 for recent Android Versions (7.0, 7.1.2, 8.0), and Java 9 for Windows 10 OS, Ubuntu Linux OS (and other Linux distributions), Macintosh OSX, and Open Solaris OS.

It is important to note that there are three primary versions of Java; **Java ME** or **Micro Edition** is optimized for embedded devices, **Java SE** or **Standard Edition**, which we'll be covering, which is used on the "client side" as well as in mobile consumer electronics devices and in iTV sets, and **Java EE**, or **Enterprise Edition**, which could be thought of as a "server side" paradigm, as large corporate computing environments are generally server-based, and not "peer to peer" (pure client side, with client to client inter-communication possible, in addition to client-server interactions).

Java 6, released in December of 2006 (over a decade ago), is still widely used in conjunction with the **Eclipse** IDE to develop applications for all 32-bit versions of Android, from version 1.0 through version 4.4. This is because this is the Java version Google originally specified for use in developing 32-bit Android applications, when Android 1.0 was released in September of 2008. It is important to note that Google created a custom version of Java 6, using the Open Java Project, but this won't effect the programming API, as the classes, methods, and interfaces still function the same way that they would if you were using Java 6 in the **NetBeans** IDE or the **IntelliJ** IDEA, instead of using the Eclipse IDE.

When Google upgraded Android to a 64-bit Linux Kernel, in Android 5.x, which uses the Android Studio IDEA based on IntelliJ, they upgraded to using Java 7, which also has a 64-bit version. Java 7 was released in July of 2011. So if you are developing Android 5-6 applications for advanced platforms, such as Android Wear, which is covered in my *Pro Android Wearables* (2015) title from Apress, or Android TV or Android Auto, covered in *Android Apps for Absolute Beginners* (2017) title from Apress, you will want to utilize Java 7. The JavaFX 8 engine found in JavaFX 8 and JavaFX 9, has been back-ported to Java 7 as well; however Java 7 was retired this year. Java 6, 7 and 8 are still used in Android.

Java 8 is the current version of Java SE, as of the writing of this book, and additionally, features the powerful JavaFX 8.0 multimedia engine, which has also been made compatible with Java 7, although JavaFX 8.0 APIs are not yet natively supported inside of the Android APIs. It is however, possible to develop JavaFX 8 or 9 applications that run on both Android OS and iOS platforms, making this book significantly more valueable to our readers! Java 8 is supported across all popular browsers, in Android 7, 7.1.2 and 8.0, and across all four of the popular OSes, including Windows 7, 8.1 and 10, in all Linux Distros, Macintosh OS/X, and Open Solaris from Oracle. Java 8 was released in March of 2014, and added a powerful new feature called **Lambda Expressions**, which we will be covering during the book, as this is a way to write more compact code, which is also often more multi-processor (and multi-thread) efficient.

Java 9 is the next major revision of Java. Java 9 was released September 22, 2017. The primary new feature in Java 9 that the Java language developers are reworking is making the Java 9 language API **modular**. This will allow Java 9 developers to "mix and match" features in "modules" (code libraries), and create their own custom, optimized versions of Java. These custom Java versions would work exactly the way that the developer will need it to for custom development environments or custom applications. As of the release of this book, **NetBeans 9** is still in development.

As a Game Developer, or as an IoT Developer, this means that you could create several Game Development customized Java Version levels, or alternately several custom IoT Development Java Version levels. Start with a Java 7 version, add Lambda Expressions (a coding shortcut which we will cover later) if needed, to create a Java 8 version, or package as custom modules (a new feature in Java 9) to create a Java

9 version for all the popular OS platforms. If you are using the JavaFX multimedia/game engine, the latest JavaFX features exist across both the Java 8 and Java 9 APIs.

I wanted to point out to readers that they can optimize their game program logic to span several versions of Java, optimizing for Java 7 (Android 5 or 6) to Java 8 (Android 7, 8 and modern OSes) to the Java 9 version which came out on September 22, 2017 before the book release. This can also be done **without any major code changes**, because the core JavaFX game processing logic, other than using Lambda Expressions, exists across all of these Java revisions.

Java Development Workstation: Required Hardware

To get the best results from all of the professional open source software we will be installing during the course of this chapter, you will want to have a powerful **64-bit** workstation, running a paid OS, such as Windows 10 or OSX, or a free OS, such as Ubuntu LTS 17. I use Windows 10 on several workstations, and Ubuntu LTS 17.10 on several workstations. You will also want a large display, preferably HD (1920 by 1080) or UHD (3840 by 2160). If you do the math, a UHD display is four HD displays in a single bezel, and UHD displays are now $300 to $500. I got one at a Thanksgiving sale for $250. The sizes I use for HD range from 32" to 43" and for UHD range from 44" to 55" yeilding a tight pixel density.

A computer workstation should feature (contain) at least 8 Gigabytes (8GB) of **DDR3** system memory (16GB or 32GB of system memory would be even better). This memory should cycle at 1333, 1600, 1866, or 2133 megahertz clock speed. Cutting-edge systems often feature **DDR4** system memory running at **2400** megahertz clock speed. DDR4 memory also comes in 16GB DIMMS, so that you can put 48GB, 64GB, or 128GB in your workstation motherboard. I'd do this for workstations running Fusion 9, DaVinci Resolve 14, Blender 2.8, JavaFX 9 or other i3D production software.

The faster your system memory runs, the faster your computer can process data, and the faster the CPU can get what it needs to process. That brings us to the "brain" or CPU/GPU for the workstation which does the processing. The same concept holds true; the more instructions a 64-bit CPU can process per second the more you're going to get done in a shorter period of time, and the smoother your i3D applications are going to perform their given functions.

Almost all 64-bit workstations these days will feature a **multi-core** processor, often called a CPU, or Central Processing Unit. Popular CPUs include **AMD** Ryzen (QuadCore, HexaCore or OctaCore), 9590 (OctaCore or eight cores), or the more expensive **Intel** i7, which comes in QuadCore, HexaCore, OctaCore, and DecaCore versions. Like the AMD Ryzen, the Intel i7 features two threads per core, so these will look like 8, 12, 16 or 20 core processors to an operating system, which is why they're more expensive than the AMD FX 9590 series of processors. I use AMD Ryzen or Intel i7 processors, depending on the application. For instance, Android Studio 3 is optimized for Intel hardware architecture, and doesn't emulate Android Virtual Devices (AVD) fast enough on AMD FX CPU for smooth development and testing.

To store your data, you will also need a hard disk drive. Computers these days will usually come with a one terabyte (1TB) hard disk drive, and you can even get a workstation with a 2TB, 3TB, 4TB, 6TB, or an 8TB HDD. Opt for the 3GB or 4GB model if you are working on games (or 3D, film, special effects, or video assets) which feature UHD, or 4K, screen resolution. If you want your system to boot (start-up) rapidly, and load your software into memory rapidly, be sure to get an SSD (Solid State Drive) as your primary (C:\ for Windows, or, C:/ for Linux) drive assignment. These are more expensive than the traditional Terabyte Hard Disk Drives, but you only really need 64GB or 128GB to hold your OS and software. I have a 256GB SSD, and 512GB SSD and 768GB SSDs are also becoming much more affordable.

Workstations with features such as these have essentially become commodity items, priced between $500 and $750, and can be purchased at WalMart or Best Buy, or on-line, at www.PriceWatch.com, where you can compare market prices on any of the components that I have mentioned in this section of the chapter. If you are new to Java 9 Game Development, and if you do not yet have an appropriate workstation, go to WalMart, or PriceWatch.com, and purchase your affordable 3D multi-core (purchase a 4, 6, or 8 core) 64-bit computer running Windows 10, or Ubuntu LTS 17, that has 8, 16 or 32 Gigabytes of DDR3 system memory, at the very least. You will also want a fairly large hard disk drive, at least a 750GB, or even a 1.5TB or 2TB hard disk drive, as well as a 3D GPU from AMD (Radeon), or nVidia (GeForce), which will be used for real-time i3D rendering for both JavaFX 9 as well as Fusion, Blender, and DaVinci Resolve.

During the rest of this chapter, I am going to proceed as if you have just purchased one of these affordable 64-bit workstations, and we're going to create a premiere Java 9 Games and IoT development workstation 100% from scratch! In case you already have an existing game development workstation, I'm going to include a short section that shows you how to remove outdated Java development software from Windows, so that we can all start from scratch.

Prepare a Workstation for Java 9 Game Development

Assuming that you already have a professional level workstation in place for new media content development and game development, you may need to remove an outdated JDK or IDE, to make sure that you have the latest software. The first thing that you will do in this section is make sure you have **removed** any of the **outdated versions** of Java, such as Java 6 or Java 7, and any outdated versions of NetBeans, such as NetBeans 6 or NetBeans 7. This involves **uninstalling** (removing, or completely deleting) outdated Java development software versions from the workstation. I had to do this on one of my QuadCore AMD workstations, to make room for the NetBeans 9.0 IDE for development of Java 9 and JavaFX 9 apps and games, so the screenshots in this section show a Windows 7 operating system. You'll do this by using an OS Software Management Utility. On Windows this is the "Programs and Features" utility. This can be found under the Windows **Control Panel**, shown highlighted in blue in the middle column (seventh row) of Figure 1-1.

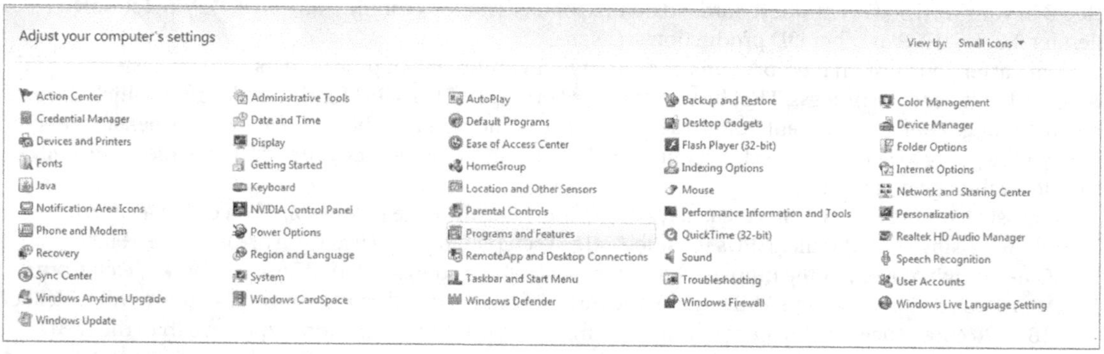

Figure 1-1. *Use the Programs and Features utility icon to uninstall or change programs on your computer workstation*

If you have a brand new workstation, you will not have to remove any previous software. There are similar software installation and removal utilities for Linux and Mac, if you happen to be using one of these OSes. Since most developers are using 64-bit versions of Windows 7, 8.1, or 10, we'll only be using this 64-bit OS platform for this book.

It's important to note that Java 9 now comes only in a 64-bit version, so you must have a 64-bit workstation, as I've specified in the previous section of this book (In fact, you cannot even buy a new 32-bit computer these days).

The way you customize Windows OS "chrome" (the windowing UI elements), as well as the desktop, and installed software packages is via the Windows **Control Panel**, and its set of more than 50 utility icons. One of these is the **Programs and Features** icon (in Windows versions 7 through 10), which can be seen selected in blue in Figure 1-1.

Note that in earlier versions of Windows (Vista or XP), this program utility icon would be labeled differently, as: **Add or Remove Programs**. It still works in the same fashion, select software, right-click, and remove old versions. I do not recommend using outdated Vista or XP, as these are **no longer supported** by advanced Java 9 JDKs and IDEs.

Click this Programs and Features link, or double-click the icon, for previous versions of Windows, and launch the utility. Scroll down, and see if you have any older versions of the Java development tools (Java 5, Java 6, or Java 7) installed on your workstation. Note that if you have a brand new workstation, you should find there are no pre-installed versions of Java or NetBeans on the system. If you find them, return the system, as it may have been used previously.

As you can see in Figure 1-2, on my Windows 7 development workstation, I had an old version of Java 8u131 installed, taking up 442 Megabytes of hard disk drive space, and installed in 2017, on April 22nd. This was used to run the "Alpha" version of NetBeans 9, which runs on Java 8. To remove a piece of software, **select it**, by clicking on it (it will turn blue), and either click the **Uninstall** button, shown at the top of Figure 1-2, or you can alternately right-click on the (blue) software package (removal) selection, and select **Uninstall** from a context-sensitive menu that appears.

I left the **tool-tip** which says: "**Uninstall**" showing in the screen shot, so that you can see that if you "**hover**" your mouse over anything in the Programs and Features utility, it will tell you what that particular feature is used for.

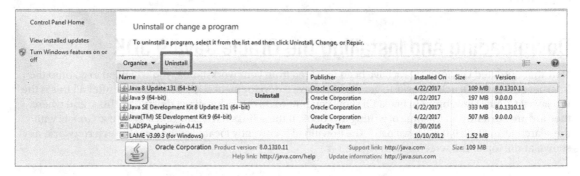

Figure 1-2. *Select versions of Java older than Java 9 and click the Uninstall option at the top, or right-click and uninstall*

Once you click on the **Uninstall** button, this utility will remove your older versions of Java 8. Remove the smaller version of Java 8 (non-JDK) first, and then remove the larger (full JDK) version, as the full JDK is required to remove the smaller JDK, as well as any old versions of NetBeans. You will need to have Java 8 installed if you want to remove NetBeans IDE, as NetBeans IDE is written in Java and requires a Java JDK to be installed in order to uninstall it.

Once you remove the full Java 8 JDK, there will only be (Alpha) versions of Java 9 (if you are me, writing this book, that is), as can be seen in Figure 1-3, labeled as Version 9.0.0.0. If you want to keep your older Java project files, make sure and back up your Java project files folder, if you haven't done that already, that is. Make sure that you back up your workstation's hard disk drive regularly, so that you do not lose any 3D, content production and coding work.

I removed any Alpha or Beta versions of Java 9 JDK software by again **selecting it** by clicking on it (it will turn blue), and either click the **Uninstall** button, seen at the top of Figure 1-3, or you can alternately right-click on the blue software package (removal) selection, and select **Uninstall** from a context-sensitive menu (opened by right-clicking).

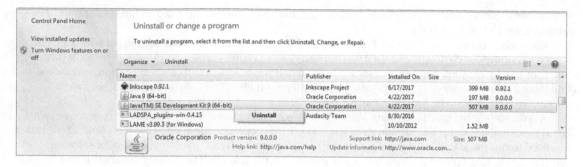

Figure 1-3. *Select Alpha versions of Java 9, and click the Uninstall option at the top, or, right-click, and select Uninstall*

Now that I have removed outdated versions of Java from my workstation, I will go and get the latest Java 9 Development Kit (JDK) versions from the Internet and install them on my Windows content development workstation.

Downloading and Installing the Oracle Java 9 JDK

Now that outdated versions of Java have been removed from your workstation, you will need to go onto the Internet and to the **Oracle** website to get the latest Java 9 development JDK and IDE, since after all this is the Pro Java 9 Games Development book. I'll show you how to do this using direct download URLs, and where they are are currently, at the time of writing this book. If these links have changed, simply use Google with the search term "Java 9 JDK Download." The download is currently located at the **Oracle Tech Network**, as is shown at the top of the screen shot in Figure 1-4.

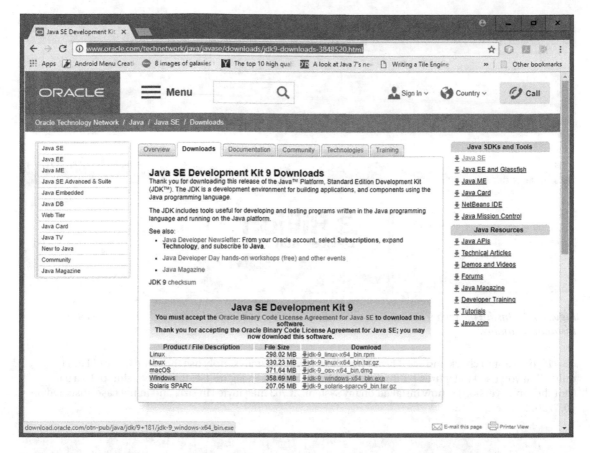

Figure 1-4. *The JDK9 Download link at oracle.com/technetwork/java/javase/downloads/jdk9-downloads-3848520.htm*

Before you can download the 360 Megabyte JDK9 installer file for Windows 64-bit, you will need to click the **radio button** next to an **Accept License Agreement** option, which can be found at the top-left of the download table.

Once you accept this license agreement, five OS-specific links will become activated for use, including Linux, Mac OS/X, Windows (7 through 10), and Solaris. Be sure to match the Java JDK software that you download to match your operating system. As you can see, there are now only 64-bit (or x64) versions available for use on 64-bit systems.

To launch a downloaded JDK9 installer, right-click on the file and use **Run as Administrator** to install it using Administrator priveledges (or as Superuser on Linux). Accept the default settings in the six dialogs, seen in Figure 1-5.

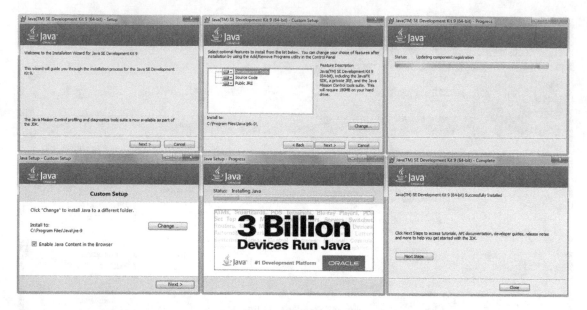

Figure 1-5. *Install the Java 9 JDK on the workstation, accepting the default settings in the six Java 9 installation dialogs*

If you want to check and see if Java 9 installed on your system simply use the same Control Panel utility that you used in Figures 1-1 through 1-3. As you can see in Figure 1-6, the real version of Java 9.0 (not the alpha version) is now installed on my system, at 763 megabytes in size, and in my case, installed on 10/7/2017.

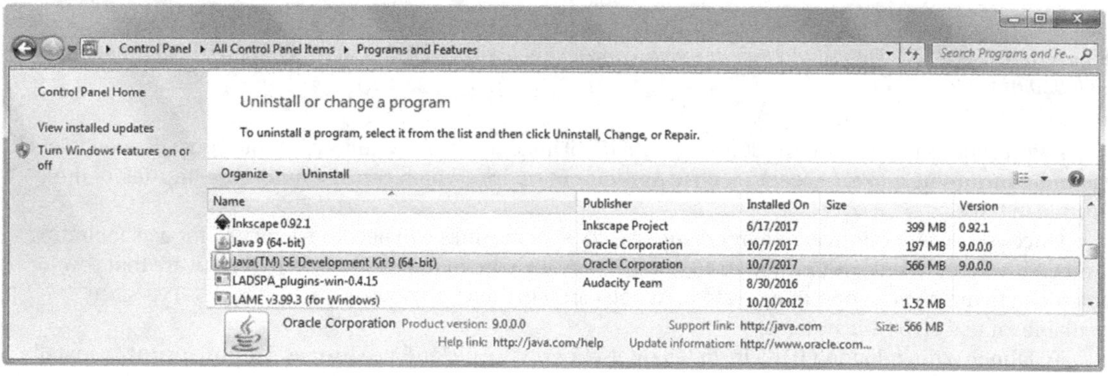

Figure 1-6. *Find the JDK-for the latest (currently 9.0.1) Java 9 version and make sure it is installed*

Next, let's install Java 8, used currently to run NetBeans 8.2 (you may already be developing using this IDE), and also used currently to run the NetBeans 9.0 IDE (beta), which I used for this book, because eventually Java 9 and NetBeans 9 will be used together to develop Java 9 Games. During the transition period, NetBeans 9.0 runs on Java 8, so I am adding a section or two on how this works, for the early adopters of the book who may use this configuration.

Downloading and Installing the Oracle Java 8 JDK

You may be wondering why we are downloading the latest version of Java 8 (currently update 152) right now, given that this is a Java 9 Games book. The reason is because although Java 9 JDK came out in September, the NetBeans 9 IDE version is still in beta (I wrote the book while it was still in alpha), meaning that NetBeans 9 (beta) still runs on top of Java 8, due to the complexity of modules in Java 9 (meaning the programmers are still modularizing NetBeans 9 so that it will be coded in Java 9). Once NetBeans 9 is released, it is likely that it will run directly on top of Java 9 JDK. There is a way to get to a webpage on the Oracle Tech Network that has links to both Java 8u144 and Java 9.0, located at the URL www.oracle.com/technetwork/java/javase/overview/index.html as seen in Figure 1-7. The download links for both JDKs are located at the very bottom of the webpage, so just click the **Download** link for the **Java SE 8 update 144** JDK (already upgraded to 8u152).

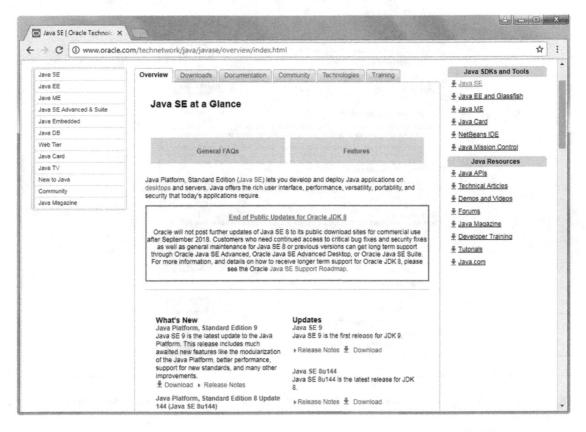

Figure 1-7. *The Oracle Tech Network Java SE Overview webpage, which has links to Java 9 JDK as well as to Java 8u144*

As you can see, there is also a red **End of Public Updates for Oracle JDK 8** admonition, circled in the middle of the webpage. Java 8 does not have a lot of bugs, as after all it has been through over 144 updates and is quite solid! Java 9 is a rewrite, in a sense, as it has been remodularized, so all the "wiring" of API classes and packages (into modules) is being redone, which is why NetBeans 9 (which was coded in Java) is not complete (coded and debugged) at the same time as Java 9. Previous versions of Java and NetBeans have come out at (or near) the same time, and had a NetBeans bundle download (shown for NetBeans 8.2 at the top of Figure 1-8, via the download icon on the right hand side).

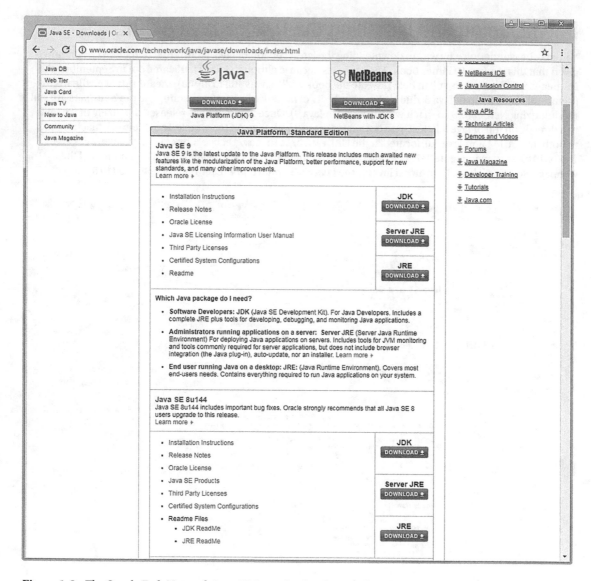

Figure 1-8. *The Oracle Tech Network Java SE Download webpage which has links to Java 8u144 JDK at the very bottom*

The Java SE downloads page seen in Figure 1-8, is the page the Download link on the previous page will take you. At the bottom of the page you will find the Java SE 8u144 section with three Download buttons in it. The first top button says JDK. This is the button you want to click to start a JDK 8u144 download. This will take you to the page for oracle.com/technetwork/java/javase/downloads/jdk8-downloads-2133151.html, which is shown in Figure 1-9.

Click an **Accept the License** radio button to enable all download links, and click the link for your OS version.

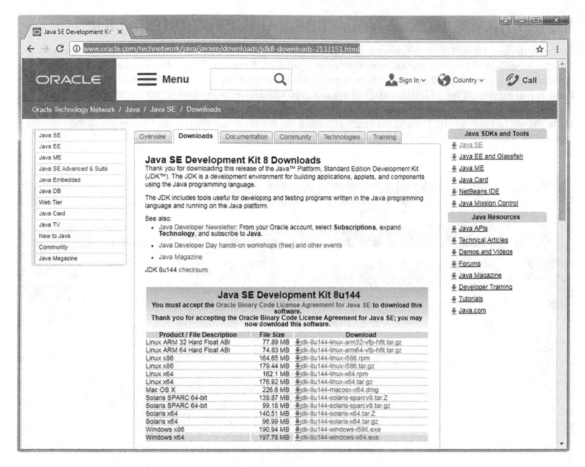

Figure 1-9. *The JDK8 Download link at oracle.com/technetwork/java/javase/downloads/jdk8-downloads-2133151.htm*

Notice that for Java 8 there are both 32-bit (i586) and 64-bit (x64) versions, as well as ARM CPU versions, which gives us over a dozen choices. Select the 64-bit version for your OS, to match what you installed for Java 9.0.

Now we can install the NetBeans 9.0 Integrated Development Environment, or IDE for short, which will use the Java 8 Run-Time Engine (JRE) that we just installed to run Java code which will create the NetBeans 9 IDE for you.

Since NetBeans 9 is transitioning from Oracle to Apache, there are actually two code repositories currently. I am going to first show you the one that I used while writing the book, which is hosted at Oracle, and second, I'll show you the one hosted at Apache, which uses a beta repository called Jenkins, and also a link to GIT where you can build the NetBeans IDE from scratch if you so desire. There will also eventually be a "bundle" of Java 9 and NetBeans 9 as a single install. This is of course the easiest and most desireable, but does not exist currently, so I am covering the more advanced ways to build and install NetBeans 9.0 since it is not yet finished. This complicates installation currently, but there is nothing that I can do about this other than to give you all of this additional extra information, so that you can get NetBeans 9.0 up and running for Java 9 and JavaFX 9 development before the final NetBeans 9 on Java 9 bundle is released. This gives you a head start on everybody else as far as Pro Java 9 Games Development is concerned.

Installing the Oracle NetBeans 9.0 (Development) IDE

Since NetBeans 9 is still in development, I am going to show you how I got the NetBeans 9 release from Oracle, as well as in the next section how the general public will eventually get the NetBeans 9 IDE from Apache. In this way you will know all of the ways to download and install NetBeans 9. The Oracle repository (which will exist until the official transfer of the software to Apache) is located at bits.netbeans.org/download/trunk/nightly/latest/ and looks like the original NetBeans download page that you are all familiar with, shown in Figure 1-10. I would recommend using the simplest (smallest) Java SE version of the software, since it includes the three APIs (NetBeans, Java and JavaFX) which we are covering in this book. Click the first **Download (Free, 97MB)** button, and start the NetBeans download process.

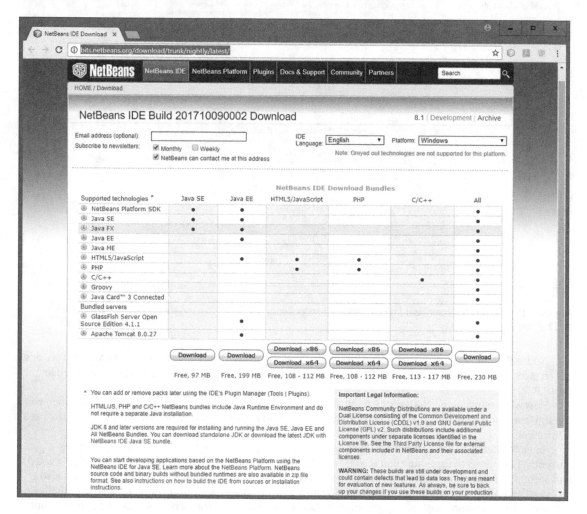

Figure 1-10. *The Oracle NetBeans 9.0 IDE download page located at bits.netbeans.org/download/trunk/nightly/latest/*

Once this installation file downloads, right-click on it, and select **Run as Administrator** (Superuser on Linux), and you will see the first **Welcome** dialog, seen at the top-left of the six dialog screenshot, shown in Figure 1-11.

Click on the **Next** button to begin the default (full) installation, and you will get the NetBeans IDE 9 **License Agreement** dialog, shown in the top middle of Figure 1-11. Select the "**I accept the terms in the license agreement**" checkbox, shown circled in red, and click the **Next** button, to advance to the **NetBeans IDE Build Installation** dialog, shown on the right side of Figure 1-11. The third dialog specifies the **install location** in the Program Files directory, and also specifies the **JDK to use** for Java development. Notice that NetBeans 9 is smart enough to pick **Java 9** over Java 8 (you have installed both, as you can have more than one Java version installed on any given workstation), and defines what version of Java you will be developing games for (this used to have to be set manually inside NetBeans). Leave these at their default setting, and click the **Next** button to advance to the **Summary** dialog, shown in the lower-left in Figure 1-11. Be sure to leave **Check for Updates** selected, so that NetBeans 9 will automatically update itself.

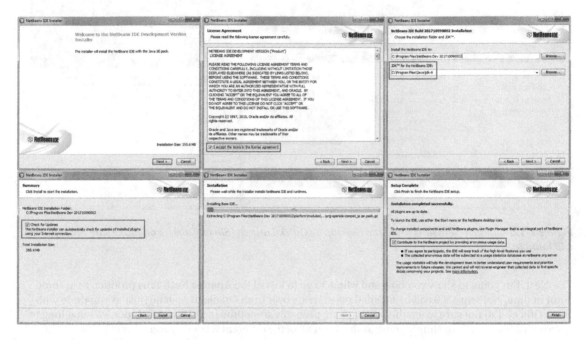

Figure 1-11. *Accept the terms of the license agreement, click the Next button (left) and do the same for JUnit (right)*

Once you click on the **Install** button, NetBeans will install the base IDE as can be seen in the bottom-middle dialog in Figure 11-1, showing you what it is doing via a progress bar and extracted files text underneath it. When the setup is complete, you will get a **Setup Complete** dialog, which will give you the checkbox option to "Contribute to the NetBeans project by providing anonymous usage data." I chose to select this option, to help the NetBeans developers.

One final step, which you should do for all of the various game development and game asset development software packages which we will be installing in this first chapter, is to test the installation by launching the software to make sure that it runs.

This is done by finding the software icon on your desktop (double-click desktop icons to launch them) or in your Taskbar (called a Quick Launch icon, which only requires a single click to launch) and launching the software. In the case of NetBeans 9 IDE, the result should look like Figure 1-12 on the left hand side.

To confirm how NetBeans 9 is set up, use the **Help ➤ About** menu sequence, which is seen on the right hand side of Figure 1-12, showing your product version, Java JDK version being used, Java Runtime Environment (JRE) being used (JRE is part of the JDK install) to run NetBeans 9.0, Operating System being used, and the User directory location and Cache directory location. If you ever have a problem installing subsequent versions of this IDE, try deleting these two (that is, deleting the \dev folder), as they contain information from the previous NetBeans installation which may misdirect the next NetBeans installation.

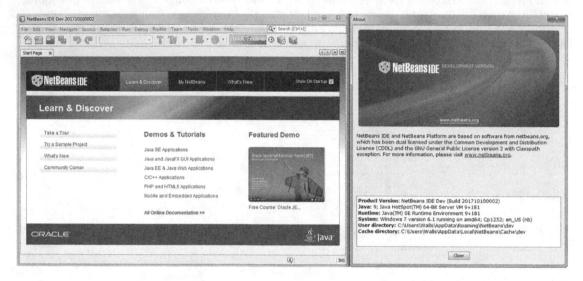

Figure 1-12. *Launch NetBeans using the Desktop or Quick Launch (Silver Cube), and make sure the software will launch*

Next, I'm going to show you how and where to go to install the **Apache NetBeans** product, as at some point in time, NetBeans 9.0 will be finished transferring over from Oracle to Apache (just as was done with Open Office). I'm not sure when this will happen, probably sometime in 2018, but I cannot wait that long to release this book, so I am simply going to show you all of the different ways that you can get NetBeans 9.0. Note that if you wanted to use 8.2, on top of Java 8, this is fine as well, as the JavaFX 8 (and JavaFX 9) classes (API) have not changed. This is because the focus for Java 9 (and NetBeans 9) was just to introduce modules into the workflow and get the IDE working, so JavaFX was left alone and the focus was on the other parts of Java (as you'll see, JavaFX is the Java multimedia/game engine).

Installing the Apache NetBeans 9 (Development) IDE

Next we are going to take a look at the **Apache Jenkins** and **GIT Repository** for NetBeans, which is where the software is going to "land" after the transfer currently underway is finished. The Apache Jenkins' NetBeans site is located at **https://builds.apache.org/job/incubator-netbeans-windows/** and is what is called an "incubator" site. An incubator is used to hatch eggs, so the inference here is that until a NetBeans 9 on Java 9 bundle is "hatched," this is where you can get the NetBeans 9 IDE software while it is still under development. You can see what the Apache Jenkins website looks like at this time (there is a chance that this could change) in Figure 1-13. As you can see it has quite a few options.

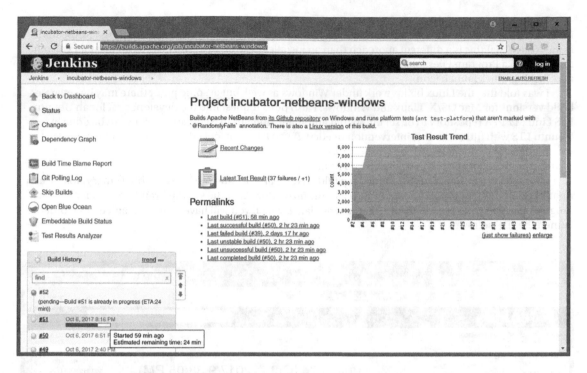

Figure 1-13. *Apache Jenkins' NetBeans is located at* `https://builds.apache.org/job/incubator-`
`netbeans-windows/`

The top left part of Jenkins has the Jenkins software incubator function navigation links, so that you can go back to the Dashboard (home page), get Development Status, see Changes amongst builds, see a Dependency Graph, get a Build Time Blame Report, see a GIT Polling Log, get the Embedded Build Status, see a Test Results Analyzer, Skip Builds and Open Blue Ocean. Blue Ocean is a free, open source, continuous update utility which essentially makes you feel like you are part of the software development team.

Underneath that is the Build History. This is a pane that contains the builds, as they are built, complete with progress bars and build times and completion estimates. If you click on one of these builds (if it is finished) it opens up another window (browser tab) with details on the build and a download link. This is shown in Figure 1-14.

To download one of these ZIP files, right-click on it, and use the **Save As** function, and save the ZIP file in the location (directory/folder) on your hard disk drive that you want to unZIP (decompress) NetBeans 9 from. Notice that this is a different approach than an installer (.exe or .msi) will take, as an installer will put the files into a Program Files folder, along with other installed applications, and will create a desktop icon and Taskbar quick launch icon.

I was told that the Linux builds work under Windows as well, but at some point there may be separate build versions for Mac OS/X, Linux and Windows. I also put a request into the developer list for an Ubuntu LTS Linux 17 PPA repository to be set up, so that automatic updates to NetBeans 9.0 IDE can be done by Ubuntu LTS with little end-user intervention needed. If you have not looked at Ubuntu LTS 17.10 or 18.04 yet you might want to do that now; you will be amazed at how far Ubuntu Linux (Debian, the other major Linux distribution is Fedora) has come relative to OSX or Windows.

Once you unzip NetBeans 9 (I named my folder NetBeans-9-Build) go into the **/bin** (binary) folder, and right-click on **netbeans64.exe**, and use **Run as Administrator**. After the startup branding screen and load progress bar, you will get a **Licensing Agreement** dialog, which you will have to accept (agree to) in order to launch the IDE software.

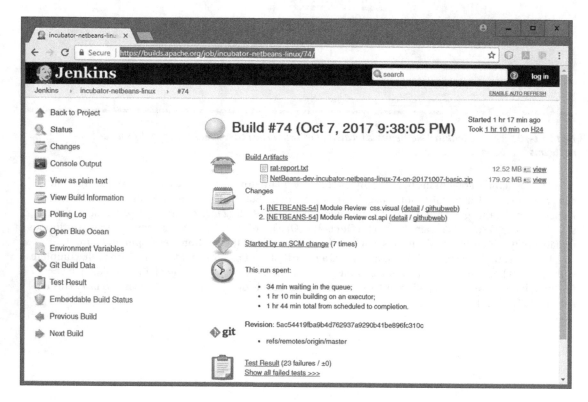

Figure 1-14. *Click a version to get a build page, shown is builds.apache.org/job/incubator-netbeans-linux/74/*

Next, let's go and download a dozen or so of the most popular (and free) open source new media content development software packages, so that you will have all of the powerful, professional tools that you will ultimately need for your Pro Java 9 Game Development business. This represents tens of thousands of (your currency here, mine is dollars) paid software packages, so this first chapter will ultimately become quite valuable to all of the readers.

After that, I'll tell you about some other impressive open source software that I use on my workstations, so that if you want to put together the ultimate software development workstation, before this chapter is over, you can do that, creating an incredibly valuable content production workstation, for the cost of the hardware (and OS) alone.

Installing New Media Content Production Software

There are a number of "genres" of new media elements, or "assets" as I call them, which are supported in JavaFX 9, which is the new media "engine" for Java 9, and therefore what you'll be using as the foundation for your Pro Java 9 Games Development. The primary genres of new media, which you will be installing leading open source software for during the remainder of this chapter, include: SVG digital illustration, digital image compositing, digital audio editing, digital video editing, VFX or Visual Effects, 3D modeling and animation, virtual world creation, character animation, songwriting, digital audio sampling, office productivity (yes, you have to sell your games as well), and much more.

Downloading and Installing InkScape for SVG Digital Illustration

Since JavaFX supports 2D or "**vector**" technology, commonly used in **digital illustration** software packages such as Adobe Illustrator and Freehand, we will download and install the popular open source digital illustration software package known as **InkScape**, which recently had a huge jump in versioning from 0.48 to 0.92, and has professional features. InkScape is available for the Linux, Windows and Macintosh operating systems, just like all of these software packages that we will be installing during this chapter, so readers can use any platform they like to develop games. If you want to learn more about digital illustration and SVG, take a look at the *Digital Illustration Fundamentals* title from Apress.

To find the InkScape software package on the Internet, use the Google Search Engine, and type in **InkScape**. Visit the website and click on the **DOWNLOAD** menu at the top left or on the **Download** icon on the right, as shown in Figure 1-15. The Download icon will represents the operating system which you are using as auto-detected by website code that polls your system for what OS it is using, and automatically gives you the correct version, with a single click.

Figure 1-15. *Google the word InkScape, go to the inkscape.org website, click on the download icon, or download menu*

Once you have downloaded the InkScape software, right-click on the filename, and **Run as Administrator** to install it on your workstation. If you like, you can use the Programs and Features utility that you used earlier in the chapter to uninstall a previous Inkscape version.

After your software is installed, create a Quick Launch Icon on your Taskbar so that you can launch InkScape with a single click of the mouse. Next, you'll install a popular digital imaging software package called **GIMP**, which will allow you to create "raster," or pixel-based, artwork for games using JPEG, PNG, WebP, or GIF digital image formats.

Downloading and Installing GIMP for Digital Image Compositing

Since JavaFX also supports 2D images that utilize "**raster**" image technology which represents images as an array of pixels. This is what is used in paid digital image compositing software packages, such as Adobe Photoshop and Corel Painter. We'll download and install the popular open source digital image editing and compositing software package known as "The Gimp." GIMP is available for the Linux, Windows, Solaris, FreeBSD, and Macintosh operating systems. If you want to learn more about digital image compositing, take a look at the *Digital Image Compositing Fundamentals* title from Apress. To find the GIMP software on the Internet, use Google Search, and type in **GIMP**. The website is shown in Figure 1-16.

Figure 1-16. *Google Search GIMP; go to gimp.org; click the Download link for 2.8.22, or for 2.10 (currently 2.9.6 beta)*

Click on the **Download** link (or right-click, and open it in a separate tab), and click on the **Download GIMP 2.8.22** (or later version such as the new 2.10 or 3.0 versions currently in beta at 2.9.6 and soon 2.9.8) which represent the operating system that you are using.

The download page will automatically detect what OS you are using, and give you the correct OS version; in my case, I am using GIMP on Windows7, Windows 10 and Ubuntu LTS Linux 17.04, as I have it installed on every single workstation I have. Needless to say, open source software has a plethora of advantages over paid software packages.

Once the software is downloaded, install the latest version of GIMP, and then create a Quick Launch Icon for your workstation Taskbar, as you did for InkScape.

Next, we'll install a powerful digital audio editing and special effects software package called **Audacity**.

Downloading and Installing Audacity for Digital Audio Editing

JavaFX supports 2D (and 3D) digital audio which utilizes digital audio technology. Digital audio represents analog audio by taking digital audio "**samples**." Digital audio content is commonly created using digital audio composition and sequencer software packages such as Cakewalk Sonar. If you want to learn more about digital audio editing, take a look at the *Digital Audio Editing Fundamentals* title from Apress. In this section, we will download and install the popular open source digital audio editing and optimization software package known as "**Audacity**." Audacity is available for the Linux, Windows and Macintosh operating systems. To find the Audacity software package on the Internet, use the Google Search Engine, and type in **Audacity**, which will show you the Audacity Team website. Go to this website, as shown in Figure 1-17, at the top-left. Click on the **Download Audacity** link (or use the Download menu) and click on the **Audacity for Windows** (or OS version which you're using). I also use Audacity 2.1.3 on Ubuntu Linux LTS OS 17.04.

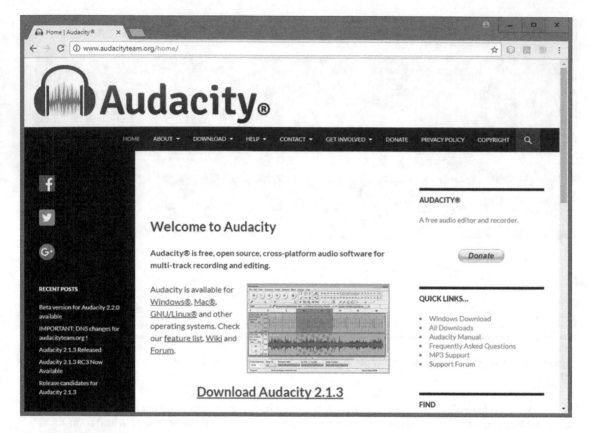

Figure 1-17. *Google the word Audacity, go to audacityteam.org, and click a Download Audacity link matching your OS*

Download and install the latest version of Audacity, currently this is 2.1.3, and create the Quick Launch Icon for your workstation Taskbar, as you did for InkScape and GIMP. Audacity 2.2.0 may be out by the time you read this, and adds a new user interface design and lots of cool new digital audio editing, synthesis, and sweetening features.

Next, you will install a professional, non-linear digital video editing and "color timing" (also known as color correction) software package used for feature films, recently upgraded from version 12.5 to version 14, called Black Magic Design **DaVinci Resolve**. This software packages used to cost thousands of dollars, just a year or two ago!

Downloading and Installing DaVinci Resolve 14 for Digital Video

JavaFX 9 supports digital video, which utilizes "raster" pixel-based motion video technology. This represents video as a sequence of frames, each of which contains a digital image based on an array of pixels. Digital video assets are usually created with digital video editing and color timing software packages such as AfterEffects and EditShare LightWorks. In this section, we will download and install the latest version of an open source digital video editing software known as **DaVinci Resolve 14**. This package is available for Windows 10, Mac OSX, and Ubuntu Linux, and other distributions. To find DaVinci Resolve, use Google Search and type in **DaVinci Resolve**. Click the **Download** button as seen in Figure 1-18 in the middle, or scroll to the bottom of the page, where you can click on the FREE **DOWNLOAD** button.

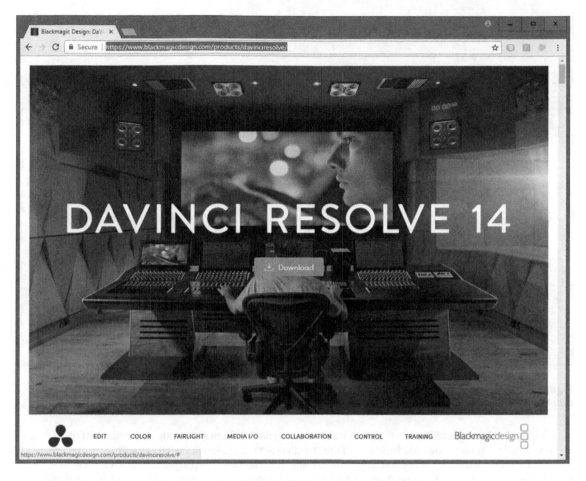

Figure 1-18. *Google the word DaVinci Resolve; go to BlackMagicDesign.com webpage; click on the Download button*

Install the software, and create a Quick Launch Icon for your Taskbar, as you did for all the other software. If you want to learn more about digital video editing, take a look at the *Digital Video Editing Fundamentals* title from Apress. Next, we'll install an advanced Special Effects, 3D modeling and animation, and VR package, called **BlackMagic Fusion**.

Downloading and Installing Blackmagic Fusion for Visual Effects

JavaFX also supports special effects pipelines, since all of the new media genres can be combined together seamlessly using Java 9 code. SFX utilizes "**raster**" pixel-based motion video technology, static image compositing, digital audio, 3D, i3D and SVG digital illustration together all at once, and is therefore as advanced as 3D modeling and animation. BlackMagicDesign's Fusion used to be a paid software package until it was made open source. There is a professional version which used to cost $999 which is now $299! If you are serious about multimedia, purchase this!

You first have to **register** on the **BlackMagicDesign.com** website to be able to download and use this software. This package is available for Linux, Windows 10, and Macintosh operating systems. To find Fusion the Internet, use Google Search Engine and type in **Fusion 9,** and you will be directed to what is shown in Figure 1-19. Click on the **DOWNLOADS** button that represents the operating system that you are using. This download page will automatically detect what OS you are using; in my case, Windows.

21

Figure 1-19. *Google the word Fusion 9; go to the blackmagicdesign.com download page; click on the download button*

Register on the BlackMagicDesign.com website, if you havn't done so already, and once you're approved, you can then download and install the latest version of Fusion 9. Install the software, and create a Quick Launch Icon for your Taskbar, as you did for the other software. If you want to learn Fusion in detail, Apress.com has a recent book entitled *VFX Fundamentals* that gets into Fusion and Visual Effects Compositing Pipelines in much greater detail.

Next, we'll install a 3D modeling and animation package, called **Blender**.

Download and Install Blender for 3D Modeling and Animation

JavaFX has recently moved to support 3D new media assets which are created outside of the JavaFX environment, which means that you will be able to create 3D models, textures and animation using third party software packages such as Autodesk 3D Studio Max or Maya and NewTek Lightwave. In this section we will download and install the popular open source 3D modeling and animation software package known as "Blender." Blender is available for the Linux, Windows and Macintosh operating systems, so readers can use any operating system platform that they like to create and optimize 3D models, 3D texture mapping and 3D animation for use in their Java 9 and JavaFX 9 games.

To find the Blender software on the Internet, using the Google Search Engine and type in **Blender** as shown in Figure 1-20. Click on the correct download link to download and install Blender, then create the Quick Launch Icon.

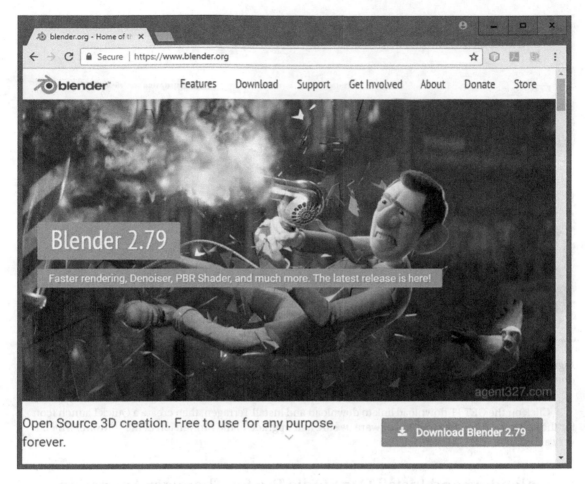

Figure 1-20. *Google the words Blender 3D, go to www.blender.org and click on the blue Download Blender 2.79 button*

Download and Install Terragen for 3D Terrain or World Creation

Another impressive (and free, for the basic version, or if you are in the education industry) 3D world generation software package is Terragen 4.1 from Planetside Software in the UK. You can download the basic version at Planetside.co.uk, as well as joining their Forum. I've used this software in a couple of my Android application development book titles as well, so I know it works well for use in projects such as multimedia applications, Interactive TV or iTV, and games. It is also used by professional filmmakers, as its quality level is extremely pristine. Since we're covering 3D in the book, you may want to look into Terragen, as it's affordable, and used by television producers and movie studios. To find the Terragen software on the Internet, use the Google Search Engine and type in **Terragen 4.1**. Click on the link, which will bring up the Planetside Software website as shown in Figure 1-21.

Figure 1-21. *Google the word Terragen; go to the planetside.co.uk website; click on a blue GET IT button to download*

Click on the GET IT download link to download and install Terragen, then create a Quick Launch Icon for the software. If you like this 3D software be sure and upgrade to the Pro version of the software, which is very affordable.

Downloading and Install Daz Studio Pro for Character Animation

For professional 3D character modeling and animation, be sure to check out the 3D software packages from DAZ 3D, located at daz3d.com, when you have the chance. The current version of DAZ Studio PRO is 4.9, and yes, it is free! You have to log in and sign up, like you did for Black Magic Design software, but that is a small price to pay! There is also a free 3D modeling software package on this website called Hexagon. The most expensive software on the DAZ 3D website is Carrara ($150) or Carrara Pro ($285). DAZ Studio makes most of their revenues selling character models of one type or another, so check them out, as they are a force to be reckoned with in the 3D content (virtual) world!

To find the Daz Studio Pro software on the Internet, using the Google Search Engine and type in **Daz Studio Pro 5 download**. The link should take you to the daz3d.com/daz_studio page, as is shown in Figure 1-22. Click on the download link to download and install the latest version of Daz Studio Pro, and then create your Quick Launch Icon.

Figure 1-22. *Google the words Daz Studio Pro, go to* www.daz3d.com, *and download the latest version of Daz Studio*

Other Open Source New Media Software Packages

There are a significant number of other professional level, open source software packages which I also use in my new media content production business. I thought it would be nice to let you know about some of these, in case you had not heard about them. These will add even more power and versatility to the new media production workstation that you have built up to this point during this chapter. It is important to note that you have already saved yourself thousands of dollars (or your native unit of currency), which would have been spent on similar paid content production software packages, during this process of doing all of this extensive downloading and installing. I guess my motto could be said to be: "do it right the first time, and be sure to go all the way," so I will go ahead and tell you about some of the other free, and even about some of the more approachable (not free, but very affordable) new media content production software packages that I usually have installed on my 3D content production workstations.

One of the best values in open source software, aside from the DaVinci Resolve package, which used to cost close to six figures (back in the day), is a **business productivity software suite** which was acquired by **Oracle** after their acquisition of Sun Microsystems and then made open source. Oracle transferred their OpenOffice software suite over to the popular **Apache** open source project, just like they are doing currently with NetBeans 9.

Open Office 4.3 is an entire office productivity software suite, which contains **six** full-fledged business productivity software packages! Since your content production agency is actually a full-fledged business concern, you should probably know about office software, as this is an exceptionally solid open source software offering. You can find it at: **OpenOffice.org**, and this popular business software package has been downloaded by savvy professionals such as yourself over one hundred million times, so, it's no joke, as they say!

For user interface (UI) design prototyping there's a free software package called **Pencil 2.0.6** from **Evolus.vn** which will allow you to easily prototype user interface designs before you create them in Java, Android or HTML5. The software is located at **pencil.evolus.vn** and is available for Linux Distros, Windows 7 and 8.1, and Macintosh OS/X.

A great compliment to the Audacity 2 digital audio editing software is the **Rosegarden** MIDI sequencing and music composition and scoring software, which can be used for music composition, and for printing out your resulting scores for music publishing. Rosegarden is currently being ported from Linux to Windows.

Note the most full featured version is for Linux, and can be seen in Figure 1-23. It can be found using Google Search, or at **RoseGardenMusic.com**, and it is currently at version 17.04 (same as Ubuntu LTS). This is popularly called the "Twice in a Blue Moon" version.

Figure 1-23. *Rosegarden is a MIDI, music scoring, and notation program for Linux which is being ported to Windows 10*

Another impressive audio, MIDI and sound design software package is called **Qtractor**, which is a hard disk drive based audio sampler, editor and sound design package, shown in Figure 1-24. So if you're running the Linux OS, be sure to Google Search, download, and install this professional level digital audio synthesis software package, which you can find on SourceForge at the **Qtractor.SourceForge.net** URL website address.

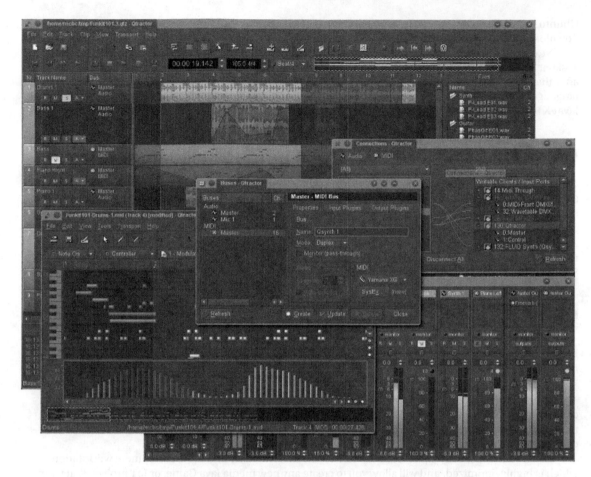

Figure 1-24. *Qtractor, the hard disk based digital audio editing software for Linux*

Another impressive free 3D modeling and animation software, which used to cost nearly a thousand dollars when it was developed by **Roman Ormandy** at Caligari Corporation (it was later purchased by Microsoft), was **Caligari TrueSpace 7.61**, which you can find on multiple sites simply by doing a Google Search for Caligari TrueSpace 3D.

Another 3D rendering software you should take a look at is **POVRay**. POV stands for "Persistence of Vision," and this software is what is known as a "raytracer," an advanced rendering engine, which works with any 3D modeling and animation software packages, to generate impressive 3D scenes using advanced ray-traced rendering algorithms. The most recent version can be found on the **www.povray.org** website. It is **3.7,** and the latest version is 64-bit, and is multi-core (multi-threaded) compatible, and can be downloaded for free, which is why I am telling you about it here.

Another sleek 3D modeling software package which was specifically designed for use with POVRay is **Bishop 3D**. The software could be used to create custom 3D objects, which can then be imported into POVRay (and then into JavaFX) for use in your pro Java games. The most recent version is **1.0.5.2,** for Windows 7, or 10. The software can be found on **www.bishop3d.com**, and the latest version is an 8MB download, and can currently be downloaded for free.

Another free 3D subdivision modeling software you should take a look at is **Wings3D**. This software could be used to create 3D objects, which could then be imported into JavaFX for use in your games. The most recent version is **2.1.5** and was released in December of 2016 for Windows 10, Macintosh OS/X and

Ubuntu Linux. The software can be found on the **wings3d.com** and the latest version is 64-bit, is a 16MB download, and can currently be downloaded for free.

Next I will show you how I organize some of the basic OS utilities and open source software on the Taskbar. Over the next few chapters, we will start to learn the principles behind using new media assets, and after that, how to use NetBeans 9 to create a JavaFX 9 project, and then we will get into the Java programming language, in the chapter after that, before we start to learn about the particulars regarding the powerful JavaFX 9.0 multimedia game engine.

Organizing Quick Launch Icons in Your Taskbar Area

There are certain operating system utilities, such as the **calculator**, **text editor** (called Notepad in Windows), and **file manager** (called Explorer in Windows), for which I keep **Quick Launch Icons** in my Taskbar, as these are used frequently in programming and new media content development work processes. I also keep a wide range of new media development, programming, and office productivity applications on my Taskbar as Quick Launch Icons, as you can see in Figure 1-25, which shows a dozen of these, including everything that we just installed, in the order that we installed it, as well as a few others, including OpenOffice 4.3, DAZ Studio Professional 4.9, and Bryce Professional 7.1.

Figure 1-25. Make Taskbar Quick Launch Icons for key system utilities, NetBeans 9 and new media production software

There are a couple of ways to create these Quick Launch Icons; you can drag and drop programs right out of the **Start** menu onto the Taskbar, or you can right-click icons on the desktop or in the Explorer file manager and select the **Pin to Taskbar** context-sensitive menu option. Once icons are in the Taskbar, you can change their position simply by dragging them to the left or to the right.

Congratulations! You've just created your new media Java Game and IoT Development workstation, which is highly optimized, and will allow you to create any new media Java Game, or IoT project, that your clients can imagine!

Summary

In this first chapter, you made sure that you had everything that you needed to develop innovative Java Games or IoT projects, complete with the latest versions of Java 9, JavaFX 9.0, NetBeans 9 and all of the latest open source new media software. This involved getting the latest Java 9 JDK and NetBeans 9 IDE software, and then we installed Java 9 and then NetBeans 9. After that, you did the same for a gaggle of professional, open source, new media content tools.

CHAPTER 2

■ ■ ■

An Introduction to Content Creation: 2D New Media Asset Fundamentals

Now that you have a pro Java game and IoT development workstation put together, thanks to the previous chapter, let's jump right in and learn about the basic 2D content development concepts and principles that most of these new media content development software packages are based on. The exception to this is Blender, which is based on more advanced 3D content development, which we will cover in the next chapter. The reason that we need to cover this foundational multimedia material before we get into Java, NetBeans, and JavaFX is because there's an incredible level of support, thanks to the JavaFX multimedia engine, for digital illustration using Scalable Vector Graphics (SVG); digital imaging using raster (bitmap) image formats such as PNG, JPEG, or GIF; and digital audio using audio formats such as MP3, MPEG4 AAC, WAV or AIFF (PCM), and 3D, using the JavaFX internal rendering engine. I assume that you are not going to be creating text-based games but rather interactive new media applications, so I wanted to cover some non-coding-related topics first. Once we start coding using the NetBeans, Java, and JavaFX APIs, we'll never stop coding.

During this chapter, you'll get a detailed overview of the concepts behind each of the 2D new media content types that are supported in JavaFX, including digital illustration (vector), digital imaging (raster), digital video (motion), and digital audio (waveform). We will do this so that you have the foundational knowledge to be able to use the free, open source, multimedia content production tools that you downloaded and installed in Chapter 1 for game design.

The first thing that I want to cover is the foundational new media asset type of **digital imagery**, as it will be used as the foundational input asset for many of the other new media asset types. For instance, your digital video is simply a series of digital images played rapidly over time to create an illusion of motion. Your 2D vector illustration assets can be filled with digital image data using the JavaFX **ImagePattern class**, and your 3D vector assets can use digital image assets for **shaders** and **texture maps**, which we will be covering in Chapter 3, including advanced 3D content creation and related JavaFX packages and classes that are used to implement these 3D content elements.

The next thing I will cover are the concepts, techniques, and "lingo" of digital video, including things such as frames, frame rates, bit rates, and other concepts that add the fourth dimension of time, making static digital image assets into animated digital video assets. These concepts also relate to animation as well, including both 2D animation and 3D animation. We will be covering 2D vector and 3D vector concepts during Chapter 3, as they are closely related.

Finally, we'll take a look at digital audio concepts; digital audio is closely related to digital video because it can be contained within a digital video file format. Digital audio can also exist on its own, and therefore we will also cover digital audio format support in JavaFX, as well as a digital audio asset data footprint

W. Jackson, *Pro Java 9 Games Development*, https://doi.org/10.1007/978-1-4842-0973-8_2

optimization work process. We will thus be covering all of the 2D (X,Y data representation) new media forms in this chapter with the exception of 2D vector illustration, which is closely related to 3D vector rendering, which we cover in the first part of Chapter 3.

Game Design Assets: New Media Content Concepts

One of the most powerful tools that you have to make your game content professional and visually desirable to your customers is the **multimedia** production software that you downloaded and installed in Chapter 1. Before I get too far into this book, I need to spend some time providing you with the basic foundational knowledge regarding the four primary types of **new media assets** that are supported in Java via the JavaFX multimedia engine. These include **digital images**, used for sprites, background imagery, and 2D animation; **vector shapes**, used in 2D illustration, collision detection, 2D shapes, paths, and curves; **digital audio**, used for sound effects, narration, and background music; and **digital video**, used in games for animated background loops (birds flying through sky, drifting clouds, etc.) and highly optimized video playback. As you can see in Figure 2-1, these four 2D genres, or areas, are all installed in your games using the JavaFX Scene Graph. There is one other new media area that I like to call **Interactive 3D (i3D)**. i3D, which we will cover in the next chapter about **OpenGL ES**, brings real-time 3D rendering to Java 8 and 9.

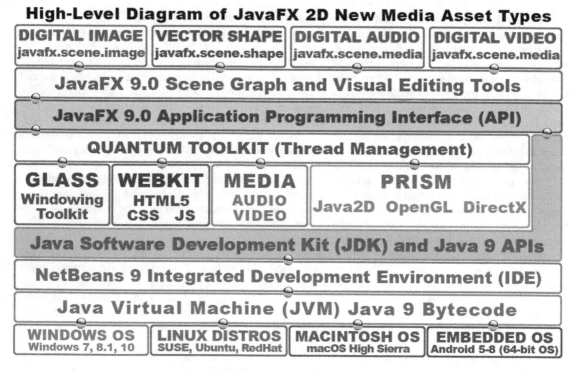

Figure 2-1. How 2D or audio new media assets are implemented in Scene Graph using JavaFX 9, Java 9, and NetBeans 9

Since you'll need to have a **technical foundation** before you can create, or properly implement, any of these new media elements in a Java game design (or programming) pipeline, I am going to go over core concepts for each of the four new media areas. The only two that are related conceptually are **2D animation** and **digital video**, as each of these involve using the fourth dimension of **time** and use **frames**, so I'll cover these together. Since digital audio also involves the fourth dimension of time, I will finish up with digital audio concepts; finally, we will take a quick look at **digital content optimization** so that your pro Java games and IoT projects are compact and download quickly.

Digital Imaging Concepts: Resolution, Color Depth, Alpha, Layers

JavaFX supports the most popular digital imaging file (data) formats, which gives us game designers a ton of flexibility. Since the JavaFX 8 API is now part of Java 8 and 9, this means Java also supports these image formats. Some of these digital image formats have been around for decades, like the CompuServe **Graphics Information Format** (GIF) or the widely used **Joint Photographic Experts Group** (JPEG) format. Some of the JavaFX digital image formats are more modern; for instance, the **Portable Network Graphics** (PNG, pronounced "ping") is the file format that we will be using for our games because it yields the highest quality level and supports image compositing, which we will be learning about soon. All of these mainstream digital image file formats supported in Java are also supported in HTML5 browsers, and since Java apps can be used inside HTML apps or web sites, this is a very logical synergy indeed! You can also use a third-party digital image library called **ImageJ**, if you need a wider range of digital image file format support.

The oldest format is a **lossless** digital image file format called CompuServe GIF. It is termed *lossless* because it does not throw away (lose) any source image data to achieve its compression result. The GIF compression algorithm is not as refined (not as powerful) as the PNG format, and GIF only supports **indexed color**, which is how it obtains its **compression** (smaller file size). We will be learning about **color depth** (indexed color versus true color) in detail later in this section. If all your game image assets are already created using the GIF format, you'll be able to use them in your Java game with no problems, rather than less efficient image compression and limited image compositing capabilities.

The most popular digital image format that Java supports via JavaFX is JPEG. JPEG uses a "true color" color depth, instead of an indexed color depth. We'll be covering color theory and color depth a bit later. JPEG uses what is termed **lossy** digital image compression. This is because the compression algorithm "throws away" image data so that it can achieve a smaller file size. This image data is lost forever, unless you are smart and save the original raw image!

If you magnify a JPEG image after compression, you will see **discolored or dirty areas**, which clearly weren't present in your original image. The degraded area or areas in an image are termed **compression artifacts** in the digital imaging industry. This will only occur in lossy image compression and is common with JPEG (and MPEG) compression.

The digital imaging format that I recommend you use for your pro Java games is the **Portable Network Graphic** file format. PNG has two true-color file versions; one is called **PNG24** and can't be used in image compositing, and the other is called **PNG32** and carries an **alpha channel** used to define transparency, which we will be covering a bit later. There is also an **indexed** (a maximum of 256; can be fewer) color version of the PNG format, called **PNG8**.

The reason I recommend PNG for your games is because it has a decent image compression algorithm and because it is a **lossless** image format. This means that PNG has great image quality as well as reasonable levels of data compression efficiency, which will make your game distribution file smaller. The real power of the PNG32 format comes in its ability to **composite** with other game imagery using **transparency** and anti-aliasing (via its alpha channel).

Digital Image Resolution and Aspect Ratio: Defining Your Image Size and Shape

As you probably know, digital imagery is made up of two-dimensional (**2D**) **arrays** of **pixels**. Pixels is short for **Picture** (pix) **Elements** (els). The number of pixels in an image is expressed by its **resolution**, which is the number of pixels in the image **Width** (or **W**, sometimes referred to as the **x-axis**) and **Height** (or **H**, sometimes referred to as the **y-axis**) dimensions. The more pixels your image has, the higher the resolution is said to be. This is similar to how digital cameras work, as the more **megapixels** there are in your image capture device (which is usually your camera's Charged-Coupled Device (CCD), which captures the image data), the higher the image quality that can be achieved.

To find the total number of image pixels, **multiply** the width pixels by the height pixels. For instance, a wide VGA 800x480 image will contain 384,000 pixels, which is exactly 3/8ths of 1MB. This is how you would find the **size** of your image, both as far as kilobytes (or megabytes) used and height and width on the display screen.

The **shape** of a digital image asset is specified using the image **aspect ratio**. Aspect ratio is the **width:height ratio** for the digital image and defines a square (**1:1** aspect ratio) or rectangular (also known as **widescreen**) digital image shape. Displays featuring a **2:1** (widescreen) aspect ratio, such as **2160x1080** resolution, are widely available.

A **1:1 aspect ratio** display or image is always **perfectly square**, as is a **2:2** or **3:3** aspect ratio image. An IoT developer might see this aspect ratio on a smart watch, for instance. It is important to note that it is the **ratio** between these two width and height numbers, or X and Y variables, that define the shape of an image or a display screen, not the actual numbers themselves. The actual numbers define the resolution, or total pixel array capability, for a screen.

An aspect ratio should always be expressed as the **smallest pair of numbers** that can be achieved (reduced) on either side of the aspect ratio **colon**. If you paid attention in high school while you were learning about the lowest common denominator, then an aspect ratio will be very easy for you to calculate. I usually do aspect ratio calculation by continuing to divide each side of the colon by 2. For instance, if you take the **SXGA 1280x1024** resolution, half of 1280x1024 is 640x512, and half of 640x512 is 320x256. Half of 320x256 is 160x128, half of that again is 80x64, half of that is 40x32, and half of that is 20x16. Half of 20x16 is 10x8, and half of that gives you the **5:4 aspect ratio** for SXGA.

Digital Image Color Theory and Color Depth: Defining Precise Image Pixel Colors

The color values for each digital image pixel can be defined by an amount of three different colors, **red**, **green**, or **blue** (**RGB**), which are present in different amounts in every pixel. Consumer electronic display screens leverage **additive** colors, which is where wavelengths of light for each RGB color channel are **summed** together in order to create **16.8** million different color values. **Additive color** is utilized in LCD, LED, or OLED displays. It is the opposite of **subtractive** color, which is used in printing. To show you the different results, under a subtractive color model, mixing red with green (inks) will yield purple colors, whereas in an additive color model, mixing red with green (light) creates a vibrant yellow coloration. Additive color can provide a much broader spectrum of colors than subtractive color can provide.

There are **256 levels** of **brightness** for each red, green, and blue color value that is held for each pixel. This allows you to set **8 bits** of data value range, or zero through 255, controlling color brightness variation for each of the red, green, and blue values. This data is represented using hexadecimal notation, from a minimum of **zero** (**#00**, or off, all dark, or a black color) to a maximum of **255** (#FF, or fully on, or a maximum RGB color contributed, making white).

The number of bits that are used to represent the number of digital image pixel colors supported is referred to as **color depth** for an image and uses "power of 2" just like 3D does for texture mapping, which we will get into in the next chapter. So, PNG8 images use 256 colors, PNG7 uses half as many as that (128),

PNG6 uses half as many as that (64), PNG5 uses half as many as that (32), PNG 4 would therefore use 16, PNG3 would use 8, PNG2 would use 4, and PNG1 would use 2, or black and white (on or off). Generally, you will want to use the full 256 colors, because JavaFX only supports PNG8, PNG4, or PNG1, so use PNG8 if you are going to use indexed color imagery at all.

Common color depths used in the digital imaging industry include 8-bit, 16-bit, 24-bit, and 32-bit. I'll outline the common ones here, along with their formats. The **lowest color depth** exists in **8-bit indexed color** images. These feature a maximum of 256 color values and use **GIF** and **PNG8** image formats to hold this indexed color type of data.

A **medium color depth** image will feature 16-bit color depths and will thus contain 65,536 colors (calculated as 256 times 256) and is supported by the TARGA (TGA) and Tagged Image File Format (TIFF) digital image formats. If you want to use digital image formats other than GIF, JPEG, and PNG in your Java 8 games, import the **ImageJ** library.

True-color color depth images will feature the **24-bit** color depth and will thus contain more than 16 million colors. This is calculated as **256 times 256 times 256** and equals **16,777,216** colors. File formats supporting 24-bit color depth include JPEG (or JPG), PNG, BMP, XCF, PSD, TGA, TIFF, and WebP. JavaFX supports three of these: JPEG, PNG24 (24-bit), and PNG32 (32-bit). Using the **true-color depth** 24-bit or 32-bit imagery will give you the highest level of quality. This is why I have been recommending that you use the PNG24 or PNG32 formats for your Java 9 games and IoT projects.

Next, let's take a look at how we represent image transparency, by using the PNG32 image's alpha channel.

Digital Image Compositing: Using Alpha Channels and Transparency with Layers

Next let's take a look at how to define digital image pixel transparency values using **alpha channels** and how these can be used for **compositing** digital imagery in real time for your Java game. Compositing is the process of seamlessly **blending** together more than one **layer** of digital imagery. As you might well imagine, this is an extremely important concept for game design and development. Compositing is useful when you want to create an image on the display that appears as though it is one single image (or animation) but is actually the seamless collection of (more than one) composited image layers. One of the principal reasons you would want to set up an image or animation composite is to allow **programmatic control** over various elements in those images, by having each element on a different layer.

To accomplish this, you need to have an **alpha channel transparency** value, which you can utilize to precisely control the blending of that pixel with the pixel in the same X,Y image location on other layers that are underneath it. In digital imaging software, transparency values for each image layer are represented by using a checkerboard pattern, which you can see on the right side of Figure 2-2.

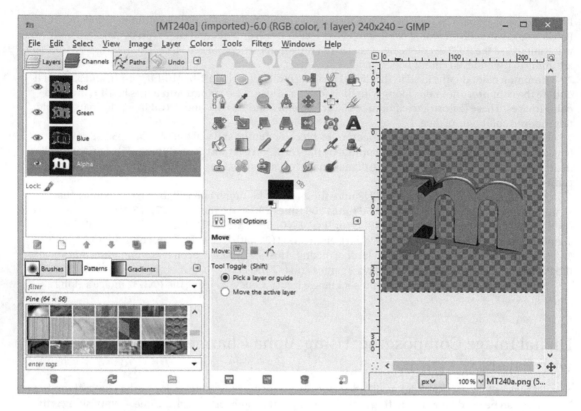

Figure 2-2. *Showing the checkerboard representation of transparent pixels in an image, as well as the RGBA channels*

On the left side of GIMP you can see **Alpha layer**, which I selected in blue. This contains the transparency values for the MindTaffy logo. The GIMP **Channels** palette, which is the tab that I selected to show you these color and alpha channels (Red, Green, Blue, Alpha), holds these color (and alpha) channels separately for each layer, allowing you an incredible level of control over each pixel in each image composite layer.

Like the other **RGB channels**, an **alpha channel** has **256 levels**, but instead of red, green, or blue, these values are transparency levels. In Java programming, the alpha channel is represented by the **first two slots** in a **hexadecimal representation** delineated in the format **#AARRGGBB** data value. We will be covering this in detail in the next section. Alpha plus color channel **ARGB** data values utilize **eight** slots (32-bit) of data, rather than the **six data slots** (**#RRGGBB**) used in a 24-bit image, which could be thought of as a 32-bit image with zero (no) alpha channel data.

Therefore, a 24-bit (PNG24) image has no alpha channel and will not be used for compositing, unless it's the **background (bottom) image plate** in your compositing layer stack. On the other hand, PNG32 imagery will be used as compositing layers on top of a PNG24 (background plate) image, or on top of lower z-order PNG32 compositing layers that will need their alpha channel capability in order to show through, via these alpha channel transparency values, in certain pixel locations in the image composite where some measure of transparency (or opacity) is required.

How do digital image alpha channels, and the concept of image compositing, factor into Java Game Design? You must be wondering! The primary advantage is an ability to break the gameplay screen, and the sprites, projectiles, and background graphic elements that it includes, into a number of **component layers**. The reason for doing this is to be able to apply Java programming logic (or JavaFX or SVG special effects) to the individual graphic image elements to control parts of your gameplay screen. Without a 2D compositing approach, you would not otherwise be able to individually control game components, as pixel-by-pixel processing is too processing intensive for most devices.

There is another part of image compositing, called **blending modes**, that also factors heavily into professional image compositing capabilities. JavaFX blending modes are applied by using the **Blend** class with **BlendMode** constant values found in a **javafx.scene.effect** subpackage that we will be covering later during this book. This JavaFX blend effect class gives Java game developers many of the same image compositing modes that Photoshop or GIMP affords to a digital imaging artisan. This turns Java and JavaFX into a powerful image compositing engine, just like GIMP, and the blending algorithms are controllable at a very flexible level, using custom Java code. Some JavaFX blending mode constants include the **ADD**, **SCREEN**, **OVERLAY**, **DARKEN**, **LIGHTEN**, **MULTIPLY**, **DIFFERENCE**, **EXCLUSION**, **SRC_ATOP**, **SRC_OVER**, **SOFT_LIGHT**, **HARD_LIGHT**, **COLOR_BURN**, and **COLOR_DODGE** constants.

Representing Color and Alpha in Java Game Logic: Using Hexadecimal Notation

Now that you know what color depth and alpha channels are and that color and transparency are represented by using a combination of four different alpha, red, green, and blue (ARGB) **image channels** within any given digital image, it is now important to understand how, as programmers, we are supposed to represent these four ARGB image color and transparency channel values in Java and in JavaFX.

In the Java programming language, color and alpha are not only used in 2D digital imagery, commonly termed **bitmap** imagery, but are also used in 2D illustration, commonly termed **vector** imagery. Colors and transparency values are also often used across a number of different color setting options. For instance, you could set a background color (or a transparency value) for the JavaFX Stage, a Scene, a layout container such as a StackPane, a vector shape fill, or a UI control, among other things, such as 3D asset characteristics. We will be covering 3D and JavaFX in future chapters.

In Java and the JavaFX API, different levels of ARGB color intensity values are represented using **hexadecimal** notation. Hexadecimal, or "hex" for short, is based on the original **Base16** computer notation. This was used long ago to represent **16 bits** of data values. Unlike the more common **Base10**, which counts from zero through 9, the Base16 notation counts from zero through F, where F represents the Base10 value of 15 (0 through 15 yields 16 data values).

Hexadecimal values in Java always start with a **zero and an x**, so the 24-bit color value for white would look like this: **0xFFFFFF**. This hexadecimal color value represents Java's **Color.WHITE** constant and uses no alpha channel. A 32-bit color value for white would look like **0xFFFFFFFF**, with the alpha channel data being fully opaque. White with a transparent alpha channel, which could not be white at all but rather would be "clear," is coded like this using hexadecimal: **0x00FFFFFF**. I usually use 0x00000000 to represent a clear (transparent) alpha+color value in Java code.

Each slot in a **24-bit hexadecimal representation** represents one Base16 value, so getting the 256 values that we need for each RGB color will take 2 slots, as 16 times 16 equals 256. Therefore, to represent the 24-bit image using hexadecimal notation, we would need to have **six slots** after the 0x to hold each of those six hexadecimal data values (data pairs representing 256 levels of values each). If you multiply 16x16x16x16x16x16, you should get the 16,777,216 colors that are possible to address by using 24-bit, also known as *true-color* digital image data.

The hexadecimal data slots represent RGB values in the following format: **0xRRGGBB**. For the Java constant **Color.WHITE**, all of the red, green and blue channels in the hexadecimal color data value representation are at the full (maximum color value) luminosity setting. If you additively sum all of these colors together, you will get white light.

The color yellow would be represented by the red and green channels being on and the blue channel being off, so the hexadecimal representation for Color.YELLOW would therefore be **0xFFFF00** where both the red and green channel slots are fully on (FF, or a 255 Base10 data value) and the blue channel slots are fully off (00, or a zero value).

The eight hexadecimal data slots for an ARGB value will hold data with the following format: **0xAARRGGBB**. Thus, for **Color.WHITE**, all alpha, red, green, and blue channels in the hexadecimal color data value representation would be at their maximum luminosity (or opacity), and the alpha channel is fully opaque, that is, not transparent, as represented by an FF value. Therefore, a 32-bit hexadecimal value for the **Color.WHITE** constant would be **0xFFFFFFFF**.

A 100 percent transparent alpha channel can be represented by the alpha slot being set to zero, creating a "clear" image. Therefore, you would represent transparent image pixel values using any data value between **0x00000000** and **0x00FFFFFF**. It is important to note that if an alpha channel value equates to this full transparency level, then it would follow that the 16,777,216 color values that will be contained in the other six (RGB) hexadecimal data value slots will not matter whatsoever, because that pixel will be evaluated as not being there, as it is transparent and, thus, will not be composited in the final image or animation composite image, so its color is moot (does not matter at all).

Digital Image Object Masking: Using Alpha Channels to Composite Game Sprites

One of the primary applications for alpha channels in game design is to **mask** out areas of an image or an animation (an image series) so that it can be utilized as a game sprite in a gameplay image compositing scenario. **Masking** is the process of "cutting" subject matter out of a digital image so that it can be placed on its own layer using alpha channel transparency values. This is done using a digital imaging software package, as shown in Figure 2-2.

Digital image compositing software packages such as Photoshop or GIMP feature tools that are included for use in masking and image compositing. You can't do effective image compositing without doing effective masking, so this is an important area to master for game designers who want to integrate graphics elements, such as image sprites and sprite animation, into their game designs. The art of digital image masking has been around for a very long time!

Masking can be done for you automatically, using professional bluescreen (or greenscreen) backdrops along with computer software that can automatically extract those exact color values to create a mask. This mask is turned into alpha channel (transparency) information (data). Masking can also be done manually by hand, by using digital image software, by using one of the **algorithmic selection** tools in conjunction with various sharpening and blur algorithms.

We'll learn a lot about this work process during the course of this book using common open source software packages such as GIMP. Masking can be a complex and involved work process, and a complete mastery of this process may need to span a couple of chapters, instead of trying to fit it all into one single chapter in the book (this one). This chapter is to expose you to foundational knowledge of the work processes we undertake during the book.

A key consideration for the masking process is getting smooth, sharp edges around a masked object (subject matter). This is so that when you place a masked object (in the case of this book, it would be a game sprite) into (over) new background imagery, it will look to a game player like it was photographed there in the first place (like it is in the video).

The key to doing this successfully lies in the **pixel selection** work process, which involves using digital image software **selection tools** such as the **scissors** tool in GIMP or the **magic wand** tool in Photoshop. These must be used in the proper fashion (order) to be completely effective. Using the correct selection work process is critical!

For instance, if there are areas of **uniform color** around the object that you want to mask (maybe you shot it against a bluescreen), you'll use a magic wand tool with a proper **threshold** setting to select everything **except** your object. Then you **invert** the **selection**, which will give you a **selection set** containing the object. Often the correct work process involves approaching something in reverse. Other selection tools contain complex algorithms that can look at color changes between pixels. These can be useful for **edge detection**, which we can use for other selection methods.

Smoothing Digital Image Composites: Using Anti-aliasing to Smooth Image Edges

Anti-aliasing is a popular digital image compositing technique, where two adjacent colors in a digital image that are on an **edge** between two areas of different color are **blended** together along that edge. This will serve to make this edge look smoother (less jagged) when an image is zoomed out. What this does is to "trick" the viewer's eye into seeing a smoother edge and gets rid of what has come to be called *image jaggies*. Anti-aliasing provides an impressive result by using averaged color values using just a few colored pixels along the edge that needs to be made smoother. By averaged color values, I mean some color range that is a portion of the way between the two colors that are coming together along an image's jagged edge. This takes only a half-dozen or so intermediate colors. I created an example of this to show you what I'm talking about; see Figure 2-3.

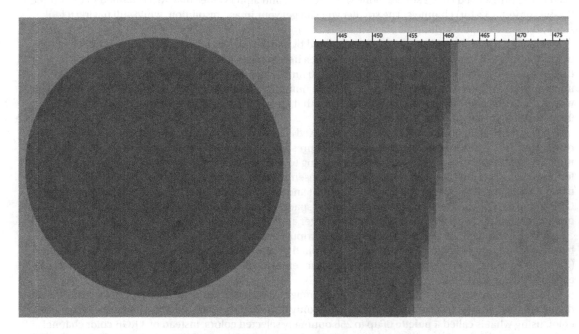

Figure 2-3. *A red circle composited on a yellow background (left) and a zoomed-in view (right) showing anti-aliasing*

As you can see, I created what appears to be a razor-sharp red circle on one layer, overlaying a yellow filling color on a background layer. I zoomed into the red circle shape's edge and took another screenshot and placed this to the right of the zoomed-out circle. This reveals a range of yellow-orange through orange to red-orange anti-aliasing color values, right on the edge that is between the red and yellow colors bordering each other at the edge of where the circle meets the background.

It is important to note that the JavaFX engine will anti-alias 2D shapes and 3D objects against the background colors and background imagery, using the Java2D software renderer or the hardware rendered i3D, using the Prism engine, which can use OpenGL or DirectX. You will still be responsible for correctly compositing, that is, providing anti-aliasing for your multilayered imagery, by effectively using the alpha channel, which we learned about earlier in this chapter.

Digital Image Data Optimization: Using Compression, Indexed Color, and Dithering

A number of factors affect digital image compression, and you can use some basic techniques to achieve a better-quality result with a smaller data footprint. This is a primary objective in optimized digital imagery; obtaining the smallest possible data footprint for your application (in this case it is a game) while at the same time achieving the highest-quality visual result. We'll start with the aspects that most significantly affect the data footprint and examine how each of these contributes to data footprint optimization for any given digital image. Interestingly, these are similar to the order of the digital imaging concepts that we have covered thus far during this section on imaging.

The most critical contributor to a resulting digital image asset file size, what I like to call the **data footprint**, is going to be the number of pixels, or the **resolution** of a digital image. This is logical, because each of the pixels needs to be stored, along with the color and alpha values that are contained in their three (24-bit) or four (32-bit) channels. The smaller you can get your image resolution, while still having it look sharp, the smaller the resulting file size will be.

Raw (or uncompressed) image size is calculated by **width times height times 3** for 24-bit RBG images, or for 32-bit ARGB images that would be **width times height times 4**. For instance, an uncompressed, true-color, 24-bit VGA image will have 640 times 480 times 3, equaling **921,600 bytes** of original (raw) uncompressed digital image data. To determine the number of **kilobytes** that is in this raw VGA image, you would divide 921,600 by 1024 (the number of bytes that are in a kilobyte), and this would give you an even **900 KB** of data in a true-color VGA image.

It is important to optimize for raw (uncompressed) image size by optimizing your digital imagery resolution. This is because once an image is decompressed out of a game application file into system memory, this is the amount of memory that it is going to occupy since the image is going to be stored pixel for pixel using a 24-bit (RGB) or 32-bit (ARGB) representation in memory. This is one of the reasons I'm using **PNG24** and **PNG32** for my game development and not indexed color (GIF or PNG8) because if the OS is going to transmute the color to a 24-bit color "space," then we should utilize that 24-bit color space for quality reasons and deal with (accept) a slightly larger application file size.

Image color depth is the next most critical contributor to the data footprint of a compressed image, because the number of pixels in the image is multiplied by one (8-bit), two (16-bit), three (24-bit), or four (32-bit) color data channels. This small file size is the reason 8-bit indexed color images are still widely used, especially using the GIF image format.

Indexed color images can simulate true-color images, if the colors that are used to make up the image do not vary too widely. Indexed color imagery uses only 8 bits of data (256 colors) to define the image pixel color, using what is called a **palette** of up to 256 optimally selected colors, instead of 3 RGB color channels, or 4 ARGB color channels, containing 256 levels of color each. Again, it is important to note that after you turn a 24-bit image into an 8-bit image by compressing it, then once it is decompressed in system memory and turned back into a 24-bit RGB or ARGB data model used for the game (the representation used out of system memory), you only have a potential (maximum) 256 colors out of the original 16.8M colors to use! This is why I am advocating using PNG24 or PNG32 imagery, rather than GIFs or PNG1 (1-color), PNG2 (4-color), PNG4 (16-color), and PNG8 (256-color) images that JavaFX also supports.

Depending on how many colors are used in any given 24-bit source image, using 256 colors to represent an image originally containing 16,777,216 colors can cause an effect called **banding**. This is where the transfer between adjoining colors in the resulting (from compression) 256 (or less) color palette is not gradual and thus doesn't appear to be a smooth color gradient. Indexed color images have an option to visually correct for banding, called **dithering**.

Dithering is an **algorithmic process** of creating **dot patterns** along those edges between any adjoining colors within an image to trick the eye into thinking there's a third color used. Dithering will give you a maximum perceptual amount of colors of 65,536 colors (256x256), but this will occur (be necessary) only if each of those 256 colors borders one of the other (different) 256 colors. Still, you can see the potential for creating additional colors, and you would be amazed at the result that indexed color formats can achieve in some compression scenarios (with certain imagery).

Let's take a true-color image, such as the one that is shown in Figure 2-4, and save it as a **PNG5** indexed color image format to show you this dithering effect. It is important to note that PNG5, although supported in Android and HTML5, is not supported in JavaFX, so if you do this exercise yourself, select the PNG1 (2), PNG2 (4), PNG4 (16), or full PNG8 (256) color options!

Figure 2-4. *This is a true-color PNG24 image created with Autodesk 3ds Max that we are going to compress as PNG5*

We will take a look at the dithering effect on the driver-side rear fender on the Audi 3D image because it contains a gray gradient to which we will apply this dithering effect. You can see the 24-bit source digital imagery in Figure 2-4.

It is interesting to note that it is permissible to use **less than the 256** maximum colors that can be used for an 8-bit indexed color image. This is often done to further reduce the imagery's data footprint. For instance, an image that can attain good results by using only 32 colors is actually a **5-bit** image and would technically be called a **PNG5**, even though the format itself is generally called PNG8 for the indexed color usage level. Remember that JavaFX supports only PNG4 (16 colors) or PNG8 (256 colors), so for this image in a Java game, you would use PNG8, or 256 colors.

I will set this indexed color PNG5 image, shown in Figure 2-5, to use 5-bit color (32 colors) using Photoshop so that you can see this dithering effect clearly. As you can see, in the Photoshop image preview area on the left side of Figure 5-4, the dithering algorithm creates **dot patterns** between adjacent colors in order to create additional colors.

Figure 2-5. *Setting dithering to the Diffusion algorithm and 32 colors (5-bit color) with 100 percent dithering for PNG5 output*

Also, notice that you can set the **percentage of dithering** used. I often select either the 0 percent or 100 percent setting; however, you can **fine-tune** the dithering effect anywhere in between these two extreme values to fine-tune your resulting file size because these dithering dot patterns introduce more data to compress and increase file size.

You can also choose between **dithering algorithms** because, as you probably have surmised already, these different dithering effects are created mathematically by using dithering algorithms that are ultimately compatible with (supported by) indexed file format compression, which uses a **palette** to hold the color values used for the pixels.

I use **diffusion** dithering, which gives a smooth effect along irregularly shaped gradients, as is seen in the car fender. You can also use a **noise** option, which is more randomized, or a **pattern** option, which is less randomized. The diffusion option usually gives the best results, which is why I use it when I am using indexed color (which is not often).

Dithering, as you might imagine, adds data patterns into your images. These are more difficult to compress. This is because smooth areas in an image, such as gradients or fill areas, will generally be easier for these compression algorithms to compress, whereas sharp transitions (anti-aliased edges), or random pixel patterns usually generated by dithering, or possibly by "noise" from a camera with a substandard CCD, for instance.

Therefore, applying the dithering option will **always** increase the data footprint by a few percentage points. Be sure to check the resulting file size with and without dithering applied (selected in an export dialog) to see whether this is worth the improved visual result that it affords. Notice that there is also a **transparency** option check box for indexed color PNG images but that an alpha channel used in PNG8 images is only **1-bit** (on/off), not 8-bit like with PNG32.

The final concept that we have learned about so far that can increase the data footprint of your image is adding the **alpha channel** to define transparency for compositing. This is because adding the alpha channel will add in another 8-bit color channel (more accurately, a transparency or alpha channel) to the image being compressed. If you need an alpha channel to define transparency for the image, most likely to support future compositing requirements such as using the image as a game sprite, there's not a whole lot of choice in the matter, so include the alpha channel.

If your alpha channel contains all zeros (that is, uses an all-black fill color, which would define your imagery as being completely transparent) or if your alpha channel contains all FF values (or uses an all-white fill color, defining your image as being completely opaque or a background plate), you would essentially (in practical use) be defining an alpha channel that does not contain any useful alpha data values.

Unused alpha channels will therefore need to be removed, and an opaque image would need to be defined as a PNG24 rather than a PNG32 to save on the data footprint.

Finally, most alpha channels that are used to mask objects that are in the RGB layers of the digital image should compress very well. This is because they are largely areas of white (opaque) and black (transparent) with some medium gray values along the edges between the two colors to anti-alias your mask (see Figure 2-2). These gray areas that contain the **anti-aliasing transparency values** in the alpha channel, which will always provide you with visually smooth edge transitions, between the object in the RGB layers of the image, and **any** background color or background images that might be used behind it. Essentially, anti-aliasing in the alpha channel provides you with **real-time compositing** for the object that the alpha channel serves because you could put video behind it, in the background plate, and the alpha anti-aliasing will in real time guarantee a smooth edge result with different edge color blending on every single frame of the video.

The reason for this is that since your alpha channel image mask uses an 8-bit **transparency gradient**, ranging from white to black and defining levels of transparency rather than color, this should be thought of as **per-pixel blending**, or **opacity strength value**. Therefore, the medium gray values, on the edges of each object in a mask that is contained in the alpha channel, will serve to essentially **average** the colors of your object's edges and any target background, no matter what color value, image asset, illustration asset, animation asset, or video asset that a background plate might contain.

This provides real-time anti-aliasing with any target background that might be used, even if your object is a static object, because the anti-aliasing provided by your alpha channel will even work using animated backgrounds.

Digital Video or Animation: Frames, Frame Rate, Loops, Direction

It is interesting to note that all the concepts that we have just covered for digital images apply equally as well to **digital video** and **2D animation** since both of these fourth-dimensional (time-based) new media formats use digital images as a foundation for their content. Digital video, as well as 2D animation, extends digital imaging into the fourth dimension of time by introducing something called **frames**. Digital video and animation are comprised of an **ordered sequence of frames**, which are displayed rapidly over time to create the illusion of movement, bringing imagery alive.

The term *frame* comes from the film industry where even today film frames are run through film projectors, at a **frame rate** of **24 frames per second** (typically abbreviated as **24 FPS**). This creates the illusion of **motion**. Since both digital video and animation are made up of a collection of frames containing digital imagery, this concept of frame rate, expressed as frames per second, is also very important when it comes to both the memory data footprint optimization work process (for animation assets) and the digital video file size data footprint optimization work process. In JavaFX, as you will soon learn, this attribute for animation is stored in the **Animation** object's **rate** variable.

The optimization concept regarding frames in an **Animation** object or digital video asset is very similar to the optimization concept regarding pixels in the image (the resolution of a digital image); the fewer used, the better! This is because the number of frames used in an animation or video multiplies both the system memory used and the file size data footprint with each frame that is used. In digital video, not only does each frame's (image) resolution greatly impact the file size, but so does the **number of frames** per second, or frame rate, that is specified in the **compression settings** dialog. Earlier in this chapter, we learned that if we multiply the number of pixels in the image by its number of color channels, we'll get the raw data footprint for the image. With animation or digital video, we will now multiply that number again by the total number of frames that will need to be utilized in order to create an illusion of motion.

Therefore, if we have an animated VGA (RGB) background plate for our game (remember that each frame is 900KB) that uses five frames to create the illusion of motion, we are using 900KB times five, or 4500KB (or 4.5MB), of system memory to hold that animation. Of course, this is too much memory to use for a background, which is why we will be using static backgrounds with sprite overlays to achieve this same

41

end result during the book in less than a megabyte. The calculation for digital video is a bit different; as with digital video, you have hundreds, or thousands, of frames. For digital video you would multiply your raw image data size by the number of frames per second (the frame rate), which the digital video is set to play back at (this frame rate value is specified during the compression process), and then multiply that result by the total number of seconds of content duration, which is contained in your video file.

To continue with the VGA example used earlier, you now know a 24-bit VGA image is 900KB. This makes the calculation to take this to the next level very easy. Digital video traditionally runs at 30 FPS, so one second of **standard definition** (SD, or VGA) raw (uncompressed) digital video in system memory prior to play back on the screen would be 30 image frames, each of which is 900KB, yielding a total data footprint in memory of 27000KB, about 27MB!

You can see why having digital video compression file formats such as the **MPEG-4 H.264 AVC** format, which can significantly compress this massive raw data footprint that digital video can create, is extremely important.

The JavaFX multimedia package uses one of the most impressive **video compression codecs** (**codec** stands for **CO**de-**DEC**ode) that is also supported in HTML5 and Android: the aforementioned MPEG-4 H.264 Advanced Video Codec (AVC). This "cross open platform support" spanning the three major "open platforms" today (Java, HTML5, and Android) is extremely convenient for developer asset optimization because one single digital video asset can be used across Java, JavaFX, HTML5, and Android applications. There is also a "native" digital video codec, called VP6, included in the JavaFX engine in case H.264 is not installed. I am going to cover the basics of digital video asset compression and data footprint optimization next, before I get into digital audio, to be thorough. Then, in the next chapter, we will get into the complexities of 3D so you have a complete foundational understanding of new media elements in games.

Digital Video Compression Concepts: Bit Rate, Data Streaming, SD, HD, and UHD

Let's start out covering the primary or standard resolutions that are used in commercial video. These also happen to be common consumer electronics device screen resolutions, probably because if the display screen pixel resolution matches the video pixel resolution that is being played "full screen" on the screen, there will be zero "scaling," which can cause **scaling artifacts**. Before HDTV or high definition came along, video was called **standard definition (SD)** and used a standard pixel vertical resolution of **480 pixels**. VGA is an SD resolution, and **720 by 480** could be called **Wide SD** resolution. **High Definition (HD)** video comes in two resolutions, **1280 by 720**, which I call **Pseudo HD**, and **1920 by 1080**, which the industry calls **true HD**. Both HD resolutions feature a **16:9** aspect ratio and are used in TV and iTV sets, smartphones, tablets, e-book readers, and game consoles. There is also an **UHD** resolution out now that features 4096 by 2160 pixels. IMAX resolution was 4096 by 4096, so UHD has IMAX resolution in the horizontal, or x-axis, resolution, which is pretty impressive since consumers can now have IMAX in their living rooms for $1,000!

Video streaming is a more complicated concept than resolution because it involves playing back video data over a wide expanse, such as the one between your Java game application and the remote video data servers that will hold your potentially massive digital video assets. Streaming is complicated because the device that your Java game app is running on will be communicating, in real time, with remote data servers, receiving **video data packets** as the video plays! This is why it is termed *streaming*; as the video is streaming from the video server over the Internet and into the hardware devices. Video streaming is supported by the MPEG-4 H.264 AVC format codec (encoder-decoder pair).

The last concept that we need to cover in this section is the concept of **bit rate**. Bit rate is the key setting used in the video compression process; bit rates represent your **target bandwidth**, or **data pipe size**, that is able to accommodate a **certain number of bits streaming through it every second**. Your bit-rate setting should also take into consideration the CPU processing power that exists within any given Java-capable device, making your digital video's data optimization even more challenging. Fortunately, most devices these days feature dual-core or quad-core CPUs!

The reason for this is because once these bits travel through a data pipe, they also need to be **processed** and **displayed** onto the device screen. Thus, bit rates for digital video assets need to be optimized not only for bandwidth but in anticipation of variances in CPU processing power. Some single-core CPUs may not be able to decode high-resolution, high-bit-rate digital video assets without **dropping** frames. Make sure to optimize low-bit-rate video assets if you are going to target older, or less expensive, consumer electronics devices, like those used in third-world nations.

Digital Video Data Footprint Optimization: Important Settings for Video Codecs

As you have learned in the previous section, digital video assets are compressed using software utilities called *codecs*. There are two "sides" to the video codec: one that **encodes** the video data stream and the other that **decodes** the video data stream. The video decoder will be part of your OS, platform (JavaFX), or browser that uses it. The decoder is primarily optimized for **speed**, as smoothness of playback is a key issue, and the encoder is optimized to **reduce the data footprint** for the digital video asset it is generating. For this reason, the encoding process can take a longer time and depends on how many processing cores a workstation contains. Most digital video content production workstations should support eight processor cores, like my 64-bit AMD OctaCore workstation.

Codecs (the encoder side) are like plug-ins, in the sense that they can be installed into different digital video editing software packages in order to enable them to encode different digital video asset file formats. Since Java and JavaFX 9 support the ON2 VP6 format natively and MPEG4, if it's installed, you'll need to make sure you're using one of the digital video packages that supports encoding digital video using one of these digital video file formats.

It's important to note that more than one software manufacturer makes MPEG4 encoding software, so there will be different MPEG4 H.264 AVC codecs that will yield different (better or worse) results, as far as encoding speeds and file size go. I prefer the **MainConcept H.264** codec. A professional solution, which I highly recommend that you secure if you want to produce digital video professionally, is called **Sorenson Squeeze Pro**, and it supports ON2 VP6.

I will show you the digital video compression setting (Presets) dialog for Sorenson Squeeze Pro in Figure 2-6, and then we will go over some of these important settings during the remainder of this section of the chapter.

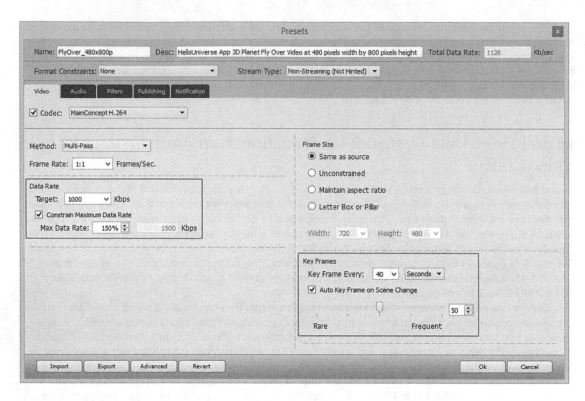

Figure 2-6. *Digital video compression Presets dialog for the Sorenson Squeeze Pro digital video compression utility*

There is also an open source solution called EditShare LightWorks 14, which is scheduled to natively support output to open source codecs (by 2018). For now, I will have to use Squeeze Pro 11 for this book, until codec support for JavaFX (and HTML5 and Android) is added to EditShare LightWorks 14 sometime during 2018. When optimizing for (setting compression settings for) digital video data file size, there are a large number of variables that directly affect the digital video data footprint. I'll cover these in the order in which they affect a video file size, from the most impact to the least impact, so that you know which parameters to tweak to obtain the result you're looking for.

As with digital image compression, the resolution, or number of pixels, in each frame of video is the optimal place to start the optimization process. If your user is using 1024x640 or **1280x720** smartphones, e-readers, or tablets, then you don't need to use true HD, 1920 by 1080 resolution, to get good visual results for your digital video assets. With today's super-fine density (small dot pitch) displays, you could scale a 1280 video up 33 percent, and it will look reasonably good. The exception to this might be HD or UHD (popularly termed 4K iTV) games targeted at iTV sets; for these huge 65- to 96-inch screen scenarios, you would want to use industry-standard true HD at **1920x1080** resolution.

The next level of optimization would come in the **number of frames used for each second** of video (or **FPS**), assuming the actual number of seconds in the digital video itself can't be shortened. This is known as the *frame rate*, and instead of setting the **video standard 30 FPS** frame rate, seen at the top left of Figure 2-6, set to 1:1, or one frame compressed for each source frame, consider using the **film standard** frame rate of 24 FPS or even a **multimedia standard** frame rate of **20 FPS**. You might even be able to use a **15 FPS** frame rate, which is half of the video standard 30 FPS, which would equate to a 1:2 setting for the Frame Rate field shown in Figure 2-6, depending upon the amount of (and speed of) movement within the content. Note that 15 FPS is **half as much data** as 30 FPS (a 100 percent reduction in data encoded).

For some video content, this will play back (look) the same as the 30 FPS content. The only way to test this is to try different frame rate settings and observe the results during your video optimization (encoding) process.

The next most optimal setting for obtaining a smaller data footprint would be the **bit rate** that you set for a codec to try to achieve. This is shown on the left side of Figure 2-6, encircled in red. Bit rate equates to the **amount of compression applied** and thus sets the **quality level** for the digital video data. It is important to note that you could simply use 30 FPS, 1920-resolution HD video and specify a low-bit-rate ceiling. If you do this, the results would not be as professional looking as they would be if you first experimented with compression using a lower frame rate and (or) a lower resolution, in conjunction with using the higher (quality) bit-rate setting. There is no set rule of thumb for this, as every digital video asset contains 100 percent different and unique data (from a codec algorithm's point of view, that is).

The next most effective setting for obtaining a smaller data footprint is the number of **keyframes**, which the codec uses to **sample** your digital video asset. This setting is seen encircled in red on the right side of Figure 2-6. Video codecs apply compression by looking at each frame and then encoding any pixel changes over the next several frames so the codec algorithm doesn't have to encode every single frame in a video data stream. This is why a talking head video will encode better than a video where every pixel moves on every frame (like video with camera panning).

A keyframe is the setting in a codec that forces the codec to take a **fresh sampling** of the video data asset every so often. There is usually an **auto setting** for keyframes, which allows a codec to decide how many keyframes to sample, as well as a **manual setting**, which allows you to specify a keyframe sampling every so often, usually a certain number of times per second or a certain number of times over the duration of the entire video (the total frames).

Some codec setting dialogs have either a **quality** or **sharpness** setting (a slider) that controls the amount of **blur** applied to the video frame before compression. In case you don't know this trick, applying a slight blur to your image or video, which is usually not desirable, can allow for better compression as sharp transitions (sharp edges) in an image are harder to encode (these take more data to reproduce) than softer transitions are. That said, I'd keep the quality (or sharpness) slider between an 85 percent and 100 percent quality level and then try to get your data footprint reduction using the other variables that we have discussed here, such as decreasing the resolution, frame rate, or bit rate.

Ultimately, there will be a number of variables that you'll need to fine-tune to achieve the best data footprint optimization for any given digital video data asset. It is important to remember that each digital video asset will "look" different (mathematically) from a digital video codec. For this reason, there can be no standard settings that can be developed to achieve any given compression result. That said, experience tweaking various settings will eventually allow you to get a better feel, over time, as to the various settings that you need to change to get the desired end result.

Digital Audio Concepts: Amplitude, Frequency, Samples, Waves

Those of you who are audiophiles already know that sound is created by sending sound waves pulsing through the air. Digital audio is complex; part of the complexity comes from the need to bridge "analog" audio technology created with speaker cones with digital audio codecs. Analog speakers generate sound waves by pulsing them into existence. Our ears receive analog audio in exactly the opposite fashion, catching and receiving those pulses of air, or vibrations with different wave lengths, and then turning them back into "data" that our brain can process. This is how we "hear" the sound waves; our brain then interprets different audio sound wave frequencies as different notes or tones.

Sound waves generate various **tones** depending on the **frequency** of each sound wave. A wide or infrequent (long) wave produces a low (bass) tone, whereas a more frequent (short) wavelength produces a higher (treble) tone. It's interesting to notice that different frequencies of light will produce different colors, so there is a close correlation between analog sound (audio) and analog light (color). There are many other similarities between digital images (and video) and digital audio that will carry through into your digital new media content production, as you will soon see.

The **volume** of a sound wave will be determined by the **amplitude** of the sound wave or the **height** (or size) of that wave. Thus, frequency of sound waves equates to how **closely together** the waves are spaced, along the **x-axis**, if you are looking at it in 2D, and the amplitude equates to how tall the waves are, as measured along the **y-axis**.

Sound waves can be uniquely shaped, allowing sound waves to "piggyback" various sound effects. A "pure," or baseline, type of sound wave is called a **sine wave**, which you learned about in high school trigonometry, using the **sine**, **cosine**, and **tangent** math functions. Those of you who are familiar with **audio synthesis** are aware that there are other types of sound waves that are utilized in sound design, such as the **saw wave** that looks like the edge of a saw (hence its name) or the **pulse wave** that is shaped using only right angles, resulting in immediate on and off sounds that translate into pulses (or bursts) of synthesized digital audio.

Even randomized waveforms, such as noise, are used in sound design to obtain "edgy" sound results. As you may have ascertained by using your recently acquired knowledge regarding data footprint optimization, the more "chaos" or noise that is present in the sound waves (and in new media data in general), the harder they will be to compress for a codec. Therefore, more complex sound waves will result in larger digital audio file sizes because of the chaos in the data.

Converting Analog Audio to Digital Audio Data: Sampling, Accuracy, and HD Audio

The process of turning analog audio (sound waves) into digital audio data is called **sampling**. If you work in the music industry, you have probably heard about a type of keyboard (or even rack-mount equipment) that is called a **sampler**. Sampling is the process of **slicing** an analog audio wave into **segments** so that you can store the **shape** of the wave as digital audio data using a digital audio format. This turns an infinitely accurate analog sound wave into a discreet amount of digital data, that is, into zeroes and ones. The more zeroes and ones used, the more accurate the reproduction of the infinitely accurate (original) analog sound wave. Each digital segment of a sampled audio sound wave is called a sample, because it samples that sound wave at that exact point in time. The **sample accuracy** determines how many zeroes and ones are used to reproduce analog sound waves, so the **precision** of a sample is determined by how much data is used to define each wave slice's **height**. Figure 2-7 shows a button sound effect that I sampled using Audacity, using a **32-bit** float sample accuracy and a **48 kHz** sampling rate, which we will cover next.

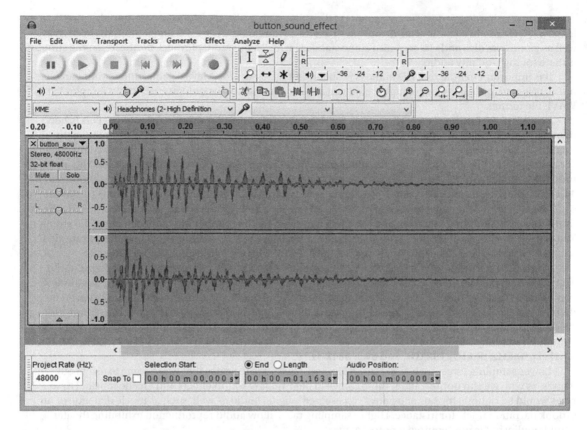

Figure 2-7. *Stereo sample of button sound effect in Audacity using 32-bit float sample accuracy and 48kHz sample rate*

Just like with digital imaging, this **sampling accuracy precision** is termed the **resolution** or, more accurately (no pun intended), the **sampling resolution**. Sample resolution is usually defined using **8-bit**, **12-bit**, **16-bit**, **24-bit**, or **32-bit** resolution. Java games mostly leverage the **8-bit** resolution for effects such as explosions where clarity is not as important, use **12-bit** resolution for crystal-clear spoken dialog and more important audio effects assets, and possibly use CD quality 16-bit resolution for background music or audio elements that need to exhibit pristine audio quality.

In digital imaging and digital video, this resolution is quantified in the number of pixels, and in digital audio, this resolution is quantified in how many bits of data are used to define each of the analog audio samples taken. Just like in digital imaging (more pixels yields better quality), a higher sample resolution yields better sound reproduction. Thus, higher sampling resolutions, using more data to reproduce a given sound wave sample, will yield a higher audio playback quality, at the expense of a larger data footprint. This is the reason why 16-bit audio, commonly termed **CD-quality audio**, will sound better than 8-bit audio. Depending on the audio involved, 12-bit can be a good compromise.

In digital audio, there is a new type of 24-bit audio sample, known as *HD audio*, in the consumer electronics industry. HD digital audio broadcast radio uses 24-bit sample resolution. Each audio sample, or slice of a sound wave, can potentially contain up to 16,777,216 bits of sound wave sampling resolution, although all the bits are rarely used.

Some new hardware devices now support HD audio, such as the smartphones you see advertised, featuring "HD-quality" audio. This means they have 24-bit audio hardware. PC and laptops these days, as well as game consoles and iTV sets, also come standard with 24-bit audio playback hardware, so the support is there for high-quality audio.

It is important to note that HD audio is probably not necessary for a Java 9 game, unless your game is music oriented and makes use of high-quality music, in which case you could use HD audio samples via a **WAVE** file format.

Besides digital audio sample resolution, we also have a digital audio **sample frequency**. This is how many of these samples at a particular sample resolution are taken during one second of sampling time frame. In digital image editing, the sampling frequency would be analogous to the number of colors that are contained within a digital image. Sampling frequency can also be called the **sampling rate**. You are probably familiar with the term *CD-quality* audio, which is defined as using a **16-bit** sample resolution and a **44.1 kHz** sampling rate. This is taking 44,100 samples, each of which contains 16 bits of sample resolution, or 65,536 bits of audio data held in each of these 44,100 samples. You can figure out raw data in an audio file by multiplying the sampling bit rate by the sampling frequency by the number of seconds in the audio snippet. You can see that it can potentially be a huge number! Audio codecs are really great at optimizing sampled sound wave data down to an amazingly small data footprint with very little audible loss in quality.

Thus, the same trade-off that we have in digital imaging and in digital video exists with digital audio. The more data that we include, the more high quality of a result that we will obtain! However, this always comes at the cost of a much larger data footprint. In the visual mediums, the amount of data footprint is defined using color depth, pixels, and, in the case of digital video and animation, frames. In a digital audio medium, it is defined with the sampling resolution, in combination with the sampling rate. The most common sampling rates in the digital audio industry currently include **8kHz, 11.25 kHz, 22.5kHz, 32kHz, 44.1kHz, 48kHz, 96kHz, 192kHz**, and even **384kHz**.

Lower sampling rates, such as 8kHz, 22kHz, and 32kHz, are the ones that we're going to use in our games, as with careful optimization, these can yield high-quality sound effects and arcade music. These rates would be optimal for sampling any "voice-based" digital audio as well, such as movie dialogue or an e-book narration track, for instance. Higher sampling rates allow audio reproduction exhibiting theater sound quality but is not required for most games.

Digital Audio Asset Playback: Captive Audio Playback vs. Streaming Audio

Just like with digital video data, digital audio data can be **captive**, held within the application distribution file (in the case of Java, this is a **JAR** file); alternately, the digital audio can be **streamed** using remote data servers. Similar to digital video, the upside to streaming digital audio data is that it can reduce the data footprint of the application file, just as streaming digital video data can. The downside is reliability. Many of the same concepts apply equally well to audio and video. Streaming audio will save data footprint because you do not have to include all of that heavy new media digital audio data in your JAR files, so if you are planning on coding a jukebox application, you may want to consider streaming your digital audio data. Otherwise, try to optimize your digital audio data so that you can include it (captive) inside the JAR file. In this way, it will always available to the application's users when they need it!

The downside to streaming digital audio is that if a user's connection (or the audio data server) goes down, your digital audio file may not always be present for your end users to play and listen to using your game application. The reliability and availability of digital audio data are key factors to be considered on the other side of this "streaming audio data versus captive digital audio data" trade-off. The same trade-off would apply to digital video assets as well.

Just like with digital video, one of the primary concepts in regard to streaming your digital audio is your bit rate for that digital audio data. As you learned in the previous section, this bit rate is defined during your compression process. As with digital video, digital audio files that need to support lower bit-rate bandwidth are going to have more compression applied to the audio data, which will result in lower quality. These will stream (play back) more smoothly across a greater number of devices because fewer bits can be quickly transferred, as well as processed, more easily.

Digital Audio Assets in JavaFX: Digital Audio Codec and Data Format Support

There are considerably more **digital audio codecs** in JavaFX than there are digital video codecs, as there are only two video codecs, which are MPEG-4 H.264 AVC or ON2 VP6. JavaFX audio support includes **MP3** (**MPEG3**) files, Windows **Wave** (**Pulse Code Modulated [PCM]** audio) **WAV** files, **MP4** (or M4A) **MPEG-4 AAC** audio, and Apple's **AIFF** (PCM) file format. The most common audio format supported by JavaFX is the MP3 digital audio file format. The reason the MP3 digital audio file format is popular is because it has a good compression to quality ratio and is widely supported.

MP3 would be an acceptable digital audio format to use in a Java game or IoT application, as long as you get the highest quality level possible out of it, using an optimal encoding work process. It's important to note that MP3 is a **lossy** audio file format, like JPEG uses for digital images, where some of the audio data, and therefore some of your original audio sample quality, is **thrown away** during your compression process and cannot later be recovered.

JavaFX does have two **lossless** audio compression codecs, called AIFF and WAVE. You are probably familiar with these digital audio formats, as they are the original audio formats used for the Apple and Microsoft Windows operating systems, respectively. These files use PCM audio, which is lossless, in this case, because there is *no* compression applied whatsoever! Pulse Code Modulated refers to the data format it holds.

PCM audio is commonly used for CD-ROM content, as well as telephony applications. This is because PCM Wave audio is an **uncompressed** digital audio format, and it has no CPU-intensive compression algorithms applied to the data stream; thus, decoding (CPU data processing) is not an issue for telephony equipment or for CD players.

For this reason, when we start compressing digital audio assets into these various file formats, we will use PCM as our **baseline** file format. Not only can we look at the difference between the PCM (Wave) and MP3 or MP4 audio compression results to get an idea of how much data footprint optimization we are getting for our JAR file, but more importantly, we can see how our sample resolution and sample frequency optimization are going to affect system memory used for our game audio effects. Even if we used MP3 or MP4 format, it would still have to be decompressed into memory before the audio asset can be used with the **AudioClip** class, and used as a sound effect, in a Java game.

Since a Wave or AIFF file will not have any quality loss because there is also no decompression needed, this Pulse Code Modulated data can be placed straight from the JAR file into system memory! This makes PCM audio great for game sound effects that are short in duration (0.1 to 1 second) and can be highly optimized, using 8-bit and 12-bit sample resolution and 8kHz, 22kHz, or 32kHz sample frequency. Ultimately, the only real way to find out which audio format supported by JavaFX has the best digital audio compression result for any given digital audio data is to actually encode your digital audio in the primary codecs that we know are supported and efficient. We will be going through this work process in Chapter 21 when we add audio to the game and will observe the relative data footprint results between the different formats using the same source audio sample. Then we will listen to the audio playback quality so that we can make our final **quality to file size** decision. This is the work process that you will need to go through to develop your JavaFX digital audio assets, for use in your pro Java game development work process.

JavaFX also supports the popular MPEG-4 **Advanced Audio Coding (AAC)** codec. This digital audio data can be contained in MPEG4 containers (.mp4, .m4a, .m4v) or file extensions and can all be played back using all operating systems. It's important to note that JavaFX does not contain an MPEG-4 decoder but instead supports what is called a "Multimedia Container." What this means is that it uses the host operating system's MPEG-4 decoder for decoding.

For this reason and because online listening studies have concluded that MP3 has better quality (for music) than the MP4 format, we will be using MP3 audio file format for **longer-form** audio (game background musical loops), which we'll use via the **Media** and **MediaPlayer** classes. We'll use the PCM Wave audio format for **short-form** audio (game sound effects, such as shots, bells, yelps, grunts, laughter, cheering, and similar, one-second long or less digital audio assets), which we will use via the **AudioClip** digital audio sequencing engine (class) that JavaFX so generously provides.

Digital Audio Optimization: Start with CD Quality Audio and Work Backward

Optimizing your digital audio assets for playback across the widest range of hardware devices in the market is going to be easier than optimizing your digital video or digital imagery (and thus animation) across hardware devices. This is because there is a much wider disparity of target screen resolutions and display aspect ratios than there is a disparity of digital audio playback hardware support across hardware devices (with the possible exception for new hardware featuring 24-bit HD audio playback hardware compatibility). All hardware plays digital audio assets well, so audio optimization is a "one audio asset hits all devices" scenario, whereas with the visual (video, image, animation) part of the equation, you have display screens as large as 4096x2160 pixels (4K iTV Sets) down to 320x320 pixels (flip phones and smart watches).

It's important to remember that a user's ears can't perceive the same quality difference with digital audio that a user's eyes can with digital imagery, 2D animation, or digital video. Generally, there are three primary "sweet spots" of digital audio support, across all hardware devices, which you should target for support for Java game audio.

Lower-quality audio, such as short narration tracks, character exclamations, or short-duration sound effects, can achieve remarkably high quality by using an **8 kHZ**, **11.25 kHz**, or **22.5 kHz** sampling rate, along with **8-bit** or **12-bit** sampling resolution. Medium-quality audio, like long narration tracks, long duration sound effects, looped background (termed: ambient) audio, and the like, can achieve a very high-quality level by using a **22.5 kHz** or **32 kHz** sampling rate along with a **12-bit** or **16-bit** sampling resolution.

High-quality audio assets, such as music, should be optimized approaching **CD-quality audio** and would use a **32 kHz** or **44.1 kHz** sampling rate, along with the **16-bit** data sampling resolution. For **HD-quality** audio, being at the ultra-high-end of this audio spectrum, you would use the **48 kHz** sampling rate, along with the **24-bit** digital audio data sampling resolution. There is also an unnamed "somewhere in the middle" high-end audio specification, using a **48 kHz** sampling rate along with a **16-bit** data sampling resolution, which just happens to be what Dolby THX used to use for its high-end audio experience technology. This was used in movie theaters "back in the day" for *Star Wars*.

Ultimately, it comes down to the quality to file size results that emerge from the digital audio data footprint optimization work process, which can yield some amazing results. Therefore, your initial work process for optimizing your digital audio assets across all of these hardware devices is going to be to create "baseline" 16-bit assets, either at 44.1 kHz or at 48 kHz, and then optimize (compress) them using the different formats supported in JavaFX. Once that work process is completed, you can see which resulting digital audio assets provide the smallest data footprint, along with the highest-quality digital audio playback. After that, you can reduce your 48 kHz or 44.1 kHz data to 32 kHz and save that out using 16-bit resolution and then using 12-bit resolution. After that, re-open the original 48 kHz data, **downsample** to 22.5 kHz sample frequency, and export that using 16-bit or 12-bit resolution, and so on, and so forth. We will be performing this work process later during this book, in Chapter 21, so that you'll have experience with the audio work process.

You'll perform this work process using the open source **Audacity 2.1.3** digital audio editing and engineering software package. You downloaded and installed this software package during Chapter 1, and ideally, you installed all of those free VST, Nyquist, LV2, and LADSPA plug-ins, as well as the LAME MPEG3 encoders and FFMPEG encoders for the AC3, AMR-NB, M4A, and WMA audio formats. You will want to do this, if you have not done so already, so that you have absolutely the most powerful digital audio editing and engineering suite possible for your Java workstation.

If you have not done this yet and don't feel like doing it now, I will show you how to do that in the chapter where we learn how to use the **AudioClip**, **Media**, and **MediaPlayer** classes to add digital audio elements to your Java 9 game environment. It's really quite simple; all that you have to do is to download these plug-ins and place them in the correct plug-ins folder underneath the primary Audacity software installation folder so it's not difficult to add effects.

Summary

In this second chapter, we took a closer look at some of the more important 2D new media concepts that we will be using in our pro Java game and IoT development work process so that you have a solid foundational knowledge for these 2D multimedia assets that JavaFX 8 support has taken care of adding to your Java 9 environment. Note that Java and JavaFX releases are not synchronized, so for instance Java 6 used JavaFX 1.*x* and Java 7 used JavaFX 2.*x*. They are getting closer to synchronizing the releases, as Java 8 used JavaFX 8, but the focus in Java 9 is modularizing the language, and not on JavaFX 9, so for now, the Java 9 platform may start out using JavaFX 8 technology.

I started out covering the most important and foundational 2D new media concepts as they relate to Java FX 8, which is the new media engine for Java 8 and Java 9, as well as to Android, iOS, Windows, Linux OS, and HTML5 development, for that matter. New media concepts are as important to understand for games developers as Java 9 and JavaFX coding practices, as new media makes your game more immersive, compelling, and visually exciting. I have a series of new media "fundamentals" books at www.apress.com if you want to dive deeper into these new media topics. Each of the books focuses specifically on one new media vertical (audio, video, VFX, illustration, painting, etc.).

Since 3D is considerably more complex, I saved that foundational information for Chapter 3; I wanted to keep the chapters in this book at reasonable lengths to optimally digest all of this technical information. 3D and i3D new media assets are distinctly different from 2D and i2D new media assets, as these add an entirely new dimension, depth data, and the z-axis to the already complex undertaking of scratch new media content creation. This serves to turn basic 2D (area) math into vector or matrix algebra (BA level to MS or PhD level); thus, 3D is an order of magnitude more complex than 2D.

We also took a look at some fairly advanced digital imaging concepts, JavaFX-supported formats, techniques, and data footprint optimization. This information will allow you to extract the maximum utility and performance from every pixel you utilize inside of your pro Java games or IoT applications.

You learned all about **pixels**, **resolutions**, and how **aspect ratios** define the shape of an image, animation, or video, as well as about **color depth**, **layers**, **channels**, and how **alpha channel** transparency allows you to implement **image compositing pipelines**. You learned how to define colors, as well as alpha channel transparency values, by using **hexadecimal notation**. We looked at advanced digital imaging concepts such as masking, dithering, anti-aliasing, and blending and transfer modes.

Next, we looked at the fourth dimension of time and learned about how frames, frame rates, and bit rates are used in conjunction with the concepts that we learned about in the digital imaging section to add motion to our new media assets, creating 2D animation or digital video. We looked at different formats and the codecs that encode them and looked at some of the software packages that will edit and encode digital video, such as DaVinci Resolve, Lightworks, and Sorenson Squeeze.

Finally, we looked at digital audio, and we learned about sampling frequency and sampling resolution, as well as the MP3 and PCM audio formats supported by JavaFX, and how to use these codecs to optimize digital audio to use the least amount of system memory. We looked at how to get the smallest data footprint for our pro Java 9 games and IoT applications, while still putting a high-quality product into the game and app stores.

In the next chapter, we're going to take a look at the **3D and i3D** concepts, principles, formats, optimization, and work processes that we will be using for your pro Java 9 games and IoT applications. You will get a feel for how complex 3D is relative to 2D new media assets, as we look at things such as 3D character modeling, bones, rigging and animation, particle systems, physical systems (physics forces), fluid dynamics, visual effects (VFX) and special effects (SFX), texture mapping, shaders, and UVW mapping coordinates.

CHAPTER 3

■ ■ ■

Advanced 3D Content Rendering: 3D Asset Concepts and Principles

Now that you have learned about the 2D (raster and audio) content development concepts and principles that your 2D new media open source content development software packages (GIMP, Lightworks, Audacity, and DaVinci Resolve) are based on, we will finish up learning about new media assets by taking a look at Inkscape (2D vector, or shapes), Blender (3D vector, or polygons), and Fusion (2D and 3D visual effects) during this chapter. The reason we are covering Inkscape 2D in this chapter, instead of in the 2D content chapter, is because we can use the basic concepts regarding how 2D vector graphics work as our conceptual bridge between 2D vector graphics and 3D vector graphics. This is because 3D vectors work just like 2D vectors do in the 2D X and Y dimensions, only in the 3D X,Y,Z dimensions. For this reason, we'll start this chapter by learning about Inkscape 2D vector illustration, or digital illustration, so that we can build onto this 2D vector knowledge and then learn about more complex 3D vector graphics software packages.

I first cover the underlying concepts of **vertices** (points) and **splines** (lines or curves connecting points) since these provide the foundation for **2D shapes** or **3D geometry**. This is important because this is the foundation you will build upon whether you decide to become a 2D vector illustrator or a 3D vector modeler (or both). Working with vertices and splines can become an entire profession, so be sure to master these first few sections.

Next, we will get into how you turn an empty 2D shape or a 3D wireframe into something solid looking. This is done using **color fills**, **gradients**, or **pattern fills** for 2D shapes (these can also be used with 3D models) and by using **texture maps** for 3D geometry. Texture maps use **UVW maps** to position the 2D texture maps onto the 3D geometry.

After we have covered all of those concepts that apply to both the 2D and 3D space, we can get into things that are encountered only in 3D. These include **3D rendering**, which is the process of turning **3D models**, which have 3D geometry along with 2D texture maps attached with 3D UVW texture mapping coordinates, into **3D imagery**. I call 3D imagery *static* 3D since the 3D technology is being used to make images that do not move and thus are static, or fixed. There's also **3D animation**, which features movement, much like digital video does, and **Interactive 3D (i3D)** where programming logic is embedded inside 3D objects or scene hierarchy, which is the most advanced level of 3D.

Animation gets into a fourth dimension of time, just like digital video does, and 3D animation adds another layer of complexity into the 3D new media asset development work process. 3D animation utilizes keyframes just like digital video does, so all of those same concepts apply, such as frame rates; it also has some other concepts, such as **motion curves**, which are supported by JavaFX and which change the rate of acceleration and deceleration to provide realistic movement to your 3D animation, as well as your 2D animation in JavaFX, as they are separate functions.

Interactive 3D involves inserting code into an object hierarchy called a **Scene Graph**, which holds the assets, as well as the code and other elements, in a hierarchical format. Scene Graphs were invented by 3D software packages back in the Amiga days. The 3D software package that originated this design and development approach was Real 3D, by Realsoft OY, which today is called Realsoft 3D. Fortunately, JavaFX 9 also has an extensive Scene Graph API, which makes it perfect for creating both Interactive 3D and Interactive 2D games and IoT applications.

Interactive 2D Assets: 2D Vector Content Concepts

There is one other type of 2D asset that we didn't cover in detail in Chapter 2 as its concepts relate directly to 3D, so I decided to logically put this information at the beginning of this chapter so the information flowed together better. 2D and 3D are very similar in their use of **vertices** and **splines**, which we will be learning about next. 2D uses the **X,Y** dimension, which is a flat plane (or **planar** area, if you will), and 3D uses the X,Y,Z dimension (which is a **cubic** area, if you will).

Therefore, in this section, we will look at how to create 2D vector illustration by placing points, or vertices, in 2D space and then connecting them together by using straight lines, or curved splines, and filling closed shapes with solid colors, color gradients, or tiling image patterns. JavaFX 9 offers a plethora of 2D classes supporting each of these 2D elements, as well as a **SVGPath** class, used for importing all of these 2D data elements, if you choose to use Inkscape.

The 2D assets or objects that you will use in Java using the JavaFX APIs are generally called *shapes*, although they are technically also *geometry* since shapes are inherently geometric! Typically in the industry, 3D is referred to as *3D Geometry*, and 2D is referred to as *2D Shapes*. The foundation of both 2D and 3D assets start with points in space called *vertices*. These are connected with (straight) lines or (nonstraight) curves. Let's look at these next.

Points on a Plane: 2D Vertices, Model Reference Origin, Pivot Point, Dummy Point

Now don't get excited—this is not the sequel to *Snakes on a Plane*; it's just a discussion regarding the foundation of 2D shapes, which, like 3D models, are based on points in space. Since 2D space consists of an X,Y plane, we place points on a 2D plane. Each point in space is called a *vertex* in professional terminology, since this is *Pro Java 9 Games Development* after all. You can use these vertices both in planar X,Y space for your 2D shape creation and in cubic X,Y,Z space for 3D geometry creation, which we will be covering later during this chapter.

The reason I subtitled this section "Points on a Plane" is because vertices are placed in 2D space using an X,Y grid on a 2D plane and in an X,Y,Z cubic area in 3D space. The **origin** of this 2D grid is located at 0,0. Usually this is the upper-left corner of the screen, and for the 3D cubic area, this referencing origin would be located 0,0,0.

For both 2D shapes and 3D objects, this origin can be **relocated**, so different packages will reference this grid from a different corner of the plane or cube. You will see this later in JavaFX, which has different ways to reference coordinates. Another reference point inside of that plane or cubic area is used for the rotation of your 2D or 3D object and is called the **pivot point**.

For instance, if you wanted your hammer 2D shape (or 3D model) to rotate near the end of the handle, as it would be rotated in real life, you would accomplish this by moving the pivot from the default (center) position in your 2D (or 3D) modeling space down toward the end of the handle of the hammer. For this application, your pivot point will then become the center for the **axis** for that object. The pivot point is a referencing origin for how the asset needs to be rotated, whereas the grid (space) origin will provide a reference for how the points will be positioned relative to each other. Thus, a rotation algorithm will use both the modeling grid origin as well as the pivot point position. These are usually different point coordinates; however, it is possible that they can be the same point, in some scenarios.

Both origins and pivots represent that point in space using an axis. This axis can be moved and looks like a star in 3D software and like a plus symbol in 2D software. In fact, an axis is really a separate object within a 2D shape or 3D geometry, and it can even be animated just like every other 2D or 3D object element can, using JavaFX and Java code, to create special effects relating to how the shape or geometry rotates over time. There's also a "dummy point" used for special effects and advanced applications that is very similar to a pivot but used for other purposes that is also represented using an axis. You'll see later during the book how important this axis element is for Java games.

Connect the 2D Dots: Vector Lines and Spline Curves Connect Your 2D Vertices

Since vertices are mathematically infinitely small, making these tiny dots essentially invisible, you will need to connect them to make something that you can visualise. The simplest incarnation of this is a straight line, known as a **vector** (also sometimes termed a **ray** in 3D rendering). A vector starts at one vertex and projects out until it hits a second vertex, which defines the **direction** of the vector. A vector is inherently straight, so it would be considered a **line**, not a curve. A curve is mathematically far more complex than a straight line is, as you are about to see.

Since we often want an **infinitely smooth** curve as part of our 2D shape or 3D geometry, we will need to use a different type of mathematical construct, called a **spline**. The reason why a spline is infinitely smooth is because it is a curvature that is defined using a mathematical equation, the resolution of which can be increased by using smaller numbers such as by using floating-point numbers rather than integers, for all of you computer programmers out there (which I am hoping is everyone, given the professional nature of this *Pro Java 9 Games Development* book).

The mathematical foundation for most types of splines is called the **Bezier** curve, which was named after the mathematician **Pierre Étienne Bézier**, who was a French engineer who lived from 1910 to 1999. Pierre was one of the founders of the fields of 3D solids, geometric modeling, and physical modeling, as well as the leader in the specialty area of representing curves, especially in CAD CAM and 3D systems. There are several mathematical formats for Bézier curves, including cubic or quadratic Bézier curves, which are defined using different types of mathematical equations that define how each curve is to be constructed.

The simplest of these curves is the **Linear Bézier** curve, which can be used to create straight-line (vector) rays and which uses only two control points to define your curve. If you can get your shapes defined using only Linear Bezier curves, less processing and memory will be used by your game or IoT application. This is because fewer control points will need to be processed. As you can see in the top part of Figure 3-1, Inkscape draws control points and their handles using blue. If you want to try this in Inkscape, click the **Spline/Line tool**, shown on the left of Figure 3-1, and click to create a point, click a second point somewhere else to add a straight line, and then click a third point and drag to create a curve! It's fairly easy once you get the hang of it; that being said, the truth is, everything you learn in this book takes tons of practice to master at a professional level.

To adjust the curvature of the Linear Bezier curve, you can move each of the two handles that come out of the vertex you just added. If you want a straight line, just click to add vertices, and straight lines will connect them. On the other hand, if you want to make a curve, click down to add the vertex, and with the mouse still clicked (keep your mouse depressed), drag out the Bezier curve control point handles.

The next most complex type of Bezier curve is a **Quadratic Bézier** curve, named after the type of quadratic mathematical algorithm that is used to prescribe it. A Quadratic Bezier has three control points instead of two, so it is more processing intensive but provides more control over "tweaking" the curvature of the curve by using the handles.

The most complex is the **Cubic Bézier** curve, named after the type of cubic mathematical algorithm that is used to prescribe it, and it has four control points, instead of three, so it is even more processing intensive, but again, it provides even more control over tweaking the curvature of the curve.

In Adobe Illustrator, control points are subdivided into using handles and anchor points. The handle positions that are used to influence the curvature are the handles. The anchor points are the vertices describing the start and end positions of the Bézier curve. Inkscape uses a different term for an anchor point, calling it a node.

There is also a 3D modeling approach called **NURBS**, or **Non-Uniform Rational B-Spline**, which is related to a Bezier spline representation but optimized for use in 3D X,Y,Z space. A NURBS is more complex and allows a smooth, organic 3D geometry representation to be created. **Moment of Inspiration 3D** by Michael Gibson is one of the really affordable NURBS modelers, at only $295; it is based on the original SGI Alias Wavefront NURBS Modeler API.

Filling the Shape Interior: Color Fills, Gradients, and Patterns

If the 2D shapes that you create using these vertices and splines (or vectors/lines) are **closed**, then they can be **filled** with various things such as solid colors, color gradients, or tiled image patterns. This is shown on the bottom portion of Figure 3-1. To close a curve, draw your final vector (line) or spline (curve) until your mouse cursor is over the starting vertex, and when that vertex changes (in Inkscape, it turns from black to red), click down to create a closed shape. To fill the shape you just closed in Inkscape, click the **Fill** tool, shown on the left along with the Spline/Line tool and their tooltips, and then click the color, along the bottom swatches, to fill the selected shape with that color.

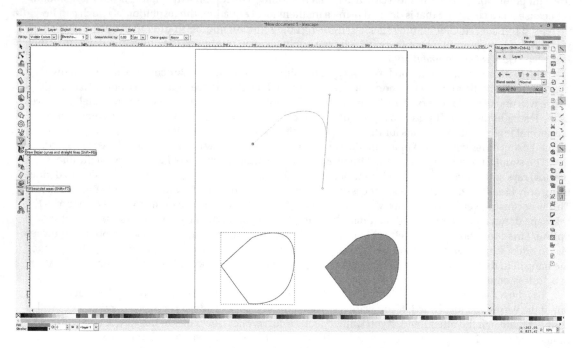

Figure 3-1. *Creating an open shape in Inkscape using vectors and splines, closing that shape, and then filling the shape*

The 2D vector shape file format used by both Inkscape and JavaFX is Scalable Vector Graphics (SVG), so if you save your Inkscape project, it will use the .svg extension, like ProjectName.svg, for instance. If you want to learn more about SVG, take a look at *Digital Illustration Fundamentals* from Apress.com. Next let's take a look at i3D media assets, which are fully supported in Java 8 and 9 using the JavaFX 9 new media engine.

Interactive 3D Assets: 3D Vector Content Concepts

The most advanced type of multimedia asset is an interactive 3D vector object, which can be created using Java and the JavaFX API (classes and methods) or using a combination of this approach with 3D modeling packages (such as those discussed in Chapter 1) or with 3D animation packages (such as Autodesk 3ds Max, which is what I have used since its first version; 3D Studio DOS; or Blender, which is nearing a similar level of professional features). i3D assets are comprised of 3D vector geometry, surfaced using 2D raster imagery (which we learned about in Chapter 2), and contain programming logic inside of their model and scene hierarchy that will bring them to life.

We will learn about how a 3D object goes from a mesh to a surfaced model during this section of the chapter. We'll also look at animation, motion curves, object hierarchies, axis placement, dummy objects, particle systems, fluid dynamics, hair and fur dynamics, rigid body dynamics, soft body dynamics, cloth dynamics, rope dynamics, and related 3D topics during this chapter. As you can see, 3D is by far the most complex and interesting new media type.

These 3D objects can further be made to be **interactive** by using programming logic inside of a Scene Graph object hierarchy, which defines what each part of the 3D object will do and which is an integral part of JavaFX 9. Let's start from the ground up. I'll show you the various attributes that take a 3D asset from being 3D geometry to being a 3D model to being a 3D hierarchy to being a 3D object. This is the most involved multimedia and is the least common new media asset type to be found in HTML5 (using WebGL2), Android 8 (using Vulkan), and Java 8 and 9 using JavaFX.

The Foundation of 3D: The Geometry of the Mesh

The lowest level of your 3D new media elements is, just as with 2D shape new media elements, the vertices and the connections between those vertices. In 3D you will still have vertices, but the connections between them become a bit more complicated. In 2D, the vertices, vectors (rays or lines), and splines (curves) between themselves are empty (nonfilled), closed shapes or open shapes, which cannot be filled because they are open and will spill over. Connections between 3D geometry (which before it is texture mapped is sometimes referred to in the 3D industry as a *mesh* or *wireframe* since that is what 3D geometry looks like before it is texture mapped, or skinned), are called "edges" between vertices and "faces" between edges.

Points in Space: Origins of the 3D Vertex

Just like with 2D vertices (or *anchor points* as they are called in Illustrator or *nodes* as they are called in Inkscape), the vertex is the foundation of 3D geometric and organic (NURBS, Catmull-Rom Splines, and Hash Patches) modeling. The vertex defines where the model's infrastructure, whether that is edges or splines, is in 3D space, and in 3D, vertex data can hold surface color data, normal data, UVW texture mapping data, and vertex XYZ location data. Those of you who are familiar with 3D scanners may be familiar with the term *point clouds*, so the vertex is still the foundation of everything that we do in the 3D industry.

For Java 8 and 9 coding, JavaFX 9 has a **VertexFormat** class that can hold vertex data, which includes your vertex location, normal information (we will cover normals soon), and UVW texture mapping coordinates. So, you can place the vertices for your Java 9 game or IoT application by using Java code or you can use a 3D modeler, such as Daz Hexagon, MoI 3D, or Nevercenter SILO, or a 3D modeling and animation package, such as Blender or Autodesk 3ds Max.

Connect the 3D Vertices: Edges Bridge 3D Vertices

Most 3D geometry uses something called an **edge** to connect two vertices. An edge is a vector, or straight line, so it looks like the edge of a razor in 3D space. Three or more edges are needed to form a **polygon**, which we are going to cover next. When you are modeling 3D geometry, you can select vertices, edges, polygons, or entire objects.

If you've created your 3D geometry using a more advanced spline-based modeling paradigm, such as NURBS using MoI 3D, Quads using SILO 2 (which is only $160), or Hash Patches using Animation:Master (which is only $80), you will need to **decimate** these formats into polygons or triangles, which we are going to cover next. The process of **decimation** turns the infinitely smooth curves used in these paradigms into a collection of straight edges. This is done using a decimation (smoothness) numeric factor (slider or setting), which is usually supplied in the **File Export** function that outputs the spline modeling format from your curve-based modeler into a polygonal geometric model format.

Creating the Surface: Three Edges Form Polygons, Four Edges Form Quads

Once you have put three edges together in the format of a **triangle**, you have a **polygon**, which can be used as a surface to host a *skin*, or *texture*, to make the 3D data look more realistic. Polygons are sometimes referred to as **Triangles**, **Tris**, or **Faces**, and some modelers use square polygons that are referred to as "Quads." If your rendering engine requires triangles as JavaFX and its **TriangleMesh** class do, you can decimate Quads into Tris. The decimation algorithm is fairly simple, in this case, as it simply inserts an edge between two opposite corners of the quad surface, creating two triangles of equal (mirrored) angle characteristics. The optimal triangle comes from a square polygon and has a 45-45-90 degree corner angle configuration. The rule of thumb is that the more uniform (square) a triangle is, the better it renders, whereas "slivered," or long, thin triangles, could cause **rendering artifacts** but usually do not.

Once you have a surface (which is usually a triangle, as shown in Figure 3-2), the faces on the basic cube are quads, and you have defined its normal (which we will learn about next), then you can apply a texture map. We will cover texture mapping in the next major section of this chapter. There is also another principle that is related to adjacent polygons or faces that is called a *smoothing group*, which we will take a look at after we cover surface normals. So, at the very least, a surface (polygon, triangle, quad, face) will host one normal, one or more texture maps, and a smoothing group.

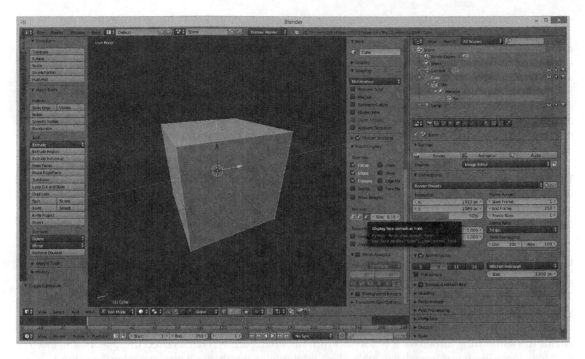

Figure 3-2. *Use the "Display face normals as lines" button to show direction normals for each quad face as light blue lines*

Specify the Direction the Surface Is Facing: The Concept of Surface Normals

If you know how to turn the "show normals" feature on in your 3D software, you can see the **face surface normals**, which will be displayed as a line coming out of the exact center of the face, as you can see in light blue in Figure 3-2.

There are also toggles (buttons) in Blender 2.8 for showing vertex normals, which point outward from the vertex, so for this model the vertex normals point out diagonally from the corners of the cube (45 degrees), the exact opposite result from the face normals, which point straight up (90 degrees, straight up, like a skyscraper) coming out of the center of the face (surface, quad). As you can see in Figure 3-2, two of the normals shown are actually aligned with the x-axis (red) and y-axis (green), which intersect the cube at 90 degrees.

The axis guide is in the lower-left corner of the 3D Edit Mode view, which is also indicated under the XYZ axis guide at the bottom left of the Blender UI. The function of this surface normal is fairly simple; it tells the rendering engine which direction the surface is facing. In this case, this cube would render as a cube, with whatever texture (skin) you give it to color it. The same logic would apply to a vertex normal; it would show the rendering engine which side of your 3D geometry to process for surface rendering.

If the normals in this cube geometry had been pointing inward instead of outward, the cube would not be visible at all when rendered. There's a **flip normals** operation (algorithm) in 3D software that is used to **reverse** your normal directions for a model universally (all normals are flipped 180 degrees). This will be utilized when you render a scene, and your imported object is not visible when you render the scene.

Flipped normals can appear when the 3D import utility points (flips) the normals for imported 3D geometry in the wrong direction or when the exporter from the other 3D tool exported them in the wrong direction, relative to the software you are importing them into. This will be a fairly common occurrence in your 3D workflow, so expect to use this flip normals function at least a few times if you are going to work in 3D, or in i3D, frequently.

If you need something (like a house, for instance) where the 3D geometry has to render from the outside as well as from the inside, which is common in i3D (virtual worlds, for instance), you would have to create the geometry, the faces in particular, to be **double-sided.** You would then need to apply a double-sided texture map and UVW map, which we will be covering in the next section of the chapter when we talk about 3D texture mapping concepts and techniques.

It is important to note that for i3D, double-sided geometry with double-sided textures requires significantly more rendering engine processing, and the rendering is being implemented in real time based on a user's exploration of the interactive 3D environment, world, or simulation, so JavaFX will be navigating, processing, and rendering an i3D scene all at the same time, which requires a lot of processor cycles to do smoothly, so data optimization is important.

Although you can assign a normal to a vertex in JavaFX, a normal is usually assigned on a per-face basis. This is why there are two formats for the **VertexFormat** class. One supports location and texture for polygons that have the normal defined once because defining the normal using three vertices is not as efficient as just using the one face, and the other is a **VertexFormat** data format for when you want to define normals using the vertices instead of the polygons.

Smoothing the Surface: Using Smoothing Groups to Make Polys Look Like Splines

You probably have seen 3D models that are rendered as solid (instead of wireframe) but still look like they are chiseled; that is, you can see the polygons (faces) rendered as if they were flat. In this case, the rendering engine has **smoothing** turned off. If you render with smoothing turned on, this effect disappears, and the geometry looks like it was intended to look, which is infinitely smooth, like it was created using splines when it actually is using polygons. It is more efficient to have the rendering engine do the smoothing, so there is something called a **smoothing group**, which is applied to each face, to tell a renderer when to smooth between two faces and when to not smooth, which leaves what is commonly referred to as a *seam.* A smoothing group uses simple integer numbers. If the numbers match on each side of a face (for each adjacent face on the opposite side of that edge), it renders as a smooth transition (color gradient). If the numbers are different, it renders as a seam; that is, the edge is clearly visible as the color gradients on each side of that edge are different (the color gradient is not seamless across the two faces, also known as *polygons*).

In some 3D software packages, such as Autodesk 3D Studio Max, you can see this smoothing group number schema in the user interface and can actually select the (integer) numbers used next to each edge. You can also select the numbers on either side of an edge, which is a much more complex approach but gives a 3D modeler much more precise smoothing control.

In others such as Blender, the numbering is hidden, and the smoothing group function is "exposed" by using commands such as **Mark Seam**, **Clear Seam**, **Mark Sharp**, and **Clear Sharp**. These commands are found in the Blender **Edges Menu**, as shown on the left side of Figure 3-3 with the **Mark Sharp** option shown selected in light blue.

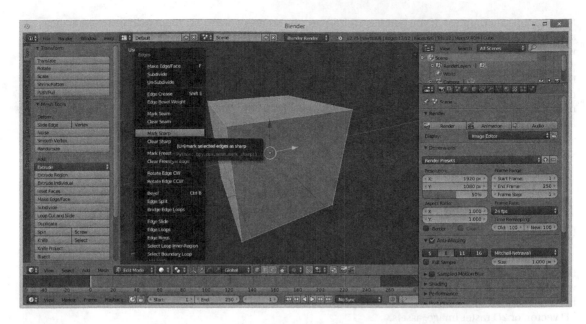

Figure 3-3. *Set edge smoothing in Blender using the Edges menu (Ctrl-E when in Edit Mode) command called Mark Seam or Mark Sharp*

In Blender, some 3D modelers (people, not software) will make the mistake of trying to expose a seam, or a sharp edge, in their 3D geometry by actually **splitting the edge** of the 3D geometry itself, which will achieve this visual effect but which could also cause a problem down the line during a 3D geometry **topology refinement** work process. If you're familiar with the term *topography* used in mapping, topology is very similar, referring to how 3D geometry is constructed and, therefore, how it will be rendered since a rendering engine is "math-based," just as 3D geometry is.

The topology of a 3D model is the construction of the 3D geometry, that is, where vertices, edges, and faces are placed relative to each other, or it's the construction of spline-based organic 3D models where control point, handles, and similar spline-based topology have been placed (and the order in which they are placed). In other words, 3D modeling is complex!

Having to split your geometry edges to achieve a seam can be avoided by instead using the **Mark Seam** or **Mark Sharp** edge modifier in Blender. These particular Blender **modifiers** are actually smoothing group based and therefore achieve this smoothing (or edge seam) effect without actually affecting the 3D geometry topology.

A Blender **modifier** is applied just before rendering and therefore does not affect the actual mathematical **topology** of your underlying 3D geometry. A Blender modifier is always a more flexible 3D content creation approach because it applies smoothing (or any other desired effect) at the rendering engine level, not at the 3D geometry topological level, leaving your 3D mesh intact. As with anything in *Pro Java 9 Games Development* (and IoT design), simpler will always be better if you can achieve a desired effect and end result because simpler equals less processor overhead.

Skinning Your 3D Model: 2D Texture Mapping Concepts

Once your 3D geometry, which is the foundation for your 3D model is completed, you can apply **texture maps** to it to create a solid appearance for your 3D model and add detail and special effects to it to make its appearance more and more realistic. If you are wondering what the difference is between 3D geometry and a 3D model, 3D geometry is just the mesh or wireframe, whereas a 3D model could have (should have) texture maps also applied. If you purchase third-party 3D models, you expect them to look like what they are when you render them, instead of just being flat gray, which is what a rendered model will look like without any texture mapping (and no vertex color) information applied. In fact, some 3D models that you will find online (free or paid) will not even have smoothing groups applied, so you will have some that are faceted, some that are smoothed, and some that are textured to various levels of detail. Some may even have their normals flipped and will not even appear in your 3D scene until you apply a flip normals operation or modifier to them. Usually you will have to do additional modeling, smoothing, and texture mapping work to any preexisting models that you do not create from scratch. I usually try to create everything from scratch, so I have control over, and familiarity with, the underlying 3D geometry topology and how my smoothing groups, UVW mapping coordinates, shaders, and texture maps are applied to a model. We will be covering all of this in this section.

Texture Map Basics: Concepts, Channels, Shading, Effects, and UVW Coordinates

Texture mapping is as complex an area of 3D as creating geometric topology correctly is; in fact, each of the areas of 3D is equally complex, which is what makes 3D the most complex new media type by far and why 3D feature films employ artists to specifically focus on (work on) and handle each of these areas we are looking at during this chapter. Texture mapping is one of the primary areas in 3D modeling that is able to use 2D vector, or 2D raster image, assets.

It is important to note that there is also a more complex area of 3D texture mapping, also called **texturing**, that uses 3D texture algorithms, commonly termed **volumetric textures**, to create texture effects that go all the way through your 3D object, as though it were a solid and not a hollow (think double-sided here) 3D object.

The basic concept behind texture mapping is taking 2D assets, such as those that we learned about during the previous chapter, and applying these 2D assets to the surface of your 3D geometry. This is accomplished by using UVW, or 3D, **mapping coordinates** to show how you want that 2D image (plane) oriented to, or projected on, your 3D geometry surface topology. Now I want you to quickly look up from the book and exclaim to those within earshot: "I really need to decimate this spline topology into a polygonal topology so that I can apply shaders using UVW texture mapping coordinates onto the resulting geometry and export this 3D model into my JavaFX Scene Graph hierarchy." Then just resume reading as though nothing has happened, even though you just established your pending interactive multimedia production genius to everyone who is currently within earshot.

You can add more than one texture map to the surface of your 3D geometry using **texture channels**, which are analogous to the layers that you use in your 2D image compositing software. JavaFX currently supports four of the most important texture channels: the **diffuse** texture map (basic ARGB color values), the **specular** texture map (where surface is shiny or dull), the **illumination** texture map (also called a glow map), and a **bump** texture map.

3D software packages support other texture map channel types for additional texture mapping **effects**. To be able to bring these into JavaFX, you'll have to use a process called *baking*. **Baking texture maps** involves rendering all of the not yet supported texture channels into a single diffuse texture map since that is what JavaFX 8 and 9 supports. This provides much of the same visual result that you get in your more advanced 3D animation packages.

As you can see in Figure 3-4, Blender 2.8 also uses a Scene Graph, just like most modern-day 3D software packages do, and JavaFX offers this Scene Graph functionality as well; we will be covering it in Chapter 8. The sphere geometry and texture mapping are grouped together in the Scene Graph hierarchy, which I expanded for you.

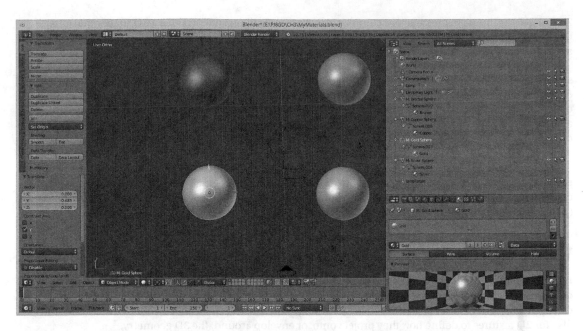

Figure 3-4. *Using a Scene Graph (right) to apply a gold texture map and shader (bottom) to a sphere object in Blender*

As time goes on, ideally JavaFX 9 will add more texture channel support and give developers more visual flexibility regarding their 3D new media asset usage, as transparency areas (opacity maps) and surface details (normal map) are two of the most important areas regarding advanced texture mapping support. These will ultimately need to be added to Java using the JavaFX API in order for developers to be able to create realistic i3D models for Java games.

The collection of texture channels and any code governing these channels' relationship to each other, as well as how they will be composited, applied, and rendered relative to each other, is called the **shader definition**. Shaders are also commonly referred to as **materials** in the 3D industry. We will be covering **shaders** and **shader languages**, as this is another specialized and complex area of 3D and i3D games development, in the next section of this chapter. I also go into shader construction in detail in my book *VFX Fundamentals* (Apress, 2016) using open source Fusion 8.2.1.

Finally, once your textures are defined inside the shaders, you will need to **orient** these 2D assets to your 3D geometry, which is done by using **texture mapping coordinates**, usually done via something called **UVW mapping**, which we will also be covering in its own specific section, before we move on to the fourth dimension and animation.

Texture Map Design: Shader Channels and Shader Language

Shader design is an art form in and of itself; thousands of shader artists work on 3D movies, games, and television shows making sure that the shaders used to "shade" or "skin" the 3D geometry make the resulting 3D model look as real as possible, which is often the objective of 3D, to replace more expensive video camera shoots (and reshoots).

The basic shader consists of a series of 2D vector shapes, 2D raster images, or volumetric textures, held in different types of channels that apply different types of effects, such as **diffuse** (color), **specular** (shininess), **glow** (illumination), **bump** (topography), **normal** (height), **opacity** (transparency), and **environmental** (surroundings) maps. Volumetric shaders are also 3D in nature and as such do not use

2D imagery as inputs but instead use complex algorithm definitions that produce a 3D shader that cuts through the 3D object, which is why it is called *volumetric*. These 3D volumetric shaders can also be animated and can change color and translucency based on their position in 3D space.

On top of this, advanced shader languages, such as **Open GL Shader Language (GLSL)**, use **code** to specify how these channels interrelate to each other, how to apply or process the data contained in these channels, and how to provide other more complex applications of the data within these channels based on complex factors such as time, orientation, or position in 3D space. The complex nature of shaders also means that the render-time processing of the shader is more time-consuming, and processing cycle consuming, the more complex a shader becomes. The processor cycles required can often be expensive because of the ability of complex shaders to produce photorealistic results.

This is probably the primary reason that JavaFX 9.0 currently supports the four basic (and easiest to process) shaders. As hardware becomes more powerful (you'll see six-, eight-, and ten-core CPUs in more consumer electronics products), JavaFX will probably add the last two important shader channels: opacity (or transparency mapping) and normals mapping.

Texture Map Orientation: Texture Map Projection Types and UVW Coordinates

It is important to **align** the detail features in your 2D texture map channels, especially the foundational **diffuse color** channel, to the 3D geometry correctly or some fairly odd or at least visually incorrect results can appear at render time. This needs to be done in 3D X,Y,Z space, especially for volumetric textures but also for 2D textures to define how they project onto, or envelop around, the 3D geometry.

One of the easiest ways this can be done is by applying **texture map projection** types, and related settings, which will then automatically set your UVW mapping numeric values for you. These UVW map coordinate values will define how the 2D imagery plane maps onto the 3D geometry in 3D space, sort of a bridge between the 2D space and the 3D space, and UVW floating point values can be set or tweaked manually in order to fine-tune your visual results.

The simplest of these is **planar projection**, which you can visualize as if your texture map were in front of the 3D object and you were shining a light through it, so it looks like the colors in the diffuse texture map are on the 3D object. Planar projection is the simplest for a computer to process, so use it if you can get the results that you'll need for your pro Java game or IoT application. However, it is usually used for static rendered 3D imagery because once you move (the camera) around to the sides of the 3D model, this type of projection mapping does not provide photoreal results.

Camera Projection is similar to planar projection. **Camera projection** projects your texture from the camera lens (100 percent parallel with the lens) onto a 3D object surface much like a slide projector would do. This could be used for projecting video backgrounds on your scene so that you could model, or eventually animate, your 3D assets in front of them. If the camera moves, the camera projection stays parallel with the front of the lens. This is sometimes termed *billboard mode* (or projection).

The next simplest is **cylindrical projection**, which provides more of a 3D application of the texture map than the (inherently) 2D planar projection of a texture map onto a 3D object from one direction. A cylinder would surround your object, in the up and down (the z-axis) dimension, projecting the image all the way around your object! So, if you walked around it, there would be unique texture detail in another dimension that planar projection does not provide.

A more complex type of projection is called a **spherical projection**. This provides an even more complete 3D application of the texture map than the cylindrical projection of a texture map onto a 3D object, from both the X and Y directions along the Z dimension. Spherical projection attempts to address all three (X,Y,Z) axis projection directions.

Similar to a spherical projection is the **cubic projection**, which is like having **six planar projections** in a cube format; this gives a result similar to the spherical projection. When you apply a cubic projection to a 3D object, the object's faces are assigned to a specific face of a **cubic texture map**, based on the orientation of the polygon normal or on the proximity to the face. The texture is then projected from each face of the cubic texture map using a planar projection method, or possibly a spherical projection map for some 3D software packages.

If you are using volumetric textures, the **spatial projection** is a three-dimensional UVW texture projection, which projects through a 3D object's volume. It is typically used with procedural or volumetric textures for materials that need to have an internal structure, such as wood, marble, sponge, agate, and so forth. If you deform a 3D object or transform the texture mapping coordinate relative to the 3D object, different parts of the volumetric or procedural texture will be revealed.

There's also a simpler texture mapping called **UV mapping** (no W dimension). This applies the texture in two dimensions, instead of three, and is easier to process because it has less data. We will probably map our 3D models outside of JavaFX using 3D software and then use a model importer to import the already texture-mapped 3D object into Java as the classes for some of this more advanced 3D map support have not been added to the JavaFX API as of JavaFX 8.

Animating Your 3D Model: Keyframes, Motion Curves, and IK

After you have created your 3D geometry and texture mapped it using shaders and mapping coordinates, you might want to make it move in some fashion, such as flying an airplane model, for instance. The concepts that you learned about for digital video assets as well as for 2D animation assets in Chapter 2 apply equally as well for 3D animation.

Linear Animation: Tracks, Keyframes, Looping, and Ranges

The simplest type of 3D animation, and 2D animation for that matter, is linear animation, which is fine for many types of animation. Figure 3-5 shows how to add a keyframe to a cube object in Blender 2.8 using the Insert Keyframe Menu.

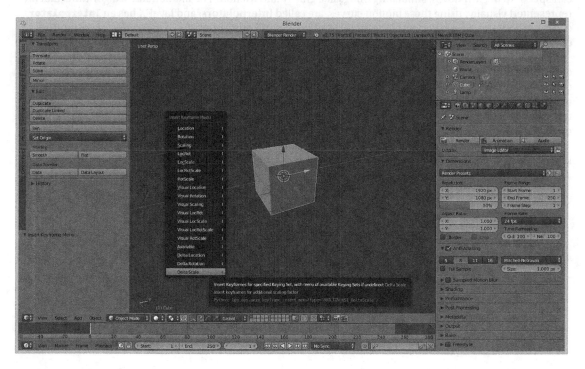

Figure 3-5. *Using the Insert Keyframe Menu in Blender 2.8 with a Cube object selected to add a Delta Scale keyframe*

The I hotkey on your keyboard is used to access this Insert Keyframe Menu, with the Cube object selected. Most 3D software packages have what are generally termed *track editors* that allow you to add keyframes and a motion curve to the tracks. Each track will relate to a 3D model, and if your 3D model uses subcomponent grouping, then there will be tracks for groups and subgroups as well as individual components inside of a group or subgroup.

Linear animation uses the least amount of processing power, so it is the most efficient. If you can use linear animation to accomplish your animation objective, use the fewest number of tracks you can, and the fewest number of keyframes, because this will use the least amount of system memory.

If the animation motion is repetitive, use a seamless loop instead of a long range. One seamless motion loop can take up less memory than a long range containing multiple copies of the same motion. Using looping is a great optimization principle where linear animation is concerned. Next, let's take a look at some of the more complex types of animation, including those that are not linear (in a straight line, with evenly spaced keyframes) as well as character animation and procedural animation, which is used for things such as rigid body or soft body physical (physics) simulations, cloth dynamics, hair and fur dynamics, particle systems, and fluid dynamics, for instance.

Nonlinear Animation: Motion Paths and Motion Curves

A more complex type of nonlinear animation, which is less regular and often looks more realistic, especially where human motion and simple physics simulation is concerned, will implement a **motion path** for the animated 3D object or element (subobject in a hierarchy) to move along. JavaFX has a **Path** class that can be utilized as a motion path for your own complex animation or game sprite movements. To add even more complexity to the motion along that path, it is possible to use a **motion curve** so that the movement itself can speed up or slow down, simulating things like gravity and friction. The mathematical algorithms that are represented visually, using these motion curves, are called **interpolators**, and JavaFX has an **Interpolator** class that contains a wide variety of the most standard (yet still quite powerful, if used effectively) motion curve algorithms.

A good example of nonlinear irregular motion keyframing would be a rubber ball bouncing down a curvy road. The curved path of the road would use your motion path to make sure the ball stays on the road curvature and that the ball floor conforms to the slope (angle) of that road. The bouncing of the ball would use a motion curve, also sometimes called a **motion interpolator**, to make each bounce look more realistic regarding the timing of the acceleration and deceleration of its movement through space over time. In this case, this would control how your ball reacts to the ground.

Figure 3-6 shows the Blender Timeline Editor at the bottom of the screen; you can see two rotation keyframes as vertical yellow lines, with the current frame setting as a vertical green line.

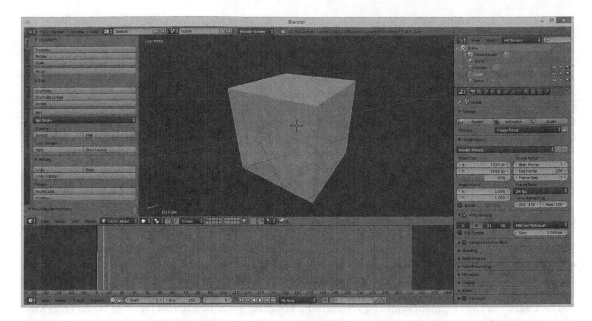

Figure 3-6. *The Blender 2.8 Timeline Editor, with two keyframes at frame 0 and frame 10, and the current frame 6 setting*

Complex physics simulations containing many interacting elements can't be done using keyframes, although it is theoretically possible if you have a massive amount of time on your hands; however, this would not be profitable (worth your time). Just like the application of motion curves to keyframe playback utilizes interpolation algorithms, a procedural animation algorithm goes one step further and also affects not only the timing of the keyframes but also the keyframe data itself (X, Y, Z data, rotation data, scale data, etc.).

Since procedural animation is in the form of an algorithm, it's quite efficient because once the algorithm has been created, it can be used again and again with no additional work. These procedural animation algorithms have created a number of special effects genres in 3D, including rigid body dynamics and soft body dynamics (physics simulations), rope and chain dynamics, cloth dynamics, hair and fur dynamics, particle systems, fluid dynamics, muscle and skin flex dynamics, lip-sync dynamics, and facial expression dynamics. We will cover procedural animation a bit later, as we are progressing from the less advanced concepts to more advanced concepts in each of these chapter sections.

Let's cover an overview of character animation next; it is the next type of animation that is likely to be supported in JavaFX because the JavaFX importers are supporting the import of more complex types of 3D data, including advanced types of animation such as character animation.

Character Animation: Skeletal, Muscles, Skin, Forward, and Inverse Kinematics

An even more complex type of animation is character animation, and character animators are one of the popular positions on a 3D film, game, or television content production team. Character animation involves a number of complex layers, including setting up a "bones" hierarchy for the character's skeleton, using inverse kinematics to control the skeletal (character) movement, attaching muscles to the skeleton and defining how they flex, attaching the muscles to the skin, and even adding clothing and cloth dynamics to dress the character. In 3D character animation, things are done in a very similar matter to how they are done in real life so as to realistically simulate real life, which is often what 3D, i3D, and VR are attempting to do.

Therefore, simulating living beings using character animation gets about as complex as animation can get without using straight coding, which as you now know is called *procedural animation*.

At the lowest level of character animation you have the **bone**; the bone uses an **inverse kinematics** algorithm that tells the bone its range of movement (rotation) so you don't have elbows that bend the wrong way or a head that spins around like in *The Exorcist*! Bones are connected in a hierarchy into, you guessed it, a **skeleton**. This skeleton is what you animate (keyframe) later to animate your character. You can also simulate **muscles** and **skin** by attaching these to the bones and defining how the bone movement will flex the muscles and stretch the skin for your character. As you might imagine, setting all of this up is a complex process; it's an area of character animation called *rigging*. If you need to add clothing, there is a new area of 3D called **cloth dynamics** that defines how clothing will move, wrinkle, and blow in the wind, and there are similar procedural animation algorithms targeted at increasing realism. Let's take a look at this next, along with some other similarly advanced procedural animation and simulation FX algorithms.

Procedural Animation: Physics, Fluid or Cloth Dynamics, Particle Systems, Hair

The most complex type of animation is procedural animation, because it needs to be done using code, and writing code that computes 3D vectors and matrices, along with physics and fluid dynamics equations, is just as complex, if not more so, than game programming code (depending on the complexity of the game). In 3D packages, this coding is usually done using C++, Python, or Java, and procedural 3D animation in your Pro Java 9 Games Development would be accomplished by using a combination of Java 9 APIs and JavaFX 8 APIs. Procedural is the most complex but also the most powerful type of 3D animation and is the reason why procedural animation programmers are another one of the more popular 3D job openings in the 3D film, gaming, IoT, and interactive television (iTV) industries currently.

There are a lot of "features" in 3D modeling and animation packages such as Blender or 3D Studio Max that are actually procedural animation algorithm plug-ins, which expose a user interface to the user to specify parameters that will control the result of a procedural animation once it is applied to 3D models or a complex 3D model hierarchy (created by using the 3D software or JavaFX Scene Graph, such as the Scene Graph shown on the right in Figure 3-4). We just discussed a complex bones-rigging-muscles-skin character model hierarchy to which cloth dynamics can be applied to make clothing move realistically with 3D characters as they run, fight, drive, dance, and so forth.

Examples of procedural animation algorithm–controlled features, many of which include real-world physics simulation support, that are often added to advanced 3D animation software packages include 3D particle systems, fluid dynamics, cloth dynamics, rope dynamics, hair and fur dynamics, soft body dynamics, and rigid body dynamics.

JavaFX 3D Support: Geometry, Animation, and Scene Packages

There are three top-level packages in JavaFX that contain all of the support for both 2D and 3D new media asset types. The **javafx.geometry** package supports the low-level 3D geometric constructs such as vertices, with the **Point2D** and **Point3D** classes, and areas, using the **Bounds** and **BoundingBox** classes. The **javafx. animation package** supports the low-level animation constructs such as timelines, keyframes, and motion curves using the **Timeline**, **KeyFrame**, **KeyValue**, and **Interpolator** classes. The **javafx.scene** package contains a number of nested packages, which I like to call *subpackages*, including **javafx.scene.shape** for 2D or 3D shape constructs, such as the **Mesh**, **TriangleMesh**, and **MeshView** classes; the **javafx.scene. transform** package supporting 2D and 3D transformations, including **Rotate**, **Scale**, **Shear**, and **Transform** classes; the **javafx.scene.paint** package containing shading classes like the **Material** and **PhongMaterial** classes; and the **javafx.scene.media** package (**MediaPlayer** and **MediaView** classes).

JavaFX API 3D Modeling Support: Points, Polygons, Mesh, Transforms, Shading

I will split the JavaFX 3D asset support into two diagrams, one for static 3D (rendered images) and one for animated 3D (3D animation). Interactive 3D will use all of the JavaFX 3D capabilities plus some of the Java API capabilities. The first diagram, Figure 3-7, shows the four major areas that are supported in JavaFX packages. These are important for creating 3D models that can be used in static 3D imagery as well as with other JavaFX APIs for animated 3D and with Java APIs for interactive 3D games, IoT applications, and 3D simulations.

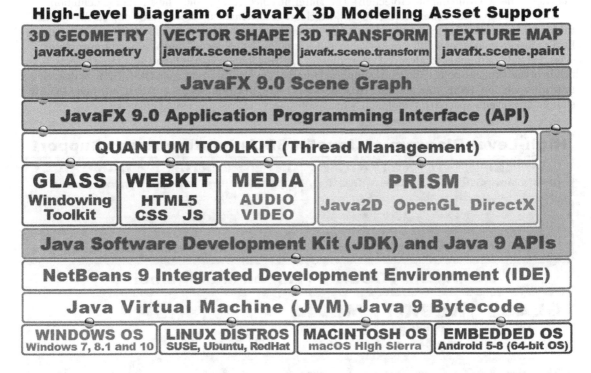

Figure 3-7. *High-level diagram of JavaFX 3D modeling asset support for geometry, shape, transform, and texture map*

The **javafx.geometry** package contains the foundation for all 3D or 2D geometry in Java and JavaFX, namely, the vertex (points) and space (bounds). The **Point2D** class supports both **vertex** (a point in 2D space) and **vector** (a line in 2D space emanating from a point) representations. A **Point3D** class also supports both **vertex** (a point in 3D space) and **vector** (a line in 3D space emanating from a point) representations. The **Bounds** superclass represents the boundaries of a JavaFX Scene Graph Node and the object that it contains. The **BoundingBox** subclass of the **Bounds** superclass contains a more specialized representation of a Scene Graph Node object's boundaries in 2D or 3D space.

The **javafx.scene.shape** package contains the **Mesh**, **MeshView** and **TriangleMesh** objects (classes) used to create 3D geometry, and the **javafx.scene.transform** package contains the Rotate, Scale, Shear and Transform objects (classes) used to apply 3D **spatial** transformations to your 3D geometry in 3D space.

69

The **javafx.scene.paint** package contains the **Material** and **PhongMaterial** objects (classes) that allow you to **texture** your 3D objects in JavaFX using different shader algorithms. Next, let's take a closer look at what the JavaFX API offers us to support the fourth dimension of time so that we can add 3D animation features to your Pro Java 9 games (or IoT applications or 3D simulations).

JavaFX API 3D Animation Support: Timeline, KeyFrame, KeyValue, Interpolator

As you might imagine, most of the key (no pun intended) classes for implementing both 2D and 3D vector animation in JavaFX are stored inside the **javafx.animation** package, as shown in Figure 3-8. The exception to this is the **Camera** superclass and its two subclasses, **PerspectiveCamera** (Perspective Projection) and **ParallelCamera** (Orthographic Projection). The **Timeline** object (class) holds the animation definition, which is made up of **KeyFrame** objects (class), which are in turn made up of **KeyValue** objects that contain the actual transformation instruction data. A KeyFrame object can hold an array of KeyValue objects, so a KeyFrame can hold several different KeyValue transformation data objects. There is also an **Interpolator** class that holds a number of advanced algorithms for applying motion curves to the KeyFrame objects inside of the Timeline object. Currently supported Interpolator algorithms include **DISCRETE**, or discrete time interpolation, **EASE_IN** and **EASE_OUT** as well as **EASE_BOTH** (easing in and also out), and **LINEAR** straight line (evenly spaced) interpolation, which is obviously the least processing intensive.

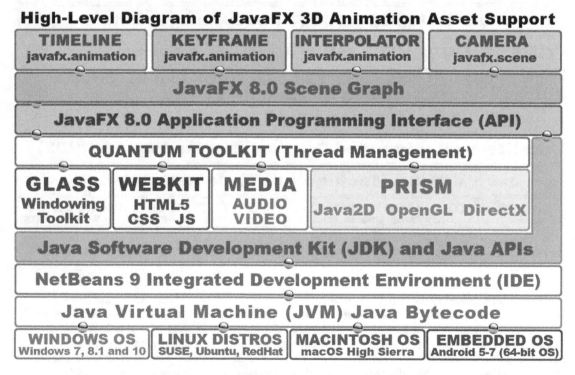

Figure 3-8. *High-level diagram of JavaFX 3D animation support, showing javafx.animation and javafx.scene packages*

Now that you have a solid (3D) overview of 2D vector illustration and 3D vector rendering and animation concepts, we'll take a little break before we get into game theory, concepts, optimizations, and the like in Chapter 4.

Summary

In this third chapter, we took a close look at some of the more important new media concepts relating to 2D vector illustration and 3D vector rendering, texturing, and animation, which you will be using in your pro Java game development work process so that you have the foundational knowledge for these things taken care of in advance.

I started out covering the 2D vector graphics concepts that also hold true for 3D vector graphics, including vertices (vertex or point), vectors (rays or straight lines), and splines (curved lines with control handles). We also took a look at how to fill these 2D shapes with solid colors, color gradients, or tiled image patterns.

Then we built on those concepts and took you into 3D vector graphics where we learned about polygons, triangles, quads, faces, and edges, all of which combine with vertices to create 3D geometry. We looked at how to make 3D geometric wireframes, also known as mesh objects, look solid using texture maps, UVW mapping, and projection mapping, as well as how all of these come together in the form of a material or shader.

Next we looked at 3D animation, which is significantly more complex than 2D animation or digital video, as on the high end this includes character animation, procedural animation, and algorithmic special effects that include physics simulation mathematics and things like controlling large amounts of particles that yield powerful types of code-based animation systems such as flocking simulations, hair and fur dynamics, crowd simulation, fluid dynamics, cloth dynamics, soft body, and rigid body dynamics. In the next chapter, we are going to take a look at game design genres.

Finally, we looked at the JavaFX 9 APIs, which we will be using during the book to implement all of the 3D concepts and principles that we learned about during the chapter. We will be taking a look at these in detail when we implement components of our Java 9 game.

In the next chapter, we'll take a global look at game theory and concepts relating to creating games, using Java 9 and new media assets to implement our gameplay design and game objectives.

CHAPTER 4

■ ■ ■

An Introduction to Game Design: Game Design Concepts, Genres, Engines, and Techniques

Let's build on the knowledge of the new media assets that we learned about in the previous two chapters here by taking a look at how these powerful pixels, frames, samples, and vectors can be utilized to create pro Java 9 games as well as IoT applications and why (or why not) to use these in certain types of pro Java 9 game development genres and scenarios. We will take a look at high-level game concepts, basic game design genres, and game design optimization concepts, as well as open source game engines that are available for the Java platform, including physics engines such as JBox2D, JBullet, Jinngine, and Dyn4J, and 3D game engines such as LWJGL and JMonkey.

The first thing that I want to cover is the underlying concept of **static** (fixed) versus **dynamic** (real time) as it applies to game genres and game design as well as to game optimization. I have already covered the concept of static (images, rendered static 3D imagery) versus dynamic (digital video, 2D and 3D animation, interactive 3D, digital audio) in Chapter 2 (image versus audio-video) and Chapter 3 (rendered 3D versus 3D animation versus interactive 3D). This simple concept is a great way to classify game genres and is a foundational principle underneath **game optimization**, as you will see. In this chapter, we get a high-level overview of gameplay design, new media incorporation, and what different game design approaches and strategies might cost in memory footprint and CPU processing cycles.

The reason why this is important, and why we are "prethinking" all of these game design factors here in the first part of the book, is because you should want your game to play smoothly across all of the different platforms and consumer electronics devices that are used to play your game, even if those devices feature a single-core processor. Single-core processors are actually exceedingly rare these days. Entry-level consumer electronics devices now feature DualCore (two-processor), QuadCore (four-processor), HexaCore (six-processor), or OctaCore (eight-processor) CPUs. The opposite of smooth gameplay would be classified as stilted or jerky gameplay, which is not a good user experience (UX). User experience results from your combination of user interface design, game concept, and new media asset and code optimization, as well as from how much each individual user is interested in, and intrigued by, your gameplay design.

The next thing I will cover are the different aspects or components of game design and development. These include the concepts, techniques, and "lingo" of game design and development that I want to make sure you are up to speed on. These include topics such as 2D sprites, 3D models, artificial intelligence, layers, levels, collision detection, physics simulation, background plate animation, gameplay logic, game design, user interface, and similar game design and development aspects that can be thought of as game "components," as each one adds different attributes and capabilities to professional Java 9 games. Finally, I'll get into the different types, or genres, of games that you could design and develop, just to get the left and right sides of your brain firing at the same time, and then I will explore some of the technical issues and asset and code optimization considerations of how the genres differ from each other.

© Wallace Jackson 2017
W. Jackson, *Pro Java 9 Games Development*, https://doi.org/10.1007/978-1-4842-0973-8_4

High-Level Concepts: Static vs. Dynamic Gaming

I want to start with a high-level concept that touches everything that I will be talking about in this chapter, from the types of games you can create to the optimization of games to the construction of your JavaFX Scene Graph. We took a look at this concept in Chapters 2 and 3, and we will look at it again in the next chapter when we look at the concept of Java **constants** that are fixed or **static** and do not change versus Java **variables** that are **dynamic** and change in real time. Similarly, user interface design in a JavaFX Scene Graph can be static (fixed or immovable) or dynamic (animated, draggable, or skinnable) which means you can change the UI look to suit your personal tastes.

The reason these concepts are so important in game design and development is because your **game engine**, which you will design to "run" or "render" your game, will need to constantly check on (process) the dynamic portions of your game to see if they have changed and therefore require a response. A response requires processing, and Java code will need to be executed (processed) to update a score, move gameboard positions, play animation frames, change a game piece's state, calculate collision detection, calculate physics, apply gameplay logic, and so forth. These dynamic checking requirements (and ensuing processing) on every gameplay cycle (called the *pulse* in JavaFX) update to make sure that variables, positions, states, animations, collisions, physics, and the like, are conforming to your Java game engine logic and can really add up. This is why a balance of static versus dynamic in your game design is important; at some point, the processor, which is doing all of this work, could get overloaded, slowing your gameplay down.

The result of this overloading of all the real-time, per-pulse checking that enhances the dynamics of the gameplay is that the **frame rate** that your game is running at could decrease. That's right, just like digital video and animation, games have frame rates too, but game frame rates are based on the efficiency of your programming logic. The lower the frame rate of the game, the less smooth the gameplay becomes, at least for dynamic, real-time games such as arcade games. How smoothly a gameplays relates to how "seamless" the **user experience** is for the customer.

For this reason, the concept of **static versus dynamic** is very important to every aspect of gameplay design and makes certain types of games easier to achieve a great user experience for than other types. We will be covering different types of games in a future section of this chapter, but as you might imagine, board games are more "static" in nature, and arcade games are more "dynamic" in nature. That said, there are game optimization approaches, which we'll be covering during this book, that can make a game remain dynamic (seem like lots is going on), when from your CPU's processing point of view, what is really going on, from a processing point of view, becomes manageable. This is one of the many tricks of game design, which, when all is said and done, is about optimization in one way or another.

One of the most significant static versus dynamic design issues that I cover in Android (Java) programming books is UI design using XML (**static design**) versus UI design using Java (**dynamic design**). The Android platform will allow UI design to be done using XML instead of Java so that nonprogrammers (designers) can do the **front-end** design for an application. JavaFX allows exactly the same thing to be done by using JavaFX Markup Language (**FXML**).

You must create FXML JavaFX apps in order to do this, as you'll see when you create your game application in NetBeans 9 during Chapter 6. This option adds the `javafx.fxml` package and classes to your application, allowing you to design UIs using FXML, and later have your Java programming logic "inflate" them so that the design becomes JavaFX UI objects. It's important to note that using FXML adds another layer of processor overhead, including FXML markup and its translation (and processing), into the application development and compilation process. For this reason and because, at the end of the day, this is a *Pro Java 9 Games Development* book, not an FXML markup title, I am going to focus during this book on how to do everything using Java 9 and the JavaFX APIs and not doing things by using FXML.

In any event, the point I am making regarding using XML (or FXML) to create the UI design is that this XML approach could be viewed as "static," because the design is created **beforehand** using XML and is "inflated" at compile time using Java. The Java inflation methods use a designer-provided FXML design to create a Scene Graph, which is filled with JavaFX UI objects, based on a UI design structure defined by using FXML. A static UI is designed to be fixed to process a user interface for the game player and is placed into memory one time when your game is loaded.

Game Optimization: Balancing Static Elements with the Dynamic

Game optimization comes down to **balancing** static elements, which do not require processing in real time, with dynamic elements, which require constant processing. Too much dynamic processing, especially when it's not really needed, can make your gameplay jerky or stilted. This is why game programming is an art form; it requires "balance," as well as great characters, a storyline, creativity, illusions, anticipation, accuracy, and, finally, **optimization**.

For instance, Table 4-1 describes some of the different game component considerations for optimization in a dynamic game. As you can see, there are a lot of areas of gameplay that can be optimized to make the processor's workload significantly less "busy." If you have even one of these primary dynamic game processing areas "run away" with the processor's precious "cycles per frame," it can greatly affect the **user experience** for your game. We will be getting into game terminology (sprites, collision detection, physics simulation, etc.) in the next section of the chapter.

Table 4-1. *Some Aspects of Gameplay That Can Be Optimized*

Gameplay Aspect	Basic Optimization Principle
Sprite Position (Move)	Move sprite as many pixels as possible while still achieving a smooth movement appearance
Sprite Animation	Minimize the number of frames needing to be cycled to create illusion of smooth animation
Collision Detection	Check for collision between objects on the screen only when necessary (in close proximity)
Physics Simulation	Minimize number of objects in a scene that require physics calculations to be performed
Flock/Crowd Simulation	Minimize number of members that need to be cycled to create an illusion of crowd or flock
Particle Systems	Minimize particle complexity and number of particles needed to create intended illusion
Camera Animation (3D)	Minimize camera animation unless it's an integral part of (absolutely required for) gameplay
Background Animation	Minimize animated background regions so entire background looks animated but is not
Digital Video Decoding	Minimize digital video use, unless it's an integral part of (absolutely required for) gameplay
Gameplay (or AI) Logic	Design/code gameplay logic, simulated, or artificial intelligence to be efficient as possible
Scoreboard Updates	Update scoreboard via binding and minimize display updates to once per second maximum
User Interface Design	Use static user interface design so that pulse events aren't used for UI element positioning

Considering all these gameplay memory and CPU processing optimization issues will make your Pro Java 9 games design, and Java coding, quite a tricky endeavor indeed. Needless to say, a lot goes into professional Java 9 games.

It is important to note that some of these work together to create a given illusion to the player; for instance, the **sprite animation** will create the illusion of a character running, jumping, or flying, but without combining that code with **sprite positioning** (movement) code, the reality of the illusion would not be achieved. To fine-tune an illusion, the speed of the animation (frame rate) and the distance moved (in pixels moved each frame) may need to be adjusted. I like to call these adjustments *tweaking*. To tweak means to interpolate a data value by hand in order to achieve the most realistic end result. Game development is an iterative process; as much as you might try to sit down and design your game up front and then create the new media assets and write the Java code, modifications will be inevitable.

We'll be getting into many of these areas of pro Java game design and development during this book, but to elucidate on these in a bit more detail here, while we are looking at these considerations, if you can move gameplay elements (primary player sprites, projectile sprites, enemy sprites, background imagery, 3D models) a greater number of pixels a fewer number of times, you will save processing cycles. It's the moving part that takes processing time, not the distance (how many pixels are moved). Similarly, with animation, the fewer frames needed to achieve a convincing animation, the less memory will be required to hold the frames. The same principle applies to the processing of digital video data, whether your digital video asset is **captive** (contained inside a JAR file) or **streaming** from a remote server. Decoding frames of digital video is processor intensive whether you are streaming the data or not and can take away valuable CPU cycles from each of the other components of the game, which probably also require a lot of processing.

It's also important to remember here that we are optimizing memory usage as well as processor cycles, and the two go hand in hand. The fewer memory locations used, the less effort the processor has to make to retrieve the data because memory locations are read and processed one memory address at a time; fewer addresses to process means less processing is going on. Therefore, memory optimization should also be considered as a processing cycle optimization.

With Flocking, Crowd Dynamics, and Particle Systems effects, fewer elements to process and less complexity per element will add up quickly when using processing-intensive special effects such as these. These types of particle-based special effects add a ton of "wow" factor to any game, movie, or television series but also require huge arrays of data to be processed in real time, which can be processing intensive. We'll cover arrays in Chapter 5.

Detecting collisions is another major part of game programming logic for a number of different game genres such as arcade games, board games, and virtual reality games such as first-person shooters. It is very important not to blindly check (process) for collisions between game elements. Be sure to exclude game assets that are not "in play" (on the screen) or are not active, that are not near each other, or that cannot ever collide with each other (static elements). As you might imagine, collision detection considerations, optimizations, and programming are art forms in and of themselves, and entire books on this topic alone have been written, so keep this fascinating topic in perspective and investigate it on your own as well, especially if you are interested in creating Pro Java 9 Games where lots of collisions could occur.

Calculating forces of nature for physics simulations is the most processor intensive, and like collisions, many books have been written on each individual area of physics programming, including rigid body or soft body dynamics, cloth dynamics, rope dynamics, hair and fur (which are actually connected cylinder particle systems), and fluid dynamics or driving dynamics (which are used in driving games). If any of these types of physics simulations have not been coded and optimized with great care, then the entire gameplay user experience may come to a grinding halt, based on how many processor cores the game player has inside the consumer electronics hardware they are playing the game with.

2D vs. 3D Rendering: Static vs. Dynamic Under the Hood

Static 3D games, such as chess, where the game board is static unless you are moving a game piece to a new location on the chessboard, may seem to be static; however, since they utilize 3D real-time rendering to create the virtual reality environment, "under the hood" the system could be busy rendering geometry, lighting, cameras, and materials in real time, depending on how you have designed all of these elements in your scene graph and how your Java game processing logic is set up. Just like we saw in Chapter 3 that the nature of 3D new media assets is an order of magnitude more complex than 2D new media assets, the same thing applies to 3D games versus 2D games. 2D games do have an element of "rendering" called *double buffering* where the next frame is composited in memory, before it is displayed on the screen. 3D rendering, however, is actually **creating** the pixel color and alpha values, not simply **organizing** them in an X,Y location. 3D rendering creates the pixel color values and X,Y locations from scratch, based on 3D geometry, transformations, materials, shaders, mapping coordinates, light position, and camera position.

Next let's take a look at the pro Java game design aspects and considerations for some of these core gaming concepts in greater detail and look at some of the core optimization principles that apply across all genres of games.

Game Components: 2D, 3D, Collision, Physics, and AI

Let's take a look at the various game design concepts, aspects, and components that you will need to understand in order to be able to build a game, as well as what Java (or JavaFX) packages and classes we can use to implement these aspects of gameplay, which I like to term **components** of gameplay design and development. These could include the gameplay elements themselves, commonly referred to in the game industry as **sprites** for a 2D game or **models** for a 3D game, as well as the processing engines, which we will either code ourselves or import preexisting Java code libraries for, such as **artificial intelligence**, **physics simulations**, **particle systems**, **inverse kinematics**, or **collision detection**. I will spend some time covering each of these and why they would be applicable to a pro Java game and some optimization considerations that you should keep in mind if you decide to use any of these game components.

2D Sprites: The Foundation of Arcade-Style Gaming

Let's start with the foundation of one of the oldest forms of electronic gameplay, the arcade game. The 2D assets, called *sprites*, define our **main character**, **projectiles** used to damage the main character, treasures collected by the main character, and the **enemies** that are firing these projectiles. Sprites are **2D graphics elements** and can be either static (fixed, a single image) or dynamic (animated, a seamless loop of several images). Sprites can be either vector (shapes) or raster (image-based) assets. If they are image based, they will usually be **PNG32** and carry an alpha channel so that they can be composited over the rest of the game design in real time and have the result look like it is digital video, that is, like it is being shot with a camera and played on the screen rather than being composited in real time based on the game player's input, which is usually a game controller, keyboard keys, or iTV set remote control.

A sprite will be moved around on the screen based on programming logic that dictates how the game is to function. Sprites need to be composited with background imagery and other gameplay elements in the Scene Graph as well as with other players' sprites, so the PNG32 graphics that are used to create the sprites will need to support **transparent backgrounds**. This is also why I covered the topic of masking 2D objects—to use as sprites for your games.

This is also why I introduced you to the concept of alpha channel transparency, in Chapter 2, as we will need to achieve this same end result with our sprites so that we achieve a seamless visual experience with our game. We'll be covering how to use **GIMP** to create graphics that use alpha channels later during this book so you can create professional-level sprites that composite seamlessly with the rest of your game graphics.

Since 3D models are all in the same rendered space together, the 3D rendering engine will take care of this transparency factor for you, and you do not have to worry about having an alpha channel for each 3D component of your game if you use 3D models instead of 2D sprites. Let's take a look at 3D models next as a follow-up to this point.

3D Models: The Foundation of the Role-Playing Style of Gaming

One of the newer forms of electronic gameplay involves real-time rendered virtual worlds, thanks to the advent of real-time rendering platforms such as OpenGL ES 3 and Vulkan, which are used in Android, HTML5, JavaFX, and DirectX (DirectX is used in Microsoft products such as Xbox and Windows). 3D models provide far more flexible, advanced, and photorealistic gameplay because they combine all of the other new media types (except for digital audio) into one; because textures, materials, and shaders can use digital imagery and digital video; and because 3D geometry mesh objects can use their actual geometry to calculate collisions with the actual object, and in three dimensions instead of two on top of that. Add in the fact that 3D assets can react in real time to multiple lights and cameras, and you have a far more powerful game design environment with i3D, albeit more complex from a mathematics and a Java coding standpoint.

Since 3D and i3D are so complex, there are a plethora of optimization considerations, such as optimizing the mesh (geometry), a process called *low-poly modeling* that involves using points, edges, and faces sparingly and then using smoothing groups to provide a smooth curvature that could also be achieved simply by adding more geometry. I also covered some of the optimization principles of using fewer pixels, lower color depth, and fewer channels that would be used for texture maps, which are images, in Chapter 2. Similarly, for 3D animation, in Chapter 2 I covered some of the optimization principles that would be used for animation data, which is similar to digital video, such as using fewer pixels, fewer frames, lower color depth, and fewer channels, along with simpler interpolation algorithms.

Another optimization for 3D and i3D games has to do with the number of lights that are utilized to light a virtual world. Light calculations tend to be expensive, so much so that most game engines, including JavaFX, limit the number of allowed lights to eight or fewer. The fewer light objects you can use, the fewer calculations the rendering engine will have to do and the higher frame rate (faster) your game will run at.

The same consideration would apply to cameras in 3D animation software. When you're rendering out to film, for instance, you can render out as many camera views of the scene as you need with no (real-time) processor penalty. When a consumer electronics device is processing that 3D (versus a massive render farm of workstations), it becomes important to minimize the number of cameras as each one is outputting the equivalent of an uncompressed raw digital video data stream. In this situation you have a 3D rendering engine generating another uncompressed 2D animation (video) asset in real time, which again takes up a lot of your processing power, so use this only if your game absolutely requires a real-time Head's Up Display (HUD), for instance, for a real-time second gameplay perspective.

Collision Detection: The Foundation of Game Asset Interaction

Another important component, or aspect, of gameplay for some types of games is **collision detection** because if your game elements simply flew right past each other on the screen and never did anything cool when they touch, or "intersect" each other, then you really would not have much of a game! Imagine a pinball game or billiards without any collision detection! Once you add a collision detection engine comprised of **intersection logic** processing routines, your game will be able to ascertain when any 2D vector sprites or 3D models are touching or overlapping each other by processing intersections of their component geometry, usually edges, lines, curves, or their bounds (**BoundingBox**).

A collision detection will call (that is, trigger) related game logic processing routines that will ascertain what happens when any given 2D sprites or 3D models, such as a projectile and the main character, intersect. For instance, when a projectile intersects the main character, damage points might accrue, a life force index might be decreased, or a death throes animation might be started. If a treasure item intersects with (that is, is picked up by) a main character, on the other hand, power or capability points might accrue, the life force index might be increased, or an "I found it" jubilation animation might be started.

As you can see, depending on the type of game you are creating, the collision detection engine for the game could well be one of the foundational design elements behind your gameplay, besides your i2D sprites or i3D models, which represent your characters, projectiles, treasures, enemies, obstacles, and props themselves, which is why I've covered these in this order. Once a collision is detected, often your physics simulation code will be triggered to show the game player how the objects need to react to each other after that collision. So, let's take a look at that next.

Physics Simulation: The Foundation of Gameplay Realism

Another important component, or attribute, to add to your gameplay is **real-world physics simulation**. The addition of things like gravity, friction, bounce, drag, wind, acceleration, deceleration, and motion curves, like the JavaFX **Interpolator** class provides, and similar forces, will each add an additional level of realism on top of the already photorealistic sprites, your synchronized animation sequences, scenic backgrounds, and highly accurate collision detection.

Gravity, friction, drag, and wind are the easiest factors to either simulate or adjust a 2D sprite or 3D model movement for in your Java code. I touch on this near the end of my book *Beginning Java 8 Games Development* (Apress, 2014). Bounce is similar to the mathematics done for acceleration and deceleration in motion curves, which could be used to simulate a single bounce, but not the decay of a bounce that a physics simulation will.

You can code your own Java methods to apply physics to your pro Java game or you can use the third-party Java libraries, which are available on sites like SourceForge, GitHub, or code.google.com. I will cover some of the libraries that are out there for 2D and 3D game engines, 2D and 3D physics simulation engines, 2D and 3D collision detection engines, forward and inverse kinematics engines, and the like. I will cover this in the next major section for this chapter, just in case you want to use these in your pro Java games or IoT applications instead of writing your own.

It is interesting to note that most of the open source third-party physics engines, which I'm going to cover in the "Java Engines: Game, Physics, and Inverse Kinematic" section of this chapter, not only implement physics simulation but also implement collision detection. This is because these two things are closely tied together in real life. To do collisions really well, the physics simulation needs to be a seamless integration in that code. There are physics involved both before and after a collision in real life, and these engines seek to re-create real-life (completely believable) implementation results. Be advised that as of Java 9 these offerings will need to be "modularized" for use with the new Java 9 module system in order to be used properly within that system.

Artificial Intelligence: The Foundation of Your Gameplay Logic

Finally, the most proprietary attribute or logic constructs (Java code) that you can add to add to your gameplay is the **custom gameplay logic**, which makes your game truly unique in the marketplace. This artificial intelligence (AI) programming logic should be kept in its own Java class and methods, separate from physics simulation or collision detection code. After all, Java makes modularization easy, and this gameplay intelligence is like the referee for your pro Java game. It oversees the player, opponents, obstacles, treasure, scoring, penalties, and similar, making sure the game experience is the same every time and for everyone! This is the same function that a referee performs at a sporting event or competition.

There are third-party AI engines for Java; however, I suggest this is an area where you may want to write your gameplay logic code from scratch so that it integrates with your user interface (UI) code, your scoring engine code, your animation engine code, your actor (sprites or models) movement code, and your collision processing code in a much more seamless fashion than any third-party AI rules engine ever could.

When you start to add all these game components together, it starts to make the game more believable, as well as more professional. One of the key objectives for a great game is "suspension of belief," which simply means that your player is "buying into" the premise, characters, objectives, and gameplay 100 percent completely. This is the same objective that any content producer, whether it be a filmmaker, television series producer, author, songwriter, game programmer, or application developer, is going for. Games these days have the same revenue generation capability as any of the other content distribution genres, if not more, and you can distribute them directly to the public without a middleman such as a movie studio, record producer, or television network. That's the most significant part, as you will get a "70 percent you, 30 percent store" split, rather than a "70 percent distributor, 30 percent you" split!

Java Engines: Game, Physics, and Inverse Kinematic

There are a number of open source third-party game engines, physics and collision engines, AI engines, and even inverse (or forward) kinematics (IK) engines that can easily be found on the Internet. Most of these are on SourceForge or GitHub or on code.google.com and can be found using a basic Google search. Most of these come in JAR format.

Game Engines: JMonkey and the Lightweight Java Game Library

LWJGL is an open source, cross-platform Java library that is useful for the development of 3D graphics (OpenGL), 3D audio (OpenAL), and parallel computing (OpenCL) applications (Figure 4-1). API access is direct and high-performance yet also wrapped in a type-safe layer appropriate for Java ecosystems. Other high-level 3D game engines may also make use of LWJGL.

Figure 4-1. *The Lightweight Java Game Library 3 is an open source Java game library compatible with Java and JavaFX*

JMonkey is also a free, open source game engine targeted at Java game developers who want to create i3D games (Figure 4-2). This software is programmed entirely in Java and is intended to provide wide accessibility and rapid deployment.

Figure 4-2. jMonkeyEngine 3.0 is an open source cross-platform game engine compatible with Java and JavaFX

It's important to note that I'm going to show you how to create games using only Java (8 or 9) and JavaFX 8 or 9 because that is what this book is about: using and learning about the native Java APIs (of which one is JavaFX) to make games or IoT applications. I just wanted to make you aware of the two leading Java games platforms before we start.

Physics and Collision Engines: Jbox2D, JBullet, Dyn4j, Jinngine

There are a large number of third-party physics engines that also include support for collision detection, so you can add collision and physics at the same time to your game using any one of these collision physics code libraries to your pro Java games or IoT application projects simply by importing a JAR file into your project and calling the proper APIs.

Jbox2D is a "port" or recoding for use in Java of the Box2D C++ physics engine. Box2D is an open source, C++-based physics and collision engine for simulating rigid body dynamics in i2D (X,Y) space. Box2D was developed by **Erin Catto** and was released under the zlib license, which does not require formal acknowledgment of usage; however, it is encouraged that you give credit to Box2D in your pro Java game if you use the Jbox2D API port from C++ Box2D.

JBullet is a partial port of the Bullet 2.7 **3D** C++ physics engine for use in Java. Bullet 2.87 is an open source, C++ physics and collision engine for simulating rigid body dynamics in 3D (X,Y,Z) space. The Bullet collision detection and physics library was developed by Advanced Micro Devices, otherwise known as AMD. It can be found at `http://bulletphysics.org` if you want more information. JBullet was released under the zlib license, which does not require formal acknowledgment of usage. However, it is encouraged that you to give credit to JBullet in your pro Java game if you use the JBullet API partial port from the Bullet 2.7 C++ physics engine.

The **dyn4j** engine shown in Figure 4-3 is a **2D** collision detection and physics engine compatible with Java 6 and 7, meaning that it works with the Java 8 and 9 versions we are covering in this book. Dyn4j was designed to be stable, extensible, optimized (fast), and relatively easy to use. Dyn4j is free for commercial use, as well as for use in noncommercial applications. It is licensed by its author, William Bittle, under the BSD licensing model.

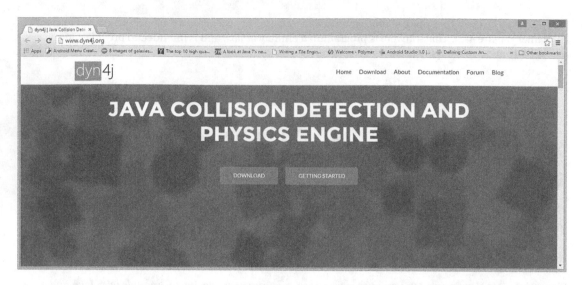

Figure 4-3. *Dyn4j is an open source, 2D collision detection and physics engine that is available under the BSD license*

Jinngine is an open source lightweight 3D physics engine written in Java that gives you real-time collisions, as well as real-time physics calculation capabilities. A user can set up and simulate physics by calling API functions to specify geometry, joints, and parameters. Friction is modeled by implementing an approximation of the Coloumb law of friction. This physics engine focuses on collision and physics only, has no rendering features, and is built using a velocity-based algorithmic approach that is solved using an efficient NCP solver. You can use jinngine as your physics engine, and you can also use other components of this engine as if it were a Java code library, for instance, if you want to only implement collision detection or if you wanted to only utilize the point-of-contact generation features. Next, let's take a look at inverse kinematics, or IK engines, which are used in character animation to define skeletal structures and their joint movement restrictions.

Inverse Kinematics and Robot Engines: JRoboOp and JavaFX-IK

JRoboOp is an open source Java library (package) designed for IK robotics simulation with visualization of a 3D robot model. The engine simulates robotic inverse kinematics as well as robot dynamics and is based upon the C++ library called ROBOOP. This library was developed by **Richard Gourdeau** of École Polytechnique de Montréal, and the library is compatible with Java 5 and later as well as with JavaFX 1.3 and later, meaning that it will work great with the Java 7, Java 8, JavaFX 9, and Java 9 versions that we will be covering during this book. This package is distributed under the GNU Public License (GPL).

The **JavaFX-IK** library was created about two years ago specifically for JavaFX and is available on GitHub at https://github.com/netopyr/javafx-ik. It is licensed under the Apache License, version 2.0. The IK software, which allows you to create **Skeleton** object structures in the JavaFX Scene Graph using **Bone** objects, was created by senior software engineer **Michael Heinrichs**, of Freiburg, Germany.

Next, let's take a look at the different types of games that can be created as well as how these differ in their application of the core game components of sprites, collision detection, physics simulation, and gameplay AI logic.

Game Genres: Puzzle, Board, Arcade, Shooter, or VR

Like everything else we have talked about in this chapter, games themselves can be categorized by using a "static versus dynamic" approach. Static games aren't "processor bound" because they tend to be "turn based" and not "hand to eye coordination based" in nature, so in a sense they are easier to get working smoothly, as only the programming logic for the "rules" of gameplay and the attractive graphics need to be put into place and debugged. A significant opportunity also exists for developing new types of game genres that use a hybrid combination of static and dynamic gameplay in creative ways that have never before been seen. I'm working on a few of these myself!

Static Games: Strategy, Knowledge, Memory, and Board Games

Since this is a pro Java games programming book at its core, I am going to approach everything from this important (for game development) static versus dynamic standpoint, and it just so happens to be a pretty slick way to categorize games into three discrete categories (static, dynamic, and hybrid). Let's cover the static (fixed graphics), turn-based games first. These would include the "move-based" or "turn-based" games such as **board games**, **puzzle games**, **knowledge games**, **memory games**, and **strategy games**, all of which should not be underestimated in their popularity and marketability, especially where families are concerned. Not all of your game customers are going to be teenage males, and this category of games is also the most likely to be used for **edutainment**, a popular buzzword these days where education and entertainment are fused together to further the success of the education part of that equation. There are a dearth of fun, effective games for educational content, so this is a significant games business opportunity.

The thing that is important to remember regarding static games is that they have the capability of being just as fun to play as dynamic games. Static games by their very nature have significantly less processing overhead, as they do not have to achieve the 60 FPS real-time processing target in order to achieve smooth, professional gameplay. This is because the nature of the game is not predicated upon continuous motion but rather on making the right **strategic moves.** Moves are made when it is your turn to do so, which is why these types of static games will often be referred to as *move-based games.*

There can be some form of basic "collision detection" involved in static games, regarding which game pieces have been moved and to which location on your game board or playing surface. With a static game, however, there is no danger of overloading the processor with collision detection because the rest of the game board is static, with the exception of the one piece that is being strategically moved during that particular player's turn. Once that process of ascertaining the collision is completed, there is no (real-time) collision detection needed until the next turn is taken by either the single player (in a single-player game) or the opponent (in a multiplayer game).

The processing logic for strategy games is more **strategy logic**–based programming, geared toward allowing the players to achieve a given end "win" given the right sequence of moves, whereas the dynamic game programming logic looks more at what collisions are taking place between game sprites. Dynamic games are focused on point score, which is generated by dodging projectiles, finding treasures, landing on targets, killing enemies, and completing those types of level objectives in order to get to the next level, where players can generate even higher point scores.

Complicated strategy games with lots of interrelated rule sets, such as chess, for instance, are even likely to have far more complex programming logic routines than dynamic games feature. However, since the execution of the code is not as time sensitive, the resulting gameplay will be smooth, no matter how powerful the platform and CPU are, because the player is willing to wait for the game to verify the validity of the move and score it, if appropriate. Of course, the game ruleset logic must be flawless for this type of game to be perceived as truly professional. Therefore, in the end, both static as well as dynamic games, the great ones at least, can be difficult to code, albeit for significantly different reasons. Next let's take a look at dynamic games, which tend to have high public profiles, appeal to younger player demographics, and tend to be played individually, instead of by groups, students, or families.

Dynamic Games: Arcade, Shooter, Platform, and Action Games

Dynamic games could be termed **Action Games** or **Arcade Games** and include a lot of movement on the display screen. These highly dynamic games almost always involve shooting things, such as in first-person shooters (*Doom* and *Half-Life*, for instance) as well as in third-person shooters (*Resident Evil* and *Grand Theft Auto*) genres, or stealing things or evading scary things. Action sports games, such as football, soccer, baseball, basketball, golf, and lacrosse, are also very popular in the dynamic games genre, and they are almost always created using a photorealistic, i3D virtual world or virtual reality game simulation environment. Driving games are another incarnation of this genre and also tend to use real-time i3D game rendering technologies to provide the driver with an ultrarealistic driving simulation.

There is also the obstacle course navigation paradigm, such as commonly seen in **platformer games** such as *Donkey Kong*, *Pac-Man*, or *Super Mario Brothers*. Platformer games are often arcade games, which are typically 2D or **2.5D**, which is called **isometric**. The arcade game *ZAXXON* was a great example of an isometric game that was 2D, and looked 3D, or *Tempest*, where geometric shapes climbed up a geometric well where the player shot down the side to prevent the climbing shapes from reaching the top.

It's important to note that any genre of game can be produced using 2D or 3D graphic assets or can even be produced using a **combination** of 2D and 3D assets, which is allowed by JavaFX 9.0 and which I would term a **hybrid**.

Hybrid Games: An Opportunity to Leverage JavaFX Creatively

From a JavaFX Scene Graph assets perspective, a hybrid game would be one that used both 2D and 3D assets, most of which we covered in Chapters 2 and 3. There is another type of hybrid, which could span different game genres, which we just covered some of in the previous section. There are so many popular game types that there is always a fantastic opportunity to create an **entirely new genre of game** by using a hybrid gameplay approach. For instance, imagine taking some of the characteristics from a static (strategic) game type, such as a board game, and adding elements of a dynamic (action) game type. A good example of this would be *Battle Chess*, where chess pieces do battle to the death when they come into each other's chess board square.

In my *Beginning Java 8 Games Development* (Apress, 2014), I used JavaFX 8.0 to create a hybrid game engine that has support for attributes of a platformer game, a shooter game, and a treasure hunting game. As you can see in Figure 4-4, the BagelToons **InvinciBagel** game engine created in that book, where I cover i2D games development, has elements normally found in different types of 2D games, including superheroes, enemies, shooting, treasures, obstacles, hiding places, buildings, cars, landscaping, magic carpet cats, safe cracking, food, and the like.

Figure 4-4. *My i2D game development book called Beginning Java 8 Games Development covers using sprites to develop games*

In summary, Java is positioned to allow game developers to deliver vanguard, hybrid games, containing both 2D and 3D assets, as well as high-quality 16-bit 48 kHz and 24-bit 48 kHz digital audio. With a little bit of creativity and the knowledge you are garnering during the course of this book, you should be able to pull off what's never been done before. This is especially true for areas that hybrid gaming will be beneficial for, such as the areas of education (edutainment) and the workplace (business process gamification). This is because Java is widely used in OSs and browsers, as well as in 64-bit platforms such as Android 5 - 8, which have a majority market share and manufacturer following in consumer electronics. That said, it is important to point out that JavaFX is not (yet) suited for i3D VR real-time 3D-rendered games with an HD or UHD high frame rate, like those created using C++ for customized game consoles such as PlayStation or Xbox.

Summary

In this fourth chapter, we took a closer look at some of the more important game design concepts that we will be using in our pro Java game development work process so that you have the foundational knowledge for these things taken care of in advance, in the first section of the book.

I started out covering the key concept of **static** versus **dynamic** and how these are important for both game design and game optimization, as too many dynamics can overload older single-core and even dual-core CPUs if game optimization is not an ongoing consideration throughout the game design, development, and optimization process.

Next, you looked at some of the key components of **game design** and development, such as **sprite position**, **sprite animation**, **collision detection**, **physics simulation**, **flocking**, or **crowd dynamics**, **particle systems**, **background animation**, **camera animation**, **digital video streaming**, **user interface design**, **scoring engines**, and **gameplay AI logic**.

We took a look at how these applied to static games, which are games without continuous movement, such as move-based strategy games, board games, puzzles, knowledge games, and memory games, and then at how these applied to dynamic games, which are games using continuous movement, such as platformers, arcade games, first-person shooters, third-person shooters, driving games, sports games, science-fiction games, and similar games where 3D real-time rendering along with various types of physical systems and particle systems simulations are heavily leveraged.

We also took a look at some of the most popular third-party game engines, physics (and collision) engines, and inverse kinematics engines. We looked at some different genres of games, and their characteristics, so that you could get your creative juices flowing and think about what types of pro Java games you want to create.

In the next chapter, we are going to take a look at the **Java** programming language and get a refresher or a primer just to make sure everyone is on the same page regarding Java programming language API components such as packages, classes, interfaces, methods, constants, variables, modifiers, and so on.

CHAPTER 5

■ ■ ■

A Java Primer: Introduction to Java Concepts and Principles

Let's make sure that all of our readers are on the same page here in Chapter 5 by reviewing the core programming language concepts and principles behind the **Java** programming language. It is important that we take this chapter to give our readers a Java "primer," or comprehensive overview, and concisely review the programming language in a single chapter. The Java 9 JDK (and JRE) that you installed in the first chapter of this book will be the foundation for your Pro Java Games and IoT applications, as well as for the NetBeans 9 IDE. (We'll cover NetBeans in the next chapter so you can see how the IDE that you will be using to code Java 9 games or IoT applications functions as a code editor and application testing tool.)

Most of the core Java constructs and principles that we will be covering during this chapter go back fairly far in the Java programming language, most as far back as Java 5 (known as 1.5) or **Java 6** (1.6). We will also be covering the features added in **Java 7** (1.7) and **Java 8** (1.8), which is the most recent release, as well as the new features planned for **Java 9** (1.9), which will be released in the third quarter of 2017. These versions of Java are used on billions of devices. **Java 6** is used in the **32-bit Android** 2.*x*, 3.*x*, and 4.*x* OS and applications; **Java 7** is used in the **64-bit Android** 5.*x* and 6 OS and applications; **Java 8** is used in Android 7 through 8, and in popular operating systems (including Microsoft Windows, Apple Macintosh, Open Solaris, and a plethora of popular Linux distributions such as SUSE, Ubuntu, Mint, Fedora, and Debian); and **Java 9** is now released to the general public.

You will of course learn about new advanced concepts of Java 8 such as **Lambda Expressions** and about Java 8 and Java 9 components, such as the **JavaFX** multimedia engine, as we progress through the book. This chapter will cover the most foundational Java programming language concepts, techniques, and principles that span the five major versions of Java that are currently in widespread use today, on computers, iTV sets, and handheld devices.

We will start out with the easiest concepts and progress to the more difficult ones, so we will be starting at the highest level of Java, which is the **API** and its modules, and then progress down to those "hands-on" parts of the Java programming constructs inside of those modules, including packages, classes, interfaces, methods, constants, and variables.

Before you get into the structural part of Java, such as packages, classes, and methods, you will take a look at Java **syntax**, including what Java **keywords** are, how to **delimit** Java programming structures, and how to add function **comments** into your Java code. Then we'll cover top-level concepts of **application programming interfaces (APIs)**, what a **package** is, and how you can **import** and use existing code provided by Java packages that are part of this API, as well as how to create custom Java packages of your own that contain your own games and IoT application code.

You will take a look at the constructs that are held inside of the Java packages, which are called Java **classes**. You will learn about the **methods**, **variables**, and **constants** that classes contain; about what superclasses and subclasses are; and about what nested classes and inner classes are and how to use them. Finally, you'll learn about Java **objects** and how they form the foundation of **Object-Oriented Programming (OOP)**. You will learn what a **constructor** method is and how it creates a Java object using a special kind of method that has the same name as a class in which it is contained.

W. Jackson, *Pro Java 9 Games Development*, https://doi.org/10.1007/978-1-4842-0973-8_5

Writing Java Syntax: Comments and Code Delimiters

There are a couple of things that you need to understand right off of the bat regarding writing Java **syntax**. Syntax controls how Java "parses" things regarding the programming language. Parsing your code syntax allows Java to understand what it is that you want to do with your programming logic. The primary syntax **rules** are important to understand because they allow the Java **compiler** to understand how you are **structuring** Java code. Java **compilation** is the part of a Java programming process where the JDK compiler (program) turns your Java code into **bytecode**. This gets **executed** (run) by the JRE Java **Runtime** Engine, which is installed on the end user's computer system. This Java compiler needs to know what parts of your code are Java programming logic and what parts are comments to yourself (or comments to other members of your project programming team); where your Java code blocks begin and end; and, inside of those Java code blocks, where your individual Java programming statements or instructions begin and end. Once this is clear to the compiler, it can **parse** the statements and turn them from code into bytecode.

Let's start with comments, as this topic is the easiest to grasp. There are two ways to add comments to Java code: **single-line** or **in-line** comments, which can be placed right after each line of Java code logic, and **multiple-line** or **block** comments, which are placed before (or after) a line of Java code or a block of Java code (a Java code structure).

A **single-line comment** is used to add a comment regarding what a line of Java code, or a Java programming **statement**, is doing. This comment explains what that line of Java code is there to accomplish within your overall code structure. Single-line comments in Java will start with a **double forward slash** character sequence. For instance, if you want to comment one of your import statements in the BoardGame bootstrap code that you will be creating later in Chapter 6, you would add double forward slashes after the line of code. This is what your line of Java code would look like once it has been single-line commented; it is also shown in Figure 5-1 at the bottom-right side of NetBeans:

```
import javafx.stage.Stage; // This line of code imports Stage class from JavaFX.stage
package
```

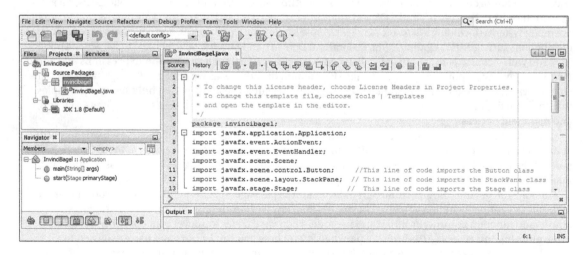

Figure 5-1. *Multiline comments (first five lines of code at the top) and single-line comments (last three lines of code at the bottom)*

Let's also take a look at **multiline comments**, shown at the top of Figure 5-1 above the **package invincibagel** statement, which we'll be learning about in the next section of this chapter. As you can see, **block** comments are done differently, using a **single forward slash next to an asterisk** to start the comment, and the reverse of that, using an **asterisk and then a single forward slash**, to end the multi-line comment (this kind of comment is also called a **block comment**). These are the two ways that you will generally add short (single-line) or long (multiline) comments to your pro Java games.

It is important to note that you cannot "nest" multiline comments. Simply use a larger multiline comment!

In case you are wondering, this InvinciBagel project was the i2D arcade game that I taught readers how to create in the *Beginning Java 8 Games Development* book I wrote for Apress covering i2D game development using Java 8 and JavaFX 8. All of the principles in that book apply to *Pro Java 9 Games Development*, so I'm using that code here.

I usually line up my single-line comments to look fairly orderly. The Java **convention** for block commenting is to line up your asterisks, with an asterisk in your beginning comment delimiter and one in your ending comment delimiter. This is shown in Figure 5-1 at the top of the **InvinciBagel.java** code editor tab in NetBeans.

There is a third type of comment called a **Javadoc** comment, which you'll not be using in your pro Java game development in this book, as the code is intended to be used to create your game and not distributed to the public. If you're going to write a Java game engine for use by others to create games, that is the point in time when you would use a Javadoc comment to add documentation to your pro Java game engine. The JDK has a Javadoc tool that is used to process the Javadoc comments and add them into the NetBeans 9 IDE. A Javadoc comment is similar to a multiline comment, but instead it uses **two asterisk characters** to create your opening Javadoc comment delimiter, as I have done here:

```
/**  This is an example of the Java Documentation (Javadoc) type of Java code commenting
     This is a type of comment that will automatically generate your Java documentation!
*/
```

If you want to insert a comment right in the middle of your Java statement or programming structure, which you should never do as a professional Java games developer, you would use the multiline comment format, like this:

```
import  /* This line of code imports the Stage class */  javafx.stage.Stage;
```

This will not generate any errors but could confuse the readers of your code, so don't comment the code in this way. The following way of commenting this, using a single-line comment format, will, however, generate errors:

```
import  // This line of code will not successfully import the Stage class  javafx.stage.Stage;
```

This is because the compiler will see only the word **import**, as this single-line comment parses to the end of the line, whereas the multiline comment is specifically ended using the block comment delimiter sequence (asterisk and forward slash). For this reason, a Java compiler will **throw** an error for this second improperly commented code, essentially asking "import what?" Since you cannot import nothing, you must import a Java class from a Java package.

Just as the Java programming language uses the double forward slash and slash-asterisk pairing to **delimit** the comments in your Java code, there are a couple other key characters that are used to delimit Java programming statements, as well as to delimit entire blocks of Java program logic. I often call Java code blocks *code structures*.

The **semicolon** character is utilized in Java (all versions) to delimit or separate Java programming statements such as the package and import statements shown in Figure 5-1. What the Java compiler does is look for a Java keyword, which starts a Java statement, and then takes everything after that keyword as being part of that Java code statement until it reaches the semicolon character, which is the way that you tell the Java compiler "I am done coding this Java statement." For instance, to declare your Java package at the top of your Java application, you would use the Java package keyword, the name of your package, and then a semicolon character, as follows (as shown in Figure 5-1):

```
package invincibagel;
```

We will be covering APIs and packages in the next section, as well as how they are accessed by using **import** statements. Import statements are also **delimited** using the semicolon character (also shown in Figure 5-1). The import statement starts with the **import** keyword, the package and class to be imported, and finally, the **semicolon delimiter**, as shown in the following Java programming statement:

```
import javafx.application.Application;
```

The next delimiters that we should take a look at are the **curly braces {...}**. Like a multiline comment delimiter, curly braces feature an opening { curly brace, which delimits (or shows the compiler) the beginning, or start, of a collection of Java statements, and a closing } curly brace, which delimits (or shows the compiler) the end of a collection of Java programming statements. Curly braces allow you to **nest** Java programming statements inside of other Java constructs. We'll be covering nesting Java constructs frequently throughout this book.

As you can see in Figure 5-2, Java code blocks delimited using these curly braces can be nested (contained) inside of each other, allowing more complex Java code structures. Figure 5-2 shows the first (outermost) code block using curly braces in your class. Inside of that is your **start()** method, inside of that is your .setOnAction() method call, and inside of that is a handle() method definition. We will be taking a look at what all of this Java code does as this chapter progresses. What I want you to visualize now, which I am helping you to do by drawing red squares in Figure 5-2, is how these curly brackets are allowing your methods (and class) to define their own code blocks (structures), each of which are a part of a larger Java structure, with the largest Java structure being an InvinciBagel class. Each left curly bracket has a matching right curly bracket, and also notice the indenting of the code so that the innermost Java code structures are indented the farthest to the right. Each block of Java code is indented by an additional four characters, or spaces. As you can see, the class is not indented (zero), the **start()** method is four spaces in, the **.setOnAction()** method is eight spaces in, and the **handle()** method is twelve spaces in. Note that NetBeans 9 will indent each of your Java code structures for you.

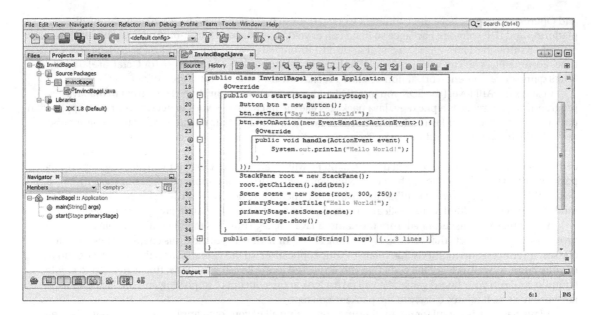

Figure 5-2. *Nested Java code blocks for InvinciBagel class, start method, setOnAction method, and the handle method*

Note that the nested Java code, inside each of these red squares, begins with a curly brace and ends with a curly brace. Now that you are familiar with the various Java code commenting approaches, as well as how your Java programming statements need to be delimited (both individually and as Java code blocks), you're going to take a look at the various Java code structures. You will see how they're used, what they can do for your applications and games, and which important Java keywords are utilized in order to implement your Java programming structures.

Java Packages: Organizing the Java API by Function

At the highest level of a programming platform, such as Google's 32-bit Android 4 (which uses Java SE 6), 64-bit Android 5 (which uses Java SE 7), or the current Oracle Java SE platform (which was recently released as Java SE 9), there is a **collection of packages** that contains classes, interfaces, methods, and constants, which collectively form the **Application Programming Interface (API).** This collection of Java code (in our case, this is currently the Java 9 API) can be used by application (in this case, games) developers to create professional-level software across many OSs, platforms, and consumer electronics devices such as computers, laptops, netbooks, tablets, HD and UHD iTV sets, e-book readers, and smartphones.

To install a given version of an API level, you install its **Software Development Kit (SDK).** The Java SDK has a special name, the **Java Development Kit (JDK).** Those of you who are familiar with Android development (Android is actually Java on top of Linux OS) know there's a different API level released every time a few new features have been added. This is because of the fact that hardware devices that run Android add new hardware features that need to be supported, not because Google feels like releasing a new SDK every couple months. Android has released over 26 different API levels in just a few years, whereas Java SE has released only nine in more than a decade. Only four of Java's API levels (Java 6, 7, 8, and 9) are in active use currently in billions of consumer electronics devices.

Java 6 is used with Eclipse's ADT IDE to develop for 32-bit Android (versions 1.5 through 4.4), Java 7 is used with Android Studio to develop for 64-bit Android (versions 5.*x*, 6, 7.*x*), Java 8 is used with the IntelliJ IDE to develop for Android Studio 3.0, and Java 9 is used across the Windows, Macintosh, Linux, and OpenSolaris OSs. I have three different workstations that are optimized for each of the Java API platforms and IDE software packages so that I can develop applications for 32-bit Android devices (Java 6), Android 5 through 6 (Java 7), HTML5 and Android 7 through 8 (Java 8), and JavaFX 9 (Java 9) at the same time. Fortunately, you can get a powerful Windows 10 or Ubuntu LTS 18 HexaCore (or OctaCore) 64-bit pro Java 9 game development workstation at www.PriceWatch.com for a few hundred dollars.

Besides the API level (the SDK you installed and are using), the highest-level construct in the Java programming language is a **package**. Java packages use the **package** keyword to declare your own application package at the top of your Java code. This needs to be the first line of code declared other than comments, as you'll see in Chapter 6 (and shown in Figure 5-1 earlier in this chapter). You can have only one package declaration and can declare only one package, and it must be the first Java statement! The **New Project** series of dialogs in NetBeans 9 that you will use in Chapter 6 will create your package for you and will import other packages that you will need to use based on what you want to do in your application. In our case, these will be JavaFX 9 packages, so we can utilize the JavaFX new media engine. Java 9 further groups packages into modules, which are added to an application outside of (externally to) your main Java program logic.

As you may have ascertained from the name, a Java package bundles together all of the Java programming constructs that you will be learning about, or reviewing, during this chapter. These include classes, interfaces, and methods that relate to your application, so the gameboard package will contain **all of your code**, as well as all of the code that you **imported** to work with your code, that is needed to create, compile, and run your board game. We will take a look at the concept of importing and the Java import keyword next, as it relates closely to the package concept.

A Java package is useful for organizing and containing all of your own application code, but it is even more useful for organizing and containing the SDK's (API's) Java code that you will utilize along with your own Java programming logic to create your pro Java games or IoT applications. As of Java 9, Java packages will now be organized by functional modules, which we will be covering at the end of this chapter, as modules do not affect your Java game programming logic; they simply organize things at a high level to allow you to optimize your distribution so that you can obtain the smallest download size for your Java game distribution to your target game-playing end users.

You can use any of the classes that are part of the API that you are developing "under," or with, by using the Java **import** keyword, which, in conjunction with the package and the classes that you want to use, is called an **import statement**. This import statement begins with the **import keyword**, the **package and class reference path** (full proper name) is next, and then the statement needs to be **terminated** using a **semicolon**. As you saw in Figure 5-1, the import statement used to import the JavaFX **EventHandler** class from the **javafx.event** package should look like this:

```
import javafx.event.EventHandler;
```

An import statement informs the Java compiler that it will need to bring a specified external package inside of your package (import it into your package), because you will be using methods (and constants) from the class that is referenced using the import keyword, as well as what package it's stored in. If you use a class, method, or interface in your own Java 9 class, such as the BoardGame class you will be creating during Chapter 6, and you have not **declared** that class for use by using an import statement, the Java 9 compiler will **throw** an error. This is because it cannot locate or reference the class that is going to be used in your package so that it can import that functionality.

Java Classes: Java Structure to Modularize the Game

The next largest Java programming structure underneath the package level is the Java **class** level, as you have seen in the import statement, which references both the package that contains the class and a class itself. Just like a package organizes all of the related classes, a class organizes all of its related methods, variables, and constants, and sometimes other **nested** classes as well, which we will cover in the next section of this chapter.

The Java class can be used to organize your Java code at the next logical level of functional organization, and therefore, your classes will contain Java code constructs that add specific functionality to a game application. These include methods, variables, constants, nested classes, or inner classes, all of which will be covered during this chapter.

Java classes can also be used to create Java **objects**, which we'll cover after we learn about classes, nested classes, methods, and data fields. Java objects are **constructed** using your Java class. They have the same name as the Java class and as that class's **constructor method**, which we will be covering a bit later during this chapter.

As you can see in Figure 5-2, you **declare** your class using a Java **class** keyword along with a name for your class. You can also preface the declaration with Java **modifier** keywords, which we will cover later in this chapter. Java modifier keywords are always placed **before** (or, in front of) the Java class keyword, using the following format:

```
<Java modifier keywords here> class <your custom class name goes here>
```

One of the powerful features of Java classes is that they can be used to **modularize** your Java game code so your core game application features can be part of a high-level class, which can be **subclassed** to create more specialized versions of that class. Once a class has been used to create a subclass, it then becomes the **superclass**, to use Java class hierarchy terminology. A class will usually subclass another superclass using a Java **extends** keyword.

Using a Java extends keyword tells the compiler that you want the superclass's capabilities and functionality added (extended) to your class, which, once it uses this "extends" keyword, becomes a subclass. A subclass "extends" the core functionality that is provided by the superclass that it is extending. To extend the class definition to include a superclass, you add to (or extend, no pun intended) your existing Java class declaration using the following format:

```
<Java modifier keywords here> class <your class name here> extends <superclass name here>
```

When you extend a superclass using your class, which becomes the subclass of that superclass, you can use all of that superclass's features (nested classes, inner classes, methods, constructors, variables, and constants) in your subclass. You can do this without having to explicitly rewrite (recode) these Java constructs in the **body** of your class, which would be redundant (and disorganized) because your class extends the superclass, making it part of your class. We'll be covering nested and inner classes in the next section of this chapter, in case you're wondering what they are.

The body of your class is coded inside of the curly braces (the outer red box, in Figure 5-2), which follow your class and javafx.application.Application superclass (in this particular case) declaration. This is why you learned about, or reviewed, Java syntax first; you are building upon that with the class declaration and then the Java syntax that holds the class **definition** (variables, constants, methods, constructors, nested classes, inner classes) constructs.

Notice in Figure 5-2 that the InvinciBagel class extends the Application superclass from a JavaFX application package. Doing this gives the InvinciBagel class everything that it needs to host, or run, the JavaFX 8 application. What this JavaFX 8 Application class does is to "construct" your Application object so that it can use system memory, call an **.init()** method (to initialize anything that might need initializing), and call the **.start()** method that you can see in Figure 5-2 (in the second red box). This .start() method is where you put Java code statements in place that will ultimately be needed to "fire up" (that is, to start or launch) the InvinciBagel i2D arcade game Java 8 application. This Java 8 game will also run under Java 9 without modification.

When the end user finishes using the i2D InvinciBagel Java Application, the Application object created by the Application class, using the Application() constructor method, will call its **.stop()** method and remove your application from system memory. This will free up memory space for other uses by an end user. We will be getting into methods, constructors, and objects soon, as we are progressing from the high-level package and class constructs to lower-level methods and object constructs so that we can approach the learning process from a high-level overview to lower levels as we go along. You may be wondering if Java classes can be **nested** inside of each other. That is, can Java classes contain other Java classes? The answer is yes, they can. Let's take a closer look at this concept of Java nested classes next.

Nested Classes: Java Classes Living Inside of Other Classes

A **nested class** in Java is a class that is defined inside of another Java class. A nested class is part of the class that it is nested inside of, and this nesting signifies that the two classes are intended to be utilized together in some way. There are two types of nested classes: **static nested classes**, which are commonly referred to simply as nested classes, and **nonstatic nested classes**, which are commonly referred to as **inner classes**.

Static nested classes, which I will refer to as nested classes, are used to create **utilities** for use with the class that contains them and are sometimes used simply to contain **constants** for use with the class that contains them. Those of you who develop Android applications are familiar with nested classes, as they're quite commonly used in the Android API, either to hold utility methods or to contain Android constants, which are used to define things like screen density settings, animation motion interpolation curve types, alignment constants, and user interface element scaling settings, among other things. In Chapter 4 we covered the concept of static as it relates to games, and for code this has the same meaning or implication. Java constants can be thought of as fixed, or not capable of being changed.

A nested class uses what is commonly referred to in Java as **dot notation** in order to reference the nested class "off of" its master (or parent) containing class. For instance, **MasterClass.NestedClass** would be the referencing format that would be used to reference a nested class using, or via, its master class (containing class) name, using generic class type names here. If you created your SplashScreen nested class to draw the splash screen for your Java board game, it would be referenced in your Java code as **BoardGame. SplashScreen** by using Java dot notation syntax.

As an example of this, let's take a look at the JavaFX Application class, which contains the **Parameters** nested class. This nested class **encapsulates**, or contains, the parameters that you can set for your JavaFX Application. Thus, this **Application.Parameters** nested class would be part of the same **javafx.application** package as your **Application** class and would be referenced as **javafx.application.Application.Parameters** if you were using an import statement.

Similarly, the constructor method (we will be learning about constructor methods soon) would be written as **Application.Parameters()** since constructor methods must have the same name as the classes that they are contained in. Unless you are writing code for other developers to use, which is where nested classes are most often utilized, like with the JavaFX Application class or the many nested (utility or constant provider) classes in the Android 8 OS, you are far more likely to utilize nonstatic nested classes. These nonstatic nested classes are commonly referred to as *inner classes* for Java games.

A nested class, technically termed a static nested class, is declared using the **static** keyword (modifier), which you will be learning about a bit later on during this chapter. So, if you were to create the BoardGame. SplashScreen nested class, the BoardGame class and the SplashScreen nested class declaration would look something like the following code:

```
public class BoardGame extends Application {
    static class SplashScreen {
        // The Java code that creates and displays your splashscreen is in here
    }
}
```

It is important to note that if you use **import javafx.application.Application.Parameters** (as an example) to import the nested class, you can reference the nested class within your class at that point, using just the **Parameters** class name, rather than having to use the full class name "path" that shows your class's code how to travel through its parent class to the nested class using the Application.Parameter (ClassName. NestedClassName) reference.

As you'll see many times throughout this book, methods can also be accessed using **dot notation**. So, instead of using **ClassName.NestedClassName.MethodName**, you could, if you had used the import statement to import this nested class, simply use **NestedClassName.MethodName**. This is because the import statement has already been used to establish the full "reference path" to this nested class, through its containing class, so you don't have to.

Next, let's take a look at nonstatic nested classes, which are more commonly referred to as **inner classes**.

Inner Classes: Different Types of Nonstatic Nested Classes

Java **inner classes** are also nested classes, but they are not declared using the **static** keyword modifier before the class keyword and class name, which is why they are called "nonstatic" nested classes. Thus, any class declaration that is inside another class that doesn't use the static (keyword) modifier would be termed an inner class in Java. There are three types of inner classes in Java: the **member** class, the **local** class, and the **anonymous** class. We'll cover what the differences are between these inner class types, as well as how they're implemented, in detail during this section.

Like nested classes, **Member classes** are defined within the body of your containing (parent) class. You can declare a member class anywhere within the body of the containing class. You would want to declare a member class when you wanted to access data fields (variables or constants) and methods belonging to the containing class without having to provide a path (via dot notation) to the data field or method (ClassName. DataField or ClassName.Method). A member class can be thought of as a nested class that does not use the Java static modifier keyword.

Whereas a nested class is referenced through its containing or "top-level" class, using a dot notation path to the static nested class, a member class, since it is not static, is "instance-specific," which means that objects (instances) created using that class can be different from each other (an object is a unique "instance" of a class), whereas a static (fixed) nested class will have only one version that doesn't change. For instance, a **private inner class** can only be used by a parent class that contains it. The SplashScreen inner class coded as a private class would look something like this:

```
public class BoardGame extends Application {
    private class SplashScreen {
        // The Java code that creates and displays your splashscreen is in here
    }
}
```

Since this is declared as private, it is for our own application usage (the containing class's usage specifically). Thus, this would not be a utility or constant class for use by other classes, applications, or developers. You can also declare your inner class without using the **private access modifier keyword**, which would look like the following Java programming construct:

```
public class BoardGame extends Application {
    class SplashScreen {
        // The Java code that creates and displays your splashscreen is in here
    }
}
```

This level of **access control** is called **package** or **package private** and is the "default" level of access control that is applied to any class, interface, method, or data field that is declared without using one of the other Java access control modifier keywords (public, protected, or private). This type of inner class can be accessed not only by the top-level or containing class but also by any other class member of the package that contains that class. This is because the containing class is declared as "public" and the inner class is declared as "package private." If you wanted an inner class to be available outside of the package, you would declare it to be public, using the following Java code structure:

```
public class BoardGame extends Application {
    public class SplashScreen {
        // The Java code that creates and displays your splashscreen is in here
    }
}
```

You can also declare an inner class to be **protected**, which means that it can be accessed by any subclasses of the parent or containing class. We'll be getting into Java modifiers after we cover Java methods and Java variables.

If you declare a class inside of a lower-level Java programming structure that is not a class, such as a method or an iteration control (commonly called a *loop*) structure, it would be technically referred to as a **local class**. This local class would be visible only inside of that block of code, and as such it does not allow (or make sense to use) class modifiers such as static, public, protected, or private.

A local class is used like a **local variable**, except that it is a more complex Java coding construct, rather than a simple data field value that is used locally. This is not often used in games, as you usually want your game to be divided "functionally," into functional classes with methods and variables that clearly are for a distinct use and reason to keep the complexity of game design and processing clearly defined using the organization or encapsulation of Java. We will be looking at this throughout the book as we design a different functional component of the game in each chapter starting in Chapter 6. In this way we are using Java's features to their best advantage to create a game design.

Finally, there's a type of inner class that is called an **anonymous class**. An anonymous class is a local class that has not been given any class name. You are likely to encounter anonymous classes far more often than you are local classes. This is because programmers often do not name their local classes (making them anonymous classes). The logic local classes contain is only used locally to their declaration, and therefore, these classes do not really need to have a name, as they are only referenced internally to that block of Java code.

Java Methods: Core Logic Function Java Constructs

Inside of classes you generally have **methods** and the **data fields** (variables or constants) that these methods utilize. Since we are going from outer structures to inner structures, or top-level structures to lower-level structures, we will cover methods next. Methods are sometimes called *functions* in other programming languages, and you can see an example of the **.start()** method in Figure 5-2, which shows how the method holds the programming logic that creates your basic Java game application. The programming logic inside of the method uses Java programming statements to create a Stage and a Scene, places a button on the screen in a StackPane, and defines event handling logic so that when the button is clicked, the bootstrap Java code writes some "Hello World" text to your NetBeans 9 IDE output area.

Declaring Your Method: Modifier, Return Type, and Method Name

The method declaration starts with an **access control modifier keyword**, either public, protected, private, or package private (which is designated by not using any access control modifier keyword at all). As you can see in Figure 5-2, your .start() method has been declared using the public access control modifier. We will be covering access modifier keywords in greater detail later during this chapter.

After this access control modifier, you will need to declare the method's **return type**. This is the type of data that the method will **return**, after it is called, or **invoked**. Since the .start() method performs setup operations but does not return any specific type of value, it uses a **void** return type, which signifies that the method performs a task but does not return any resulting data to the calling entity. In this case, the calling entity is the JavaFX Application class since the .start() method is one of the key methods (the others being the .stop() and .init() methods) provided by the Application superclass that we extended, which controls the life-cycle stages for your i3D BoardGame JavaFX application.

After the return type, you will supply your method name, which, by convention (programming rules), should start with a **lowercase letter** (or word, preferably a verb), with any subsequent (internal) words (nouns or adjectives) starting with a capital letter. For instance, a method to display the splash screen would be named .showSplashScreen() or .displaySplashScreen() and, since it does something but does not return a value, would be declared using this code:

```
public void displaySplashScreen() { method Java code to display splashscreen goes in here }
```

If you need to pass parameters, which are named data values that need to be operated on within the body of your method (the part inside of the curly braces), these go inside of the **parentheses** that are attached to the method name. In Figure 5-2, the .start() method for your bootstrap HelloWorld JavaFX application receives a **Stage** object, named **primaryStage**, using the following Java method declaration syntax:

```
public void start(Stage primaryStage) { bootstrap Java code to start Application goes in here }
```

You can provide as many parameters using the data type and parameter name pairs as you like, with each pair separated by a comma character. Methods can also have no parameters in which case the parameter parentheses are empty and the opening and closing parentheses are right next to each other; this is how I am writing method names in this book so that you know that they are methods. I am using the dot (notation) before, and the parentheses characters after, the method name, like .start() or .stop() and so forth, so that you know I am referencing a Java method.

The programming logic that defines your method will be contained inside the "body" of the method, which as you have already learned is inside the curly braces that define the beginning and the end of the method. The Java programming logic inside of methods can include variable declarations, program logic statements, interative control structures, and iterative loops, among other things, all of which we will be leveraging to create our Java game during this book.

Overloading Your Methods: Providing Unique Parameter Lists

There is another concept in Java that applies to methods that I will cover in this section before I move on, called **overloading** Java methods. Overloading the Java method specifically refers to using the same method name but using different parameter list configurations. What overloading signifies is the Java compiler will be able to figure out which of your overloaded methods to use, if you have defined more than one method with the same name.

The Java compiler differentiates overloaded methods by looking at your parameter data types as well as the order in which they are being passed into the method being called. The Java compiler then uses the uniqueness of the parameter list as a fingerprint of sorts to discern which of the identically named methods (that have the same names) to utilize. Therefore, your parameter list configurations must all be completely unique from each other in order for a Java method overloading feature to be able to work correctly.

We will be learning how to use and how to code Java methods during the course of this book, from Chapter 6 introducing NetBeans 9 and onward until the end of the book, so I am not going to spend too much time on them here, other than to define what they are and the basic rules for how they are declared and utilized inside Java classes.

Constuctor Methods: Turning a Java Class into a Java Object

There is one specialized type of Java method I'm going to cover in detail in this section of this chapter called a **constructor method**. This is a special type of method that can be used to create (construct) Java **objects**, which we will be covering a bit later in the chapter, after we cover all of the different types of Java syntax and programming structures that can be used to create, define, and interface with these Java objects. Java objects just happen to be the foundation of **Object-Oriented Programming (OOP)**, so we will be taking a look at constructor methods here; it is important to have an understanding of this before we cover the Java object itself later in the chapter. Since we are covering methods in this section, this is the most logical place to take a look at **constructors**, as constructor methods are sometimes called (for short) by veteran Java game developers, which you are on your way to becoming.

Creating a Java Object: Invoking the Class Constructor Method

A Java class can contain a constructor method with the same name as the class and can be used to create Java objects using that class. A constructor method uses its Java class as a blueprint to create an **instance** of that class in system memory, which creates the Java object. A constructor method will always **return** a Java object and thus does not use any of the other **Java return types** that other methods will typically use (void, String, float, int, byte, etc.). We will be covering these Java return types later during the chapter. The constructor method should be invoked by using the Java **new** keyword since you are creating a new Java object.

You can see an example of this in the bootstrap JavaFX code shown in Figure 5-2, in line numbers 20, 28, and 30. These lines are where the Button, StackPane, and Scene objects are created, respectively, by using the following object declaration, naming, and creation Java code structure, as follows:

```
<Java class name> <object instance name> =
                    new <Java constructor method name><parameter list><semicolon>
```

The reason that a Java object is declared in this fashion—using the class name, the name of the object you're constructing, the Java new keyword, and the class's constructor method name (and parameters, if any) in a single Java statement terminated (finished) with a semicolon character—is because each Java object is an **instance** of a Java class.

To use the Button object creation from line 20 of your current Java code as an example, what you are telling the Java language compiler using the part of the Java statement on the left side of the equals "operator" is that you want to create a **Button type object** named **btn** using a JavaFX Button class as the object blueprint. This "declares" the Button class (object type) and gives it a unique name. (We will soon be covering operators, a bit later on in the chapter.)

The first part of creating the object is thus called the **object declaration**. The second part of creating your Java object is called the **object instantiation**, and this part of the object creation process can be seen on the right side of the equals operator and involves a constructor method and the Java new keyword.

What you do to instantiate a Java object is that you **invoke**, or utilize, the Java **new** keyword in conjunction with an object constructor method call. Since this takes place on the right side of the equals operator, the result of the object instantiation is placed into the declared object, which is on the left side of the Java statement. As you will see a bit later in the chapter when we discuss operators, this is what an equals operator does, and a useful operator it is.

This completes a process of **declaring** (class name), **naming** (object name), **creating** (using a **new** keyword), **configuring** (using a constructor method), and **loading** (using the equals operator) your very own custom Java object.

It's important to note that the declaration and instantiation part of this process can be coded using separate lines of Java code. For instance, the Button object instantiation (Figure 5-2, line 20) could be coded as follows:

```
Button btn;        // Declare a Button object named btn
btn = new Button(); //  Instantiate btn object using Java new keyword and Button()
constructor
```

The reason this is significant is because coding an object creation in this way allows you to declare an object at the top of your class, where each of the methods inside of the class that use or access these objects can "see" the object. In Java, unless declared as otherwise using modifiers, which we will be covering next, an object or data field is only visible inside of the Java programming construct (class or method) that it is declared inside of.

If you declare an object inside of your class, and therefore outside of all the methods contained in the class, all of the methods in your class can access (see and use) that object. Similarly, anything declared inside of a method is "local" to that method and is only "visible" to other "members" of that method, meaning all Java statements inside of that method scope that is inside of the {...} delimiters. If you wanted to implement this separate object declaration in the class, outside of the methods and object instantiation inside of the .start() method, in a current BoardGame class, the first few lines of Java code for your class would change to look like the following Java programming logic:

```
public class BoardGame extends Application {
    Button btn;
    @Override
    public void start(Stage primaryStage) {
        btn = new Button();
        btn.setText("Say 'Hello World'");
        // other programming statements continue here
    }
}
```

When the object declaration and instantiation are split up, they can be placed inside (or outside) of methods as needed for visibility. In the previous code, other methods of the BoardGame class could call a **btn.setText()** method call shown earlier without the Java compiler "throwing" an error. The way the Button object is declared in Figure 5-2, only the .start() method can "see" the object, so only the .start() method can implement the **btn.setText()** method call.

Creating a Constructor Method: Designing and Coding a Java Object Structure

A constructor method is a specialized type of method that is utilized to create an object in system memory. This differs significantly from other methods (if you use a different programming language, you are used to referring to them as functions). Nonconstructor methods in Java are used to perform some sort of complex calculation or encapsulated (modularized) processing of one form or another. The constructor method's usage for creating Java objects in memory, rather than performing some other programming functionality, as evidenced by the use of the Java **new** keyword in conjunction with the constructor method, which creates a new Java object of that unique class type in memory. For this reason, a constructor method will therefore define an internal structure of a unique type of Java object. If you want to configure the Java object at the same time as you instantiate it, you can define the constructor method **parameter list** to allow the calling entity to **populate** the object structure with specific (custom) data values. That way, you can create different types of that object by passing in different attributes in the constructor's parameter list.

We will create a couple of sample constructor methods in this section to show you the basics regarding how to create a constructor method and what it usually contains. Let's say you were creating an object for the game. You could declare a **public BoardGame()** constructor method by using this following Java code structure, for instance:

```
public BoardGame() {
    int      healthIndex = 1000;    // Defines units of Health
    int      scoreIndex  = 0;       // Defines units of Scoring
    int      boardIndex  = 0;       // Current Game Board Location
    boolean  turnActive  = false;   // Flag showing if current turn
}
```

A constructor method, called using the **BoardGame playerName = new BoardGame();** constructor method call, creates a BoardGame game player object named **playerName**. The object has 1,000 units of Health, has no current score because the object is on the first square of the game board, and is not currently moving because it is not currently their turn.

Next, let's explore the concept of **overloading** this constructor method, which we learned about earlier, and create another constructor method that has parameters that will allow us to define your healthIndex and turnActive variables of the BoardGame object at the same time that you're creating it. A constructor method would look like this:

```
public BoardGame(int startingHealthIndex, boolean isTurnActive) {
    int healthIndex = startingHealthIndex;
    int scoreIndex;
    int boardIndex;
    boolean turnActive = isTurnActive;
}
```

In this version, I still initialize the scoreIndex and boardIndex variables to **zero**, which is the **default value** for an Integer value, so I do not have to use lifeIndex = 0 or hitsIndex = 0 in this code, just to show you an optional way to code these two statements. Since the Java programming language accommodates method overloading, if you use the **BoardGame playerOne = new BoardGame(1250, true);** method call to instantiate a BoardGame object, the correct constructor method will be utilized to create the object. This BoardGame object named **playerOne** will have a healthIndex of 1250 units of Health, would have a zero score, would be on the first game board location, and would currently be at their turn.

The Java keyword this can be used to access data fields created using a constructor method. For instance, within an object's code, this.startingHealthIndex = value; sets that object's own internal data field to the value that you specify. You can also use this() to invoke another constructor method within the same class construct.

You can have as many (overloaded) constructor methods as you like, as long as they are each 100 percent unique. This means that **overloaded constructors** must have different parameter list configurations, including parameter list length (the number of parameters), order, and/or different parameter list types (different data types). As you can see, it is your parameter list (number of parameters, parameter data types, and parameter order) that allows a Java compiler to differentiate your overloaded methods from one another.

Java Variables and Constants: Values in Data Fields

The next level down, from API to package to class to method, are the actual **data values** that are being operated upon in these Java classes and methods. In Java this is called the **data field**. Data is held inside of something that is called a field, just like in database design. Java data fields can be dynamic, or **variable**, which is why they are often referred to as "variables," and can change during the operation of your Java game or IoT application. Alternatively, they can be static (fixed), which makes that data permanent, in which case it would be called a **constant**. A constant is a special type of variable, which we will cover in the next section, because declaring a constant correctly in the Java programming language is a bit more involved (advanced) than declaring a Java variable.

As far as Java lingo (convention) goes, variables declared at the top of a class are called **member variables**, **fields**, or **data fields**, although all variables and constants can be considered to be data fields at a fundamental level.

A variable declared inside of a method, or other lower-level Java programming structure (nested inside of a class or a method), is called a **local variable** because it can only be "seen" or used locally, inside of that programming construct that has been delimited by using curly {...} braces. Finally, variables passed inside of a parameter list area of a method declaration, constructor method definition, or a method call are, not surprisingly, called **parameters**.

A variable is a data field that holds an **attribute** of your Java object or software, which can (and will) change during the course of the execution of your software. As you might imagine, this can be especially important for game programming. The simplest form of variable declaration can be achieved by using one of the Java **data type keywords** along with the name that you want to use for that particular variable within the Java program logic. In the constructor method in the previous section, we declared an integer variable named scoreIndex to hold the score that your object will accumulate during gameplay. We defined the variable data type and named it using the following Java variable declaration programming statement:

int scoreIndex; // This could be coded as: **int scoreIndex = 0;** (default integer value is zero)

As you also saw in the previous section on constructor methods, you can initialize your variable to a starting value, using the equals operator, along with a data value that matches up with the data type declared. Here's an example:

boolean turnActive = false; // Could be: **boolean turnActive;** (default boolean value is false)

This Java statement declares a **boolean** data type variable and names it **turnActive**, on the left side of your equals operator, and then sets a declared variable to a value of false, which will signify that player's turn is not active. This is similar to how an object is declared and instantiated, except the Java new keyword and constructor method are replaced by the data value itself since now a variable (data field) is being declared instead of an object being created. We will be covering the different data types (we've already covered integers, Boolean, and Object) in a future section of this chapter.

You can also use Java modifier keywords with variable declarations, which I will do in the next section of the chapter when I show you how to declare an **immutable** variable, also known as a **constant**, which is fixed or **locked** into place in memory and which cannot be changed or altered in any way so that it remains, you guessed it, constant.

We will be covering the Java access modifier keywords, as they pertain to all Java constructs, in the sections that follow the next section on constants. So, now that I'm almost finished going from the largest Java constructs, or packages, to the smallest, or data fields, we will start to cover those topics that apply to all levels (classes, methods, data fields) of Java. These Java concepts will increase in complexity as we progress through the end of this Java primer chapter, as I wanted to start with easier high-level concepts and drill down to more complex lower-level ones. At the end of the chapter, we will also cover packaging your Java project for distribution using the new Java 9 modules feature, which will allow you to optimize the data footprint for your Pro Java 9 game and make it more secure as well. Java 9 should be released at around the same time that this book is released to the public, so I am making this book a Java 9 book. Everything in the *Beginning Java 8 Games Development* book would still apply to Java 9 development.

Fixing Data Values in Memory: Defining a Data Constant in Java

If you are already familiar with computer programming, you will know that there is often a need to have data fields that will always contain the same data value and that will not change during the duration of the application's run cycle. These are termed **constants** and are defined, or declared, using a special combination of Java access modifier keywords that are used to fix things in memory so that they cannot be changed. There are also Java modifier keywords that will restrict (or unrestrict) object instances, or access to certain classes inside or outside of a Java class or package. We will be getting into these in detail in the next section of the chapter, covering Java modifier keywords.

To declare Java variables as "fixed," you must use Java's **final** modifier keyword. Final means the same thing as when your parents say something is final; it is fixed in place, a fact of life (FOL), and not going to change, ever. Thus, the first step in creating a constant is to add this final keyword in front of the data type keyword in your declaration.

A convention when declaring a Java constant (and constants in other programming languages, as well) is to use **uppercase characters** with **underscore characters** between each word, which signifies a constant in your code.

If we wanted to create **screen width** and **screen height** constants for your game, you would do so like this:

```
final int SCREEN_HEIGHT_PIXELS = 480;
final int SCREEN_WIDTH_PIXELS = 640;
```

There is also a "blank" final, which is a nonstatic final variable whose initialization will be deferred to your constructor method body. It is also important to note that each object gets its own copy of a nonstatic final variable.

If you wanted all of the objects created by your class's constructor method to be able to "see," and use, this constant, you would have to also add the Java **static** modifier keyword in front of the final modifier keyword, like this:

```
static final int SCREEN_HEIGHT_PIXELS = 480;
static final int SCREEN_WIDTH_PIXELS = 640;
```

If you wanted only your class and objects created by this class to be able to see these constants, you would declare the constants using the Java **private** modifier keyword in front of the static modifier keyword, using this code:

```
private static final int SCREEN_HEIGHT_PIXELS = 480;
private static final int SCREEN_WIDTH_PIXELS = 640;
```

If you wanted any Java class, even those outside of your package (that is, anyone else's Java classes), to be able to see these constants, you would declare the constants using the Java **public** modifier keyword in front of the static modifier keyword using the following Java code:

```
public static final int SCREEN_HEIGHT_PIXELS = 480;
public static final int SCREEN_WIDTH_PIXELS = 640;
```

As you can see, declaring the constant can be a significantly more detailed Java statement construction than declaring a simple variable for use in your class. Next we should take a deeper look at Java's access modifier keywords since they allow you to control things (like **access** to classes, methods, constants, and variables, allowing you to **lock** a Java code structure from being modified) and similar high-level Java code control concepts that are fairly complicated.

Now that you understand the primary Java programming logic constructs or structures, you're ready to learn about (or review) more complicated language features, such as **modifiers**, **operators**, **data types**, and **statements**.

Java Modifier Keywords: Access Control and More

Java **modifier keywords** are **reserved** Java keywords that modify the **access control**, **visibility**, or **longevity** (how long something exists in memory, during the execution of your application) for code or data structures inside of the primary types of Java programming structures that you have learned about (reviewed) thus far. The modifier keywords are the first Java reserved words that are "declared" or utilized on the "outside" and "head" (beginning) of your Java code structures since the Java logic for the structure, at least for classes and methods, is contained within the curly braces {...} delimiters, which come after the class keyword and class name or after the method name and parameter list. Modifier keywords come before any of these and can be utilized with your Java classes, methods, data fields (variables and constants), and Java interfaces, which we will be covering a bit later.

As you can see at the bottom of Figure 5-2 for the .main() method, which was created by NetBeans 9 for the BoardGame class definition (which uses the **public** modifier that we are going to be covering next), you can use more than one Java modifier keyword. The **.main()** method first uses a **public** modifier keyword, which is the access control modifier keyword, and then it uses a **static** modifier keyword second, which is a **nonaccess control** modifier keyword. Let's cover the Java access control modifiers next, and after that, we will get into the much more complex nonaccess control modifiers. These access control modifiers become much more important with the extra security protection in Java 9 afforded by the Java Modules feature, which controls how your packages and API are bundled and distributed.

Access Control Modifiers: Public, Protected, Package, or Private

Let's cover access control modifiers first since they are declared first before any nonaccess control modifier keywords and before any return type keywords; they are easier to understand conceptually as well. There are four access control modifier levels that can be applied to any Java programming structure. If you do not declare any access control modifier keyword, a "default" access control level of **package private** will be applied to that Java code structure, which allows it to be "visible to," and thus usable by, any Java programming structure inside of your Java package. In this case, that would be the **boardgame** package.

The other three Java access control modification levels all have their own access control modifier keywords, including the **public**, **private**, and **protected** keywords. These are aptly named for what they do, so you probably have a fairly good idea of how to apply these to either share your code publicly or protect it from public usage already, but let's cover each of these in detail here, just to make sure. As you know, access control, as in **security**, is the important issue for Java software these days, both inside of your code and in the outside world, which is why Java 9 added modules. We will start with the least amount of access control (security) first, with the public access control modifier.

Java Public Modifier: Variables or Methods That Exist Independently of Instances

The Java **public** access modifier keyword can be used by classes, methods, constructors, data fields (variables and constants), and interfaces. If you declare something as public, it can be accessed by the public. This means it can be imported and utilized by any other class, in any other package, as long as it is exported in a module. Essentially this means your code can be used in any software that is created using the Java 9 language. As you will see in the classes that you use from the Java and JavaFX programming platforms

(APIs), the public keyword is most often used in open source programming Java platforms or packages that are used to create custom applications, including games.

It is important to note that if a public class that you are trying to access and utilize exists in another package other than your own package (in our case, your own package will be named boardgame), then you will need to use the Java import keyword to create an import statement to be able to utilize that public class. This is why, by the end of this book, you will have dozens of import statements at the top of your **JavaFXGame.java** class. You will be leveraging preexisting Java and JavaFX classes in code libraries, which have already been coded, tested, refined, and made public, by using a public access control modifier keyword so that you can create pro Java 9 games and IoT apps that leverage Java APIs.

Because of **class inheritance** in Java, all of the public methods and public variables inside a public class will be **inherited** by the subclasses of that class (which, once it is subclassed, becomes a superclass). You can see an example of a public access control modifier keyword in front of the Invincibagel class keyword, as shown in Figure 5-2.

Java Protected Modifier: Variables and Methods Allow Access by Subclasses

The Java **protected** access modifier keyword can be used by **data fields** (variables and constants) and by **methods**, including **constructor** methods, but cannot be used by classes or interfaces. We will be covering Java interfaces later in this chapter. The protected keyword allows variables, methods, and constructors in a superclass to be accessed only by subclasses of that superclass in other packages (such as your boardgame package) or by any class within the same package as the class containing those protected members (Java constructs). Using this access control modifier is like putting a lock on the original Java code; to use the original code (much less to add to it and thus modify its intended usage), you are forced to **extend**, or **subclass**, the protected class, and then you can **override** its methods.

This access modifier keyword therefore essentially **protects** methods or variables in a class that is intended to be (is hoped to be) used as a superclass by being subclassed (extended) by other developers. Unless you **own** this package, which these protected Java constructs are defined inside (which you don't), you must **extend** this superclass and create your own subclass **implementation** in order to be able to utilize these protected methods and variables.

You might be wondering when would one want to do this and protect Java code structures like this? When you are designing a larger project, such as the Android operating system API, for instance, you will often want to have the highest-level methods and variables not be used directly, right out of the class, or directly from within that class.

In this situation, where others are using your code structures, you would rather that your original Java code be used within a separately defined, developer-coded subclass structure. This "isolates" the superclass code so that it will remain directly untouched, in a sense, guaranteeing that the original methods, fields, and intent are maintained as they were originally intended by the Java code author or authors (package owner or owners), protected from others' modifications. This ensures that your API and its superclasses remain, ad infinitum, as a "blueprint" for other Java 9 developers to utilize to create their own (Android, JavaFX, etc.) games, business utilities, and IoT applications.

You can achieve this direct use prevention by protecting methods and variable constructs from being used directly so that they become only a **blueprint** for more detailed implementations in other classes and are not able to be used directly. Essentially, protecting a method or variable turns it into a blueprint, or "implementation road map."

Java Private Modifier: Fields, Methods, or Constructors Allowed Local Access

The Java **private** access control modifier keyword can be used by data fields (variables or constants) and by methods, including constructor methods and interfaces, but cannot be used by classes. We will be covering Java interfaces later in this chapter. The private access control keyword allows variables, methods, and constructors in a class to be accessed only inside of that class, and as of Java 9, private interfaces are now allowed. This private access control keyword allows Java to implement a concept called *encapsulation*, where a class (and objects created using that class) can encapsulate itself, hiding its "internals" from the outside Java universe, so to speak. This encapsulation is further enhanced in Java 9 using modules, which we'll be covering toward the end of this chapter. The OOP concept of encapsulation can be used to allow teams to create (and debug) their own classes and objects. In this way, no one else's Java code can break code that exists inside of a class because its methods, variables, constants, interfaces, and constructors are private. Encapsulation can also be utilized to protect code and resources (assets) from public access.

This access modifier keyword essentially "privatizes" methods or variables in a class so that they can be used locally only within that class or by objects created by that class's constructor methods. Unless you own the class that these private Java constructs are inside of, you cannot access, or utilize, these methods or data fields. This is the **most restrictive** level of access control in Java. A variable declared as private can be accessed outside of the class, if a public method that accesses a private variable from inside of the class, called a public .get() method call, is declared as public and thus provides a pathway (or doorway) through that public method to the data in the private variable or constant.

Java Package Private Modifier: Variables, Methods, or Classes in the Package

If no Java access control modifier keyword is declared, then a **default** access control level, which is also referred to as the **package private** access control level, will be applied to that Java construct (class, method, data field, constructor, or interface). This means that these package private Java constructs are visible, or available, to any other Java class that is inside of that Java package that contains them. This package private level of access control is the easiest to apply to your classes, interfaces, methods, constructors, constants, and variables since it is applied as a default action by simply not explicitly declaring any Java access control modifier keyword before your Java construct.

You will use this default package private access control level quite a bit for your own pro Java games and IoT applications programming, as usually you are creating your own application in your own package for your users to use in a completed, compiled, executable state with Java 9's new enhanced security Java Module System (Project Jigsaw).

As of Java 9, you will also install your package into one of the core JavaFX modules, probably javafx. media or javafx.graphics. As you will see in the final section in this chapter, using the public and private keywords correctly will allow you to fully leverage the power of Java 9's new module features. We'll be covering modules in detail at the end of this chapter, after we cover all of the other core Java programming language features that have existed in many of the previous versions of Java and that are still in use today in Java 6 (32-bit Android), Java 7 (64-bit Android 5 through 6), and Java 8 (64-bit Android 7 through 8 and the current version of Java, until Java 9 is released, during the last quarter of 2017).

If you were developing game engines for other game developers to use, however, you would most probably end up using more of the other three access control modifier keywords that we have been discussing in this section so that you would be able to control precisely how others would implement your game engine's Java code structures. Next, let's take a look at the nonaccess control modifier keywords, which are even more intellectually challenging!

Non Access Control Modifiers: Final, Static, and Abstract

The Java modifier keywords that do not specifically provide access control features to your Java constructs are termed **nonaccess control modifier keywords**. These include the often used **static**, **final**, and **abstract** modifier keywords, as well as the not so often used **synchronized** and **volatile** modifier keywords, which are used for more advanced **thread** control, which I will be covering later during this professional-level programming title. I will cover those keywords in this section so that you will know what they mean if you encounter them in your Java programming before then.

I will cover these concepts in order of their complexity, from the easiest for developers to wrap their minds around to the most difficult for the object-oriented programming developers to wrap their minds around. OOP is like surfing, in that it seems very difficult until such time as you have practiced doing it a large number of times and then suddenly one day you just get it.

Java Final Modifier: Variable Reference, Method, or Class Cannot Be Modified

We have already looked at the **final** modifier keyword, as it is used to declare a constant along with a static keyword. A final data field variable can be initialized (set) one time. A final **reference variable**, which is a special type of Java variable that contains a reference to an object in memory, cannot be changed (reassigned) to refer to a different object. The data that is held inside of the (final) referenced object can be changed, however, as only the reference to the object itself is the final reference variable, which is essentially "locked in" using a Java final keyword.

A Java method can also be "locked" using the final modifier keyword. When a Java method is made "final," it means that if the Java class that contains that method is subclassed, that final method cannot be **overridden**, or modified, within the body of the subclass. This essentially "locks" what is inside of the method code structure. For example, if you wanted the .start() method for your JavaFXGame class (were it to ever be subclassed) to always do the same things that it does for your JavaFXGame superclass (prepare the JavaFX staging environment), you would do this:

```
public class JavaFXGame extends Application {
    Button btn;
    @Override
    public final void start(Stage primaryStage) {
        btn = new Button();                              // other Java statements can be added
    }
}
```

This would prevent any subclasses (public class JavaFXGame3D extends JavaFXGame) from changing anything regarding how the JavaFXGame game engine (JavaFX) is set up initially, which is what the .start() method does for your game applications, as you'll see in Chapters 7 and 8, covering the JavaFX 9 multimedia engine. A class that is declared using a final modifier keyword can't be extended (also called subclassed), locking that class against any future usage.

Java Static Modifier: Variables or Methods That Exist Independently of Instances

As you have seen already, the **static** keyword can be used in conjunction with the final keyword to create a constant. The static keyword is used to create Java constructs (methods or variables) that exist independently or "outside of" any object instances that are created using the class that static variables or static methods are defined in. A static variable in a class will **force all instances of the class to share the data in that variable**. In other programming languages, this is generally referred to as a *global variable*, one everything created by the code can access and share.

Similarly, a static method will also exist outside of instanced objects for that class and will be shared by all of those objects. A static method will not reference variables "outside of" itself, such as an instanced object's variables.

Generally, the static method will reference its local, or static, variables and constants from its declaring class and will also take in variables using that method's parameter list. It will then provide processing or computation based on those parameters, as well as using the method's own static or local constants or variables, and programming logic.

Since static is a concept that applies to **instances** of a class and is thus inherently at a lower level that any class itself, a **Java class would therefore not ever be declared using the static nonaccess control modifier keyword**.

Java Abstract Modifier: Classes or Methods to Be Extended or Implemented

The Java **abstract** modifier keyword has more to do with protecting your actual code than it has to do with code that has been placed into memory (object instances and variables and so on) at run time. The abstract keyword allows you to specify how the code will be utilized as a superclass, that is, how it is implemented in a subclass once it is extended. For this reason, the abstract modifier keyword would only apply to classes and methods and would not apply to data fields (variables and constants), as these data structures hold values and are not code (programming logic) constructs.

A class that has been declared using the abstract modifier keyword cannot be instanced, and it is intended to be used only as a superclass (blueprint) to create (extend) other classes. Since a final class cannot be extended, you will not use the final and the abstract modifier keywords together, at a class level. If a class contains any method that has been declared using the abstract modifier keyword, that class must then itself be declared to be an abstract class. An abstract class does not have to contain any abstract methods, however.

A method that has been declared using the abstract modifier keyword is a method that has been declared for use in subclasses but that has **no current implementation**. This means it will have zero Java code inside of its "method body," which, as you know, is delineated in Java by using the curly braces. Any subclass that extends an abstract class must implement all of these abstract methods, unless that subclass is also subsequently declared to be abstract, in which case the abstract method is passed down to the next subclass level to eventually be implemented.

Java Volatile Modifier: Advanced Multithreading Control Over Your Data Fields

The Java **volatile** modifier keyword is used when you are developing **multithreaded** applications, which you are not going to be doing for Java 9 game development, as you want to optimize your game well enough so that it only uses the JavaFX threads. What the volatile modifier does is to tell the Java Virtual Machine (JVM) that is running your application to merge the private (that thread's) copy of the data field (variable or constant) that has been declared as volatile with the master copy of that variable in system memory.

Volatility is associated with the property of visibility to the running app. When a variable is declared volatile, a write will affect the main memory copy of a variable so that any thread running on any CPU or core will observe the change. When a variable is not declared to be volatile, that write is made to a cached copy, so only the thread making that change will be able to observe that change. Only use volatile when it's absolutely necessary for your Java 9 game.

This is similar to the static modifier keyword, with the difference that a static variable (data field) is shared by more than one object instance, whereas a volatile data field (variable or constant) is shared by more than one thread.

Java Synchronized Modifier: Advanced Multithreading Control Over Methods

The Java **synchronized** modifier keyword is also used when you're developing multithreaded applications, which we are not going to be doing for your Java 9 game development engine in this particular book. What the synchronized modifier does is to tell the Java Virtual Machine (JVM) that is running your application that the method that has been declared as synchronized can be accessed by only one thread at a time. This concept is similar to the concept of synchronized in database access, so you don't have data record access **collisions**. A synchronized modifier keyword thus also prevents these collisions between threads accessing your method (in system memory) by "serializing" the access to one at a time so simultaneous access (collision) of a method in memory by multiple threads can never occur. The synchronized keyword is associated with the properties of visibility and mutual exclusion for the running app. Many multithreading scenarios do not require mutual exclusion, only visibility, and therefore using a synchronized keyword instead of a volatile keyword in those situations would be considered overkill (the opposite of optimization).

Now that we have covered primary Java constructs (classes, methods, and fields) and basic modifier (public, private, protected, static, final, abstract, etc.) keywords, let's journey inside of the curly braces: { } now, learning about the tools that are used to create the Java programming logic that will eventually define your pro Java 9 gameplay.

Java Data Types: Defining Data Types in Applications

Since we have already covered variables and constants, you have encountered a few of the Java data types already. Let's get into that topic next, as it's not too advanced for our current progression from easy-to-comprehend to more difficult topics! There are two primary data type classifications in Java: **primitive data types**, which are the ones that you are probably the most familiar with if you have used different programming languages, and **reference (object) data types**, which you are probably familiar with if you have used another Object-Oriented Programming language, such as LISP, Python, Objective-C, Ruby, Groovy, Modula, Object COBOL, ColdFusion, C++, and C# (C Sharp and .NET).

Primitive Data Types: Character, Numbers, and Boolean

There are **eight primitive data types** in the Java programming language, as shown in Table 5-1. We will be using these during the book to create our JavaFXGame i3D Java 9 game, so I am not going to go into a high level of detail regarding each one of these now, except to say that boolean data is usually used in games to hold "flags" or "switches" (on/off), char data is usually used to contain Unicode characters or is used to create more complex String objects (which are essentially are an array of char), and the rest are used to hold numeric values of different sizes and resolutions. Integer values hold whole numbers, while a floating-point value holds fractional (decimal point value) numbers.

It's important to use the right numeric data type for a variable's "scope" or range of use, because as you can see in Table 5-1, large numeric data types can use up to eight times more memory than the smaller ones. Notice that a Boolean data value can be 64 times smaller than a long or double numeric value, so designing your Java 9 games to utilize lots of Boolean values can be an incredible memory optimization technique. Don't use any more numeric value resolution than you absolutely need to accomplish your game processing objective, as memory is a valuable resource.

Table 5-1. *Primitive Data Types in Java 9 Along with Their Default Values, Size in Memory, Definition, and Numeric Range*

DataType	Default	Binary Size	Definition	Range
boolean	false	1 bit (or 8 in 1 byte)	A true or false value	0 to 1 (false or true)
char	\u0000	16 bit	A Unicode character	\u0000 to \uFFFF
byte	0	8 bit	A signed integer value	-128 to 127 (256 total values)
short	0	16 bit	A signed integer value	-32768 to 32767 (65,536 total values)
int	0	32 bit	A signed integer value	-2147483648 to 2147483647
long	0	64 bit	A signed integer value	-9223372036854775808 to 9223372036854775807
float	0.0	32 bit	IEEE 754 floating-point value	±1.4E-45 to ±3.4028235E+38
double	0.0	64 bit	IEEE 754 floating-point value	±4.9E-324 to ±1.7976931348623157E+308

Next, let's take a look at reference data types, which are termed this because they reference more complex data structures in memory, such as objects and arrays, both of which contain far more complex data structures that will either hold complex data and method substructures (objects) or will hold more extensive lists of data (arrays). I will logically cover Java operators, which "operate" on these Java data structures, in the section right after data types.

Reference Data Types: Objects and Arrays

Object-Oriented Programming (OOP) languages also have **reference data types**, which provide a reference in memory to another structure containing a more complex data structure, such as an **object** or an **array**. These more complex data structures are created using code. In the case of Java, this is a class. There are Java Array classes of one type or another that create arrays of data (like simple databases), as well as the constructor method in any Java class, even custom classes that you create, which can create the object structure in memory, which can contain both Java code (methods) as well as data (fields).

Since a reference data type is a reference to a memory location, the default value is always null, which will signify that the object has not been created yet, as there is no reference in place. Since there are different Array and DataSet classes, arrays are also reference objects, but since they are created by class constructor methods, they are actually objects. The bottom line is that reference data types are created using classes and are always an object of one type or another, which is referenced in memory. Usually this reference is static and/or final so that the memory location is fixed and memory use is therefore optimized. Next, let's take a look at Java operators that are utilized to operate on (that is, perform operations on or with) the different Java data types that we have just covered.

Java Operators: Manipulating Data in the Application

In this section we are going to cover some of the most often used **operators** in the Java programming language, especially the ones that are the most useful for programming games. These include the **arithmetic** operators, used for mathematical expressions; the **relational** operators, used to ascertain relationships (equal, not equal, greater than, less than, etc.) between data values; the **logical** operators, used for boolean logic; the **assignment** operators, which do the arithmetic operations and assign the value to another variable in one compact operation (operator); and the **conditional** operator, also known as a **ternary** operator, which assigns a value to a variable based upon the outcome of a true or false (boolean) evaluation.

There are also the conceptually more advanced **bitwise** operators, used to perform operations at the **binary** data (zeroes and ones) level, the application of which is beyond the scope of the book. The use of binary data is not as common in JavaFX game programming as these other more mainstream types of operators, each of which you will be using during this book to accomplish various programming objectives in your pro Java games and IoT application logic.

Java Arithmetic Operators: Basic Mathematics

The Java **arithmetic operators** are the most commonly used operators in pro Java game programming, especially in dynamic action-type games, where things are moving on the screen by a precise, highly controlled number of pixels. Don't underestimate simple arithmetic operators, as in the framework of a OOP language. Far more complex mathematical equations can be created using Java structures, such as methods, that leverage these basic arithmetic operators using the other powerful tools that Java offers, which we are reviewing (learning about) during this chapter.

The only arithmetic operators, shown in Table 5-2, that you might not be that familiar with are the **Modulus** operator, which will return the **remainder** (what is left over) after a divide operation is completed; and the **Increment** or **Decrement** operator, which adds or subtracts one, respectively, from a value. These operators are sometimes used to implement your **counter** logic. Counters (using increment and decrement operators) were originally used for **loops**, which we will be covering in the next section; however, increment and decrement operators are also extremely useful in game design as well, for point scoring, life-span loss, game piece movement, and similar linear numeric progressions.

Table 5-2. *Java Arithmetic Operators, Their Operation Type, and a Description of That Arithmetic Operation*

Operator	Operation	Description
Plus +	Addition	Operation adds the operands on either side of the operator
Minus -	Subtraction	Operation subtracts the right operand from the left operand
Multiply *	Multiplication	Operation multiplies the operands on both sides of the operator
Divide /	Division	Operation divides the left operand by the right operand
Modulus %	Remainder	Operation divides the left operand by the right operand, returning the remainder
Increment ++	Adding One	Increment operation will increase the value of the operand by one
Decrement --	Subtract One	Decrement operation will decrease the value of the operand by one

To implement the arithmetic operators, place the data field (variable) that you want to receive the results of the arithmetic operation on the **left side** of your **equals assignment operator** (we will cover assignment operators during this section of the chapter as well) and the variables that you want to perform arithmetic operations on the right side of the equals sign. Here's an example of **adding** an X and a Y variable and assigning the result to a z variable:

```
Z = X + Y;   // Using the Addition Operator
```

If you wanted to **subtract** Y from X, you would use a **minus** sign rather than a plus sign, and if you wanted to **multiply** the X and Y values, you would use an **asterisk** character, rather than a plus sign. If you wanted to **divide** X by Y, you would use a **forward slash** character, instead of using a plus sign. If you wanted to find the **remainder** of divide X by Y, you would use a **percentage sign** character. Here is how these basic arithmetic operations would look in code:

```
Z = X - Y;   // Subtraction    Operator
Z = X * Y;   // Multiplication  Operator
Z = X / Y;  //    Division      Operator
Z = X % Y; //     Modulus       Operator
```

You should be careful if your Java code involves division by zero (0). Dividing an integer by 0 will result in an ArithmeticException. Dividing a floating-point value by 0 will result in +Infinity, -Infinity, or NaN. In game development environments, it is possible that you might encounter this scenario, and you will have to redesign your programming logic to make sure that these scenarios do not interfere with your gameplay.

You will be using these arithmetic operators quite a bit during this book, so you will get some great practice with these before you're done with your game! Let's take a closer look at relational operators next, as sometimes you will want to compare values rather than calculating values precisely.

Java Relational Operators: Making Comparisons

The Java **relational operators** can be used to make **logical comparisons** between two variables or between a variable and a constant, in some circumstances. These should also be familiar to you from junior high school, and they include equals, not equal, greater than, less than, greater than or equal to, and less than or equal to. The greater than uses the open end of the arrow (chevron) since the open span is greater than the closed span, and the less than uses the closed end of the arrow (chevron) since the closed span is less than the open span. This is a great way to look at this visually; when you do, you can immediately see that in the relational operator **X > Y**, X is (on the) greater than (side of) Y. In Java, the **equal to** relational operator uses **two equals signs, side by side,** between the data fields being compared and uses an **exclamation point** before an equals sign is used to denote **not equal**, as you can see in Table 5-3, which shows the relational operators along with an example and a description of each.

Table 5-3. *Java Relational Operators, an Example Where A=10 and B=20, and a Description of the Relational Operation*

Operator	Example	Description
==	(A == B) **not** true	Comparison of two operands: if they are **equal**, then the condition equates to **true**
!=	(A != B) **is** true	Comparison of two operands: if they are **not equal**, the condition equates to **true**
>	(A > B) **not** true	Comparison of two operands: if left operand is **greater** than right operand, equates to **true**
<	(A < B) **is** true	Comparison of two operands: if left operand is **less** than right operand, equates to **true**
>=	(A >= B) **not** true	Compare two operands: if left operand is **greater** or equal to right operand equates to **true**
<=	(A <= B) **is** true	Compare two operands: if left operand **less** than or equal to right operand, equates to **true**

The greater-than symbol is the right-facing arrowhead, and the less-than symbol is a left-facing arrowhead. These are used before the equals sign to create greater than or equal to and less than or equal to relational operators, respectively, as you can see at the bottom of Table 5-3.

These relational operators return a boolean value of true or false. As such, they are also used in control (loop) structures in Java quite a bit and are used in gameplay programming logic as well to control the path (result) that the gameplay will take. For instance, let's say you want to determine where the left edge of the game board is so that the GamePiece 3D object does not fall right off of the board when it is being moved to the left. Use this relational comparison:

```
boolean gameBoardEdge = false;    // boolean variable gameBoardEdge initialized to be false
gameBoardEdge = (GamePieceX <= 0); //  boolean gameBoardEdge set to TRUE if left side reached
```

Notice that I have used <= **less than or equal to** (yes, Java supports negative numbers too), so that if the GamePiece has gone past the **(x=0)** left side of the screen, the **gameBoardEdge** boolean flag will be set to the value of true, and the game movement programming logic can deal with the situation by changing the direction of movement (so GamePiece does not fall off GameBoard) or stopping its movement entirely (so the GamePiece stops at the edge).

You will be getting a lot of exposure to these relational operators during this book as they are quite useful in creating gameplay logic, so we are going to be having a lot of fun with these soon enough. Let's take a look at logical operators next so we can work with Boolean sets and compare things in groups, which is also important for gaming.

Java Logical Operators: Processing Groups and Opposites

The Java **logical operators** are somewhat similar to the Boolean operations (union, intersection, etc.) in that they compare Boolean values to each other and then make decisions based upon these comparisons. Java logical operators will allow you to determine whether two Boolean variables hold the same value, which is called an **AND** operation, or whether one of the Boolean variables is different from the other, which is called an **OR** operation. There is also a third logical operator called the **NOT** operator, which will reverse the value of any of your compared boolean operands, or even reverse the value of a boolean operand that is not being compared, if you simply want to flip a switch or reverse a boolean flag in your gameplay programming logic. As you may have guessed, the AND operator uses two of the AND symbols, like this: &&. The OR operator uses two vertical bars, like this: ||. The NOT operator uses the exclamation point, like this: !. So, if I were to say I was not joking, I would write **!JOKING** (hey, that would be a great programmer's T-shirt). Table 5-4 shows Java logical operators, with an example of each, along with a brief description.

Table 5-4. *Java Logical Operators, an Example Where A=true and B=false, and a Description of the Logical Operation*

Operator	Example	Description:
&&	(A && B) is false	A logical **AND** operator equates to **true** when **BOTH** of the operands hold the true value.
‖	(A ‖ B) is true	A logical **OR** operator equates to **true** when **EITHER** of the operands hold the true value.
!	!(A && B) is true	A logical **NOT** operator **reverses** the **logical state** of the operator (or set) it is applied to.

Let's use logical operators to enhance the game logic example I used in the previous section to ascertain whether a player has fallen off of the game board (moved beyond the edge) while they are moving the game piece (that is, while it is their turn).

The modified code for doing this will include a logical AND operator, which will set the **fellOffBoard** boolean variable to a value of true, if gameBoardEdge = true AND turnActive = true. The Java code to ascertain this will look like the following Java statements:

```
boolean gameBoardEdge = false;    // boolean variable gameBoardEdge is initialized to be false
gameBoardEdge = (GamePieceX < 0);  // boolean gameBoardEdge set TRUE if past (before) left side
fellOffBoard = (gameBoardEdge && turnActive) // It's your turn, but you fell off the left edge!
```

Now you have a little practice declaring and initializing variables and using relational and logical operators to determine the turn, boundary, and location of your game pieces. Next, let's take a look at Java assignment operators.

Java Assignment Operators: Assigning a Result to a Variable

The Java **assignment operators** assign a value from a logic construct on the right side of the assignment operator to a variable on the left side of the assignment operator. The most common assignment operator is also the most commonly used operator in the Java programming language, the **equals** operator. The equals operator can be prefixed with any of the arithmetic operators to create an assignment operator that also performs an arithmetic operation, as shown in Table 5-5. This allows a "denser" programming statement to be created when the variable itself is going to be part of the equation. Thus, instead of having to write **C = C + A;**, you can simply use **C+=A;** and achieve the same end result. We'll be using this assignment operator shortcut often during our game logic design.

Table 5-5. *Java Assignment Operators, What That Assignment Is Equal to in Code, and a Description of the Operator*

Operator	Example	Description
=	C=A+B	Basic assignment operator: assign value from right-side operands to left-side operand
+=	C+=A equals C=C+A	ADD assignment operator: add right operand to left operand; put result in left operand
-=	C-=A equals C=C-A	SUB assignment operator: subtract right operand from left operand; put result in left operand
*=	C*=A equals C=C*A	MULT assignment: multiply right operand and left operand; put result in left operand
/=	C/=A equals C=C/A	DIV assignment operator: divide left operand with right operand; result in left operand
%=	C%=A equals C=C%A	MOD assignment: divide left operand with right operand; put remainder in left operand

Finally, we're going to take a look at conditional operators, which also allow us to code powerful game logic.

Java Conditional Operator: Set One Value If True, Another If False

The Java language also has a **conditional operator** that can **evaluate** a condition and make a variable assignment based upon the resolution of that condition for you, using only one compact programming construct. The generic Java programming statement format for a conditional operator always takes the following basic format:

```
Variable = (evaluated expression) ? Set this value if TRUE : Set this value if FALSE ;
```

So, on the left side of the equals sign, you have the variable that is going to change (going to be set) based on what is on the right side of the equals sign, which conforms to what you have learned during this section thus far.

On the right side of the equals sign, you have an **evaluated expression**. For instance, "x is equal to three," and then you have the **question mark** character. After that you have two numeric values that are separated from each other using the **colon** character, and finally, the conditional operator statement is terminated using the **semicolon**. If you wanted to set a variable **y** to the value of **25** if **x** was equal to **3** and otherwise set its value to **10** if x was not equal to 3, you would write that conditional operator programming statement by using the following Java programming logic:

```
y = (x == 3) ? 25 : 10 ;
```

It is important to note that the data types of the expression after the ? and after the : must agree with the type of data variable on the other side of the equals operator. As an example, you cannot specify the following:

```
int x = (y > z) ? "abc" : 20;
```

Next we're going to look at Java logic control structures that leverage the operators you just learned about.

Java Conditional Control: Loops or Decision Making

As you have just seen, many of the Java operators, especially the conditional operator, can have a fairly complex program logic structure and provide a ton of processing power using very few characters of Java programming code. Java also has several more complicated **conditional control** structures, which can **make decisions** automatically for you or automatically **perform repetitive tasks** for you once you have set up the conditions for Java to make those decisions. You can also carry out those task repetitions by coding what is popularly called a Java **logic control** structure.

In this section of the chapter, we will first take a look at decision-making control structures, such as the Java **Switch-Case** structure and the **If-Then-Else** structure, and then we will take a look at Java's looping control structures, including the **For**, **While**, and **Do-While** iterative (looping) control structures.

Decision-Making Control Structures: Switch - Case and If - Else

Some of the most powerful Java logic control structures, especially when it comes to pro Java games development, are those that allow you to define gameplay **decisions** that you want your gameplay program logic to make for you as your game application is running. One of these, called a *switch*, provides a case-by-case "flat" decision matrix, and the other, called an *if-else*, provides a cascading decision tree, evaluating "if this, do this, if not, else do this, if not, else do this, if none of these, else do this." Both of these can be used to create a type of evaluation structure where things are evaluated in precisely the order and in the fashion that you want them to be evaluated.

Let's start by looking at the Java **switch** statement, which uses the Java switch keyword and an expression at the top of this decision tree. Inside of the decision tree the switch construct uses a Java **case** keyword to provide Java statement blocks for each outcome for the switch statement expression's evaluation. If none of these cases inside the switch statement's structure (that is, inside the curly {} braces) is used by the expression evaluation, you can provide a Java **default** keyword and a Java statement code block for what you want done if none of these cases is invoked.

The **general format** for your switch-case decision tree programming construct would look like the following:

```
switch(expression) {
    case value1 :
        programming statement one;
        programming statement two;
        break;
    case value2 :
        programming statement one;
        programming statement two;
        break;
    default :
        programming statement one;
        programming statement two;
}
```

The variable used in case statements can be one of five Java data types: **char** (character), **byte**, **short**, **string**, or **int** (integer). You will generally want to provide the Java **break** keyword, at the end of each of your case statement code blocks, at least in the use case where the values being switched between need to be "exclusive" and only one is viable (or permissible) for each invocation of the switch statement.

The default statement does not need to use any break keyword.

If you do not provide a Java break keyword in each of your case logic blocks, more than one case statement can be evaluated, in the same pass, through your switch statement. This would be done as your expression evaluation tree progresses from top (the first case code block) to bottom (last case code block or default keyword code block).

The significance of this is that you can create some fairly complex decision trees based upon case statement evaluation order and whether you put the break keyword at the end of any given case statement's code block.

Let's say you want to have a decision in your game as to what GamePiece moving animation is called when the GamePiece is moved (walk, jump, dance, etc.). The GamePiece animation routine (method) would be called based on what the GamePiece is doing when he (or she) is moved, such as Walking (**W**), Jumping (**J**), Dancing (**D**), or Idle (**I**). Let's say these "states" are held in the data field called **gpState** of type **char** that holds a single character. Your switch-case code construct for using these game piece state indicators to call a correct method, once a turn has been taken, and movement needs to occur. This should look something like the following Java pseudocode (prototyping code):

```
switch(gpState) {            // Evaluate gpState char, execute case code blocks accordingly
    case 'W' :
        gamePieceWalking(); // Java method controlling Walk sequence if GamePiece is walking
        break;
    case 'J' :
        gamePieceJumping(); // Java method controlling Jump sequence if GamePiece is jumping
        break;
```

```
    case 'D' :
        gamePieceDancing(); // Java method controlling Dance sequence if GamePiece is dancing
        break;
    default :
        gamePieceIdle();    // Java method controlling processing if a GamePiece is idle
```

This switch-case logic construct evaluates the **gpState** char variable, inside of the evaluation portion of the **switch()** statement (notice that this uses a Java **method** structure), and then provides a case logic block for each of the game piece states of Walking, Jumping, and Dancing. It also implements a default logic block for the Idle state. This is the most logical way to set this up because the game piece is usually idle unless it is that user's turn.

Since a game piece cannot be Idle, Walking, Running, and Dancing at the same time, I need to use the **break** keyword to make each of the branches of this decision tree unique (mutually exclusive) to the other branches (states).

The switch-case decision-making construct is generally considered to be more efficient and faster than the if-else decision-making structure, which can use just the **if** keyword for simple evaluations, which would look like this:

```
if(expression == true) {
    programming statement one;
    programming statement two;
}
```

You can also add an **else** keyword to make this decision-making structure evaluate statements that would need to execute if the boolean variable (true or false condition) evaluates to false rather than true, which makes this structure more powerful (and useful). This general programming construct would then look like the following:

```
if(expression == true) {
    programming statement one;
    programming statement two;
} else {                            // Execute this code block if (expression == false)
    programming statement one;
    programming statement two;
}
```

You can also nest **if-else** structures, thereby creating **if-{else if}-{else if}-else{}** structures. If these structures get nested too deeply, then you would want to **switch**, no pun intended, over to using the switch-case structure. This structure will become more and more efficient, relative to the nested if-case structure, the deeper your if-else nesting goes. Here's an example of how the switch-case statement that I coded earlier for the BoardGame game could translate into a nested if-else decision-making construct in a Java programming structure:

```
if(gpState = 'W') {
    gamePieceWalking();
} else if(gpState = 'J') {
    gamePieceJumping();
  } else if(gpState = 'D') {
      gamePieceDancing();
    } else {
        gamePieceIdle();
    }
```

As you can see, this if-else decision tree structure is quite similar to the switch-case that we created earlier, except that the decision code structures are **nested** inside of each other, rather than contained in a "flat" structure. As a general rule of thumb, I would use an if, and the if-else, for one- and two-value evaluations, and I would use a switch-case for three-or-more-value evaluation scenarios. I use a switch-case structure extensively in my books covering Android, such as *Android Apps for Absolute Beginners* (Apress, 2017) and *Pro Android Wearables* (Apress, 2015).

Next, let's take a look at the other types of conditional control structures that are used extensively in Java, the "looping" or iterative programming structures. These iterative conditional structures will allow you to execute any block of programming statements a predefined number of times by using the **for** loop or until the Java programming objective has been achieved by using either the **while** or **do-while** loop.

As you might imagine, these iterative control structures can be extremely useful for your game control logic.

Looping Control Structures: While, Do - While, and the For Loop

Whereas the decision tree type of control structure is traversed a fixed number of times (once all the way through, unless a break [switch-case], or resolved expression [if-else], is encountered), a **looping** control structure keeps executing over time, which for the **while** and **do-while** structures makes them a bit dangerous as an **infinite loop** could be generated if you are not careful with your programming logic! The **for** loop structure executes for a finite number of loops specified in the definition of the loop, as we will see during this section of the chapter.

Let's start with the **finite** loop and cover the **for loop** first. A Java for loop uses the following general format:

```
for(initialization; boolean expression; update equation) {
    programming statement one;
    programming statement two;
}
```

The three parts of the evaluation area for the for loop, inside the parentheses, are separated by semicolons, and each contains a programming construct. The first is a variable declaration and initialization, the second is a Boolean expression evaluation, and the third is an update equation showing how to increment the loop during each pass.

If you wanted to move the GamePiece 40 pixels diagonally on the board, your for loop would be as follows:

```
for (int x; x < 40; x = x + 1) { // Note: the x = x + 1 statement could also be coded as x++
    gamePieceX++;  // Note: gamePieceX++ could be coded gamePieceX = gamePieceX + 1;
    gamePieceY++;  // Note: gamePieceY++ could be coded gamePieceY = gamePieceY + 1;
}
```

The **while** (or **do-while**) type of loop, on the other hand, does not execute over a finite number of processing cycles but rather executes the statements inside of the loop until a condition is met, using the following structure:

```
while (boolean expression)  {
    programming statement one;
    programming statement two;
    expression incrementation;
}
```

Coding your for loop that moves the GamePiece 40 pixels, using a while loop structure, would look like this:

```
int x = 0;
while(x < 40) {
    invinciBagelX++;
    invinciBagelY++;
    x++;
}
```

The only difference between a do-while loop and a while loop is that in a do-while loop the loop logic programming statements are performed **before** the evaluation, instead of after the evaluation, as they are in the while loop. Thus, the previous example would be written with a **do-while** loop programming structure that has a Java programming logic structure inside of curly braces, after the Java **do** keyword, with the **while** statement **after** the closing brace, coded as follows:

```
int x = 0;
do {
    invinciBagelX++;
    invinciBagelY++;
    x++;
    }
while(x < 40);
```

You should also take notice that for the do {...} while(...); construct, the while evaluation statement (and thus the entire do-while programming construct) needs to be finished with a **semicolon**, whereas the while(...){...} structure does not.

If you wanted to make sure that the programming logic inside of the while loop structure is at the very least performed one time, use the **do-while**, as the evaluation is performed **after** the loop logic is executed. If you wanted to make sure that the logic inside of the loop is executed only after, or whenever, the evaluation is successful (which is the safer way to code things), use the while loop structure.

Java Objects: Virtualizing Reality Using OOP in Java

The reason I saved the best for last, Java Objects, is because they can be constructed in one fashion or another using all of the concepts that I have covered thus far in the chapter and because they are the foundation of the Object-Oriented Programming (OOP) language, in this case, Java 7, 8, and 9. Everything in the Java programming language is based on the Java language's Object superclass (I like to call it the *master class*), which is in the **java.lang** package, so an import statement for it would reference java.lang.Object, which is the full pathname to the Java Object class. All other Java classes are created, or rather, subclassed using this class because everything in Java is an Object.

Note that your Java compiler **automatically imports** this java.lang package for you! Java objects are used to "virtualize" reality by allowing objects you see around you in everyday life (or, in the case of your game, objects that you are creating out of your imagination) to be realistically simulated. This is done by using data fields (variables and constants) and the methods that you've been learning about during this chapter. These Java programming constructs will make up the object **characteristics** or **attributes** (constants), **states** (variables), and **behaviors** (methods).

The Java **class** construct will organize each object definition (constants, variables, and methods) and will give birth to an **instance** of that object. It does this by using the **constructor** method for the class, which designs and defines your object, and by using the various Java keywords and programming constructs that you have learned about during this chapter. In this section I will give you an idea as to how this can be done, and I think you will find it very interesting if you are new to Java 9.

One way to think about Java objects is like they are nouns, that is, things (objects) that exist in and of themselves! The object behaviors, created using methods, are like verbs, that is, things that the nouns can do. As an example, let's consider that very popular object in all of our lives: the car. We could very well add this car to our board game as one of the GamePieces or as another component of the board game altogether.

Let's define the Car object attributes next. Some characteristics, or attributes, that do not change and are held in constants could be defined as follows:

- Color (Candy Apple Red)

- Engine type (gas, diesel, hydrogen, propane, or electric)

- Drivetrain type (2WD or 4WD)

Some states that change, define the car in real time, and are held in variables could be defined as follows:

- Direction (N, S, E, or W)

- Speed (15 miles per hour)

- Gear setting (1, 2, 3, 4, or 5)

The following are some things that a car should be able do, that is, the car's behaviors, defined as methods:

- Accelerate

- Shift gears

- Apply the brake

- Turn the wheels

- Turn on the stereo

- Use the headlights

- Use the turn signals

You get the idea. Now stop daydreaming about your new GamePiece, and let's get back down to learning about Objects!

Figure 5-3 shows the Java object structure, using this car as an example. It shows the characteristics, or attributes, of the car that are central to defining the Car object and the behaviors that can be used with the Car object.

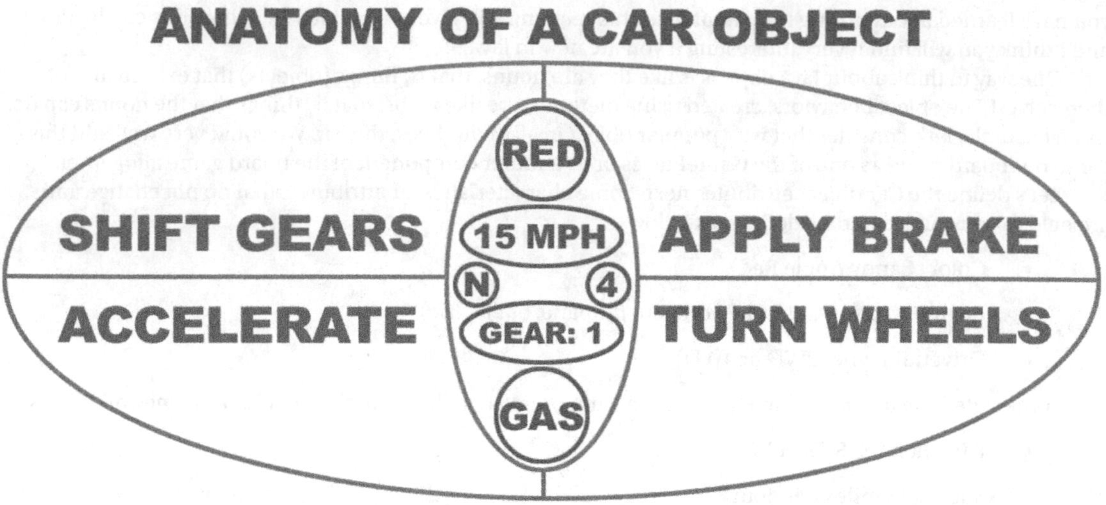

ANATOMY OF A CAR OBJECT

Figure 5-3. *The anatomy of a car GamePiece object, with methods encapsulating variables or constants inside a class*

These attributes and behaviors will serve to define a car to the outside world, just like your pro Java 9 game application objects will do for your Java 9 and JavaFX 9 game applications.

Objects can be as complicated as you want them to be, and Java objects can also nest, or contain, other Java objects within their object structure or their object hierarchy. An object hierarchy is like a tree structure, with a main trunk, branches, and then subbranches as you move up (or down) the tree structure, very similar to a JavaFX or a 3D software Scene Graph, which you saw in Chapter 3 (on the right of Figure 3-4).

A good example of a hierarchy that you use every day would be the multilevel directory or folder structure, which is on your computer's hard disk drive.

Directories or folders on your hard drive will contain other directories or folders, which can, in turn, contain yet other directories and folders, allowing complex hierarchies of organization to be created.

You'll notice that, in real life, objects can be made up of other objects. For example, a car engine object is made up of hundreds of discrete objects that function together to make the engine object work as a whole.

This same construction of more complicated objects out of simpler objects can be done in OOP languages, where complex hierarchies of Java objects can contain other Java objects. Many of these Java objects may have been created using preexisting or previously developed Java code, which is one of the objectives of modular programming.

As an exercise, you should practice identifying different complex objects in the room around you and then break their definition or description down into states (variable states or constant characteristics) as well as behaviors (things that the objects can or will do) and object and subobject hierarchies.

This is a great exercise to perform because this is how you will eventually need to start thinking to become more successful in your professional object-oriented game programming endeavors using the JavaFX engine, inside of the larger Java programming language framework.

Coding the Object: Turning Your Object Design into Java Code

To illustrate this further, let's construct a basic class for our Car object example. To create a Car class, you use the Java keyword class, followed by your custom name for the new class that you are writing, and then curly brackets that will contain your Java code class definition. The first things that you usually put inside of a class (inside the curly {} brackets) are the data fields (variables). These variables will hold the states, or characteristics, of your Car object. In this case, you will have six data fields, which will define the car's current gear, current speed, current direction, fuel type, color, and drivetrain (two-wheel or four-wheel drive), as specified earlier for this Car object. So, with six variables from Figure 5-3 in place, a Car class definition will initially look something like this:

```java
class Car {
    int speed = 15;
    int gear = 1;
    int drivetrain = 4;
    String direction = "N";
    String color = "Red";
    String fuel = "Gas";
}
```

Notice how the example spaces out the curly braces: { } on their own lines, as well as indenting certain lines. This is done as a Java programming convention so that you can visualize the organization of the code constructs that are contained within your Java class structure inside of those curly braces more easily and more clearly, analogous to a "bird's eye view" of your Java 9 code construct.

Since we specified a starting value using the equals sign for all of these variables, remember that these variables will all contain this default or starting data value. These initial data values will be set (in the system memory) as the Car object's default values at construction since these are set as your class's "starting" variable data values.

The next part of your Java class definition file will contain your methods. Java methods will define how your Car object will function, that is, how it will "operate" on the variables that you defined at the top of the class that hold the Car object's current "state of operation." Method "calls" will invoke the variable state changes, and methods can also "return" data values to the entity that "calls" or "invokes" the method, such as data values that have been successfully changed or even the result of an equation.

For instance, there should be a method to allow you to shift gears by setting the object's gear variable or attribute to a different value. This method would be declared as void since it performs a function but does not return any. In this Car class and Car object definition example, we will have four methods, as defined in Figure 5-3.

The **.shiftGears()** method will set the Car object's **gear** attribute to the **newGear** value that was passed into the .shiftGears() method. You should allow an integer to be passed into this method to allow "user error," just as you would have when you are driving your car in the real world when a user might accidentally shift from first to fourth gear.

```java
void shiftGears (int newGear) {
        gear = newGear;
}
```

The **.accelerateSpeed()** method takes your object **speed** state variable and then adds your **acceleration** factor to that speed variable, which will cause your object to accelerate. This is done by taking your object's current speed setting, or state, and adding an acceleration factor to it and then setting the result of this addition operation back into the original speed variable so that the object's speed state now contains the new (accelerated) speed value.

```java
void accelerateSpeed (int acceleration) {
        speed = speed + acceleration;
}
```

The **.applyBrake()** method takes the object's **speed** state variable and subtracts a **braking factor** from the current speed, which causes the object to decelerate, or to brake. This is done by taking the object's current speed setting and subtracting the **brakingFactor** from it and then setting the result of the subtraction back to the original speed variable so that the object's speed state now contains the updated (decelerated) braking value.

```java
void applyBrake (int brakingFactor) {
        speed = speed - brakingFactor;
}
```

The **.turnWheel()** method is straightforward, much like the .shiftGears() method, except that it uses a **String** value of N, S, E, or W to control the direction that the car turns. When .turnWheel("W") is used, a Car object will turn to the left. When .turnWheel("E") is used, the car will turn to the right, given, of course, that the car object is currently heading to the north, which according to its default direction setting, it is.

```java
void turnWheel (String newDirection) {
        direction = newDirection;
}
```

The methods that make a Car Object function go inside the class, after the variable declarations, as follows:

```java
class Car {
    int speed = 15;
    int gear = 1;
    int drivetrain = 4;
    String direction = "N";
    String color = "Red";
    String fuel = "Gas";

    void shiftGears (int newGear) {
        gear = newGear;
    }

    void accelerateSpeed (int acceleration) {
        speed = speed + acceleration;
    }

    void applyBrake (int brakingFactor) {
        speed = speed - brakingFactor;
    }

    void turnWheel (String newDirection) {
        direction = newDirection;
    }
}
```

This Car class will allow you to define a Car object, even if you don't specifically include the Car() constructor method, which we will cover next. This is why your variable settings will become your Car object defaults. It is best to code your own constructor method, however, so that you take total control over your object creation and so that you don't have to pre-initialize your variables to one value or another. Therefore, the first thing that you'll want to do is to make the variable declarations undefined, removing the equal sign and initial data values, as shown here:

```
class Car {
    String name;
    int speed;
    int gear;
    int drivetrain;
    String direction;
    String color;
    String fuel;
    public Car (String carName) {
        name = carName;
        speed = 15;
        gear = 1;
        drivetrain = 4;
        direction = "N";
        color = "Red";
        fuel = "Gas";
    }
}
```

Instead, the Car() constructor method itself will set data values as part of the construction and configuration of the Car object. As you can see, I added a **String name** variable to hold the Car object's name (**carName** parameter).

A Java constructor method will differ from a regular Java method in a number of distinct ways. First of all, it will not use any of the data return types, such as void and int, because it is used to create a Java object rather than to perform a function. It does not return nothing (void keyword) or a number (int or float keywords) but rather returns an object of type java.lang.Object. Note that every class that needs to create a Java Object will feature a constructor with the same name as the class itself, so a constructor is the one method type whose name can (and should always) start with a **capital letter**. As I mentioned, if you do not code a constructor, the Java compiler will create one for you!

Another difference between constructor methods and any other method is that constructors need to utilize the **public** access control modifier and can't use any non-access-control modifiers. If you're wondering how to modify the previous Car() constructor method, say if you wanted to not only name your Car object using the constructor method but also define its speed, direction, and color using an overloaded Car() constructor method call, you might accomplish this more advanced objective by creating a longer parameter list for your constructor by using this following code:

```
class Car {
    String name;
    int speed;
    int gear;
    int drivetrain;
    String direction;
    String color;
    String fuel;
    public Car (String carName, int carSpeed, String carDirection, String carColor) {
        name = carName;
        speed = carSpeed;
        gear = 1;
```

```
        drivetrain = 4;
        direction = carDirection;
        color = carColor;
        fuel = "Gas";
    }
}
```

It is important to note here that constructor methods can be declared **without using the public keyword**, as long as the classes containing nonpublic constructors do not need to be instantiated from beyond their packages. If you wanted to code one constructor invoking another constructor using this(), you could do this as well. For example, Car() might execute the constructor method call this("myCar", 10, 1, 4, "N", "red");, and this would be legal Java code.

To use the overloaded Car() class constructor and the Java new keyword to create a new Car object, you would use like the following Java code:

```
Car carOne = new Car();                       // Creates a Car object using default values
Car carTwo = new Car("Herbie", 25, "W", "Blue"); // Creates a customized Car object
```

The syntax for constructing an object is similar to declaring a variable but also uses the Java **new** keyword:

- Define the object type Car.

- Give a name to the Car object (carOne, carTwo, etc.) that you can reference in the class Java code.

- Use the default Car() constructor method to create your generic or default Car object, or...

- Use an overloaded Car(name, speed, direction, color) constructor with different value parameters.

Invoking the Car object methods using these Car objects requires the use of something called **dot notation**, which is used to chain or reference Java constructs to each other. Once the Java object has been declared, named, and instantiated, you can then call methods "off of it." This would be done, for example, using the following Java code:

```
 objectName.methodName(parameter list variable);
```

So, to shift to third gear, for the Car object named carOne, you would use this Java programming statement:

```
carOne.shiftGears(3);
```

This "calls" or "invokes" the .shiftGears() method "off of" the carOne Car Object and "passes over" the gear parameter, which contains an integer value of 3, which is then placed into the newGear variable, which is utilized by the .shiftGears() method internal code to change a gear attribute of that Car object instance, setting a new value of 3.

Java dot notation "connects" the Java method call to the Java object instance, which then invokes, or "calls," that method off of (or from or for) that Java object instance. If you think about it, how Java works is logical and cool.

Extending a Java Object Structure: Java Inheritance

There is also support in Java for developing different types of enhanced classes (and therefore objects). This is done by using an OOP technique called **inheritance**. Inheritance is where more specialized classes (more uniquely defined objects) can be **subclassed** using the original **superclass**; in this case, it would be Car. The inheritance process is shown in Figure 5-4. Once a class is used for inheritance by "subclassing" it, it then becomes the superclass. Ultimately, there can be only one superclass at the very top of the chain, but there can be an unlimited number of subclasses. All of the subclasses inherit the methods and fields from the superclass. The ultimate example of this in Java is the java.lang.Object superclass (I sometimes call this the *master class*), which is used to create all other classes in Java 9.

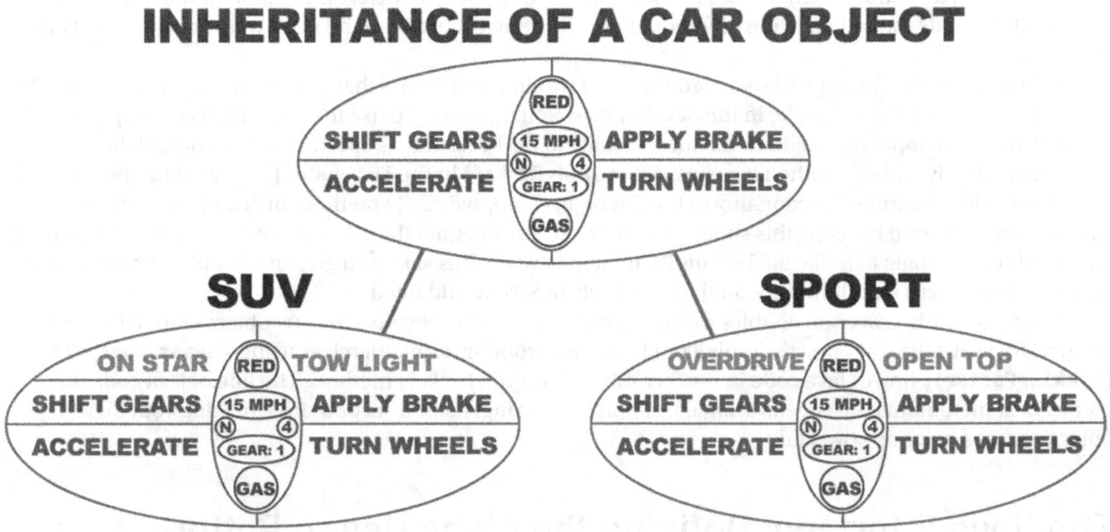

Figure 5-4. The inheritance of a Car object superclass will allow you to create an SUV Car object and a Sport Car object

As an example of inheritance using the Car class, you could "subclass" the **Suv** class from the Car class, using the Car class as the superclass. This is done using the Java **extends** keyword, which extends the Car class definition, to create an Suv class definition. This Suv class will define only those additional attributes (constants), states (variables), and behaviors (methods) that apply to an SUV type of Car object, in addition to **extending** all attributes (constants), states (variables), and behaviors (methods) that apply to all types of Car objects. This is the functionality that the Java extends keyword provides for this subclassing (inheritance) operation, which is one of the more important and useful features for code modularization within the Java 9 OOP language. You can see this modularization visually in Figure 5-4, with additional Car features for each subclass added in orange. This is a great way to organize your code!

The Suv Car object subclass might have additional **.onStarCall()** and **.turnTowLightOn()** methods defined, in addition to inheriting the usual Car object operation methods, allowing the Car object to shift gears, accelerate, apply the brakes, and turn the steering wheel.

Similarly, you might also generate a second subclass, called the Sport class, which creates Sport Car objects. These might include an **.activateOverdrive()** method to provide faster gearing and maybe an **.openTop()** method to put down the convertible roof. To create the subclass using a superclass, you extend the subclass from the superclass by using a Java extends keyword inside of the class declaration. The Java class construct would thus look just like this:

```
class Suv extends Car {
    void applyBrake (int brakingFactor) {
        super.applyBrake(brakingFactor);
        speed = speed - brakingFactor;
    }
}
```

This extends the Suv Object to have access to, essentially to contain, all of the data fields and methods that the Car Object features. This allows the developer to only have to focus on the new, or different, data fields and methods that relate to the differentiation of the Suv Object from the regular or "master" Car Object definition.

To refer to one of the superclass's methods from within the subclass that you are coding, you can use the Java **super** keyword. For example, in the new Suv class you may want to use the Car superclass .applyBrake() method and then apply some additional functionality to the brake that is specific to Suv. You call the Car object's .applyBrake() method by using **super.applyBrake()** in the Java code. The Java code shown earlier will add additional functionality to the Car object's .applyBrake() method, inside of the Suv Object .applyBrake() method by using this super keyword to access the Car Object's .applyBrake() method and then add in additional logic to make the brakingFactor apply twice. This serves to give the Suv object twice the braking power that a standard car would have, which an SUV would need.

The reason this Java code doubles the SUV's braking power is because the Suv object's .applyBrake() method first calls the Car object's .applyBrake() method from the Car superclass using a **super.applyBrake (brakingFactor);** line of Java code in the Suv subclass's .applyBrake() method. The line of Java code that comes next increments the speed variable by applying brakingFactor a second time, making your SUV object's brakes twice as powerful.

The Java Interface: Defining the Class Usage Pattern

In many Java applications, Java classes must conform to a certain usage pattern. There is a specialized Java construct that is called an **interface** that can be implemented so that application developers will know exactly how to **implement** those Java classes, including alerting developers that methods are required for a proper implementation of the class. Defining an interface will allow your class to inform other developers using that class that behaviors (which Java methods) for your class must be implemented in order to correctly utilize your Java class's infrastructure.

Interfaces in essence prescribe a **programming contract** between the class and the rest of the development community. By implementing a Java interface, a contract can be enforced at build time by the Java compiler. If a class "claims" to implement a public interface, all of the methods that are "defined" by that Java interface definition must appear in the source code for the class that implements that interface, before that class will successfully compile.

Interfaces are especially useful when working within a complex, Java-based programming framework, such as Android uses, that is utilized by developers who build applications on the Java classes that the Google Android OS developer team members have written specifically for that purpose. A Java interface should be used like a road map, showing developers how to best implement, and utilize, the Java code structure that is provided by that Java class within another Java programming structure.

Basically, a Java interface guarantees that all methods in a given class will get implemented together as an interworking, interdependent, collective programming structure, guaranteeing that any individual function needed to implement that functional collective does not get inadvertently left out. This public interface that a class "presents" to other developers who are using the Java language makes using that class more predictable and allows developers to safely use that class in programming structures and objectives where a class of that particular end-usage pattern is suitable for their implementation. As of Java 9 you can also define **private** interfaces to be used internally to your app.

The following is an **ICar** interface, which forces all cars to implement all of the methods that are defined in this interface. These methods must be implemented and exist even if they're not utilized, that is, no code exists inside the curly braces. This also guarantees that the rest of the Java application knows that each Car object can perform all of these behaviors because implementing an ICar interface defines a public interface for all Car objects. The way that you would implement the ICar public interface, for those methods that are currently in your Car class, is as follows:

```java
public interface ICar {
    void shiftGears (int newGear);
    void accelerateSpeed (int acceleration);
    void applyBrake (int brakingFactor);
    void turnWheel (String newDirection);
}
```

To implement an interface, you need to use the Java **implements** keyword, as follows, and then define all of the methods exactly as you did before, except that the methods must now be declared using the **public** access control modifier in addition to the void return data type. So, you will add the public keyword before the void keyword, which will allow other Java classes to be able to call or invoke the methods, even if those classes are in a different package. After all, this is a **public interface**, and any developer (or more accurately, any class) should be able to access it. Here is how your Car class should implement this ICar interface by using the Java implements keyword:

```java
class Car implements ICar {
    String name = "Generic";
    int speed = 15;
    int gear = 1;
    int drivetrain = 4;
    String direction = "N";
    String color = "Red";
    String fuel = "Gas  ";

    public void shiftGears (int newGear) {
        gear = newGear;
    }
    public void accelerateSpeed (int acceleration) {
        speed = speed + acceleration;
    }
    public void applyBrake (int brakingFactor) {
        speed = speed - brakingFactor;
    }
    public void turnWheel (String newDirection) {
        direction = newDirection;
    }
}
```

A Java interface cannot use any of the other Java access control modifier keywords, so it cannot be declared as private (prior to Java 9) or protected. It's important to note that only those methods declared in an interface definition will need to be implemented. The data fields that I have at the top of the class definition

127

are optional. These are in this example to show it's parallel to the Car class, which I declared earlier without using an interface. There is not too much difference, other than using the implements keyword, except that implementing an interface tells the Java compiler to check and make sure that all of the necessary methods that make the Car class work properly are included by the developer.

What's New in Java 9: Modularity and Project Jigsaw

You might be wondering why I am covering Java 9 and its new modules last, and there are a couple of reasons for this, which I will explain first before we get into what is new in Java 9. None of what is new in Java 9 affects your game code, which is great because you can write the same basic Java game code in Java 6, Java 7, and Java 8; this means your game can go places that are not yet using Java 9 and probably won't be for a while. Since 32-bit Android uses Java 6 and 64-bit Android uses Java 7 (Android 5 and 6) and Java 8 (Android 7, 8 and later), this means you can write game logic in Java that spans a decade worth of platforms. Since Java 9 is a couple of years late in its release originally planned for the fourth quarter of 2015, I had to develop the code for this book, which releases the same time as Java 9, using Java 8. Fortunately, **Project Jigsaw** (Java 9's primary feature) affects the modularity of the programming language and not the code inside of the modules, which stays the same as Java 8 and JavaFX 8. So for the purposes of what this book is about, writing Pro Java Game Logic, there is no significant change between Java 8 and Java 9. Whether or not a game is modularized using the Java 9 features does not affect performance (gameplay), only its distribution, so I'm covering this modularity feature last during this chapter, as it is the least important Java aspect regarding game performance.

I did want to include this coverage of **modules** in Java because as of Java 9 modules are now a core feature, even though they only affect the packaging of a Pro Java Game and not how games are actually coded and optimized for memory and processor usage.

The Definition of a Java 9 Module: A Collection of Packages

The defining feature of Java 9 is JEP 200 (Modular JDK), which stands for JDK Enhancement Proposal 200. This is an "umbrella" JEP over JEP 201 (Modular Source Code), JEP 220 (Modular RunTime), JEP 260 (Encapsulate APIs), and JEP 261 (Module System), which encapsulate what needs to be accomplished to achieve a Modular JDK (JEP 200).

Currently, Java 8 and JavaFX 8.0 are like having two different programming languages in one. The first thing that is therefore going to be modularized for Java 9 JDK is JavaFX 8 (now renamed JavaFX 9), and since that is what you are going to be using to create games, we'll get into that in detail in this section. If you are an enterprise (business apps) Java 9 developer, this Java 9 module system will allow you to exclude all of the "heavy" JavaFX API libraries, packages, classes, and so on. However, the knife also cuts the other way as well, so if you are only going to be developing an i2D or i3D Java game, you will only need to declare and include the **javafx.graphics** module, and your distribution package (module) for your game will not need to include the plethora of other Java APIs that a game does not need, as it just focuses on graphics and event processing (multimedia visuals on the screen and how they interact with the player).

A Java module contains a collection of Java packages, so Java modules add another hierarchical level above the Java package-class-method-variable hierarchy that exists currently. A Java package can belong to only one module, and you cannot split Java packages between modules. This makes your organization of packages even more important both for your own game and for JavaFX, which has been organized into packages and modules for you in Java 9. We will be learning about that later during this section of the chapter.

Whereas Java packages allow you to organize by function, modules allow you to organize by features. This allows data (and code) footprint optimization. For instance, we will not be using JavaFX Swing, Standard UI Controls, FXML, or WebKit for our Pro Java 9 Game; thus, we will not need to include these code modules in our distribution.

The Properties of Java Modules: Explicit, Automatic, or Unnamed

There are three ways to create Java modules: explicitly, implicitly, and anonymously. An **Explicit Module** is created on purpose by the developer by specifying a **module-info.java** file that defines what other modules and packages will be in the explicit module. The explicit module defines **requires:inputs** (needed API packages) and **exports:outputs** (published packages). Exported packages are visible to the Java environment and can thus be executed. Only requires (input or read packages) packages specified in the module definition file can be accessed (utilized) by that module. I will show you the format for this definition a bit later during this section of the chapter.

The Java 9 environment can also create an **Implicit Module**, which is also known as an **Automatic Module**, if the developer has not supplied a **module-info.java** file and if it finds a JAR file on a module-path that does not contain a **module-info.java** definition file, so the Java 9 environment automatically creates an implicit module for the JAR file's contents. In this case, it will automatically export all packages needed, require (input or read) all modules needed, and include any unnamed modules as well, which we will cover next.

Finally, the Java 9 environment may also create an **Unnamed Module** by adding classes on a classpath that are not in JAR files and do not have developer-supplied **module-info.java** files. This allows the Java 9 environment to accommodate older Java 6 through 8 projects by making them into Unnamed Modules so that they will still function in the Java 9 environment even though they were created in earlier versions of Java where **module-info.java** did not yet exist. An explicit module cannot require an unnamed module, meaning developers of older versions of their Java software must create a **module-info.java** definition file to bring their software into the Java 9 modularity realm.

If an application's main classes are in the unnamed module, all default modules will be loaded to make sure that the Java 9 application can function, and the benefits of modularity (data footprint reduction of the distribution) will be lost. If you do optimally define a **module-info.java** file with the minimum packages needed to run your Pro Java 9 Game, the **javapackager** utility will be able to produce a bundled application for you with only the needed modules.

An Example of a Java 9 Module Hierarchy: JavaFX Modules

Since JavaFX was the first API that Oracle modularized and the native Java multimedia API that we will need to use to create Pro Java 9 Games, it makes sense to use this as the example of how modules work, which at the same time will show us how JavaFX is modularized and which JavaFX modules we could need to "require" (input) for our own Java 9 module definition file. With Java 9 modules, JavaFX can be linked directly into the JDK "image," and there will be no need to reference an external JFXRT.JAR file. Third-party JARs such as JFXSWT.JAR would become automatic modules. This JFXSWT.JAR will be renamed JAVAFX-SWT.JAR for Java 9 so that when the automatic module derives its name, using the JAR file, it will become JAVAFX.SWT.

The Java 9 Runtime Environment (JRE) contains seven JavaFX modules that you can "require" in your own game module as needed. The fewer of these you require, the more optimized your data and memory footprint would be for your game, and the more system resources will be available to your game processing requirements.

Table 5-6 shows you the new JavaFX module hierarchy, which modules (base and graphics) are required for any JavaFX usage, and which of the nonbase and nongraphics JavaFX modules require the other JavaFX modules.

Table 5-6. *Seven Core JavaFX Modules Contained in the Java 9 Runtime Environment for Use in New Media Applications*

Module Name	Required?	Used For	Required JavaFX 8 Modules
javafx.base	Yes	Events, Utilities, Beans, Collections	None (this is a Foundational JavaFX Library)
javafx.graphics	Yes	Stage, Images, Geometry, Animation	javafx.base
javafx.controls	No	User Interface Controls Module	javafx.graphics (require will also import base)
javafx.media	Yes	Audio/Video MediaPlayer Module	javafx.graphics
javafx.fxml	No	JavaFX Markup Language Module	javafx.graphics
javafx.swing	No	Java Swing Compatibility Module	javafx.graphics
javafx.web	No	WebKit Support Module	javafx.controls, javafx.media, javafx.graphics

For example, javafx.web (the WebKit API WebEngine) will require javafx.controls (used for the UI elements for the audio and video transport bar user interface element), javafx.media (audio or video playback codec support), and javafx.graphics (application, stage, scene, geometry, image, shapes, canvas, effects, text, and animation support).

Since modular applications need to list dependencies in that **module-info.java** file, let's take a look at how that would look for an application that uses the WebKit support API in JavaFX. Here's the **module-info.java** syntax:

```
module myWebKitApp.app { requires javafx.web; }
```

You might be wondering why you do not explicitly have to require those other modules that the javafx.web module requires in the **module-info.java** file's module myWebKitApp.app { ... } module use declaration, which one might suspect should look more like this:

```
module myWebKitApp.app        {
    requires javafx.base;
    requires javafx.graphics;
    requires javafx.controls;
    requires javafx.media;
    requires javafx.web;
}
```

This is because modules required by modules further down the chain are imported (required) automatically as part of the syntax. So, if we created a JavaFX game that did not use "canned" UI elements (called *controls* in JavaFX) or WebKit, FXML, or Java Swing, we could get away with using just base, graphics, and media modules.

Since the javafx.graphics module requires javafx.base and the javafx.media module requires javafx.graphics, you can simply write the entire module declaration Java file in one line of code, which would look like the following:

```
module ProJava9GamesDevelopment.app { requires javafx.media; }
```

Between these three JavaFX modules (base, graphics, and media) you have everything you need for games in Java 9, as long as you make your own user interface element control graphics, which is **standard practice** in games development. We'll be taking a look at what packages, classes, and methods are contained within these core modules over the course of the book. When I cover a given package and classes, I will let you know what module it is a part of.

The Purpose of Java 9 Modules: Secure, Strong Encapsulation

One of the biggest complaints over the years has been that Java is not as secure as other platforms, and that has prevented widespread use as a digital content distribution avenue. Like all the distribution formats (Kindle, Android, HTML5, etc.), secure DRM is also needed and on the way next year, but internal security of the API itself is also an issue that needs to be addressed in Java in particular, and as you'll see in this section, Java 9 Modules **Strong Encapsulation** rules will go a long way toward doing this by preventing access to the Java internal API as well as private encapsulation.

Applications previous to Java 9 will have to be modularized to "lock them down" using the **module-info.java** definition file discussed previously. Only explicitly exported packages will be visible; the internal API used to create an application will not be visible (accessible) anymore. Attempting to access any type in a package not explicitly exported will throw an error. Advanced programmers will not be able to use reflection to call a .setAccessible() method to force access. For testing, there is currently a command-line switch that will allow access to nonexported packages. This will be called --add-exports and should be used only when absolutely necessary.

There is also increased security within exported packages because now only types declared using a **public** access control modifier will be accessible. Attempting to access any type in an explicitly exported package not declared using public access control throws an error. Programmers will not be able to use reflection to call a .setAccessible() method to force access. For testing, there is currently a command-line switch that will allow access to nonpublic types. As you might have guessed, this will be called --add-exports-private and should be used only when absolutely necessary.

Strong encapsulation allows you to selectively support or expose only portions (modules) of the API. In this case, we are using the JavaFX API, and I am going to show you how to create a robust i3D game in this book using only the two core JavaFX packages (base and graphics) and the MediaPlayer (media) package, along with highly optimized new media assets. We will not need to include the "heavy" WebKit (web), Swing (swing), FXML (fxml), or UI (controls) packages, which will reduce the distribution file data footprint and increase the security of this Pro Java 9 Game. Each module you access (require) will list its publicly exported packages, and your public classes and methods will be part of the API.

Creating a Pro Java 9 Game Module: Using the Exports Keyword

Let's continue looking at how to set up the Java 9 Game we will be creating using the JavaFX API by looking at how we use the exports keyword to add your BoardGame package to the rest of the Java (JavaFX) APIs we are going to be using to create the game. The JavaFX launcher will construct an instance of your application subclass, which will be called BoardGame or something similar. You can see this in Figure 5-4 for the InvinciBagel i2D game created in *Beginning Java 8 Games Development*. You can export the package that contains this Application subclass to the javafx.graphics module (which contains the majority of the packages and classes that will comprise this game) using an exports keyword and package name and a to keyword and module name. Here's the Java code:

```
module BoardGame.app {
       requires javafx.media;
       exports  boardgame.pkg to javafx.graphics;
}
```

It's important to note that if you use FXML, which allows nonprogrammers to design the UI layouts, this will require the javafx.fxml module, which needs the ability to access your private variables and methods. This will require the **exports private** keyword string in your **module-info.java** declaration file, which would then look like the following:

```
module BeginnerBoardGame.app {
    requires javafx.media;
    requires javafx.fxml;
    exports private beginnerboardgame.pkg to javafx.fxml;
}
```

We are not using FXML in this *Pro Java 9 Games Development* book because we will be doing everything with Java and external new media content development applications, just like a professional Java 9 game developer would. This will keep your application more secure and more compact because the library for using FXML is massive in size and scope; the same goes for the library for using CSS, HTML5, and JavaScript (javafx.web) as well as the libraries for using generic user interface control or widget collections (javafx.swing and javafx.controls).

Resource Encapsulation: Further Module Security Measures

Java 9 modularity not only covers your Java code but also your application resources, which in the case of a Java 9 game include audio, video, image, vector (SVG), and animation assets. As you probably know, security can be breached through these file formats as easily as it can through text file formats. The only issue preventing Java from taking off in web, e-mail, apps, e-books, or iTV sets is the security issue, and it looks like Oracle is determined to fix this very soon. Another issue with Java has been the deployment of a huge Java runtime and the many different versions of this runtime. The new module feature will allow developers to optimize their distribution to only include needed Java components.

Resources are encapsulated using the **java.lang.Class** class, and resources can be retrieved using only the **Class.getResource()** method. As of Java 9, there is no **ClassLoader.getResource()** method call access, as there was in previous Java versions.

You cannot use URLs to access resources in a class anymore either, so /path/name/voiceover.mp3 will no longer work. This again makes the Java 9 distribution more secure. Some of the other modules still allow URL access, such as javafx.web and javafx.media; however, we are going to use **captive** (that is, internal to your JAR) media assets, and we are not going to open up our game to the Internet by not requiring the javafx.web (WebKit API) module. The package containing the resource must be accessible (exported) for the resources to be "visible" and not hidden from public view. This is done via your **exports boardgame. pkg to javafx.graphics;** line of code. Since javafx.media is also dependent on javafx.graphics, **exports boardgame.pkg to javafxmedia;** should also work since your chain of module requirements goes from **javafx.media ➤ javafx.graphics ➤ javafx.base**, as you can see in Table 5-6.

If you wanted to externalize your new media and design assets (which I never do, for my Android and Java 9 development), there are several JavaFX APIs that will still take a URL object or a URL specified using a String URL value. These include CSS (Cascading Style Sheets in javafx.web); FXML (JavaFX Markup Language in javafx.fxml); image, audio, and video assets (javafx.media and javafx.graphics); and HTML and JavaScript (WebKit WebEngine javafx.web).

Summary

In this fifth chapter we reviewed some of the more important concepts and structures found in the Java programming language. Certainly I cannot cover everything about Java in one chapter, so I stuck with key concepts, constructs, and keywords that you will be using to create a game during this book. Most Java books are 1,000 pages or more, so if you want to get really deep into pure Java, I suggest the *Pro Java Programming* book from Apress. Of course, we'll be learning more about Java as we progress through this book, as well as learning about the JavaFX 9.0 engine's classes.

We started by taking a high-level view of Java by looking at the syntax of Java, including Java **comments** and **delimiters**, and then we took a look at what **Application Programming Interfaces (APIs)** are. We also learned about the Java **packages** that a Java API contains.

Next, we covered Java **classes**, including **nested** classes and **inner** classes, since these Java packages contain Java classes. We learned that a Java class has a **constructor** method that can be used to **instance** objects from a class.

The next level down in Java is the **method**, which is like the functions you are familiar with in many of your other programming languages, and we looked at a required type of Java method called the **constructor** method.

Next we took a look at how Java represents data using fields, or data fields, and we looked at the different types of data fields such as constants (fixed data fields) and variables (or data fields that can change their values).

After that, we took a closer look at Java **access control modifier keywords**, including **public**, **private**, and **protected** access control keywords, and then we looked at the nonaccess modifier keywords, including the **final**, **static**, **abstract**, **volatile**, and **synchronized** nonaccess control modifier keywords.

After we finished covering the basic code structures and how to modify them to do what we wanted them to do, we looked at the primary Java data types, such as **boolean**, **char**, **byte**, **int**, **float**, **short**, **long**, and **double**, and then we looked at the Java operators that are used to process or "bridge" these data types over to our programming logic. We looked at **arithmetic** operators for use with numeric values, **logical** operators for use with boolean values, **relational** operators to look at relationships between data values, **conditional** operators to allow us to establish any conditional variable assignments, and **assignment** operators that allow us to assign values to (or between) variables.

Next, we looked at Java **logic control** structures, including decision-making (I like to call them decision trees) control structures and looping, or **iterative** logic control structures. We learned about the Java **switch-case** structure, the **if-else** structure, the **for** loop structure, and the **do-while** loop structure.

Next, we looked at Java objects and learned how to define object attributes, states, and behaviors using a Java class, methods, and constructor methods, and we looked at the Java OOP language concepts of inheritance and the public Java interface and learned how to implement these using Java code.

Finally, we looked at Java modules, added in Java 9, and learned how to define module hierarchies and module types using an example of how this was done for the JavaFX API, the first major Java API to be modularized. We learned about the advantages of Java 9 modules and how this was a major step in reworking the Java language to obtain the security level that the public has come to expect from the language and that we've all been waiting for.

In the next chapter, we're going to look at the **NetBeans 9** integrated development environment (IDE) and how to create the foundation (project and core APIs) for your game development during the rest of this book.

CHAPTER 6

■ ■ ■

Setting Up Your Java 9 IDE: An Introduction to NetBeans 9

Let's get started here in Chapter 6 by learning about the important features and characteristics of the **NetBeans 9** Integrated Development Environment (**IDE**) since that is the primary piece of software that you are going to be using to create your Pro Java 9 Games and IoT Applications. Even though the Java 9 JDK is the foundation for your Pro Java 9 Games as well as for the NetBeans 9 IDE, we will start on our Java game coding journey by learning about NetBeans, which is the "front end" (or window through which you look at and work on) for your Java Game Projects.

NetBeans 9 is the **official IDE** for the Java 9 JDK, and as such, it is what you will be using for this book. That is not to say you cannot use another IDE, such as Eclipse or IntelliJ, which are the official IDEs for 32-bit Android 4.4 and for 64-bit Android Studio 3.0, respectively. I prefer to use NetBeans 9 for my new media apps and game development for my Java 9 and JavaFX games and IoT application software development programming paradigm.

This is not only because NetBeans 9 can integrate third-party plug-ins, such as the **JavaFX Scene Builder** from Gluon, but because it is an HTML5+CSS4+JS IDE, and I usually create everything I design for my clientele using Java 9, JavaFX, Android 4.4, and Android 8.0, using HTML5 as well. I do this so that the content works across or on closed and proprietary operating systems and platforms, which will hitherto remain unnamed. As most of you know, I prefer open (source) software and platforms, as you might have observed as recently as during Chapter 1, as they are "inherently" open, free for commercial use, widely available, supported by 99 percent of the major manufacturers, and do not require an approval process, or that I publish applications for only one specific hardware platform or just one operating system.

It's important to note that NetBeans 9 supports many other popular programming languages such as C, C++, Groovy, and PHP, for instance. I use NetBeans 9 for HTML, CSS, and JavaScript web sites and applications development, as NetBeans is rapidly moving to become a premiere Java, JavaFX, and HTML5 applications development environment.

The first thing we'll do is take a look at what is new in NetBeans version 9. NetBeans 8.2 was released in the fourth quarter of 2016, about a year and a half after Java 8 was released. This version number synchronization is no coincidence, as NetBeans 8.0 was released right after Java 8, and NetBeans 9 will probably be released right after Java 9 in the fourth quarter of 2017. We'll look at why you'll want to use NetBeans 9, rather than an older version of NetBeans, during this chapter.

The next thing that we will do is take a look at the various attributes of the NetBeans 9 IDE that make it an invaluable tool for Pro Java 9 Games Development. We will look at all the amazing features that it will be providing to you during the course of this book; you will not be able to get hands-on experience with some of these features during this chapter, as we also need to get started creating your game and therefore put the bootstrap codebase or application infrastructure in place so that you can really give some of these NetBeans 9 IDE features a good workout.

© Wallace Jackson 2017

W. Jackson, *Pro Java 9 Games Development*, https://doi.org/10.1007/978-1-4842-0973-8_6

Therefore, during the latter part of this chapter, you will be learning how to create your Java 9 and JavaFX 9 project using NetBeans 9. This is so that you can start making solid progress toward and making your Pro Java 9 Games Development a reality by creating a real-world i3D board game, which you will be developing during the course of this book.

New NetBeans 9 Features: Java 9 Module Integration

NetBeans 9 is the next major revision of the software after the stable edition 8.2 and now features integration of the Java 9 Module System, Java 9 Runtime Edition (JRE), and JUnit Java Testing Suite, so these do not have to be downloaded separately. If you're downloading NetBeans 9 for HTML5+CSS+JS, PHP, or C++, you no longer have to download the JDK or JRE. This can be seen on the NetBeans IDE Download Bundles page, shown in Figure 6-1, and is the reason why there are 32-bit (x86) or 64-bit (x64) precompiled NetBeans 9 versions for HTML5/JS, PHP, and C/C++.

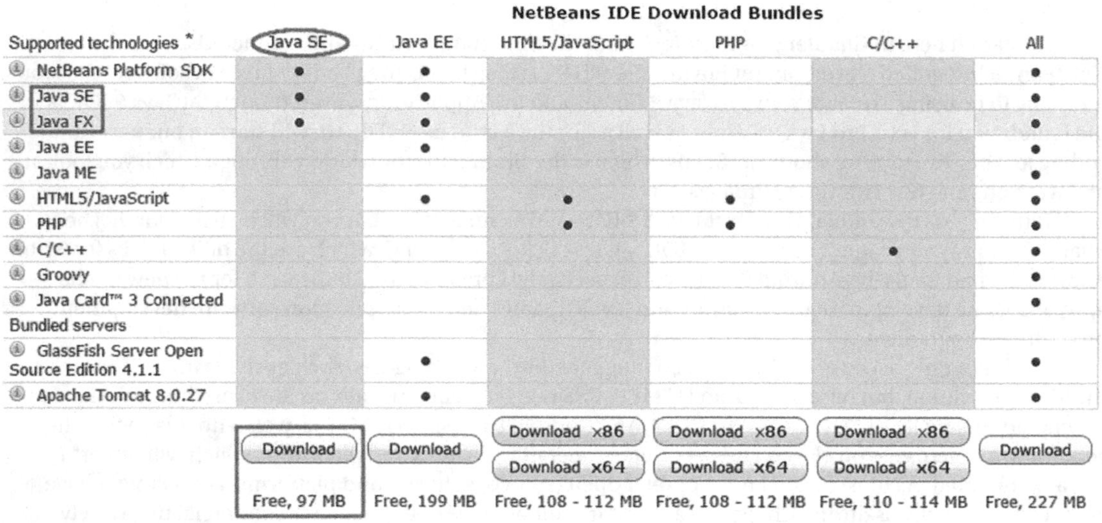

NetBeans IDE Download Bundles

Supported technologies *	Java SE	Java EE	HTML5/JavaScript	PHP	C/C++	All
ⓘ NetBeans Platform SDK	•	•				•
ⓘ Java SE	•	•				•
ⓘ Java FX	•	•				•
ⓘ Java EE		•				•
ⓘ Java ME						•
ⓘ HTML5/JavaScript		•	•	•		•
ⓘ PHP			•	•		•
ⓘ C/C++					•	•
ⓘ Groovy						•
ⓘ Java Card™ 3 Connected						•
Bundled servers						
ⓘ GlassFish Server Open Source Edition 4.1.1		•				•
ⓘ Apache Tomcat 8.0.27		•				•
	Download	Download	Download ×86 / Download ×64	Download ×86 / Download ×64	Download ×86 / Download ×64	Download
	Free, 97 MB	Free, 199 MB	Free, 108 - 112 MB	Free, 108 - 112 MB	Free, 110 - 114 MB	Free, 227 MB

***Figure 6-1.** The Java SE Edition NetBeans download bundle contains the NetBeans platform, Java SE, and JavaFX SDKs*

That said, if you are using any of the other (Java SE, Java EE, or All) versions, as we are for this book, the JRE is **not included**. This is because you'll be downloading the JDK, as you did in Chapter 1, to be able to use these Java SE (or EE, for large corporations) versions, and the JRE is included in the download and installation process, as you have already seen. NetBeans 9 also includes support for the latest revisions of the Apache Ant and Maven repositories. I'll cover some of the new features in NetBeans since version 8.0 came out more than three years ago in the first quarter of 2014 during the rest of this section of the chapter. I'll classify these using subsections to organize them by relevant topic for readers.

Java 9 Support: Modules, Ant, Java Shell, Multirelease

NetBeans 9 will release around the same time as Java 9, so its main objective will be supporting the Java SE 9 release in all of its features and capabilities. This will include the new Java 9 modules feature, which will improve security and give developers the capability of optimizing the data footprint of their Java 9 game distribution. This will include Ant-based and Maven-based Java 9 projects, so the Ant and Maven Build Systems will be upgraded to support Java 9 modules.

The Java 9 SE application project will initially support single-module development (all modules included) as well as a new project type that will support multimodule development, so you can pick and choose Java 9 modules. We will eventually be using just a few of the core JavaFX modules (base, graphics, and media) so that our distribution data footprint will be significantly reduced, but we'll do that at the end of this book, as this is a more advanced topic.

Apache Ant is being updated to get support for JDK 9 covering the basic Ant tasks, and all the tools in Java 9 SE distribution will work correctly when NetBeans 9 is running on JDK 9 or while JDK 9 is set to be your project's Java Platform. The NetBeans Profiler now works with JDK 9 applications, and Java shell support and integration with the NetBeans 9 IDE has been added at every level of NetBeans 9 projects. Multirelease JAR files are now handled properly by NetBeans 9 and its integrated Java 9 support.

Finally, the NetBeans 9 project will soon be moved over to Apache. The proposal for this can be reviewed at https://wiki.apache.org/incubator/NetBeansProposal. The proposal covers how the change will impact the NetBeans 9 releases. This moving of source, bugs, build jobs, and related services will happen during the NetBeans 9.0 and 9.0.1 releases.

IDE User Experience: More Information and Intelligent Coding

NetBeans 8.1 introduced an improved **Code Navigator pane**, which now distinguishes the **superclasses** or **interfaces** that your game's Java methods are contained in, along with the method name and its return type. Code completion, which we'll be covering in the next major section of this chapter, has also been significantly improved in almost all of the areas of NetBeans 8.1 (and in later versions such as 8.2 and 9), including improved preselection of the most relevant Java code insertion item, improved prefix autocompletion, improved subword autocompletion, and improved autocompletion of Java enum values.

Java Code Profiling: Completely Redesigned Java Profiling Suite

NetBeans did a complete overhaul of its **Java Code Profiling Suite** in version 8.1, including a simplified profiler setup, new single-click Java code profiling without having to set up anything in advance, and the ability to select methods or classes for detailed profiling simply by selecting check boxes next to the code profiling results. There is an improved ability to attach to running processes, and selected PIDs are remembered for subsequent sessions. New features include the monitoring of CPU utilization, an ability to dump threads from the profiled application, the ability to display merged results for selected threads in CPU profiling views, and an improved live application profiling view.

Other new profiler features include live forward and live reverse call trees in your CPU profiling results, live allocation trees in your System Memory profiling results, and simplified tweaking of settings during a profiling session.

This NetBeans Profiling Engine has the most improvements of any area of the 8.1 (and later) IDEs, including a significantly faster connection speed when connecting to an already running process, a limit on outgoing calls from your currently profiling methods, and the ability to profile your System Memory performance for certain preselected classes. All of these will be useful for optimizing Pro Java 9 Games Development as games require peak performance.

The profiler User Interface (UI) is now much more polished and professional, featuring one unified profiling window with all actions, settings, and results in one single customizable, managed view. There is a separate Snapshots window pane, which you can use to manage persistent profiling data.

There are also a completely new, 100 percent reimplemented profiler tables and tree tables area, which delivers a native-looking profiling appearance, allowing developers to seamlessly integrate code development and optimization.

There's also much improved profiler integration with the rest of the NetBeans IDE; in addition, there is a more polished profile menu, a new action called the **Attach to Project** action has been added, and **Profile Class** and **Profile Method** actions have been added into the Code Navigator. We will be taking a look at the NetBeans 9 Profiler later during this book, when we need to implement system memory and CPU optimizations into your Java 9 game.

Primary Attributes of NetBeans 9: An Intelligent IDE

In this section I will give you a comprehensive overview of all the amazingly powerful features of NetBeans 9 so that you understand just how powerful this IDE tool is that you have installed on your development workstation and how important it is that you master all of its features so that you can wield all of this power as a Pro Java 9 games or IoT applications developer. The IDE is the interface between the Java 9 code you are writing using the JavaFX APIs and your computer; it allows you to visualize your code, organize it into logical methods, test it on your computer, profile how optimally it is functioning relative to your system memory and processor cycles, and package it for distribution on the Internet via web sites or as a stand-alone application for Windows, OS/X, Linux, or OpenSolaris for Desktop Computers or even as an embedded device application for Android OS or Tizen OS. Ideally, iOS, Opera OS, and Chrome OS will also move to support Java 9 applications by 2018 since Android and Tizen already have the largest market share for Java-on-top-of-Linux-kernel (Android OS) and HTML5-on-top-of-Linux-kernel (Tizen OS) platforms.

NetBeans 9 Is Intelligent: Put Your Code Editing in Hyperdrive

Although it's true that an IDE is quite similar to a word processor, only optimized for creating modular code constructs rather than writing business documents, an integrated development environment such as NetBeans 9 is able to assist developers significantly more in their programming work process than a word processor will help an author in their writing and document authoring work process. Word processors are mostly for formatting text to make it look presentable using desktop publishing features, correcting spelling errors, and correcting grammar and sentence structure.

For instance, your word processor does not make suggestions in real time regarding the content that you're writing for your business, whereas the NetBeans 9 IDE will actually look at what you are coding while you are writing that code in real time and help you finish writing the Java code statements and Java code construct that you are coding **as you create them**. Therefore, NetBeans 9.0 could be said to have a higher **artificial intelligence quotient** than work processors, such as Microsoft Office, Corel WordPerfect, Apache Open Office, or Ubuntu Libre Office currently feature.

One of the things that NetBeans will do is to finish lines of Java code for you, as well as **applying color** to the code statements to highlight different types of constructs (classes, methods, variables, constants, arrays, references), as shown in Figure 6-2. NetBeans will apply the industry-standard **code indenting** to make Java code much easier to read, for both yourself and for the other members of your Pro Java 9 game and IoT application development team.

Figure 6-2. *NetBeans includes Files, Services, Projects, Navigator, and Output Panes (left top to bottom) as well as a Java editor*

NetBeans will also provide **matching** or **missing** code structure elements such as **brackets**, **colons**, and **semicolons** so that you don't get lost when you are creating complex, deeply nested, or exceptionally dense programming constructs. You will be creating advanced Java constructs with these characteristics, as you progress in your Java code complexity throughout this book as I take you from Java Game Developer to Pro Java 9 Game Developer, and I will be sure to point out Java 8 and Java 9 code that is dense, complex, or deeply nested as we implement it in your games.

NetBeans can also provide **bootstrap** code, such as the JavaFX game application bootstrap code that we will be creating a bit later during this chapter, since I know you are eager to get started creating your Pro Java 9 Game. NetBeans 9 provides code templates that you can fill out and customize, coding tips and tricks, and **code refactoring** tools. As your Java 9 code becomes more complex, it becomes a logical candidate for code refactoring, which can make code easier to understand, easier to upgrade, and more efficient. NetBeans can also refactor your code automatically.

In case you're wondering what **code refactoring** is, it is **changing the structure** of existing computer code to make it more efficient or scalable, without changing its external behavior (that is, what it accomplishes). For instance, NetBeans can take legacy Java 7 code and make it more efficient by implementing the **Lambda Expressions** introduced in Java 8.

NetBeans 9 will also provide **pop-up helper dialogs**, of one type or another, containing **methods**, **constants**, asset **references** (all of which you will be learning about as you code your Pro Java 9 game during this book), and even **suggestions**, regarding how to construct your Java statements. For instance, NetBeans 9 will suggest when it might be appropriate to use the Java 8 **Lambda Expressions** to make your code streamlined and multithreading compatible.

NetBeans 9 Is Extensible: Code Editing with Many Languages

Another thing that your word processor can't do is allow you to add features to it, which NetBeans 9 can do with its **plug-in** architecture. The term that describes this type of architecture is **extensible**, which means that, if needed, it can be extended to include additional features. So if you wanted to extend NetBeans 9 to allow you to program in Python, for instance, you could. NetBeans 9 can also support older languages such as COBOL or BASIC in this fashion as well, although since the majority of popular consumer electronics devices use Java, XML, JavaScript, SVG, and HTML5 these days, I'm not really sure why anyone would want to take the time do this. I Googled it and found there are people coding in Python and COBOL in NetBeans, so there's real-world proof that this IDE is indeed extensible.

Probably because of its extensibility, the NetBeans 9 IDE supports a number of popular programming languages, including **C**, **C++**, **Java SE**, **Javadoc**, **JavaScript**, **XML**, **HTML5** and **CSS** on the **client side**, and **PHP**, **Groovy**, **Java EE**, and **Java Server Pages** (**JSP**) on the **server side**. Client-side software is run on the device that the end user is holding or using (in the case of an iTV set), and server-side software is running **remotely** on a server somewhere and talking to the end user over the Internet or similar network while the software is running on the server.

Client-side software will be more efficient, as it is **local** to the hardware device that it is running on, and thus it is more **scalable**, as there is no server involved to experience any overload. Server overload will always occur as more and more people use the server-side software at any given point in time. The Java SE 9 and JavaFX games or IoT deliverables you create will tend to be on the client side, delivered in and using a web site, but also downloadable for use on the client side via JNLP or downloading a JAR or a compiled executable file for a given operating system platform.

NetBeans 9 Is Efficient: Organized Project Management Tools

Clearly, project management features must be extremely robust in any mainstream IDE, and NetBeans 9 contains a plethora of project management features that allow you to look at your pro Java game development projects, and their corresponding files and the interrelationships between those files, in a number of different analytical ways for this very reason. There are six primary project management views, or *panes*, that you can use to observe the various types of **interrelationships** within your project. Figure 6-2 shows the bootstrap pro Java 9 games development JavaFX project that we will be creating a bit later during this chapter.

Figure 6-2 shows the six primary project management panes or windows opened up for this new project so that you can see exactly what they will show you. A great programming IDE needs to be able to manage projects that can grow to become quite massive, involving well over a million lines of code and contained in hundreds of folders in your project folder hierarchy. This can potentially involve thousands of text (Java 9 code) files, along with hundreds of new media assets in the form of files, some text-based (SVG, XML) and some in binary data format (JPEG, MPEG).

The **Projects** pane shows the Java Source Packages, Libraries, and Modules that make up your Java 9 game project. This can be seen on the bottom left in Figure 6-2. The pane at the top is the **Files** pane and shows the project folder and its file hierarchy on your hard disk drive.

The **Services** pane underneath that shows Databases, Servers, Repositories, Docker, and Build Hosts so that these can be used in a project. These are primarily server-side technologies, and these technologies are generally used with a large development team, so we're not going to get into these in detail as this is a book for solo game designers.

The Projects pane should always be left open, on the left side of your IDE, as you will see in all of the figures in this chapter from Figure 6-7 onward. The Projects pane, or window, provides you with a primary access point for all of the project source code and assets (content) in your Java 9 game project. The Files pane not only shows the project folder and file hierarchy but also shows the data, JavaFX new media assets, and Java 9 code hierarchy inside each file.

The **Navigator** pane, shown on the bottom of the NetBeans IDE underneath the Files, Projects, and Services panes, shows the **relationships** that exist inside your Java code structures. In this case, that is the JavaFXGame class, the .start() method, and the .main() method, which we will be learning about in Chapter 7, after we learn all about the NetBeans 9 IDE and how to use it to create a Java 9 game project called JavaFXGame, which we are going to do soon.

NetBeans 9 Is UI Design Friendly: User Interface Design Tools

NetBeans 9's extensible plug-in capabilities support the **design-your-UI** drag-and-drop design tools for a number of platforms, including Java SE, Java EE, Java ME, JavaFX, and Swing, as well as C, C++, PHP, HTML5, and CSS4. NetBeans 9 supports visual editors that write application UI code for you, so all you have to do is make the visual on the screen look like what you want it to look like in the game application. Since games use the JavaFX new media game engine, NetBeans supports the Gluon **JavaFX Scene Builder Kit**, an advanced JavaFX user interface design visual (drag-and-drop) editor.

Since JavaFX has the PRISM game engine as well as 3D (using OpenGL ES or Embedded Systems) support, we will be focusing primarily on i3D for this book since I covered i2D in *Beginning Java 8 Games Development* (Apress, 2014). The assumption for the book is that readers will want to build the most advanced pro Java games possible, which would equate to 3D and i3D leveraging a JavaFX engine, which is now part of Java 8 and 9 (along with Lambda Expressions). The most efficient way to accomplish this is by using Java code and not a drag-and-drop code generator.

The fastest way to develop pro Java 9 games is to leverage advanced code and programming constructs that the Java and JavaFX environments generously provide to you for your use in creating cutting-edge applications. In this case, that would be pro Java games that contain powerful new media elements, such as 2D vectors, 3D vectors, digital audio, video, and digital images, assembled together as one single unified 2D and 3D hybrid content creation pipeline.

NetBeans 9 Is Not Bug Friendly: Squash Bugs with the Debugger

There is a general assumption that applies across every computer programming language that the negative impact to a programming project of a "bug," or code that does not do exactly what you want it to, will increase in magnitude the longer it remains unresolved. For this reason, these bugs need to be "squashed" as soon as they are "born," so to speak. NetBeans 9 has extensive bug-finding **code analysis** tools that can be accessed using an integrated **NetBeans Debugger**. NetBeans 9 also supports integration with the third-party **FindBugs 3.0.1** project, which can be found on SourceForge.net, which is located at findbugs. sourceforge.net if you want to download the stand-alone version.

These tools take the real-time "as you type" code correction and coding efficiency tools we discussed at the beginning of this section of the chapter to the next level of advanced debugging.

Your Java code won't be getting that complicated until a bit later in the book, so we will cover how these advanced tools work when we need to use them in later chapters, when your knowledge base is a bit more advanced.

NetBeans 9 Is a Speed Freak: Optimize Your Code with a Profiler

NetBeans also has something that is called a **Profiler**, which is one of the areas that the NetBeans IDE overhauled in release version 8.1, as I pointed out in the "NetBeans Code Profiling" section earlier. The NetBeans Profiler Tool will look at your Java 8 or Java 9 code while it is actually running and will tell you how **efficiently** it uses **memory** as well as **CPU cycles**. This profiling analysis will allow you to refine your code and will make it more efficient in its use of critical system resources, such as **Threads**, **System Memory**, and **Processing Cycles**. This can become quite important for Pro Java 9 Game Development, as profiling complex games can help you to optimize the "smoothness" of your game play on embedded systems, which are not as powerful (on single-core or dual-core CPUs, for instance), or on less powerful computer systems using dual-core or quad-core CPUs, for instance, versus commonplace six- and eight-core CPUs.

This Profiler is a **dynamic** software analysis tool, as it looks at your Java code **while it is running**, whereas the **FindBugs** code analysis tool could be said to be a **static** software analysis tool, as it simply **looks at your code** in the editor, when it is not "compiled" and running in system memory. Since I have already gone into the significance of static versus dynamic in Chapter 4, you know how much more powerful and CPU-intensive dynamic processing can be for your pro Java games development work process. The same considerations also apply here to real-time debugging. The NetBeans Debugger will also allow you to **step** through your code while it is running, so that tool could be viewed as a "hybrid," which spans the gap that exists between static (editing) and dynamic (executing) code analysis modes.

After you create a project foundation for a Pro Java 9 Game and its JavaFX PRISM Engine, in the next section of this chapter, you can run the Profiler if you like using the Profile menu at the top of the IDE. However, if you do this, you won't really see much at all, as the Hello World bootstrap application does not really do much of anything.

Therefore, we will get into the NetBeans Profiler as we add things such as real-time rendered 3D assets. I'm going to try to expose you to as many of these key features of NetBeans 9 as possible "up front" during this chapter, without using a lot of pages, so that you get comfortable with the software and are not surprised or "blindsided" by anything IDE related when it pops up (sometimes literally) over the course of this book.

Without further ado, let's fire up NetBeans 9 and create your bootstrap JavaFX API–based Pro Java 9 Game project so that we can make some Java 9 and JavaFX programming progress toward your pro Java 9 game during this chapter.

Creating the Pro Java 9 Game Project: JavaFXGame

Let's get down to business and create a project foundation for the pro Java 9 game that you are going to create over the course of the book so that you make progress toward your ultimate goal during every chapter of this book yet to come. I am going to show you how to create an original game during the course of this book so you see the process involved in creating a game that does not exist, rather than most game programming books that replicate a game that already exists in the market or drag and drop assets into a prebuilt game engine. For *Beginning Java 8 Games Development* (Apress, 2014), I got permission from my client to allow readers to see the process of creating the i2D InvinciBagel game during the course of that book. For this book, I'm going to create the i3D board game engine for use on my own iTVboardgame.com web site.

Click the Quick Launch Icon on your Taskbar, or double-click the icon on your desktop to launch NetBeans 9, and you will see the NetBeans 9 startup screen. This screen shows a progress bar and will tell you what's being done to configure the NetBeans 9 IDE for use. This involves loading the various components of the IDE into your computer's system memory so that the IDE can be used smoothly and in real time during your pro Java 9 games development.

After the NetBeans 9 IDE has been loaded into the system memory, the initial NetBeans 9 **Start Page** will be displayed on your display screen, as shown in Figure 6-3. Click the **x** at the right side of the Start Page tab. This will close this introductory page (tab) and will reveal the NetBeans 9 IDE, shown on the left of Figure 6-4.

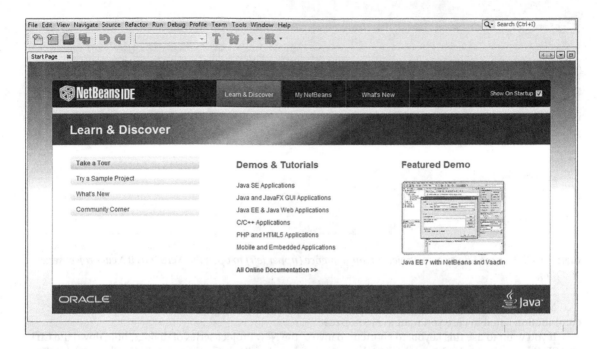

Figure 6-3. *Close the Start Page tab (upper left) by clicking the x on the right side of the tab to reveal NetBeans 9 IDE*

This will display what I term a "virgin" IDE, with no projects active in the IDE. Enjoy this now, as soon we will be filling this IDE with windows (I call these floating palettes *panes*, as the entire IDE is in what I call a *window*) for your project components. You can see part of this empty IDE in Figure 6-4, and there is not much to see, as currently there are only top menus and shortcut icons, also at the top of the IDE, and not much else is currently visible.

In case you are wondering, the Start Page that you exited displays only the first time you start the NetBeans IDE, although if you wanted to open this Start Page tab up later, perhaps so that you could explore the Demos and Tutorials sections, you can! To open this Start Page at any time, you would use the NetBeans 9.*x* Help menu and then select the Start Page submenu. I will usually denote a menu sequence like **Help ➤ Start Menu** just for your future reference. If you see a structure like this later in the book, it is a cascading menu sequence of nested submenus.

The first thing that you will want to do in the NetBeans 9.0 IDE is to create a new JavaFXGame Java Project. To do this, we will use the NetBeans 9.0 **New Project** series of dialogs. This is one of those helpful Java programming features that I was talking about in the previous section, which creates your bootstrap project with the correct JavaFX libraries, .main() and .start() methods, java statements, and import statements, all of which you'll be learning about in the next chapter. Click the **File** menu in the upper-left corner of your NetBeans 9 IDE, as shown in Figure 6-4, and then select the **New Project** menu item, which happens to be the first menu item.

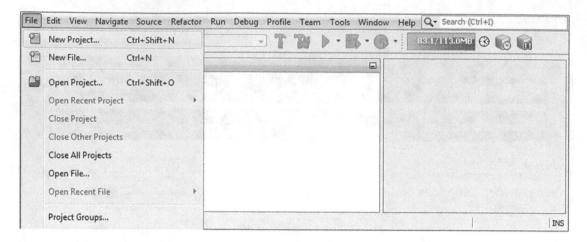

Figure 6-4. *Use the File ➤ New Project menu sequence (upper left) to open the NetBeans 9 New Project series of dialogs*

Notice on the right side of the New Project menu item that there's a **Ctrl+Shift+N** shortcut keystroke combination listed in case you want to memorize it.

If you want to use this keyboard shortcut to invoke the New Project series of dialogs, hold down the **Ctrl** and **Shift** keys on your keyboard (both at the same time), and while they are depressed (held down), hit the **N** key. This will do the same thing as selecting the **File ➤ New Project** menu sequence using your mouse.

The first dialog in the series is the **Choose Project** dialog and is shown on the right side of Figure 6-5. Since you are going to use the powerful JavaFX new media engine in your game, select the **JavaFX** category from the list of all of the programming language categories in the **Categories** selector pane on the left, labeled with a red number 2 for step 2.

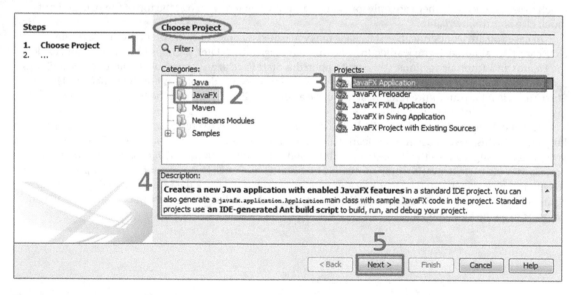

Figure 6-5. *Use the Choose Project dialog to specify a JavaFX Application for your Pro Java Game*

Next, select **JavaFX Application** from the **Projects** selector pane on the right, labeled with the red number 3, for step 3. We are selecting this because your pro Java 9 game is going to be a type of JavaFX API application. You can read the description of each project type in the **Description** pane (shown as a red number 4) and finally click the **Next** button to advance to the next dialog, which is shown as a red number 5 in Figure 6-5.

Remember that Oracle made a decision to integrate the JavaFX API (then libraries, now modules) back in Java 7 and then in Java 8, and so a JavaFX Game is now simply a Java Game, whereas before Java 7 (in Java 6), JavaFX 2.0 was its own separate programming language! The JavaFX engine, which you will learn more about during the next chapter, had to be completely recoded to be a Java 7 (and Java 8) API, or collection of libraries (and now in Java 9 it becomes modules), in order for it to become the seamless, integrated component of the Java 9 programming language that it is currently.

The JavaFX API will replace Abstract Windowing Toolkit (AWT) and Swing (UI elements), and although these older UI design libraries can still be utilized in Java projects, they are normally used only by legacy (older) Java code so that those projects will still compile and run under Java 1.02, 2, 3, 4, 5, 6, 7, 8, and 9. You'll be compiling and running this new JavaFX API–based project that you are creating during this section of the chapter, so you will see JavaFX is running under Java 9. The current version of JavaFX is 9, because Oracle made the version number match with Java 9, however, the classes are the same ones used in my *Beginning Java 8 Games Development* book.

Notice there is a **Description** pane underneath the other panes that will tell you what you have selected will give you. In this case, that would be **a new Java application with enabled JavaFX features**, where "enabled" means that the JavaFX 9 API libraries will be included (and started) in the Java application project's class and methods, as you will soon see in the code, via a series of import statements. You will learn what all of this Java 9 and JavaFX 9 code does in Chapter 7, which will cover JavaFX 9 and its many user interface design and multimedia-related features.

Click the **Next** button to advance to the next dialog in the New Java Project series of dialogs, which is the **Name and Location** dialog, as shown in Figure 6-6. This dialog allows you to set an application **Project Name**, which will be used to create both a Class Name and a Package Name, as well as where you want the project stored on the hard disk drive, using the **Project Location** and **Project Folder** data fields, which are also shown in Figure 6-6.

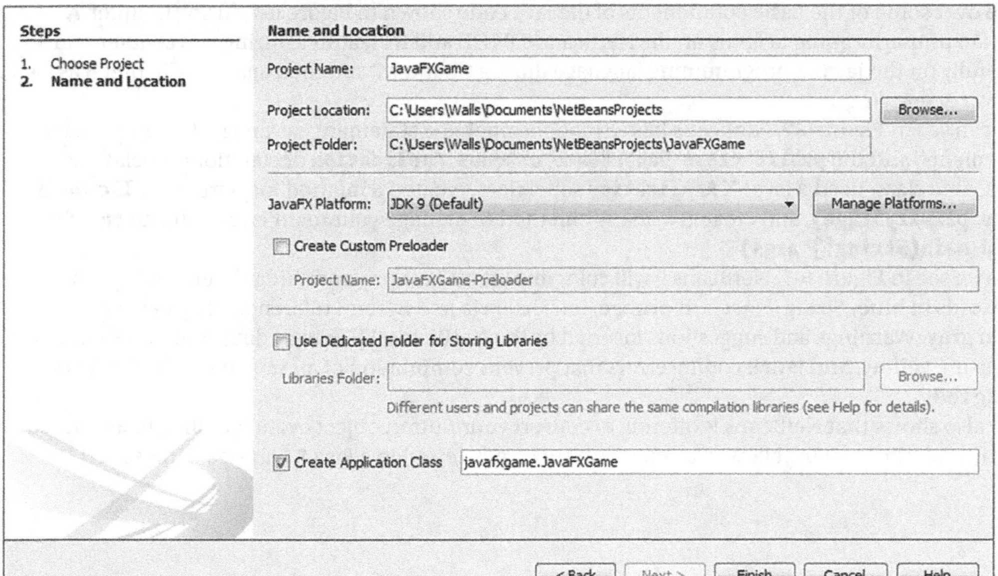

Figure 6-6. Name the project JavaFXGame, and leave all other naming conventions the way NetBeans set them

Name the project **JavaFXGame**, and leave the default **Project Location**, **Project Folder**, **JavaFX Platform** and **Create Application Class** settings exactly the way that NetBeans has configured them for you, as this NetBeans dialog will implement all of your class and package naming conventions for you automatically, based upon the Project name.

Once you are done, you can click the Finish button, which will tell NetBeans 9 to create the JavaFX game application for you and open it up in the NetBeans 9 IDE so you can start working on it and learning about the JavaFX API.

It's usually a good idea to let NetBeans 9.0 do things for you in the way that they should be done. As you can see in Figure 6-6, NetBeans creates the logical **C:\Users\Walls\Documents\NetBeansProjects\ JavaFXGame** folder for your user folder and Documents subfolder using the Project Location and Project Folder data fields from this dialog.

For the Project Folder data field, NetBeans will (logically) create the subfolder named JavaFXGame. This will be underneath a NetBeansProjects folder, just as if you had created it yourself, only NetBeans 9 has done it for you.

For the JavaFX Platform selection drop-down, NetBeans 9 defaults you to the very latest Java 9 JDK, which is also known as JDK 1.9 and has the latest JavaFX API (which is now an integrated part of the Java 7, 8, and 9 languages).

We are not going to be implementing a custom preloader project at this point, although if I have time and any page count left, I may revisit this later during the book. Thus, leave this option unchecked so you can learn to create this preloader Java 9 project code on your own, rather than having NetBeans 9 do it for you.

Since you are not creating multiple applications that will share libraries, leave the **Use Dedicated Folder for Storing Libraries** check box **unchecked**, and lastly, make sure that the **Create Application Class** is configured correctly. The Java 9 Class should be named **JavaFXGame**, and it should be contained in the **javafxgame** package.

In this configuration, the package path and class name will be **javafxgame.JavaFXGame**. This will follow the **PackageName.ClassName** Java class and package name paradigm, camelCase capitalization, and path, using your dot notation period character to concatenate the Package Name to the head of the Class Name, showing where it is kept.

I will go over some of the basic components of the Java code shown in Figure 6-7 during Chapter 7, because we are primarily going to focus on the NetBeans 9.0 IDE and its features during this chapter and concentrate fully on the JavaFX programming language during Chapter 7 and then again in Chapter 8 as well when we cover Scene Graph.

As you can see in Figure 6-7, NetBeans has written the **package** statement, seven JavaFX API package **import** statements, and the **public class JavaFXGame extends Application** declaration; subclassed your JavaFXGame class, used a JavaFX **Application** superclass, created a method for startup **public void start(Stage primaryStage)**, and created a .main() method to manage your main JavaFX thread **public static void main(String[] args)**.

As you can see in Figure 6-7, NetBeans 9 will color important Java programming statement keywords, putting keywords in **blue**, String Objects in **orange**, internal Java and System references in **green**, and comments in **gray**. Warnings and suggestions inserted by the NetBeans 9 IDE regarding your Java 9 code are colored using **yellow**, and Java 9 coding errors that prevent compilation of an executable (JAR) will be colored using **red**.

Line 20 also shows that NetBeans is offering to convert your Button object event handling to a Lambda Expression by underlining it in yellow (warning: this can be converted to a Java 8 Lambda Expression).

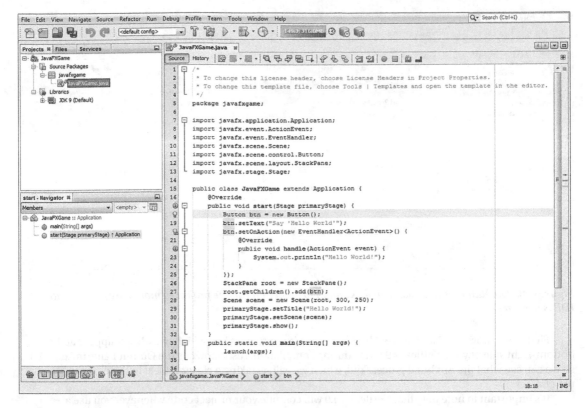

Figure 6-7. *Examine the bootstrap JavaFX code NetBeans created for you, based on the Name and Location dialog*

You can also change these colors, if you like, but I suggest you use the industry-standard coding colors implemented by Oracle NetBeans 9 and earlier versions, as these have become standardized over time.

Before you can **run** this bootstrap code to make sure that NetBeans 9 wrote bootstrap Java 9 code for you that actually works, you will need to **compile** this code into an **executable** format that will be run using system memory. NetBeans 9 also manages the compilation and run processes for you, even though these operations actually utilize utilities provided by the Java Development Kit (JDK).

Let's take a look at how this is done using NetBeans 9 next, using the NetBeans 9 **Run** menu, which contains Run, Test, Build, Clean, Compile, Check, Validate, Generate JavaDoc, and other Run-related Java compilation functions.

Compiling a Pro Java 9 Game Project in NetBeans 9

In the interest of showing you how to compile your Java game code before you run and test it, I am showing you the step-by-step work process here so you are exposed to every step of the compile/build/run/test Java code testing process. Click the **Run** menu and the **Run Project (JavaFXGame)** (first) menu item in order to build, compile, and run your Java 9 and JavaFX code, as shown in Figure 6-8. You can also use the **F6** shortcut key, as indicated on the right side of the menu item selection. Now your project is ready to test!

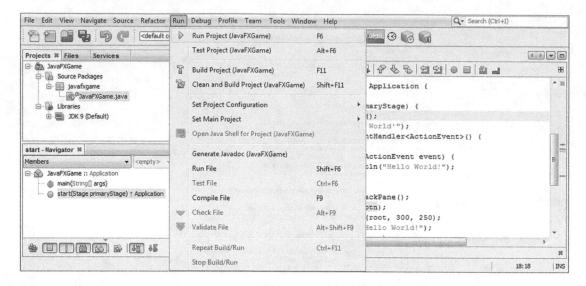

Figure 6-8. *Use Run ➤ Run Project (JavaFXGame) to build and run the project to make sure the NetBeans IDE is working*

Figure 6-9 shows the NetBeans 9.0 build/compile/run progress bar, which will always appear at the bottom-right side of your NetBeans 9.0 IDE during compilation. Also shown is the Output Pane, maximized so we can see what the Ant build process did, which we will be taking a closer look at in the next section of the chapter.

It's important to note here that NetBeans 9.0 will compile your project code whenever you use a **File ➤ Save** menu sequence or the **Ctrl-S** keyboard shortcut, so if you had used the **Save** feature of the NetBeans IDE right after the bootstrap code had been created, you would not have needed to undertake this compilation process, which I just showed you how to do manually, as this process will be done automatically every time you save a Java game project.

Also shown in Figure 6-9, right above the Output Pane or window, is the .start() method in the Java code editing pane or window. At the left is a minus icon with a square around it. This should be used to **collapse or hide the contents of this method. This is done** simply by clicking this **minus icon** at the left side of the code editing window.

A minus icon will turn into a plus icon so that a collapsed code block can be "expanded" (uncollapsed). Now that we have looked at how to compile the project in NetBeans 9, as well as how to collapse and expand the view of your logical method code blocks (logical functional components of your Java class) in your **JavaFXGame.java** project's code, it's time to run this code and see if it works. If it does, we can proceed to Chapter 7 and start to learn about the JavaFX API and what it brings in new media development power to the Java 9 programming environment.

Running Your Pro Java Game Project in NetBeans 9

Now that you have created and compiled your bootstrap Java 9 with JavaFX game project, it is time to run or execute the bootstrap code, to see what it does. As you have already learned, you can access the Run Project menu item using the **Run ➤ Run Project** menu sequence at the top of NetBeans, or, as shown at the top left of Figure 6-9, you can use the shortcut icon that looks like a green video transport **play** button. If you mouse over this, you will get a pale yellow tooltip, showing a **Run Project (JavaFXGame) (F6)** pop-up helper message. I will generally use the longer menu sequences rather than the shortcut icons when writing Java 9 and

Android Studio books just to be thorough. This shows readers where everything is located in the IDE menuing system, so everything gets covered. If you haven't already, run your new JavaFXGame Application now. Once you run your compiled Java 9 and JavaFX code, a window will open up over the NetBeans IDE with your software running in it, as shown on the right of Figure 6-9. Currently it uses the popular **Hello World** sample application.

Figure 6-9. *Drag up the separator bar to reveal the Output area of the IDE (running application seen at right)*

Click and **hold** your left mouse button down on top of the **divider line** between the Java 9 code editing pane and the **Output tab** at the bottom of the code editor pane and **drag** this divider line up, resizing your relative window space. The space is shared between the **JavaFXGame.java** code editing pane and an Output - JavaFXGame information pane. Doing this resizing operation will reveal your **Output** tab and its compile info contents, as is shown in Figure 6-9.

This Output tab will contain different types of output for NetBeans 9, such as compile operation output, run operation output (which is shown in Figure 6-9), profiler operation output (which we will be taking a look at later in the book when we have something to profile), and even output from your application itself (which we will look at here).

You may have noticed, in Figure 6-7, that your code for a bootstrap Java and JavaFX application uses a **green** System.**out**.println("Hello World!"); Java statement on line **23**, so if you wanted to see the application that you are currently running print to the Output Pane (this is what **out** means and is often referred to as the **Output Console**), you would click the **Say "Hello World"** button in the Hello World app that is currently running on top of your IDE.

Once you click the button, the words "Hello World!" should appear in the Output tab under the red text that says that it is executing your **JavaFXGame.jar** file. A JAR file is a **Java ARchive** (J for Java, and AR for Archive) file and is one of the **distributable formats available** for your Java 9 application.

Part of the compile process involves creating this file, so if your compiled version works, you can have your JAR file ready to distribute when all of your application design, programming, testing, and optimization is complete.

A JAR file does not contain your actual JavaFX code but rather a compressed, encrypted, "Java bytestream" version of your application, which the JRE can execute and run (like NetBeans 9 is doing now). The "path" that is attached to the front of the JavaFXGame.jar file tells you where NetBeans 9 has compiled your JAR file to on your HDD and where it is accessing it from currently to be able to run it. On my system, this location was as follows:

`C:\Users\Walls\Documents\NetBeansProjects\JavaFXGame\dist\run1381287366\`**`JavaFXGame.jar`**

Let's take a look at some of the other Output tab text in order to see what NetBeans did to get to the point where it could run the JAR file for the project. First the Ant Build System is invoked using **`ant -f source-path jfxsarun`**, and since the Java executable is not found in the JDK, it finds one in the runtime instead. It then initializes (init:) and in the JAR Dependencies (deps-jar:) section creates a **`\build`** directory and updates the built-jar-properties file. It then creates the **`\build\classes`**, **`\build\empty`**, and **`\build\ generated-sources\ap-source-output`** directories. Ant will then compile the project to the **`\build\classes`** directory, and if the build (compile) is successful (error-free), Ant will create the **`\dist`** distribution folder and deposit your JAR file there.

Ant then uses the JavaFX Ant API to launch **`ant-javafx.jar`** and deploys the JavaFX API, copying the JavaFX JAR files into a **`\dist\run1381287366`** folder. Finally, Ant runs the JavaFX project using **`jfx-project- run:`**, executing the Java 9 and JavaFX code, which is the equivalent of running (and testing) it, as shown on top of the NetBeans 9 IDE.

Ant is the "build engine" or **build tool** that creates your JAR file, and there are other build engines, such as **Maven** and **Gradle**, that can also be used in NetBeans if you like because, as you now know, NetBeans is extensible. Since Ant goes back the furthest and is the "legacy" build system, we will be using that during the course of this book.

Summary

In this sixth chapter we took a look at the NetBeans 9 "official" Integrated Development Environment (IDE) that you will use as the foundation and primary tool for your Java 9 Game Development work process. This is because this IDE is where your Java 9 (and JavaFX API) code is written, compiled, run, tested, and debugged, as well as where your new media (imagery, audio, video, 3D geometry, textures, fonts, shapes, etc.) assets are stored and referenced using your NetBeansProject folder and its subfolders. We started by taking a high-level view of NetBeans 9 and its new features such as Java 9 module support, as well as some recent legacy features, and added in NetBeans 8, 8.1, and 8.2. These are the powerful features that make NetBeans 9.0 the official IDE for Java 9. These features will help programmers to develop Pro Java 9 game code quickly, efficiently, and effectively, the first time. After this overview, we created a Pro Java 9 Game Project using the New Project series of dialogs and the JavaFX Application bootstrap Java code template.

We went through the **New ➤ Java Application** series of dialogs and created a JavaFX framework for our game, which will allow us to use new media assets. After that we took a look at how to **compile** (build and run) the app using NetBeans 9 and then at how to **run** an application using NetBeans. We looked at the **Output** tab and how this is used for compiler output and looked at the Ant build process to see what it does to combine Java 9 with its JavaFX APIs.

In the next chapter, we are going to take a tour of the JavaFX programming language, a "JavaFX primer," if you will, and examine the JavaFX code that is in your JavaFX bootstrap application (shown in Figure 6-7) so that you will know what this JavaFX code is doing. We will also look at the modular components of the comprehensive JavaFX API.

CHAPTER 7

■ ■ ■

Introduction to JavaFX 9: Overview of the JavaFX New Media Engine

Let's build on the knowledge of the Java 9 programming language and the NetBeans 9 IDE that you reviewed in the previous two chapters here in Chapter 7; we'll review in detail the capabilities, components, and core classes that comprise the **JavaFX 9** new media engine. This JavaFX 9 new media UI and UX API was added to Java using the **javafx** package that you saw in Chapter 6 when you created your bootstrap pro Java 9 game application. The previous JavaFX 8 API was released with Java 8 and was also compatible with Java 7, as well as Android and iOS. The JavaFX packages are significant to game programming because they contain advanced new media classes that you will need to harness for game programming, including classes for organizing scene components into a hierarchy using a **Scene Graph**, classes for **user interface** layout and design, classes for **2D digital illustration** (known as vector graphics), and classes for **digital imaging** (known as raster graphics), **2D animation (vector and raster)**, **digital video**, **digital audio**, **3D rendering**, a **web page rendering engine** (WebKit), and much more. We'll be touching on all of this in this chapter so you'll know what you have available for Java 9 games now that JavaFX has been added into Java as an API.

The rationale for going into the API detail overview early in the book is to get the creative side of your brain firing so you can start to think about how the JavaFX new media engine features support your pro Java game concept and design. Not only is it important that you know what JavaFX can do for your games development, but all of the API classes are interrelated, so you need an overview of how the various components of the JavaFX new media engine are put together. JavaFX uses a complex set of APIs that I like to call the **engine** to implement incredible "front-end" power. This is because of the inherent power that it brings to implementing User Interface (UI) and User Experience (UX) "wins" to your pro Java games and IoT applications. So, bear with me regarding these "foundational" chapters that cover how to master your IDE (NetBeans 9), your foundational programming language (Java 9), and a new media engine (JavaFX 8), which is now an integrated Java platform API and which is rapidly growing in browser support, power, and popularity.

In this chapter you will review the JavaFX **QUANTUM** toolkit, the **PRISM** rendering technology, the **WebKit** web engine, the **GLASS** windowing technology, the JavaFX **Media Engine**, the JavaFX **Scene Graph**, and the JavaFX API.

Once you take a look at how JavaFX comes together at the highest level, like you did in Chapter 5 for Java 9, you will take a look at some of the key classes that you will be using to construct pro Java games. These include Node, as well as the following: Group, Scene, Stage, Layout, Control, StackPane, Shape, Geometry, Media, Image, Camera, Effect, Canvas, Paint, and Animation. We already looked at the JavaFX Application class in Chapter 6; we will continue to learn about this class, as well as about the various classes that can be used to build complex multimedia projects such as games.

© Wallace Jackson 2017

W. Jackson, *Pro Java 9 Games Development*, https://doi.org/10.1007/978-1-4842-0973-8_7

Finally, you'll take an in-depth look at the bootstrap JavaFX application code that you generated in Chapter 6 and look at how the Java **.main()** method and the JavaFX **.start()** method create the primaryStage Stage object using the **Stage()** constructor method and, inside of that, create a Scene object named scene using the **Scene()** constructor method. You'll look at how to use methods from the Stage class to set the Scene, title the Stage, and show the Stage. You'll learn how to create and use **StackPane** and **Button** class objects and how to add an **EventHandler** to a Button.

Overview of JavaFX: From SceneGraph Down to OS

As I did in Chapter 2 and Chapter 3 covering new media, I want to start at the highest level with JavaFX, which is the **Scene Graph**. This is the level right under the new media asset types that were shown on the very top level in Figure 2-1 and Figure 3-7. JavaFX API's Scene Graph Java code can also be built by using the Gluon drag-and-drop JavaFX Scene Builder, which can be integrated into NetBeans 9, as you learned in Chapter 6, or used as a stand-alone. We will be looking at how to "scratch-code" all of these scene structures since this is *Pro Java 9 Games Development*.

As you can see in Figure 7-1, the JavaFX Scene Graph Architecture sits on top of the **JavaFX API**, a collection of JavaFX packages such as **javafx.scene** or **javafx.application**, which is what ultimately allows you to build your Scene Graph and design your JavaFX new media creations. In this case, it will be a pro Java game. Notice that the JavaFX API is connected (using steel bearings on this diagram to denote bridges) not only to the Scene Graph Architecture above it but also to the Java API and its JavaFX Quantum toolkit below it. As you can see, the Java JDK (and API) connects the JavaFX new media engine to NetBeans 9 and to the JVM. The JVM allows Java to distribute your Pro Java Game across the various platforms that Java currently supports, as well as future (native support) platforms like Android 8 and iOS.

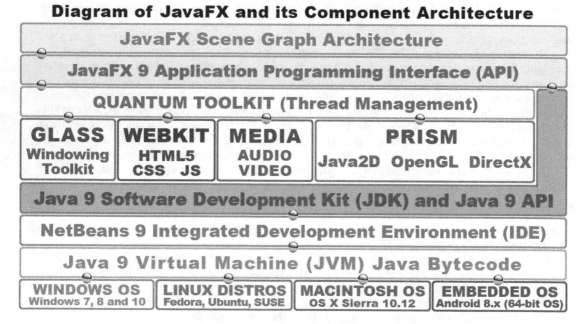

Figure 7-1. JavaFX Component Architecture from Scene Graph at the top down through Java, NetBeans, JVM, and OSs

The **Quantum toolkit** that is connected to the JavaFX API ties together all of the powerful new media–related engines that I'm going to talk about next. The Quantum toolkit handles **thread management** for all these engines so that your game code, which is on the JavaFX primary (main) thread, and your game's new media assets (audio, video, 3D vector, 2D vector), which are on their own thread (A/V uses a dedicated thread, as does WebKit, Windowing, or 3D rendering), can use separate processors via separate threads (or processes) on those dual-core, quad-core, hexa-core and octa-core CPUs, which are now commonplace in today's computers and embedded consumer electronics devices. I have shown new media engines that are important enough to have their own threads in the fourth tier of Figure 7-1.

The **Glass Windowing Toolkit** controls **window management** for JavaFX. This is responsible for the control of any discrete areas of your display, such as your **Stage** or **Popup** windows, such as dialogs. Glass also manages the **events processing queue** and passes events up to JavaFX for processing, and it also sets up **timers**, which you will learn about later in the book when we get into gameplay and how pulse milliseconds can control the timing for your games.

As you can see in the middle of Figure 7-1, there is also a **WebKit** engine and a **Media Player** engine. These are also managed by the Quantum toolkit. The WebKit engine can render HTML5, CSS3/4, and JavaScript content. This means you can create web content that runs seamlessly inside your JavaFX games. The Media Player media playback engine offloads (handles) the playback, UI controls for, and navigation of your Digital Audio and Digital Video assets.

The most important new media engine underneath the Quantum toolkit is the **PRISM** engine, which I like to call the "Prism Game Engine," as it renders 2D content using **Java2D** and renders 3D content using either **OpenGL** (Macintosh, Linux, or Embedded OS) or **DirectX** if users are using the Windows 7, 8, or 10 platforms. I use Windows 7.2 and 10 on some of my production workstations. Windows XP and Vista support was discontinued, as most of the computers and consumer electronics devices are now 64-bit capable (Windows XP is 32-bit and only addresses 3.24 GB of memory).

What PRISM does is to "bridge" the powerful game engines (DirectX and OpenGL) that are on the major OS platforms, as well as on consumer electronics embedded devices so that JavaFX can "offload" complex rendering task processing to **GPU hardware** from nVidia (GeForce), AMD (Radeon), ARM, Qualcomm, or Intel. This makes JavaFX/Java games faster and allows games to use less of the CPU processing power for rendering game assets to the screen. This in turn allows more of the CPU processing power to be used for gameplay logic, such as AI or collision detection. We'll be getting into these areas of game design after we master the JavaFX engine features and its Scene Graph Hierarchy and Architecture during the next two chapters of the book, this JavaFX primer, and Chapter 8 on Scene Graph design.

It is important to note that game developers do not need to understand the inner workings of the Quantum (threading), Glass (windowing), or Prism (rendering) engines to be able to leverage their powerful new media features. Throughout this book, you are going to be focusing on the top-level Scene Graph Architecture, as well as the JavaFX and Java API levels of this diagram. You'll also be covering the NetBeans 9 IDE level, which we just took care of in Chapter 6, but whose features we will also be exploring in further detail throughout the remainder of this book.

As far as the lower levels of the diagram in Figure 7-1 are concerned, NetBeans 9.0 will generate a Java ByteCode file that is read by the custom JVM or Java 9 Virtual Machine, for each of the OS platforms. This JVM, shown at the bottom of Figure 7-1, can be installed for any given OS platform by downloading the Java 9 **Java Runtime Engine (JRE)**, which you have already encountered in Chapter 1, when you installed it as part of your Java 9 JDK installation.

This JVM layer allows your game to be installed as an application across all popular OS platforms, as well as on embedded devices, which will also be moving to support JavaFX. You should also generate your pro Java game as a Java "applet" that can be embedded into a web site, and there's even a deployment model where the application can be dragged out of the web site and onto the desktop, where it is then installed as a full-fledged Java game application.

There is also already a work process used to run JavaFX apps on iOS 8 and Android 8, although the support is not "native" as yet, so JavaFX applications can't yet run directly inside those OSs. If you are interested in the latest information regarding this, simply Google "JavaFX on Android" or "JavaFX on iOS," and you can bet that by 2018 that Android OS, iOS, BlackBerry, and Tizen OS devices will be running JavaFX applications "natively." This will allow you to "code once, run everywhere" with this Java and JavaFX dynamic duo! What I mean by native is that you will someday be able to export Java (and JavaFX engine) apps directly to Android 8 using **JetBrains IntelliJ 2017 Android Studio** or to iOS or Tizen OS, or possibly even directly to Android 8, using NetBeans 9. This will add to the Windows, Mac, Open Solaris, and Linux distributions support currently afforded by NetBeans 9.

■ **Note** The **JetBrains IntelliJ IDEA** is now the official IDE used for creating 64-bit Android 8 applications. This IDE is covered in my *Android Apps for Absolute Beginners* (Apress, 2017), which covers developing 64-bit Android 5 to 8 applications using the IntelliJ IDEA using Java 8. IntelliJ is also covered in my *Pro Android Wearables* (Apress, 2015). I expect Java 9 will also feature support for wearables and appliances by the end of 2018.

Let's start at the top of the diagram shown in Figure 7-1 and take a look at the JavaFX Scene Graph and the **javafx.scene** package, which implements the Scene Graph in the JavaFX API using 16 powerful and useful Java classes.

The JavaFX Scene Package: 16 Java Scene Classes

The first thing that I want to do after our high-level overview is take a look at one of the most important JavaFX packages, the **javafx.scene** package. As you have seen in Chapters 2 and 3, there is more than one JavaFX package. As you can see at the top of Figure 6-7, your **JavaFXGame.java** application is already using four different JavaFX packages. The javafx.scene package contains **16** powerful Java classes (remember JavaFX was recoded in native Java) including **Camera**, **ParallelCamera** and **PerspectiveCamera**, **Cursor** and **ImageCursor**, **LightBase**, **PointLight**, and **AmbientLight**, as well as the Scene Graph classes (**Node**, **Parent**, **Group**, **Scene**, and **SubScene**) and some utility classes seen in Figure 7-2. As you can see, I have grouped these 16 javafx.scene package classes logically. I have the Scene class inside of the Scene Graph section of this diagram because Scene objects that are created using this Scene class will contain Scene Graph objects that are created using the other four Node, Parent, Group, and SubScene Scene Graph–related classes, and their subclasses. We'll be covering all of these Scene Graph classes in detail a bit later during the chapter.

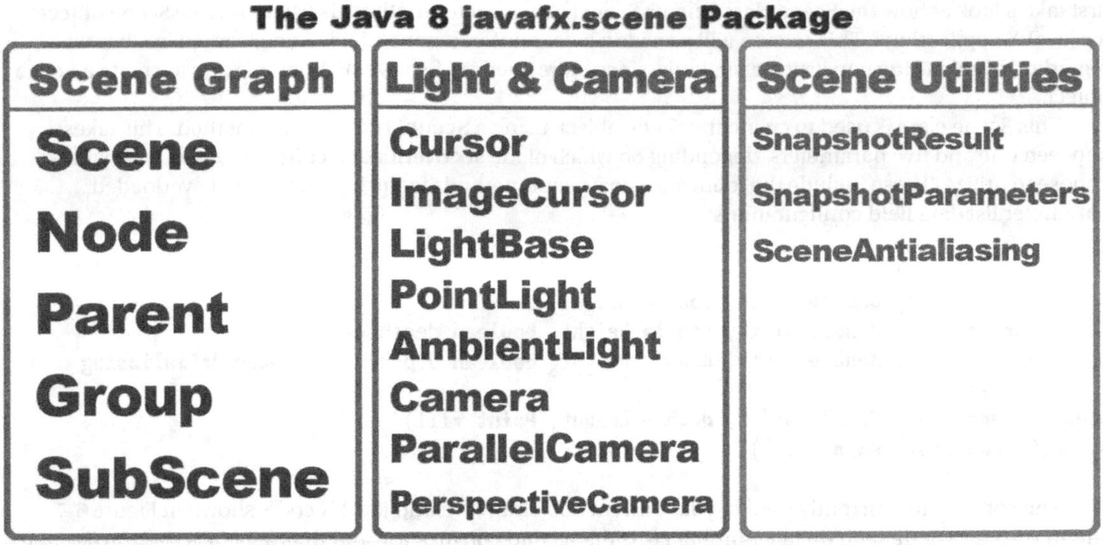

The Java 8 javafx.scene Package

Scene Graph	Light & Camera	Scene Utilities
Scene **Node** **Parent** **Group** **SubScene**	**Cursor** **ImageCursor** **LightBase** **PointLight** **AmbientLight** **Camera** **ParallelCamera** **PerspectiveCamera**	**SnapshotResult** **SnapshotParameters** **SceneAntialiasing**

Figure 7-2. *The Java javafx.scene package and 16 core Scene Graph, Scene Utility, Lighting, Camera, and Cursor classes*

Scene Graph Architecture classes for JavaFX start at the highest level with the **Node** superclass, along with its **Parent** and SubScene subclasses and the **Group** subclass of the Parent class, which we will be using later during this book to create our game Scene Graph hierarchy. These core Node classes are used to create the game's JavaFX Scene Graph hierarchy and are used to organize and group objects that have been created using JavaFX media asset and graphic design packages, which are contained in the **javafx.media** and **javafx. graphics** Java 9 modules.

There are three Scene utility classes, as I call them, which allow you to take a **Snapshot** (like a screenshot) of your Scene or any of its Scene Graph nodes at any time, as well as to turn **Scene AntiAliasing** on or off, if you are using 3D primitives (geometry defined using math rather than a mesh) in a Scene. The other half (eight) of the classes in the javafx.scene package are utilized for scene lighting, scene cameras, and cursor control for your scene.

We'll be covering these javafx.scene classes in future chapters as we create your game, after we take a look at the Scene Graph classes that are used to create, group, manage, and manipulate your JavaFX scene content. Thus, I will be covering the javafx.scene package's classes, shown in Figure 7-2, from the left side of the diagram and moving to the right side of the diagram, in the order of the classes that you are likely to use the most often to those used the least often. That said, all of these classes (with the possible exception of Snapshot) are very important for i3D games.

JavaFX Scene Class: Defining Dimension and Background Color

The two primary classes in the javafx.scene package are the **Scene** class and the **Node** class. We will be covering the Node class and its **Parent**, **Group**, and **SubScene** subclasses in the next section, as those classes, along with their subclasses (such as the **StackPane** class used in the JavaFXGame class), can be utilized to implement the Scene Graph architecture in JavaFX. Also, in a sense, and in my diagrams shown in Figure 7-2 and 7-3, the Node class and its subclasses can be viewed as being "below" the Scene class, although the Node class is not a subclass of the Scene class. In fact, the Node (Scene Graph) class and its subclasses, or rather the objects created using these classes, are actually contained **inside** of the Scene object itself, just like things are grouped by scene in real-life stage productions. For this reason, we will first take a look at how the Scene class, and its **Scene()** constructor method, is used to create Scene objects for JavaFX applications. This section will provide a great reinforcement for what you learned in Chapter 5 regarding **overloading** constructor methods, since there needs to be several different ways to create a Scene object.

This Scene class is used to create the Scene object, using a **Scene()** constructor method. This takes between one and five parameters, depending on which of the **six** overloaded constructor methods you choose to utilize. These include the following constructor methods featuring six different overloaded parameter list data field configurations:

```
Scene(Parent root)
Scene(Parent root, double width, double height)
Scene(Parent root, double width, double height, boolean depthBuffer)
Scene(Parent root, double width, double height, boolean depthBuffer, SceneAntialiasing
      aAlias)
Scene(Parent root, double width, double height, Paint fill)
Scene(Parent root, Paint fill)
```

The constructor currently used in your current bootstrap Java and JavaFX code, shown in Figure 6-7 and in your Java code seen on line number 28, is the second constructor, and thus far, it has been structured (called) as follows:

```
Scene scene = new Scene(root, 300, 250);
```

If you wanted to add a **Black** background color to the scene, you would use the **fifth** overloaded constructor method using a **Color.BLACK** constant from the **Color** class (this is a **Paint** object because Color is a Paint subclass) as your fill data, in this case a fillColor. This would be done by using the following Scene() object constructor method call:

```
Scene scene = new Scene(root, 300, 250, Color.BLACK);
```

Notice that the **root** object is a **Parent** subclass, called the **StackPane** class, and is created using the **StackPane()** constructor method, two lines above the Scene() constructor method call, by using the following line of Java code:

```
StackPane root = new StackPane(); // StackPane subclassed from Parent; so Parent root node
type
```

As you can see, any class can be used in the constructor that is a subclass of the object (class) type that is declared (required) for that constructor parameter position (data). This is why we are able to use Color and StackPane objects in our parameter list, because they have the superclass origins from the Paint and Parent classes, respectively.

In case you are wondering what the **boolean depthBuffer** parameter is, it is used for **i3D** scene components. Since these scene components are 3D and have depth (a "Z" component, in addition to a 2D "X" and "Y" components), you will need to include this parameter and set it to a value of **true**, if you are creating 3D scenes, or combining 2D and 3D scene components. Finally, if you are wondering what the **SceneAntialiasing** object (and class) that is passed in the parameter list for the fourth constructor method is, it provides **real-time smoothing** for 3D scene components. So, for a 3D Scene object, which is what we will be needing, the constructor method call would look like the following:

```
Scene 3Dscene = new Scene(root, 300, 250, true, true);
```

JavaFX Scene Graph: Organizing Scenes by Using Parent Nodes

The Scene Graph, which is not at all unique to JavaFX, can now be seen in quite a few genres of new media content creation software packages, such as 3D, digital audio, sound design, digital video, and special effects, for instance. A Scene Graph is a visual representation for a **content data structure** that resembles an upside-down tree, with the **root node** at the top and **branch nodes** and **leaf nodes** coming off of the root node. The first time I saw the Scene Graph approach to scene design was when I was 3D modeling, rendering, and animating using a software package on the Amiga 4000 called Real3D from RealSoft OY in Finland. This approach has since been copied by a plethora of 3D, digital video, and special effects software packages since then and is now the way that JavaFX organizes the content in its scenes. For this reason, many of you may be familiar with, and therefore comfortable with, this design paradigm. Not only does the Scene Graph data structure allow you to architect, organize, and design your JavaFX scene and its content, but it also allows you to apply **opacity**, **states**, **event handlers**, **transformations**, and **special effects** to entire logical branches of your Scene Graph hierarchy if you set your Scene Graph up correctly. Figure 7-3 shows a basic Scene Graph tree, with the **root node** at the top and **branch nodes** and **leaf nodes** underneath that root node.

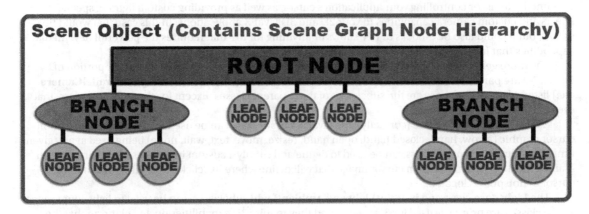

Figure 7-3. *JavaFX Scene Graph hierarchy, starting with the root node and progressing to branch nodes and leaf nodes*

The root node is the topmost node, which is why it is called the *root*, even though it is at the top, rather than at the bottom, like a root would be in the plant life world. A root node has no **parent**, that is, nothing above it in the Scene Graph hierarchy. A root node is itself a parent to the branch nodes and leaf nodes that are underneath it.

The next most powerful (and complex) construct in the Scene Graph tree is called the *branch* node, which uses the **javafx.scene.Parent** class as its superclass and can contain **children**, which is logical since it extends a class that is aptly named **Parent**. A branch node can contain other branch nodes, as well as "leaf" nodes, so it can be used to create some very complicated and very powerful Scene Graph hierarchy (or Scene Graph architecture) constructs.

The last level in the hierarchy is the "leaf" node, and a leaf node is the end of the branch. As such, a leaf node can have **no children**. It is important to notice that leaf nodes can come directly off the root node, as you can see in Figure 7-3. Branch nodes can be created by using the **Parent**, **Group**, or **SubScene** classes, shown in Figure 7-2, or using any of their subclasses, such as the **WebView**, **Region**, **Pane**, or **StackPane** classes, for instance.

Examples of objects that would be at the very end of the branches, that is, leaf nodes, include JavaFX classes (instantiated as objects) that can be **configured using parameters**. Examples would include shapes, text, or controls. These are design or content components in and of themselves, and therefore not designed to have any children (child object), so they inherently have to be at the end of the tree and branches by the nature of their class function design.

A leaf node will therefore always contain a JavaFX class that has not been subclassed (extended) from the Parent class or from the Group, Region or SubScene class and that has not itself been specifically designed to have any child elements (child objects) within it (or below it) within your JavaFX Scene Graph hierarchy.

The three subclasses of the Parent class can be utilized as branch nodes. These include the **Group** class for grouping child (leaf node) objects so that opacity, transforms, and special effects can be applied to Group nodes all at once; the **Region** class for grouping child (leaf node) objects in 2D to form screen layouts, which could be styled using CSS3, if you like; and the **WebView** class, which is used to manage the **WebEngine** class, which renders HTML5, JS, and CSS content in a WebView.

JavaFX Scene Content: Lights, Camera, Cursor, Action!

Next, let's take a look at the eight classes listed in the center of Figure 7-2 that provide some powerful multimedia tools for controlling your application's cursor, as well as providing custom lighting special effects and custom camera capabilities to your 2D and 3D JavaFX applications. In this case that would be games, but it could also be e-books or iTV shows or anything for IoT that requires the powerful new media capabilities that JavaFX provides for the Java 9 APIs.

The more generalized classes (**Cursor**, **LightBase**, **Camera**) that are listed in the center portion of Figure 7-2 are parent classes, and the more specialized ones (**ImageCursor**, **PointLight**, **ParallelCamera**, etc.) listed after each of those are the subclasses of those parent classes. Except for the LightBase class, that seems to be stating the obvious!

As you might have guessed (correctly), the JavaFX **Cursor** class can be used to control the application cursor graphic (arrow, hand, closed hand, open hand, resize, move, text, wait, none) being used at any given time. The **ImageCursor** subclass can be used to define and supply a custom image-based cursor, using an X and Y location within a custom cursor image that will define where its "click point," also known as the cursor's "hotspot," is located.

The **LightBase** class, and its **PointLight** and **AmbientLight** subclasses, can be used to light your scenes. These classes are primarily used for 3D scenes, and they require 3D capabilities on any platform that the game is running on, which is not really a problem these days as most of the major CPU manufacturers also make (and include) GPUs. Also, it is important to note, the Prism game engine will simulate the 3D environment (GPU) using 3D processing emulation if a GPU is not available on the hardware platform that is rendering your game. This is termed *software rendering*.

If you set it up correctly, you could also use these lighting classes with your 2D games, or use lighting with a "hybrid" 2D and 3D game, which we will be taking a look at later during this book as well, since JavaFX supports it.

The **Camera** class, and its **ParallelCamera** and **PerspectiveCamera** subclasses, can be used to photograph or video your scene and can be used in 3D, 2D, and hybrid game applications. Two of the camera classes, Camera and ParallelCamera, do not require that 3D (GPU) capabilities be present on the platform that is playing your JavaFX application, in this case, a game. A Parallel Camera view is sometimes called **Orthographic Projection** in 3D software.

The subclasses of the Camera class provide two different specialized types of Cameras. The ParallelCamera class can be utilized for rendering scenes without any depth perspective correction, which in the 3D industry is called an **orthographic projection**. This means this class is perfect for use with 2D scenes (and for 2D games).

The PerspectiveCamera class provides a far more complex camera used for 3D scenes, which will support 3D viewing volumes. Like the LightBase class, and its subclasses, a PerspectiveCamera class will require 3D capabilities for the hardware platform that your pro Java 9 game (or IoT application) will be running on (called the *target* platform).

A PerspectiveCamera class has a **fieldOfView** attribute (state or property). This can be used to change your viewing volume, just like a real camera zoom lens can, when you zoom it in from a wide angle to a zoom. The default setting for the fieldOfView attribute is an acute angle of **30 degrees.** If you remember your geometry class from high school, you can visualize this field of view by looking down the y-axis (the up and down one) at the camera. As you might expect, there are **.getFieldOfView()** and **.setFieldOfView(double)** method calls to control this camera class attribute.

Next, let's take a closer look at the Scene utility classes. After that, we will take a closer look at some of the nine javafx.scene **subpackages**, such as javafx.scene.text, javafx.scene.image, javafx.scene.shape, and javafx.scene.layout.

JavaFX Scene Utilities: Scene Snapshots and Anti-aliasing

Finally, we should take a quick look at the three utility classes that are shown on the right side of Figure 7-2, as they can be used to increase the quality of your scene output on your user's device screen (using anti-aliasing), as well as to provide screen capture capabilities to either your user (for social media sharing) or your gameplay logic.

Let's get the **SceneAntialiasing** class out of the way first. You learned about **anti-aliasing** in Chapter 2, and I showed you how it uses an algorithm to smooth jagged edges where two different colors come together, usually on a diagonal line or circular area of an image composite. An **image composite** is where two separate images are placed in **layers** to form one resulting image. Sometimes the edges that differ between the image components that are in these two (or more) image layers will need to be **smoothed**. Smoothing (anti-aliasing) is needed so a final image composite looks like it is one seamless image, which is the intention of the artist or game designer. Interestingly, we are already implementing the JavaFX "layer engine" in our JavaFXGame application using the **StackPane** class (**panes** are **layers**). The "layer stack" image compositing approach is common in games as well as in software such as Photoshop or GIMP.

What the SceneAntialiasing class does is to provide **anti-aliasing processing** (algorithm) to 3D scenes so that they can be composited over your scene's 2D background, whether that is the default **Color.WHITE** or any other color value, a 2D image (creating a hybrid 2D and 3D app), or anything else, like Digital Video. The SceneAntiAliasing class allows you to set the **static SceneAntialiasing** data field to a value of **DISABLED** (turns anti-aliasing off) or **BALANCED** (turns anti-aliasing on). The balanced option provides a balance of quality and performance, which simply means that more anti-aliasing quality will be processed the more processing power that the device hardware brings to the table.

Next let's take a look at the **SnapshotParameters** class (object), which is used to set up (contain) a rendering attribute parameter that will be used by your **SnapshotResult** class (object). The parameters include what type of **Camera** (parallel or perspective) object will be used, whether the **depthBuffer** used for 3D is on (true for 3D) or off (false for 2D), a **Paint** object used to contain a resulting snapshot image data, a **Transform** object used to contain any transform data, and a **Rectangle2D** object that is used to define the viewport area that is to be rendered. This would be the snapshot **dimensions** and what X,Y **location** on the screen the upper-left corner of the SnapshotResult is set to.

This SnapshotResult class (and the object created using this class, more importantly) contains your resulting snapshot image data, requested parameters, and source node in the Scene Graph that it was generated from. For this reason, three methods supported by this class would be obvious: a **.getImage()** method will get the snapshot image, a **.getSource()** method will get the source node, and a **.getSnapshotParameters()** method will get the SnapshotParameters.

Scene Subpackages: Nine Scene-Related Packages

You might be thinking "Whew! That was a lot to cover in that javafx.scene package overview!" and indeed the core javafx.scene package has a lot of classes in it covering scene creation, scene graph organization, and scene utilities such as lighting, cameras, cursors, screenshots ("sceneshots"), and settings utilities.

There is a lot more in the javafx.scene package, in "subpackages" as I call them, which are packages that are underneath the javafx.scene package that are referenced using another dot with another package name (description). In fact, there are nine more javafx.scene packages, as you can see in Table 7-1, which cover things such as canvas drawing, texture painting, special effects, UI layout, digital imaging, event handling, text and fonts, shapes (2D and 3D geometry), and 2D and 3D transforms. We'll be looking at all of these javafx.scene subpackage classes and concepts during this chapter, as well as using many of them during the course of this book. This section of the chapter goes over javafx.scene subpackages in greater detail, and much of the functionality that you'll be using for your game development will be found in these subpackages. This is why I'm giving you an overview of what JavaFX provides so that it's done all in one place and we can start Pro Java 9 Games coding using JavaFX 9 APIs and use all this multimedia power to create game experiences.

Table 7-1. *The Nine Second-Level JavaFX Scene Subpackages with Primary Function and Description of the Functional Classes*

Package Name	Function	Package Contents and Functional Description
javafx.scene.**canvas**	Direct drawing	Provides the Canvas class (and Canvas object) for a custom drawing surface
javafx.scene.**effect**	Special effects	Special effects classes: Glow, Blend, Bloom, Shadow, Reflection, MotionBlur
javafx.scene.**image**	Digital imaging	Digital imaging classes: Image, ImageView, WritableImage, PixelFormat
javafx.scene.**input**	Event handling	Provides classes related to getting input from the user into the JavaFX app
javafx.scene.**layout**	UI layouts	User interface layout container classes: TilePane, GridPane, FlowPane, etc.
javafx.scene.**paint**	Texture (paint)	Paint classes: Paint, Color, LinearGradient, RadialGradient, Stop, Material, etc.
javafx.scene.**shape**	Geometry	2D and 3D geometry classes: Mesh, Shape, Shape3D, Circle, Line, Path, Arc, etc.
javafx.scene.**text**	Text and fonts	Provides text rendering and font rendering classes: TextFlow, Text, Font, etc.
javafx.scene.**transform**	Transforms	Provides transform classes: Transform, Affine, Rotate, Scale, Shear, Translate

Let's start with the packages that contain the fewest classes and get those out of the way first. Even though the table lists subpackages alphabetically, the first one, **javafx.scene.canvas**, contains two classes: a Canvas class that is used to create a Canvas object and a GraphicsContext class that is used to control calls to draw onto that Canvas.

The next subpackage, **javafx.scene.effect**, contains the **special effects** classes. These can be very useful for pro Java 9 games development, so this is one of the subpackages that I'm going to cover in detail during this section.

The **javafx.scene.image** subpackage is used to implement digital imagery within JavaFX, and it contains your **ImageView**, **Image**, **WritableImage**, **PixelFormat**, and **WritablePixelFormat** classes. The ImageView class is what you'll normally use to hold your digital image assets, and the more advanced **PixelFormat** classes allow you to create digital imagery on a **pixel-by-pixel basis** if you want to do more advanced (algorithmic) pixel-based digital image creation.

The **javafx.scene.input** subpackage contains classes that are used to get **input** from the JavaFX app's user, including mouse and keyboard input, gestures, touchscreen, scrolling, zooming or swipes input, and clipboard content, among other types of input. Input and actions are processed using the **event-handling** capabilities, which you will be looking at in great detail during this book and which you have already experienced in your Pro JavaFX 9 application, as seen in your bootstrap Java 9 code in lines 20 through 25 (shown in Figure 6-7).

The **javafx.scene.layout** subpackage contains classes that are used to create user interface design **layouts** and can be used for your screen layout designs as well. These layout classes include classes that control and manage backgrounds, add and style borders, and provide UI **Pane** management classes such as **StackPane**, **GridPane**, **TilePane**, **FlowPane**, and **AnchorPane**. These **Pane** subclasses provide automatic screen layout algorithms for UI controls in JavaFX. The **Background** class provides **screen background** utilities, and the **Border** class provides **screen border** utilities, which can be used for spicing up graphics for your user interface screens.

The **javafx.scene.paint** subpackage contains a **Stop** class; a **Paint** superclass and **Color**, **ImagePattern**, **LinearGradient**, and **RadialGradient** subclasses; and the 3D **Material** superclass and its **PhongMaterial** subclass. Those of you who are familiar with 3D content production will recognize this Phong shader algorithm, which will allow different **surface** looks (plastic, rubber, etc.) to be simulated. These Material and PhongMaterial classes need the i3D capabilities to be present on the playback hardware in order to function successfully, just like the SceneAntialiasing, PerspectiveCamera, and LightBase classes and subclasses. These need GPU hardware acceleration or software rendering.

The abstract **Paint** class creates subclasses that paint objects, the **Color** class colors these objects (fills them with color), **LinearGradient** and **RadialGradient** are Paint subclasses that fill objects with color gradients, and the **Stop** class allows you to define where a gradient color starts and stops inside of the gradient, which is where its name comes from. Finally, there is your **ImagePattern** class, which can fill a Shape object with a tileable image pattern, which can be quite useful for games.

The **javafx.scene.shape** subpackage contains classes for 2D geometry, commonly called **shapes**, as well as for 3D geometry, commonly called **meshes**. A **Mesh** superclass and its **TriangleMesh** subclass handle 3D geometry, as do the **Shape3D** superclass and its **Box**, **Sphere**, **Cylinder**, and **MeshView** subclasses. The **Shape** superclass has a lot more subclasses (12); these are 2D geometry elements, and they include the **Arc**, **Circle**, **CubicCurve**, **QuadCurve, Ellipse**, **Line**, **Path**, **Polygon**, **Polyline**, **Rectangle**, and **SVGPath** classes. There is also "path" support, which a path being defined as an "open" shape (I like to call it a "spline" since I am a 3D modeler) provided by the **PathElement** superclass, and its **ArcTo**, **ClosePath**, **CubicCurveTo**, **HLineTo**, **LineTo**, **MoveTo**, **QuadCurveTo**, and **VLineTo** subclasses, which allow you to draw spline curves to create your own custom Scalable Vector Graphics (SVG) shapes.

The **javafx.scene.text** subpackage contains classes for rendering text shapes and fonts into your scenes. This includes the **Font** class for using any fonts that you may want to use that are not the JavaFX "system" font, as well as the **Text** class for creating a Text Node that will display the text values using this font. There's also a specialized layout container class called **TextFlow**, which is used to "flow" text, much like you would see done in a word processor.

The **javafx.scene.transform** subpackage contains classes for rendering 2D and 3D **spatial transformations**, such as the **Scale**, **Rotate**, **Shear**, **Translate**, and **Affine** (3D rotation) subclasses of the **Transform** superclass. These can be applied to any Node object in the Scene Graph. This allows anything in your Scene Graph (text, UI controls, shapes, meshes, images, media, etc.) to be transformed in any way that you like, which affords JavaFX game developers a ton of creative power when it comes to transforming things. Translation, in case you are wondering, is a linear movement of an entire object. Shear is linear movement on a 2D plane in two different directions or movement in one direction when another part of the 2D plane is fixed. Imagine moving the top of a plane, while the bottom remains fixed, so the square becomes a parallelogram, or moving the top and bottom of the same plane (a square) in different directions.

Now that we have looked at a plethora of important and useful classes (objects) in the javafx.scene package and its related subpackages, let's take a look at the other 18 top-level JavaFX packages to get an idea of the other key capabilities that JavaFX offers for application development, and of course we will focus on those that can be utilized for game development as we have been doing so far during this chapter and will continue to do throughout the book.

The javafx.graphics Module: 18 Multimedia Packages

There are 18 top-level **javafx.graphics module** packages that are the most often used packages (besides the core javafx.base module packages). These follow a **javafx.packagename** name format (not javafx.graphics. packagename). Some of these, such as scene and css, have subpackage levels as well. We saw this with the nine javafx.scene package and its subpackages, which we looked at previously, so we won't look at these here. The javafx.graphics module is one of three key modules to include for creating Pro Java 9 Games, with the others being **javafx.base** and **javafx.media**. Since nine javafx.graphics module packages are included in Table 7-2, this essentially means that from a JavaFX API module perspective, the javafx.graphics module has a total of 18 package categories, as nine are listed in Table 7-1. These module packages have been reorganized since JavaFX 8 by the JavaFX 9 development team at Oracle to allow better modularization (function optimization). For instance, if you don't need audio or video in your 3D game, you could just use the base and graphics modules. Since we want audio, we will use base, graphics, and media modules, or three of the seven JavaFX API modules (a 57 percent JavaFX API package code reduction right off the bat). I wanted to give you an overview of these 18 functional areas in the javafx.graphics module's packages, as shown in Table 7-1 and 7-2, and take a closer look at what each of the graphics areas (vector, raster, animation, CSS) will do.

Table 7-2. *javafx.graphics Module Top-Level (Nonscene) Packages, with Primary Functions and Description of Function*

Package Name	Functions	Package Contents Description
javafx.animation	Animation	Classes: AnimationTimer, Timeline, Transition, Interpolator, KeyFrame, KeyValue
javafx.application	Application	Provides Application (init, start, stop methods), Preloader, Parameters, Platform
javafx.concurrent	Threading	Provides threading classes: Task, Service, ScheduledService, WorkerStateEvent
javafx.css	CSS	Provides classes related to implementing Cascading Style Sheets (CSS) in JavaFX
javafx.css.converter	CSS	Provides classes related to implementing CSS in JavaFX
javafx.geometry	3D geometry	Provides 3D geometry
javafx.print	Printing	Provides printing
javafx.scene	Scene control	Classes related to scene creation, organization, and control (see Table 7-1)
javafx.stage	Stage creation	Provides Stage creation

Some of these we have covered already, such as the **javafx.application** package, which we learned about in Chapter 6, and the **javafx.scene** package and its subpackages, which we covered in the previous section.

The first package in Table 7-2 is the **javafx.animation** package. Since animation is important for Java games, let's cover that in the next section of the chapter. I'll also cover **javafx.geometry** and **javafx.stage**, as the core packages from Table 7-2 that are needed for a Java 9 game are animation, application, geometry, scene, and stage.

JavaFX Animation for Games: Using javafx.animation Classes

The javafx.animation package contains the **Animation** superclass and **Timeline**, **AnimationTimer**, **Interpolator**, **KeyFrame**, and **KeyValue** classes. It also contains the **Transition** superclass and ten transition subclasses, all of which we are going to take a look at during this section of the chapter, as animation is an important design element for pro Java 9 games development. Since these animation classes are already coded for us, thanks to the JavaFX 9 API, all that we have to do to add animation to games is use these classes properly. You'll be spending a lot of time with these classes, so I'm going to go into each one in detail so you know how each one works, which ones work together, and which ones you'll need to implement your own Java 9 game logic solution.

The JavaFX Animation Class: A Foundation for Animation Objects in JavaFX

The **Animation** class or more accurately the Animation object, provides the core functionality for animation in JavaFX. The Animation class contains two (overloaded) Animation() constructor methods. They include `Animation()` and `Animation(double targetFramerate)`, and they will create the Animation object in memory, which will control your animation, and its playback characteristics and life cycle, from a high-level object that contains other subobjects.

The Animation class contains the **.play()** method, the **.playFrom(cuePoint)** or **.playFrom(Duration time)** method, and a **.playFromStart()** method. These methods are used to start playback for the Animation object. There is also the **.pause()** method, which can pause the animation playback, and a **.stop()** method, which can stop animation playback. There are **.jumpTo(Duration time)** and **.jumpTo(cuePoint)** methods to jump to predefined positions in an animation.

You can set the animation **playback speed** (some call this the frame rate, or FPS) by using the **rate** property. The **cycleCount** property (variable) allows you to specify how many times an animation will **loop**, and the **delay** property allows you to specify a delay time before the animation starts. If your animation is looping, this delay property would specify your delay time used between loops, which can be used to create some realistic effects.

You can specify a **seamless** animation **loop** by setting the **cycleCount** attribute or property (variable) to be **INDEFINITE** and then using the **autoReverse** property (set to **false**), or you can use **pong** (back and forth) animation looping by specifying the **true** value for the autoReverse property. You can also set cycleCount to a **numeric value** such as 1 if you want the animation to play only one time and not loop indefinitely.

There is a **.setRate()** method to set the animation playback rate property, a **.setDelay()** method to set the delay property, and **.setCycleCount()** and **.setCycleDuration()** methods for controlling the cycling characteristics. As you might imagine, there are also similar **.get()** methods to "get" the currently set values for these **Animation** objects variables (or properties, attributes, parameters, characteristics; however you prefer to look at your data fields is fine).

You can assign an action to be executed when the animation has completed playback using the **onFinished** property, loaded with an ActionEvent object. This will be executed when the animation reaches the end of each loop, and as you can imagine, some very powerful things can be triggered in a pro Java game using this particular capability.

There are **read-only** variables (properties) that you can "poll" at any time, to find the **status**, **currentTime**, **currentRate**, **cycleDuration,** and **totalDuration** for each Animation object. For instance, you can use this **currentTime** property to see the position of the playback head (frame pointer) at any point in time in the animation playback cycle.

The JavaFX Timeline Class: An Animation Subclass for JavaFX Properties Timeline Management

The JavaFX **Timeline** class is a subclass of the JavaFX Animation superclass, so its inheritance hierarchy would look like the following, starting with the Java masterclass java.lang.Object and progressing on downward to the Timeline class:

```
> java.lang.Object
  > javafx.animation.Animation
    > javafx.animation.Timeline
```

Timeline objects can be used to define a special kind of Animation object that is comprised, or made up of, JavaFX values (properties) of object type **WritableValue**. All JavaFX properties are of type WritableValue, so this class can be used to animate anything in JavaFX, which means what you can do with it is limited only to your imagination.

Timeline animations are defined using **KeyFrame** objects, created via the KeyFrame class mentioned earlier. This KeyFrame class, not surprisingly, allows you to create and manage the KeyFrame objects that live inside the Timeline object. Those familiar with animation know keyframes set the different interpolated data values for different points in the animation of an object or data value to create smooth movements.

KeyFrame objects will always be processed by Timeline objects according to a **time** variable (accessed using **KeyFrame.time**) and by properties to be animated, which are defined using the KeyFrame object's values and accessed using the **KeyFrame.values** variable.

It is important to note that you need to set up your KeyFrame objects before you start running the Timeline object, as you cannot change a KeyFrame object within a running Timeline object. This is because it has been put into system memory once it has been started. If you wanted to change a KeyFrame object in a running Timeline object in any way, first stop the Timeline object, then make the change to the KeyFrame, and then restart the Timeline object. This will reload the Timeline object and its revised KeyFrame objects into memory along with their new values.

An **Interpolator** class, which you will be using during the book, interpolates these KeyFrame objects in your Timeline object based on the Timeline **direction**. Interpolation is a process of creating in-between, or "tween," frames based on the beginning and ending values. In case you're wondering how the **direction** is inferred, it is kept in the rate property and the read-only currentRate property of the Animation superclass, which is part of the extended Timeline subclass.

Inverting the value of the rate property (i.e., making it **negative**) will reverse (toggle) the playback direction, and the same principle would hold when reading the currentRate property (the negative value signifies the reverse, or backward, direction). Finally, a **KeyValue** class (object) is used to hold the data values inside of each KeyFrame object. A KeyFrame object stores multiple (as many as needed) KeyValue objects, using one KeyValue object per data value.

The JavaFX Transition Class: Animation Subclass for Transitions and Special Effects Application

The JavaFX **Transition** class is a subclass of the JavaFX Animation superclass, so its inheritance hierarchy would look like the following, starting with a Java master class called java.lang.Object and progressing downward to a Transition class:

```
> java.lang.Object
  > javafx.animation.Animation
    > javafx.animation.Transition
```

The Transition class is a **public abstract** class, and as such, it can only be utilized (subclassed or extended) to create transition subclasses. In fact, there are ten of these subclasses that have already been created for you to use, to create your own transition special effects. These include your **SequentialTransition**, **FadeTransition**, **FillTransition**, **PathTransition**, **PauseTransition**, **RotateTransition**, **ScaleTransition**, **TranslateTransition**, **ParallelTransition**, and **StrokeTransition** classes. The Java 9 class inheritance hierarchy for these subclasses would look similar to the following:

```
> java.lang.Object
  > javafx.animation.Animation
    > javafx.animation.Transition
      > javafx.animation.PathTransition
```

As a subclass of Animation, the Transition class contains all the functionality of Animation. Chances are you will end up using the ten custom transition classes directly, since they provide the different types of transitions you are likely to want to use (fades, fills, path based, stroke based, rotate, scale, movement or translate, etc.). We'll be learning how to use some of these as the book progresses, so I'm going to move on to the AnimationTimer class.

The JavaFX AnimationTimer Class: Frame Processing, Nanoseconds, and Pulse

The JavaFX **AnimationTimer** class is **not** a subclass of the JavaFX Animation superclass, so its inheritance hierarchy would look like the following; it starts with the Java master class called java.lang.Object and ends with AnimationTimer:

```
> java.lang.Object
  > javafx.animation.AnimationTimer
```

This means the AnimationTimer class was **scratch-coded** specifically to provide AnimationTimer functionality to JavaFX and that it is not related to the Animation (or Timeline or Transition) class or subclasses in any way. For this reason, the name of this class might be somewhat misleading if you are mentally grouping it in with the Animation, Interpolator, KeyFrame, and KeyValue classes that occupy the javafx.animation package with it; it has no relation to these classes whatsoever! This class allows you to implement your own animation (or game engine) timer and scratch-code everything yourself! I showed how to do this for i2D games in *Beginning Java 8 Games Development*.

This AnimationTimer class has also been declared to be a **public abstract** class, just like the Transition class. Since it's an abstract class, it can be utilized (subclassed or extended) only to create AnimationTimer subclasses. Unlike the Transition class, it has no subclasses that have been created for you; you have to create your own AnimationTimer subclasses from scratch.

The AnimationTimer class is deceptively simple, in that it has only one method that you must "override," or replace, which is contained in the public abstract class: the **.handle()** method. This method contains the programming logic that you want to have executed on every frame of the JavaFX engine's stage and scene processing cycle, which is optimized to play at **60 FPS** (60 frames per second), which just happens to be perfect for games. JavaFX uses a **pulse** system, which is based on the new Java **nanosecond** unit of time (versions previous to Java 7 used **milliseconds**).

JavaFX Pulse Synchronization: Asynchronous Processing for Your JavaFX Scene Graph Elements

A JavaFX **pulse** is a type of timing, or **synchronization event**, which synchronizes the states of your elements that are contained within any given Scene Graph structure that you create for your Pro Java 9 game or IoT application. The pulse system in JavaFX is administered by the Glass Windowing Toolkit. Pulse uses the high-resolution (nanoseconds) timers, which are also available to Java programmers using the **System. nanoTime()** method, introduced as of Java 7.

The pulse management system in JavaFX is "capped" or "throttled" to 60 FPS. This is an optimization so that all the JavaFX threads we discussed earlier have enough "processing headroom" to do what they need to do. A JavaFX application will automatically **spawn** up to three threads, based on what you're doing in your pro Java 9 game logic. A basic business application would probably only use the **primary JavaFX thread**, but an i3D game would also spawn the **Prism rendering thread** and if that pro Java 9 game also uses audio and or video, which it usually will, it would also spawn a **Media playback thread**, and if it also implements a social media interface or element, it would also spawn the **WebKit rendering thread**. So, as you will see, robust Java 9 games will require careful processor time management.

We will be using audio, 2D, 3D, and possibly video during the course of our game development journey, so our JavaFX game application will certainly be multithreaded! As you will see, JavaFX has been designed to be able to create games with multithreading and nanosecond timing capabilities and i3D PRISM rendering hardware support.

When something is changed in your Scene Graph, such as UI control positioning, a CSS style definition, or an Animation is playing, a pulse event is scheduled and is eventually "fired" to synchronize the states of elements in the Scene Graph. The trick in JavaFX game design is to **optimize pulse events** so that they are focusing on gameplay logic (animation, collision detection). For this reason, for pro Java 9 games, you'll want to minimize nongameplay changes (UI control location, style changes) that the pulse engine needs to process. You will do this by using a Scene Graph for a **Static** design system, that is, to design the fixed visual elements (UI, background imagery, etc.) that are not altered by the pulse engine. This will save "pulses" for use on dynamic elements of the game that animate or are interactive.

What I mean by this is you will use the Scene Graph to design your game's structure but will not manipulate static design Nodes (UI, background, decoration) in real time via the Scene Graph, using **dynamic** programming logic, as the pulse system would need to be utilized to perform these UI updates, and we'll most likely need those real-time processing events to use for our Pro Java 9 gameplay processing. There it is again: static versus dynamic game design.

The JavaFX pulse system allows developers to handle events **asynchronously**, or out of order, and schedules tasks on the nanosecond level. Next, we will take a look at how to schedule code in a pulse using a **.handle()** method.

Harnessing JavaFX Pulse Engine: Extending AnimationTimer Superclass to Generate Pulse Events

Extending your AnimationTimer class is a great way to get the JavaFX pulse engine to process Java code on every pulse that it processes. Your real-time game programming logic will be placed inside of your **.handle(long now)** method and can be started and stopped at will by using the other two AnimationTimer methods, **.start()** and **.stop()**.

The **.start()** and **.stop()** methods are called from the AnimationTimer superclass, although the two methods can also be overridden; just make sure to eventually call **super.start()** and **super.stop()** in the overridden code methods. The code structure for this might look like the following, if you were to add it as an inner class inside of your current JavaFX **public void .start()** method structure (which you can reference in Figure 6-7, to refresh your memory):

```
public void start(Stage primaryStage) {
    Button btn = new Button;
    btn.setText("Say 'Hello World'");
    btn.setOnAction(new EventHandler<ActionEvent>() {
        @Override
        public void handle(ActionEvent event) {
            System.out.println("Hello World!);
        }
    }
    new AnimationTimer() {
        @Override
        public void handle(long now) {
            // Program logic that gets processed on every pulse which JavaFX processes
        }
    }.start();
            // Rest of start() method code regarding Stage and Scene objects is in here
}
```

The previous programming logic shows how the AnimationTimer inner class could be constructed "on the fly," as well as how Java **dot chaining** works, as a .start() method call to the AnimationTimer superclass is appended to the end of a new AnimationTimer() constructor. In one statement, you have the AnimationTimer creation (new keyword), declaration (constructor method), and execution (start() method call chained to the AnimationTimer object construct).

If you want to create a more complex AnimationTimer implementation for something central to your game logic, such as **Collision Detection**, it would be a better approach (that is, a better pro Java 9 game design) to make game timing logic into its own (custom) AnimationTimer **subclass**, instead of an inner class. This is especially true if you are going to be creating more than one AnimationTimer subclass so that you can implement custom pulse event processing. You can have more than one AnimationTimer subclass running at the same time, but I recommend that you don't get carried away and use too many AnimationTimer subclasses but instead optimize your Java code and just use one.

To create your own AnimationTimer class called **BoardGamePulseEngine** using the Java **extends** keyword in conjunction with an AnimationTimer superclass, implement this AnimationTimer class definition and these required AnimationTimer superclass methods to create your "empty" JavaFX pulse board game logic timing engine.

```
public class BoardGamePulseEngine extends AnimationTimer {
    @Override
    public void handle(long now) {    // Program logic here that gets processed on every pulse
    }
    @Override
    public void start() {
        super.start();
    }
    @Override
    public void stop() {
        super.stop();
    }
}
```

167

We will be creating animation code later in the book after we learn the basics about Java 9, NetBeans 9, JavaFX 9, and SceneGraph (Chapter 8). The code examples in this chapter are just examples to show you how these JavaFX animation implementations would be accomplished. Next, let's take a look at the JavaFX Stage classes, where I will actually show you some code to make your JavaFX environment transparent so your games can float over the OS desktop, an effect in Windows called a "Windowless ActiveX Control," which allows you to create virtual i3D objects.

JavaFX Screen and Window Control: Using javafx.stage Classes

The **javafx.stage** package contains classes that can be considered to be "top level" where the display that your JavaFX application uses. In your use case, this is pro Java 9 games. This stage is at the "top" of your resulting gameplay, because it shows your game's scenes to the end user of your application. Inside of your **Stage** object you have **Scene** objects, and inside of these are SceneGraph **Node** objects, which contain the elements that comprise a Java 9 game or a Java 9 IoT application. Thus, a JavaFX Stage object is the highest-level object you'll be using in your Java 9 game.

The classes that are in this package, on the other hand, could be considered to provide **low-level** services, from an operating system's perspective. These would include **Stage**, **Screen**, **Window**, **WindowEvent**, **PopupWindow**, **Popup**, **DirectoryChooser**, and **FileChooser**, as well as the **FileChooser. ExtensionFilter** nested class. These classes will be utilized to interface with device display hardware, operating system windowing management, file management, and directory (folder) management functionality. This is because a Stage class (object) asks the OS for these features, rather than actually implementing them using Java or JavaFX APIs, so the OS is actually spawning these services at the request of your Java 9 game or Java 9 IoT application's request for the OS to provide these OS front-end utilities.

The **Screen** class is what you will want to use if you want to get a description of the display hardware that is being used by the hardware device that a JavaFX application is running on. This class supports **multiscreen** (*second screen* is the common industry term) scenarios by providing a **.getScreens()** method that can access **ObservableList** objects (a list object that allows listeners to track changes when they occur), which will contain a list array containing all of the currently available screens. There is a "primary" screen that is accessed using the **.getPrimary()** method call. You can get the **physical resolution** for the current screen hardware by using a **.getDpi()** method call. There are also **.getBounds()** and **.getVisualBounds()** method calls for usable resolution.

The **Window** superclass, and its **Stage** and **PopupWindow** subclasses, can be used by the JavaFX end user to interact with your application. This is done using the **Stage** object named primaryStage that is passed into your .start() method (see Figure 5-2) or using a **PopupWindow** (dialog, tooltip, context menu, notification, etc.) subclass, such as a **Popup** or **PopupControl** object.

You can use the Stage class to create secondary stages within your JavaFX application programming logic. A **primary** Stage object is always constructed by the JavaFX platform, using the **public void start(Stage primaryStage)** method call (as you have seen already in Chapter 6 in your bootstrap JavaFX 9 application created by NetBeans 9). All JavaFX Stage objects must be constructed using, and modified inside of, the primary JavaFX Application Thread, which I talked about earlier, when we looked at pulse event processing. Since a Stage equates to a window on the operating system platform it is running on, certain attributes, or properties, are **read-only** and need to be controlled at your OS level. These are **boolean** properties (variables), and they include **alwaysOnTop**, **fullScreen**, **iconified**, and **maximized**.

All Stage objects have a **StageStyle** attribute and a **Modality** attribute, which can be set using constants. The stageStyle constants include the **StageStyle.DECORATED**, **StageStyle.UNDECORATED**, **StageStyle. TRANSPARENT**, **StageStyle.UNIFIED**, and **StageStyle.UTILITY** constants. The Modality constants include the **Modality.NONE**, **Modality.APPLICATION_MODAL**, and **Modality.WINDOW_MODAL** constants. After we finish discussing the javafx.stage package, in the next section, I will show you how to do something really impressive using this StageStyle attribute and the TRANSPARENT constant that will set your JavaFX-based Java 9 games and IoT applications far apart from everyone else's in the marketplace.

The **Popup** class can be used to create custom popup notifications, or even custom game components, from scratch. Alternately, you can use the **PopupControl** class and its **ContextMenu** and **Tooltip** subclasses to provide predefined (that is, precoded for your own implementation) JavaFX graphical user interface (GUI) controls.

The **DirectoryChooser** and **FileChooser** classes provide support for passing through the standard OS file selection and directory navigation dialogs into your JavaFX applications. The **FileChooser. ExtensionFilter** nested class provides a utility for filtering the files that will come up in the FileChooser dialog based on file type (file extension).

Next, let's take your current JavaFXGame Application's Stage object to the next level and show you how to make your Java 9 (JavaFX 9) game a **windowless** (floating) application! This is one of the many impressive features of JavaFX 9 that you can leverage in your Pro Java 9 Games Development pipeline.

Using the JavaFX Stage Object: Creating a Floating Windowless Application

Let's make the primaryStage Stage object, created by our `.start(Stage primaryStage)` method constructor, for our JavaFXGame application **transparent** so that the HelloWorld Button (UI control) floats right on top of your OS desktop (or in this case, on top of NetBeans 9). This is something that JavaFX can do that you don't see utilized very often, and it will allow you to create i3D games that will appear to "float" right on top of your user's OS desktop. For i3D virtual objects, at least on the Windows 7, 8, and 10 OS, this would be called a "windowless ActiveX control." Removing the window "chrome" or decorations should also be supported in other advanced OSs such as Linux and Mac as well, and there is a program call to determine whether this "remove everything except my content using alpha channel (transparency)" capability is in place, so you can implement a fallback plan to a solid color or background image. This cool little trick (I thought I'd show you something cool and powerful early on in the book) is accomplished in part by using the **StageStyle. TRANSPARENT** constant, which you have just learned about, in conjunction with the **.initStyle()** method from the **Stage** class. StageStyle is a "helper" class filled with stage (or OS window, ultimately) decoration constants, one of which is TRANSPARENT. The fallback we'll use is UNDECORATED (a normal OS window).

Adding a StageStyle Constant: Using the .initStyle(StageStyle style) Method Call

As you can see in Figure 7-4, I have added a new **line 26** in the Java 9 code (highlighted in light blue) and typed in the primaryStage Stage object name; then I hit the period key to insert a Java dot chain to the method that I want to use. At this point, NetBeans 9 will open a pop-up method selector helper dialog (more of a chooser UI, actually); look for the .initStyle(StageStyle style) method, as shown in Figure 7-4. Clicking the method will select it in blue, and double-clicking it will insert it into your code. We will do the same thing for the parameter for the method next using the same work process of allowing (or enticing) NetBeans 9 into doing the Java coding work for you.

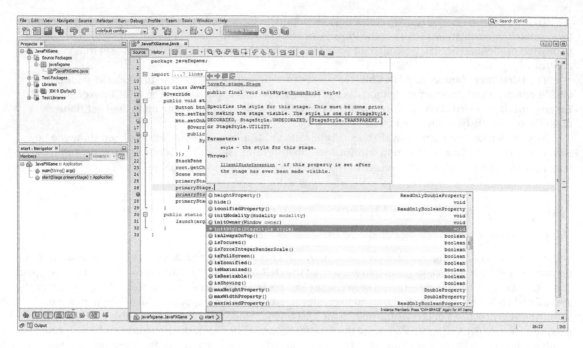

Figure 7-4. *Call an .initStyle() method off of the primaryStage Stage object, using dot notation to invoke a helper menu*

As you can see in Figure 7-4, I clicked the initStyle(StageStyle style) option in the NetBeans 9 helper, and this brings up a Javadoc window above the line of code you are crafting with documentation about the method. You can use this as a way to learn what methods an object supports by typing the object name, hitting the period key, and then selecting each method to see what it does.

As you can see in Figure 7-5, the Stage object is created using the **.start(Stage primaryStage)** method call declaration and is set up (titled, styled, loaded with a scene, and then displayed) using the **.setTitle()**, **.initStyle()**, **.setScene()**, and finally the **.show()** method calls inside of the .start() method structure.

I'm going to leave a .setTitle() method call in the Java 9 code for now, but make a mental note that once you get this windowless application treatment working, this title is part of the window's **chrome** (titlebar UI element). Once these are gone (including the titlebar), this setting of the title attribute will amount to being a moot point.

If you were focusing on memory optimization at this point in the application development work process, you would remove this .setTitle() method call because the title attribute would take up memory space and wouldn't even be seen because of your use of the StageStyle.TRANSPARENT constant for the StageStyle (actually window style) attribute.

Inside of the .initStyle() method type, type the required StageStyle class (object) and a period to bring up the next helper selector. This time it is a constant selector, as shown in Figure 7-5. Select the TRANSPARENT option, read the Javadoc information on it, and then double-click it to complete the code statement, which should look like the following:

```
primaryStage.initStyle(StageStyle.TRANSPARENT); // Insert StageStyle Class TRANSPARENT
Constant
```

As you can see in Figure 7-5 in the Javadoc information pop-up, a fallback (downgrade) method automatically will be coded for a TRANSPARENT window (stage) decoration style to be UNDECORATED. This features a background color of white and still removes the standard OS windowing chrome (title bar, minimize, maximize, close, resize, etc.). Next, let's test our code and see if the button is now floating over whatever is behind it (in this case, this is NetBeans).

Figure 7-5. *Type StageStyle and a period in the method parameter area to pop up a constant selector NetBeans helper*

Next use the Run icon (or the Run menu) and run the application. As you can see in Figure 7-6, what we are trying to achieve did not work, and the Window chrome elements are gone, but the transparency value is not evident.

Figure 7-6. *Run Project to see if the Stage object is transparent; clearly there is an object set to off-white background color*

As you can see, there is an off-white color value (used in iTV set applications, as some iTV sets don't support a 255,255,255 White) that is evident against the full 255,255,255 white that NetBeans 9 uses for its code editor pane.

There must be something else in your processing pipeline that is not yet defining your Stage's **background** using the **transparency** value. Transparency is defined using the hexadecimal value of **0x00000000**, which signifies all **AARRGGBB** (Alpha, Red, Green Blue) transparency and color values being turned off. You need to start thinking about the JavaFX components within your application as being **layers** (currently these are Stage, Scene, StackPane, Button).

You learned about digital imaging concepts, such as color depth, alpha channels, layers, blending, dithering, and all of that fun technical information that relates to processing pixels in a 2D plane during Chapter 2 of this book.

The next thing that we should try to set to this transparent value is the next level down in your JavaFX Scene Graph hierarchy from the Stage, which contains the Scene Graph itself. The next most top-level component, as you've learned during this chapter, is the **Scene** object, which also has a background color value parameter or attribute.

Therefore, the next step is to try to set that attribute to zero opacity and color using the hexadecimal value of 0x00000000 or a Java 9 Color class constant that will accomplish this same exact objective.

Your Scene class (object) does not have the style constant of TRANSPARENT like the Stage class (object) has, so you will have to approach setting the Scene object's background to a transparency value in a different way, using a different method and constant. One thing that you should realize is that everything in JavaFX that writes itself to the screen will in some way or another support transparency. This allows multiple layer **compositing** within JavaFX apps.

If you look at the Scene class documentation, you will notice that there is a **.setFill(Color value)** method that takes a **Color** (class or object) value, so let's try that next. As you see in Figure 7-7, I called the .setFill() method off of the Scene object named scene using a **scene.setFill();** method, which NetBeans lets me select from the drop-down helper.

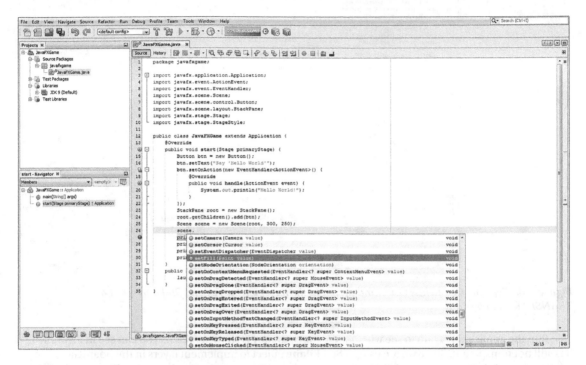

Figure 7-7. *Add a new line of code and type in the scene's Scene object and a period to invoke a method helper selector*

Select and double-click the **.setFill(Paint value)** method and then type the Java 9 **Color** class name in the parameter area (Color is a subclass of Paint). Next, type a period to bring up the constants contained in the Java 9 Color helper class, as shown in Figure 7-8, and find and select a TRANSPARENT constant. As you can see in the Javadoc helper pane, the ARGB color value is the desired #00000000.

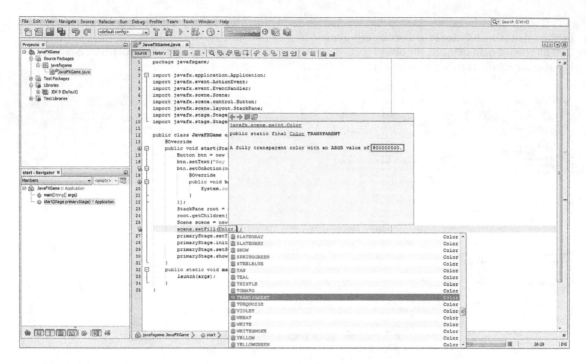

Figure 7-8. *Type the Color class name and period in the parameter area, and find and select a TRANSPARENT constant*

Run the application again to see whether the transparency is showing yet. As you can see in Figure 7-9, it is still not transparent. Since we are using a **StackPane** object to implement layers in the BoardGame application, this is the next level up that we need to try to set a transparency value at. JavaFX uses a Color class constant to determine a default background color value for all its UI objects. If I were on the JavaFX 9 team, I'd be arguing for this to be changed to the Color.TRANSPARENT constant, but of course, this might confuse new users, as alpha channel and compositing layers are advanced concepts and topics, which is why they are at the beginning of this pro Java 9 games development book in Chapter 2 covering digital image compositing and related concepts. Notice in Figure 7-9 that NetBeans has imported the Java Color class for you since you used it in the **scene.setFill(Color.TRANSPARENT);** Java statement.

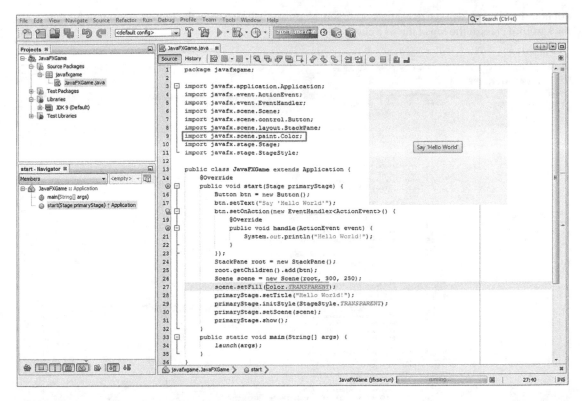

Figure 7-9. *Set the Scene object fill color to TRANSPARENT, and notice that NetBeans codes a Color class import statement*

The **javafx.scene.layout.StackPane** class is subclassed from the **javafx.scene.layout.Region** class, which has a **.setBackground()** method to set the **Background** (class or object) value. Again, there must be a TRANSPARENT value constant available, or something similar to that such as Background.EMPTY, as you need to always set the background values to be transparent, especially for pro Java 9 game design, where you need the flexibility to achieve advanced 2D and 3D compositing and rendering pipelines. This support for transparency also holds true for Android UI containers.

It is interesting to note that things are not always as straightforward and consistent as we would want them to be in Java programming, as we've used three different method calls, passing three custom object types, thus far, to achieve exactly the same end result (installing a transparent background color/image **plate** for the design element): .initStyle(StageStyle object), .setFill(Color object), and .setBackground(Background object). This time, you are going to call a .setBackground(Background value) method with yet another Background class (object) constant called **EMPTY**.

NetBeans 9 will help you to find the constant once you call the method off of the StackPane object named root, using the **root.setBackground(Background.EMPTY);** Java statement. This time it is easier as the Background.EMPTY constant happens to be the default configuration setting for the .setBackground() method call. If you want to see all of the Background helper class constants, type **root.setBackground(Background.** into NetBeans 9 and look at the results that appear in the constants pop-up helper selector pane.

As you can see in Figure 7-10, NetBeans 9 provides a method selector drop-down, and once you select and double-click the .setBackground(Background value) method, NetBeans 9 will write the code statement for you, automatically inserting the default EMPTY constant called off of the Background class using

175

dot notation. As you will see in Figure 7-11 in red, NetBeans will also code the import statement for the Background class at the top of the Java class.

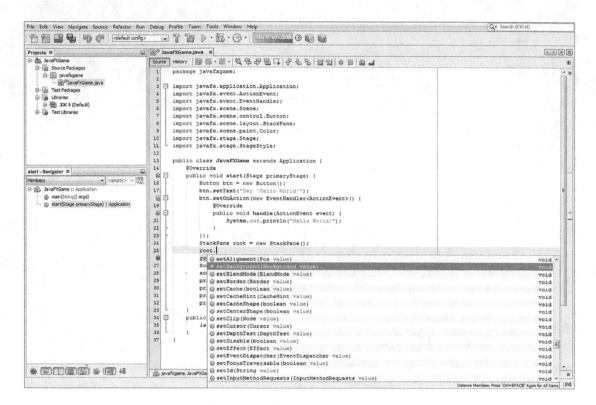

Figure 7-10. *Add a line of code after the root StackPane object, type root and a period, and select setBackground()*

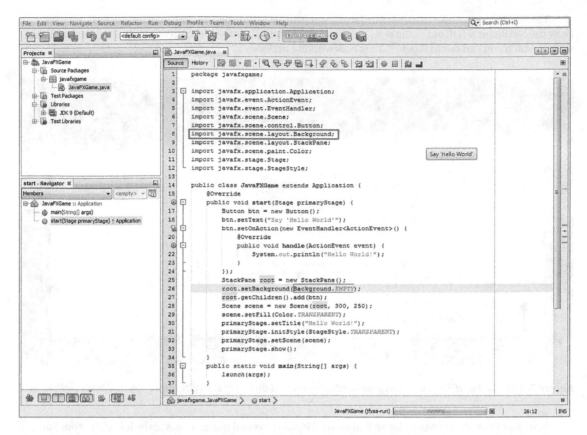

Figure 7-11. *The transparency now goes through all objects (layers), and the button is now rendered on the OS directly*

You're now ready to again test your windowless (transparent) JavaFX application version by using your **Run Project** work process, either via the Run menu or via the green play transport icon at the top left of the NetBeans IDE.

As you can see in Figure 7-11, we've now achieved our objective, and just the Button object is visible on top of the NetBeans IDE Java code editing pane, which is the next application under the running Java code window. Under that is the OS desktop.

You can also see that NetBeans added your Background class import statement and the nine lines of the StackPane (root) and Scene (scene) objects Java 9 code, which we added to make this end result happen in lines 25 to 33 of Figure 7-11. Be sure to understand the progression of the creation of these objects and how they link, or "wire up," as I like to call it, into each other, becoming inexorably functionally intertwined. Understand that the order of the Java 9 programming statements is nearly as important as the construction of the Java 9 statements themselves.

For instance, you can't code line 28 until you have coded line 25, where you instantiate your root StackPane object, so that you can use it to create the scene's Scene object.

I clicked the root object in NetBeans 9 to tell the IDE to show me the usage of that object in the class, which, as you'll see in Figure 7-11, is tracked using yellow highlighting on the root object in the Java 9 code. This cool feature becomes more and more important the more complex and complicated your pro Java 9 games code becomes. As I mentioned in Chapter 6, we will be covering handy NetBeans 9 features during many of the chapters in this book.

The last test is to make sure that our JavaFX application is transparent on top of the OS desktop itself. Drag the NetBeans 9 IDE out of the way, and see your Button UI element on top of the desktop background image, which you can see in Figure 7-12 is now working perfectly.

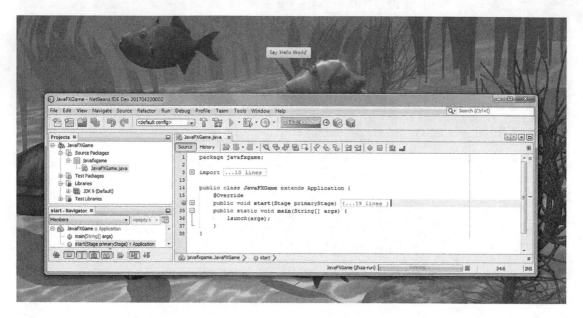

Figure 7-12. *The JavaFX application seamlessly composited on top of the Windows 7 OS desktop's wallpaper*

You can also see the code collapse and expand icons (plus and minus icons at the left of the code) at work. I have closed (collapsed) the .start() method and opened the .main() method. Clicking the minus will close the .main() method, and clicking the plus icons will open the import statements and .start() method code bodies.

I closed the import statements block and .start() method code block to show you the five primary areas for this class: your javafxgame package declaration, your import statements block, your JavaFXGame Application subclass declaration, and the two primary methods needed for any JavaFX 9 games (or IoT) application, which are .start() and .main().

Using 2D, 3D, and alpha channels, some crazy cool apps can be created using this StageStyle. TRANSPARENT capability, so I thought I would show this to you early on during the book so that I could get some cool tricks and tips pertaining to enhancing your JavaFX IoT application and pro Java games coding experience into this JavaFX "overview" chapter. Defining a game or i3D virtual object that floats right on an OS desktop is a rare and visually impactive result.

Now that we've taken a fun coding break from reviewing all of the JavaFX 9 APIs that most directly relate to pro Java 9 games development, let's get back into looking at some of the other JavaFX modules, packages, and class offerings that you may want to know about regarding interactivity, UI design, charting, audio, or video media assets, as well as about interfacing with the Internet and social media platforms. We'll also briefly cover some of the APIs you won't use!

Now that we have taken a look at the javafx.stage package, let's look at the **javafx.geometry** package next.

JavaFX Bounds and Dimensions: Using javafx.geometry Classes

Even though the term *geometry* technically applies to 2D and 3D assets, these are contained in a **javafx. scene.shape** package, which we have already covered earlier in the chapter. The **javafx.geometry** package can be considered to be more of a "utility" package, containing foundational classes for building 2D or 3D constructs from scratch. As such, the package contains classes such as a **Bounds** superclass and its **BoundingBox** subclass, as well as **Insets**, **Point2D**, **Point3D**, **Dimension2D**, and **Rectangle2D** geometry content creation utility classes. All of these classes in this **javafx.geometry** package, except for the BoundingBox class, were extended directly from the java.lang.Object master class, meaning that they were each developed (coded from scratch) for providing points (also called *vertices*), rectangles, dimensions, boundaries, and insets (inside boundaries) for use as geometric utilities for your Java 9 games.

The Point2D and Point3D classes (objects, ultimately) hold **X,Y coordinates** for a 2D point on a 2D plane, or **X,Y,Z coordinates** for a 3D point in 3D space, respectively. These Point objects will ultimately be utilized to build more complex 2D or 3D structures, made up of a collection of points, such as a 2D path, or a 3D mesh. The Point2D and the Point3D constructor method calls are not overloaded, and they use the following standard format, respectively:

```
Point2D(double X, double Y)
Point3D(double X, double Y, double Z)
```

The Rectangle2D class (object) can be used to define a rectangular 2D area, often referred to as a "plane," and has many uses in graphics programming, as you might well imagine.

A Rectangle2D object has a **starting point** on the **upper-left** corner of the rectangle, specified using an X and Y coordinate location, as well as a **dimension** (width by height). A constructor method for a Rectangle2D object has the following standard format and is not overloaded:

```
Rectangle2D(double minX, double minY, double width, double height)
```

There is also a Dimension2D class (object) that specifies only the width and height dimension and does not place the dimension (which would make it a rectangle) on the screen using an X, Y location. Its constructor method is as follows:

```
Dimension2D(double width, double height)
```

The Insets class (object) is like a Dimension2D class, in that it does not provide a location value for the inset but does provide **offsets** for a rectangular inset area based on **top**, **bottom**, **left**, and **right** offset distances. The Insets method is, in fact, overloaded so that you can specify an equidistant inset, or a customized inset, using the following:

```
Insets(double topRightBottomLeft)
Insets(double top, double right, double bottom, double left)
```

The Bounds class is a **public abstract** class and will never be an object but instead is a **blueprint** for creating Node boundary classes such as its BoundingBox subclass. The Bounds superclass also allows a **negative** value, which is used to indicate that a bounding area is **empty** (think of it as **null**, or **unused**). A BoundingBox class uses the following (overloaded) constructor methods to create a **2D** (first constructor) or a **3D** (second constructor) BoundingBox object:

```
BoundingBox(double minX, double minY, double width, double height)
BoundingBox(double minX, double minY, double minZ, double width, double height, double depth)
```

Next, let's take a look at Event and ActionEvent processing in JavaFX, as this adds interactivity to your game.

JavaFX Input Control for Games: Using the javafx.event Classes

Since games are interactive by their very nature, let's take a look at the **javafx.event** package next, since it provides us with the **Event** superclass and its **ActionEvent** subclass for handling **ACTION** events like UI elements use or animation KeyFrame processing events use, for instance. Since you are going to be using ActionEvent in pro Java 9 games (or IoT applications), I am going to look at its cross-package (Java to JavaFX) class inheritance hierachy here, as that will also show you the origin of the JavaFX Event class. This is possible because JavaFX API is part of (underneath) the Java API.

```
Java.lang.Object
  > java.util.EventObject
    > javafx.event.Event
      > javafx.event.ActionEvent
```

The JavaFXGame application is already using this **ActionEvent** class (object) with the **EventHandler interface** and its **.handle()** method, which you'll implement in order to tell the Java application what to do to **handle** that Event, which is an ActionEvent once it has occurred (the programming term is *fired*). This .handle() method then "**catches**" the **fired** event and processes it, according to the Java 9 programming logic inside of the "body" of this .handle() method.

As you know from Chapter 5, a Java **interface** is a type that provides **empty** methods that are declared for use but do not yet contain any Java constructs. The **unimplemented methods** will, at the time of their use, need to be implemented by you, the Java programmer. This Java interface defines only which methods need to be implemented; in this case, it's a single method that will "handle" the ActionEvent so that this event gets processed in some fashion.

It is important to note that the Java interface defines a method that needs to be coded but does not write the method code for you, so it is a "road map" of what you must do to complete, or **interface with**, the programming structure that is in place. In this case, this is a Java programming structure for handling ActionEvent objects, or, more accurately, a programming structure for handling ActionEvents once they have been fired.

As with everything else covered in this JavaFX new media engine overview chapter, you will soon be getting deeper into the details of how to use these packages, classes, nested classes, interfaces, methods, constants, and data fields (variables) during the course of this pro Java 9 games and IoT applications development book as you apply these JavaFX 9 programming structures, JavaFX scene graph construction, and new media asset design concepts.

JavaFX UI Elements: Using the javafx.scene.control Classes

The **javafx.scene.control** package, along with the javafx.scene.chart package, which we will cover next, is in the **javafx.controls module**. This package contains all the user interface control (they are called "widgets" in Android, and I like to call them UI "elements") classes, like Alert, Button, Cell, CheckBox, ChoiceDialog, ContextMenu, Control, DatePicker, ColorPicker, Label, ProgressBar, Slider, Label, RadioButton, ScrollBar, and TextField. Since there are more than 100 classes in javafx.scene.control, I am not even going to attempt to cover them all here, as an entire book could be written about this one Java 9 module. If you wanted to review these classes, simply reference javafx.control module using Google, or on the Oracle Java web site, and you can peruse what these classes can do for days on end. For this module, "reference" is the key word, as you will want to reference this package, and its classes, individually, at the time you need to implement a given UI element. I will be attempting to create the i3D game in this book (eventually) using my own 3D UI elements and code so that I do not have to include this javafx.controls module in the distribution, saving the overhead of having to include more than 100 control classes (not to mention well over a dozen charting classes) in the distribution that are not even utilized.

JavaFX Business Charting: Using the javafx.scene.chart Classes

The **javafx.scene.chart** package is in the javafx.controls module with the predefined UI controls (UI elements). This package contains the business charting classes, such as Chart, ScatterChart, StackedAreaChart, XYChart, PieChart, LineChart, BarChart, StackedBarChart, AreaChart, BubbleChart and the like, for use in business applications, which is a different book entirely, so we won't be covering charting during this book. In fact, for my games I'm going to use a 3D UI approach, which would mean that I don't need to include the javafx. controls module (a massive amount of classes) at all, meaning my game module would only have to include javafx.base, javafx.media and javafx.graphics, making the distribution a significantly smaller download (base has only 10 packages, media has 9, while graphics has 18 as you have seen throughout this chapter).

JavaFX Media Control: Using the javafx.scene.media Classes

The **javafx.scene.media** package is contained in the javafx.media module and contains classes that are used for the playback of audio and video media assets, including the Media, MediaPlayer, and MediaView classes, as well as the AudioClip, AudioEqualizer, EqualizerBand, Track, VideoTrack, and SubtitleTrack classes. The Media class (or object) references or contains an audio or video media asset, the MediaPlayer plays that asset, and the MediaView, especially in the case of video, displays the digital audio or video media asset along with a transport used for media playback.

We will be using the AudioClip class later in this book when we add digital audio sound effects for your pro Java 9 game, and as long as we are using the digital audio portions of this module, if we have to include it in your application (modules) distribution, we might as well leverage the digital video asset (video classes) features as well.

JavaFX Web Rendering: Using the javafx.scene.web Classes

The javafx.scene.web package is contained in the javafx.web module and contains classes for rendering web (Internet) assets in a scene. This package contains a collection of classes, including WebEngine, WebView, WebEvent, WebHistory, and HTMLEditor. The WebEngine class (hey, someone else calls these algorithms engines), as you might imagine, does the processing for showing HTML5, CSS3, CSS4, and JavaScript in JavaFX Scenes, and the WebView creates the Node to display the WebEngine output in a JavaFX Scene Graph. The WebHistory class (object, ultimately) holds the Internet "session," from WebEngine instantiation to removal from memory, which is a history of web pages visited, and the WebEvent class "bridges" the JavaScript web event processing with the JavaFX 9 event processing. We will not be using the javafx.web module for the i3D game that we will be creating over the course of this book, as I am going to focus on the core APIs that can be used to provide the most visually professional i3D gameplay results.

Other JavaFX Packages: Print, FXML, Beans, and Swing

There are a few other JavaFX packages that you should take a closer look at before you are done with this JavaFX overview chapter, as they are packages that contain classes that you may want to use in your pro Java games development but that provide more specialized capabilities such as printing, using third-party Java code, using older UI paradigms such as AWT and Swing, and offloading UI design to nonprogrammers using XML (specifically FXML). These APIs include the javafx.print package (javafx.graphics module), javafx.fxml package (javafx.fxml module), javafx.beans package (javafx.base module), and javafx.embed.swing package (javafx.swing module). You are not likely to use these in your Java game design and development work process unless you have a specialized need for your project. The most obvious of these is javafx.print used to allow printers to work with your pro Java 9 games. If you need to use older Swing UI elements, there is a javafx.swing module that will allow this but will add a bigger data footprint to your Java 9 game distribution. The javafx.beans package will allow you to use Java Beans (third party or added-in classes), and the javafx.

fxml module will allow you to use Java FXML, the XML language that allows user interface and graphics design to be offloaded to XML instead of Java coding. This allows non-Java-savvy designers to work on a game project. This approach is also used by the Android OS and Android Studio IDE, which uses XML for many top-level design tasks so the designers don't also have to be programmers.

Summary

In this seventh chapter, you got an overview of some of the most important packages, concepts, components, classes, constructors, constants, and variables (attributes, parameters, data fields) that can be found in the **JavaFX 9 API**. This is an impressive collection of seven Java 9 modules containing **36** packages, many of which I outlined succinctly using tables and then covered one by one. I did this as most, if not all, of the packages and classes outlined during this chapter will eventually be needed, in one way or another, for new media, 2D, 3D, and hybrid 2D+3D pro Java 9 games development. When I say a comprehensive overview, I mean let's take a look at everything we'll need for game development using JavaFX 9 under Java 9.

Certainly, I can't cover every functional class in the JavaFX 9 API in one chapter, so I started with the overview of the JavaFX API new media engine in Figure 7-1 and how it integrates with the JavaFX **Scene Graph** above it and with the **Java 9** APIs, **NetBeans 9**, and the target operating systems below these APIs. Your Java 9 game distribution and the OSs are bridged using the Java Virtual Machine (JVM). This serves to give JavaFX its expansive OS support across so many popular platforms and consumer electronics devices, from smartphones to tablets to iTV sets, as well as all of the leading web browsers (Chrome, Firefox, and Opera) that are based on the popular WebKit engine.

You took a high-level technical view of JavaFX by looking at the structures that make up your JavaFX engine, including a JavaFX **Scene Graph**, the **JavaFX APIs**, **Quantum**, **Prism**, **Glass**, **WebKit**, and the **Media Player** engine. You looked at how these multithreading, rendering, windowing, media, and web engines interface with the **Java 9 APIs** and the **JDK**, as well as with **NetBeans 9** and the **JVM** bytecode that it generates, which is supported by all the various operating system platforms that are currently running on top of more than a dozen different consumer electronics device types from 96-inch UHD iTV sets down to 4-inch smartphones.

I covered JavaFX core concepts, such as using the JavaFX Scene Graph, and the JavaFX **pulse** events system, which we'll be leveraging to create a pro Java 9 game throughout the course of the book, starting in the next chapter, when we start to design the game and cover how to use the JavaFX Scene Graph to develop the processing hierarchy.

I dove into some of the key JavaFX packages, subpackages, and classes used for pro Java 9 game design, such as application, scene, shape, effect, layout, control, media, image, stage, animation, geometry, event, fxml, and web, as well as their related Java 9 modules, packages, subpackages, classes, and subclasses. In some cases, I even covered their interfaces, nested (helper) classes, and data constants.

You took a break from this JavaFX 9 API review to add some code to the JavaFXGame application that allowed it to be a "windowless" application, which is able to "float" over any popular OS desktop. You learned about how to make the Stage, Scene, and StackPane objects' background attribute transparent by using the alpha channel with a hexadecimal setting of **0x00000000** or by using the equivalent constant representing 100 percent alpha transparency, such as Color.TRANSPARENT, StageStyle.TRANSPARENT, or Background.EMPTY. You also saw that the Group (Node) class and object inherently have a transparent background; when you changed your top-level Node for your Scene Graph from a StackPane to a Group (a much better top-level Node), the Group background transparency did not need to be set at all.

I had to get some work using the NetBeans 9 IDE, the Java 9 programming language, and the JavaFX 9 API into this chapter, so we can start to gradually add more and more code until (soon) the remaining chapters are completely coding, as all of this foundational material, covering new media asset design, API, IDE, game concepts, JVM, UI, UX, 3D rendering engines, 2D playback engines, WebKit, static versus dynamic, game optimization, and so forth, have all been put firmly into place in your minds, as you will need to build upon this advanced knowledge throughout the duration of the book.

In the next chapter, you're going to look at the **JavaFX** 9 **Scene Graph**. You'll begin to construct your Scene Graph structures that you learned about during this chapter and start to build the foundation for the game, including a UI "panel" of Button elements used to start your game. I'll also explain your game's rules, display high scores, give production credits, and include legal disclaimers. I know you're eager to get started building your pro Java 9 game infrastructure, which you'll begin doing in earnest in the next chapter, creating custom methods and adding new Java code using JavaFX APIs to start creating the top level for your JavaFXGame class. Actually, you started doing this a little bit during this chapter by learning how to implement transparency inside of (and through) your JavaFX 9 Scene Graph layers (Application to Scene to Group to StackPane to VBox to Button).

CHAPTER 8

■ ■ ■

JavaFX 9 Scene Graph Hierarchy: A Foundation for Java 9 Game Design

Let's build on our newfound knowledge of JavaFX, game design, multimedia, and Java that we learned about in the previous chapters here in Chapter 8 by starting to design the infrastructure of our i3D JavaFXGame game, from both a **User Interface** and **User Experience** standpoint and an "under the hood" **game engine**, **3D sprite engine**, **collision engine**, and **physics engine** standpoint. We will keep optimization in mind, as we must do during the rest of the book, so that we don't get a **Scene Graph** that is so extensive or complicated that the **pulse** system cannot update everything efficiently. This means keeping primary game UI screens (**StackPane Node**) to a minimum (four or five) to leave most processing power for the 3D game rendering (**Group Node**) and making sure the Media Player (digital audio or digital video) uses its own thread, if this type of media is used at all. (Audio and especially video is very data heavy and can be very processing intensive.) You will also need to make sure that the functional "engines" that drive the game are all coded modularly and logically, use their own classes, and utilize the proper Java programming conventions, structures, methods, variables, constants, and modifiers that you learned about in Chapter 5. It will be a massive undertaking and will take hundreds of pages to implement, starting with this chapter, now that I have made sure you are all on point with your knowledge of Java, JavaFX, NetBeans, 2D, and 3D new media concepts.

The first thing that I will cover is a **top-level**, **front-facing** user interface screen design, which your game will offer to the user when launching the Java application. This will include the BoardGame "branding" splash screen that a user sees when launching the application. This screen will have Button controls on one side that access information screens containing instructions, credits, legal disclaimers, and the like. These UI screens, which we want to minimize in number, will be StackPane Node layers. A StackPane object is designed to contain stacked image (compositing) layers. These game support screens will contain information that a user needs to know in order to play the game effectively. This includes text-based information, such as game instructions, credits, legal disclaimers, and a high score screen. We will include legal disclaimers to keep the legal department happy and will feature a credits screen highlighting the contributions of programmers and new media artisans who worked on creating the game and game assets.

The next level down of this BoardGame design foundation that we will conceptualize during this chapter is the **under the hood**, **back-facing** game engine component Java class design aspects for the BoardGame. These will be unseen by the game user but are still very important. They might include a **GamePlay Engine** to control gameplay updates to the game using JavaFX pulse, a **3D Sprites Engine** to manage 3D game sprites for the game, a **Collision Engine** that detects and responds when any collision has occurred between two sprites, a **Physics Engine** that will apply force and similar physics simulations to the gameplay so the 3D sprites **accelerate** and **bounce** realistically, and finally the **3D Actor Engine** that will

© Wallace Jackson 2017

W. Jackson, *Pro Java 9 Games Development*, https://doi.org/10.1007/978-1-4842-0973-8_8

manage the characteristics for individual Actors that have been instantiated for your JavaFXGame game. You will modify the existing **JavaFXGame.java** class to implement a UI, with **Button controls** accessing functional information screens needed to provide the top-level user interface gameplay information features. You'll learn about several new JavaFX classes used for organization and positioning, including the **Group**, **VBox**, **Insets**, and **Pos** classes.

Game Design Foundation: Primary Function Screens

One of the first things you will want to design for your game is the top-level, or **highest-level**, **user interface screens** with which your game's users will interface. This defines the **user experience** when the user first opens your game. These screens will be accessed using your JavaFXGame Splash (Branding) Screen, contained in the primary **JavaFXGame.java** class code. As you have seen already, this Java code will extend the **javafx.application.Application** class and will launch the application, displaying a splash screen, along with options to review the instructions, play the game, see the high scores, or review the game legal disclaimers and game creator credits (programmer, artist, writer, composer, sound designer, etc.). Figure 8-1 shows a high-level diagram of the game starting with functional UI screens at the top and progressing down to the **JavaFXGame.java** code and then to the APIs, to the JVM, and to the OS level.

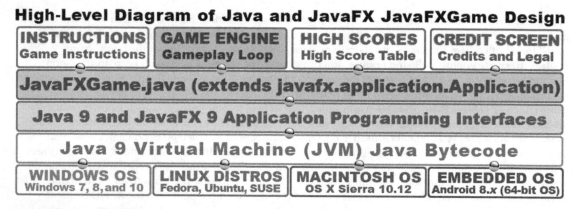

Figure 8-1. *JavaFXGame functional screens and how they'll be implemented in Java 9 and JavaFX 9 by using the JVM*

This will require you to add four more **Button** nodes to the **StackPane** layout container **Parent** branch node and eventually (in Chapter 9) an **ImageView** node to serve as a SplashScreen image container. This ImageView node will have to be added to the StackPane "backplate" in order to be the **first child node** in the StackPane (**z-order=0**), as the ImageView holds what I term the **background plate** for your Splashscreen UI design. Since it is in the background, the image needs to be behind Button UI Control Node (SceneGraph) elements, which will have z-order values of 1 to 5.

This means that initially you'll be using only eight JavaFX SceneGraph Node objects: one Parent root **Group** Node, a second **StackPane** layout "branch" Node, and five "leaf" **Button Control** Nodes in a **VBox** UI container Node to create your JavaFXGame (functional) info screens. Your instructions, legal disclaimers, and credit screens will utilize a **TextFlow** and **ImageView** Node, so we'll be at ten Node objects after Chapter 9. You can use the **VBox** Node to contain UI Buttons, which we will be doing during this chapter to put game UI navigation infrastructure in your game application. This is before we even consider adding a Group "branch" Node, and branch and leaf Node objects under that, to contain the 3D gameplay screen. This is, of course, where you want to get the best pulse update performance for your Java game.

This really isn't so bad if you think about it, as these UI screens are all **static** and do not need to be updated. That is, the UI elements contained in these Node objects are fixed and do not require any updating using a pulse system, so you should still have **99 percent** of the power of the JavaFX **pulse** engine left over to process the JavaFXGame gameplay engine we'll be coding during the book. You always need to remain aware of how many **SceneGraph Node** objects you're asking the pulse engine to process because if this number gets to be too large, it will start to affect the game's i3D performance. If the i3D game performance suffers, gameplay won't be smooth, which will affect your user experience (UX). The more Node objects we keep static, the fewer have to be processed on each pulse.

Java Class Structure Design: Game Engine Support

Next let's take a look at the functional structure of how the JavaFXGame code will need to be put together "under the hood," so to speak. This will be done using your Java 9 game programming code, which we will be creating during this book. There is really no correlation between what the front-facing UI screens look like and what your underlying programming logic will look like, as the majority of the programming code for your game will always go toward creating the gameplay experience on the gameplay screen. The game instruction and legal and credits screens will just be text (held in a TextFlow object) composited over background imagery (held in an ImageView object). The scoreboard and high score screens will take a little bit more programming logic, which we will do toward the end of the book since the game logic needs to be created (and played) for a scoring engine and high scores to be able to be generated.

Figure 8-2 shows the primary functional game components that will be needed for your JavaFXGame to be complete. The diagram shows a **JavaFXGame.java** Application subclass at the top of the hierarchy. This creates the top-level JavaFXGame Scene object and the SceneGraph it contains, underneath or inside of, the JavaFXGame application. These functional areas can either be implemented as methods or as classes. In this book, we implement an i3D game using methods.

Figure 8-2. *Primary game engine functions, representing Java methods that you will need to code for your game*

Underneath the JavaFXGame Scene object, which is created inside the **JavaFXGame.java** Application subclass, is a broader structural design for functional Java 9 classes that you'll need to code during the remainder of the book. These engines (classes), shown in Figure 8-2, will create your game functions, such as **game engine** (gameplay processing loop), **logic engine** (gameplay logic), **sprite engine** (3D geometry management), **actor engine** (character's attributes), **score engine** (game score logic), **render engine** (real-time rendering), **collision detection**, and **physics simulation**. You will need to create all of these Java methods in order to implement a comprehensive game engine for an i3D BoardGame.

The Game Engine class, which I'll call GamePulse.java, is the primary class that creates an **AnimationTimer** object that processes your game logic at a high level based on pulse events that continually trigger the gameplay loop. This loop, as you know, will call a **handle()** method that will in turn contain method calls that will ultimately access your other classes that you will be creating to manage 3D geometry (sprite engine), move the 3D objects around the screen (actor engine), detect collision (collision engine), apply game logic after all collisions have been detected (logic engine), and apply the forces of physics to provide realistic effects, such as friction, gravity, and wind (physics engine) to your gameplay. During the remainder of this book you will be building some of these engines, which will be used to create the gameplay experience for your players. We'll logically stratify chapter topics based on each of the engines and what they need to process, so everything is structured logically from a learning, as well as a coding, perspective.

JavaFX Scene Graph Design: Minimizing UI Nodes

The trick to **minimizing** the Scene Graph is to use as few Nodes as possible to implement a complete UI design, and as you can see in Figure 8-3, I've accomplished this with one Group **root** Node object, one StackPane layout "branch" Node object, one VBox **branch** Node object, and eight **leaf** (children) nodes (one **TableView**, one **ImageView**, one **TextFlow**, and five **Button** UI controls). As you will see when we get into coding the Scene Graph next, I will use only 12 objects and import only 12 classes to make the entire top-level UI for the JavaFXGame class that we designed in the previous section a reality. The TableView and TextFlow objects will be overlaid on top of the ImageView object, which contains the background imagery for the UI design. This TableView object will be added later in the book and will be updated with code from the Score Engine, shown in Figure 8-2, which you'll be coding in a future chapter.

Low-Level Diagram of JavaFX Scene Graph Design and Nodes for JavaFXGame

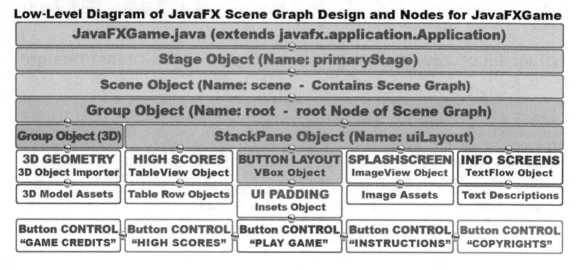

Figure 8-3. *Game Scene Graph Node hierarchy, objects that Nodes contain, and new media assets they reference*

The ImageView **backplate** will contain the BoardGame artwork, and you can use the ImageView container to hold different digital image assets, if you want. In this way, based on your ActionEvent objects, processing clicks on Button controls, you can use different background image assets for each of the information screens. The **VBox** Parent UI layout container will control the layout (spacing) for your five Button controls. There is also the **Inset** object, which you will create to hold the UI button **Padding** values to fine-tune how the Button objects align, relative to each other.

Since a Button object can't be positioned individually, I had to use the **VBox** class along with the **Insets** class to contain and position the Button controls professionally. We will be going over the classes that you will be using to create this high-level design during this chapter so that you have an overview of each class that you are going to be adding to your JavaFXGame in order to create this top-level UI design for your **JavaFXGame.java** Application subclass.

The way we optimize your Scene Graph use for the five different screens needing to match the five different buttons is to use one ImageView as a **backplate** to contain the BoardGame splash screen artwork on game startup. When a user clicks your UI buttons, you can use Java code to have the ImageView reference different images using one single ImageView Scene Graph Node object. Your TextFlow object will overlay your text assets on the ImageView.

Finally, there may be a SceneGraph Node that will contain the data structure for a High Score Table. This will be created via a Score Engine that we'll be creating later when we cover game score approaches and techniques. For now, we'll leave score and gameplay code unimplemented. Let's look at some new JavaFX UI design classes next.

JavaFX Design: Using VBox, Pos, Insets, and Group

Before we dive into coding, let's take an in-depth look at some of the new JavaFX classes we are going to utilize to complete these top-level game application UI and SceneGraph designs. These include the **Pos** class (positioning), the Insets class (padding), the VBox class (a vertical UI layout container), and the Group class (Scene Graph Node grouping). In the next chapter, we will cover the Image (image asset holder), ImageView (image backplate display), and TextFlow (text data display) classes. We will look at these in order from the simplest (Pos) to the most complex (Group), and then you will code fairly extensive changes to your bootstrap JavaFX project code, which will add these new classes (and objects) to your JavaFX Scene Graph hierarchy, as well as reorganizing it to better suit your game.

JavaFX Pos Class: Generalized Positioning Using Constants

The **Pos** class is an **Enum<Pos>** class, which is short for enumeration. It contains a list of constants that are actually translated into integer values for use in your code. The constant values make it easier for programmers to use these values in their code. In this case, it would be positioning constant prefixes like **TOP**, **CENTER**, or **BASELINE**, for instance.

The Java class extension hierarchy for the Pos class starts at the java.lang.Object master class and progresses through the java.lang.Enum<Pos> class, ending with the **javafx.geometry.Pos** class. You are referencing Pos in line 56 in the code in Figure 8-10. Pos is in the **javafx.geometry** package and uses the following subclass hierarchy structure:

```
java.lang.Object
  > java.lang.Enum<Pos>
  > javafx.geometry.Pos
```

As you'll see in the next section, you will have to use the Insets class and object to obtain the pixel-accurate positioning that you desire. Since this is an Enum class, there is not too much to learn in this section, other than what the constants are that the Pos class offers to you to use for generalized and relative positioning in your Java games.

Therefore, the Pos class is great for general positioning, using top, bottom, left, and right, as well as baseline (this is for positioning relative to fonts, primarily). Each of these also has a CENTER option for centering, so by using the dozen constants provided for in this helper class, you can implement any kind of generalized positioning you will need.

For an example of generalized position, refer to your web site design experience where you can design a web page so that it will scale to fit different window sizes and shapes. This is quite different from pixel-accurate positioning where you start at location 0,0 on a fixed screen size and shape and place elements precisely where you want them!

Game design more often than not uses pixel-precise positioning, but in this chapter I am going to show you how to position a bank of UI buttons in a general location (such as the top right or bottom left of the user's screen) so that you are exposed to as many of the JavaFX API utility classes (this one is in the **javafx. geometry** package) as possible.

You will be using the TOP_RIGHT constant, as shown on line 56 in Figure 8-10, to position your Button control bank in the top-right corner of your BoardGame user interface design, out of the way of the primary central 3D view.

The Pos class provides a set of constants, which I will summarize in Table 8-1, for providing "generalized" horizontal and vertical positioning and alignment.

Table 8-1. *The Pos Class Enum Constants That Can Be Used for Positioning and Alignment in JavaFX*

Pos Class Constant	General Positioning Result
BASELINE_CENTER	Positions an object on the baseline vertically and at the center horizontally
BASELINE_LEFT	Positions an object on the baseline vertically and on the left horizontally
BASELINE_RIGHT	Positions an object on the baseline vertically and on the right horizontally
BOTTOM_CENTER	Positions an object on the bottom vertically and at the center horizontally
BOTTOM_LEFT	Positions an object on the bottom vertically and on the left horizontally
BOTTOM_RIGHT	Positions an object on the bottom vertically and on the right horizontally
CENTER	Positions an object at the center vertically and at the center horizontally
CENTER_LEFT	Positions an object at the center vertically and on the left horizontally
CENTER_RIGHT	Positions an object at the center vertically and on the right horizontally
TOP_CENTER	Positions an object at the top vertically and at the center horizontally
TOP_LEFT	Positions an object at the top vertically and on the left horizontally
TOP_RIGHT	Positions an object at the top vertically and on the right horizontally

The Pos class provides generalized positioning; it can be used in conjunction with the Insets class to provide a more pixel-precise positioning. Let's take a look at the Insets class next, as it is also in the **javafx. geometry** package.

JavaFX Insets Class: Providing Padding Values for Your UI

The **Insets** class is a **public** class that directly extends the java.lang.Object master class, meaning that the Insets class was "scratch-coded" to provide insets, or **offsets**, inside of a rectangular area. Imagine a picture frame where you leave a "matte," or attractive border, between the frame on the outside and the picture on the inside. This is what the Insets class does with two constructor methods; one provides **equal** or even insets, and one provides **unequal** or uneven insets.

We will be using the constructor that provides **unequal** inset values, which would look very unprofessional if we were framing a picture! The Java class hierarchy for the Insets class starts with the **java. lang.Object** master class and uses this class to create the **javafx.geometry.Insets** class. As you will see later in this chapter in code line 58 in Figure 8-11, the Insets class is set to provide zero pixels on two sides and ten pixels on two sides. This pushes the Button bank away from the corner of your user's display screen. The JavaFX Insets class is contained in the javafx.scene.geometry package, just like the Pos class, and uses the following Java 9 class hierarchy structure:

```
java.lang.Object
  > javafx.scene.geometry.Insets
```

The Insets class provides a set of four double offset values specifying the **top**, **right**, **bottom**, and **left** sides of a rectangle and should be specified in that order within a constructor method, as you saw when you wrote your code. You will be using this Insets class (object) to "fine-tune position" your Button control bank, which you will be creating using the VBox layout container (which you will be learning about in the next section). Think of these Insets objects as a way to draw a box inside of another box, which shows the spacing that you want the objects inside of the rectangle to "respect" around its edges. This is often called *padding*, especially in Android Studio and HTML5 programming.

The simplest Insets() constructor for use in creating your Insets object would use the following format:

```
Insets(double topRightBottomLeft)
```

This constructor uses **a single value** for all the spacing sides (topRightBottomLeft), and an overloaded constructor allows you to specify each of these values **separately**, which looks like the following:

```
Insets(double top, double right, double bottom, double left)
```

These values need to be specified in this order. A great way to remember this is to think of an analog clock. The clock has 12 at the top, 3 at the right, 6 at the bottom, and 9 at the left. So, simply remember to specify clockwise starting at high noon (for you Western film genre lovers out there), and you will have a great way to remember how to specify the Insets values when using the "uneven values" constructor method.

You are using the Insets class to position your Button control bank, which would initially be "stuck" in your bottom-left corner of the BoardGame user interface design. The Insets object will allow you to push the Button controls away from the right side of your screen and away from the top of your VBox, using two of these four Insets parameters.

JavaFX VBox Class: Using a Layout Container for Your Design

Since Button objects cannot be positioned easily, I will be placing the five Button objects into a **layout container** from the **javafx.scene.layout** package called **VBox**, which stands for **vertical box**. This **public** class arranges things into a column, and since you want the buttons aligned at the side of your BoardGame, it is the Parent Node that you will use for five Button control Nodes, which will become children **leaf** nodes of this VBox **branch** node. This will create a "bank" of UI Button controls that can be positioned (moved around) together as a single unit of the UI and splash screen design.

A **VBox** class is a **public** class that directly extends the javafx.scene.layout.Pane superclass, which in turn extends a javafx.scene.layout.Region superclass, which extends the javafx.scene.parent superclass, which extends a javafx.scene.Node superclass, which extends the java.lang.Object master class. As you can see in line 55, in Figure 8-10, you will use VBox as a Button control positioning user interface layout container. This VBox class is contained in the **javafx.scene.layout** package, just like the StackPane class, and it uses the following Java class hierarchy structure:

```
java.lang.Object
  > javafx.scene.Node
    > javafx.scene.Parent
```

```
> javafx.scene.layout.Region
 > javafx.scene.layout.Pane
  > javafx.scene.layout.VBox
```

If the VBox has a **border** or **padding** value specified, the contents inside of your VBox layout container will "respect" that border and padding specification. A padding value is specified using the Insets class, which we covered earlier and which you will be using for this fine-tuned user interface Control Button bank application.

You are using the VBox class (object), along with the Pos class constant and the Insets class (object), in order to group your UI Button objects together and, later, to fine-tune position them as your Button control bank. This VBox layout container will thus become a Parent Node (as well as a branch node) for the UI Button controls (or leaf nodes).

Think of a VBox object as a way to **vertically array** child objects together using a column. This could be your image assets, arranged on top of each other, which would use the basic VBox constructor (with zero pixels spacing) or UI controls, such as Buttons arranged on top of each other, spaced apart, using one of the overloaded constructors.

The simplest constructor for a VBox object creation would use the following **empty** constructor method call:

```
VBox()
```

The overloaded constructor that you'll be using for your VBox object creation will have a spacing value to put some space in between your child Button objects inside of a VBox. It uses the following constructor method call format:

```
VBox(double spacing)
```

There are also two other overloaded constructor method call formats. These will allow you to specify your children Node objects (in our case, these are Button objects) inside of the constructor method call itself, as follows:

```
VBox(double spacing, Nodes... children)
```

This constructor would specify zero pixels of spacing value in between the Array of Node objects:

```
VBox(Nodes... children)
```

We're going to be using the "short form" and **.getChildren().addAll()** method chain in our code to show you how this is done, but we could also declare our VBox, and its Button Node objects, by using the following constructor:

```
VBox uiContainer = new VBox(10, gameButton, helpButton, scoreButton, legalButton,
creditButton);
```

Your VBox layout container will control the resizing of child elements based on different screen sizes, aspect ratios, and physical resolutions if the child objects are set to be resizable. If the VBox area will accommodate the child object preferred widths, they will be set to that value. There is a boolean **fillWidth** attribute (property), which is set to **true** as its default value. This specifies whether a child object should fill (scale up to) the VBox width value.

The alignment of a VBox is controlled by the **alignment** attribute (property or variable), which defaults to the **TOP_LEFT** constant from the Pos class (**Pos.TOP_LEFT**). If the VBox fillWidth property is false and

VBox is sized above its specified width, the child objects use their preferred width values, and the extra space will go unutilized. The default setting of fillWidth is true, and the children widths will be resized to fit the VBox width. It is important to note that the VBox UI layout engine will lay out the managed child elements regardless of their **visibility** attribute (also called a property, characteristic, or object variable) setting.

You will also notice that the classes we are adding during this chapter have inherently transparent or empty backgrounds (I call them backplates), so we don't have to do any extra work like we did in Chapter 7 to maintain alpha.

Now that we have taken several pages to discuss some of the classes from the javafx.scene.layout and **javafx.geometry** packages, which you are using to create your UI (bank of Button objects) Design, let's take a close look at the SceneGraph grouping-related classes from the javafx.scene package. These classes will allow us to implement the high-level SceneGraph hierarchy that you will need to put into place next to the five JavaFX Button Control UI elements (objects) held inside your VBox UI layout container object, which is inside of your StackPane UI layer compositing object. This Group (Node) container object will hold your i3D game object hierarchy when we get into 3D and i3D later during this book.

JavaFX Group Class: High-Level Scene Graph Node Grouping

The **Group** class is a **public** class that directly extends the javafx.scene.Parent superclass, which extends the javafx.scene.Node class, which extends the java.lang.Object master class. The Group object is therefore a type of Parent (branch) Node object in the JavaFX Scene Graph, which is used for grouping other branch and leaf node objects. The Group class uses the following Java class inheritance hierarchy structure:

```
java.lang.Object
  > javafx.scene.Node
    > javafx.scene.Parent
      > javafx.scene.Group
```

The Group Parent Node object contains an ObservableList of children Node objects, which will be rendered in a predetermined order whenever this Group Parent Node object is rendered. A Group Node object will take on the collective (summary) bounds of its children; however, it is not directly resizable. Any transform, effect, or state applied to a Group will be applied to (passed through to) all of the children of that Group Node but not to the Group itself.

This means that these applied transforms and effects will not be included in the Group Parent Node's layout bounds; however, if transforms and effects are set directly on the child Node objects inside of this Group, those will be included in this Group's layout bounds. So, to affect a Group Parent Node's layout bounds, you will do it from the inside out by transforming the members of the Group ObservableList, rather than by transforming the Group object itself.

By default a Group Parent Node will automatically scale its managed child objects set to be resizable to their preferred sizes during the layout pass. This ensures the Region or Control child objects will be scaled properly as their state changes. If an application needs to disable this autosizing behavior, then it should set **autoSizeChildren** to **false**. It is important to note that if the preferred size attribute of any of the child objects is changed, they won't be resized automatically because autoSizeChildren has been set to false. This **Group()** constructor will create an empty group.

```
Group()
```

The overloaded **Group(Collection<Node>)** constructor method will construct a Group consisting of a Java Collection<Node> containing a given Java collection of Node object children, using the following constructor method:

```
Group(Collection<Node> children)
```

The second overloaded **Group(Node...)** constructor method will construct a Group consisting of a Java List of child Node objects, constructed as a comma-delimited list inside of the constructor method parameter area. This can be accomplished by using the following constructor method format:

```
Group(Node... children)
```

Now that you have taken an overview of the various classes you are using during this chapter, let's get back to organizing the code for the JavaFXGame class so that it conforms to what we're doing with the game SceneGraph.

Scene Graph Code: Optimize the JavaFXGame Class

I know you are eager to work on the JavaFXGame class code, so let's clean up, organize, and optimize the existing Java 9 code to implement the majority of this top-level user interface and SceneGraph design shown in Figure 8-3 so that you make some progress toward creating your top-level Java 9 game framework during this chapter. The first thing you're going to do is to put all the object declaration and naming statements at the top of the JavaFXGame class, after the import block and the Java class declaration. These object declarations will come before all of your methods. Many of you programmers are used to declaring global variables at the top of your code, and an empty object declaration can be declared for use at the top of your Java code in much the same fashion. This approach is more organized, and all the methods that are inside of this class will be able to "see" (access or reference) these objects, without using any Java modifier keywords. This is because the object declarations are at the top of the JavaFXGame class and not inside any of the methods contained in the class, so all of the declarations done in this way are "visible" to all of the methods declared "underneath" them. As you can see in Figure 8-4, I am adding a new Group object, which I am naming **root** because it will become the new SceneGraph root. Notice the wavy red underline error under Group because there is no import statement telling Java 9 that you want to use the Group class. Use the **Alt+Enter** keystroke combination to bring up the NetBeans helper pop-up and select the **Add import for javafx.scene.Group** option, as shown in Figure 8-4.

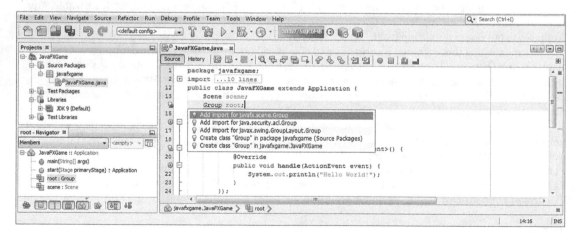

Figure 8-4. *Declare the scene Scene object and the root Group object at the top of the JavaFXGame class before .start()*

As you can see, I also moved the declaration for your existing scene Scene object to the top of the class, so, instead of **Scene scene = new Scene();**, we now have the following Scene object declaration Java code structure, which can be seen in Figure 8-5:

```java
public class JavaFXGame extends Application {
    Scene scene;
    public void start(Stage primaryStage) {
        scene = new Scene(root, 300, 250);
    }
}
```

Figure 8-5. *Organize the .start() method by creating createBoardGameNodes() and addNodesToSceneGraph() methods*

Next, we will do the same thing for the StackPane object, which I am going to rename **uiLayout**, as the **root** object is now a **Group** Node class object. Add a **StackPane uiLayout;** declaration, as shown in Figure 8-5, and then change the Java code shown in Figure 8-5 in a red box to use the uiLayout name instead of the root name, as follows:

```java
uiLayout = new StackPane;
uiLayout.setBackground(Background.EMPTY);
uiLayout.getChildren().add(btn);
```

I placed the uiLayout StackPane code right before the scene Scene instantiation. We are going to be moving the object instantiations, with the exception of the Stage object (which needs to be part of the .start() method), into their own .createBoardGameNodes() method, after we create the block of object declarations and naming at the top of the **JavaFXGame.java** class.

Remember that if you declare any object by using its class name at the top of your class and a wavy red underline appears underneath it, you can simply use the Alt+Enter keystroke combination and select the import javafx.packagename.classname option to have NetBeans code the import statement for you.

As you can see in Figure 8-4, there is often more than one possible import statement in a pop-up helper dialog, so be sure to select the classes from the JavaFX API since that is what we will be using for rich media, IoT, and games development; that is where all of the multimedia production features are now kept in the Java 9 APIs.

In the case of our new top-level Group SceneGraph Node subclass, there is also the java.security.acl. Group class and a second javafx.swing.GroupLayout.Group helper class. Since we are not using Swing UI elements (Java 5) and ACL security here, we know that the correct import statement for us to select is the **javafx.scene.Group** option.

JavaFX Object Declarations: Global Class Access for Methods

Let's add JavaFX object declarations and names for the new classes we've covered and the ImageView and TextFlow objects we'll be needing in the next chapter on designing the UI visuals and splash screen elements for the game. Add a VBox object (button alignment) named **uiContainer**, an Insets object named **uiPadding**, an ImageView object named **boardGameBackPlate**, a TextFlow object named **infoOverlay**, and five Image objects named **splashScreen**, **helpLayer**, **legalLayer**, **creditLayer**, and **scoreLayer**. Add four more Button objects to your Button declaration named **helpButton**, **legalButton**, **creditButton**, and **scoreButton**, and change the bootstrap code–generated btn Button object to instead be named **gameButton**. You can see the block of nine lines of declaration code, some of which will be **compound declarations** with one class name and multiple object names (such as Image and Button below, and soon, we'll also have multiple Group objects named root and gameBoard), in the following Java 9 code, as well as in Figure 8-6:

```
Scene scene;
Group root;
StackPane uiLayout;
VBox uiContainer;
Insets uiPadding;
ImageView boardGameBackPlate;
TextFlow infoOverlay;
Image splashScreen, helpLayer, legalLayer, creditLayer, scoreLayer;     // Compound
Declaration
Button gameButton, helpButton, legalButton, creditButton, scoreButton; // a Compound
Declaration
```

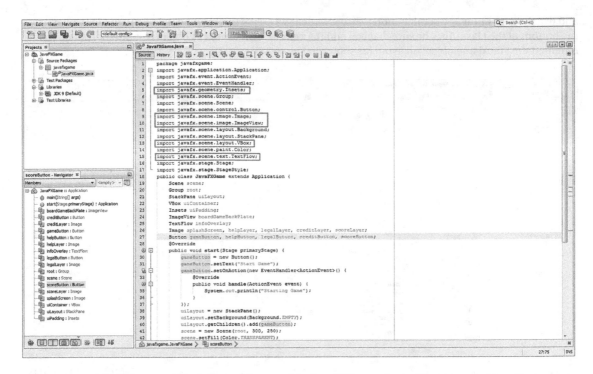

Figure 8-6. *Declare five new object types at the top of the JavaFXGame class and rename the btn object gameButton*

As you can see in Figure 8-6 outlined in red, NetBeans will code five new import statements for you, as long as you hit Alt+Enter as you type these object declaration and naming statements at the top of the JavaFXGame class.

As you can see highlighted in yellow, I have renamed the bootstrap btn Button to gameButton and changed its **.setText("Hello World")** to **.setText("Start Game")** to more directly reflect what this Button UI element will eventually accomplish, as we continue to refine this Java 9 class code throughout the course of this book.

I also changed **uiLayout.getChildren().add(btn);** to **uiLayout.getChildren().add(gameButton);** to reflect this name change throughout all of the Java 9 code in this class that currently affects this Button object. All of this is shown highlighted in Figure 8-6 using red boxes, blue line selection, and yellow object reference selection.

NetBeans 9 will write these five new import statements for you as long as you utilize an **Alt+Enter** keystroke combination. Be sure to select the option with the correct **javafx package** class path. Next, let's optimize your .start() method by offloading game object instantiation (with the exception of Stage, which is part of your **.onCreate(Stage primaryStage)** method) so that all non-Stage object creation is done using the **.createBoardGameNodes()** method.

Scene Graph Design: Optimizing the BoardGame .start() Method

Now we can optimize the .start() method so that it uses less than a dozen lines of code (see Figure 8-16 if you want to look ahead). The first thing that I want to do is to modularize the Scene Graph Node creation Java constructs into their own **createBoardGameNodes()** method, which will be called at the top of the .start() method, as shown in Figure 8-7. Add a line of code at the top of the method, type **createBoardGameNodes();**, and use the **Alt+Enter** key combination to have NetBeans 9 create this method infrastructure for you at the bottom of the class. Also, be sure that you add the **root = new Group();** object instantiation since you renamed the StackPane object uiLayout (as shown in Figure 8-5).

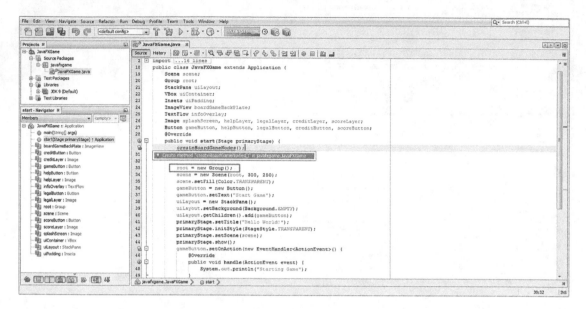

Figure 8-7. *Add a createBoardGameNodes() method call at the top of the .start() method and add root = new Group()*

Cut and paste your object instantiation and configuration code currently in the .start() method (you will be adding to this later) into the createBoardGameNodes() method to replace the "Not Supported Yet" line of error code in the bootstrap method, as shown (selected) in Figure 8-8. The new .createBoardGameNodes() method should look like the following once you are finished with this Java 9 code reconfiguration operation:

```
private void createBoardGameNodes() {
    root = new Group();
    scene = new Scene(root, 640, 400);
    scene.setFill(Color.TRANSPARENT);
    gameButton = new Button();
    gameButton.setText("Start Game");
    uiLayout = new StackPane();
    uiLayout.setBackground(Background.EMPTY);
    uiLayout.getChildren().add(gameButton);
}
```

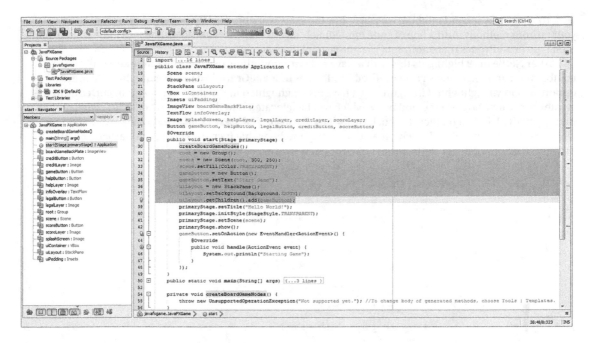

Figure 8-8. *Select all non-Stage and non-event-handling code in the start() method and cut and paste it in new method*

Notice that we are taking everything out of the .start() method that is not required to be "hosted" there. As the primaryStage Stage object is created by the .start() method parameter passed in, we'll leave all primaryStage object references inside of this method, as well as all of the event-processing structures, which need to be put into place on application startup. Everything else will be going in createBoardGameNodes() and another addNodesToSceneGraph() method we'll be creating later in the chapter to hold the .getChildren.add() or .getChildren().addAll() method call.

So, in the .start() method, we will call createBoardGameNodes() first to create all of your SceneGraph Node objects (that is, all the subclasses of Node, Parent, or Group) and then call the addNodesToSceneGraph() method to add all of these to the SceneGraph using the .getChildren().add() method chain or the .getChildren().addAll() method call chain. This organizational method allows us to add new nodes to your SceneGraph as we build your Java 9 game.

Next, let's create a second addNodesToSceneGraph() method that we can use to organize, reconfigure, and expand the SceneGraph Node building part of the JavaFX game application development work process.

Add Scene Graph Nodes: addNodesToSceneGraph()

Next, you need to create a method that will add the SceneGraph Node objects that we have created, and the ones we are about to instantiate using the VBox constructor, to the Scene Graph root object, which in this case is now a Group object. This new higher-level SceneGraph root Group object will hold your StackPane UI Panel for your high-level game functions, as well as another Group object that we will be creating to hold the 3D game branch of the SceneGraph. In a sense, we are already using JavaFX 9 to create a hybrid application, as the game UI (StackPane) branch will be 2D and the game itself (Group) will be 3D. We will use the .getChildren().add() method chain or the .getChildren().addAll() method chain to add the "children" Node (subclasses of Node, Parent, or Group) objects to the "parent" Group object named root, which is now the "root" of the JavaFX SceneGraph.

199

To create this second method, we will follow the same work process that we used to create the first of your custom methods. Add a line of code immediately after the **createBoardGameNodes();** line of code and then type in addNodesToSceneGraph(); as the second line of code.

After NetBeans 9 highlights this with a wavy red error underline, use the **Alt+Enter** keystroke combination and select the **Create method "addNodesToSceneGraph" to javafxgame.JavaFXGame** option, as shown highlighted in Figure 8-9. I have also highlighted in red the one statement currently in the createBoardGameNodes() method body, which will be relocated into this new addNodesToSceneGraph() method body. This will replace the stock **throw new UnsupportedOperationException()** Java statement, which NetBeans puts into all newly created bootstrap methods that it creates using this particular work process where you can get NetBeans to write your new method code for you.

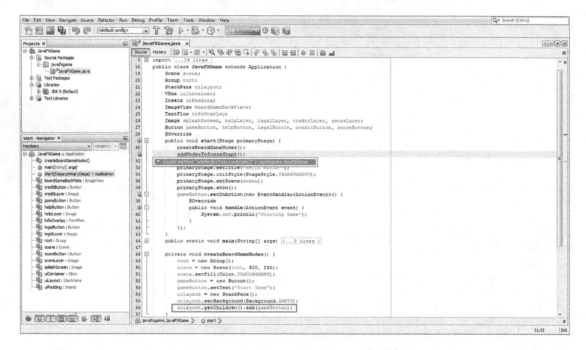

Figure 8-9. *After creating addNodesToSceneGraph() method, copy the uiLayout.getChildren() method chain to new method*

Cut the uiLayout.getrChildren().add(gameButton); statement at the end of createBoardGameNodes() and paste it over the placeholder throw new UnsupportedOperationException() line of code, replacing that code. We will be adding more nodes to the SceneGraph using this method once we instantiate those new nodes in the next section.

Adding New UI Scene Graph Nodes to createBoardGameNodes()

Let's add those new UI design and positioning JavaFX class objects (VBox, Pos, Insets) that we learned about earlier in the chapter to the JavaFXGame class and the createBoardGameNodes() method we created that contains our JavaFX 9 SceneGraph Node object creation (and configuration) Java 9 statements.

Create a **new VBox** named **uiContainer** by using the following Java object instantiation code, which uses the Java **new** keyword in conjunction with the **VBox()** constructor method:

```
uiContainer = new VBox();  // Create a Vertical Box UI element container named "uiContainer"
```

Set the alignment of the VBox to the **Pos.TOP_RIGHT** constant from the Pos helper class using the **.setAlignment()** method by using the following Java statement, shown under construction in Figure 8-10:

```
uiContainer.setAlignment(Pos.TOP_RIGHT); // Set VBox Alignment to TOP_RIGHT via Pos helper
class
```

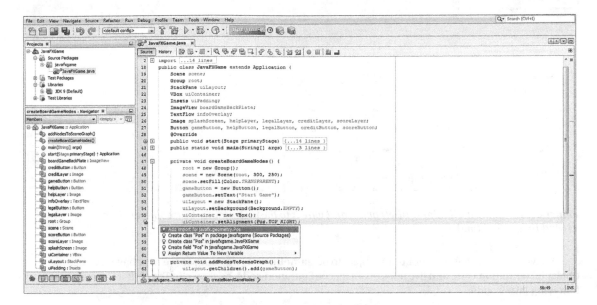

Figure 8-10. *Inside of the .setAlignment() method parameter area, type Pos.TOP_RIGHT and hit Alt+Enter to import*

Use the **Alt+Enter** keystroke combination to eliminate the wavy red error underlining, and be sure to select the correct solution to the problem, which in this case is an **Add import for javafx.geometry.Pos** option, which is listed first (most likely to be the correct solution) and which is the solution that allows a Pos class to be used in your code.

In the next step, we will create the uiPadding Insets object using the **uiPadding = new Insets(0,0,10,10);** Java instantiation statement, shown in line 58 in Figure 8-11. Finally, we will "wire up" the uiPadding Insets object to the uiContainer VBox object by using the **uiContainer. setPadding(uiPadding);** method call. This connection is shown in yellow in Figure 8-11 and shows a connection between the Insets declaration, instantiation, and implementation.

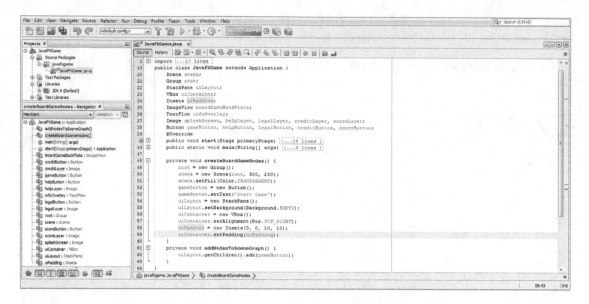

Figure 8-11. *Create a uiPadding Insets object and wire it to the uiContainer VBox object using .setPadding(uiPadding);*

We've already renamed our Button object to be **gameButton** (was btn), so we now have six lines of object instantiation code and five lines of object configuration code, as shown in Figure 8-11, using the following Java 9 code:

```
private void createBoardGameNodes()  {
    root = new Group();
    scene = new Scene(root, 300, 250);
    scene.setFill(Color.TRANSPARENT);
    gameButton = new Button();
    gameButton.setText("Start Game");
    uiLayout = new StackPane();
    uiLayout.setBackground(Background.EMPTY);
    uiContainer = new VBox();
    uiContainer.setAlignment(Pos.TOP_RIGHT);
    uiPadding = new Insets(0,0,10,10);
    uiContainer.setpadding(uiPadding);
}
```

It is important to note that since your root Group object is used in the constructor method call for the scene Scene object, this line of code will need to come first so that the root Group object is created before it is utilized.

Next, let's take the handy programmer's shortcut and cut and paste your two gameButton instantiation and configuration lines of code underneath the **uiContainer.setPadding(uiPadding);** method call and then copy and paste that code four times underneath itself, as shown highlighted at the bottom of Figure 8-12, to create all ten of your user interface button elements using the modified gameButton (btn) bootstrap UI element created in Chapter 6.

Figure 8-12. *Create 10 Button object instantiation and configuration statements at the end of* *createBoardGameNodes()*

This will allow you to change gameButton to be **helpButton**, **scoreButton**, **legalButton**, and **creditButton**, respectively, to create five unique UI Button objects. Your Java 9 game code for your Buttons should look like this:

```
gameButton = new Button();
gameButton.setText("Start Game");
helpButton = new Button();
helpButton.setText("Game Rules");
scoreButton = new Button();
scoreButton.setText("High Scores");
legalButton = new Button();
legalButton.setText("Disclaimers");
creditButton = new Button();
creditButton.setText("Game Credits");
```

Adding the New UI Design Nodes in addNodesToSceneGraph()

As you can see in Figure 8-13, the Java code is error-free, and I have now declared and instantiated another Group object named **gameBoard**. This will hold the 3D game elements branch of the SceneGraph, so the Group object declaration has now become a compound statement at the top of your class. I clicked the **gameBoard** object in the code to create a highlighted tracking of this object's declaration, instantiation in createBoardGameNodes(), and use in addNodesToSceneGraph(), showing that if you declare at the top of the class, you can use objects anywhere you need to. This **click object name to track** is a useful NetBeans 9 trick and is one you will want to use whenever you want to track object usage. I will be using it often in screenshots to highlight what I'm doing (and why) as I add new Java code.

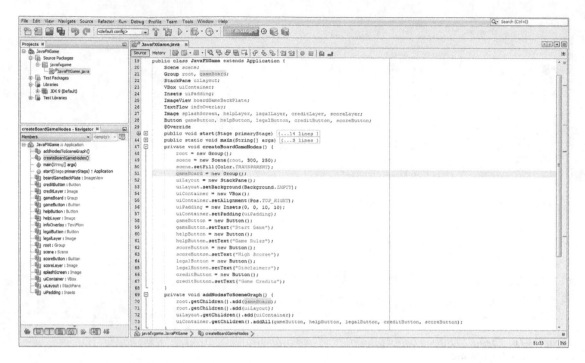

Figure 8-13. *Add gameBoard Group object and add Node objects to SceneGraph using .getChildren().add and .addAll()*

Next, let's make sure our nodes are added to the SceneGraph correctly. Out of the root (top) of the Scene Graph, which is a Group object, we will have another gameBoard Group object to hold the i3D game elements and assets, as well as the uiLayout StackPane object. These are added to the root Group using the following statements:

```
root.getChildren().add(gameBoard);    // Add new i3D Game Group Node to root Group Node
root.getChildren().add(uiLayout);     // Add uiLayout StackPane Node to root Group Node
```

Next, we add the uiContainer VBox layout container branch node to the uiLayout StackPane branch node and add five Button UI element leaf nodes to the uiContainer VBox. This is done using two lines of Java 9 code, like this:

```
uiLayout.getChildren().add(uiContainer);      // Add VBox Vertical Layout Node to StackPane
Node
uiContainer.getChildren().addAll(gameButton,  // Add All UI Button Nodes to the VBox Node
                                 helpButton,
                                 legalButton, creditButton, scoreButton);
```

Figure 8-13 shows this SceneGraph construction code. I used color fills on the object hierarchy, which is visualized to show Node objects (Node subclassed objects, more accurately), which are Scene, root, or branch nodes. (This is shown in Figure 8-3 if you want to review these JavaFX root, branch, and leaf Node object hierarchies.)

The important thing to observe here is the **order** that you have added the Node objects to the Group root Scene Graph object. The order affects the compositing layer order for the scene render compositing, as well as for the UI element compositing, on top of your 3D elements. The first Node added to the root Group will be on the **bottom** of the scene compositing (rendering) stack. Therefore, this needs to be the **gameBoard** Group Node object, which will hold the i3D game so that Node is added to the Scene Graph root first and is at the bottom, if you are looking down, or at the back, if you are looking forward, of the Scene compositing and rendering stack. You can see this in Figure 8-13.

The next Node to add will be your **uiLayout** StackPane Node object because your 2D user interface (floating) panel will need to overlay right on top of your 3D GameBoard. After these top-level Node objects are placed into your Scene Graph hierarchy, we can add the **uiContainer** VBox Node object, which will contain all of the Button Control leaf Node objects, to the StackPane Node object. Note that we are using the **.getChildren().addAll()** method chain to add Button Control objects to the VBox because we can more easily add them using a Java List object or comma-delimited list in the parameter area of the .addAll() method call (chain) called off of the .getChildren() method.

In Chapter 9 we'll also add an ImageView object named boardGameBackPlate and a TextFlow object named infoOverlay. I will also need to instantiate five Image objects to hold digital image assets in memory during Chapter 9 so that the image objects we declared in this chapter can be implemented. As you know, we named these splashScreen, helpLayer, legalLayer, creditLayer, and scoreLayer using a compound Java statement, as we did for the Button objects.

Interactivity: Creating the BoardGame Button UI Control

The next thing you need to do is to copy the **gameButton.setOnAction()** event-handling Java code structure in your .start() method and then paste it four more times underneath itself to create your helpButton, legalButton, creditButton, and scoreButton Button Control object event-handling structures. For testing purposes, at this stage, you will want to change the System.out.println statements to each print a unique message to your Output console window, so you can make sure that each of the five Button UI elements is unique to itself and is handling its Button events properly. It is important to always make sure that your Java 9 code constructs work at each stage (that is, after each change or enhancement) before proceeding to add even more Java code and thus more application complexity. This takes a little bit longer during development than writing all your code at once but saves time in debugging.

In case you are wondering what the wavy yellow underline warning (or suggestion) is in Figure 8-14, along with the pop-up message I generated by putting my mouse over this yellow highlighting found under your event handler ActionEvent processing construct `EventHandler<ActionEvent>() { public void handle(){...} });`, it is because this expression can be turned into a lambda expression using less code. Be aware that doing this will ensure your code works only under Java 8 and Java 9. If you want to use your code in Android, which uses Java 6 and Java 7, you may just want to leave these slightly longer Java code structures in place, as they do exactly the same thing.

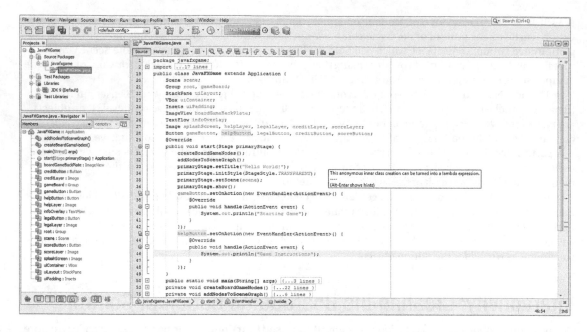

Figure 8-14. *Copy the gameButton event processing code and paste it underneath itself and create your helpButton event handling*

When you are finished, your new event-handling structures should look like the following Java code shown in the middle of Figure 8-15:

```java
gameButton.setOnAction(new EventHandler<ActionEvent>() {
    @Override
    public void handle(ActionEvent event) {
        System.out.println("Starting Game");
    }
});
helpButton.setOnAction(new EventHandler<ActionEvent>() {
    @Override
    public void handle(ActionEvent event) {
        System.out.println("Game Instructions");
    }
});
scoreButton.setOnAction(new EventHandler<ActionEvent>() {
    @Override
    public void handle(ActionEvent event) {
        System.out.println("High Score");
    }
});

legalButton.setOnAction(new EventHandler<ActionEvent>() {
    @Override
    public void handle(ActionEvent event) {
        System.out.println("Copyrights");
    }
});
```

```
creditButton.setOnAction(new EventHandler<ActionEvent>() {
    @Override
    public void handle(ActionEvent event) {
        System.out.println("Credits");
    }
});
```

As you can see in Figure 8-15, your event-handling code is error-free, and you are ready to run and test your **JavaFXGame.java** game application to make sure that your Scene Graph hierarchy is rendering to the screen and that your Button UI Control objects are handling event processing correctly. Once you make sure that your Scene Graph is constructed at this high level for your game and your core user interface processing Java 9 code structures are also in place and working properly, you can proceed, during the next chapter, to add digital image assets and fine-tune all of the UI element positioning so that you can make everything look and function correctly at the top level of your game.

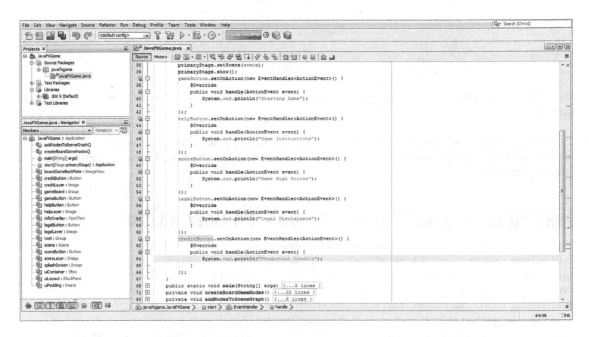

Figure 8-15. *Copy the gameButton and helpButton and paste them to create your scoreButton, legalButton, and creditButton*

As you can see in Figure 8-16, after you **duplicate** the **.setOnAction()** event-handling constructs for each of your Button objects, when you collapse the EventHandler routines using the minus icons at the left side of the screen (shown circled in red on the left side of Figure 8-16), you'll have fewer than a dozen lines of code in the .start() method. Your first line of code will call a method to create Node objects and configure them, your second line of code will call a method to add these Node objects to your Scene Graph hierarchy, lines 3 through 6 will configure your Stage object, and lines 7 through 11 will set up your UI Button Control object event handling. This is relatively compact if you consider the amount of functionality that you are adding to the top level of your game infrastructure, including creating your top-level (root and branch node) Scene Graph structure and user interface design elements for your gameplay, instructions, legal disclaimers, credits, and scoreboard display.

Figure 8-16. *Click the Run (Play) icon at the top of NetBeans and test your code to make sure your UI design is working*

Next, it's time to test the code that reorganizes the JavaFXGame class and creates your UI design structure and Scene Graph hierarchy for your game application. Let's make sure all these UI Button elements (objects) function.

Testing Your BoardGame: Process the Scene Graph

Click the green **Play** arrow shown at the top of the NetBeans 9 IDE circled in red in Figure 8-16 and **Run** your JavaFXGame **project**. This will bring up the VBox UI layout container that is shown encircled in red on the top-middle part of Figure 8-16. As you can see, you are getting a professional result, with no crashes, using around a dozen-and-a-half import statements (external classes), a few dozen lines of Java code, and less than a dozen child Nodes underneath your Scene Graph root Group Node object. It is important to optimize your Scene Graph hierarchy because each pulse event that JavaFX will use to process your game design structure will have to traverse this hierarchy, so the more compact it is, the better your game will perform, and the smoother your user experience will be. Therefore, you should optimize everything from the get-go. As you can see circled in red in the **Output-JavaFXGame** tab at the bottom of Figure 8-17, I have tested the event-handling structures attached to all Button UI Control objects.

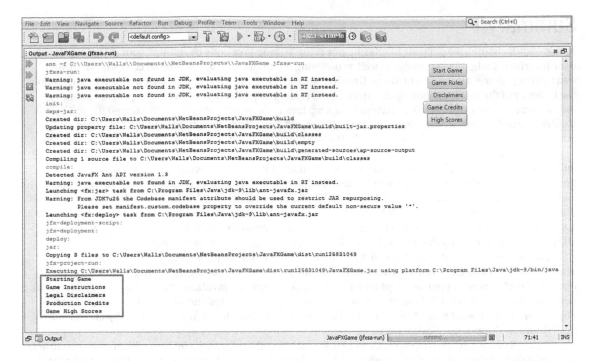

Figure 8-17. *Click each of the Button objects and make sure your event-handling code is printing the right messages*

I did this to make sure each button is implementing its own event handling and is printing out the correct **System.out.println()** text message when I click each of the five UI Button Controls.

Later we can replace this System.out.println() method call with a different one that controls the ImageView reference to the Image object, allowing us to switch between your digital image assets for your user interface design ImageView digital image backplate holder.

Since we only copied and pasted the EventHandler routines for each Button and changed only your Button objects names and the code that is executed inside of these routines, these Button objects should still work properly (writing text to the console) and not cause any compiler errors. However, they will not ultimately do what you want them to, which is to change the Image object, which is referenced in the ImageView object (UI backplate) underlay, or to place the proper text over this using the TextFlow. This is what you are going to be coding in the next chapter; you'll also do some UI design tweaking that will put the Button bank in the proper location on the display screen. As you can see in Figure 8-16, although the Button Control objects are indeed aligned at the TOP_RIGHT position inside the VBox UI container Node, the VBox itself is not yet aligned within its Parent (branch) StackPane Node object. Just like with the transparency in Chapter 7, the VBox (in StackPane) and StackPane (in a Group) must be positioned correctly.

Congratulations, you have maintained the improvements added in Chapter 7 and put in place new methods for organizing your Scene Graph hierarchy and improved this Scene Graph to include your i3D game branch, which we will start to add objects and assets into during the second half of the book.

Summary

In this eighth chapter, we got your hands into our **JavaFXGame.java** code by refining your actual **top-level user interface design** for our game, as well as outlining the underlying **game engine component design** and figuring out the most efficient **Scene Graph Node design** using fewer than a dozen nodes to implement the majority of the top-level game user interface structure. You got back into Java game programming by redesigning the existing **JavaFXGame.java** bootstrap Java code, which was originally created for you by NetBeans 9 in Chapter 6. Since the NetBeans 9–generated Java 9 code design was not optimal for your purposes, you rewrote it significantly to make it more modular, streamlined, and organized.

You did this by creating two new Java methods: **.createBoardGameNodes()** and **.addNodesToSceneGraph()**. You did this so you could **modularize** your Scene Graph Node creation process and also so that you could modularize the adding of the two Parent branch Node and five Control leaf Node objects to your Scene Graph **root**, which in this case happens to be the **Group** Node object. Under that you have your StackPane branch Node named **uiLayout**, which you are using for its multilayer UI object compositing capability, and a Group branch Node named **gameBoard**, which you will be using to hold the i3D game object hierarchy that you will be building during the remainder of this book.

You learned about some of the JavaFX classes that we're going to implement in these new methods. These included a **Pos** class and an **Insets** class from the **javafx.scene.geometry** package, the **VBox** class from the **javafx.scene.layout** package, and the **Group** class from the **javafx.scene** package. You coded your new .createBoardGameNodes() method that instantiated and configured the VBox object using the Inset object, the StackPane uiLayout branch Node object, the Group gameBoard branch Node object, and your five UI Button Control leaf Node objects.

Once all of your Scene Graph Nodes were instantiated and configured, you were able to then construct your .addNodesToSceneGraph() method to add your Scene Graph Node objects to your Group root object. You did this so that the correct Scene Graph Node hierarchy would be displayed inside of your Stage object, which will reference and load your Scene Graph root Group Node object and the hierarchy that we are building underneath it.

Finally, you created the other four Button UI Control objects and added ActionEvent EventHandler program logic. This completed our programming tasks for this chapter that are related to setting up your Scene Graph hierarchy and user interface design infrastructure for the **JavaFXGame.java** Java 9 game application.

Once this was all coded, you tested your top-level Java 9 game application user interface design and Scene Graph hierarchy in NetBeans 9.

In the next chapter, you are going to add cool digital image assets to your user interface design and work on the positioning and alignment, as well as getting everything working with your UI Button objects.

CHAPTER 9

■ ■ ■

JavaFX 9 User Interface Design: The Front End for Java 9 Game Design

Let's build upon the top-level Scene Graph architecture that you built during Chapter 8 by continuing to design the front-end user interface infrastructure of your i3D BoardGame. This will be done inside of your StackPane branch Node, using three primary nodes underneath that Node. The VBox branch Node holds the Button leaf Nodes, the ImageView leaf Node displays different Image objects, and the TextFlow leaf Node displays (flows) different text descriptions that are overlaid on top of the ImageView Node. These seven leaf nodes will work together to form your game's top-level user interface design. The StackPane Node will serve as the background image plate (holder), and the ImageView leaf node will hold five different Image objects that reference your digital image section assets for each of the five buttons. The StartGame background image asset will be what's considered to be the splash screen. On top of the ImageView in the StackPane hierarchy will be the TextFlow leaf node, which will serve as the foreground text information holder and will reference different text data based on which Button Control object has been clicked. On top of the TextFlow layer will be the VBox branch Node layer, which will hold five Button leaf nodes. This will hold, align, and position your five Button Control objects, which will eventually use event handlers to swap different Image objects into your ImageView object, as well as different text data into your TextFlow object.

The first thing that I will cover since you have already **declared** your five background **Image** objects (as well as your **ImageView** and **TextFlow** objects for use at the top of the **JavaFXGame.java** class) is how you're going to finish implementing your user interface design using your Scene Graph hierarchy that you started building during Chapter 8.

The next thing that we will need to cover are the four new JavaFX classes from the **javafx.scene.image** and **javafx.scene.text** packages, which you are going to be instantiating and configuring for use in your Java game during this chapter. These will include the Image class, the ImageView class, the **Text** class, and the TextFlow class.

The next thing that you will need to do is to create the background imagery that will be loaded in the Image objects so that you have something to test your Java code with later so you can make sure it is working properly.

After that, you will learn a cool trick to add another compositing layer to your compositing pipeline without adding another Node object to your Scene Graph hierarchy. This will involve learning about how to utilize your JavaFX **Background** class (object) along with the JavaFX **BackgroundImage** class (object) to utilize the Background attribute of Node subclasses as another Image object holding layer within your pro Java game digital image compositing pipeline.

W. Jackson, *Pro Java 9 Games Development*, https://doi.org/10.1007/978-1-4842-0973-8_9

All of this will involve adding new Java statements to both your **.createBoardGameNodes()** method and your **.addNodesToSceneGraph()** method to put the ImageView background image plate and TextFlow information text overlay into place, behind your VBox Button Control bank. You will also be adding two new Java methods into the JavaFXGame class to load the Image assets (the loadImageAssets() method) and to create your Text assets (the createTextAssets() method). You have a lot of coding, recoding, rewiring (object referencing changes), and parameter adjustments to do to get your user interface a lot more organized and professional, and we'll get started on that after we look at some of the JavaFX API classes that we will be leveraging over the course of this chapter on user interfaces.

UI Design Foundation: Finishing the Scene Graph

One of the first things that you are going to do in this chapter is to finish up your Scene Graph design for the top-level **user interface screens**. This means instantiating your **ImageView** digital image display backplane, which will hold your background Image objects that will reference your digital image assets. You will be referencing these digital image assets during this chapter that were created using GIMP 2.10. On top of the ImageView in the Scene Graph hierarchy, you will be adding a **TextFlow** information container; therefore, your text content will be on top of the background image and not underneath it. Finally, on top of these two leaf Node objects will be the VBox Button Control branch Node object, which you already created and implemented during Chapter 8. Figure 9-1 shows the final Scene Graph hierarchy (expanding on the generic root, branch, and leaf Scene Graph diagram that you saw in Chapter 7 in Figure 7-3). This time, I have customized it for your pro Java 9 game application. Notice there are no connectors on the i3D Group branch Node leaf Node objects, as we have not yet implemented them in the Java code.

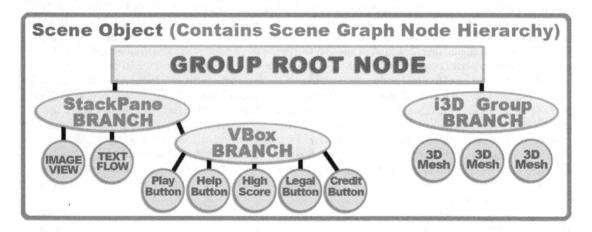

Figure 9-1. *BoardGame user interface design Scene Graph hierarchy, showing the root, branch, and leaf Node objects*

This will require you to add two more leaf Nodes to your **StackPane** layout container **Parent** branch Node, as shown on the lower left in Figure 9-1. Before we get into the Java coding to instantiate these two leaf Node objects in the .createBoardGameNodes() method and to add them in your Scene Graph hierarchy, let's get an overview of each of the classes that you'll be using in the new Java statements that you will be putting into place during this chapter.

JavaFX 9 UI Compositing: ImageView and TextFlow

Next, let's take a look at the primary JavaFX classes that can be used to create the basic compositing pipeline for the game splash screen and text information screens that will be next to (and underneath) the UI Button bank that you created during the previous chapter. The game instructions, high scores, and legal and credits screens will essentially be text (held inside your TextFlow object) composited over background imagery (held in an ImageView object). The splash screen will be associated with the Start Game Button and will display on launch of the game application; it will become invisible when the Start Game Button is pressed. This is because the StackPane UI construct is on a higher-level z-order than the root Group and gameBoard Group Node objects, which are above it on the Scene Graph. This means that anything that is opaque in the StackPane will overlay (block from view) the i3D gameBoard Group that is directly underneath the Scene Graph root, as shown in Figure 8-3. Let's take a look at the Image class first.

JavaFX Image Class: Referencing Digital Imagery in Your Design

The **Image** class is a **public** class that directly extends the java.lang.Object master class, meaning that the Image class was also "scratch-coded" to provide image loading (referencing) and scaling (resizing). You can **lock the aspect ratio** for scaling and specify the scaling (algorithm) quality as well. All URLs that are supported by the **java.net.URL** class are supported. This means you can load images from the Internet (www.domainname.com/imagename.png), from the OS file system (**file:imagename.png**), or from your JAR file using a forward slash character (/imagename.png).

The JavaFX Image class is part of the **javafx.scene.image** package. The class hierarchy for the JavaFX Image class originates with the **java.lang.Object** master class and uses the following Java class hierarchy:

```
java.lang.Object
  > javafx.scene.image.Image
```

The Image class provides six different (overloaded) **Image()** constructor methods. These take anything from a simple URL to a set of parameter values specifying the **URL**, **width**, **height**, **aspectRatioLock**, **smoothing**, and **preload** options. These should be specified in this order within your constructor method. You'll see this soon when you code an Image() constructor using the most complicated of all of these constructor methods, which uses the following format:

```
Image(String url, double requestedWidth, double requestedHeight,
      boolean preserveRatio, boolean smooth, boolean backgroundLoading)
```

The simplest constructor for an Image object specifies only the URL and would use the following format:

```
Image(String url)
```

If you wanted to load the image and also have the constructor method scale the image to a different width and height (usually this would be smaller, for better quality) using the highest-quality resampling (smooth pixel scaling) while also locking (preserving) the aspect ratio, you would utilize the following format for the Image object constructor:

```
Image(String url, double scaleWidth, double scaleHeight, boolean preserveAspect, boolean
smooth)
```

If you wanted to load an image using its "native" or "physical" (default) resolution and native aspect ratio and have it load the image in the background (**asynchronously**), you would use the following format for the Image() constructor:

```
Image(String url, boolean backgroundLoading)
```

There are also two Image() constructor methods that use the **java.io.InputStream** class. This class provides a lower-level Java input stream of input data to the Image() constructor method. Generally, you'll use a URL to reference your digital image files. These two Image object constructor formats take the following formats. The simple format is as follows:

```
Image(InputStream is)
```

The complex InputStream constructor method allows you to specify the width, height, aspect ratio lock, and image scaling interpolation smoothing algorithm (on/true or off/false). The second format will look like the following:

```
Image(InputStream is, double newWidth, double newHeight, boolean preserveAspect, boolean smooth)
```

The Image class (object) is thus used to prepare a digital image asset for use, that is, to read its data from a URL, resize it if necessary (using whatever smoothing and aspect ratio lock you like), and even load it asynchronously while other things are going on within the application. It is important to note that this Image class (or object) does not display your image asset; it just loads it, scales it if needed, and places it into system memory, to be used in your app.

To display an Image object, you'll need to utilize a second class (object), called an ImageView, which we are going to cover in the next section of this chapter. This ImageView object is implemented as a leaf Node in your Scene Graph and references and then "paints" your Image object data onto the layout container, which contains this ImageView Node. In our case, this is the uiLayout StackPane Parent (or branch) Node above the leaf ImageView Node.

From a digital image compositing perspective, the StackPane class (object) is the layer compositing engine, or the layer manager if you will, and the ImageView object represents one single digital image layer in the layer stack. An Image object contains the digital image data that is displayed inside of the ImageView layer or in more than one ImageView, if that is required, since the Image objects and the ImageView objects are decoupled and therefore exist independently of each other. I am trying to minimize Scene Graph Node use, so I'm using one ImageView image plate and one text information compositing plate to create the user interface screens and then using code to switch them.

JavaFX ImageView Class: Display Digital Images in Your Design

The **ImageView** class is a **public** class that directly extends the javafx.scene.Node superclass, which is an extension of the java.lang.Object master class. The ImageView object is therefore a type of Node object in the JavaFX Scene Graph that is used for painting a graphic viewport using the data contained in an Image object. The class has methods that allow image resampling (resizing), and like with the Image class, you can lock aspect ratio for scaling, as well as specify the resampling algorithm (the smoothing quality, through the use of pixel interpolation).

As you can see in line 24 of your Java code, shown in Figure 8-6, you will be using an ImageView object named **boardGameBackPlate** to display your Image object data. This ImageView class, like your Image class, is also contained in the **javafx.scene.image** package. The Java class hierarchy for the ImageView class starts out with the **java.lang.Object** master class and uses this class to create a **javafx.scene.Node** class, which is then used to create the javafx.scene.image.ImageView Node subclass. An ImageView class uses the following Java class inheritance hierarchy:

```
java.lang.Object
  > javafx.scene.Node
    > javafx.scene.image.ImageView
```

The ImageView class provides three different (overloaded) **ImageView()** constructor methods. These range from the empty ImageView constructor (which is the one you are going to use later in your code) to one that takes an Image object as its parameter to one that takes a URL String object as the parameter and creates the Image object automatically. The simplest, empty parameter list ImageView() constructor method will create an (empty) ImageView object (that is, one with no Image object to display but can hold Image objects). It will use this following format:

```
ImageView()
```

We will be using this constructor method so that I can show you how to use the **.setImage()** method call to load your Image object into an ImageView object. If you wanted to avoid using the .setImage() method call, you could use another overloaded constructor method. That ImageView object constructor would use this following format:

```
ImageView(Image image)
```

So, the way that I'm going to explicitly set up an ImageView and wire it to the Image object will look like this:

```
boardGameBackPlate = new ImageView();        // This uses empty constructor method approach
boardGameBackPlate.setImage(splashScreen);
```

This could be condensed into one line of code using an overloaded constructor method, structured like this:

```
boardGameBackPlate = new ImageView(splashScreen);  // using the overloaded constructor method
```

If you also want to bypass the process of creating and loading an Image object, there is another constructor method for that as well, which uses the following format:

```
ImageView(String url)
```

If you wanted to load an image using its "native" or "physical" (default) resolution and native aspect ratio and have it load the image in the background (**asynchronously**), the Image() constructor would use the following format:

```
backPlate = new Image("/backplate8.png", 1280, 640, true, false, true);
boardGameBackplate = new ImageView();
boardGameBackplate.setImage(backPlate); // use empty ImageView constructor method approach
```

If you didn't want to specify the image dimensions, background image loading, or smooth scaling and you wanted to lock the aspect ratio for any scaling, you could condense the previous three lines of Java code into the one following constructor:

```
boardGameBackPlate = new ImageView("/backplate8.png");   // uses third constructor method
```

215

At least initially, for learning purposes, I am going to do this the long way, and I will always "explicitly" load Image objects using the Image() constructor method so that we can specify all of the different attributes and so that you can see all of the different image assets that you're using in your Java 9 programming logic. I wanted to show you the shortcut code here because you might want to use this shortcut approach later if you start using ImageViews as 2D sprites. You can use this shortcut approach with your sprites because you will not be scaling them and because they are so highly optimized that the background loading option, which saves long loading times, won't be necessary.

JavaFX TextFlow Class: Use Text Objects (Content) in a Design

The **TextFlow** class is a **public** class that allows the developer to create a text paragraph. A text paragraph is a container for multiple lines of text, each of which is delimited using a "new line" character, denoted using an "escape n" sequence in your Java code.

The TextFlow class would therefore use the following Java class inheritance hierarchy:

```
java.lang.Object
  > javafx.scene.Node
    > javafx.scene.Parent
      > javafx.scene.layout.Region
        > javafx.scene.layout.Pane
          > javafx.scene.text.TextFlow
```

This TextFlow object is the type of Node object in the JavaFX Scene Graph that can be used for rendering text paragraphs using the data contained in a Text object, in much the same way an ImageView can render data contained in an Image object. The TextFlow can handle more than one Text object at a time, however, allowing you to style different Text objects differently using method calls like .setFill() and .setFont(). TextFlow is a specialized text layout class designed to render what's commonly referred to as *rich text format* (RTF). Some call this *desktop publishing*, and it involves using different fonts, styles, or color to enhance the presentation of text-based content. It's interesting to note that javafx.scene.text is kept in the javafx.graphics module and not in the javafx.controls module. This is significant, because if you wanted to optimize out (not use) the JavaFX 9 UI Control classes (100 classes or more), you could still create your own UI elements using Image, ImageView, Text, and 3D geometry objects using only the javafx.base and javafx.graphics modules, which give you everything you need to create pro Java 9 i3D games.

A TextFlow object can be used to lay out a number of Text nodes within a single TextFlow object. A TextFlow object uses the text and the font and style settings for each of the Text Node objects inside of it, plus its own maximum width and text alignment style properties, to determine the location for rendering each child Text object.

A single Text node can span several lines because of the wrapping capability of the TextFlow object, and a visual location of a Text node can differ from the logical location because of bidirectional (bidi) reordering. The Java Bidi object provides information on the bidirectional reordering of the text used to create it. This is required, for example, to properly display Arabic or Hebrew text, which is read from right to left (RTL) instead of left to right (LTR).

Any other Node object type, other than a Text Node object, of course, will be treated as an embedded "rich content" object within the TextFlow object's layout. It will be inserted in the content using its preferred width, height, and baseline offset values to space and align it relative to the other Text objects within the parent TextFlow object.

When a Text Node object is inside of a TextFlow object, some its properties will be ignored. For example, the X and Y properties of a Text Node object will be ignored since the location of the child Text Node is determined by the Parent TextFlow object. Likewise, the wrapping width in the Text node will be ignored since the maximum width used for wrapping will inherit the TextFlow object's maximum width property.

The wrapping width of a TextFlow layout will be determined by the Region object's current width. This can be specified by your application by setting the TextFlow object's preferred width property. If no wrapping feature is desired, the application can set the preferred width to either **Double.MAX_VALUE** or, alternately, **Region.USE_COMPUTED_SIZE**. Paragraphs should be separated using the **new line**, or **\n (escape character)**, inside of any of your child Text Node objects, shown in the following bold code example.

The value of the **pickOnBounds** property of a Text Node object will be set to **false** when it is rendered in the TextFlow object. This happens because your content in a single Text Node object can become divided by the TextFlow algorithm and be placed in different locations in the TextFlow because of line breaking and bidi reordering. TextFlow algorithms will lay out each managed child Text Node object regardless of that child's visibility property value, leaving gaps for Text Node objects that are set to be invisible. Here is an example of the TextFlow object creation workflow:

```
Text titleText = new Text("Welcome to iTVboardgame! \n");
titleText.setFill(Color.RED).setFont(Font.font("Helvetica", FontPosture.ITALIC, 40));
Text pressPlayText = new Text("Press the Start Game Button to Start!");
pressPlayText.setFill(Color.BLUE).setFont(Font.font("Helvetica", FontWeight.BOLD, 10));
TextFlow gameTextFlow = new TextFlow(titleText, pressPlayText);
```

The TextFlow class has two properties: the **DoubleProperty lineSpacing** attribute, which defines the vertical space using pixels between the lines of Text, and the **ObjectProperty<TextAlignment> textAlignment** attribute, which defines the horizontal text alignment constant such as **LEFT**, **RIGHT**, **CENTER**, or **JUSTIFY**.

The TextFlow class has two constructor methods; the first has an empty parameter area and constructs an empty TextFlow text layout object. This constructor method would use the following format:

```
TextFlow()
```

The second TextFlow constructor method used previously creates a TextFlow with the child Text (or rich media) Node objects that are passed into the parameter area using a comma-delimited list, using the following format:

```
TextFlow(Node... children)
```

The reason this second constructor method takes a parameter **list Array of Node** objects is because the TextFlow object supports "Rich Text Layouts," which is the combination of Text objects and other supported Node objects that support rich media (images, shapes, geometry, mesh, animation, video, etc.).

Let's get back to coding and instantiate and configure the Image, ImageView, Text, and TextFlow objects so that you can add them into your existing Scene Graph hierarchy to achieve what is shown in Figure 9-1. After that, in Chapter 10 we can write code in your Button ActionEvent handlers that will customize your UI based on clicks.

Coding the User Interface: A UI Compositing Pipeline

To get the User Interface Design dialed in, you will need to instantiate the ImageView and TextFlow objects, add them to your Scene Graph in the proper position in the hierarchy, import digital images into your project, create a method to load your Image objects with your digital image assets, create a method to create your Text objects with the proper information, and finally tweak your SceneGraph and UI elements to fine-tune your UI end result.

Instantiating the Compositing Layers: .createBoardGameNodes()

Since you have already declared the boardGameBackPlate ImageView and infoOverlay TextFlow and coded the import statements for these classes in Chapter 8, the next thing that you will need to do is to instantiate them into objects using the Java **new** keyword along with their basic (empty parameter list) constructor methods. You will do this in your createBoardGameNodes() method to keep things highly organized. To mirror the Scene Graph hierarchy, you will instantiate them after the StackPane and before the VBox since that will be the compositing (layer) order you will be using. As you can see in Figure 9-2, the Java code is error-free, and you have a SceneGraph root, i3D gameBoard branch, and UI layout branch instantiated using only a root and three branch Node objects in system memory, including one Group Node, a StackPane, and a VBox (the Insets object is a utility object and not a SceneGraph Node).

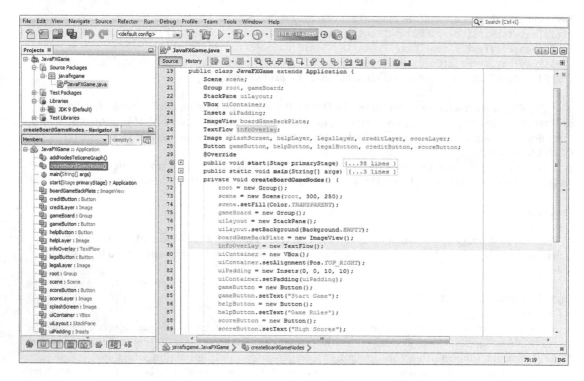

Figure 9-2. *Instantiate boardGameBackPlate and infoOverlay objects inside of your createBoardGameNodes() method*

If you count the Scene object holding the SceneGraph, there are five game organization objects in memory. Add to this the Stage object, which was created using the .start() method, and your Application object, created by the JavaFXGame class extends Application declaration, and you have created the top-level infrastructure for your pro Java 9 games development using a mere seven objects in system memory. With the ImageView and TextFlow displays, we are still under ten objects in system memory. Once we load your five Image objects with digital image assets and set up five UI Button objects, you still have fewer than 20 objects in memory, which is still quite well optimized. You will also be adding eight Text objects later during the chapter, but these are not pixel-centric, so they will not take up much memory footprint at all. We'll also be using some utility objects, like Insets, but even with those you'll still be under 30 objects before you start adding the core 3D objects that will make up your i3D BoardGame. Let's add your ImageView and TextFlow to the Scene Graph next, placing them behind the VBox UI Button bank so they render first.

Adding UI Backplate to Scene Graph: addNodesToSceneGraph()

For the ImageView compositing layer and the TextFlow information plate to be on top of the Scene, 3D gameBoard, and StackPane but behind the VBox Button bank, you will need .getChildren().add() method calls off of the uiLayout StackPane object, after the root method calls, and before the uiContainer method call. This is shown in Figure 9-3 and will use the following two Java statements inside of your addNodesToSceneGraph() method structure:

```
uiLayout.getChildren().add(boardGameBackPlate); // Add ImageView backplate behind TextFlow Node
uiLayout.getChildren().add(infoOverlay);         //  Add TextFlow information overlay second
```

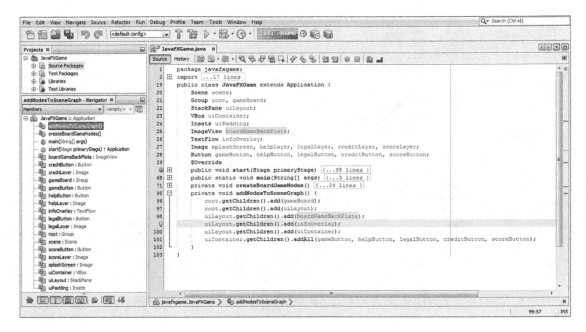

Figure 9-3. *Add boardGameBackPlate and infoOverlay to your Scene Graph in the addNodesToSceneGraph() method*

Since a Button object can't be positioned individually, I had to use the **VBox** class, along with an **Insets** class, to contain and position a vertical bank of Button controls. Now we are ready to code our two asset-loading methods.

Asset Load Methods: loadImageAssets() and createTextAssets()

The next thing that we want to do to keep things organized as we create this game over the course of the book is to create another two dedicated methods for loading Image object assets and creating Text object assets. This creates a dedicated "method-based work process" for adding elements to your game. Instantiate in .createBoardGameNodes(), add to SceneGraph in .addNodesToSceneGraph(), reference Image objects in .loadImageAssets(), and create Text objects in .createTextAssets(). As you can see in Figure 9-4, I have placed these two new method calls at the top of the .start() method, as well as having NetBeans create empty methods for them, which we'll add Java code to, as we add assets to your game. I placed these at the top of the start method so that your application can load these assets into system memory first thing so they are there when the rest of your pro Java game code needs them and so that we do not have to use any specialized preloader. Also, these objects must be in place before they can be called by other methods, so they need to be called first, before the methods that set up more advanced objects and add them to the SceneGraph hierarchy. Later, we can make sure this asset loading is taking less than a second using the NetBeans 9 profiler, once we have things like 3D object rendering and game processing logic that we need to make sure is highly optimized and not taking up too many of the Pulse engine's 60 FPS interrupts (time slices) processing the SceneGraph.

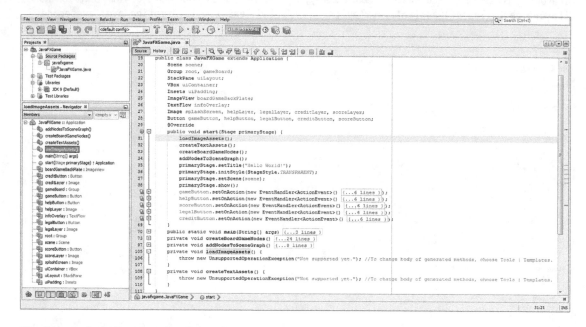

Figure 9-4. *Create empty methods for loadImageAssets() and createTextAssets() to create your image and text assets*

Before we can continue, we need to create some new media assets to use with the Image objects, which we are going to instantiate and reference (load) with PNG32 digital image assets, which will leverage alpha channels. This alpha channel data will allow us to composite these logos or screen captions on top of any background image or even over the i3D gameBoard itself if we choose to down the line. In the next section, I will create an iTVBoardGame logo in Autodesk 3D Studio Max and then export it as an OBJ file and render it using a cool (or maybe, hot) rock texture. Then we will have a pro Java 9 game 3D splash screen title for use later on during the chapter as you refine your UI design.

Creating SplashScreen Assets: Using 3D Assets in a 2D Pipeline

As you can see in Figure 9-5, I have created a "quick and dirty" iTVBoardGame 3D logo using the **2D Text** tool and then **extruding** it, using the **Bevel** modifier, as you can see in the Autodesk 3D Studio Max version of the Scene Graph hierarchy (called a Modifier List in 3D Studio Max) on the top-right portion of the screenshot. I later used the **File ➤ Export** function to output a WaveFront .OBJ 3D file format, which is one of the several 3D file import formats supported by JavaFX 9. We may be using this format, or one of the others, depending on what types of 3D data we need to import, as each format supports different types of 3D data and features, such as texture maps, UVW maps, inverse kinematic (IK) skeletal animation data, mesh morphing, animation, camera data, lighting data, and the like. JavaFX has the capability to import quite a few advanced 3D formats, such as Collada (DAE), FrameBox (FBX), 3D Studio 3DS and OBJ.

Figure 9-5. *I created an iTVBoardGame logo with 3D Studio Max, exported it to an OBJ file format, and rendered it*

I will import this mesh data into the rendering engine, add a burled walnut texture map, render it, and then export the 2D pixel data as a 2D image asset. I will make sure that it has an alpha channel, so it will still look like it is a 3D object, even though in fact it is not. This is what is termed in the industry as 2.5D.

If we want to spin it around and so on later, we can always import it as a 3D asset later in the book when we have learned more about the i3D content production pipeline in JavaFX. One of the advantages of the hybrid 2D+3D environment (API) that JavaFX gives you is the ability to decide what 3D is an "illusion" (like 2.5D, or stereoscopic) and what 3D is "real" i3D. Stereoscopic 3D (film, primarily) is not really 3D, as you cannot walk behind the scene and all its characters. In an i3D game, such as *Halo* or *Madden Football*, you can, as it is a completely virtual reality.

Next let's take some of the UI screen title digital Image objects I've created for use inside of your ImageView object, and I will show you how to add these into the proper folder in your NetBeansProject folder hierarchy. After NetBeans 9 can "see" these PNG32 digital image assets, you will then be able to code the loadImageAssets() method, which will load PNG32 data into Image objects in system memory so the ImageView can reference and display them.

Adding Image Assets to Your Project: Using the \src\ Folder

As you can see at the top of Figure 9-6, the path on my Windows 7 64-bit QuadCore AMD workstation starts with the **Users** folder and looks like **C:\Users\Walls\MyDocuments\NetBeansProjects\JavaFXGame\src\ credits.png**. As you can see, I named the PNG32 files after what was inside of them, and even though they look like they are on a white background, they're actually transparent. Copy the files from the book assets repository to your project folder, and then you will be able to reference them in your code.

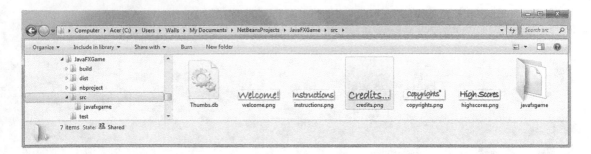

Figure 9-6. *Copy the PNG32 files for the digital image titles for the UI screens to /NetBeansProjects/ JavaFXGame/src/*

A Method for Loading Image Assets: .loadImageAssets()

Open your empty loadImageAssets() method structure to add five Image() constructor methods, instantiating and loading your Image objects with the correct image asset and its specifications, as shown highlighted in Figure 9-7.

Figure 9-7. *Instantiate and reference your five Image objects inside of the loadImageAssets() method you just created*

The Java code, shown in Figure 9-7, should look like this:

```
splashScreen = new Image("/welcome.png", 1280, 640, true, false, true);
helpLayer = new Image("/instructions.png", 1280, 640, true, false, true);
legalLayer = new Image("/copyrights.png", 1280, 640, true, false, true);
creditLayer = new Image("/credits.png", 1280, 640, true, false, true);
scoreLayer = new Image("/highscores.png", 1280, 640, true, false, true);
```

What this constructor method format does is to load the Image with the digital image asset in your JAR file, referenced using the "root" or forward slash character, since the file is in the /src/ folder. The second and third entries represent the image **X and Y resolution**, and the fourth true entry turns on **aspect ratio locking**. The fifth false entry turns off **bilinear interpolation**, and a sixth true entry turns on **background image loading**, as a speed optimization.

A Method for Creating Text Assets: .createTextAssets()

Open your empty createTextAssets() method structure and add eight Text() constructor methods, instantiating and loading your Text objects with correct information. The code, shown in Figure 9-8, should look something like this:

```
playText = new Text("Press the Start Game Button to Start! \n");
moreText = new Text("Use other buttons for instructions, copyrights, credits and high scores.");
helpText = new Text("To play game roll dice, advance gamepiece, follow gameboard instruction.");
cardText = new Text("If you land on square that requires card draw it will appear in UI area.");
copyText = new Text("Copyright 2015 Wallace Jackson, All Rights Reserved. \n");
riteText = new Text("Visit the iTVboardGame.com website on the Internet: www.iTVboardGame.com");
credText = new Text("Digital Imaging, 3D Modeling, 3D Texture Mapping, by Wallace Jackson. \n");
codeText = new Text("Game Design, User Interface Design, Java Programming by Wallace Jackson.");
```

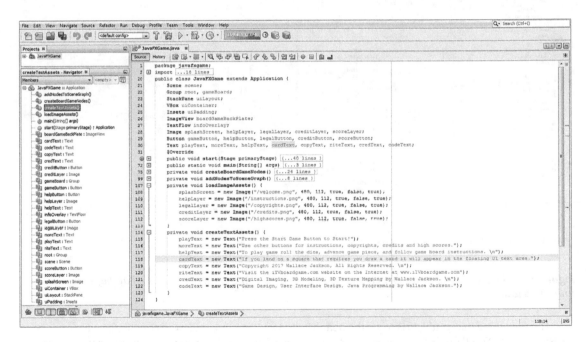

Figure 9-8. *Declare eight Text objects at top of class; instantiate and load Text objects in the createTextAssets() method*

The next thing you may want to do is to make the Button Controls uniform in width, which you'll accomplish by using a Button.setMaxWidth() method. When you upgrade your Scene object constructor to support iTV 1280x720, you'll be able to see the TOP_RIGHT Pos constant in action, and a uniform block of buttons will look more professional.

Using a Button.setMaxWidth() Method: Making Buttons Uniform

The first thing that you will need to do is to set the scene Scene object to an iTV width of 1280 and a height of 640 so that you are using a wide 2:1 aspect ratio and have the minimum supported iTV screen resolution for your pro Java 9 game application. As you can see in Figure 9-9, I upgraded the Scene() constructor method to use these new application window screen dimensions in the following Java code, shown on line 83 at the top of Figure 9-9:

```
scene = new Scene(root, 1280, 640);
```

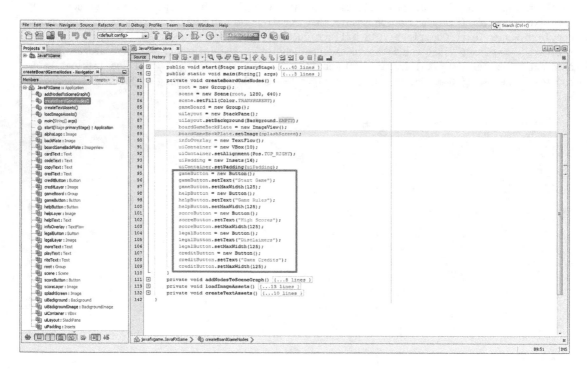

Figure 9-9. *Use the .setMaxWidth() method call to set your Button UI objects to 125 so that they have a uniform width*

The next thing that you'll do is to set the boardGameBackPlate ImageView to contain the welcome message image. You'll do this using a **.setImage()** method with the splashScreen Image, using this code on line 89 in Figure 9-9:

```
boardGameBackPlate.setImage(splashScreen);
```

Finally, to make the Button objects 125 pixels in uniform width, use the **.setMaxWidth(125)** method call, called off of each of the five Button UI objects (as shown in Figure 9-9, on code lines 97, 100, 103, 106, and 109).

I configured the VBox to space its children out by 10 pixels, placing a value of 10 in the **VBox(10)** constructor method call. I increased the Insets() spacing value to **Insets(16)**. Run the project to view the changes, shown in Figure 9-10.

Figure 9-10. *Use the Run ➤ Project work processing to see your Button bank design improvements in spacing and width*

Next, copy the backplate8.png and alphalogo.png image assets to the source folder, as shown in Figure 9-11.

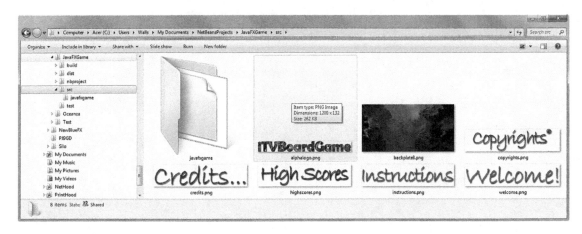

Figure 9-11. *Use your file management utility to copy the backplate8.png and alphalogo.png assets to your / src folder*

225

Next, let's use the Background Image capability of the StackPane. Currently we're using the EMPTY constant from the Background class, so let's replace that with a BackgroundImage object, which your Background class will also support. Let's take a look at how to wire this up next so we can optimize your SceneGraph further by using an unused feature (a StackPane background) rather than by adding another ImageView object, which most will be inclined to do.

Using StackPane Background: Leverage All Compositing Layers

The JavaFX StackPane class supports a **.setBackground(Background background)** method call, which, in turn, supports a BackgroundImage object, which can be loaded with an Image object or used with the EMPTY constant. This means you can reference an image asset in the background of a StackPane UI layout container object, so let's take a look at how to use this to your advantage so that you have five compositing layers (Stage background, Scene background, ImageView, TextFlow, StackPane) you can utilize, using only the nodes you have added to the Scene Graph. All these are currently set to EMPTY or TRANSPARENT or contain a PNG32 with alpha. Add the backPlate and alphaLogo object names to your existing Image declaration compound Java statement at the top of the class, using the following code:

```
Image splashScreen, helpLayer, legalLayer, creditLayer, scoreLayer, backPlate, alphaLogo;
```

Next, declare a **BackgroundImage** object named **uiBackgroundImage** at the top of your class and use Alt+Enter to have NetBeans 9 write your import statement for you. Next, add a **Background** object named **uiBackground** (notice that the Background class was already imported during Chapter 6, so you can utilize the Background.EMPTY constant) at the top of your JavaFXGame class, as shown in the following Java code, as well as highlighted in Figure 9-12:

```
BackgroundImage uiBackgroundImage;  // Object Declaration at the top of the JavaFXGame class
Background uiBackground;             //  Object Declaration at the top of the JavaFXGame class
```

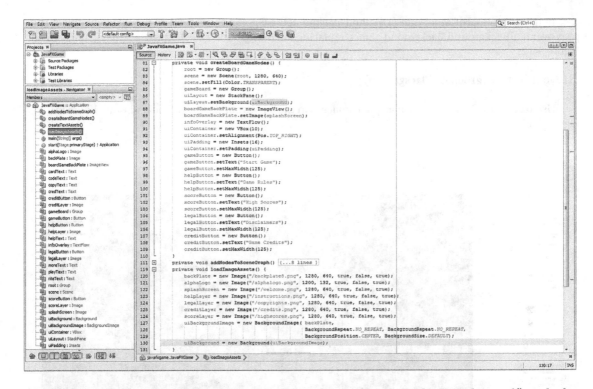

Figure 9-12. *Add a backgroundImage object named uiBackgroundImage; use the .setBackground() method to load it*

In the beginning of the loadImageAssets() method, instantiate the **backPlate** and **alphaLogo** Image objects and then load them with their associated digital image assets using the following Java code, as shown in Figure 9-12:

```
backPlate = new Image("/backplate8.png", 1280, 640, true, false, true);
alphaLogo = new Image("/alphalogo.png",  1200, 132, true, false, true);
```

At the end of this same loadImageAssets() method, instantiate your uiBackgroundImage object and load it with the backplate Image object, which we will use as an optimized, 8-bit PNG8 background image for the composite splash screen image we're creating using Node subclasses (StackPane, ImageView, and VBox); you can do this using the following Java code, also shown in Figure 9-12:

```
uiBackgroundImage = new BackgroundImage(backPlate,
                          BackgroundRepeat.NO_REPEAT, BackgroundRepeat.NO_REPEAT,
                          BackgroundPosition.CENTER, BackgroundSize.DEFAULT);
```

Finally, you will need to instantiate the uiBackground Background object and, using its constructor method, load it with the uiBackgroundImage BackgroundImage object you just created in the previous line of Java code. This would be done using the following line of code, shown highlighted in the loadImageAssets() method in Figure 9-12:

```
uiBackground = new Background(uiBackgroundImage);
```

In the createBoardGameNodes() method, call the .setBackground() method off the uiLayout object and pass over a uiBackground Background object, replacing the Background.EMPTY constant, using the code in Figure 9-12:

```
uiLayout.setBackground(uiBackground);
```

Use **Run ➤ Project** to see if a backplate image is in the background of your StackPane, as shown in Figure 9-13.

Figure 9-13. *Use the Run ➤ Run Project (JavaFXGame) menu sequence to test your new compositing pipeline Java code*

Now we're ready to add your text layer into your compositing pipeline using the TextFlow and Text objects.

Using TextFlow: Setting Up Your Information Overlay Object

Open your createTextAssets() method, add two method calls off of each of the playText and moreText objects, make sure that they use the **Color.WHITE** constant to fill the font, and select a widely supported **Helvetica** font, using its REGULAR font face and setting a large **50** pixels for the font height. Use the **FontPosture** helper class (font face constants) to set the playText and moreText objects to use the regular font style. Add the escape newline, or \n character sequence, inside of the moreText object to split it into two lines. The new Text objects configuration highlighted in the middle of Figure 9-14 should look like the following Java code:

```
playText = new Text("Press the Start Game Button to Start! \n");
playText.setFill(Color.WHITE);
playText.setFont(Font.font("Helvetica", FontPosture.REGULAR, 50));
moreText = new Text("Use other buttons for instructions, \n copyrights, credits and scores.");
moreText.setFill(Color.WHITE);
moreText.setFont(Font.font("Helvetica", FontPosture.REGULAR, 50));
```

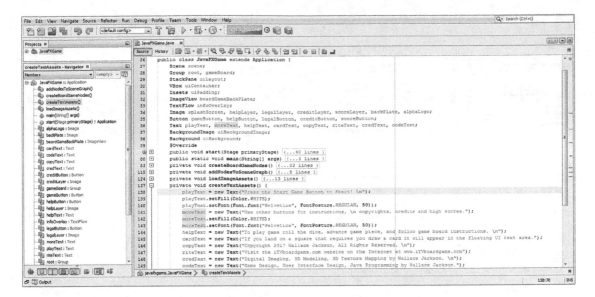

***Figure 9-14.** Add .setFill() and .setFont() methods to your SplashScreen text*

Open the createBoardGameNodes() method, and after your infoOverlay object instantiation, add a line of code and call the .setTranslate X() method with a value of 240 off of the infoOverlay object. Then add another line of code and call the .setTranslateY() method with a value of 420. This will position the TextFlow container underneath the ImageView object (currently a welcome message) so that your block of composited text will be at the bottom of the screen. The Java code for these statements should look like the following (and are shown highlighted in Figure 9-15):

```
infoOverlay.setTranslateX(240);
infoOverlay.setTranslateY(420);
```

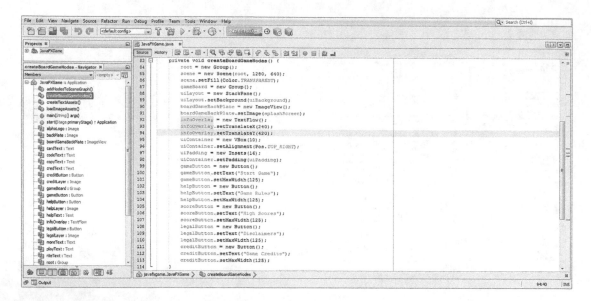

Figure 9-15. *Add Text objects to your TextFlow object and .setTranslateX() and .setTranslateY()*

Open the addNodesToStackPane() method. At the end of the method add an infoOverlay object and call the .getChildren().addAll() method, with the playText and moreText objects separated by commas, as shown in Figure 9-16.

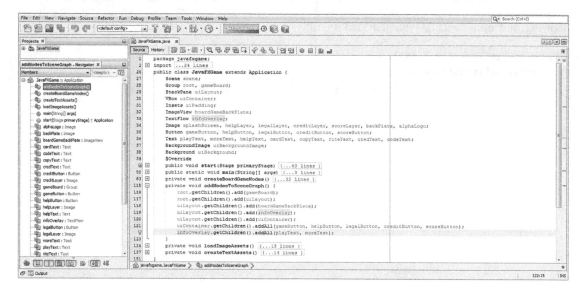

Figure 9-16. *Add infoOverlay object to end of .addNodesToSceneGraph() and use .addAll() to add playText and moreText objects to infoOverlay*

The Java code for this statement should look like the following and is shown highlighted in Figure 9-16:

```
infoOverlay.getChildren().addAll(playText, moreText);
```

As you can see in Figure 9-17, the white text objects look cool, and your image compositing pipeline looks as if it is being created using professional digital imaging software. Next, let's add an image compositing layer for a logo.

Figure 9-17. *Run the project and check the result of adding a TextFlow object to the splash screen compositing pipeline*

This UI design is starting to look more professional, with the Buttons positioned over the outcropping of the rock and the "Welcome!" text centered in the screen design. However, the UI design still needs a branding logo, and there is an extra space pushing the third line to the right that needs to be fixed (removed). Let's do this in the next section.

Using StackPane: Add More Digital Image Compositing Layers

Let's add another ImageView object declaration named logoLayer at the top of the JavaFXGame class, turning the ImageView declaration into an **ImageView boardGameBackPlate, logoLayer;** compound Java statement. Open your createBoardGameNodes() method, add an object instantiation for this object, and then a .setImage() method call wiring this to the alphaLogo Image object you created earlier when you imported this digital image asset. Next, you will add two method calls off of the logoLayer object, one for X scaling and one for Y scaling, using the same 80 percent value of 0.8, so that we **lock the aspect ratio** (also called **uniform scaling**) for this scaling operation. Finally, you will move the logo up the y-axis 225 pixels from the center of the screen, using a **-225** value, as StackPane uses a 0,0 center screen referencing model rather than the standard 0,0 upper-left corner pixel referencing model. We will also pull the logo 75 pixels back toward the left using an

X translation value of -75 pixels. The new logoLayer ImageView object instantiation, asset referencing, and transformation (location/translation and scale) configuration code can be seen highlighted in the middle of Figure 9-18 and should look like this following Java 9 code statement block:

```
logoLayer = new ImageView();
logoLayer.setImage(alphaLogo);
logoLayer.setScaleX(0.8);
logoLayer.setScaleY(0.8);
logoLayer.setTranslateX(-75);
logoLayer.setTranslateY(-225);
```

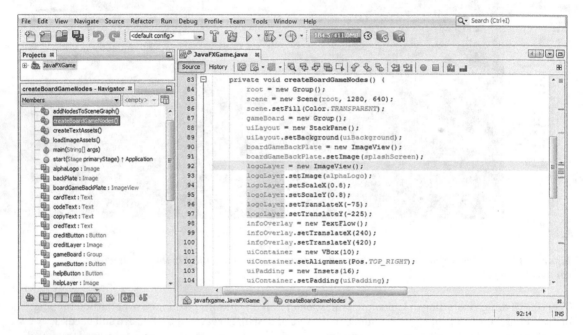

Figure 9-18. *Create a logoLayer ImageView referencing the alphaLogo image; set scale to 80 percent and position to -75,-225*

Next, you'll have to add this new logoLayer ImageView to the StackPane uiLayout container of compositing layers in your addNodesToSceneGraph() method. While we're there, since we are adding multiple Node subclasses to the root and uiLayout SceneGraph hierarchy, we'll switch from using the .getChildren().add() method chain to using a .getChildren().addAll() method chain to reduce the number of Java statements in this method from eight to four.

The order added affects the compositing layer order, so for .add() statements, this equates to top to bottom. The first statements added (top) are on the bottom of the compositing layer stack (sort of counterintuitive, isn't it?).

With the .addAll() method, this changes to become left to right, so the objects added first (left) are on the bottom of the compositing layer stack. A new addNodesToStackPane() method structure using .getChildren().addAll() method calls would therefore look like the following, as shown highlighted at the bottom of Figure 9-19:

```
private void addNodesToSCeneGraph() {
    root.getChildren().addAll(gameBoard, uiLayout);
    uiLayout.getChildren().addAll(boardGameBackPlate, logoLayer, infoOverlay, uiContainer);
    uiContainer.getChildren().addAll(gameButton, helpButton, legalButton,
                                     creditButton, scoreButton);
    infoOverlay.getChildren().addAll(playText, moreText);
}
```

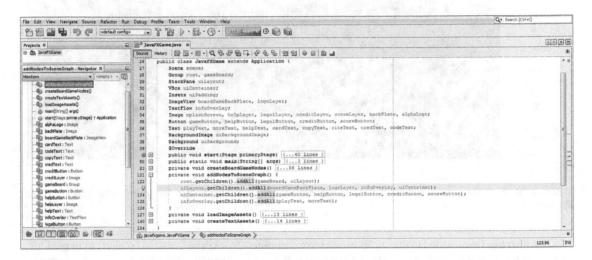

Figure 9-19. *Consolidate six .add() method calls into two .addAll() method calls off of a SceneGraph root and UI branch*

As you can see in Figure 9-20, I have added the logo and fixed the text paragraph (left) alignment, removing that space after the\n, which is counterintuitive because it leaves\ncopyrights and there is no escape ncopyrights. You as a Java programmer would need to know in this situation that the compiler will look at the escape (\) character, and only one letter thereafter (in this case n or newline), and then continue parsing characters as part of your text content.

Figure 9-20. *Run the project and check the result of adding ImageView object to the splash screen compositing pipeline*

The logo has been added to the compositing layer container (StackPane), resized (scaled) to fit next to the Button bank, and moved up (translated) to center with your Button bank. This all looks well-balanced and professional; it uses very few nodes in the SceneGraph and very few objects in system memory, so it's optimized.

Since we're not using the transparency (trick) that I showed you back in Chapter 7 for this UI, let's replace the OS chrome by reverting to the default DECORATED StageStyle class constant, which I could do by removing the primaryStage.initStyle() method call. Instead, I will leave that Java statement in place and change the TRANSPARENT constant use to a DECORATION constant use in case we want to decorate the Stage object differently in the future. This is done by changing this line of code, shown in line 46 in Figure 9-21, to the following Java code:

primaryStage.**initStyle**(StageStyle.**DECORATED**);

Figure 9-21. *Revert to StageStyle.DECORATED and add an iTVBoardGame (JavaFX 9 Game) title for your OS window*

Next, add your title for your OS window chrome by replacing the "Hello World" placeholder text from the bootstrap code that was created for you in Chapter 6. I'm going to use **iTVBoardGame** to match the 3D logo and add "JavaFX 9 Game" using parentheses to clarify to the user what platform this application is built on. The code for doing this is shown in orange in Figure 9-21 above the .initStyle() method and should look like the following Java statement:

```
primaryStage.setTitle("iTVBoardGame (JavaFX 9 Game)");
```

As you can see in Figure 9-22, we now have an initial application startup splash screen with logo, background image, user interface button bank, and sectional title image layer. In the case of the splash screen, this is "Welcome!"

Figure 9-22. *Run the project to make sure the OS chrome has been replaced and the window title is in place and correct*

The only thing that we have left to do is to finish implementing the Image objects for the other four sections and implement font style and color in the other four TextFlow objects. All of these objects will be called in your event-handling code, which we'll be adding in Chapter 10 (which covers event handling and effects in JavaFX 9 and Java 9 games).

After all of this 2D screen design and UI design and event handling has been coded, we can start getting into 3D and i3D during the second half of the book.

Finishing Up Your UI Design Object Creation and Configuration

Let's open your createTextAssets() method and add the .setFill() and .setFont() method calls off of the other six Text objects to set their color to match the boardGameBackPlate ImageView that holds the handwriting text images and to set their Font style to Helvetica Regular. This is a relatively straightforward exercise; the resulting method body is shown in Figure 9-23 and should look like the following Java method body and Java statements:

```java
private void createTextAssets(){
    playText = new Text("Press the PLAY GAME Button to Start!\n");
    playText.setFill(Color.WHITE);
    playText.setFont(Font.font("Helvetica", FontPosture.REGULAR, 50));
    moreText = new Text("Use other buttons for instructions,\ncopyrights, credits and
scores.");
    moreText.setFill(Color.WHITE);
    moreText.setFont(Font.font("Helvetica", FontPosture.ITALIC, 50));
    helpText = new Text("To play game roll the dice, advance\ngame piece and
                        follow game board\ninstructions. ");
    helpText.setFill(Color.GREEN);
```

```
        helpText.setFont(Font.font("Helvetica", FontPosture.REGULAR, 50));
        cardText = new Text("If you land on a square\nthat requires you draw a card, it
                             will\nappear in the floating UI text area.");
        cardText.setFill(Color.GREEN);
        cardText.setFont(Font.font("Helvetica", FontPosture.REGULAR, 50));
        copyText = new Text("Copyright 2015 Wallace Jackson.\nAll Rights Reserved.\n");
        copyText.setFill(Color.PURPLE);
        copyText.setFont(Font.font("Helvetica", FontPosture.REGULAR, 50));
        riteText = new Text("Visit the iTVboardGame.com website on\nthe Internet
                             at www.iTVboardgame.com");
        riteText.setFill(Color.PURPLE);
        riteText.setFont(Font.font("Helvetica", FontPosture.REGULAR, 50));
        credText = new Text("Digital Imaging, 3D Modeling, 3D\nTexture Mapping
                             by Wallace Jackson.\n");
        credText.setFill(Color.BLUE);
        credText.setFont(Font.font("Helvetica", FontPosture.REGULAR, 50));
        codeText = new Text("Game Design, User Interface Design,\nJava Programming
                             by Wallace Jackson.");
        codeText.setFill(Color.BLUE);
        codeText.setFont(Font.font("Helvetica", FontPosture.REGULAR, 50));
}
```

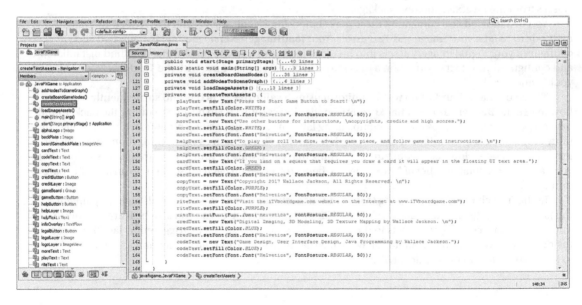

Figure 9-23. *Finish configuring your Text objects using .setFill() and .setFont() methods with Color and Helvetica values*

You have made a lot of progress toward putting together your professional Java game splash screen design, user interface design, and top-level SceneGraph and class (and method) infrastructure during this chapter. You have also learned about the Image, ImageView, Text, TextFlow, Background, and BackgroundImage classes. Pat yourself on the back, if you are that flexible, and then take a little break from Java 9 programming!

You are by no means finished with this user interface design part of your pro Java 9 game development. Be prepared to refine it even more later in the book, when we make it interactive (Chapter 10) and make it a 2D plane when we convert your now 2D Scene into a 3D Scene by adding a PerspectiveCamera to the Scene root (Chapter 11), all of which will necessitate changes to the StackPane object compositing layer pipeline attributes as well as to the coordinate referencing system. As I said, this book is going to get more and more complex with each chapter, until your knowledge of Java 9 and JavaFX and NetBeans 9 is good enough to create any i3D game design you can imagine!

Summary

In this ninth chapter, you added even more code to your **JavaFXGame.java** class by adding to the compositing pipeline for your actual **top-level user interface design** for your game using the JavaFX Image, ImageView, Background, BackgroundImage, Text, and TextFlow classes. The first thing that you did was to finish the JavaFX Scene Graph hierarchy design, which I visualized in Figure 9-1, showing how the SceneGraph uses one root Node object, three branch Node objects, and seven leaf Node objects (five Button objects, one ImageView object, and one TextFlow object). Later, you will add more branch and leaf Node objects for the 3D part of the game, primarily to hold 3D objects (primitives) offered by JavaFX or your own 3D mesh geometry. During the chapter you added a second ImageView node for logo compositing.

Next, you learned about some of the JavaFX classes that we were going to implement in these new methods during this chapter as well as the next one. These included the **Image** class, as well as the **ImageView** class, both from the **javafx.scene.image** package. You also looked at the **Text** and **TextFlow** classes from the **javafx.scene.text** package.

You instantiated and configured these new compositing Node objects and then coded two new methods to handle your Image and Text assets. Your **loadImageAssets()** method instantiated and configured your digital imagery assets into Image objects, and a **createTextAssets()** method instantiated and configured your text information assets into Text objects for later use with the TextFlow Node object in your Scene Graph.

Then you made your Button widths uniform using a **value of 125 pixels** and subsequently learned how to use the **Background** and **BackgroundImage** classes (objects) to be able to utilize the background property of the StackPane as another compositing layer in your compositing pipeline without adding any more Node objects to your JavaFX Scene Graph hierarchy. This reinforces my optimization approach for pro Java games development of utilizing everything that each Node in your Scene Graph gives you so that you can keep the total number of Nodes that are being traversed on each pulse event to an absolute bare minimum.

In the next chapter, you are going to learn about event handling classes in JavaFX and implement the Java code inside of your ActionEvent EventHandler program logic. You will also be learning how to implement some cool special effects in the process, as some of these will be triggered by Java 9 statements, inside of your event handlers. After that, we will be getting into 3D and the classes and assets you will need to know about to enter the realm of 3D.

CHAPTER 10

■ ■ ■

User Interface Design Interactivity: Event Handling and Imaging Effects

Now that you have finished the Scene Graph hierarchy for the splash screen and user interface design, let's get back into our **JavaFXGame** primary application class coding here in Chapter 10 and finish implementing the **event handling** framework that you have in place but that is essentially "empty" (except for a few System. out.println calls to test your Button Control Node objects). The Java and JavaFX event handling that we will take an overview of during this chapter will implement the user interface that the player will use to learn about and start your Java 9 game. During the book you will use other types of event handling (keystroke and mouse) that we will look at during this chapter. You will be adding Java game UI programming logic that could be looked at as an **interactivity engine** for your game. There are many ways to interface with a game, including **arrow keys**, known as the **DPAD** (direction pad) for consumer electronics devices and modern remote controls; a **keyboard**; a **mouse**; a **trackball**; a **game controller**; a **touchscreen**; or even advanced hardware, including **gyroscopes** and **accelerometers**. One of the important choices that you will make for your pro Java 9 game development will be how your players will **interface** with your Java game using hardware devices that they are playing your game on and the **hardware input capabilities** the game supports.

During this chapter you will be learning about the different types of JavaFX event types that are contained in the **javafx.event**, javafx.scene.input, and the **java.util** packages. You will cover **ActionEvent** since you are using this in your user interface design currently, as well as **Input Events** such as **MouseEvent** and **KeyEvent**.

Besides continuing to work on your JavaFXGame Java code by adding event handling, you'll be learning about **JavaFX Special Effects** during this chapter, just to make sure I cover everything that is cool in Java during this book. These JavaFX special effects are stored in the **javafx.scene.effect** package and give JavaFX, and thus Java, a lot of the same special effects advantages that a digital image compositing software package such as GIMP gives you.

Event Handling: Adding Interactivity to Your Games

One could argue that event handing is the foundation of game development. This is because if you don't have a way to interface with gameplay logic and game elements, you really don't have much of a game. I'm going to cover JavaFX event handling classes during this section of the chapter, and you will implement your ActionEvent handing structures so that your users can utilize your user interface that you have been designing over the past several chapters. The first thing I want to talk about before we start dissecting

Java and JavaFX packages, classes, interfaces, and methods is the different types of input hardware events that can be handled for pro Java games. These can be generated using the arrow keys on your iTV remote or smartphone DPAD, to your keyboard, to your mouse or trackball, and to the touchscreen on your smartphone and tablet or iTV set. There is also custom input hardware, including game controllers on game consoles and now on iTV sets, gyroscopes and accelerometers in smartphones and tablets, and freeform hand gesture and motion controllers such as the Leap Motion, VR Glove, and Razer Hydra Portal.

Types of Controllers: What Types of Events Should We Handle?

One of the key things to look at is what is the most logical approach to supporting gameplay-related events, such as arrow keys, mouse clicks, touchscreen events, game controller buttons (A, B, C, and D), and more advanced controllers, such as gyroscopes and accelerometers available on Android, Kindle, Tizen, HTML5 OS, and iOS consumer electronics devices. This decision will be driven by the hardware devices that a game is targeted to run on; if a game needs to run everywhere, then code for handling different event types, and even different programming approaches to event handling, will ultimately be required. We will be taking a closer look at what input events are currently supported in Java and JavaFX during this section of the chapter to give you an overview for your game development.

It is also interesting to note that Java and JavaFX apps can already be run on two popular embedded platforms, Android and iOS, and I would put money on **native support** on **open source platforms** (Opera, Tizen, Chrome, Ubuntu, and Firefox) and proprietary platforms that currently support Java 8 or 9 technology (Windows, Samsung Bada, RIM Blackberry, LG WebOS, OpenSolaris) at some point in the near future. The future of Java 9 is bright, thanks to JavaFX, the momentum of the Java platform over several decades, and new advanced i3D hardware platform support!

Java and JavaFX Event Packages: java.util and javafx.event

As you have seen in your event handling structure's **new EventHandler<ActionEvent>** declaration, the **javafx.event** package's **EventHandler** public interface, which extends the **java.util** package's **EventListener** interface, is the way that **Event** objects are created and handled, either using an anonymous inner class (Java 7) structure, which we are using as it is compatible with Android, or using a lambda expression (Java 8). You have become familiar now with how to code this type of event handling structure, and I will continue during this book to code methods using the Java anonymous inner class approach. That said, you can mouse over the wavy yellow underline highlight under any Java 7 code and have NetBeans 9 convert it to use a more streamlined Java 8 lambda expression. In this way, you can create games that are compatible with Java 7 (64-bit Android 5 and 6), Java 8 (64-bit Android 7 and 8), and Java 9 (PC OSs and future versions of Android) game code delivery pipelines. In this section, we will look at ActionEvent and InputEvent EventObject subclass categories so that you have an understanding of what the major events are in JavaFX. These come from the java.util.EventObject superclass, and we will take a look at how they would be applied to handling actions, keystrokes, mouse events, touch events, and similar advanced input event types.

JavaFX ActionEvent Class: Created from the java.util.EventObject Superclass

The **ActionEvent** class (and objects) that you've used thus far during the book for your user interface Button control event handling is a subclass of the **javafx.event** package's **Event** superclass, which is itself a subclass of the **java.util** package's **EventObject** superclass, which is a subclass of the java.lang.Object master class.

This class also has one known direct subclass, the MediaMarkerEvent class. The class hierarchy structure therefore looks like the following:

```
java.lang.Object
   > java.util.EventObject
      > javafx.event.Event
         > javafx.event.ActionEvent
```

The ActionEvent class is contained in the **javafx.event** package along with the EventHandler public interface. An ActionEvent object, as you might have guessed, is an Event object that represents some type of action. This type of Event object can be used to represent a wide variety of things. As you have seen, it is used when a Button has been fired and is also used, for instance, when a KeyFrame has finished playing and in other similar internal software usage. The ActionEvent was introduced to JavaFX in version 2.0 and was not available in the JavaFX 1.*x* versions (1.0 to 1.3). It remains in JavaFX 7 for Java 7 (both now discontinued), in JavaFX 8 for Java 8, and now in JavaFX 9 for Java 9.

There are two data fields (attributes) of an ActionEvent object. The first is a static EventType<ActionEvent> ACTION characteristic, which is the only valid EventType for the ActionEvent. There is also, however, a supertype for an ActionEvent object that takes the form of static EventType<ActionEvent> ANY that provides developers with a common supertype that is able to represent **all action event types**. Thus, if you want your Java code to process *any* ActionEvent object, use this data field, and if you want your Java code to process specific ActionEvent objects, use the ACTION data field.

There are also two constructor methods supported by this ActionEvent class. The default empty parameter list **ActionEvent()** constructor method creates a new ActionEvent object with the default event type of **ACTION**. There is also an **ActionEvent(Object source, EventTarget target)** constructor method, which will create the new ActionEvent with the specified event Object source and EventTarget target.

There are also two methods supported by this ActionEvent class. The first is an **ActionEvent copyFor(Object newSource, EventTarget newTarget)** method, which is used to create and return a copy of the event using a specified event source and target. The second is an **EventType<? extends ActionEvent> getEventType()** method, which will get the event type for the event object that it has been called off of.

All the other event-related classes that we'll be using for the i3D component of the gameplay are contained in the **javafx.scene.input** package. I'm going to focus on the javafx.scene.input package for the rest of this section, as you have already learned how to code your **new EventHandler<ActionEvent> { ... }** structure for Java 7. If you instruct NetBeans 9 to turn this into a **Lambda Expression**, it will take the **(ActionEvent) -> { ... }** code structure format for Java 8.

Now it's time to learn how to use other types of events, called *input events*, in your Java game development work process. Let's take a look at the **javafx.scene.input** package and its 25 input event-related classes.

JavaFX Input Event Classes: The javafx.scene.input Package

Even though the java.util and **javafx.event** packages contain the core **EventObject**, **Event**, and **EventHandler** classes that "handle" your events, at the foundational level of making sure that the events get processed (handled), there is another JavaFX package called **javafx.scene.input** that contains the classes that you'll be interested in using to process (handle) your player's input for the different types of games that you might be creating. These are called *input events*, and they are different events than the ActionEvents and pulse events, which you learned about already.

It's interesting to note that a number of the input event types that are supported in the javafx.scene. input package are more suited to consumer electronics (the industry term is *embedded*) devices such as smartphones and tablets. This tells me that JavaFX is being positioned (designed) for use on open source platforms, such as Android OS, Firefox OS, Tizen OS, Bada OS, Opera OS, Ubuntu OS, or Chrome OS. JavaFX 9 has "specialized" events, such as **GestureEvent**, **SwipeEvent**, **TouchEvent**, and **ZoomEvent**, that support specific features in the new embedded devices marketplace. These input event classes support advanced touchscreen device features, such as gestures, page swiping, touchscreen input handling, and multitouch display features, such as two-finger "pinching" or "spreading" touch input, for instance, for zooming in and out of the content on the screen, respectively.

We will be covering the more "universal" input types in this book, which are supported across both personal computers (desktops, laptops, notebooks, netbooks, and the newer "pro" tablets, such as the Surface Pro 4) and embedded devices, including smartphones, tablets, e-readers, iTV sets, game consoles, home media centers, set-top boxes (STBs), and so forth. These devices will also process these more widespread (in their implementation) **KeyEvent** and **MouseEvent** types of input events, as mouse events and key events will always be supported for legacy software packages. For example, mouse click events are supported by touchscreens, but touchscreen events are not supported with positioning devices (mouse, trackball, controller, DPAD, etc.). So if you can, use keyboard and mouse events!

It is interesting to note that a touchscreen display will "handle" mouse events as well as touch events, which is quite convenient as far as making sure that your game works across as many different platforms as possible. I often use this approach of using mouse event handling in my Android books so that both the touchscreen and a DPAD center (click) button can be used by the user to generate a mouse click event, without having to specifically use touch events. Another advantage of using mouse (click) events, when possible, for touchscreen users is that if you use touch events, you cannot go in the other direction. That is, your game application will only work on touchscreen devices and not on devices (such as iTV sets, laptops, desktops, netbooks, and the like) that feature mouse hardware of some type.

This same principle applies to key events, especially the arrow keys developers use for their games, as these keys can be found on the arrow keypad on keyboards and remote controls, on game controllers, and on the DPAD on most smartphones. I will also show you how to include **alternate key mappings** so that your player can decide which input method they prefer to use to play your pro Java 9 game. Let's take a look at KeyCode and KeyEvent classes next.

The KeyCode Class: Using Enum Constants to Define Keys Players Use for Game

Since a lot of games use the **arrow keypad** for navigation (usually the **A, S, D, and W** keys) and sometimes use alternate mappings for these to the game controller's **GAME_A**, **GAME_B**, **GAME_C**, and **GAME_D** buttons, let's take a closer look at the JavaFX **KeyCode** class first. This class is a public **Enum** class, which holds **enumerated constant** values for keys that are evaluated when a key is pressed or released. This class is where the **KeyEvent** class goes to get the keycode constant values that it uses (processes) to determine which key was used by the player for any particular key event invocation. The Java and JavaFX class hierarchy for the KeyCode class will look like the following:

```
java.lang.Object
  > java.lang.Enum<KeyCode>
    > javafx.scene.input.KeyCode
```

The constant values contained in the KeyCode class use **capital letters** and are named after the key that the keycode supports. For instance, a, s, w, and d keycodes are **A**, **S**, **W**, and **D**. The arrow keypad keycodes are **UP**, **DOWN**, **LEFT**, and **RIGHT**, and the game controller button keycodes are **GAME_A**, **GAME_B**, **GAME_C**, and **GAME_D**.

You will be implementing KeyCode constants along with the KeyEvent object in an EventHandler object later in this book, so I am covering these event-related packages and classes for input event handling here. As you'll see, this is done in much the same way that an ActionEvent is set up to be handled. Your KeyEvents can also be coded using the Java 7 inner class approach or via Java 8 lambda expressions. Your KeyEvent object handling should be done in a **modular** fashion so your KeyCode evaluation structure sets Boolean flag variables for each KeyCode mapping. The Boolean flags will provide an accurate view of what keys are being pressed, or released, by a player in any millisecond.

These Boolean values can then be read and acted upon by using Java game programming logic in your other game engine classes, which will then process these key events in real time so that your pro Java gameplay works well and your user experience is good. Next, let's take a look at the KeyEvent objects that process these KeyCode objects.

The KeyEvent Class: Using KeyEvent Objects to Hold KeyCode Constants

Next, let's take a closer look at the **KeyEvent** class. This class is designated **public final KeyEvent**, and it extends the **InputEvent** superclass, which is used to create all of the input event subclasses that are in the javafx.scene.input package. The KeyEvent class is set into motion using the EventHandler class and handles **KeyCode** class constant values. This class's hierarchy starts with the java.lang.Object master class and goes through the java.util.EventObject event superclass to the **javafx.event.Event** class, which is used to create the javafx.scene.input.InputEvent class that the KeyEvent class extends (subclasses). It is interesting to note that we are spanning **four different packages** here.

The Java and JavaFX class hierarchy for the KeyEvent class jumps from the java.lang package to the java.util package to the **javafx.event** package to the javafx.scene.input package. A KeyEvent hierarchy looks like the following:

```
java.lang.Object
  > java.util.EventObject
    > javafx.event.Event
      > javafx.scene.input.InputEvent
        > javafx.scene.input.KeyEvent
```

The generation of a KeyEvent object by an EventHandler object indicates that a keystroke has occurred. This KeyEvent is often generated using one of your Scene Graph Node objects such as an editable text UI control; however, in the case of your game, you're probably going to attach the key event handling above the Scene Graph Node object hierarchy level directly to the Scene object named scene. This will serve to minimize the Scene Graph pulse processing overhead by not attaching any KeyEvent handling to any of the Node objects in your Scene Graph. In the case of your game, this is the root Group object containing the uiLayout StackPane object and the gameBoard Group object.

A KeyEvent object is generated whenever a key is **pressed** and held down, **released**, or **typed** (pressed and immediately released). Depending on the nature of this key pressing action itself, your KeyEvent object is passed into an **.onKeyPressed()**, **.onKeyTyped()**, or **.onKeyReleased()** method for further processing inside a .handle() method.

Games typically use key-pressed and key-released events, as users typically press and hold keys to move the actors in the game. Key-typed events on the other hand tend to be "higher-level" events and generally do not depend upon the OS platform or the keyboard layout. Typed key events (.onKeyTyped() method calls) will be generated when a Unicode character is entered. They are used to obtain character input for UI controls such as text fields and are used for business applications, such as calendars, calculators, e-mail clients, and word processors, for instance.

In a simple case, the key-typed event will be produced by using a single key press and its immediate release. Additionally, alternate characters can be produced using combinations of key press events. For instance, a capital A is produced using a Shift key press and an "a" key-type (press and immediate release).

A key-release is not usually necessary to generate a key-typed KeyEvent object. It is important to notice that there are some fringe cases where a key-typed event is not generated until the key is released; a great example of this is the process of entering **ASCII character code sequences** using that old-school

Alt-key-with-numeric-keypad entry method that was used "back in the day" with DOS and held over into Windows OSs. It is important to note that no key-typed KeyEvent objects will be generated for computer keyboard keys that do not generate Unicode (visible, printable) characters, such as the Shift, Control (Ctrl), or Alternate (Alt) keys, commonly referred to as **modifier** keys.

The KeyEvent class has a **character** variable (I am tempted to call this a character characteristic, but I won't) that will always contain a valid **Unicode character** for a key-typed event or **CHAR_UNDEFINED** for a key-pressed or key-released events. Character input is reported only for key-typed events, since key-pressed and key-released events are not necessarily associated with character input. Therefore, your character variable is guaranteed to be meaningful only for key-typed events.

For key-pressed and key-released KeyEvent objects, the **code** variable in the KeyEvent class will contain your KeyEvent object's keycode, defined using the KeyCode class you learned about earlier. For key-typed events, this code variable always contains the constant **KeyCode.UNDEFINED**. So as you can see, key-pressed and key-released are thus designed to be used differently than key-typed, and that is the reason you will probably be using key-pressed and key-released events for game event handling. Key-pressed and key-released events are low level and are generated whenever a given key is pressed or released. They are the only way to "poll" the keys that do not generate character input. Your key being pressed or released is indicated to the OS using the **code** variable, which contains a virtual **KeyCode**.

Adding Keyboard Event Handling: Using KeyEvents

I think that is enough background information for you to understand a basic example of how to implement KeyEvent processing for pro Java games. It's fairly straightforward, so I'm going to give you a quick overview of how it is done here, since we are covering the KeyEvent class. This is also covered in my *Beginning Java 8 Games Development* book. The first thing that you would do is to add a line of code at the top of your JavaFXGame class and declare four Boolean variables, named up, down, left, and right, using a single compound declaration statement, shown here:

```
boolean up, down, left, right;
```

Since the default value of a boolean variable is **false**, this will signify a key that is not being pressed, that is, a key that is currently released, or unused. Since this is also the default state for keys on a keyboard, this would be the correct default value for this application. Since in Java, boolean variables default to false, you do not have to **explicitly initialize** these variables.

I put an event handling foundation for a KeyEvent (key-pressed, in this instance) object in place by using the .setOnKeyPressed() method call off of the Scene object named scene, which I have already instantiated. Inside of this method call, I create the **new EventHandler<KeyEvent>** just like is done for the ActionEvent. The code looks like this:

```
scene.setOnKeyPressed( new EventHandler<KeyEvent>() { a .handle() method will go in here } );
```

KeyEvent object processing just happens to be the perfect application for implementing the highly efficient Java **switch** statement. You can add a **case** for each of the JavaFX KeyCode constants that you want to process. These are contained inside of the KeyEvent object named **event** that is passed into this .handle() method via its parameter area.

The KeyCode is then extracted from the KeyEvent object inside of the switch() evaluation area by using your **.getCode()** method call, off of an **event** KeyEvent object. This can be done by using the following Java switch-case Java code programming structure:

```java
scene.setOnKeyPressed(new EventHandler<KeyEvent>() {
    @Override
    public void handle(KeyEvent event) {
        switch (event.getCode()) {
            case UP:    up    = true; break;
            case DOWN:  down  = true; break;
            case LEFT:  left  = true; break;
            case RIGHT: right = true; break; // No break; statement is needed here, if there
                                             // are no more case statements to be added later
        }
    }
});
```

This will give you the basic **key-pressed** event handling structure, which you can add to your pro Java games and poll these four boolean variables with your code to find out what your user is doing with their arrow keys. If you instruct NetBeans 9 to turn this Java 7 structure into a Java 8 lambda expression for you, you'll get a compact structure. A number of things, such as the **public void handle()** declaration and the **new EventHandler<KeyEvent>()** declaration, will become implied or assumed (but still exist to the compiler) in the lambda expression Java 8 code structure. Using a lambda expression will simplify code, reducing it from a three-deep nested code block to one that is nested only two deep and from eleven lines of code to eight. Lambda expressions can really be elegant for writing tighter code but do not show you everything that is going on with the classes (objects), modifiers, and return types that are being used. This is the reason why I am opting to utilize the more explicit Java 7 (and earlier) code structure, utilized in Java 5 through 7 and prior to the introduction of Lambda Expressions in Java 8. Both approaches are supported in Java 9.

Your resulting Java 8 lambda expression code structure would look like the following Java code structure:

```java
scene.setOnKeyPressed(KeyEvent event) -> {
    switch (event.getCode()) {
        case UP:    up    = true; break;
        case DOWN:  down  = true; break;
        case LEFT:  left  = true; break;
        case RIGHT: right = true; break;
    }
});
```

The next thing that you'll want to do is to create the polar opposite of the OnKeyPressed structure and thus create an OnKeyReleased structure. This will use the same code structure, except the true values would become false values, and the .setOnKeyPressed() method call will instead be a .setOnKeyReleased() method call. The easiest way to do this is to select the .setOnKeyPressed() structure and copy and paste it underneath itself. The Java code would look like the following:

```java
scene.setOnKeyReleased(new EventHandler<KeyEvent>() {
    @Override
    public void handle(KeyEvent event) {
        switch (event.getCode()) {
            case UP:    up    = false; break;
            case DOWN:  down  = false; break;
```

```
                    case LEFT:  left  = false; break;
                    case RIGHT: right = false; break;
            }
        }
});
```

One of the interesting things that using lambda expressions does by "implicitly" declaring and using classes, such as the EventHandler class in the instances in this chapter, is that it **reduces the number of import statements** in the top of your class code. This is because if a class is not specifically used (its name written) in your code, the import statement for that class does not have to be in place at the top of your code with the other import statements. You'll also notice that your code-collapsing plus or minus icons in the left margin of NetBeans 9 will disappear if you convert into the lambda expression. This is because a lambda expression is a basic Java code statement, and not a construct or structure such as an inner class or a method, which is what it was before you converted it to a lambda expression.

Now that you have taken a look at how KeyEvent handling structures would be put in place, let's take a look at how easy it is to add an alternate key mapping to the ASDW keys that are often used in gameplay. This is done by adding in a few more case statements for the A, S, D, and W characters on the keyboard and setting these to the UP, DOWN, LEFT, and RIGHT boolean equivalents (up, down, left, and right variables) that we have set up already.

This will allow users to use the A and D characters with their left hand and the UP and DOWN arrows with their right hand for easier gameplay, for instance. Later if you wanted to add more features to the gameplay using your game controller and its support for the KeyCode class **GAME_A**, **GAME_B**, **GAME_C**, and **GAME_D** constants, all that you will have to do to add these new features into your game would be to add another four boolean variables (a, b, c, and d) to the up, down, left, and right variables at the top of the class and add in another four case statements.

These four W (UP), S (DOWN), A (LEFT), and D (RIGHT) case statements, once added to the switch statement, would make your KeyEvent object and its event-handling Java code look like the following 15 lines of Java code:

```
scene.setOnKeyPressed(new EventHandler<KeyEvent>() {
    @Override
    public void handle(KeyEvent event) {
        switch (event.getCode()) {
            case UP:    up    = true; break;
            case DOWN:  down  = true; break;
            case LEFT:  left  = true; break;
            case RIGHT: right = true; break;
            case W:     up    = true; break;
            case S:     down  = true; break;
            case A:     left  = true; break;
            case D:     right = true; break;
        }
    }
});
```

As you can see, now the user can use either set of keys, or both sets of keys at the same time, to control the gameplay. Now do the same thing to the .setOnKeyReleased() event-handling structure using a copy-and-paste work process and change the value to false. The .setOnKeyReleased() event-handling Java code will look like the following:

```
scene.setOnKeyPressed(new EventHandler<KeyEvent>() {
    @Override
    public void handle(KeyEvent event) {
        switch (event.getCode()) {
            case UP:    up    = false; break;
            case DOWN:  down  = false; break;
            case LEFT:  left  = false; break;
            case RIGHT: right = false; break;
            case W:     up    = false; break;
            case S:     down  = false; break;
            case A:     left  = false; break;
            case D:     right = false; break;
        }
    }
});
```

Next, let's switch back into Java coding mode and implement event handling for your user interface design.

Finishing Your UI Design: Coding the Event Handling

Let's finish your top-level UI design by writing Java statements inside of your ActionEvent EventHandler structures inside of the .handle() method. This method clears and then adds Text objects to the infoOverlay TextFlow object and sets the correct section imagery in your compositing pipeline using the .setBackground() and .setImage() method calls. As you can see in Figure 10-1, I always clear the TextFlow object first using the **.getChildren().clear()** method call, and then I use the **.getChildren.addAll()** method call to add the correct Text objects to the TextFlow object. I then use the .setTranslateX() and .setTranslateY() method calls off the infoOverlay TextFlow to position that container (and layer). After that, I use the **.setBackground()** method call to set the uiLayout VBox object background image (for the SplashScreen) or Background.EMPTY for the other four Button objects, which allows the **Color.WHITE** background color to show through. Finally, I use the **.setImage()** method call to set the boardGameBackPlate ImageView object with the correct Image object. In the case of the Game Rules (Help) Button, this is a helpLayer Image object reference. For the first helpButton event handler, this .handle() method code body would include the following Java statements:

```
helpButton.setOnAction(new EventHandler<ActionEvent>() {
    @Override
    public void handle(ActionEvent event) {
        infoOverlay.getChildren().clear();
        infoOverlay.getChildren().addAll(helpText, cardText);
        infoOverlay.setTranslateX(130);
        infoOverlay.setTranslateY(360);
        uiLayout.setBackground(Background.EMPTY);
        boardGameBackPlate.setImage(helpLayer);
    }
} );
```

Figure 10-1. *Implement the code in the handle() method to reconfigure your helpButton UI compositing layer objects*

Now when you use your **Run ➤ Project** work process, the Game Rules Button UI control will trigger the user interface design that is optimized for showing your game players your instruction (help) screen, as shown in Figure 10-2. We will be doing further design "tweaks" to this design using Java code during this chapter.

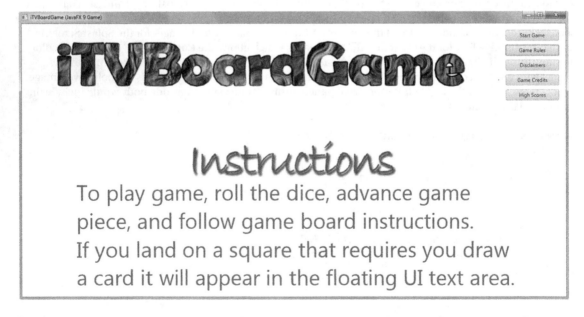

Figure 10-2. *Test your UI Button event handling with the Start Game and Game Rules buttons, switching back and forth*

This code configures the different objects in the compositing stack (Stage ➤ Root ➤ StackPane ➤ ImageView ➤ TextFlow) to display the default white background for the OS, which is the Scene (and Stage) object, by installing transparency in a StackPane object using Background.EMPTY. The boardGameBackPlate ImageView contains a transparent Instructions script font drop-shadowed PNG32 image, which lets the white background color through. The TextFlow and two Text objects also support transparency and add the game instructions, so the Information screen is a nice, readable white color with the text preset to Color.GREEN. If you click the Start Game Button (which we'll be coding next, to reset itself to the default settings), you can switch between the SplashScreen and the new help text, albeit with some mistakes on the SplashScreen because the gameButton event handler needs to reset characteristics, which we'll do next to restore the white text, text location, splash screen image, and welcome image, since this Button changes the object characteristics.

Next, let's copy and paste these Java statements into the gameButton event handling structure, and then we will configure your method call parameter areas using the correct Text, Background, and Image objects and pixel location values. Clear your TextFlow object and then load your TextFlow object with your **playText** and **moreText** Text objects using the .addAll() method. Next, set the TextFlow container X,Y pixel location (its position on the screen) using a 240 Integer value for your .setTranslateX() method call and a 420 Integer value for your .setTranslateY() method call. Load your uiLayout StackPane object's background with the uiBackground Background object by using the .setBackground() method call and then load the boardGameBackPlate ImageView with the splashScreen Image object by using the .setImage() method call. This is all accomplished using the following Java code structure inside the .handle() method, as shown highlighted in the middle of Figure 10-3:

```java
gameButton.setOnAction(new EventHandler<ActionEvent>() {
    @Override
    public void handle(ActionEvent event) {
        infoOverlay.getChildren().clear();
        infoOverlay.getChildren().addAll(playText, moreText);
        infoOverlay.setTranslateX(240);
        infoOverlay.setTranslateY(420);
        uiLayout.setBackground(uiBackground);
        boardGameBackPlate.setImage(splashScreen);
    }
} );
```

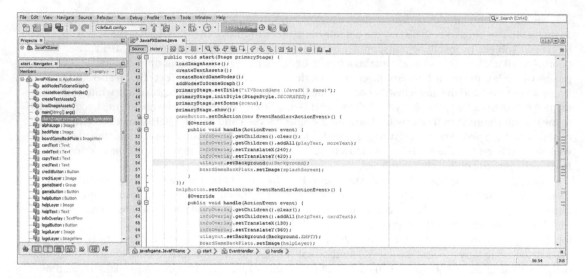

Figure 10-3. *Implement the code in the handle() method to configure gameButton default UI compositing layer objects*

Notice in Figure 10-3 that I left both the gameButton and helpButton event handling structures open in the NetBeans 9 IDE using the plus (+) icons in the left margin of the code editing pane so that you can see from a Java code perspective how these Java 9 code blocks inside of your .handle() methods set all of your compositing pipeline object characteristics to control each different Button object's screen designs using only a handful of different variable and object settings. This is an example of how powerful Java can be when you set up your JavaFX Scene Graph optimally.

Use your **Run ➤ Project** work process, and again toggle between the **Start Game** and **Game Rules** Button UI controls. You'll see that the Game Rules button no longer messes up your Start Game screen, as shown in Figure 10-4.

Figure 10-4. Test your UI Button event handling with the Start Game and Game Rules, switching back and forth

Next, let's copy and paste the helpButton Java statements into the legalButton event handling structure and then configure these method call parameter areas by using the correct Text, Background, and Image objects and pixel location values. Again, clear your TextFlow object and then load your TextFlow object with your **copyText** and **riteText** Text objects using the .addAll() method. Next, set the TextFlow container X,Y pixel location (its position on the screen) using a 200 Integer value for the .setTranslateX() method call and a 370 Integer value for the .setTranslateY() method call. Load your uiLayout object background with the Background.EMPTY constant using your .setBackground() method call and then load your boardGameBackPlate ImageView with your legalLayer Image object by using the .setImage() method call. This is all accomplished using the following Java code structure inside the .handle() method, as shown highlighted in the middle of Figure 10-5:

```
legalButton.setOnAction(new EventHandler<ActionEvent>() {
    @Override
    public void handle(ActionEvent event) {
        infoOverlay.getChildren().clear();
        infoOverlay.getChildren().addAll(copyText, riteText);
        infoOverlay.setTranslateX(200);
        infoOverlay.setTranslateY(370);
        uiLayout.setBackground(Background.EMPTY);
        boardGameBackPlate.setImage(legalLayer);
    }
} );
```

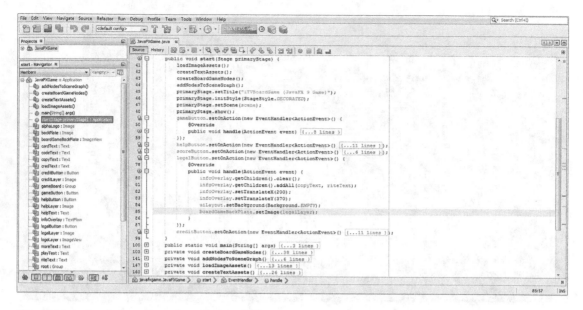

Figure 10-5. *Implement the code in the handle() method to reconfigure your legalButton UI compositing layer objects*

Next, use your **Run ➤ Project** work process, and make sure your **Disclaimers** Button is configuring your Text objects in a readable, organized format on a white background. As you'll see in Figure 10-6, your UI screen looks good, and you can move on to create a **Game Credits** Button object event handling structure by again using copy and paste.

Figure 10-6. *Test UI Button event handling with the Start Game, Game Rules, and Disclaimers, switching back and forth*

Next, let's copy and paste the helpButton Java statements into the legalButton event handling structure and then configure these method call parameter areas by using the correct Text, Background, and Image objects and pixel location values. Again, clear your TextFlow object and then load your TextFlow object with your copyText and riteText Text objects using the .addAll() method. Next, set the TextFlow container's X,Y pixel location (its position on the screen) using a 240 Integer value for the .setTranslateX() method call and a 370 Integer value for the .setTranslateY() method call. Load your uiLayout object background with the Background.EMPTY constant using your .setBackground() method call and then load your boardGameBackPlate ImageView with your legalLayer Image object by using the .setImage() method call. This is all accomplished using the following Java code structure inside the .handle() method, as shown highlighted in the middle of Figure 10-7:

```java
creditButton.setOnAction(new EventHandler<ActionEvent>() {
    @Override
    public void handle(ActionEvent event) {
        infoOverlay.getChildren().clear();
        infoOverlay.getChildren().addAll(credText, codeText);
        infoOverlay.setTranslateX(240);
        infoOverlay.setTranslateY(370);
        uiContainer.setBackground(Background.EMPTY);
        boardGameBackPlate.setImage(creditLayer);
    }
} );
```

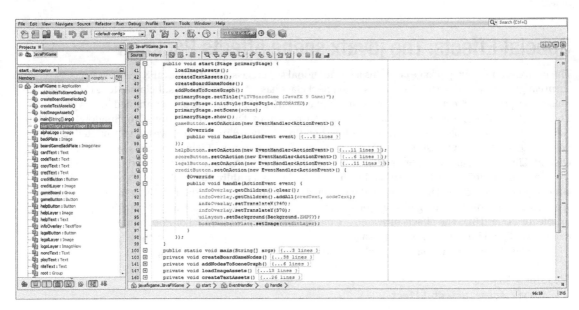

Figure 10-7. *Implement the code in the handle() method to reconfigure your creditButton UI compositing layer objects*

Next, use your **Run ➤ Project** work process and make sure your Credits TextFlow object is positioning all its Text objects in a readable format on the screen. As you can see in Figure 10-8, your UI screen looks great. We'll leave the High Scores Button unimplemented for now, as we'll be creating a scoring engine and high score table a bit later.

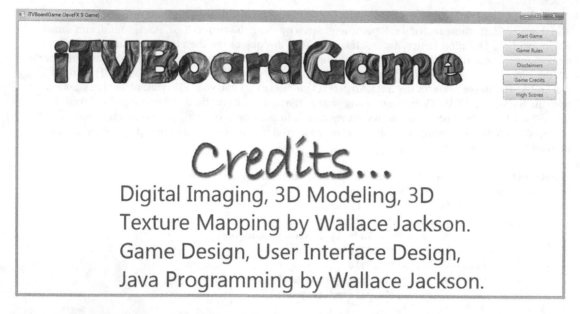

Figure 10-8. *Implement the code in the handle() method to reconfigure the creditButton UI compositing layer objects*

Special Effects: The javafx.scene.effects Package

The javafx.scene.effect package contains a foundational superclass for all the JavaFX special effects. Not surprisingly, this is called the Effect class. The Effect class has 17 known direct subclasses for 2D digital image compositing effects, such as you would find in GIMP 2.10, which are also contained in this package. These include Blend, Bloom, BoxBlur, ColorAdjust, ColorInput, DisplacementMap, DropShadow, FloatMap, GaussianBlur, Glow, ImageInput, InnerShadow, Lighting, MotionBlur, PerspectiveTransform, Reflection, SepiaTone, and Shadow classes. For 2D, this package also contains the Light superclass and the Light. Distant, Light.Point, and Light.Spot subclasses, which we'll use later, during the 3D part of this book.

Let's cover the JavaFX Effect superclass first. This class is a **public abstract** class, extending a java. lang.Object master class. This means that it was created, from scratch, by the JavaFX development team, specifically for providing image-based (pixel-based) special effects in JavaFX and to provide lighting support, usable for 2D and 3D. The effects provided are much like those that GIMP 3 or Photoshop provide in their respective digital imaging software packages.

The JavaFX Effect Java class hierarchy would therefore look like the following:

```
java.lang.Object
 > javafx.scene.effect.Effect
```

The Effect class provides an abstract or "base" class for the creation of all special effects implementations in JavaFX. An Effect object (and subclass) in JavaFX will always contain a pixel graphics algorithm that produces an Image object. This will be an algorithmic modification of the pixels in your source Image object and works in both 2D and 3D.

An Effect object can also be associated with a Scene Graph Node (rather than an Image object) by setting an attribute called **Node.effect**, that is, the effect attribute for the Node class (or object created from a Node subclass).

Some effects, such as ColorAdjust, will change the color characteristics (hue, lumination, and saturation) for the source pixels, while others such as Blend will combine multiple images together algorithmically (via Porter-Duff).

The DisplacementMap and PerspectiveTransform special effects classes will warp, or move, the pixels of the source image around in 2D space to simulate 3D space, commonly called "2.5D" or "isometric" spatial optical effects.

All JavaFX special effects have at least one input defined. Additionally, this input can be set to another Effect object, allowing developers to **chain** the Effect objects together. This allows developers to combine the Effect results, allowing compound or hybrid special effects to be created. This input can also be left "unspecified," in which case the effect will apply its algorithm to the graphical rendering (pixel representation or rendering result) of the Node object that it has been attached to using a .setEffect() method call or back onto the Image object that has been provided.

It's important to note that special effects processing is a conditional feature. The ConditionalFeature. EFFECT enum class and constant will define a set of conditional (supported) special effects features. These features may not be available on all operating system or on all embedded platforms, although "modern-day" consumer electronics devices can usually support effects processing as well as i3D rendering using their hardware GPU graphics-processing abilities.

If your pro Java games application wanted to poll the hardware platform to ascertain whether any particular effect feature is available, you may query effects support using the **Platform.isSupported()** method call. If you use any conditional feature on a platform that does not support it, it will not cause an exception. In general, the conditional feature will simply be ignored so that you don't have to code any specific error-trapping or error-handling Java code.

Next, let's take a look at how you would implement one or two of these special effects in the UI design and add drop shadows to the TextFlow object so the text that it displays is made more readable using increased contrast. After that, we will take a look at the way that you can shift your digital image color around the visible color spectrum.

Creating Special Effects: Add a createSpecialEffects() Method

Let's follow our trend of organizing your Java code and create a method for setting up all of your special effects called .createSpecialEffects(). Have NetBeans 9 create an empty **private void createSpecialEffects() {...}** infrastructure by adding a line of code to call it in the start() method, after the createTextAssets() method call, as shown highlighted in Figure 10-9. The logic here is that we will first load images, then define effects, and then create text.

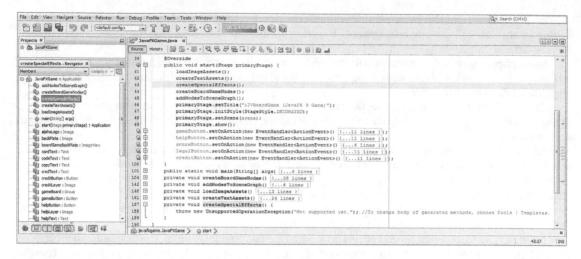

Figure 10-9. *Add a createSpecialEffects() method call at the top of .start() so that NetBeans creates the method body*

Next, we will replace the bootstrap code inside this createSpecialEffects() method with special effects code.

Drop Shadows: Adding Drop Shadows to Your TextFlow Object

Now it is time to add Java code into the empty createSpecialEffects() method to set up the **drop shadowing** effect. You will apply this to your TextFlow objects later by using the .setEffect() method call. The first thing that you will need to do is to declare a DropShadow object named dropShadow at the top of your class and use an Alt+Enter work process to have NetBeans generate an import statement for you. Next, inside the createSpecialEffects() method, instantiate this object using the Java new keyword and the DropShadow() constructor method. Next, use the .setRadius() method call off of the dropShadow object to set a shadow radius (how much it spreads out from the source) of 4.0 pixels. Next, use the .setOffsetX() and .setOffsetY() method calls with a setting of 3.0 pixels to offset the shadow diagonally to the right (use negative values to go the other direction). Finally, use a .setColor() method call to specify a **DARKGRAY** Color class constant. The code, shown highlighted in Figure 10-10, should look like the following:

```
DropShadow dropShadow;
...
private void createSpecialEffects() {
    dropShadow = new DropShadow();
    dropShadow.setRadius(4.0);
    dropShadow.setOffsetX(3.0);
    dropShadow.setOffsetY(3.0);
    dropShadow.setColor(Color.DARKGRAY);
}
```

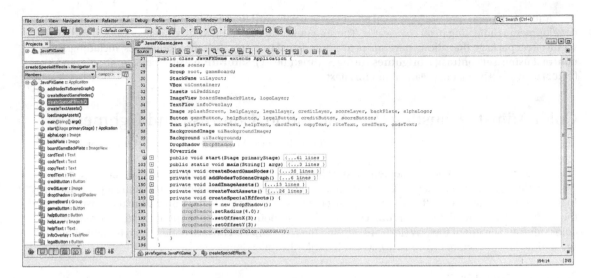

Figure 10-10. *Code your private void createSpecialEffects() method body to create and configure a DropShadow object*

Next, open your createTextAssets() method body and add a **.setEffect(dropShadow)** method call off each Text object to wire them to the DropShadow effect and the settings you've set for the object, as shown in Figure 10-11.

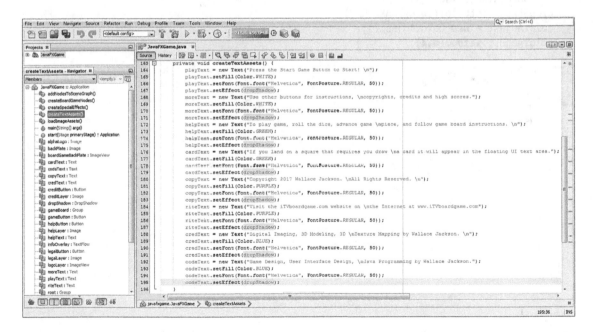

Figure 10-11. *Add a .setEffect(dropShadow) method call to each of your Text objects in the createTextAssets() method*

Another popular and useful special effect that you will want to use in your pro Java 9 games development is adjusting pixel color value. There's a powerful ColorAdjust special effect class in the javafx. scene.effect package that allows developers to adjust digital imaging attributes for images, including **contrast** using .setContrast(), **brightness** using .setBrightness(), **saturation** using .setSaturation(), and hue (color) using .setHue(). Let's learn about this next.

Color Adjust: Adjusting Hue, Saturation, Contrast, and Lightness

Let's use the .setHue() method call off of a ColorAdjust object to allow us to "color shift" the color temperature of our PNG32 transparent logo digital image asset so that it will match up visually with the color of all of your other screen design element color values for each of the Button Control user interface designs we are refining during this chapter. Declare a ColorAdjust object named **colorAdjust** at the top of your class. Inside of your createSpecialEffects() method, instantiate the object using the **ColorAdjust()** constructor and then call a .setHue() method off this object using a floating-point **0.4** value to color shift the current image color value 40 percent of the way (forward) around the color wheel. The Java code, which is highlighted in the middle and bottom of Figure 10-12, would look like the following:

```
DropShadow dropShadow;
ColorAdjust colorAdjust;
...
private void createSpecialEffects() {
    dropShadow = new DropShadow();
    dropShadow.setRadius(4.0);
    dropShadow.setOffsetX(3.0);
    dropShadow.setOffsetY(3.0);
    dropShadow.setColor(Color.DARKGRAY);
    colorAdjust = new ColorAdjust();
    colorAdjust.setHue(0.4);              }
```

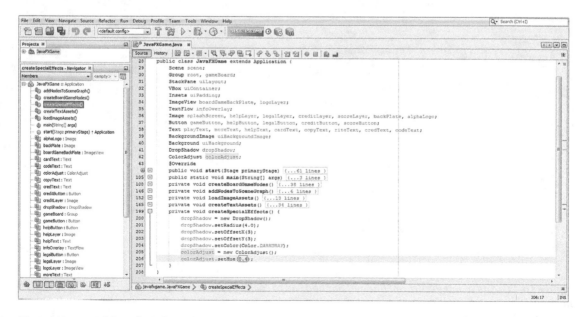

Figure 10-12. *Add a colorAdjust object instantiation and use a .setHue(0.4) method call off of the object to configure it*

The next step in this implementation of your ColorAdjust Effect object is to add the
.setEffect(colorAdjust) method call off of your **logoLayer** ImageView object, inside the helpButton.
setOnAction() event handler. This will shift the brown colored pixels in the transparent logo PNG32 image
to be green, while leaving the transparent pixels alone, as they have zero color value (and maximum
transparency value). If these pixels had been defined using a partial color value and a partial transparency
value, then the partial color values would be shifted forward 40 percent.

I have added this .setEffect() method call right after your **boardGameBackPlate.setImage(helpLayer);**
method call since we now need to color shift the logo image composite layer, as you can see highlighted in
Figure 10-13. The logoLayer object's Effect object is set to the colorAdjust object, which is then set to a Hue
value of 0.4 (40 percent).

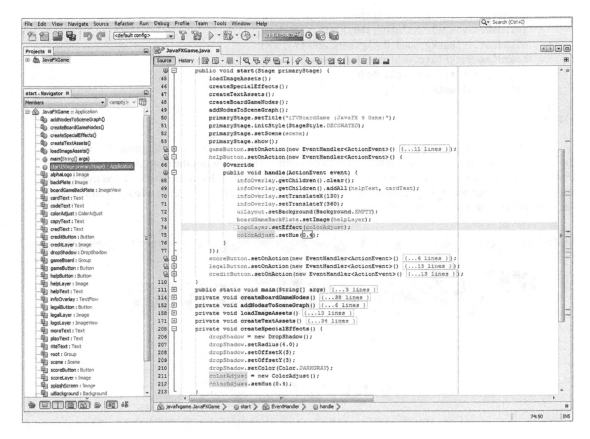

Figure 10-13. *Use a Run ➤ Project work process to make sure that the drop shadow special effects are working
well*

You may be wondering why I set Hue to 40 percent (again) when I did this already in the createSpecialEffects() method. The reason for this is that the setting in the createSpecialEffects() method could be viewed to be a "default" setting, and the reason I have to specify it (again) in the helpButton event handler code is that other Button handlers will set different Hue values. Your helpButton.setOnAction() event-handling code should now look like the following:

```
helpButton.setOnAction(new EventHandler<ActionEvent>() {
    @Override
    public void handle(ActionEvent event) {
        infoOverlay.getChildren().clear();
        infoOverlay.getChildren().addAll(helpText, cardText);
        infoOverlay.setTranslateX(130);
        infoOverlay.setTranslateY(360);
        uiLayout.setBackground(Background.EMPTY);
        boardGameBackPlate.setImage(helpLayer);
        logoLayer.setEffect(colorAdjust);
        colorAdjust.setHue(0.4);
    }
});
```

Now it's time to use the **Run ➤ Project** work process and make sure the drop shadow effect on the TextFlow object is making your Text objects more readable and matches the drop shadow on the screen caption image. You can see in Figure 10-14 that something is amiss in the Java code, as the JavaFX application runs but is not drop shadowing the text. Let's check the order our Java code is executing our statements in to see if there is something out of order!

Figure 10-14. *Declare and instantiate a ColorAdjust object named colorAdjust and use .setHue() to shift the color 40 percent*

Since the Java code is in the right order inside of the methods, I suspect that the order the methods are called in is most likely the source of this problem. Let's take a look at the order of the method calls inside of the start() method, shown at the top of Figure 10-9. Notice that createSpecialEffects() is called **after** createTextAssets(), and yet we're using the .setEffect(dropShadow) method call inside of the createTextAssets() method, so we have to move the createSpecialEffects() method call **above** the createTextAssets() method call, as shown in Figure 10-13, so your effect is set up **before** you utilize it. Java code is pretty logical if you trace that logic through the process of what you're doing!

As you can see in Figure 10-16, this solved the problem, and your drop shadow effect is rendering correctly.

The next modification you will need to make is to your legalButton.setOnAction() event-handling structure to make everything on the screen a nice shade of purple. This can be achieved by color shifting the hue of your logo 40 percent, this time in the **negative direction** around the color wheel. Using floating-point numbers, the right positive 180 degrees of a color wheel ranges from 0.0 to 1.0, and the left negative side ranges from 0.0 to -1.0.

The Java code for your legalButton event-handling Java statements is shown, highlighted, at the bottom of Figure 10-15. It should look like the following Java code:

```java
legalButton.setOnAction(new EventHandler<ActionEvent>() {
    @Override
    public void handle(ActionEvent event) {
        infoOverlay.getChildren().clear();
        infoOverlay.getChildren().addAll(copyText, riteText);
        infoOverlay.setTranslateY(200);
        infoOverlay.setTranslateY(370);
        uiLayout.setBackground(Background.EMPTY);
        boardGameBackPlate.setImage(legalLayer);
        logoLayer.setEffect(colorAdjust);
        colorAdjust.setHue(-0.4);
    }
} );
```

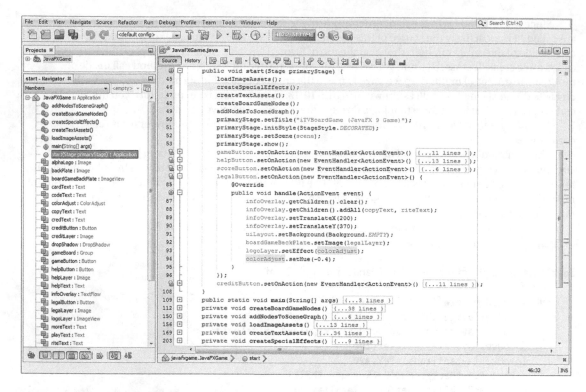

Figure 10-15. *Add a .setEffect(colorAdjust) method call off logoLayer and call .setHue(-0.4) to change the color shift*

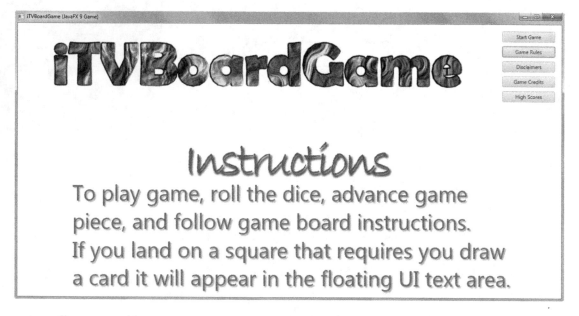

Figure 10-16. *Use the Run ➤ Project work process and make sure that the drop shadow effect is rendering correctly*

Figure 10-17 shows my **Run ➤ Project** Button handler testing work process, showing both a drop shadowing effect and the hue (color) shifting in place in the **Disclaimers** Button control, refining the design even further. I clicked back and forth between all the different Button elements to make sure that all of the attributes are not resetting any other Button screen design attributes in a way that is not desirable, which is the reason that I put all of the correct variables in all the event handling code bodies so that no method call has a setting overlooked (not specified/passed).

Figure 10-17. *Use the Run ➤ Project work process and make sure that the color hue shift matches the rest of the design*

The final modification you will need to make is to your creditButton.setOnAction() event handling structure to make everything on the screen a nice shade of blue. This can be achieved by color shifting the hue of your logo 90 percent in the negative direction around a color wheel. The code for your creditButton event handling Java statements is shown highlighted in the middle of Figure 10-18 and should look like the following:

```
creditButton.setOnAction(new EventHandler<ActionEvent>() {
    @Override
    public void handle(ActionEvent event)    {
        infoOverlay.getChildren().clear();
        infoOverlay.getChildren().addAll(credText, codeText);
        infoOverlay.setTranslateY(240);
        infoOverlay.setTranslateY(370);
        uiLayout.setBackground(Background.EMPTY);
        boardGameBackPlate.setImage(creditLayer);
        logoLayer.setEffect(colorAdjust);
        colorAdjust.setHue(-0.9);
    }
});
```

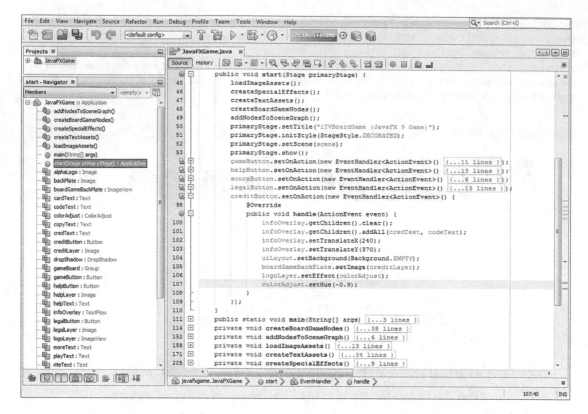

Figure 10-18. *Copy and paste the colorAdjust.setHue(-0.9) and logoLayer.setEffect(colorAdjust) Java code in creditButton*

Use your **Run ➤ Project** work process, and make sure that this 90 percent negative shift around the color wheel is now turning the logo into a vibrant blue color, which looks good with the rest of your user interface design. As you can see in Figure 10-19, the Credits Button Control screen now matches up in both color and drop shadowing effects.

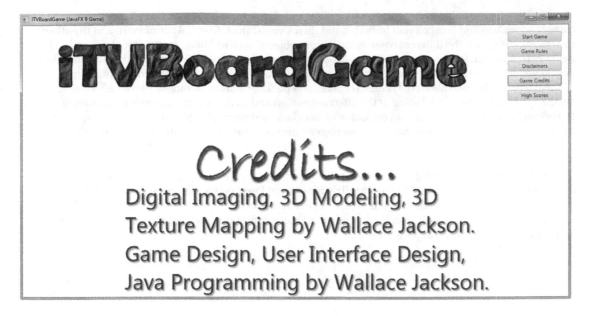

Figure 10-19. *Use the Run* ➤ *Project work process and make sure that the color hue shift matches the rest of the design*

We will code the interior of the scoreButton.setOnAction() event handler when we cover implementing the scoring engine and high scores UI design later in the book when you have a board game that you can score in place.

The work process to implement dozens of other special effects in your pro Java 9 game development can be implemented in much the same way—by declaring a class for the effect you want to utilize, instantiating it inside of the createSpecialEffects() method, setting parameters for the effect configuration by using methods from the class, and finally applying the effect to whatever Node object, Control object, ImageView object, 3D object, or Text object that you want by using the .setEffect(effectClassNameHere) method call off of the object name you're applying it to.

You will find that the JavaFX special effect package and classes are especially flexible in this implementation approach, as you can apply all of the popular special effects found in most software packages to almost any object or Scene Graph Hierarchical structure in JavaFX 9, usually using around a dozen lines of code and sometimes even fewer.

Once you know how to create and apply these special effects in JavaFX, your pro Java 9 games development creative power goes up by an order of magnitude. This is because these effects can be applied anywhere in the Scene Graph hierarchy, as well as anywhere in the 2D, imaging, and 3D rendering pipeline.

I will try to use more of these JavaFX 9 Effect subclasses later during this book as I add more and more complexity to each chapter and as we progress throughout the book.

Summary

In this tenth chapter, we added interactivity to your user interface design using ActionEvent handling structures, learned about InputEvent objects and MouseEvent and KeyEvent object processing, and learned how to apply the special effects contained in the **javafx.scene.effects** package that leverage the JavaFX **Effect** superclass.

Next you learned about how events, which allow interactivity, are handled in Java 9 and JavaFX by using the **java.util** and **javafx.event** packages and their **EventObject**, **Event**, **ActionEvent**, and **InputEvent** classes. We discussed the different types of InputEvent objects, such as MouseEvents, TouchEvents, and KeyEvents, and then you implemented your ActionEvent handling to make the (middle three) Instructions, Legal Disclaimers, and Production Credits sections (Button objects) of your user interface interactive.

Finally, you learned about the **javafx.scene.effects** package and the dozens of special effects that JavaFX offers developers. We looked at the Effect superclass and went over how to implement both the **DropShadow** class (and object) and the **ColorAdjust** class (and object) so that you can spruce up your user interface by adding shadows to your TextFlow objects, improve readability (contrast), and color shift your top logo digital image asset to match the color schema for each of your Button Control object user interface designs.

In Chapter 11, we're going to take a look at how to configure your JavaFX game to utilize 3D assets. This involves the **Camera** superclass and its **ParallelCamera** and **PerspectiveCamera** subclasses. We're also going to learn how to create light in your 3D Scene so that the Camera object can "see." We will look at the LightBase superclass and its AmbientLight and PointLight subclasses, which are specifically provided for lighting design in 3D Scene applications.

■ ■ ■

3D Scene Configuration: Using the PerspectiveCamera and PointLight

Now that you have finished the 2D SceneGraph hierarchy for the splash screen and user interface design, let's get back into our JavaFXGame primary application class coding here in Chapter 11 and start to design the 3D GameBoard Scene Infrastructure that will be the foundation for the rendering and lighting of the board game and its gameplay. We will learn about the basic 3D scene components that you will find pre-installed (for all default or empty scenes) in 3D software packages like Blender or Autodesk 3D Studio Max. After that, we can get into JavaFX Primitives (Box, Plane, Cylinder, Disk, Sphere, and Pill) during Chapter 12 and shading with materials and texture maps in Chapter 13.

During the chapter you'll be learning about the different types of JavaFX 9 **Camera** and **LightBase** subclasses that are contained in the core **javafx.scene** package, which, in turn, is contained (as of Java 9) in the **javafx.graphics** module. We will cover **PerspectiveCamera** since you will be using this in the basic 3D scene infrastructure that we'll be creating during this chapter, as well as **ParallelCamera**, another Camera subclass that is better suited for your 2D or 2.5D game development pipeline. Camera is an **abstract** superclass and cannot be utilized directly. We'll also learn about the public **LightBase** abstract superclass and its two core lighting subclasses, **AmbientLight** and **PointLight**.

We will also continue to work on your JavaFXGame Java code by adding 3D rendering, camera, and lighting to the JavaFX SceneGraph so that you can start to add 3D elements to your 3D game, which we will do after we cover the JavaFX Shape3D class and its primitive subclasses (in Chapter 12) and using shaders and applying materials and texture maps to that 3D geometry (in Chapter 13).

We have a lot to learn about what is needed for JavaFX to even be able to visualize (render) your game's 3D geometry assets and their texture maps in your 3D scene, so let's get started learning about the scene camera object.

Use a 3D Camera: Adding Perspective to 3D Games

The top level of any 3D rendering pipeline is the scene camera, as this is what processes everything in the 3D scene and then hands that data over to the rendering engine. In this case, that's the PRISM software renderer (in the absence of a GPU), or it could be the OpenGL hardware rendering engine on the consumer electronic device (PC, phone, tablet, iTV set, laptop, game console, set-top box) that your 3D game is playing on. If you are still using Windows, it might also include DirectX 3D rendering. The Camera object (in our case, this will be a PerspectiveCamera object) is used specifically for 3D scene rendering; we will be looking at it during this section of the chapter. It is so integral to the JavaFX 9 SceneGraph that it has its own Scene. setCamera(Camera) method call. This method call is used to add the Camera object to the SceneGraph root to make sure it is at the very top (the root) of the SceneGraph rendering hierarchy. It does not use the

W. Jackson, *Pro Java 9 Games Development*, https://doi.org/10.1007/978-1-4842-0973-8_11

.getChildren().add() method chain, and therefore, it will be set up inside of your createSceneGraphNodes() method, as you will see a bit later during this section of the chapter when we set up this Camera object for your pro Java 9 game. We'll also cover ParallelCamera, which is better suited for 2D games.

JavaFX Camera Class: An Abstract Superclass Defining Camera

The public JavaFX Camera superclass is an abstract class, used only to create different types of cameras. Currently there is an orthographic or ParallelCamera subclass (object) or a PerspectiveCamera subclass (object). Your application should not attempt to extend this abstract Camera class directly; if you attempt this, Java will throw an UnsupportedOperationException, and your pro Java 9 game will not compile or run. The Camera class is kept in the javafx.graphics module in the core javafx.scene package and is a subclass of Node, as it is ultimately a Node at the top of your SceneGraph. The Camera class implements the Styleable interface so it can be styled, and it contains the EventTarget interface so it can process events. The Java 9 class hierarchy for the JavaFX Camera class thus looks like the following:

```
java.lang.Object
 > javafx.scene.Node
   > javafx.scene.Camera
```

The Camera class is the base class for any camera subclass that is used to render scenes. A camera is used to define how the scene's coordinate space is rendered on the 2D window (Stage) that a user is looking at. The default camera (if you don't create one specifically, which we'll be doing later in this section) will be positioned in a scene such that its projection plane in a scene's coordinate space is at Z=0 (in the exact middle) and is looking into the screen in the positive Z direction. For this reason, we'll be backing our camera 1,000 units away from (-1000) the center of the screen in the code since the i3D GameBoard will be at "center stage" and located at 0, 0, 0 (X, Y, Z).

The distance in Z units from the camera to the projection plane can be determined by the width and height of the Scene to which it is attached (which is also the resulting projection plane) and the fieldOfView parameter for a Camera object. The nearClip and farClip properties for a Camera object are the only two properties or characteristics defined in this abstract class and are specified in what JavaFX calls *eye coordinate space*. This space is defined with the viewer's eye at the Camera object's origin, and the projection plane is one unit in front of the eye in the positive Z direction. The nearClip and farClip properties for any Camera subclass, such as PerspectiveCamera, can be set using the .setNearClip() and .setFarClip() method calls. These are two PerspectiveCamera class (object) method calls that we will be utilizing later during this section of the chapter to configure our SceneGraph camera object.

JavaFX PerspectiveCamera Class: Your 3D Perspective Camera

The JavaFX PerspectiveCamera class extends the Camera class and is used to create a PerspectiveCamera (object) that is used to render your i3D scene. The PerspectiveCamera class is also kept in the javafx. graphics module in the core javafx.scene package; it is a subclass of Node and is a Node at the top of your JavaFX SceneGraph. The PerspectiveCamera class also implements the Styleable interface so it can be styled and the EventTarget interface so it can process events. The Java 9 class hierarchy for the JavaFX PerspectiveCamera class looks like the following:

```
java.lang.Object
 > javafx.scene.Node
   > javafx.scene.Camera
     > javafx.scene.PerspectiveCamera
```

The PerspectiveCamera object defines the viewing volume for a perspective projection. Imagine a truncated right-facing pyramid, as most cameras are represented visually in 3D software such as Blender or 3D Studio Max.

There are two (overloaded) constructor methods for this class. One has an empty parameter area, like this:

```
camera = new PerspectiveCamera();
```

The second uses the boolean value fixedEyeAtCameraZero attribute (or parameter or characteristic), which is the one we are going to use in our camera object declaration, instantiation, and configuration Java code, like this:

```
camera = new PerspectiveCamera(true);
```

Of course, we will also declare a PerspectiveCamera camera at the top of the class, and use Alt+Enter to have NetBeans 9 write an import statement for this class for us. The PerspectiveCamera has a fieldOfView value, which can be used to change the field of view (FOV) angle for a camera projection and is measured in degrees. I will leave the FOV at its default value and assume that this default FOV gives the best visual result, as determined by the JavaFX Development Team.

My tendency in using i3D for games and for simulations is to "dolly," or move the camera along the Z (in and out of the scene) transformation axis rather than to use FOV value changes, as even in real life changing a camera lens (like going from 24mm to 105mm) tends to change perspective more drastically. In my experience, using different 3D virtual cameras, this change in perspective is even more drastic in virtual 3D than it is when using real-life cameras.

By default, your PerspectiveCamera is located at center of your scene on creation (instantiation) and looks along (is pointed down) the positive z-axis. If you construct a PerspectiveCamera using PerspectiveCamera(false), then the coordinate system defined by the camera will have its 0,0 origin located in the upper-left corner of the panel, with the y-axis pointing down and the z-axis pointing away from the viewer (into the screen). If a PerspectiveCamera node is added to the scene graph, the transformed position and orientation of the camera will define the position of the camera and the direction that the camera is looking. In the default camera, where fixedEyeAtCameraZero is false, the eye position Z value is adjusted in Z such that the projection matrix generated using the specified fieldOfView will produce units at Z = 0 (on the projection plane) using device-independent pixels. This matches your characteristics for a ParallelCamera. When the Scene is resized, the objects in the scene on the projection plane (Z = 0) will stay the same size, but more or less content in your scene is viewable, which is more appropriate for 2D camera and 2D scroller use than 3D camera use, where resizing a camera will instead zoom your scene. This is why a PerspectiveCamera is usually instantiated using the PerspectiveCamera(true), as we will be doing later during this section of the chapter.

When fixedEyeAtCameraZero is set to true, the eye position is fixed at (0, 0, 0) in the local coordinates of the camera. The projection matrix will be generated using the default (or specified) fieldOfView attribute, and a projection volume will be mapped on the window (viewport or Stage object) such that it will be "stretched" (zoomed) over more or fewer device-independent pixels at the point of the projection plane. When the Scene size attribute is changed, the objects in a scene will shrink or grow proportionally, but the visible extent (bounds) of the content will be unchanged.

The JavaFX Development Team recommends setting this fixedEyeAtCameraZero to true if you're planning to transform (move or dolly) your camera object. Transforming your camera when fixedEyeAtCameraZero is set to false may lead to results that are not intuitive to the end user.

Note that the PerspectiveCamera is a conditional 3D feature. You can poll the ConditionalFeature. SCENE3D boolean variable to ascertain if a given user's device supports this feature (in this case, supports i3D). This would be done using the following Java code structure, which sets a boolean variable to reflect system support for 3D rendering:

```
boolean supportFor3D = Platform.isSupported(ConditionalFeature.SCENE3D);
```

Finally, there is a Boolean property for this class called verticalFieldOfView, which is used to define whether the fieldOfView property will apply to the vertical dimension of the projection. This logically means that increasing or decreasing the FOV will change the width of the projection but not the (vertical) height if this is false, and if this is true, it will change (scale) both the horizontal (width) and vertical (height) dimensions of the camera projection, which would ostensibly maintain aspect ratio better than changing only one dimension of the camera's projection plane.

Next, let's take a look at the ParallelCamera class, which we'll cover to be consistent in our Camera subclass coverage, even though this camera is more useful for use with 2D games and possibly Orthographic 3D applications.

JavaFX ParallelCamera Class: Your 2D Space Parallel Camera

The JavaFX ParallelCamera class also extends the Camera class and is used to create a ParallelCamera (object), which is used to render your i2D scene. This ParallelCamera class is also kept in the javafx.graphics module in the core javafx.scene package; it is a subclass of Node and is a Node at the top of your JavaFX SceneGraph. The ParallelCamera class also implements the Styleable interface so it can be styled and the EventTarget interface so it can process events. The Java class hierarchy for the JavaFX ParallelCamera class will therefore look like the following:

```
java.lang.Object
  > javafx.scene.Node
    > javafx.scene.Camera
      > javafx.scene.ParallelCamera
```

The default camera created by JavaFX 9 will always be a ParallelCamera, which is why we are coding specific Camera and LightBase object creation during this chapter. For instance, if you simply created a Sphere object without creating any Camera subclass object or any LightBase subclass object, the JavaFX runtime would automatically create a ParallelCamera object and an AmbientLight object so that the Shape3D subclass (Sphere) would be visible to the renderer.

If a scene contains only 2D transforms, then it does not require a PerspectiveCamera and would thus utilize a ParallelCamera, which doesn't render all of a 3D object's characteristics. The ParallelCamera would be better suited for what is covered in *Beginning Java 8 Games Development* (Apress, 2014). This camera defines a viewing volume for a parallel, also called an *orthographic* projection in the 3D industry. Essentially an orthographic projection would equate to being a rectangular plane.

The ParallelCamera is always located at center of the window and will look along the positive z-axis. What is different about the ParallelCamera (relative to the PerspectiveCamera) is that the scene coordinate system defined by this camera has its origin in the upper-left corner of the screen, with a y-axis running down the left side of the screen, the x-axis running to the right along the top of the screen, and the z-axis pointing away from the viewer (into the distance in the screen representation).

The units used in a ParallelCamera object are represented using pixel coordinates, so this is exactly like a 2D digital imaging software package and the 2D StackPane image compositing layer object we are using for 2D UI design, which also references coordinates from the upper-left corner of the screen at 0,0 (X,Y). This is yet another indicator of the fact that this is a more logical Camera subclass to use for your i2D games, rather than your i3D games.

There is one sole constructor method for this class that uses an empty parameter area and looks like this:

```
Camera2D = new ParallelCamera();
```

Next, let's take a look at how to create the PerspectiveCamera object, which we'll be using for our pro Java 9 game. We'll see how we will initially configure it for use and how we will add it to the root of our JavaFX SceneGraph.

Adding a PerspectiveCamera to Your Scene: Using .setCamera()

The first thing that we need to add to the top of the JavaFXGame class is a declaration of the PerspectiveCamera object using the PerspectiveCamera camera; Java statement, which will then present a wavy red underline indicator underneath the PerspectiveCamera object (class usage). Use the Alt+Enter keystroke shortcut to have NetBeans 9 write the import statement for you and then open up the createSceneGraphNodes() method so you can add that camera object to the top (root) of the SceneGraph. Instantiate this camera object underneath the root Group instantiation using the camera = new PerspectiveCamera(true); constructor statement. Then, on the next line, call a .setTranslateZ() method with a -1000 value to move the camera 1,000 units away from the 0,0,0 center of the 3D scene.

Set the nearClip Camera object attribute to **0.1** by using a **.setNearClip()** method call off the camera object, and set the **farClip** attribute to **5000.0** by using the **.setFarClip()** method call. Finally, wire this camera object into your scene object (root), using the **.setCamera()** method call off of the scene object, and pass the **camera** object over using a camera object as the parameter in the .setCamera(**camera**) method call. Set your scene object **Background** value to **Color.BLACK** by using the .setFill() method call so your 3D objects will stand out well, using these Java statements:

```
PerspectiveCamera camera;
...
createSceneGraphNodes() {
    camera = new PerspectiveCamera(true);
    camera.setTranslateZ(-1000);
    camera.setNearClip(0.1);
    camera.setFarClip(5000.0);
...
    scene.setFill(Color.BLACK);
    scene.setCamera(camera);
```

As you can see in Figure 11-1, your code is error-free, and the camera is now set up and attached to your 3D scene, which we have now converted into being a 3D scene. It is now a 3D Scene because it uses a PerspectiveCamera at the top of its rendering pipeline (that is, at its root), so all objects underneath it will now use the 3D perspective.

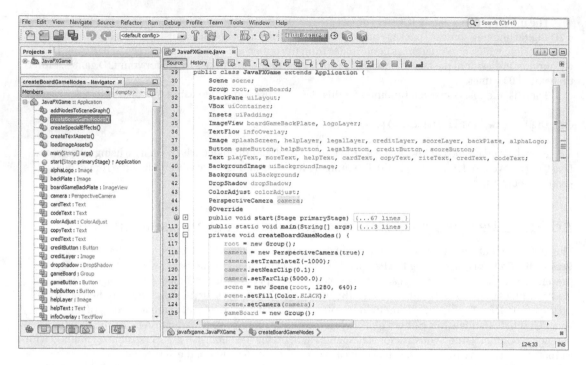

Figure 11-1. *Add a PerspectiveCamera object declaration at the top of the class and then instantiate it and configure it*

Next, let's use the Run ➤ Project work process to see how the new 3D Scene you have created by adding a PerspectiveCamera is affecting your existing 2D UI design; this is now a "hybrid" 2D and 3D application, which is the most advanced type of JavaFX application. This is true because we need to combine 2D and 3D assets in one seamless compositing environment, which is an extremely complicated undertaking. Two of the most advanced film and special effects compositing software packages available, Fusion and Nuke, accomplish this fusion of 2D with 3D. In fact, if you want to learn more about combining 2D and 3D assets into one pipeline, check out *VFX Fundamentals* (Apress, 2016). As you can see in Figure 11-2, the StackPane branch of your SceneGraph root, and everything underneath it, is being carried (correctly) with it and is now referencing (visually) from PerspectiveCamera at the top of the hierarchy and its 0,0,0 center of the screen that you learned about earlier in the chapter.

Figure 11-2. *Run the Project and notice that the StackPane is now located at the PerspectiveCamera 0,0,0 center origin*

The first thing I tried was to place the StackPane origin in the upper-left corner by using .setTranslateX(-640) and .setTranslateY(-320), which worked to some extent as the result looked like Figure 11-2; however, it was up in the upper-left corner, with the entire StackPane layout visible, and it was scaled down 200 percent (four times, or one-quarter screen).

What this told me was that the StackPane was a 2D object, technically a "plane," that was in "perfect parallel" with the camera projection plane, facing the z-axis of the camera object. By contrast, now the StackPlane is part of the 3D rendering pipeline because it's a child of (underneath the renderer processing pipeline) PerspectiveCamera.

This means that the StackPane and all of its children (VBox, ImageView, and TextFlow) are being processed through the PerspectiveCamera object. This includes all of its algorithms and coordinate systems (and similar "rules of engagement" if you will), all of which change how and where it will be rendered to the screen (the Scene object).

The next thing I tried was logically setting the uiLayout object X and Y coordinates back to the 0,0 origin settings using the .setTranslateX(0) and .setTranslateY(0) method calls. This is accomplished by adding the following two Java statements to relocate your StackPane to 0,0 inside of the .start() method somewhere after your uiLayout StackPane object instantiation Java statement.

This Java code is shown here, as well as being highlighted in blue near the middle of Figure 11-3:

```java
uiLayout = new StackPane();
uiLayout.setTranslateX(0);
uiLayout.setTranslateY(0);
```

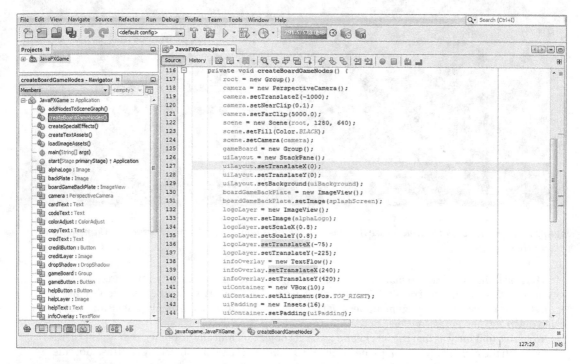

Figure 11-3. *Add the .setTranslateX() and .setTranslateY() method calls off the uiLayout StackPane object, both set to zero*

Notice in Figure 11-3 that you are using .setTranslateX() and .setTranslateY() on your logoLayer ImageView, as well as on your infoOverlay TextFlow, each of which retain their positioning relative to your uiLayout StackPane.

This preservation of relative positioning is because of the parent-child relationships that you have established in your SceneGraph hierarchy, which is why this is a powerful scene construction tool for any type of Scene whether it's i2D, i3D, or hybrid. This will also be very important as we develop the i3D portion of your pro Java 9 game during this book, as we will need to do even more integral transformations in the 3D portion of your gameplay than simply centering your UI control panel in front of the camera so that it blocks the view of the 3D game (at least for now; we may change this UI design later as we continue to refine the Java code and the game design). This is exactly how game design, and coding, transpires in real life; game development is a journey, not a destination.

Use a **Run ➤ Project** work process to see whether we're getting closer to synchronizing your 2D UI overlay with the 3D scene behind it. As you can see in Figure 11-4, the UI panel is now in the center of your screen, albeit scaled down. Therefore, we will continue to refine our object attributes. Next, we will use the camera object's Z translation variable to bring the camera closer in to the 3D scene in order to achieve our desired end result.

Figure 11-4. *Run the project; your StackPane is now centered, but your camera object Z translation is too far out*

I expect that this is because the Z translation of the camera is set **1,000 units away** from the center of this new 3D Scene. Therefore, the next thing I am going to try to do is to reduce the camera.setTranslateZ() method call parameter, from -1000 to -500, to see what the resulting change in the 2D inside of 3D composite will be.

The Java code to accomplish this modification should look like the following and can be seen highlighted in blue at the top of Figure 11-5:

```
camera.setTranslateZ(-500);
```

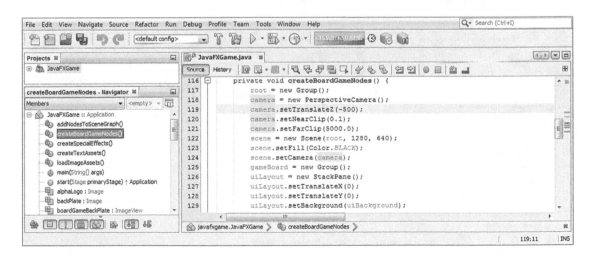

Figure 11-5. *Move the camera object 50 percent closer to the 3D scene projection plane by setting .setTranslateZ() to -500*

Again, use your **Run ➤ Project** work process. As you can see in Figure 11-6, your UI screen is now 50 percent larger, so we need to reduce our .setTranslateZ() to **zero** to synchronize your StackPane with the 3D Scene projection plane.

Figure 11-6. *Run the project to see that the StackPane is still centered, but the camera Z translate value is still too far out*

The Java code to accomplish this looks like the following and can be seen highlighted in blue in Figure 11-7:

```
camera.setTranslateZ(0);
```

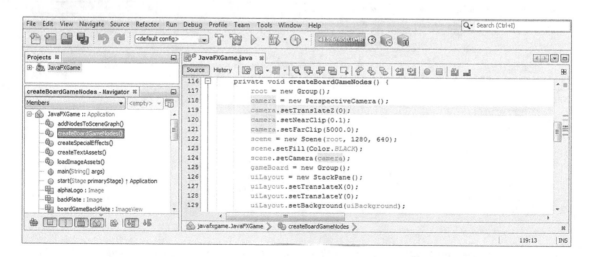

Figure 11-7. *Set the camera.setTranslateZ() method call to zero to synchronize the StackPane and projection plane*

Next, use the **Run ➤ Project** work process to see whether you've accomplished the visual objective of synchronizing your StackPane Node branch and its children with the 3D camera object's projection plane. As you can see in Figure 11-8, your UI screen looks great and the buttons are working.

Figure 11-8. *Use Run ➤ Project to see that your StackPane is perfectly synchronized (visually) with the camera projection plane*

Before we get into learning about the LightBase (superclass) object and the AmbientLight and PointLight subclasses, let's make sure all of our other previous 2D UI code is still working and doing what we want it to do. When adding a major feature or change to your Java 9 code, it is always important to take the time to do this.

StackPane UI Testing: Making Sure Everything Else Still Works

Click the **Game Rules** Button, shown in Figure 11-8, and make sure the UI screen for your game instructions is still readable and professional in appearance, even though we are going to refine this UI further, before the game is published. As you can see in Figure 11-9, the Instructions screen in indeed still readable; however, the **Color.WHITE** background color has been replaced with Color.BLACK since we set our new 3D Scene object to use this for its Fill Color value, as shown in Figure 11-1, using a scene.**setFill**(Color.**BLA CK**); Java statement. This means that we need to now set the Background Color value for our StackPane to **Color.WHITE** to fill our UI screen with a white color somewhere farther up in the scene compositing (now rendering) pipeline. Since the StackPane is above the Scene and below the VBox, ImageView, and TextFlow, this is the logical object to set to a **Color.WHITE** Background Fill color. This will involve placing only one Java statement in the three active Button event handling structures located in the .start() method, rather than changing dozens of Java statements relating to setting Text object Color and DropShadow attributes, not to mention lightening the ImageView using the .setLightness() method call to brighten the heading image text elements. This will also give me a chance to show you how to get around the limitation of the StackPane object (class) not having a .setFill() method, which means we have to create a complex method chain with two nested "object instantiation inside of a method" Java constructs, where we create a new Background object and a new BackgroundFill object inside of a .setBackground(Background) method call and configure the BackgroundFill to white.

277

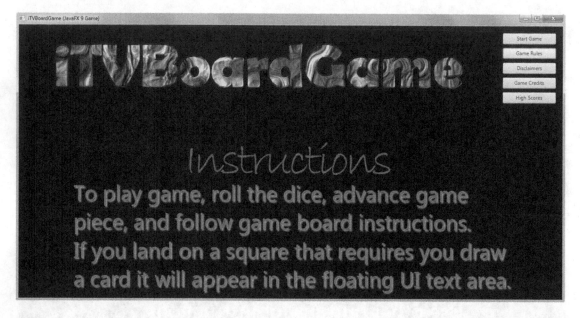

Figure 11-9. *Click the Game Rules Button control to see whether the Instructions section is rendering correctly. It is now black!*

The basic Java 9 programming statement structure for this method call, which contains two nested object instantiations, will look like the following (initially; we will configure it further next) Java 9 programming structure:

```
uiLayout.setBackground( new Background( new BackgroundFill(Color.WHITE) ) );
```

This is shown in Figure 11-10, albeit with a wavy red underline under the **BackgroundFill**, as we will need to use an **Alt+Enter** keystroke combination to have NetBeans import the BackgroundFill class from **javafx. scene.layout** (package). This is also shown highlighted in blue in the figure as "Add import for javafx.scene. layout.BackgroundFill," which you will double-click to have NetBeans 9 write this import statement for you.

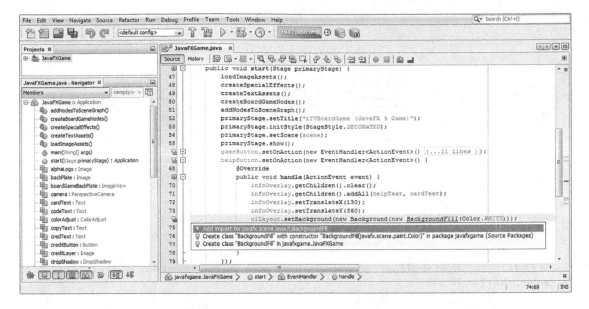

Figure 11-10. *Code your private void createSpecialEffects() method body to create and configure a DropShadow object*

NetBeans evaluates problems from the most basic (no import statement) on down. Thus, once you have the import statement in place for the BackgroundFill object, NetBeans continues to evaluate the statement to see whether there are any other problems with your Java programming constructs, from the inside (the BackgroundFill) out (to the new Background object, to the .setBackground() method call).

It turns out the constructor method for the BaclgroundFill class requires several parameters, not just the **Color.WHITE** color fill specification. This is because the BackgroundFill class will create rounded corners and supports an Insets object specification as well, so the proper constructor method format for the BackgroundFill constructor should look like the following:

```
backgroundFill = new BackgroundFill(Paint, CornerRadii, Insets);
```

Therefore, for our usage, a complete white color background fill constructor method would use the **EMPTY** constant to not have any padding or rounded edges and would therefore look like the following Java instantiation:

```
new BackgroundFill( Color.WHITE, CornerRadii.EMPTY, Insets.EMPTY );
```

Once a BackgroundFill class is imported, NetBeans shows us that the **new BackgroundFill(Color. WHITE)** object instantiation has a problem with it, indicated by a wavy red underline underneath the entire code structure, as shown in Figure 11-11. I placed my mouse over the section of the Java statement I am constructing, and NetBeans 9 pops up an explanation for the problem, which is shown in the pale yellow box with a black outline around it.

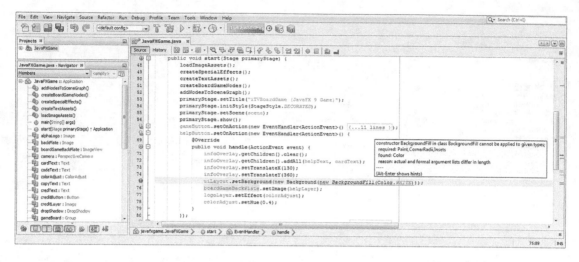

Figure 11-11. *Set uiLayout StackPane background to white using .setBackground(new Background(new BackgroundFill(Color.WHITE)));*

I want a white fill, so I used CornerRadii.**EMPTY** and Insets.**EMPTY** for the last two parameters, in that order, as required by the constructor method parameter. The final method call looks like this, as shown in Figure 11-12:

```
.setBackground(new Background(new BackgroundFill(Color.White,CornerRadii.EMPTY,Insets.EMPTY) ));
```

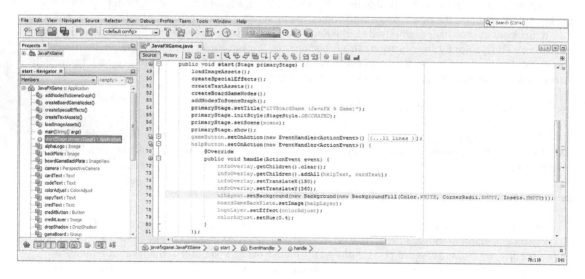

Figure 11-12. *Add BackgroundFill constructor method parameters (Paint, CornerRadii, and Insets) to the method call*

Finally, use the **Run ➤ Project** work process to see whether you've acomplished the objective of a white StackPane background color fill. As you can see in Figure 11-13, your UI screen again looks great, and the UI Buttons are working.

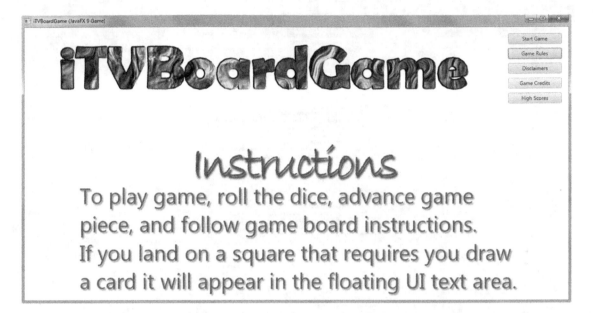

Figure 11-13. *The StackPane now has a Color.WHITE background fill, preventing scene Color.BLACK from showing*

Let's implement this fix in the Legal and Credits Button event handling structures and bring our application back to 100 percent working condition. As you can see in Figure 11-14, I have copied and pasted this uiLayout StackPane object Background attribute configuration Java 9 code structure into both your legalButton as well as your creditButton event handling infrastructures, and the code is compiling error-free.

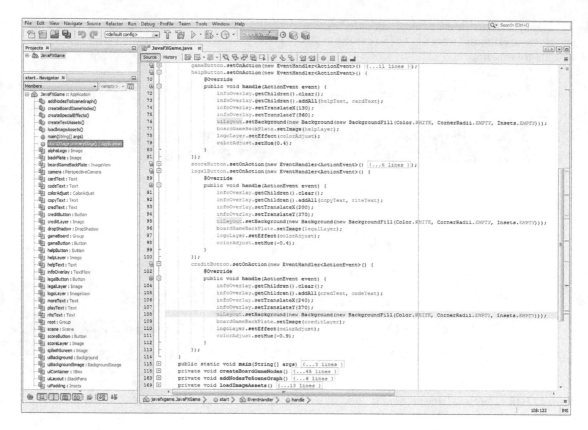

Figure 11-14. *Copy and paste the uiLayout.setBackground() construct from helpButton to legalButton and creditButton*

If you use your **Run ➤ Project** work process and test these three Button UI elements, you will see that all of your hard design work from the previous chapters has been completely restored thanks to our use of the StackPane's backplate (Background object) to hold the Paint object set to a Color helper class constant of **Color.WHITE**.

Implementing the Start Game Button: Hiding Your UI

The next thing that we want to do is to comment out all the code in the gameButton event handler code (so we can restore these later, if we want to) and then add some new statements that will hide (set visibility to false) the StackPane branch of the SceneGraph; we will also set the camera.setTranslateZ() method call to the -1000 value we wanted to use originally. As we build the game, we will be adding additional configuration and control statements into this Button regarding the i3D game, which, as you can now see, will "live" behind the StackPane UI Control Panel.

As you can see in Figure 11-15, I have commented out the code relating to your StackPane UI compositing pipeline; I have added statements relating to removing the UI control panel from view and to setting the 3D Scene Camera object to the position we want to have it is when the game is initially started. The new code statements look like the following Java code and are shown highlighted in the middle of Figure 11-15:

```
uiLayout.setVisible(false);
camera.setTranslateZ(-1000);
```

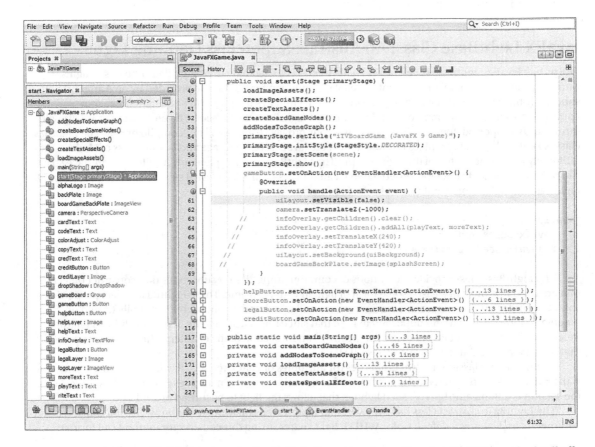

Figure 11-15. *Add a .setVisible(false) method call off of uiLayout and a .setTranslateZ(-1000) method call off the camera*

Now when you use your Run ➤ Project work process and click the Start Game Button, your StackPane will disappear and the empty (black) 3D scene will be revealed.

Now it is time to learn about 3D Scene lighting using the JavaFX 9 LightBase superclass and its AmbientLight and PointLight subclasses. We will cover these in detail before implementing them in our JavaFXGame class, before we end this chapter on core 3D Scene elements (Camera and LightBase) that need to be at the root of our SceneGraph in our i3D pro Java 9 game design and development pipeline. Getting excited yet? Lights, Camera...ActionEvents!

Using 3D Lighting: Adding Illumination to 3D Games

There are two different sets of lighting APIs in JavaFX 9. One is for 3D Scene usage and is contained in the javafx.scene package featuring an abstract **LightBase** superclass and the "concrete" (usable in your code as objects you can construct) subclasses AmbientLight and PointLight. The other is the abstract Light superclass and is contained in the javafx.scene.effect package; this package contains 2D digital imaging effects, as we covered earlier during this book. For 3D use we are going to focus on the LightBase, AmbientLight, and PointLight classes and use the PointLight class initially as we can obtain the most dramatic and realistic results using that class.

JavaFX LightBase Class: An Abstract Superclass Defining Light

The public JavaFX LightBase superclass is an abstract class, used only to create different types of lights. Currently there is a general or "ambient" level of illumination for a 3D scene provided by an AmbientLight subclass (object) or a PointLight subclass (object) that emulates the properties of a light bulb. Your application should not attempt to extend the abstract LightBase class directly; if you attempt this, Java will throw an UnsupportedOperationException, and your pro Java 9 game will not compile or run. The LightBase class is kept in the javafx.graphics module in the core javafx.scene package and is a subclass of Node, as it is ultimately a Node at the top of the SceneGraph. The LightBase class implements a Styleable interface so it can be styled and an EventTarget interface so it can process events. The Java 9 class hierarchy for the JavaFX LightBase class therefore would look like the following:

```
java.lang.Object
  > javafx.scene.Node
    > javafx.scene.LightBase
```

The LightBase class provides definitions of common properties for subclasses that construct objects that are used to represent ("cast") some form of light in your 3D Scene. These LightBase object properties should include your initial color for the light source and whether the light source is initially turned on (enabled) or off (disabled). It's important to note that since this is a 3D feature, it is a conditional feature. Reference the example I laid out in the PerspectiveCamera section of the chapter as to how to set up code that detects the ConditionalFeature.SCENE3D flag.

LightBase subclasses have two properties (or attributes or characteristics if you prefer those terms); one is the color or ObjectProperty<color> that specifies the color of light emanating from the light source, and the second is a BooleanProperty called lightOn that allows the light to be turned on and off.

The LightBase abstract class has two overloaded protected constructor methods. One has no parameters and creates a default **Color.WHITE** light source, using this constructor method call format:

```
protected LightBase()
```

The second overloaded protected constructor method allows the subclass to specify a color value for the light, using the following constructor method call format:

```
protected LightBase(Color color)
```

The LightBase class has seven methods that will all be available to (inherited by) every LightBase subclass, including the AmbientLight and PointLight subclasses, so pay attention to these here as I will cover them only once.

The **colorProperty()** method specifies the **ObjectProperty<Color>** for the light source, while the **getColor()** method gets the **Color** value property for the light source. The **getScope()** method will get an **ObservableList<Node>** containing a List of **Nodes** that specifies the **hierarchical scope** for the LightBase subclass (object).

The **isLightOn()** method call returns the **boolean** value of on (true) or off (false) for the light source, and the **lightOnProperty()** method call will set the **boolean** data value for the light source **BooleanProperty lightOn**.

Finally, the **void setColor(Color value)** method will set the data value of the light **color** property, and the **void setLightOn(boolean value)** method will set the data value of the LightBase subobject **lightOn** boolean value property.

Next, let's take a closer look at the AmbientLight and PointLight concrete classes individually.

JavaFX AmbientLight Class: Lighting Your 3D Scene Uniformly

The public JavaFX AmbientLight class is a concrete class, used to create a general or "ambient" level of illumination for a 3D scene. There is generally only one instance of AmbientLight defined for a given 3D Scene instance. The AmbientLight class is kept in the javafx.graphics module in the core javafx.scene package and is a subclass of LightBase, which is a Node subclass, as it is ultimately a Node at the top of the SceneGraph. The AmbientLight class also implements a Styleable interface so it can be styled and an EventTarget interface so that it can process events. The Java class hierarchy for the JavaFX AmbientLight class therefore would look like the following:

```
java.lang.Object
  > javafx.scene.Node
    > javafx.scene.LightBase
      > javafx.scene.AmbientLight
```

The AmbientLight class defines the ambient light source object for your 3D Scene, if needed. Ambient light can be defined as a global or general amount of illumination of an area from an unseen light source that appears to be coming into the scene from every direction. All AmbientLight object properties are inherited from the LightBase superclass and should include an initial color for the light source and whether the light source is initially turned on (enabled) or off (disabled). It's again important to note that since this is a 3D feature, it is a conditional feature.

AmbientLight has two overloaded constructor methods; the first one creates an unconfigured AmbientLight object class using the (default) **Color.WHITE** light source, using the following Java instantiation programming format:

```
AmbientLight ambient = new AmbientLight();
```

The second overloaded constructor method creates a new instance of PointLight using a specified color that is not **Color.WHITE**, using the following Java instantiation programming format:

```
AmbientLight ambientaqua = new AmbientLight(Color.AQUA);
```

Next, let's take a look at the PointLight concrete class in detail, and then we can add a PointLight object into your 3D Scene before we finish up with this chapter on setting up a 3D rendering scene environment that we can drop 3D objects into over the duration of the rest of this book.

JavaFX PointLight Class: Lighting Your 3D Scene Dramatically

The public JavaFX PointLight class is a concrete class, used to create a local or "point source" instance of illumination for a 3D scene. There is often more than one PointLight instance in a 3D Scene to allow the artist to implement complex lighting models simulating real-world light sources. The PointLight class is kept in the javafx.graphics module in the core javafx.scene package and is a subclass of LightBase, which is a Node subclass, as it is ultimately a Node at the top of the SceneGraph. The PointLight class also implements a Styleable interface so it can be styled and an EventTarget interface so that it can process events. The Java class hierarchy for the JavaFX PointLight class therefore would look like the following:

```
java.lang.Object
   > javafx.scene.Node
      > javafx.scene.LightBase
      > javafx.scene.PointLight
```

The PointLight class defines the point light source (think lightbulb) objects for your 3D Scene, as are needed. Try to use as few PointLight objects as possible as they are expensive to render (calculate, or process, their algorithm). Point lights are defined as a local light emanation point and can be animated to create a wide range of special effects. All PointLight object properties are inherited from the LightBase superclass and should include an initial color for the light source and whether the light source is initially turned on (enabled) or off (disabled). It's again important to note that since this is a 3D feature, it is also a conditional feature.

The PointLight has two overloaded constructor methods. The first one creates an unconfigured PointLight object class with the default **Color.WHITE** light source, using the following Java instantiation programming format:

```
PointLight light = new PointLight();
```

The second overloaded constructor method creates a new instance of PointLight using a specified color that is not **Color.WHITE**, using the following Java instantiation programming format:

```
PointLight aqualight = new PointLight(Color.AQUA);
```

Next, let's take a closer look at the work process for adding a PointLight object to use as a light source for your JavaFXGame class infrastructure.

Adding Light to the Game's 3D Scene: Using PointLight Objects

Next, let's add a point light source into your JavaFXGame code so that we can learn about 3D primitives in the next chapter. Declare a PointLight object named light at the top of your JavaFXGame class; then use the **Alt+Enter** keystroke combination to bring up the helper pop-up and select the "Add import for javafx.scene. PointLight" option, as highlighted in yellow and blue at the bottom of Figure 11-16.

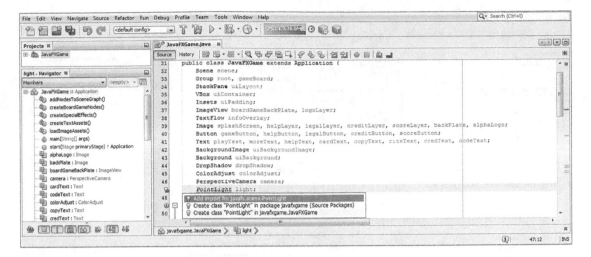

Figure 11-16. *Declare a PointLight named light at the top of your JavaFXGame class and hit Alt+Enter and Add Import.*

Since you'll also need something for the light to illuminate, add a **Sphere sphere** declaration after your PointLight light declaration so that we have something to test our code with, as shown highlighted in yellow at the top of Figure 11-17. Next, instantiate your PointLight after the scene.setCamera(camera); method call. I have used the second more explicit constructor method but given it the default **Color.WHITE**, which we might change later, after we look at materials and how they interact with light color values. Move the light down a bit so it's not inside of the Sphere (at 0,0,0) using a **light.setTranslateZ(-25);** method call. Next, use a **light.getScope().add(sphere);** method chain and add the sphere object to the scope of what the PointLight object "sees." Notice that this allows you to have **different light objects affect different 3D objects** in the 3D Scene, which is quite a powerful feature. The Java code for your PointLight and Sphere object declarations, instantiation, and configuration Java statements is highlighted at the bottom of Figure 11-17 and should look something like the following Java code:

```
PointLight light;
Sphere sphere;
...
private void createBoardGameNodes() {
    ...
    light = new PointLight(Color.WHITE);
    light.setTranslateY(-25);
    light.getScope().add(sphere); // "Wire" the Sphere and Light together via .getScope().add()
    sphere = new Sphere(100);
    ...
}
```

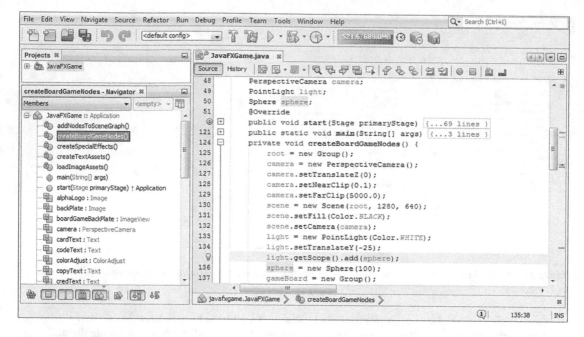

Figure 11-17. *Declare a sphere and light object, and in createBoardGameNodes instantiate and configure them for use.*

The final thing that you will need to do to wire your PointLight and Sphere to each other, to the camera, and to the GameBoard 3D branch of the SceneGraph is to add your sphere Node object to your gameBoard Group object using the .getChildren().add() method chain in the proper order inside of your .addNodesToSceneGraph() method.

The code for your addNodesToSceneGraph() method Java statements is highlighted in the middle of Figure 11-18 and should look like this Java method body:

```
private void addNodesToSceneGraph() {
    root.getChildren().addAll(gameBoard, uiLayout);
    gameBoard.getChildren().add(sphere);
    uiLayout.getChildren().addAll(boardGameBackPlate, logoLayer, infoOverlay, uiContainer);
    ...
}
```

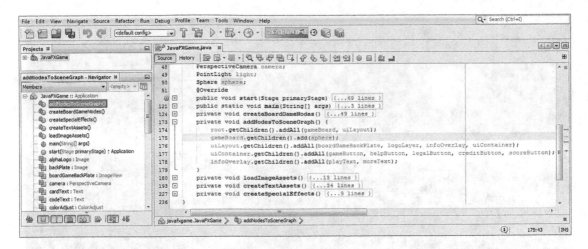

Figure 11-18. *Add the sphere to the gameBoard branch of the root Node so the primitive is added to your scenegraph.*

Use your **Run ➤ Project** work process, and make sure that all of these code upgrades and additions that we have accomplished during this chapter are working properly and giving you the end result that should be expected at this early stage of your pro Java 9 game development.

Make sure the three (middle) Game Rules, Disclaimers, and Game Credits buttons have been restored to full working capacity (now have a white background fill again). In addition, the High Scores Button should still print out a text message to the Output Console in NetBeans 9, and the Start Game should now remove the StackPane uiLayout overlay panel and show the 3D Scene.

Inside of that 3D Scene should be a 3D Sphere object primitive, which we will be learning about during the next chapter on 3D objects in your 3D Scene, called Models, Geometry, Mesh, and Primitives in the 3D industry. Since the 3D primitive has no texture mapping or color value yet and since the PointLight object is set to **Color.WHITE**, this should be a light gray sphere lit with white light.

As you can see in Figure 11-19, the Start Game Button Control now hides the entire 2D compositing pipeline for the splash screen, UI design, Button controls, and TextFlow and Text elements and formatting with one simple Java statement of **uiLayout.setVisible(false);** and because of the StackPane parent Node and VBox, ImageView, and TextFlow child hierarchy that we have set up thus far in the book. Once the pipeline is hidden from view, we see the 3D Scene, to which we've temporarily added a Sphere object primitive in order to test the PerspectiveCamera and PointLight objects.

Figure 11-19. *Use your Run ➤ Project work process and test the 3D Scene infrastructure that you have put into place*

We are now in a position to be able to work on 3D modeling and 3D texture mapping using the JavaFX APIs.

Summary

In this eleventh chapter, we added 3D Scene capabilities to **JavaFXGame.java** by adding a PerspectiveCamera object, which allows the rendering of 3D assets using X, Y, and Z dimensions, and a 3D perspective to the Scene object. We also added a PointLight object to simulate a lightbulb light source to illuminate these 3D assets, as well as a Sphere object (a "primitive") to test our basic 3D Scene setup.

You learned about the abstract Camera superclass and its ParallelCamera (for 2D or Orthographic 3D Scene usage) and PerspectiveCamera, which we are going to use for the most effective 3D or i3D Scene rendering. We then learned how to declare, instantiate, and configure a PerspectiveCamera in the JavaFXGame, changing how it operates.

We then tested our 2D UI elements and hierarchy and observed that these are now on a 2D "plane" in 3D space. We corrected the Java code to compensate for this change in coordinate space, restoring your UI to full-screen.

We then tested all the UI Button objects and found our new 3D Scene black background color was affecting our information screens and very cleverly used a complex nested Java statement to create and insert a **Color.WHITE** BackgroundFill object into your StackPane object's Background object. This solved the problem by replacing one of the compositing layer's transparency with a white color fill and adding another opaque layer to our now hybrid 3D and 2D compositing pipeline. Once that problem was solved, we changed the logic in the gameButton event handler and allowed the end user to start the game by hiding the UI overlay and reveal the test Sphere primitive, correctly lit.

In the next chapter, we are going to take a look at the JavaFX Shape3D superclass and its subclasses as we continue to begin working on the foundation knowledge needed to create the i3D portions of your pro Java 9 game.

■ ■ ■

CHAPTER 12

3D Model Design and Primitives: Using JavaFX 9 Shape3D Classes

Now that you have finished setting up a basic (empty) 3D Scene by adding a Camera object to the Scene root and a PointLight object specifically designed to work with 3D assets, let's start to get some foundational knowledge about the 3D assets themselves. These assets come in the form of predefined basic 3D shapes, called *primitives*, as well as more custom 3D geometry assets commonly referred to in the industry as *mesh* or *wireframe* 3D assets. JavaFX 9 comes with seven classes in the **javafx.scene.shape** package in the **javafx. graphics** module that specifically create 3D geometry (primitives or mesh) for you, and we are going to take a look at them during this chapter. We will also get back into our **JavaFXGame** primary application class coding here in Chapter 12 and start to add 3D primitives to the **gameBoard Group Node** of our SceneGraph to get some practice adding 3D assets to our JavaFXGame application. Whereas we could do this in a 3D software package such as Blender, a board game is simple enough (squares, spheres, cylinders) that we can do this entirely in JavaFX code, which means we do not need to import (and distribute) 3D models but can rather write code to model your i3D game "out of thin air." This will also teach you a lot more about the 3D APIs in Java 9 and JavaFX 9, as you can learn how to model complex objects (such as your board game's gameboard) using only the latest Java and JavaFX APIs.

During this chapter, you will be learning about the different types of JavaFX 3D classes contained in the **javafx.scene.shape** package. We will cover **Sphere**, which can be used to create **a Sphere** primitive and which you have used already to test your 3D Scene setup in Chapter 11. We will also look at the other two primitive classes, **Box** and **Cylinder**, which can be used to create your **Plane** and **Disk** primitives. These primitives are based on the Shape3D superclass, which we will be looking at first. We will also look at the more advanced **TriangleMesh** class that allows you to build a polygon-based Mesh object and, finally, at the **Mesh** and **MeshView** class hierarchy, which will allow you to render the 3D Mesh objects that you'll have created in external 3D modeling and rendering software packages such as Blender 2.8 (open source) or Autodesk 3D Studio Max (a paid software package).

JavaFX Shape3D Superclass: Primitive or MeshView

The **public abstract Shape3D** superclass is used to create the four primary 3D classes: **Box**, **Sphere**, **Cylinder**, and **MeshView**. You'll use these classes to create and display the 3D assets for your pro Java 9 games development. Three of these subclasses create **primitives**, which are predefined 3D objects created algorithmically, and the MeshView subclass allows more detailed complex 3D models based on **polygonal** geometry to be rendered inside your 3D Scene. It is important to note that there is also a javafx.scene.shape. Shape superclass that is not related (class hierarchy wise) to javafx.scene.shape.Shape3D; it is used for 2D shapes like those commonly found in the SVG 2D digital illustration language, which is covered in *Beginning Java 8 Games Development* (Apress, 2014) and *Digital Illustration Fundamentals* (Apress, 2016).

The Shape3D superclass is a subclass of Node, as are most of the concrete classes that we will be using in your JavaFXGame code. Like the Camera and LightBase superclasses, this Shape3D superclass implements both the Styleable and EventTarget interfaces so that its subclasses (objects) can be styled and process events (can be interactive). The Java 9 class hierarchy therefore spans both Java and JavaFX APIs and looks like the following:

```
java.lang.Object
  > javafx.scene.Node
    > javafx.scene.shape.Shape3D
```

The Shape3D base (abstract or not directly instantiated) class was created to provide definitions of common properties for 3D objects that represent 3D geometric shapes. The three primary 3D properties include the "Material" (or shader and texture maps) to be applied to the fillable interior of the shape or the outline of the shape, which we'll be covering during Chapter 13; the "Draw Model" properties, which define how the JavaFX 9 rendering engine will represent the geometry to the viewer (as a solid or a wireframe model); and the "Face Culling" properties that define which faces to cull. Face culling is an optimization that a rendering engine will utilize to get better performance (faster FPS) by not rendering all of the polygons in the models in the scene. Since a renderer is taking a 3D Scene and rendering a 2D view from the Camera, this "backface culling" will not render any faces (polygons) on the part of a model facing away from (not visible to) the Camera. Front-face culling will do the opposite, rendering only the back-facing polygons, which basically renders the inside of the polygon, with the model front faces (polygons) becoming hidden or invisible. There is also the **CullFace.NONE** constant that **turns off** the Face Culling Optimization Algorithm. **CullFace.BACK** is the default setting and is what you'll usually want to use, unless you are using **CullFace. FRONT** to get some special inside volume rendering effect, which, after this chapter is over, you will know exactly how to experiment with, if you so desire.

As you know, 3D rendering, and therefore any of the Shape3D subclasses, is a conditional feature that you can check for in your code, as we covered in the previous chapter. Let's get into the three object settings (properties, attributes, characteristics) for any Shape3D subclassed object that define how the 3D rendering engine will render it.

The **cullFace** ObjectProperty<CullFace> will define which CullFace optimization algorithm (FRONT, BACK, or NONE) will be used on this Shape3D object. This could very well affect the performance of a pro Java 9 3D game.

The **drawMode** ObjectProperty<DrawMode> will define the draw mode used to render the Shape3D object. Your two options include **DrawMode.FILL** for a solid 3D object and **DrawMode.LINE** for a wireframe representation.

The **material** ObjectProperty<Material> defines the material the Shape3D object will be utilizing as a "skin." We'll be learning all about shading algorithms, materials, and texture maps in Chapter 13, which covers materials.

The **protected** (not directly usable) constructor for the abstract Shape3D superclass looks like the following:

```
protected Shape3D()
```

Now let's get into methods that are going to be part of all your Shape3D subclasses. This is convenient because we can cover all these methods here in one place. These can be used on any primitive 3D shape or MeshView.

The **.cullFaceProperty()** method defines the ObjectProperty<CullFace> for the Shape3D object, whereas the **.getCullFace()** method allows you to poll the Shape3D object for its current CullFace constant setting. There is also the **.setCullFace(CullFace value)** method, which allows you to change the CullFace constant setting for a Shape3D object.

The **.drawModeProperty()** method defines the ObjectProperty<DrawMode> for a Shape3D object, whereas the **.getDrawMode()** method allows you to poll the Shape3D object for its current DrawMode constant setting. There is also the **.setDrawMode(DrawMode value)** method, which allows you to change the DrawMode constant setting for the Shape3D object.

The **.materialProperty()** method defines the ObjectProperty<Material> for a Shape3D object, whereas your **.getMaterial()** method allows you to poll the Shape3D object for its current Material object setting. There is also the **.setMaterial(Material value)** method, which allows you to change the Material object setting for the Shape3D object.

Next, let's take a look at the Shape3D subclasses individually as we'll be leveraging them in the JavaFXGame.

JavaFX Sphere: Creating Sphere Primitives for Your 3D Games

Since we already created a Sphere object named sphere in the previous chapter to test the PerspectiveCamera and PointLight 3D Scene setup Java code, let's cover that Shape3D subclass here first. This class is kept in the **javafx.scene.shape** package and is a subclass of Shape3D, as you know, so it has the following Java class hierarchy:

```
java.lang.Object
  > javafx.scene.Node
    > javafx.scene.shape.Shape3D
      > javafx.scene.shape.Sphere
```

The Sphere class defines a three-dimensional sphere with the specified size. A Sphere is a 3D geometry primitive created algorithmically using the input by the programmer of a **radius** dimension (size). This Sphere is always initially centered at the 3D origin 0,0,0. The Sphere object therefore has one radius DoubleProperty that defines the radius of the Sphere as well as three cullFace, drawMode, and material properties inherited from javafx.scene.shape.Shape3D.

The Sphere class contains three overloaded constructor methods, including one with no parameters, which creates an instance of a Sphere with a radius of **1.0**. This would look like the following Java 9 Sphere instantiation:

```
sphere = new Sphere();
```

The second constructor method, which is the one we used in Chapter 11, allows you to specify a radius using a **double** numeric value. This would look like the following Sphere instantiation Java code:

```
sphere = new Sphere(100);
```

The third constructor allows you to specify a radius and a mesh density via a number of divisions parameter, which looks like the following Java statement that creates a 100 unit radius Sphere with 24 divisions:

```
sphere = new Sphere(100, 24)
```

The Sphere class has some of its own unique methods in addition to the ones it inherits from the Shape3D class, including the .getDivisions() method, which polls the Sphere object to see how many divisions it is using; the .radiusProperty() method, which defines the radius of the Sphere object; the .getRadius() method, which gets the value of the current radius; and the .setRadius(double value) method, which sets the value for the radius to a different value.

JavaFX Cylinder: Creating Cylinder or Disk Primitives for Games

Next, let's cover the **public Cylinder** Shape3D subclass, which can be used to create cylindrical 3D objects as it is a concrete (usable) class that also implements the Styleable and EventTarget interfaces. This class is kept in the **javafx.scene.shape** package and is a subclass of Shape3D, so it will have the following Java class hierarchy:

```
java.lang.Object
  > javafx.scene.Node
    > javafx.scene.shape.Shape3D
      > javafx.scene.shape.Cylinder
```

The Cylinder class is used to define a three-dimensional cylinder with a specified radius and height. A Cylinder is a 3D geometric primitive algorithm that takes a radius (double) property and a height (double) property. It is initially centered at the 0,0,0 origin with the radius using the z-axis direction and the height using the y-axis direction.

Besides the radius and height properties, it will also inherit the Shape3D cullFace, drawMode, and material properties. It has three overloaded constructor methods, with one the default (empty), one with a radius and height, and the third with a radius, height, and divisions.

The first empty constructor method creates a new instance of a Cylinder object with a radius of 1.0 and height of 2.0. It has the following Java statement format:

```
cylinder = new Cylinder();
```

The second constructor method creates a new instance of a Cylinder object with a developer specified radius and height. It has the following Java statement format:

```
cylinder = new Cylinder(50, 250);
```

The third constructor method creates a new instance of a Cylinder object with a developer-specified radius, height, and resolution (number of divisions to determine smoothness). It has the following Java statement format:

```
cylinder = new Cylinder(50, 250, 24);
```

There are three methods for radius, three methods for height, and one **.getDivisions()** method used to poll the divisions property, which must be set using the third constructor method format as there is no .setDivisions() method call or divisionsProperty() method call.

The double .getHeight() method will poll for (get) the value of the height property for a Cylinder object. The DoubleProperty heightProperty() method defines the height attribute for, or the Y dimension of, the Cylinder object. Finally, a void setHeight(double value) method allows developers to set the value of the height property for a Cylinder object.

The double getRadius() method will poll for (get) the value of the radius property for a Cylinder object. The DoubleProperty radiusProperty() method defines the radius attribute for, or the Z dimension of, the Cylinder object. Finally, a void setRadius(double value) method allows developers to set the value of the radius property for a Cylinder object.

Finally, let's take a look at a Box primitive class, which allows the creation of a wide range of useful shapes.

JavaFX Box: Creating Boxes, Posts, and Planes for 3D Games

Next, let's cover the **public Box** Shape3D subclass, which can be used to create square, rectangular, and planar 3D objects as it is a concrete (usable) class that also implements the Styleable and EventTarget interfaces. This class is kept in the **javafx.scene.shape** package and is a subclass of Shape3D, so it will have the following Java class hierarchy:

```
java.lang.Object
  > javafx.scene.Node
    > javafx.scene.shape.Shape3D
      > javafx.scene.shape.Box
```

A Box class defines a three-dimensional box, often called a *cube* primitive, with a specified size. A Box object is a 3D geometric primitive with three double properties(**depth**, **width**, and **height**) in addition to the three inherited cullFace, drawMode, and material Shape3D properties. Upon instantiation, it is initially centered at the origin.

The Box class has two overloaded constructor methods. One creates a default 2,2,2 cube and looks like the following Java code:

```
box = new Box();
```

A second constructor method allows you to specify dimensions for the cube and looks like the following:

```
box = new Box(10, 200, 10); // Creates a Post (or Tall Rectangle) Primitive
box = new Box(10, 0.1, 10); // Creates a Plane (or a Flat Surface) Primitive
```

As you might have guessed, there are nine methods, three for each property, available in the Box class. This is the class we will use to create the majority of our gameboard infrastructure, so we could be using these quite often.

The **DoubleProperty depthProperty()** method is used to define the depth, or the Z dimension, for the Box. A **double getDepth()** method can be used to get (poll) the value of the depth property from the Box object. The **void setDepth(double value)** method can be used to set or specify a new value for the depth property for a Box object.

The **DoubleProperty heightProperty()** method is used to define the height, or the Y dimension, for the Box. A **double getHeight()** method can be used to get (poll) the value of the height property from the Box object. The **void setHeight(double value)** method can be used to set or specify a new value for the height property for a Box object.

The **DoubleProperty widthProperty()** method is used to define the width, or the X dimension for your Box. A **double getWidth()** method can be used to get (poll) the value of the width property from your Box object. The **void setWidth(double value)** method can be used to set or specify a new value for the width property for your Box object.

Next, let's take a look at what it takes to actually implement different primitives in your JavaFXGame code!

Using Primitives: Adding Primitives to Your JavaFXGame Class

Let's add the other two primitive objects, Box and Cylinder, to your JavaFXGame class, so we can learn about Face Culling and Draw Modes. We'll save Material for its own Chapter 13, as shaders and texture maps deserve their own chapter and focused discussion. Declare a **Box** object named **box** at the top of your class and use **Alt+Enter** to have NetBeans 9 help you write the import statement. As you can see in Figure 12-1, it is important that you add the correct class to your Java 9 game because there is also a javax.swing.Box class (second in the pop-up helper drop-down list) that is used for 2D UI design and at the top of the list is (NetBeans best guess) the javafx.scene.shape.Box that is for use as a 3D primitive! Double-click the first (correct) class and have NetBeans write the import statement for you.

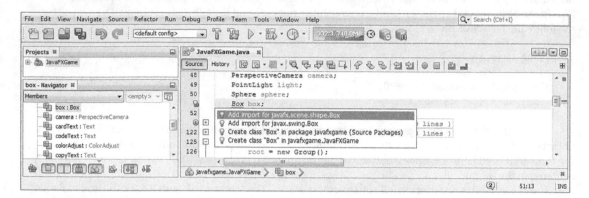

Figure 12-1. *Declare a Box object at the top of the class; use Alt+Enter, and select Add import for javafx.scene. shape.Box*

Instantiate the box object in the createBoardGameNodes() method using the second constructor, as shown in Figure 12-2. Remember, you need to add this box Node to the SceneGraph in the .addNodesToSceneGraph() method.

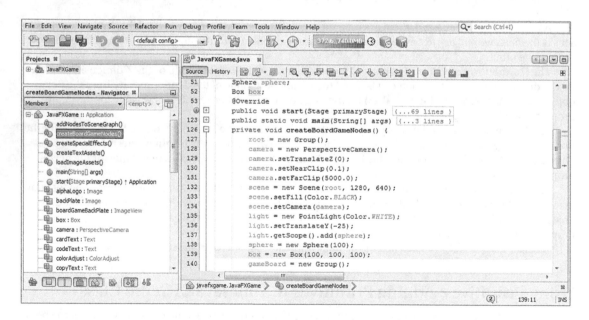

Figure 12-2. *Instantiate the Box in createBoardGameNodes, and set the depth, height, and width to 100, 100, 100*

This can be easily accomplished by modifying your current **gameBoard.getChildren().add(sphere);** Java statement to instead be **gameBoard**.getChildren().**addAll**(sphere, **box**);, as shown here and in Figure 12-3:

```
box = new Box(100, 100, 100);                      // in .createBoardGameNodes() method
gameBoard.getChildren().addAll(sphere, box);       //  in .addNodesToSceneGraph() method
```

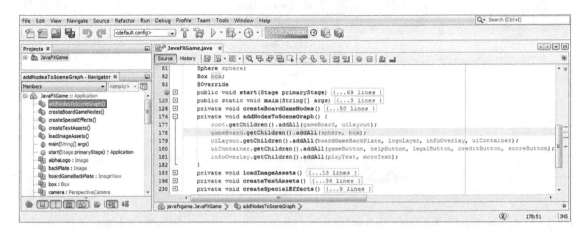

Figure 12-3. *Use the .addAll() method to add a box object to the SceneGraph in the addNodesToSceneGraph() method*

After declaring the Box object, instantiate the object inside of your createBoardGameNodes() method using the same 100 units value that you used for the Sphere. You will be able to see how the sizes relate to each other since they will both be created at 0,0,0. For the Box constructor method, this takes three (double) values, which should all be 100.

Next, declare a Cylinder named pole at the top of your class, and instantiate it inside of the .createBoardGameNodes() method, using a width of 50, a height of 250 and 24 for the number of sections or divisions used for the mesh (LINE) draw representation.

This should all look like the following Java code, which is shown highlighted in yellow and blue in Figure 12-4:

```
Cylinder pole;                   // Declare object for use at the top of your class
...
pole = new Cylinder(50, 250, 24);      // in .createBoardGameNodes() method
```

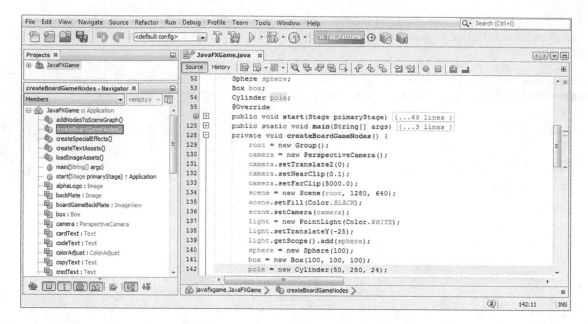

Figure 12-4. *Create a Cylinder object named pole and instantiate it with a radius of 50, a height of 250, and 24 divisions*

If you used your Run ➤ Project work process at this point, you would not see the pole object, as you have not added it to the JavaFX SceneGraph yet. Open the addNodesToSceneGraph() method and add the pole object to the end of the Java List contained inside of the parameter area (parens). This is all accomplished using the following Java code structure inside the .handle() method, as is shown highlighted in the middle of Figure 12-5:

```
gameBoard.getChildren().addAll(sphere, box, pole);      // in addNodesToSceneGraph() method
```

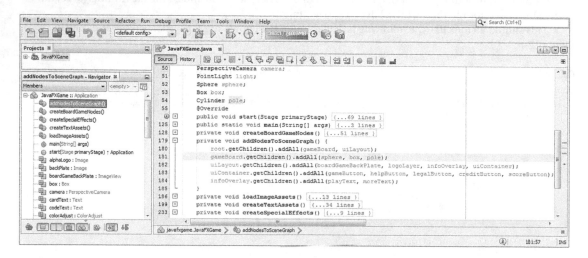

Figure 12-5. *Add a pole Cylinder object to SceneGraph, at the end of the gameBoard.getChildren().addAll() method call*

As you will see when we render this code in the 3D Scene, the order you add objects to your SceneGraph in 3D compositing turns out to be similar to what happens regarding 2D asset layer order in a 2D compositing StackPane as the 3D primitives will appear to be "in front of each other." The later that objects are added to the gameBoard Group in the SceneGraph, the later they will be rendered to the screen. Thus, the last primitive added to a SceneGraph will be rendered on top of all of the other primitives before it, and the first primitive added to a SceneGraph will be rendered first (that is, below or behind all of the other 3D primitives).

In most 3D software packages, three primitives located at 0,0,0 (Scene center) would render **inside** of each other. This tells us something very important as 3D artists regarding JavaFX, which is that you cannot perform **Constructive Solids Geometry (CSG)** modeling using JavaFX primitives. CSG was one of the early forms of modeling in 3D and involves using the basic 3D primitives in conjunction with boolean operations in order to create more complex 3D models.

Let's use your **Run ➤ Project** work process and see how JavaFX is rendering these three primitives located at 0, 0, 0. As you can see in Figure 12-6, the Cylinder object is in front of a Box object, which is in front of a Sphere object. Most 3D software packages would render this as a Box inside of a Sphere, possibly with the corners of the Box poking through the Sphere (depending on scale) and the ends of the Cylinder would be coming out of the top and bottom of the Sphere. I did this exercise in this particular order because it is critical for the developer to realize what they can do and what they **cannot** do as they build their Java 9 game. You can achieve this boolean effect in JavaFX by using a mesh object imported from a 3D modeler such as MOI3D, SILO or Blender where the Boolean operations have been done outside of JavaFX 9.

Figure 12-6. *Use the Run ➤ Project to see these three primitives in the Z-order that you added them to the SceneGraph*

Next, let's use some of the 3D primitive modification (move and rotate) method calls to move these away from center Scene and rotate the cube so that it does not look like a 2D object. This can all be accomplished using the .setTranslateX() and setRotate() method calls off the box and pole objects, as is shown at the bottom of Figure 12-7:

```
box.setTranslateX(500);
box.setRotate(45);
pole.setTranslateX(250);
```

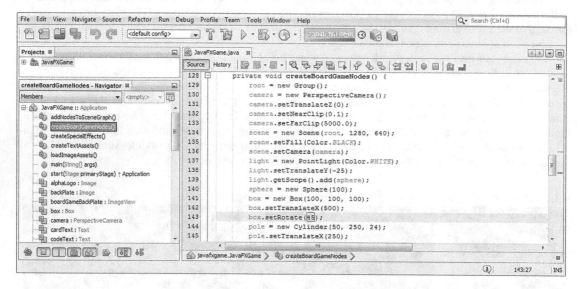

Figure 12-7. *Use setTranslateX(250) to move primitives 250 units apart and use setRotate(45) to rotate the box 45 degrees*

Next, use a **Run ➤ Project** work process to view the primitives individually. As you can see in Figure 12-8, the .setRotate() method is using the z-axis for its rotation, so your 3D object is still rendering as a 2D object. Let's fix that!

Figure 12-8. *All three primitives are now spaced apart; the box still looks 2D*

To change the rotation axis that your .setRotate() method uses to configure its rotation algorithm, there is a second **.setRotationAxis()** method that you can use to change the default **Rotate.Z_AXIS** setting to the **Rotate.X_AXIS** constant, which as you can see by the dot notation in the **Rotate** class.

Obviously, as you have learned by now, the .setRotationAxis() method call will have to take place **before** the .setRotate(45) method call so that the rotation axis will be changed before the rotate algorithm is actually utilized.

Add a .setRotateAxis() method call off your box object after the box.setTranslateX(500); method call, using the Rotate.X_AXIS constant to configure the Rotate algorithm for use. The Java statement sequence should look like the following Java code and can be seen near the bottom of Figure 12-9:

```
box.setTranslateX(500);
box.setRotationAxis(Rotate.X_AXIS);
box.setRotate(45);
pole = new Cylinder(50, 250, 24);
pole.setTranslateX(250);
```

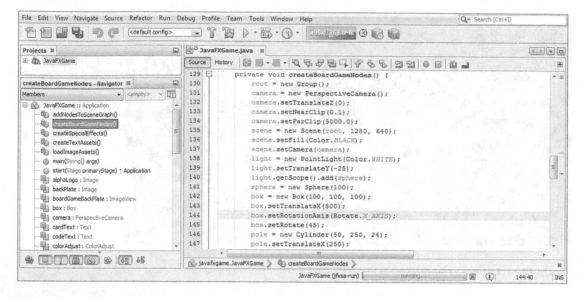

Figure 12-9. *Add a .setRotationAxis() method call off box after the box.setTranslateX(500); and set it to Rotate.X_AXIS*

Next, use a **Run ➤ Project** work process and again view your primitives individually. As you can see, in Figure 12-10, the .setRotate() method is now using the z-axis for its rotation, so your 3D object is now rendering as a 3D object, and you can see the shading (color or lightness difference on the different faces).

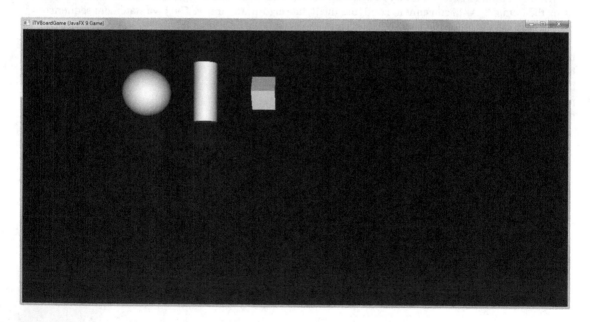

Figure 12-10. *Now all primitives are oriented in such a way that their default light gray shading is visible in the renderer*

There are more complex ways to rotate 3D objects in JavaFX that we will get into as the book progresses because rotation is quite a complex subject in 3D that doesn't seem to be "on the surface" (no pun intended). Rotation uses a more complex set of mathematics in its algorithms than translation, and some of this complexity will percolate to the surface and therefore will have to be dealt with, and comprehended by, all you pro Java 9 3D game developers.

Now that we have the three basic primitives offered in JavaFX separated and facing in a way that will show you more of their faces and edges in the rendered view, we'll take a closer look at what Face Culling and Draw Modes do to your geometry. We will save Material object creation and application for its own in Chapter 13; Material object creation is a core 3D topic (texture mapping) and should be treated as its own topic, as a 3D object's shading determines its visual quality.

Next, let's take a look at Draw Modes (called *rendering modes* in most 3D software packages) so that you can look at the 3D wireframe representations of your objects as you develop your pro Java 9 games.

Shape3D Draw Mode Property: Solid Geometry and Wireframe

Now that we have the three primary JavaFX primitives arrayed across our screen, let's take a look at the drawMode property of the Shape3D superclass, which is inherited by each of these primitives. This property uses a constant from the DrawMode class, as you may have guessed already, and the two constants available currently are **DrawMode.FILL** and DrawMode.LINE. The **FILL** constant gives you a Solid Model Geometry representation, and the **LINE** constant gives you a Wireframe Model Geometry representation. We are going to use the .setDrawMode(drawMode) method call in this section to change our three primitives from being solid models to being wireframe models so that we can change the resolution or divisions of the wireframe and see what that does and so that we can rotate the Sphere around the X dimension to see how its wireframe construction looks and how the divisions attribute changes how it looks (renders) in your 3D Scene. First, however, I am getting a bit tired of looking at these primitives in the upper-left corner of the 3D scene, so we are going to use .setTranslateZ(-500) to move the Camera object 100 percent closer (or scale the primitives up in size 100 percent) and use the .setTranslateY(300) method to center the primitives in the horizontal center of the view. Later we will use the .setTranslateX(-300) method call to center the primitives in the vertical center of the view.

Open your .start() method and your gameButton event handling code block and change the .setTranslateZ() method call value from -1000 to -500. Then add a .setTranslateY() method call off the camera object and pass it a -300 scene units data value, as shown in Figure 12-11 as well as in the following Java code statements:

```
camera.setTranslateZ(-500);
camera.setTranslateY(-300);
```

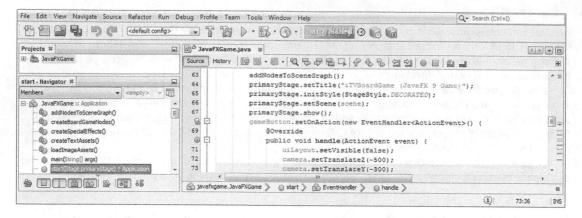

Figure 12-11. *Zoom the camera object in 100 percent using .setTranslateZ(-500), and move it down with .setTranslateY(-300)*

Next, let's open the createBoardGameNodes() method and add a **.setDrawMode**(DrawMode.**LINE**) method call to each of the primitives, setting their rendering mode from solid geometry to wireframe geometry so we can see their underlying construction. Your Java statements, which are highlighted in yellow in Figure 12-12, should look like the following:

```
sphere.setDrawMode(DrawMode.LINE);
box.setDrawMode(DrawMode.LINE);
pole.setDrawMode(DrawMode.LINE);
```

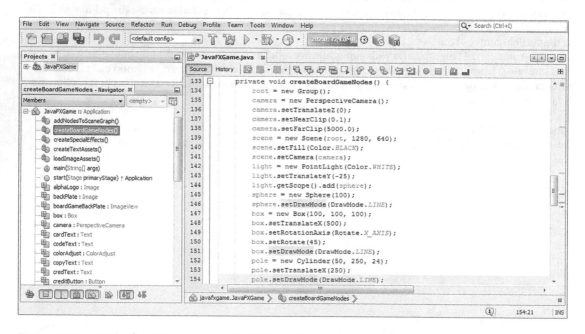

Figure 12-12. *Set the drawMode property to LINE for all primitives with a .setDrawMode(DrawMode.LINE) method call*

Next, use a **Run ➤ Project** work process and again view your primitives. As you can see, in Figure 12-13, your primitives are being rendered using a wireframe representation and are centered in the Y dimension in the 3D Scene.

Figure 12-13. *All three primitives are now rendered in wireframe mode and are centered vertically*

Center the camera in the X dimension using .setTranslateX() with the following code, shown in Figure 12-14:

```
camera.setTranslateX(-300);
```

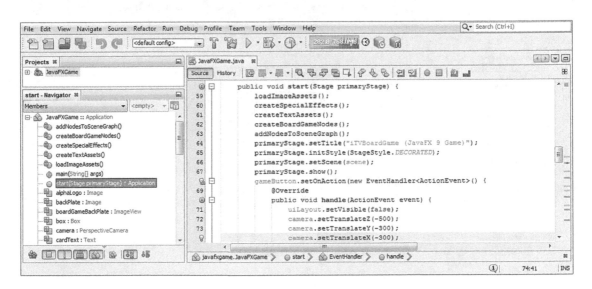

Figure 12-14. *Add a .setTranslateX(-300) to move your primitives to the vertical (X dimension) center of your 3D Scene*

Notice when you move the Camera object, it stays looking straight ahead, whereas in 3D software packages, there is a Camera "target" that stays locked in the center of the scene or on a 3D object in the Scene. In JavaFX, the Camera object is "fixed" with a straight line (called a *ray* or *vector*) that emanates from the back of the camera out through the front, going out to infinity in the direction the camera object is pointed in. So, in 3D software, if you move the camera up, its field of view rotates down, and there is a link (or line) between the camera and its subject.

If you wanted this behavior in JavaFX, you would have to rotate the camera manually, as the JavaFX Camera superclass currently has no specifyTarget attribute (target functionality). We will be looking at the PerspectiveCamera object and how to leverage it in a more advanced way in your 3D Scene as the book progresses because cameras are an important aspect of an i3D scene and an important tool for use in the pro Java 9 i3D games development process.

Before we render the 3D Scene again, since we know from our code that it is now going to be centered well enough for us to look at attributes such as divisions and face culling and see how these affect the polygons that make up the 3D primitives, let's use the overloaded (second) **Sphere(size, divisions)** constructor method format and reduce the mesh resolution of the Sphere object to optimize the amount of memory that it takes to hold this 3D object. You will also rotate it forward so that you can see the top of the Sphere's construction and also reduce the resolution of the Cylinder by 100 percent, from 24 to 12 divisions. I always use a division value that is divisible by four (90 degrees times 4 is 360), and half of the divisions are not even rendering if face culling is turned on. This can all be accomplished by using the following Java statements, which are highlighted in (and at the bottom of) Figure 12-15:

```java
sphere = new Sphere(100, 12);
sphere.setRotationAxis(Rotate.X_AXIS);
sphere.setRotate(90);
sphere.setDrawMode(DrawMode.LINE);
```

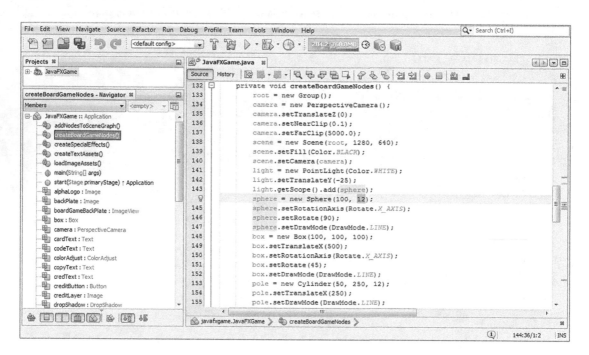

Figure 12-15. *Construct your Sphere with 12 divisions, X rotate it 90 degrees, and reduce your Cylinder to 12 divisions*

Now it's time to use a **Run ➤ Project** work process and render our Scene. As you can see in Figure 12-16, our 3D primitives are closer to the center of the 3D Scene, are easily viewable, and are using far less data to construct. As you saw in Figure 12-13, the Sphere was using 48 divisions to construct. This uses several hundred polygons and can be calculated as $48 \times 48 \times 2 = 192$; 192 polygons takes a lot of memory to process (storing and rendering) as each polygon has a lot of data to define it (location in model, size, orientation, color, normal direction, smoothing groups).

Figure 12-16. *Your primitives are now centered in the 3D Scene Camera view, and you can see the Sphere construction*

When we render these primitives in the next section on face culling, you will see the cube and cylinder have not really changed in appearance, so the cylinder's 100 percent decrease in divisions (24 to 12) was a successful optimization. The Sphere reduction of 200 percent (from 48 to 12) was a bit drastic, and the illusion of smoothness falls apart a bit around the perimeter of the Sphere, especially when rendered from the top, which is why I rotated it forward (X) 90 degrees.

Next, let's take a look at optimization for the rendering algorithm using back-face culling and how a lower resolution (fewer divisions) can affect the visual quality of the 3D primitives once they are rendered using solid mode.

Shape3D Face Culling Property: Optimize the Rendering Pipeline

The Shape3D cullFace property and the CullFace class are used to control face and polygon rendering optimization for your 3D Scene. The default is CullFace.NONE, so you will need to turn this optimization on using code, which I'm going to show you how to do in this section of the chapter. I think the models look better (more contrast) with face culling off, and if you optimize your pro Java 9 game well enough, it should play well on all platforms and devices without having to cull half the faces off of your model. That said, once you know how to do this, it should be easy enough for you to experiment during the testing phase to see how it affects **visual quality versus smoothness of gameplay**.

Let's continue to add code to the createBoardGameNodes() method to set backface culling for the primitive objects. First, we will need to change the **drawMode** property for your primitives back to FILL for solid modeling using **.setDrawMode**(DrawMode.**FILL**) on each of your sphere, box, and pole objects. Right after this method call on each of your primitive objects, add a .setCullFace(CullFace.BACK) method call on that object. If you use the pop-up helper work process in NetBeans 9, you will see that it writes your code using the default CullFace.NONE setting, so you will have to change this to CullFace.BACK in order to turn on this rendering pipeline optimization algorithm.

The Java code for your backface culling statements are highlighted at the bottom of Figure 12-17 and should look like the following Java code:

```
sphere.setDrawMode(DrawMode.FILL);
sphere.setCullFace(CullFace.BACK);
box.setDrawMode(DrawMode.FILL);
box.setCullFace(CullFace.BACK);
pole.setDrawMode(DrawMode.FILL);
pole.setCullFace(CullFace.BACK);
```

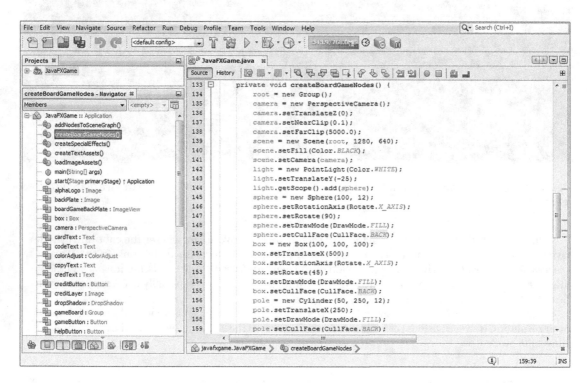

Figure 12-17. *Add method calls to .setCullFace() with the value CullFace.BACK off of all of the primitives in your Scene*

Figure 12-18 shows a **Run ➤ Project** Java code testing work process, showing the backface culling algorithm installed and operating on the 3D Scene primitives. Notice on your Sphere that a reduced geometry resolution (fewer divisions) causes some smoothing problems on the mesh where the mesh topology is showing through the smoothing algorithm. I'd increase Sphere divisions to 24 to mitigate this, which is still a 100 percent optimization on the default setting.

Figure 12-18. *The renderer is now rendering half as much 3D data, and your lower resolution can be seen on the Sphere*

Also notice that the shading contrast on the cube (Box) primitive has far less contrast (difference in shading color between faces) when backface culling is turned on. This will become less of a problem (less noticeable) the more custom texture mapping you do (covered in the next chapter and thereafter), but it may be why the default is NONE for the FaceCull class, and for this method call, because the face culling optimization may be affecting contrast (quality) in some way in the current algorithm code. I set up the chapter in this way so that you could see this because one of the most basic primitives is showing a distinct reduction in contrast between faces, using a default medium gray shader color, as you can see if you compare Figure 12-10 and Figure 12-18, where contrast goes from high to almost none whatsoever.

Next, let's take a look at the three mesh-related classes, Mesh, TriangleMesh, and MeshView, to see what these do, and how they interrelate, as they will allow you to render complex mesh objects created using 3D software.

JavaFX Mesh Superclass: Construct a TriangleMesh

It is important to understand the abstract **Mesh** superclass and how it relates to its **TriangleMesh** subclass, which can be used to "hand-code" complex mesh objects into existence, and how it relates to the **MeshView** class, which is actually a subclass of **Shape3D** and not of Mesh! This is so that MeshView can inherit (extend) the cullFace, drawMode, and material properties of Shape3D, which are, of course, crucial to making a mesh object realistic (especially the **material** property and **Material** class). The MeshView constructor takes a Mesh object, as you will see. That is the core class (algorithm) that complex 3D objects is based on, so Mesh and MeshView are the most key classes to use for pro Java 9 games development. If, for some reason, you want to **code** complex polygonal geometry, also called "a triangle mesh," which is not an optimal workflow, you can use TriangleMesh, which we will cover in detail.

A better workflow is to use an external 3D software package and import your 3D object directly into a Mesh object, which is then referenced by a MeshView object. This is a much faster way to get an advanced i3D game up and running quickly and efficiently, as well as a way to bring specialized artisans into an i3D game development workflow.

JavaFX Mesh Superclass: Your Raw 3D Model Data Container

The public abstract Mesh superclass is deceptively simple with only a Mesh() constructor method and a TriangleMesh subclass (for loading it with mesh data using Java code), so we'll cover it here first. It is essentially an object used to contain 3D data and is contained in the **javafx.scene.shape** package with the other 3D model-centric classes. The Java class hierarchy looks like the following, as the Mesh class was scratch-coded to be a Java class holding a representation of a 3D Mesh:

```
java.lang.Object
  > javafx.scene.shape.Mesh
```

This is a base class for representing complex 3D geometric surfaces that are not JavaFX Shape3D primitives. Note that this is obviously a conditional feature as complex 3D geometry will require a 3D rendering pipeline to be in place to be useful to your pro Java 9 games development. Polling the ConditionalFeature.SCENE3D will be necessary.

As stated initially, the constructor method is very basic and will look like the following Java code:

```
protected Mesh() // Protected Code Cannot Be Used Directly (but can be used by a subclass)
```

Next, let's take a look at the MeshView class, which will reference, hold in memory, and display this Mesh object in the 3D Scene using the rendering engine. This class is the "bridge" between the Mesh engine and Shape3D.

JavaFX MeshView Class: Format and Present Your 3D Mesh Data

The public MeshView class is almost as simple as the Mesh class, with only two overloaded MeshView() constructor methods and no subclasses, so I'll cover it here next. It is a subclass of Shape3D and stored in the **javafx.scene.shape** package. It implements the Styleable and EventTarget interfaces just like the three primitives classes do. It is used to define a 3D surface using the raw 3D model data held in a Mesh object. The Java class hierarchy for the MeshView class looks like the following, as a MeshView class needs to inherit all of those key Shape3D rendering characteristics:

```
java.lang.Object
  > javafx.scene.Node
    > javafx.scene.shape.Shape3D
      > javafx.scene.shape.MeshView
```

The MeshView object has one ObjectProperty<Mesh> mesh property that specifies the 3D mesh data for the MeshView, which it gets from the second overloaded constructor method parameter or using a .getMesh(mesh) method call. This class (object) also inherits the core Shape3D properties from the class javafx.scene.shape.Shape3D, which you have already covered (except for material) and which are cullFace, drawMode, and material.

There are two overloaded constructor methods. One creates an empty MeshView to be loaded with Mesh object (3D data) in the future, which would of course utilize the following Java statement format:

```
meshView = new MeshView();
```

The second overloaded constructor method call both instantiates the MeshView object and loads it with a Mesh object (3D geometry data) at the same time, using the following object instantiation Java statement format:

```
meshView = new MeshView(yourMeshNameHere);
```

The MeshView class has three method calls for working with Mesh objects, including a **getMesh(Mesh)** method call that will get the **Mesh** object value of the property **mesh**, the **ObjectProperty<Mesh> meshProperty()** method call that will specify the 3D mesh (Mesh object) data for any MeshView that this method is called off of, and the **void setMesh(Mesh value)** method call that will set the Mesh object value for the MeshView property **mesh**.

Before we cover the TriangleMesh class, let's take a look at the **VertexFormat** class, which will define vertex data, by specifying a vertex data format to use with a given 3D model (that is, the Mesh object and its 3D model data).

JavaFX VertexFormat Class: Define Your 3D Vertex Data Format

The **public final VertexNormal** class also extends the Java Object master class, which means the class was scratch-coded to define a format for the Array of data points, their texture coordinates, and their normals, if any are provided by the external 3D models exported in a variety of data formats supported by JavaFX import/export software. This class is a utility class for the Mesh, TriangleMesh, and MeshView classes, as you can tell by its final modifier, which means that it cannot be subclassed. As with the other six we have covered, it is kept in the **javafx.scene.shape** package in the javafx.graphics module, and its class hierarchy looks like the following:

```
java.lang.Object
  > javafx.scene.shape.VertexFormat
```

The VertexFormat class (object) defines two different data format constants that reflect the type of 3D data that is contained in each vertex in a 3D Mesh object. The **static VertexFormat POINT_NORMAL_TEXCOORD** field will specify a format for a vertex that contains data for the **point coordinates**, a **normal**, and **texture coordinates**. A **static VertexFormat POINT_TEXCOORD** field will specify a format for a vertex that contains data for the **point coordinates** and for **texture coordinates**. I recommend using the format that supports normals as the more data that you can use to define your 3D models, the more the renderer can render them accurately and, therefore, more professionally.

There are five methods in this class for working with vertices and their normal, point, and texture coordinate data components. The .getVertexIndexSize() method will return the integer number of component indices that will represent a vertex index. The .getNormalIndexOffset() method will return the integer index offset for the face array of the normal component within a given vertex. The .getPointIndexOffset() method will return your integer index offset in the face array of the point component within a given vertex. The .getTexCoordIndexOffset() method will return the index offset in a face array of the texture coordinates component within a vertex. The String toString() method will return the string (text) data for the VertexFormat, allowing you to look at the vertex data in a readable format.

Next, let's take a look at the TriangleMesh object, which is the most complicated; it allows you to do 3D model creation using Java code. We will not be looking at an example of this during this chapter because it is not the most efficient way to get quick, professional i3D game development 3D model creation result.

This is because using professional 3D modelling, texturing, rendering, and animation software packages such as the open source Blender.org, Autodesk 3D Studio Max, Maya, or NewTek Lightwave is the most logical work process to create a professional 3D model.

Because of the significant number of 3D data import file formats, 3D models can more quickly be created, and then pro Java 9 game developers can use one of the JavaFX 9 importer formats to bring that high-quality 3D data into JavaFX as a Mesh object.

We will look at this work process during Chapter 14, after we look at texture mapping in Chapter 13, so that we understand more about what texture mapping is since it is also used in third-party 3D modeling software packages. Using third-party development tools such as Fusion, Blender, Audacity, Gimp, and Inkscape often yields better results.

JavaFX TriangleMesh Class: Create a 3D Polygonal Mesh Object

The public TriangleMesh class is a subclass of the Mesh superclass and does not implement any interfaces as it is used to create 3D data intended to be stored inside of the Mesh object, much like 3D models that are imported into JavaFX using a number of popular 3D file format importers that we'll be covering in Chapter 14. The TriangleMesh is stored in the **javafx.scene.shape** package in the javafx.graphics module, and its Java class hierarchy looks like the following:

```
java.lang.Object
  > javafx.scene.shape.Mesh
  > javafx.scene.shape.TriangleMesh
```

A TriangleMesh object is used to define a 3D polygonal mesh. This object will use one of two VertexFormat constants and include a set of separate data array objects containing vertex components, including points, normals, texture coordinates, and an array of faces that define the individual triangles of the mesh. As I have mentioned in this chapter more than once, this low-level complexity can be avoided altogether, and accelerated past, by using an external 3D software package that supports modeling, such as Blender, Hexagon, Lightwave, Maya, or 3D Studio Max.

Note that the JavaFX term **point** equates to the 3D software term **vertex**. JavaFX 9 uses *vertex* to refer to the vertex (point) and all of its associated attributes, including its normal position and associated UV texture map coordinates. So, the point referred to in the TriangleMesh method names and method descriptions that we will be covering later during this section of the chapter actually refers to 3D point (x, y, z) locational data in 3D space, representing the spatial positioning for one single vertex.

Similarly, the term *points* (or a collection of point) is used to indicate sets of 3D points representing multiple vertices. The term *normal* is used to indicate a 3D vector (nx, ny, nz) in 3D space that represents a direction of a single vertex, which tells the rendering engine which way the face is facing so it can render the texture on the correct side of the face. The term *normals* (or a collection of normal data) is used to indicate sets of 3D vectors for multiple vertices.

The term *texCoord* is used to indicate one single pair of 2D texture coordinates (u,v) for a single vertex, while the term *texCoords* (a collection of texCoord) is used to indicate sets of texture coordinates across multiple vertices.

Finally, the term *face* is used to indicate a set of three interleaving points, normals (these are optional and will depend on the associated VertexFormat field type specified), and texture coordinates that together would represent the geometric topology of one single triangle. The term *faces* (a collection of face) is used to indicate a set of triangles (each represented using a face), which is generally what a 3D polygonal model is comprised of. Confused yet? As I said, using an import/export workflow and letting the advanced 3D modeling software user interface do all of the work is a better way to get incredible results rather than trying to use Java to place points, normal, and UV coordinates into 3D space. What I am trying to do in this book is show you the fastest, easiest, and most optimized way to create a hybrid 2D and 3D game so that you can create the pro Java 9 game on the market which has never been experienced before by any game player.

This TriangleMesh class (object) has one **ObjectProperty<VertexFormat> vertexFormat** property, which will be used to specify the vertex format of this TriangleMesh, using the VertexFormat utility class, and therefore this will be either **VertexFormat.POINT_TEXCOORD** or **VertexFormat.POINT_NORMAL_TEXCOORD**.

A TriangleMesh class has two overloaded constructor methods. The first (empty) one creates an instance of TriangleMesh class using the default VertexFormat.POINT_TEXCOORD format type and looks like the following:

```
triangleMesh = new TriangleMesh(); // Creates Points & Texture Map Only Polygonal Mesh Object
```

The second constructor method creates a new instance of TriangleMesh using the VertexFormat that is specified in the parameter area of the method call. This looks like the following Java instantiation statement:

```
normalTriangleMesh = new TriangleMesh(VertexFormat.POINT_NORMAL_TEXCOORD) // Includes Normals
```

There are a dozen methods used for working with TriangleMesh object construction; let's look at them next.

The **.getFaceElementSize()** method will return the number of elements that represent a given face. Use this method to determine what data (point, normal, texturemap) is being used for any given face.

The **ObservableFaceArray getFaces()** method will get the entire array of faces in a TriangleMesh object, including indices into the points, normals (only if VertexFormat.**POINT_NORMAL_TEXCOORD** is specified for a mesh), and texCoords arrays. Use this to extract the polygon data from your TriangleMesh object.

The **ObservableIntegerArray getFaceSmoothingGroups()** method will get a **faceSmoothingGroups** data array from a TriangleMesh object. Smoothing groups define where seams appear in your surface shading (smoothing) for the rendered 3D object. We covered this topic earlier in the book in Chapter 3.

The **.getNormalElementSize()** method will return the number of elements that represent a normal in your TriangleMesh object. This tells you how many normals are being used to represent surface direction.

The **ObservableFloatArray getNormals()** method will get your normals array for a TriangleMesh object.

The **.getPointElementSize()** method will return the number of elements representing XYZ points in your TriangleMesh object. This will tell you how many vertices (vertex count) in the 3D model in your TriangleMesh.

The **ObservableFloatArray getPoints()** method is used to get the points data array for a TriangleMesh.

The **.getTexCoordElementSize()** method will return a number of data elements that represent texture coordinates within a TextureMesh object. Use this to determine the number of UV mapping coordinates in the model.

The **ObservableFloatArray getTexCoords()** method will get your texCoords array for your TriangleMesh object. Use this to extract the texture coordinate data (only) from your TextureMesh 3D polygonal object.

The **VertexFormat getVertexFormat()** method will get the value of your vertexFormat property from inside your TriangleMesh object. Use this to ascertain if Normals are supported (or not) with this 3D model data.

The **void .setVertexFormat(VertexFormat value)** method is used to set the value of the vertexFormat property for the TriangleMesh object. Be sure the data arrays inside the object match up correctly with this setting.

The **ObjectProperty<VertexFormat> vertexFormatProperty()** method can be used to specify the vertex format for the TriangleMesh; it can be either VertexFormat.POINT_TEXCOORD or VertexFormat. POINT_NORMAL_TEXCOORD.

After we learn more about shaders, textures, and mapping in the next chapter, we'll get into 3D software and learn the import workflow that allows us to bridge powerful 3D software over to the JavaFX 9 game engine.

Summary

In this twelveth chapter, we learned about the classes in the **javafx.scene.shape** package that allow you to work with 3D models, including primitives with the Box, Sphere, and Cylinder classes and polygonal objects with the MeshView, VertexFormat, and TriangleMesh classes. These classes all are based on the abstract Mesh and Shape3D superclasses.

You learned how to create 3D primitives and how to set their properties, you learned about face culling and wireframes, and you observed how the Camera object works when you move (translate) it around the 3D Scene.

You learned about the difference between algorithmically (code) generated primitives and more advanced polygonal mesh objects and about the different workflows for creating 3D models for your pro Java 9 game design and development pipeline, which we will be continuing to learn about over the next several chapters.

In the next chapter, we are going to take a look at the JavaFX texture mapping using the abstract **Material** superclass and its **PhongMaterial** subclass, as well as learn more about shaders, textures, texture mapping, and related topics such as ambient, diffuse, specular, and self-illumination attributes.

■ ■ ■

CHAPTER 13

3D Model Shader Creation: Using the JavaFX 9 PhongMaterial Class

Now that you have learned about the 3D assets, called *primitives*, that are included in the JavaFX API, let's start to get some foundational knowledge about how to "dress up" those 3D assets using 2D image assets, which we will turn into *materials* that we can apply to the 3D surface using a *shader*. JavaFX supports the Phong shader, which contains several *channels* that accept special images called *texture maps* that apply different effects such as coloration, illumination, surface bumps, surface shininess, and so forth. JavaFX comes with two core shader classes in the **javafx.scene.paint** package in the **javafx.graphics** module that specifically "shade" or surface 3D geometry (primitives or mesh) for you, and we are going to take a look at them during this chapter. We will also look at how to use GIMP 2.8.22 to create texture maps rapidly and accurately based on pixels and mathematics so they provide an accurate texture mapping result. We will also get back into our **JavaFXGame** primary application class coding and start to add Phong shader materials to 3D primitives to get some practice. You could do this in 3D software packages like Blender, but a board game is simple enough (squares, spheres, cylinders) that we can do this using only JavaFX code. This means we do not need to import (and distribute) 3D models but can rather write code to model your i3D game "out of thin air." This will also teach you a lot more about the 3D APIs in Java 9 and JavaFX, as you will learn how to model complex 3D objects using only Java 9 and its JavaFX APIs.

During this chapter, you will be learning about the JavaFX 3D shader class hierarchy, which is contained in the **javafx.scene.paint** package. In Java 9 and Android 8, the **Paint** class applies pixel colors and attributes to the Canvas and in this case the surface of 3D primitives. The paint package contains classes that are related to this "skinning," or texture mapping objective. You will cover **Material**, a superclass that holds the top-level shader definition, and the **PhongMaterial** class, which can be used to create **a texture map, or "skin," for 3D** primitives (covered in Chapter 12).

JavaFX Material Superclass: i3D Shader Properties

The **public abstract Material** superclass is used to create the **PhongMaterial** class that you will use to create a **material** attribute used by the Shape3D subclasses for the i3D primitives that you use in your pro Java 9 games design and development. The advanced models that you import from external 3D software packages will already have materials (sometimes called *shaders*) and texture maps applied to them in the 3D software production environment, and after import, they will be in Mesh objects displayed using MeshView objects, so you will not always directly use the PhongMaterial class at this low level to shade advanced 3D objects in most practical applications. The Material superclass is even more of an empty shell than Mesh, as it has only one empty constructor and no properties or methods! The Material class is part of the **javafx.scene.paint** package and has the following Java class hierarchy:

```
java.lang.Object
  > javafx.scene.paint.Material
```

The one empty constructor method is **protected**, which means that it is not instantiated directly. However, this constructor method functionality is implemented in the PhongMaterial subclass, as PhongMaterial(), which we will be covering in the next section of this chapter.

```
protected Material()
```

Next, let's take a look at the PhongMaterial subclass, which represents the **Phong** shader rendering algorithm. This is what we will be using (and learning about) directly during the chapter to color our 3D primitives we created during Chapter 12.

JavaFX PhongMaterial: Phong Shading Algorithm and Attributes

The **public PhongMaterial** class extends the Material class to define **Phong** (algorithm) shader materials, their color settings, and their texture maps for your JavaFX 3D Scene. This class is kept in the **javafx.scene. paint** package in the **javafx.graphics** module and is a subclass of Material, as you know, so you will have the following Java class hierarchy:

```
java.lang.Object
 > javafx.scene.paint.Material
 > javafx.scene.paint.PhongMaterial
```

The Phong shading (materials and texture rendering) algorithm in JavaFX 9 describes the interaction between your PointLight object(s) and AmbientLight object (if present) and the surface of the 3D primitive that the PhoneMaterial object is applied to. The PhongMaterial object reflects light while applying a diffuse and specular color tinting, just like light in real life. When it bounces off a colored object, the light itself becomes colored. The PhongMaterial algorithm supports the AmbientLight object settings, if present, and supports self-illumination, or "glow" mapping, so that you can apply special effects to further enhance the shader realism.

According to the JavaFX 9 PhongMaterial documentation, the coloration of any given point on a geometric surface is a mathematical function of these four components: ambient, diffuse, specular, and self-illumination map. Subcomponents (algorithm input) for these include AmbientLight (Object), PointLight (Object), Diffuse Color (setting), Diffuse Color Map (Image Object), Specular Color (setting), Specular Power (setting), Specular Map (Image Object), Self Illumination, or Glow Map (Image Object).

The final color for an AmbientLight source if there is more than one AmbientLight object, in which case their values will simply be summed (which is why I suggested using one), will be computed using the following equation:

```
For each AmbientLight (Object) Source [i]: { ambient += AmbientLightColor[i] } // Color Summed
```

The PointLight source algorithm calculation is far more advanced, which is why I suggested using PointLight for your use in Pro Java 9 3D Games, as it allows fine-tuned control over how PhongMaterial objects perform, as well as adding more dramatic lighting (fall-off, shadows, higher contrast, etc.) to your 3D Scene, making it more photoreal. It is important to note that the period used in these equations is referencing the **dot product** mathematical operation.

```
For each PointLight (Object) Source [i]:
{    diffuse += (SurfaceToLightVector . Normal) * PointLightSourceColor[i]

     specular += ( (NormalizedReflectionVector . NormalizedViewVector)
              ^ (specularPower * intensity(specularMap)) )
              * PointLightSourceColor[i]
}
```

The color values in your rendered result will be calculated using the following input components algorithm:

```
color = ((ambient + diffuse) * diffuseColor * diffuseMap
     + specular * specularColor * specularMap
     + selfIlluminationMap
```

These are outlined here for the sake of completeness and because they are outlined in the PhongMaterial documentation, not because you need to become an advanced shader mathematician in order to develop pro Java 9 games. That said, this will give you an idea of how the shader input components we are going to be exploring during this chapter interact with each other in the Phong shader algorithm and how, with enough map and parameter tweaking, fine-tuning any one of these inputs can allow you to achieve any professional surface rendering result you desire!

There are seven properties in the PhongMaterial class that tell you what types of texture maps and color specifications you can use to surface your 3D primitives with. These are also available in all standard 3D packages, so models created and textured externally to JavaFX 9 also have access to these (and more, actually).

The **ObjectProperty<Image> bumpMap** is an Image object that's used to simulate bumps or slight variations in surface height on a 3D model. This can be used to add **fine surface details** to a 3D model that are not actually part of a model's geometry surface topology, but a bump map will make it **appear** to be part of the model's physical topology. A bump map is sometimes incorrectly called a normal map, as it is in the JavaFX 9 documentation. The documentation says "the bump map of the PhongMaterial is a normal map stored as an RGB Image," so I wrote to Oracle asking them if the bumpMap property was a bump map or a more advanced normal map! What I'm hoping is that it was originally a bump map algorithm that was upgraded over time to support a more complex normal map algorithm while leaving the property name bumpMap, so as to not break existing code. Normal maps can create far superior surface effects.

The **ObjectProperty<Color> diffuseColor** represents the diffuse, or base (foundational), surface color of the material. The color can be changed over the surface of the object by using a Diffuse Color Map or Diffuse Map. If your 3D software has more advanced shading map types than can be imported into JavaFX, a technique called *baking* can be used, where the 3D renderer's shader pipeline and texture map result can be rendered into a diffuse map image and then exported (as a TIFF, BMP, PNG, or TGA 24-bit RGB image) and used as a diffuse map Image object in JavaFX. Let's take a look at that next, in fact, since we've basically covered it already!

The **ObjectProperty<Image> diffuseMap** property references an Image object whose data defines a diffuse map that will be mapped using the UV texture coordinates onto the surface of a 3D primitive using a PhongMaterial.

The **ObjectProperty<Image> selfIlluminationMap** property references an Image object whose data defines a glow or illumination map (using a grayscale Image object representing lighting intensity) that will be mapped onto a 3D primitive using the UV texture coordinates onto the surface of the primitive using a PhongMaterial.

The **ObjectProperty<Color> specularColor** property specifies the specular color for the PhongMaterial. This is the color for the specular highlight (see Figure 13-5) that refines the visual characteristics for a 3D primitive surface.

The **ObjectProperty<Image> specularMap** property references an Image object whose pixel data defines an area on the surface of the 3D primitive that will respond to specular color using the specular map (a grayscale Image object representing where specular color will or will not be applied). This should be mapped onto a primitive using UV texture coordinates and will affect how shiny (or not shiny) specular mapped areas of the primitive surface will be.

The **DoubleProperty specularPower** property is used to specify a power (I like to think of it as focus) for the specular highlight. This attribute will be especially noticable on sphere and cylinder (curved) primitives, as shown in Figure 13-8, which has a high (tight or focused) specular highlight power value of 100 applied to the phongMaterial.

The PhongMaterial class has three overloaded constructor methods. The first one creates a new instance of a PhongMaterial object using the default **Color.WHITE diffuseColor** property. This would use the following Java code:

```
phongMaterial = new PhongMaterial();
```

The second constructor will create a new instance of a PhongMaterial object using a specified **diffuseColor** property. This would use the following Java code and the Color class **GOLD** constant, as we will in our code later:

```
phongMaterial = new PhongMaterial(Color.GOLD);
```

The third constructor allows you to specify the diffuse color and four different types of effects maps. This is the most convenient constructor method, which we will use once we get to more advanced stages of our game design and development. This advanced constructor method will take the following Java code statement format:

```
phongMaterial = new PhongMaterial(Color diffuseColor, Image diffuseMap, Image specularMap,
                                  Image bumpMap, Image selfIlluminationMap)
```

Finally, let's take a look at the 22 methods that allow you to work with all of these PhongMaterial components. These allow you to change a PhongMaterial on the fly, or interactively, using Java code. This will allow you to create some pretty impressive effects on your 3D and i3D game properties, as you will see during this book.

The **ObjectProperty<Color> diffuseColorProperty()** method call will return the **diffuseColor** property for the PhongMaterial that it is called off of. This is a **Color** value that sets the foundational (or base) color for the primitive.

The **ObjectProperty<Color> specularColorProperty()** method call returns a **specularColor** property for the PhongMaterial that it is called off of. This is a **Color** value that sets the specular (or highlight) color for the primitive.

The **DoubleProperty specularPowerProperty()** method call returns a double **specularpower** property for a PhongMaterial that it is called off of. This is a **Double** value that sets a specular (or highlight) power for a primitive.

The **ObjectProperty<Image> bumpMapProperty()** method call will return the **bumpMap** property for the PhongMaterial that it is called off of. This is a normal map that is stored as an RGB **Image** object.

The **ObjectProperty<Image> diffuseMapProperty()** method call will return the **diffuseMap** property for the PhongMaterial that it is called off of. This is a diffuse color map that is stored as an RGB **Image** object.

The **ObjectProperty<Image> selfIlluminationMapProperty()** method call will return a **selfIlluminationMap** property for the PhongMaterial that it is called off of. This self-illumination map is stored as an RGB **Image** object.

The **ObjectProperty<Image> specularMapProperty()** method call returns the **specularMap** property for the PhongMaterial that it is called off of. This specular color map is stored as an RGB **Image** object.

The **getBumpMap()** method call gets the **Image** object for the PhongMaterial property **bumpMap**.

The **getDiffuseColor()** method call gets the **Color** value for the PhongMaterial property **diffuseColor**.

The **getDiffuseMap()** method call gets the **Image** object for the PhongMaterial property **diffuseMap**.

The **getSelfIlluminationMap()** method call gets the **Image** object for the property **selfIlluminationMap**.

The **getSpecularColor()** method call gets the **Color** value for the PhongMaterial property **specularColor**.

The **getSpecularMap()** method call gets the **Image** object for the PhongMaterial property **specularMap**.

The **getSpecularPower()** method call gets a **double value** for a PhongMaterial property **specularPower**.

The **void setBumpMap(Image image)** method call sets the **Image** reference for the property **bumpMap**.

The **void setDiffuseColor(Color color)** method call sets the **Color** value for the property **diffuseColor**.

The **void setDiffuseMap(Image image)** method call sets an Image reference for the property **diffuseMap**.

The **void setSelfIlluminationMap(Image)** method call sets the Image for the property **selfIlluminationMap**.

The **void setSpecularColor(Color color)** method call sets the Color value for the property **specularColor**.

The **void setSpecularMap(Image image)** method call sets an **Image** object for a property **specularMap**.

The **void setSpecularPower(double value)** method call sets the value of the property **specularPower**.

The **toString()** method call converts any data in a nontext (binary, numeric, etc.) format into a text format.

Next, let's implement some of the core color attributes in our JavaFXGame class and see how they function.

Implementing PhongMaterial: Assigning Color and Power Values

Let's get down to business now that we've perused the PhongMaterial class. Let's declare a PhongMaterial object at the top of the JavaFXGame class and name it phongMaterial. In the createBoardGameNodes() method after the light object code, add a PhongMaterial instantiation using the second overloaded constructor method and set the diffuse color to Color.GOLD, as shown highlighted in Figure 13-1 as well as in the following Java code statement:

```
PhongMaterial phongMaterial;                  // Declared at the top of the JavaFXGame class
...
phongMaterial = new PhongMaterial(Color.GOLD);  // In the createBoardGameNodes() method body
```

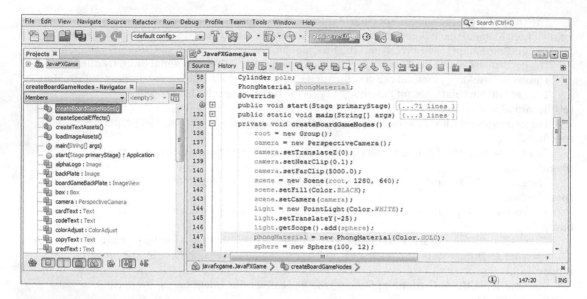

Figure 13-1. *Declare and instantiate your phongMaterial object and configure its diffuse color value to be Color.GOLD*

As you know, your PhongMaterial object can be configured with color values and loaded up with cool effect texture maps (Image objects), but unless you utilize the Shape3D class setMaterial(Material) method call (which you learned about in the previous chapter) to wire the 3D primitive and the Phong shader definition together, you won't see the shader applied to the 3D object's surface.

After the sphere object instantiation, add a setMaterial(phongMaterial) method call off of the sphere object using dot notation, as shown highlighted in yellow in Figure 13-2. Add this same method call to your pole Cylinder object and the box Box object as well. I clicked the phongMaterial shader object to highlight all of the uses of it, from declaration to instantiation to usage, in yellow in NetBeans 9 before I took the screenshot. The Java code for the statements that you have added should look like the following:

```
sphere.setMaterial(phongMaterial);
box.setMaterial(phongMaterial);
pole.setMaterial(phongMaterial);
```

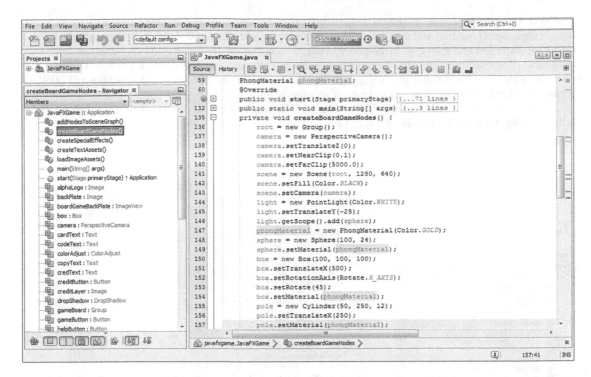

Figure 13-2. *Wire the phongMaterial to the three primitives, using a setMaterial(phongMaterial) method call off each*

Use your **Run ➤ Project** work process, and view the phongMaterial rendering, which is shown in Figure 13-3.

Figure 13-3. *Showing the phongMaterial object with the diffuseColor property set to a Color.GOLD value*

Next, let's add a specular (highlight) color to your phongMaterial shader object using the setSpecularColor() method and the **Color.YELLOW** constant. Add a line of code after the phongMaterial object instantiation and then type in the phongMaterial object name. Hit the period key, select the setSpecularColor(Color value) option from a pop-up helper selector, and double-click it to insert it into your Java statement. Type **Color** inside the parameter area and then a period key, and select the **YELLOW** constant, either by scrolling down or by typing **Y** to jump to the Y color constants.

Your resulting Java statement should look like the following Java code, which is shown highlighted in yellow and light blue in the middle of Figure 13-4:

```
phongMaterial.setSpecularColor(Color.YELLOW);
```

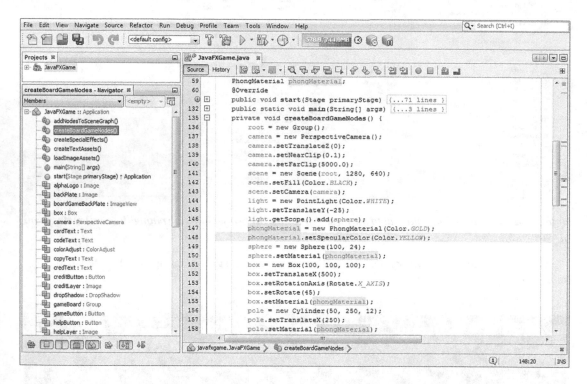

Figure 13-4. *Call the setSpecularColor() method off of the phongMaterial object, passing the Color.YELLOW constant*

If you use your **Run ➤ Project** work process, at this point, you will see that the appearance of the surface of your primitives has changed drastically the more rounded edges the primitive has. In fact, if you compare Figure 13-3 and Figure 13-5, you'll see that the Box primitive is not affected by specular color highlights at all, unless you animate it, in which case an occasional face would be colored with the specular color when it is parallel to the PointLight.

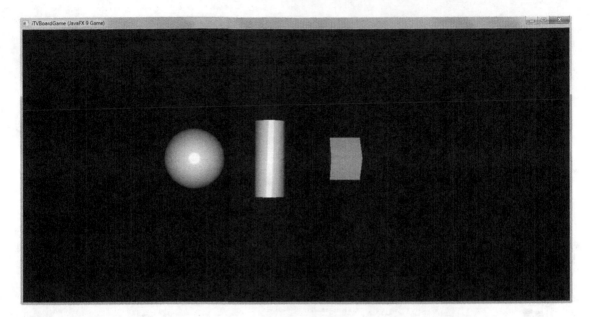

Figure 13-5. *Run your project to see the PhongShader object configured to use a Color.YELLOW specularColor property*

The appearance of the Cylinder and Sphere class (object) primitives has changed drastically, however, with the addition of a specular highlight using the specularColor property. I used YELLOW to give it a metallic look, but if you use WHITE (the default), it will look more normal. Notice that the PointLight can be set to WHITE, and you can intercede (add a color filter) to the PointLight before it hits the primitive surface.

Therefore, if you are seeking photorealism, make sure you match your PointLight and specularColor values!

The specularPower property (attribute) of the PhongMaterial class (object) controls how shiny your surface is, at least on curved objects. Having zero specular highlights, as shown in Figure 13-3, creates what is called a *matte* surface. It is important to note that calling setSpecularPower(0) will not remove the specular highlight. In fact, that would do just the opposite and give you a huge "blown-out" specular highlight, which looks terrible. Let's play around with this property next, and then we can move on to look at all the other properties. The rest of the properties involve Maps and their Image objects, which will involve digital imaging software, in our case GIMP 2.10 (or 3.0 if it has been released).

Let's add a **specularPower** property setting to the phongMaterial shader object using a **setSpecularPower()** method call with the double data value of 12. Technically, this is annotated in your Java code as "12.0d." However, since an Integer (just 12) data value fits into (conforms with) the Double specification, you can just use 12 and the Java build and compile process will understand what you are doing and make sure it's configured as a Double value (at runtime).

Add a line of code after the PhongMaterial object instantiation and type in the phongMaterial object name. Hit the period key, select the setSpecularPower(Double value) option from a pop-up helper selector, and double-click it to insert it into your Java statement. Type **12** or **12.0d** inside the parameter area.

Your resulting Java code will look like one of the following two Java statements, shown in the bottom third of Figure 13-6:

```
sphere.setSpecularPower(12);    // If you use Integer (simpler) format Java will convert for
                                   you
sphere.setSpecularPower(12.0d); // You can also use the 12.0d (double) required numeric format
```

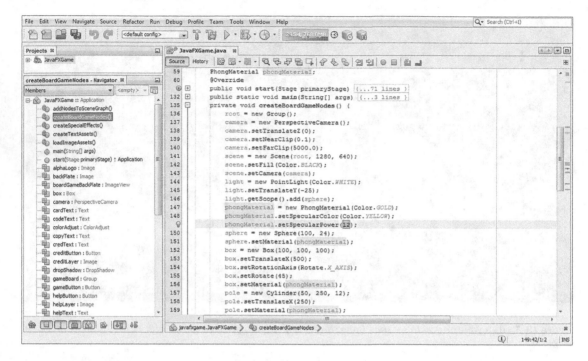

Figure 13-6. *Call the setSpecularPower() method off of the phongMaterial object, passing the double value of 12*

I fooled around with this value, changing it and rendering via Run ➤ Project. The default, shown in Figure 13-5, seems to be around 20, or 20.0d. Changing this value gives very subtle changes; lower numbers will serve to widen the specular highlight (try a zero setting, but don't use it in your games other than for special effects), and high numbers will constrict it to a pinpoint on any curved surface. Flat surfaces will not be affected much by this, if at all.

Use a Run ➤ Project work process to see how a specularPower setting of 12 will expand a specular highlight. This can be seen in Figure 13-7.

Figure 13-7. *A specularPower property set to 12 will expand the specular highlight on the surface*

Next, change your setSpecularPower() method call value to 100 (or 100.0d) and then use the **Run ➤ Project** work process to view your primitives with a higher specular power, which will make them **shinier**, or more "glossy," as you can see in Figure 13-8.

Figure 13-8. *A specularPower property set at 100 will actually contract or reduce the specular highlight on the surface*

Now that we have covered basic diffuse color and specular color and specular power attributes in the first part of this chapter, let's get more advanced and get into applying images created in GIMP to learn advanced texture mapping using the four texture map effects (bump/normal, diffuse, specular, and glow or self-illumination) channels.

Using External Image Assets: Creating Texture Maps

The most powerful capabilities of the PhongMaterial class and its algorithms are the four texture map properties that are supported. This gives you four **shader channels** to affect your surface color (diffuseMap): shininess (specularMap), illumination (selfIlluminationMap), and height (bumpMap or normal map). Think of this kind of like digital image layer compositing, where these four channels will be combined by the Phong Shader Rendering Algorithm before your specular color and power are applied to the surface (as guided by your specularMap property Image object, if present in the PhongMaterial shader pipeline).

Using External Third-Party Software: Creating Maps Using GIMP

Java 9 and JavaFX are designed to be flexible enough to allow you to use advanced (professional) third-party software such as GIMP (digital image compositing), Blender (3D modeling), Fusion (special effects), Inkscape (SVG content), or Audacity (digital audio editing). Texture maps are usually best crafted and refined in professional pixel editing and layer compositing software such as the free open source GIMP 2.8 (soon to be GIMP 3.0), which is extremely powerful.

Download GIMP at www.gimp.org and install it. Then launch it so you can follow along with me in creating some texture maps that will aptly demonstrate the four different types of texture map channels you learned about during the first few pages of this chapter. Use a **File ➤ New** menu sequence and access the **Create a New Image** dialog, shown in Figure 13-9 with a red 1, and set the Width and Height fields to a Power of Two size. The renderer works best with numbers that are binary or power of two, which would include 2, 4, 8, 16, 32, 64, 128, 256, and so forth. Most games use 256-pixel texture maps, so I'll use that size here. Set the **Color space** drop-down to **RGB** and set the Background Color **Fill with** drop-down to **White**. Create a new layer by using the Layer ➤ New Layer menu series or by right-clicking the Background layer in the Layers palette (red 3) and selecting New Layer, which accesses the New Layer dialog shown as the red 2 in Figure 13-9. Set **Layer name** to **Grayscale Map**, leave **Layer Fill Type** set to **Transparency**, and click the **OK** button to create a layer. Use this same work process to create a second layer, called **Color Map**, as shown by the red 3. Select the **Grayscale Map** layer to show GIMP where to apply your next image creation "moves" (operations), and select a **Rectangle Select Tool**, shown depressed at the top middle of the right section in Figure 13-9. A Rectangle Select tool option (red 4) will appear as shown at the bottom-right corner of the figure, where you can precisely (pixel accurately) set the **Position** and **Size** settings of the selection.

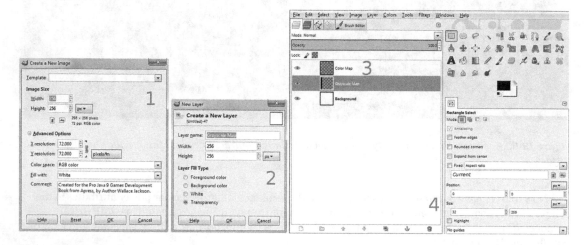

Figure 13-9. *Create a 256-pixel image, add layers to hold your color and grayscale maps, and create eight striped areas*

Next, draw out any size rectangle selection on the GIMP canvas, which is shown on the right in Figure 13-10. In the Position fields, set 0, 0, and in the Size fields, set 32, 256. This will put the selection at one-eighth span and at the left side of the canvas. Click the tiny black-over-white icon next to the foreground/background color swatch under the GIMP tool icons to set FG Color to Black and BG Color to White; then use your **Edit ➤ Fill with FG Color** menu sequence and fill the first of four stripes with Black. Since that layer is transparent and the background is White, the resulting composite will be a black-and-white texture map (eventually four alternating black-and-white stripes). Next, drag the selection to the right and position it for the second stripe fill; then edit the Position fields to set 64, 0 and leave the Size fields set at 32, 256. Again, use an Edit ➤ Fill with FG Color and drag the selection to position (or set Position fields to) 128, 0, select Fill with FG Color, and drag the selection to position (or set Position fields to) 192, 0. Finally, select Fill with FG Color one last time to complete the black-and-white effect (bump, specular) application texture map. The black and white (or transparent) texture map can be seen in the second layer named Grayscale Map in Figure 13-10.

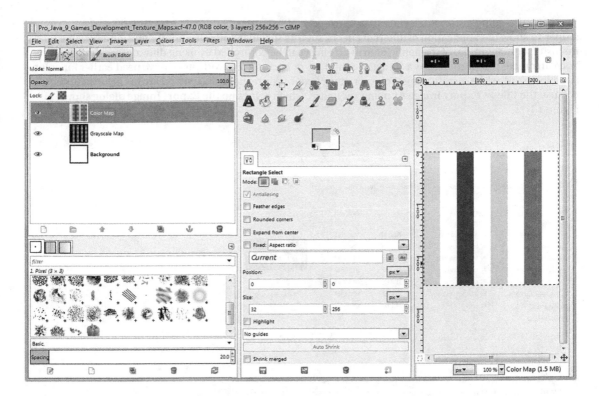

Figure 13-10. *Create a beach ball texture in the Color Map layer and an on/off (black/white) grayscale striped texture*

Now that we have created the (easier) specular or bump map effect Image asset, let's create one with color to show how a diffuse color map will work. Later, we will use these in conjunction with each other (in different shader channels) and experiment with what these PhongMaterial properties can do for our pro Java 9 games development.

To make sure your color data is separate from your effect (grayscale) data, select the Color Map layer, which will turn blue to show it is selected, as shown on the left in Figure 13-10. If you like, you can turn your Grayscale Map layer's visibility off by clicking the eye icon at the left side of the layer. In the Position fields, set 0, 0, and in the Size fields set 32, 256. This will again put the selection at one-eighth span and at the left side of the canvas. Click the Black color square on the FG/BG color swatch (color selector) to bring up the color picker dialog and set a green color, as shown in Figure 13-10. Once you click OK, this will set FG Color to Green, and BG Color will remain White. Use the **Edit ➤ Fill with FG Color** menu sequence, and fill the first of four stripes with green. Since the layer is transparent and the background is White, the resulting composite will be a green-and-white texture map (eventually four alternating color-and-white stripes). Next, drag the selection 64 pixels to the right and position it for the second stripe fill; then edit the Position fields to set 64, 0 and leave the Size field set to 32, 256. Use the color picker to set a blue color, and again use the Edit ➤ Fill with FG Color to create a second blue stripe. Next, drag 64 pixels to the right to position 128 (or set the Position fields to 128, 0), use a color picker to select a yellow foreground (FG) color, and use Fill with FG Color to fill your third stripe. Finally, drag the selection to position 192,0 (or set using the Position fields), use your color picker to select a red foreground (FG) color, and then use the Edit ➤ Fill with FG Color menu sequence one last time to complete the beach ball color (diffuse, glow) application texture map creation. Figure 13-10 shows the finished result in GIMP.

I am also going to create a texture map to use with **alternating 25 percent gray and 50 percent gray** stripes to show the application of different effects, such as specular and self-illumination, and how the intensity, or magnitude, of the application of an effect can be controlled by using different shades of gray. You can create this third map as a "practice round" in re-creating the work process we used earlier for color and black-and-white texture maps. To export any of your texture maps that you create in GIMP 2.10, you can use the **File ➤ Export Image As** menu sequence, which brings up the **Export Image** dialog shown in Figure 13-11.

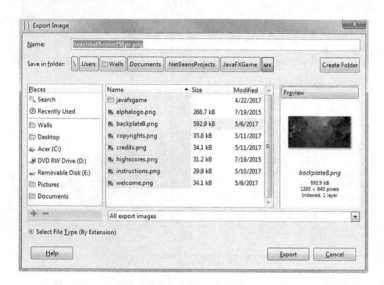

Figure 13-11. *Export to C:\Users\Name\Documents\NetBeansProjects\JavaFXGame\src*

As you can see in Figure 13-11, you can use the file navigation part of this dialog, at the top, to locate your NetBeansProjects folder. I named the files with a description, number of colors, and number of pixels in the file name. Be sure to use your **JavaFXGame** folder and **\src** subfolder, which holds your source assets for the game, as we have been doing thus far during the book. Once the files are in the proper folder, they will be visible to NetBeans 9, and we can use them as Image object assets in our code. Next, let's get back into PhongMaterial object coding and explore shader pipeline creation even further, as this is one way to make your Pro Java 9 i3D games look really spectacular.

Using Texture Maps in a PhongMaterial: Shader Special Effects

The first step in using an Image object in JavaFX is to add the name of the Image object to an Image object compound declaration statement at the top of your class. I will name the Image objects the same as the properties they will be used for. Next, since we have a loadImageAssets() method, we'll add four Image instantiation statements that reference PNG files that contain the texture mapping data. The Java code, shown in Figure 13-12, should look like the following:

```
Image diffuseMap, specularMap, glowMap, bumpMap // plus the other Image objects already in
use
...
diffuseMap = new Image("/beachball5color256px", 256, 256, true, true, true);
specularMap = new Image("/beachball3grayscale256px", 256, 256, true, true, true);
```

```
glowMap = new Image("/beachball2grayscale256px", 256, 256, true, true, true);
bumpMap = new Image("/beachball3grayscale256px", 256, 256, true, true, true);
```

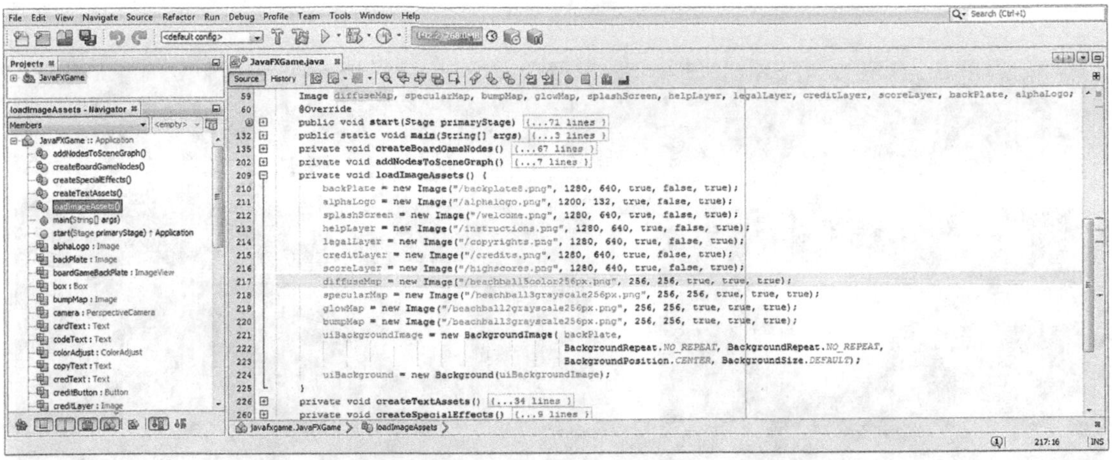

Figure 13-12. *Declare and instantiate Image objects to hold texture map data for a diffuse, specular, glow, or bump map*

Next, go into the createBoardGameNodes() method, change the diffuse and specular color settings to a **Color.WHITE** value, and add a setDiffuseMap(diffuseMap) method call off of the phongMaterial object. The Java code for the diffuse color texture map statements, highlighted in blue in Figure 13-13, should look like the following:

```
phongMaterial = new PhongMaterial(Color.WHITE);
phongMaterial.setSpecularColor(Color.WHITE);
phongMaterial.setSpecularPower(20);
phongMaterial.setDiffuseMap(diffuseMap);
```

Figure 13-13. *Add a diffuseMap to the shader pipeline to add some surface color and set the specular and diffuse colors to white*

Next, use a **Run ➤ Project** work process and again view your primitives. As you can see, in Figure 13-14, your primitives' surfaces are now being rendered using a diffuse map to control their surface coloration, and the Sphere 3D primitive now looks like a beach ball.

Figure 13-14. *A diffuse color texture map is now painting the surface of the primitive, making a sphere into a beach ball*

Next, let's rotate your Sphere primitive 25 degrees so that the delineation between the yellow and white stripe happens in the specular highlight, which we broadened back to its default setting of 20 in the previous code.

We will use the **beachball3grayscale256px.png** image asset; it has eight stripes, four of which are 100 percent on (white), two of which are 75 percent on (25 percent gray), and two of which are 50 percent on (half power, or 50 percent gray). What this will do is to "mute," or diminish, the specular flare on the white portion of the beach ball since a specular map defines the power or amount of the specular effect (shininess).

We will leave the setDiffuseMap(diffuseMap) method call off phongMaterial in place as we are attempting to construct an advanced shader rendering pipeline in this chapter to push the PhongMaterial class to the limits of a professional shader effect creation pipeline, as we would in 3D software but by using only JavaFX API and Java 9 statements.

Therefore, after the setDiffuseMap() method call, we will add a line of Java code calling setSpecularMap() off of the phongMaterial object and then pass in the specularMap Image object, which has been set to a **beachball3grayscale256px.png** image asset in the loadImageAssets() method, as shown in Figure 13-12. This would all be accomplished by using the following Java statements, which is highlighted at the bottom of Figure 13-15:

```
phongMaterial = new PhongMaterial(Color.WHITE);
phongMaterial.setSpecularColor(Color.WHITE);
phongMaterial.setSpecularPower(20);
phongMaterial.setDiffuseMap(diffuseMap);
```

```
phongMaterial.setSpecularMap(specularMap);
sphere = new Sphere(100, 24);
sphere.setRotationAxis(Rotate.Y_AXIS);
sphere.setRotate(25);
sphere.setMaterial(phongMaterial);
```

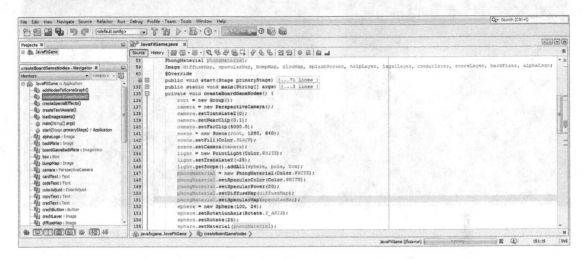

Figure 13-15. *Add a SpecularMap Image reference to the shader pipeline to control the specular highlight intensity*

It's time to again use the **Run ➤ Project** work process and render this shader pipeline into your 3D Scene. As you can see in Figure 13-16, the specular highlight on the Sphere primitive seems to get cut off with the line between the yellow and the white color. This is caused by the specular map (turning down the specular highlight intensity) for alternating areas of the texture map. This can be seen on the Cylinder primitive as well. You may have noticed by now that I decreased the Camera object distance from the center of the Scene, from 250 units away to 100 units away, to zoom into the view, and I increased the size of the 3D primitives so we can see the texture mapping effects more clearly.

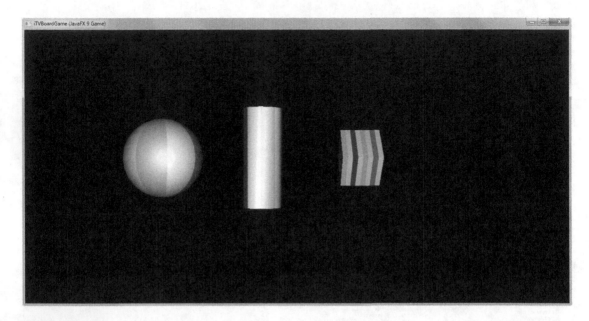

Figure 13-16. *The specular highlight on the curved surface sphere and pole objects is now brighter on the colored area*

Next, let's rotate your Sphere primitive back to **5** degrees so your yellow portion is centered in the specular highlight, with white stripes on either side. This will more accurately show you the power of the self-illumination map.

We will use the **beachball2grayscale256px.png** image asset, which has eight stripes. Four of these are 100 percent on (white) and four are 100 percent off (black), which is about as extreme as you can get as far as effect processing texture mapping is concerned, as this equates to fully apply (white or all on 255 value) or do not apply (black or zero).

What this self-illumination map (commonly called a *glow map* in 3D software) will do is to turn sections of the 3D primitive mapped with white on like a light source, whereas black areas will not be illuminated and will use the existing texture map pipeline. More gray will add more light, so 25 percent gray would simulate 25 percent illuminated (25 percent light intensity). We will leave the setDiffuseMap() and setSpecularMap() method calls off phongMaterial in place as we're attempting to construct an advanced shader rendering pipeline and to push the PhongMaterial class to the limits of a professional shader effect creation pipeline as we would in 3D software, but by using only JavaFX API and Java 9 statements.

Therefore, after the setSpecularMap() method call, we'll call a **setSelfIlluminationMap(gl owMap)** method off the phongMaterial object and pass in the **glowMap** Image object, set to the **beachball2grayscale256px.png** image asset instantiated in the loadImageAssets() method, as shown in Figure 13-12. This would all be accomplished by using the following Java statements, which are highlighted in yellow and light blue at the bottom of Figure 13-17:

```
phongMaterial = new PhongMaterial(Color.WHITE);
phongMaterial.setSpecularColor(Color.WHITE);
phongMaterial.setSpecularPower(20);
phongMaterial.setDiffuseMap(diffuseMap);
phongMaterial.setSpecularMap(specularMap);
phongMaterial.setSelfIlluminationMap(glowMap);
sphere = new Sphere(100, 24);
sphere.setRotationAxis(Rotate.Y_AXIS);
```

```
sphere.setRotate(5);
sphere.setMaterial(phongMaterial);
```

Figure 13-17. *Add the SelfIlluminationMap Image reference to the shader pipeline to control self-illumination intensity*

Figure 13-18 shows the **Run ➤ Project** Java code testing work process with the self-illumination mapping on all three primitives. The white areas have turned into light sources, with the colored areas still showing the diffuse and specular mapping characteristics. There seems to be a bit of a problem with the anti-aliasing algorithm portion of the selfIlluminationMap property code, as you can see on the perimeter edges of the Sphere primitive.

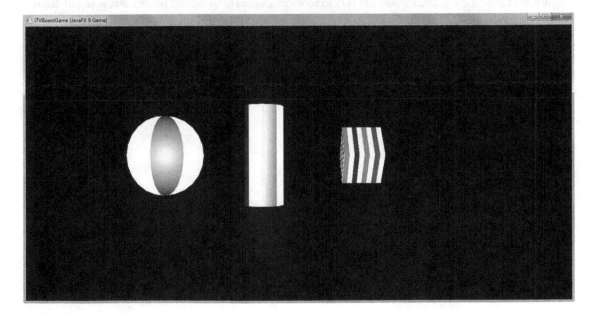

Figure 13-18. *The self-illumination map turns white area on 3D primitives into a light source, leaving color areas alone*

Next, let's take a look at how to use what we have learned thus far and create some of the shader's texture map components in GIMP 2.8.22, for use in the gameBoard Group Node hierarchy that we are going to create in Chapter 14 as we start to build our i3D game using the JavaFX 9 APIs in Java 9.

GameBoard Texturing: Creating a GameBoardSquare

It is important to understand the abstract **Mesh** superclass and how it relates to its **TriangleMesh** subclass (which can be used to "hand-code" complex mesh objects into existence) and how it relates to the **MeshView** class, which is actually a subclass of **Shape3D** and not of Mesh! This is so that MeshView can inherit (extend) the cullFace, drawMode, and material properties of Shape3D, which are, of course, crucial to making a mesh object realistic (especially the **material** property and **Material** class). The MeshView constructor takes a Mesh object, as you will see, so that is the core class (algorithm) that complex 3D objects are based on; therefore, Mesh and MeshView are the key classes to use for pro Java 9 games development. If, for some reason, you want to **code** complex polygonal geometry, also called "Triangle Mesh" (which is not an optimal workflow), you can use TriangleMesh, which we will cover in detail.

A better workflow is using an external 3D software package and "importing" your 3D object directly into a Mesh object, which is then referenced by a MeshView object. This is a workflow we will dedicate an entire chapter to how to "model" a 3D game using these JavaFX classes, so that you do not have to import any "data heavy" mesh objects. Importing 3D assets can be a much faster way to get an advanced i3D game up and running quickly and efficiently, as well as a way to bring specialized artisans into an i3D game development workflow.

Getting Ready to Create the GameBoard: Code Reconfiguration

Let's get ready for what we are going to be doing in the next chapter (building our i3D game board) and reconfigure our Java code bodies for our gameButton event handler, createBoardGameNodes() method, addNodesToSceneGraph() method, and loadImageAssets() method. Let's switch from Camera object dollying, set Camera Z = 0, and instead use FOV to zoom in and out of the scene. Since we're going to delete the Sphere and Cylinder primitives for now, we'll set the X and Y translate properties to -500 and rotate the camera around the x-axis 45 degrees so that it looks down onto the game board. The Java code to do these camera adjustments is shown in Figure 13-19 and looks like the following:

```
camera.setTranslateZ(0);
camera.setTranslateY(-500);
camera.setTranslateX(-500);
camera.setRotationAxis(Rotate.X_AXIS);
camera.setRotate(-45);
camera.setFieldOfView(1);
```

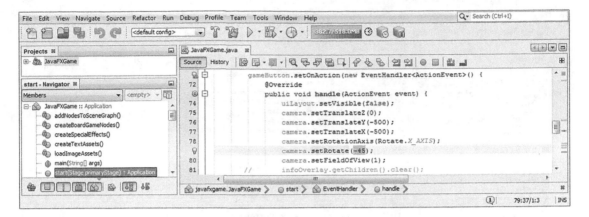

Figure 13-19. *Reconfigure your camera object to dolly to Z = 0, rotate 45 degrees, and zoom in with FOV = 1*

Next, let's remove the sphere Sphere and pole Cylinder instantiations and configuration statements; you can leave the declarations at the top of the class if you want to as we will use these later.

To make a game board square, which will be used around the perimeter of the game board and will be 150 units square and 5 units thin (tall), we will leave the Box box object and construct it with the Box(150,5,150) method call. I will also rotate it 45 degrees for now so the point (corner) is facing the camera object. We can keep the PhongMaterial code because all we have to do to change the diffuseMap once we create it in GIMP is to change the file name in the loadImageAssets() method, which we will do after we create the game board square texture map. Don't forget, if you forget to remove the objects we've removed from the SceneGraph node, you will get a fatal error during compile.

As stated initially, a Box constructor method is very basic and looks like the Java code in Figure 13-20:

```java
box = new Box(150, 5, 150);
box.setRotationAxis(Rotate.Y_AXIS);
box.setRotate(45);
box.setMaterial(phongMaterial);
```

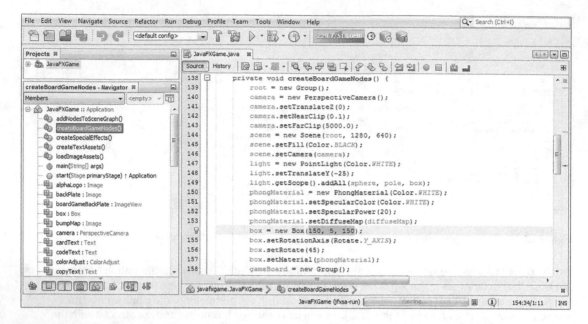

Figure 13-20. *Remove sphere and pole instantiations and configurations and change the box dimensions to 150, 5, 150*

Next, let's take care of removing these (currently) unused pole and sphere primitives from your gameBoard Group object, which will change our addAll() method call back into an add() method call. If you forget to do this and try to select Run ➤ Project, it will not compile. The resulting Java statement, shown in Figure 13-21, looks like this:

gameBoard.getChildren().**add(box)**;

Figure 13-21. *Remove the pole and sphere objects from your gameBoard.getChildren().addAll() method call for now*

Now let's go back into GIMP and add a layer to our texture map composite and create a game board square.

Creating Your Game Board Square Diffuse Texture: Using GIMP

Let's get some of our game board square design done during this chapter, so in the next chapter all we have to do is to design the center of the board, create the perimeter squares, and color shift the image to create a delineation for the squares from each other. We will do this in GIMP using the same approach that we used earlier in this chapter, with the same 32x256 stripes, only this time the four stripes will be located around the perimeter of the game board square. We'll use RGB 255,0,0 (pure red) so we can color shift this value with the algorithms in GIMP.

Open your multilayer GIMP XCF file, right-click the top layer, and use the **New ➤ Layer** menu item to create an empty transparent layer. Turn all of the visibility (eye) icons in the other layers, other than the white Background layer, off. Set **Layer name** to **GameBoardTile**. Make sure to select this layer so it turns blue to show GIMP where to apply your next image creation "moves" (operations).

Select your **Rectangle Select Tool**, shown depressed near the top-middle of Figure 13-22. Rectangle Select Tool options will appear, underneath the tool icons, as shown at the bottom middle of the figure, where you can (again) precisely (pixel accurately) set the **Position** and **Size** settings of your selections.

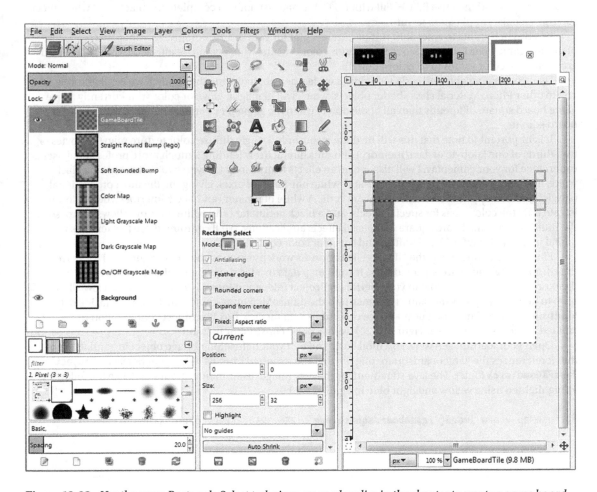

Figure 13-22. *Use the same Rectangle Select technique we used earlier in the chapter to create a game board square*

Next, draw any size rectangle selection on the GIMP canvas, which is shown on the right of Figure 13-22. In the Position fields, set 0, 0, and in the Size fields, set 32, 256. This will put the selection at one-eighth span and at the left side of the canvas. Click the large foreground/background color swatch, located under the GIMP tool icons, on the top color, and set **FG Color** to **Red**. Then use your **Edit ➤ Fill with FG Color** menu sequence and fill the first four stripes with red. Since this layer is transparent and the background is white, the resulting composite will be a red-and-white texture map (eventually four overlapping red perimeter stripes).

Next, drag the selection to the right and position it for the second stripe fill. Then edit the Position field, leaving it set to 0, 0, and reverse the Size fields to set them at 256, 32, as shown in Figure 13-22. Again, select **Edit ➤ Fill with FG Color**. Half of the game board square diffuse color texture map has been created in only a few moves!

Let's finish the other two perimeter stripes by again dragging the selection to position (or, set the Position fields to) 224, 0 on the right side of your 256-pixel texture map canvas. Be sure to set your Size data fields back to 32, 256 (width, height), and then again use **Edit ➤ Fill with FG Color** to fill the right perimeter stripe with **red** (also a Color class constant in JavaFX). Finally, drag the selection to position (or set Position fields to) 0, 224 and then use Edit ➤ Fill with FG Color, one last time, to complete the black-and-white effect (bump, specular) application texture map.

Besides being able to color shift this perimeter color for your diffuse color texture map, to create dozens of unique game board squares, since the interior color is white, which won't be affected (white, black, and grays have no color values to be color-shifted).

Using other concepts and code techniques we learned about during the chapter, we would be able to create other PhongMaterial class shader objects, which will highlight, glow, or color your currently active game board square differently than all of the others when the game piece lands on that particular game board square.

It is important to note that this will be done, using only a single diffuse color texture map (680 bytes or two-thirds of one kilobyte of data/memory) and thus interactively lending a much more professional user experience for your gameplay. I will also create an effects texture map (maybe two or three) using black, white, and gray, which will match the red-and-white one pixel for pixel, giving me the most processional (surgical) effects application within the game code. A white perimeter (and black interior) would allow me to isolate only the color areas for special effects, and a black perimeter (and white interior) allows me to isolate the interior of a game board square for special effects applications. We'll combine these few textures with digital imaging (Chapter 2) and diffuse and specular color control.

Finally, make sure to use the GIMP's File Export As work process, as shown in Figure 13-11, to save the completed game board square diffuse texture map data in a file named **gameboardsquare.png** in the correct source assets folder in your **NetBeansProject** folder and **JavaFXGame** subfolder. Now all we have to do is to swap this file name reference into the diffuseMap Image object instantiation inside of the **loadImageAssets()** method body, and we can utilize it on the new box Box object configuration that we created earlier (see the earlier Figure 13-20) using a Box() constructor method.

Open your loadImageAssets() method body and edit your diffuseMap Image object instantiation so that it references the gameboardsquare.png file that you exported from GIMP to your **NetBeansProject\ JavaFXGame\src** folder. The Java statement for the new Image instantiation should look like the following, as highlighted using yellow and light blue in Figure 13-23:

```
diffuseMap = new Image("/gameboardsquare.png", 256, 256, true, true, true);
```

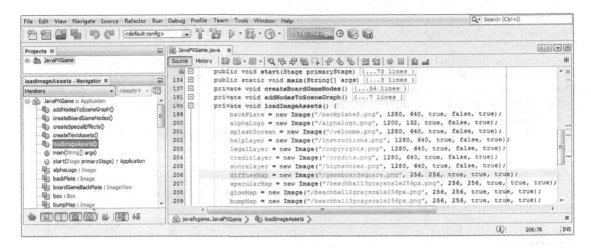

Figure 13-23. *Change your diffuseMap Image object instantiation statement to reference your gameboardsquare.png file*

Figure 13-24 shows the **Run ➤ Project** Java code testing work process; you can see the new game board square box Box object mapped with the new diffuse color texture map that you just created using GIMP 2.8.22 (or later).

Figure 13-24. *We now have a game board square, which will be duplicated around the perimeter (in the next chapter)*

There's a little white on the edges (JavaFX currently does not allow per-side Box object mapping), which we'll minimize in future chapters by adjusting the **camera.setRotate()** method call value until this becomes less evident.

There's one last point I want to make, before I finish up with shader pipeline creation and texture maps for this chapter, on how to skin your 3D primitives with JavaFX. You're probably wondering why I used a **PNG24** (24-bit) image format for this texture, instead of the more optimized PNG8 format. Well, this PNG24 codec did a pretty great job of compressing 256 × 256 × 3 (196,608) bytes into 680 bytes, which is a 290 : 1 or 99.67 percent reduction in data!

On the more technical side of the equation, Java will use a 24-bit RGB color representation **in memory**, and therefore, if we had used an indexed 8-bit color image, it would have simply been **transmuted** back into a 24-bit color value image when it was loaded into memory. Therefore, my inclination is to use PNG24 and PNG32 images whenever possible, especially for 3D texture maps that are primarily going to be 32x32, 64x64, 128x128, 256x256, and 512x512 for pro Java 9 game design and development applications anyway. For photographic imagery, you can also use JPEG.

Summary

In this thirteenth chapter, we learned about the classes in the **javafx.scene.paint** package that allow you to work with 3D shaders, texture maps, and materials, including the **PhongMaterial** class based on the abstract **Material** superclass. We learned that the Material class is basically an "empty" class or a "shell" to hold a "material" object (attribute in the Shape3D class) and that the heavy lifting (algorithms) is in a PhongMaterial subclass. We looked at the properties, constructors, and method calls in this class in a fair amount of detail so that you would know what the PhongMaterial object can do, and then we looked at how to implement these in Java code (other than bumpMap, which isn't working in the current JavaFX 9 code base I am using, so we'll revisit this later during the book).

You learned how to create texture map assets using GIMP (currently at version 2.8.22 for this book, but I am expecting 2.10 to be out in 2017 and 3.0 to be out in 2018) and how to be surgically accurate by using GIMP's tools in an optimal workflow to create balanced, pixel-precise, power-of-two texture maps optimized for professional 3D game development.

We then took a look at how to implement these texture map assets in four current texture map "channels," which are currently afforded to us via the JavaFX 9 PhongMaterial class. We saw how these texture map channels allow us to fine-tune how our material attribute is rendered, allowing us to create a far more professional appearance for our Java 9 games.

Finally, we created the diffuseColor property texture map for our game board square, transmuted the box Box object into one of these game board squares, and applied the new texture map to the new 3D primitive "plane" object in preparation for what we are going to be doing in the next chapter (creating our gameBoard branch in the SceneGraph) so that it will look like a game board as we are creating it. As you know, I recommend going about your pro Java 9 games development in such a way that you see what JavaFX 9 is going to do as you are writing your Java 9 code, creating your new media assets, and "morphing" your pro Java 9 game content and deliverable into what you ultimately want it to be. Pro Java 9 Games Development is a refinement process, so that is how I am writing this book. I'm showing you how I actually "vaporize a 3D board game application out of thin air" using the NetBeans 9 IDE and the Java 9 and JavaFX 9 APIs.

In Chapter 14, we are going to further refine our Java code organization, creating new methods and reorganizing some existing methods, to create and incorporate the core of our i3D board game, the gameboard. We will create a nested Group 3D hierarchy under the gameBoard Group Node (branch) and look at 3D primitive X,Y,Z positioning and related concepts that apply to seamlessly laying out a 3D gameboard in such a way that future Java code can access and reference its components and subcomponents in a logical, optimal fashion. Just like database design, how you design your SceneGraph greatly affects how your Pro Java 9 3D Game functions in the future. The simpler and more straightforward we can keep the design, hierarchy, and 3D object naming schema, the better shape we will be in when crafting future code for interactivity, animation, movement, collision detection, and the like. At this point, you should be starting to get excited about the possibilities that Java 9 and JavaFX 9 afford you.

CHAPTER 14

■ ■ ■

3D Model Hierarchy Creation: Using Primitives to Create a Game Board

Now that you have learned how to "skin" your 3D primitives using the JavaFX Phong shader algorithms and their various color and effects mapping channels and you have created colorful, highly optimized game board square texture maps, it's time to add some more custom methods for building the game board and setting up the Phong shader objects with the texture maps. We'll need to create a **createGameBoardNodes()** method to organize the 3D primitive assets that comprise our 3D gameboard, as the **createBoardGameNodes()** method should (and does) contain higher-level Node subobject instantiation and configuration, such as the Scene, Root, UI StackPane, 3D gameBoard Group, Camera, and Lighting, as well as four game board Quadrant Group objects named Q1 through Q4 (quadrants 1 through 4). We will also create the other 19 game board square objects, named Q1S1 through Q1S5, Q2S1 through Q2S5, Q3S1 through Q3S5, and Q4S1 through Q4S5 to keep object names short. Naming the objects the abbreviated version of Quadrant1Square1 (Q1S1) will make the Java code that uses these abbreviated terms much more readable.

During this chapter, you will be building your **gameBoard Group** branch of your SceneGraph, which is under your SceneGraph root, next to the **uiLayout** branch, which you've already built. Under your gameBoard Group branch, we'll segment the game board into **four quadrants**, so the middle of the game board can have four larger 300x300 unit areas we can use for gameplay, with each of the quadrants having 5 of your 20 perimeter game board squares as child objects. With a three-tiered 3D primitive object hierarchy, we can access your entire game board as a whole (to rotate it, for instance), access each quadrant as a unit (to levitate it or apply shader effects, for instance), and access individual game board squares at the bottom (leaf Node subobjects) of the hierarchy. Let's get to work! We have hundreds of lines of new Java code to write during this chapter implementing primitives, shaders, images, and SceneGraph hierarchy nodes.

Primitive Creation Method: createGameBoardNodes()

Since creating the 24 primitives (4 center board quadrants and 20 perimeter squares) is going to take over 100 Java statements (instantiate using new, setTranslateX(), setTranslateZ(), setMaterial(), etc.), let's create a method specifically to hold our game board objects and their instantiation and configuration statements. In this way, a createBoardGameNodes() method will create the global and top-level Node subclass objects (scene, root, camera, light, uiLayout branch, gameBoard branch, Q1 through Q4 branches, etc.). Later in the chapter, we will also extract the PhongMaterial shader creation logic to another custom createMaterials() method, where we will create a couple dozen custom shader objects to use to skin various components

© Wallace Jackson 2017
W. Jackson, *Pro Java 9 Games Development*, https://doi.org/10.1007/978-1-4842-0973-8_14

of this game board. To get NetBeans 9 to create this new method for you, add a line of code after the createBoardGameNodes() method call, in the first portion of your start() method, and then type in the following Java method call, naming your new method:

createGameBoardNodes();

NetBeans will realize this is not a valid method call and will highlight it by using a wavy red underline.

Use your **Alt+Enter** work process, and double-click your **Create method "createGameBoardNodes()" in javafxgame.JavaFXGame** option, highlighted in Figure 14-1, to have NetBeans create an empty method body structure for you. Next, remove the box Box object–related code from createBoardGameNodes() and place this code in this new method. We'll also remove the pole Cylinder and sphere Sphere so they don't interfere with your game board design.

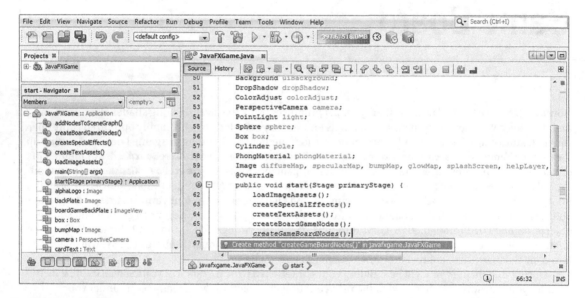

Figure 14-1. *Open the start() method; type a createGameBoardNodes() method call after createBoardGameNodes()*

Cut and paste your Box primitive code from **.createBoardGameNodes()** to **.createGameBoardNodes()** and rename the box to **Q1S1**. Delete all the Java statements, except an instantiation and shader method call, as shown in Figure 14-2:

```
Q1S1 = new Box(150, 5, 150);
Q1S1.setMaterial(phongMaterial);
```

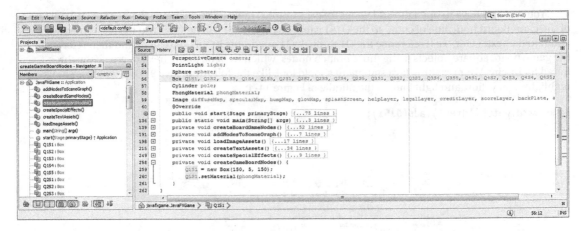

Figure 14-2. *Copy the primitive code to createGameBoardNodes(); delete everything except the instantiation and .setMaterial*

Change your Java code referencing the box to reference Q1S1 using the following code, which is also shown in Figure 14-3:

```
light.getScope().addAll(Q1S1);
```

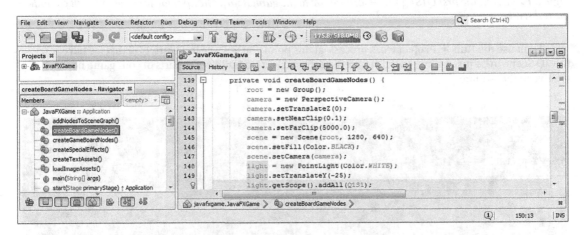

Figure 14-3. *Be sure to change all referencing from the box to Q1S1 in createBoardGameNodes() and addToSceneGraph()*

You will also have to open the addNodesToSceneGraph() method and change the box to Q1S1, inside of the gameBoard node line of code, so the Q1S1 game board square will be visible in the test render we are about to do next. Later, we'll reference the Q1 through Q4 quadrants in this statement and then reference the game board square objects using those branch nodes, which we'll be doing next, to create the three-tiered hierarchy. Your resulting Java statement should look like the following Java 9 code, which is shown highlighted in yellow and light blue in the middle of Figure 14-4:

```
gameBoard.getChildren().add(Q1S1);
```

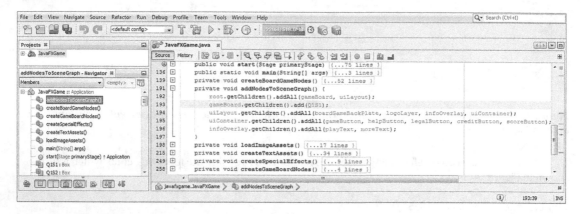

Figure 14-4. *Add the first Q1S1 game board square to the gameBoard Group node for now so it will compile the test render*

If you use the **Run ➤ Project** work process, at this point you will see in Figure 14-5 that we have reset the 3D Scene to be just a game board square, and we can start to build other parts of your game board relative to that square.

Figure 14-5. *Use the Run ➤ Project work process to test render the reconfiguration of the 3D Scene from Box to square*

Now it is time to start constructing the SceneGraph hierarchy underneath the 3D **gameBoard Group** branch of the SceneGraph. The gameBoard Group will contain four quadrant Group branches named Q1 through Q4. Each of these quadrant Group Node objects will contain a Box primitive quadrant (one-quarter of the game board center) and that quadrant's attached five game board squares. The q1 through q4 quadrant planar objects will also be Box primitives that are four times (300x300) the size of a game board square.

I am going to move the gameBoard Group object instantiation under the root Group instantiation and then add the Q1 through Q4 Group object instantiations under that at the top of the createBoardGameNodes() method so that the Java code order reflects the parent-child hierarchy. Your leaf objects (bottommost nodes) will be created inside of your **createGameBoardNodes()** method, including the q1 through q4 quadrant planar objects, which are leaf nodes of the Q1 through Q4 Group (branch) nodes.

If you like, you can use the handy copy-and-paste programmer's trick and type in the first Q1 Group object's instantiation statement and then copy and paste it three more times underneath itself, changing Q1 to be Q2 through Q4, since at this point, we are just creating four empty quadrant group nodes, which we will reference to a gameBoard Group node above them and to the Q1S1 through Q4S5 (and q1 through q4) leaf nodes below them. The resulting Java code should look like the following, as highlighted in yellow, red, and blue at the top of Figure 14-6:

```
gameBoard = new Group();
Q1 = new Group();
Q2 = new Group();
Q3 = new Group();
Q4 = new Group();
```

Figure 14-6. *Add four Group branch node object instantiations under your gameBoard Group, named Q1 through Q4*

Now we need to remove your Q1S1 leaf node from the gameBoard branch node and replace it with the Q1 through Q4 branch nodes. For the Q1S1 Box primitive to show up when we select Run ➤ Project (render) for the 3D Scene, you'll need to create a second "node builder" **.getChildren().add()** method chain off of Q1 (Q1S1 object's parent branch) so that the gameBoard node references the Q1 node, which references Q1S1 node.

Your reconfigured addNodesToSceneGraph() method statements will now number six Java statements, and your gameBoard SceneGraph hierarchy, from root to game board squares, now spans three Java 9 statements, which should look like the following Java statements inside of the addNodesToSceneGraph() method, as shown highlighted in yellow and blue at the middle (with related declarations also highlighted the top) of Figure 14-7:

```
root.getChildren().addAll(gameBoard, uiLayout);
gameBoard.getChildren().addAll(Q1, Q2, Q3, Q4);
Q1.getChildren().add(Q1S1);
```

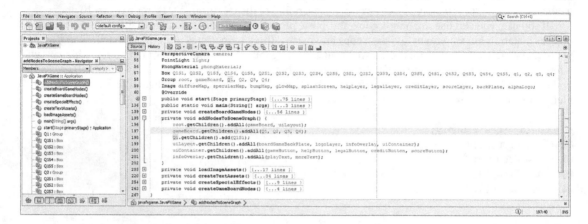

Figure 14-7. *Replace a Q1S1 reference in the gameBoard node builder with Q1 through Q4, and add a Q1 node builder*

Next, let's add the **q1** Box game board center quadrant, which will be the parent to the Q1S1 game board square; thus, this is the next logical thing to add. Since you have already declared the q1 through q4 Box objects at the top of your class, shown in Figures 14-6 through 14-8, you can add this q1 object to your Q1 branch node first, or you can instantiate it first, in the **createGameBoardNodes()** method with a 300, 5, 300 (X, Y, Z) parameter, and then add it to the addNodesToSceneGraph() method later, as you can see in Figure 14-8 and in the following Java code:

```
Q1.getChildren().addAll(q1, Q1S1);    // In addNodesToSceneGraph() method body
q1 = new Box(300, 5, 300);            // In createGameBoardNodes() method body
```

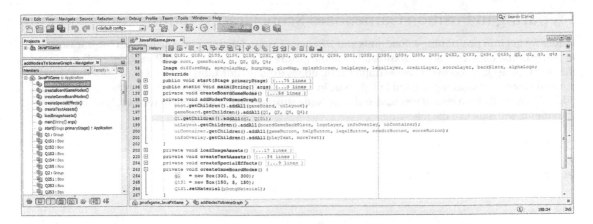

Figure 14-8. *Change the .add() method call to an .addAll() method call; add the q1 Box primitive for your first quadrant*

Figure 14-9 shows a Run ➤ Project work process showing a game board square and quadrant rendered at 0,0.

Figure 14-9. *Select Run ➤ Project and render your 3D Scene; both the quadrant and game board square are at 0,0,0*

Preparing to Position Gameboard SceneGraph Nodes

Before we get into positioning 4 quadrants and 20 squares around their perimeter, let's put the infrastructure in place for the rest of the SceneGraph and all of the texture maps for the shader (PhongMaterial) to use. Add the other three Q2 through Q4 SceneGraph Group nodes to your addNodesToSceneGraph() method using cut and paste, as shown highlighted in light blue in Figure 14-10. Notice that you can use the .getChildren(). addAll() method chain even if you have only one Node subclass object element in the List! Your Java statements will look like the following:

```
Q2.getChildren().addAll(q2);
Q3.getChildren().addAll(q3);
Q4.getChildren().addAll(q4);
```

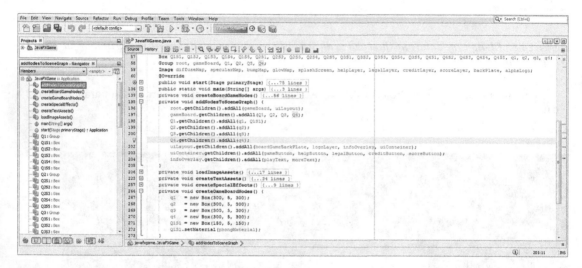

Figure 14-10. *Instantiate your other three quadrant Box primitives and your other three quadrant branch node objects*

While we're at it, create the other three q2 through q4 game board center quadrants so that we can add them to the Q2 through Q4 node construction statements. Again, since these objects are declared at the top of your class, you can construct these statements in any order that you want; just don't use Run ➤ Project to render the Scene, as you won't see the objects until they are instantiated and added to the SceneGraph hierarchy. The Box instantiation Java code should look like the following, as shown at the bottom of Figure 14-10:

```
q2 = new Box(300, 5, 300);
q3 = new Box(300, 5, 300);
q4 = new Box(300, 5, 300);
```

As you can see in Figure 14-9, quadrant 1 is underneath game board square 1 and not in a position where their corners are touching. So, move quadrant 1's **q1** Box object diagonally **225** units. This equates to the length of the board game square side plus another 50 percent, or 225 units. If you use only 150 units, the quadrant corner will be centered in the game board square. The code to create this alignment looks like the following .setTranslateX() and .setTranslateZ() Java method calls, as shown highlighted in yellow and blue in the middle of Figure 14-11:

```
private void createGameBoardNodes() {
    q1.setTranslateX(225);
    q1.setTranslateZ(225);
    Q1S1 = new Box(150, 5, 150);
    Q1S1.setMaterial(phongMaterial);
    q2 = new Box(300, 5, 300);
    q2.setVisible(false);
    q3 = new Box(300, 5, 300);
    q3.setVisible(false);
    q4 = new Box(300, 5, 300);
    q4.setVisible(false);
}
```

Figure 14-11. *Move the q1 quadrant to the X,Z location 225,225 so that it is internal to square Q1S1 with the corners touching*

Also notice that I have "hidden" quadrants 2 through 4 using the .setVisible(false) method call so that I can work on quadrant 1's q1 Box and its five game board square children first, as I am going to do quadrant 1 first to show you the work process I am using, then quadrant 2, then quadrant 3, and so forth. It is useful to break any complex tasks into subtasks if possible so you don't get overwhelmed during development. Since the SceneGraph hierarchy is set to use four board quadrants under the gameBoard branch, this is how I am going to go about building the game board, one quadrant (in this case, Q1) at a time. Notice my game board square names also match this, so I have an advantage, as my game board square objects, in this case Q1S1 through Q1S5, match up with the quadrant Group object name Q1. Since I can't duplicate the Q1 Group object name for the Box quadrant object name, I have to use a lowercase q1 through q4 for my quadrant planar primitives, which is fine, as I still know what is going on and because the quadrant portions of the game board are not nearly as important as the game board squares themselves.

Let's render the 3D Scene using the **Run ➤ Project** work process and see if the two Box primitives are still overlapping or if they are positioned correctly. As you can see in Figure 14-12, the corners of the game board square and the first quadrant are now aligned corner to corner, and you can begin to see how the game board will be laid out.

Figure 14-12. *Use the Run ➤ Project work process to see if the two 3D primitives are precisely aligned corner to corner*

Although this is the result I wanted to see, in thinking ahead about how I am going to access each quadrant and its child squares, I want to keep the squares in QxSy 1 through 5 order going around the game board, and this would not work if I started with square 1 on the corner of each quadrant! Think about it! Therefore, I actually need to move this square location from 0, 0 (X, Z) to 300, 0 (X, Z). I will do this after I create the custom method body to hold my shaders next.

Since I'm going to have a couple dozen shaders, I'm going to quickly create another custom method to keep the shader creation separate and organized so that I can collapse and expand the shader-related code as needed.

Coding a Phong Shader Creation Method: createMaterials()

Since shaders are an important part of a pro Java 9 game design pipeline, let's give them their own method body and move the PhongMaterial object code from createBoardGameNodes() to this new createMaterials() method. Add a line of code at the top of your start() method after loadImageAssets() as these are used in the shaders and before **createGameBoardNodes()**; these objects will use the shaders created in this createMaterials() method body. Type in **createMaterials()** and a semicolon to call the nonexistent method; then use your **Alt+Enter** keystroke combination and select the "add the createMaterials() method in javafxgame.JavaFXGame" option. Let's also change our PhongMaterial name to **Shader1**. We can name these first 20 shaders in this method body, as well as at the top of your class where I have added declarations for Image objects named diffuse1 through diffuse 20 and Shader1 through Shader 20, in anticipation of the code we are about to write. Cut and paste the PhongMaterial code to "live" in createMaterials() and delete the specular attributes. The code, shown in Figure 14-13, should look like the following:

```
Image          diffuse1 ... diffuse20;       // Object Declarations at top of class
PhongMaterial Shader1  ... Shader20;
...
Shader1 = new PhongMaterial(Color.WHITE);  // Create Diffuse Shader in createMaterials()
Shader1.setDiffuseMap(diffuse1);
```

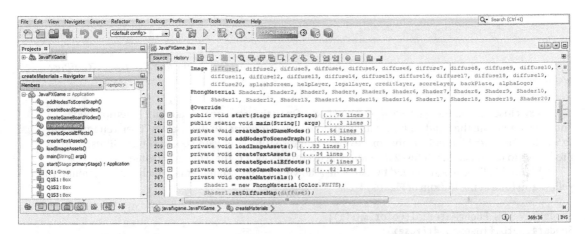

Figure 14-13. *Add Image object declarations diffuse1 through diffuse20 and create a createMaterials() shader method*

Next, let's remove all the special effects map-related code in loadImageAssets() that we created in Chapter 13, except for diffuseMap, which you will rename **diffuse1**. Copy and paste the diffuse1 instantiation four times, and reference the next four game board square texture maps, **gameboardsquare2.png** through **gameboardsquare5.png**.

You're now ready, from a shader standpoint, to construct the first quadrant of your game board. You should now have five (diffuseMap) Image objects, named diffuse1 through diffuse5, in the last half of your loadImageAssets() method. These will hold the diffuseMap property texture maps defining where the warm colors (red, orange, yellow) will be mapped onto your game board squares that are the children of quadrant (1) for the game board, which we will lay out first. We'll lay out the green quadrant second and then the blue and purple quadrants last.

These first five of the (eventual) 24 diffuse color texture map (diffuseMap property) Image objects should be added using the following Java statements, which are highlighted at the bottom of Figure 14-14:

```
diffuse1 = new Image("/gameboardsquare.png",  256, 256, true, true, true);
diffuse2 = new Image("/gameboardsquare2.png", 256, 256, true, true, true);
diffuse3 = new Image("/gameboardsquare3.png", 256, 256, true, true, true);
diffuse4 = new Image("/gameboardsquare4.png", 256, 256, true, true, true);
diffuse5 = new Image("/gameboardsquare5.png", 256, 256, true, true, true);
```

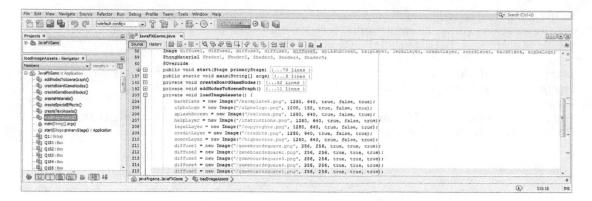

Figure 14-14. *Instantiate diffuse1 through diffuse5 in loadImageAssets() using your first five PNG diffuse texture maps*

Next, close the loadImageAssets() method body. Open the new createMaterials() method body and copy and paste the Shader1 Java statements four times underneath themselves. Then rename them to Shader2 through Shader5. Set the Image objects representing your game board square diffuseMap properties to reference the diffuse2 through diffuse5 Image objects that you just created.

This could all be accomplished by using the following ten Java statements, which are highlighted in yellow and blue at the bottom of Figure 14-15:

```
Shader1 = new PhongMaterial(Color.WHITE);
Shader1.setDiffuseMap(diffuse1);
Shader2 = new PhongMaterial(Color.WHITE);
Shader2.setDiffuseMap(diffuse2);
Shader3 = new PhongMaterial(Color.WHITE);
Shader3.setDiffuseMap(diffuse3);
Shader4 = new PhongMaterial(Color.WHITE);
Shader4.setDiffuseMap(diffuse4);
Shader5 = new PhongMaterial(Color.WHITE);
Shader5.setDiffuseMap(diffuse5);
```

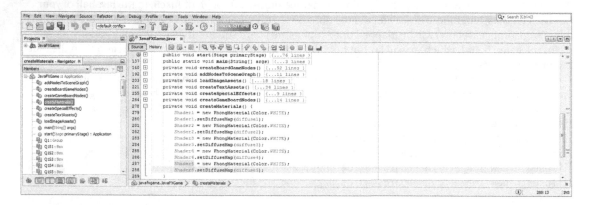

Figure 14-15. *Copy and paste the Shader1 Java code block four times underneath itself to create Shader2 through Shader5*

Finishing Your GameBoard Construction: Quadrants 2 Through 4

Close your createMaterials() method and reopen your **createGameBoardNodes()** method. Add the **location** statement to the Q1S1 object using Q1S1.setTranslateX(**300**) to position the first child square where we want it to be, at the beginning of the quadrant, going in the clockwise direction.

Next, copy and paste your three Q1S1 game board square statements four times underneath themselves to create the rest of the square objects, which we will also have to reconfigure, as far as X, Z location parameters go and as far as the shader object referencing is concerned.

Q2S2 only needs to position itself **150 units** from the 0,0 origin, because your squares are 150 by 150. This is done by changing the location method call to .setTranslateX(**150**). Be sure to also set .setMaterial(**Shader2**) to reference the correct shader that then references (and applies) the **diffuse2** Image object as a diffuseMap property.

Q2S3 is the only square that doesn't need repositioning, as it will be at the 0,0 origin. I've added the method call .setTranslateX(**0**) in the sample code (but not in NetBeans 9). Be sure to also set .setMaterial(**Shader3**) to reference the correct shader, which then references (and applies) the **diffuse3** Image object as a diffuseMap property.

Q2S4 only needs to position itself **150 units** from the 0,0 origin, but this time, in the **Z direction**. This is done by changing the location method call to .setTranslateZ(**150**). Be sure to set .setMaterial(**Shader4**) to reference the correct **Shader4** object, which then references (and applies) the **diffuse4** Image object as a diffuseMap property.

Q2S5 needs to position itself **300 units** in the **Z direction** from 0,0. This is done using a location method call to .setTranslateZ(**300**). Be sure to set .setMaterial(**Shader5**) to reference the correct **Shader5** object, which then references (and applies) the **diffuse5** Image object as a diffuseMap property. The Java code, which is also shown highlighted in Figure 14-16, should look like the following:

```
private void createGameBoardNodes() {
    q1.setTranslateX(225);
    q1.setTranslateZ(225);
    Q1S1 = new Box(150, 5, 150);
    Q1S1.setTranslateX(300);
    Q1S1.setMaterial(Shader1);
    Q1S2 = new Box(150, 5, 150);
    Q1S2.setTranslateX(150);
    Q1S2.setMaterial(Shader2);
    Q1S3 = new Box(150, 5, 150);
    Q1S3.setTranslateX(0);          // This statement can be omitted, as default X location is 0
    Q1S3.setMaterial(Shader3);
    Q1S4 = new Box(150, 5, 150);
    Q1S4.setTranslateZ(150);
    Q1S4.setMaterial(Shader4);
    Q1S5 = new Box(150, 5, 150);
    Q1S5.setTranslateZ(300);
    Q1S5.setMaterial(Shader5);
    q2 = new Box(300, 5, 300);
    q2.setVisible(false);           // Set q2 through q4 quadrant objects to visible=false for now
}
```

Figure 14-16. *Copy and paste the Q1S1 statements four times underneath themselves and reconfigure their method calls*

Before we can see these new objects rendered in the 3D Scene, we'll need to add them to the SceneGraph hierarchy in your addNodesToSceneGraph() method body. Add the Q1S2 through Q1S5 Box objects to the Q1 Group object, as highlighted in yellow and light blue in Figure 14-17.

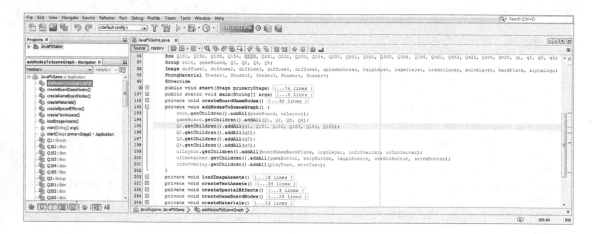

Figure 14-17. *Add your other three Q2 to Q4 Group objects to the gameBoard Group and the other four squares to Q1*

Let's also finish the second level (Q2 through Q4 branch nodes) of the SceneGraph hierarchy and add the q2 through q4 Box planar primitives to the other three Q2 through Q4 Group nodes to add the interior quadrants for the game board to the SceneGraph hierarchy. We're doing this at this point in the work process so that we will be able to work on the center portion of the game board since we are building it one quadrant at a time.

Since we are basically finished with the first quadrant, we are putting the other three into the SceneGraph so they will render (be visible) as we build out the rest of the game board quadrants and their game board squares, which will attach to them around the perimeter of each respective quadrant.

From an optimization standpoint, we have created a relatively complex SceneGraph hierarchy for the 2D UI and 3D GameBoard components using only **nine** .getChildren().addAll() method chain Java programming statements, as shown in Figure 14-17. This is relatively compact as we are referencing dozens of 2D and 3D game component leaf nodes in a highly organized fashion and using only nine SceneGraph hierarchy construction statements.

Adding the other four squares and the other three quadrants could be accomplished by using the following Java programming statements, which are shown highlighted in yellow and light blue at the bottom of Figure 14-17:

```
root.getChildren().addAll(gameBoard, uiLayout);
gameBoard.getChildren().addAll(Q1, Q2, Q3, Q4);
Q1.getChildren().addAll(q1, Q1S1, Q1S2, Q1S3, Q1S4, Q1S5);
Q2.getChildren().addAll(q2);
Q3.getChildren().addAll(q3);
Q4.getChildren().addAll(q4);
```

Figure 14-18 shows the **Run ➤ Project** JavaFX 9 code testing work process. As you can see, we already have a quarter of the game board in place, and it looks very good for a first go-round at assembling all these assets, including 3D Box primitives and 2D texture map images, which we have declared at the top of our class and are about to create.

Figure 14-18. *Use the Run ➤ Project work process to see if the completed 3D game board quadrant is aligning properly*

Copy and paste the five diffuse Image statements and create diffuse6 through 20, as shown in Figure 14-19.

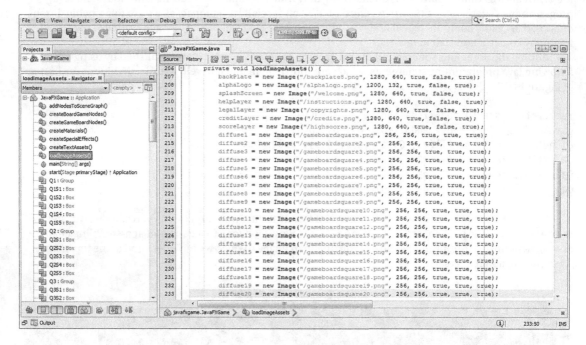

Figure 14-19. *Copy and paste 5 diffuse texture Image instantiations 3 times and create all 20 diffuse Image objects*

Close the loadImageAssets() method body now that the diffuse Image instantiation is in place, open the createMaterials() method, and do the exact same thing, copying the first five shader Java statement pairs and pasting them three more times underneath themselves. Change the numbering portion of each statement so that you create your Shader6 through Shader20 Java statement pairs. This can all be seen highlighted in yellow in Figure 14-20.

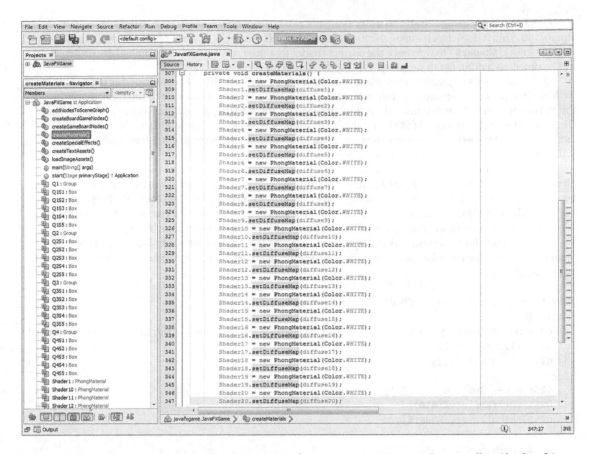

Figure 14-20. *Copy and paste 5 Shader PhongMaterial instantiations 3 times and create all 20 Shader objects*

Now let's create the second quadrant of our game board by going back into the
createGameBoardNodes() method body and creating the second section of code for Box primitives
Q2S1 through Q2S5 by copying the Q1S1 to Q1S5 statements, pasting them again underneath themselves,
and then changing the object names and method call parameters (so that you do not have to type the
majority of these Java statements into the NetBeans 9 IDE again).

The q2 Box object (second quadrant) will need to be moved by **300** units (quadrants are 300x300 in size)
out along the z-axis, so the q2.setTranslateZ() method parameter needs to be incremented from 225 to **525**
to accomplish this second quadrant game board component positioning, as shown in Figure 14-22, if you
wanted to look ahead.

Q2S1 needs to position itself **450 units** along the z-axis (from the 0,0 origin) because Q1S5 is at 300 plus
150, which is 450. This is done by changing the location method call to `.setTranslateZ(450)`. Be sure to set
`.setMaterial(`**Shader6**`)` to reference the correct shader, which references (and applies) the **diffuse6** Image
object as a diffuseMap property.

Q2S2 needs to position itself **600 units** along the z-axis (from an 0,0 origin) because 450 plus 150
equals 600. This is done by changing the location method call to `.setTranslateZ(600)`. Be sure to also set
`.setMaterial(`**Shader7**`)` to reference the correct shader that then references (and applies) the **diffuse7**
Image object as a diffuseMap property.

Q2S3 needs to position itself **750 units** along the z-axis (from an 0,0 origin) because 600 plus 150 equals 750. This is done by changing the location method call to .setTranslate**Z**(**750**). Be sure to also set .setMaterial(**Shader8**) to reference the correct shader that then references (and applies) the **diffuse8** Image object as a diffuseMap property.

Q2S4 also needs to position itself **750 units** along the z-axis from the 0,0 origin, but this time, we'll need to push this square over 150 units in the **X direction** in order to move it to the right, along the top of your game board layout. This is done by changing over to using two location method calls. One would be .setTranslate**X**(**150**), and the other would be .setTranslation**Z**(**750**). Be sure to set .setMaterial(**Shader9**) to reference the correct **Shader9** object, which then references (and applies) the **diffuse9** Image object as a diffuseMap property.

Q2S5 needs to position itself **300 units** in the **X direction** from 0,0, as well as 750 units in the Z direction, so that this square is located near the top middle of this game board, on the other side of the game board from square 1. This is again done using two location method calls, to .setTranslate**Z**(**750**) and to .setTranslate**X**(**300**). Be sure to set .setMaterial(**Shader10**) to reference the correct **Shader10** object, which then references (and applies) the **diffuse10** Image object as a diffuseMap property.

The Java code for the construction of the second quadrant of the game board, which is shown in Figure 14-21 after the code for the construction of the first quadrant, should look like the following (spaced out for readability):

```
private void createGameBoardNodes() {
    ...
    q2 = new Box(300, 5, 300);        // Java code creating a second quadrant for the gameboard
    q2.setTranslateX(225);
    q2.setTranslateZ(525);

    Q2S1 = new Box(150, 5, 150);
    Q2S1.setTranslateZ(450);
    Q2S1.setMaterial(Shader6);

    Q2S2 = new Box(150, 5, 150);
    Q2S2.setTranslateZ(600);
    Q2S2.setMaterial(Shader7);

    Q2S3 = new Box(150, 5, 150);
    Q2S3.setTranslateZ(750);
    Q2S3.setMaterial(Shader8);

    Q2S4 = new Box(150, 5, 150);
    Q2S4.setTranslateZ(750);
    Q2S4.setTranslateX(150);
    Q2S4.setMaterial(Shader9);

    Q2S5 = new Box(150, 5, 150);
    Q2S5.setTranslateZ(750);
    Q2S5.setTranslateX(300);
    Q2S5.setMaterial(Shader10);
```

```
    q3 = new Box(300, 5, 300);
    q3.setVisible(false);
    ...                              // The third quadrant configuration code will go in here
    q4 = new Box(300, 5, 300);
    q4.setVisible(false);
}
```

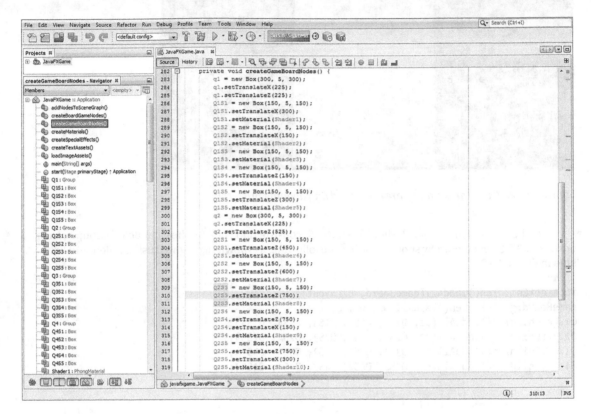

Figure 14-21. *Instantiate and configure game board squares Q2S1 through Q2S5 inside of createGameBoardNodes()*

As you can see in Figure 14-22, use **Run ➤ Project** to confirm that the construction of the game board is halfway done!

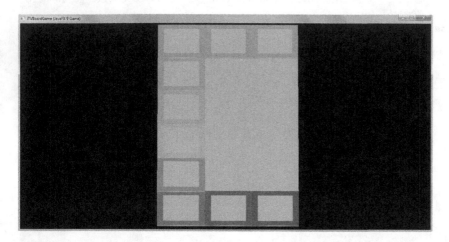

Figure 14-22. *Quadrants 1 and 2 are now coded and aligning properly*

Add the Java statements for the final SceneGraph construction code for the gameBoard Group branch next. Your 3D Scene hierarchy should look like the following, as shown highlighted using yellow and light blue in Figure 14-23:

```
root.getChildren().addAll(gameBoard, uiLayout);
gameBoard.getChildren().addAll(Q1, Q2, Q3, Q4);
Q1.getChildren().addAll(q1, Q1S1, Q1S2, Q1S3, Q1S4, Q1S5);
Q2.getChildren().addAll(q2, Q2S1, Q2S2, Q2S3, Q2S4, Q2S5);
Q3.getChildren().addAll(q3, Q3S1, Q3S2, Q3S3, Q3S4, Q3S5);
Q4.getChildren().addAll(q4, Q4S1, Q4S2, Q4S3, Q4S4, Q4S5);
```

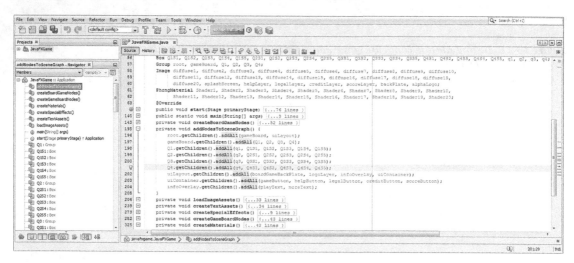

Figure 14-23. *Add all remaining SceneGraph Node object "wiring" code to add the rest of the squares to the quadrants*

Next, let's create the third quadrant for your game board by going back into the **createGameBoardNodes()** method body and creating the third section of code for the Box primitives Q3S1 through Q3S5 (as well as for your q3 center quadrant). Just copy the Q2S1 to Q2S5 statements and paste them again underneath themselves (and after the q3 instantiation and configuration statements to keep grouped nodes together logically in the Java code body). Next, you will again change your object names and method call parameters (so that you do not have to type the majority of these Java 9 statements into your NetBeans 9 IDE again) to position your squares diagonally, from your first quadrant.

The q3 Box object (third quadrant) will need to be moved by **300** units (quadrants are 300x300 in size) out along **both** the x- and z-axes, so the q3.setTranslateX() method parameter also needs to be incremented from 225 to **525** to accomplish this third quadrant game board component positioning, as shown in Figure 14-24.

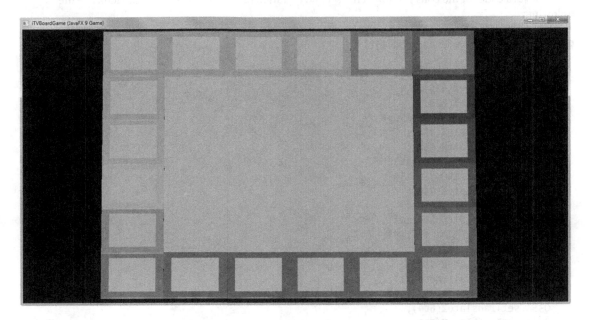

Figure 14-24. *Use your Run ➤ Project work process to see that quadrants 1 to 4 are now coded and aligning properly*

Q3S1 needs to position itself **450 units** along the **x-axis** from the 0,0 origin and **750** units out along the **z-axis**. This is done by changing your locational method call to .setTranslateX(450) and leaving (or adding w, which depends on which Java code you copied) .setTranslateZ(**750**). Be sure to also set .setMaterial(**Shader11**) to reference the correct shader number, which then references (and applies) the **diffuse11** Image object as the diffuseMap property.

Q3S2 needs to position itself **600 units** along **x-axis** from the 0,0 origin and **750** units out, along the **z-axis**. This is done by changing the location method call to .setTranslateX(**600**) and leaving (or adding, depending on the block of Java code you have copied) .setTranslateZ(**750**). Be sure to also set .setMaterial(**Shader12**) to reference the correct shader number, which then references (and applies) the **diffuse12** Image object as a diffuseMap property.

Q3S3 needs to position itself **750 units** along the **z-axis** from the 0,0 origin, as well as **750** units along **x-axis**, which puts it diagonal to an 0,0 origin. This is done by changing the location method call to .setTranslateZ(**750**) and then adding a second .setTranslateX(**750**) method call. Be sure to also set .setMaterial(**Shader13**) to reference your correct Phong shader object number, which references (and applies) the **diffuse13** Image object as your diffuseMap property.

361

Q3S4 also needs to position itself **750 units** along **X** from the 0,0 origin, but this time, we'll also need to pull this square back **down** another **150** units in the **Z direction** in order to move it down along the right side of your game board layout. This is done by again using two location method calls. One would be .setTranslateZ(**600**), and the other would still be set to .setTranslationX(**750**). Again, be sure to set .setMaterial(**Shader14**) to reference the matching **Shader14** object, which then references and applies a **diffuse14** Image object as a diffuseMap property.

Q3S5 needs to position itself **750 units** in the **X direction** from 0,0 and **450** units in the **Z direction** so that this square is located near the middle right of this game board. This is again done using two location method calls, to .setTranslateX(**750**) and to .setTranslateZ(**450**). Be sure to set .setMaterial(**Shader15**) to reference your correct **Shader15** object, which then references (and applies) the **diffuse15** Image object as the diffuseMap property.

The Java code for the construction of the second quadrant of the game board should look like the following:

```
private void createGameBoardNodes() {
    ...
    q3 = new Box(300, 5, 300);      // Java code creating a third quadrant for the gameboard
    q3.setTranslateX(525);
    q3.setTranslateZ(525);
    Q3S1 = new Box(150, 5, 150);
    Q3S1.setTranslateZ(750);
    Q3S1.setTranslateX(450);
    Q3S1.setMaterial(Shader11);
    Q3S2 = new Box(150, 5, 150);
    Q3S2.setTranslateZ(750);
    Q3S2.setTranslateX(600);
    Q3S2.setMaterial(Shader12);
    Q3S3 = new Box(150, 5, 150);
    Q3S3.setTranslateZ(750);
    Q3S3.setTranslateX(750);
    Q3S3.setMaterial(Shader13);
    Q3S4 = new Box(150, 5, 150);
    Q3S4.setTranslateZ(600);
    Q3S4.setTranslateX(750);
    Q3S4.setMaterial(Shader14);
    Q3S5 = new Box(150, 5, 150);
    Q3S5.setTranslateZ(450);
    Q3S5.setTranslateX(750);
    Q3S5.setMaterial(Shader15);
    ...                             // Your fourth quadrant configuration code will go in here
    q4 = new Box(300, 5, 300);
    q4.setVisible(false);
}
```

Finally, let's create the fourth quadrant of our game board by going back into the **createGameBoardNodes()** method body and creating the fourth section of code for Box primitives Q4S1 through Q4S5. Just copy your Q3S1 to Q3S5 statements (and q4 statements) and paste them again underneath themselves; then change the object names and method call parameters (so that you do not have to type all these Java statements into NetBeans 9 again).

The q4 Box object (fourth quadrant) will need to be moved back down by **300** units along the z-axis, so your q4.setTranslateZ() method parameter needs to be **decremented**, from 525 to **225**, to accomplish this fourth quadrant game board component positioning, as shown in Figure 14-24.

Q4S1 needs to position itself **300 units** along **Z** (from the 0,0 origin) and **750** units along **X** at the right. This is done by changing the location method call to .setTranslate**Z**(**300**). Be sure to set .setMaterial(**Shader16**) to reference the correct shader that then references and applies the **diffuse16** Image object as a diffuseMap property.

Q4S2 needs to position itself **150 units** along Z (from the 0,0 origin) and the full 750 units along X. This is done by changing the location method call to .setTranslate**Z**(**150**). Be sure to set .setMaterial(**Shader17**) to reference the correct shader that then references and applies the **diffuse17** Image object as a diffuseMap property.

Q4S3 only needs to position itself **750 units** along X from the 0,0 origin because it is at the right corner. This means the only location method call needed is .setTranslate**X**(**750**). Be sure to set .setMaterial(**Shader18**) to reference the correct shader that then references and applies the **diffuse18** Image object as a diffuseMap property.

Q4S4 only needs to position itself **600 units** along X from the 0,0 origin to pull this square back 150 units in the **direction**, of the origin, in order to move it to the left, along the bottom of your game board layout. This is done by using only the .setTranslate**X**(**600**) method call. Be sure to set .setMaterial(**Shader19**) to reference the correct **Shader9** object, which references (and applies) the **diffuse19** Image object as a PhongMaterial diffuseMap property.

Q4S5 needs to position itself **450 units** in the **X direction** from 0,0 so your last game square is located near the bottom middle of this game board. This is again done using one location method call to .setTranslate**X**(**450**). Be sure to set .setMaterial(**Shader20**) to reference the correct **Shader20** object, which then references (and applies) the **diffuse20** Image object as a diffuseMap property. The Java code for the construction of this final quadrant of the game board should look like the following Java code:

```
private void createGameBoardNodes() {
    ...
    q4 = new Box(300, 5, 300);      // Java code creating a second quadrant for the gameboard
    q4.setTranslateX(525);
    q4.setTranslateZ(225);
    Q4S1 = new Box(150, 5, 150);
    Q4S1.setTranslateX(750);
    Q4S1.setTranslateZ(300);
    Q4S1.setMaterial(Shader16);
    Q4S2 = new Box(150, 5, 150);
    Q4S2.setTranslateX(750);
    Q4S2.setTranslateZ(150);
    Q4S2.setMaterial(Shader17);
    Q4S3 = new Box(150, 5, 150);
    Q4S3.setTranslateX(750);
    Q4S3.setMaterial(Shader18);
    Q4S4 = new Box(150, 5, 150);
    Q4S4.setTranslateX(600);
    Q4S4.setMaterial(Shader19);
    Q4S5 = new Box(150, 5, 150);
    Q4S5.setTranslateX(450);
    Q4S5.setMaterial(Shader20);
}
```

Figure 14-24 shows the **Run ➤ Project** Java code testing work process, showing a completed 3D game board.

There are one or two rendering anomalies visible, such as the Q1S2 square, which looks like it is lying over the Q1S1 square. This is strange, as the code is precise and based on multiples of 150, so it should be aligned precisely like the others. Since this problem is not with the code, we will take a look at how we can deal with this rendering anomaly in the next chapter. Use the .setRotationAxis(Rotate.Y_AXIS) and .setRotate(30) methods to rotate the game board 30 degrees, as you have done before, to see what **pivot point** is being used to rotate this gameBoard hierarchy. This Java 9 test code should be placed in your **createBoardGameNodes()** method, as shown highlighted in Figure 14-25.

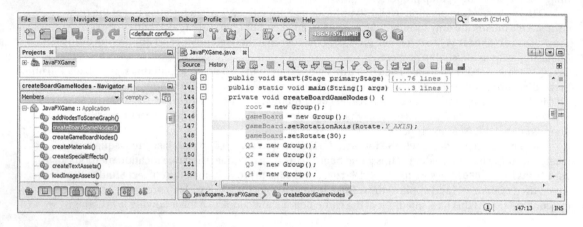

Figure 14-25. *Add .setRotationAxis(Rotate.Y_AXIS) and a .setRotate(30) method call to the gameBoard Group object*

The reason that we're doing this is that we need to check, before we leave this chapter, whether or not this game board is working as a hierarchy. That is, if we rotate it around the y-axis, will it use the center of the gameBoard Group as the pivot point, or will it pivot (rotate) around the center of the 0,0 origin corner square of the game board?

As you can see in Figure 14-26, the gameBoard Group object is indeed defining its own 0,0 center, using the average center of all of its Group Node's children. As we know from the 6 × 150 (900) construction of the game board, this 0,0 center is offset **450** (half of 900) in X and Z (450, 450) or **625** (450 + 1/2 of 450) in linear units (on the diagonal) between origins. By constructing things in evenly divisible whole numbers, we will be able to use **integers** (int) for our gameplay code in later chapters, which saves on memory and processing for the JavaFX game engine.

Figure 14-26. *Rotate the gameBoard Group Node object 30 to 45 degrees to see where it defines its center for rotation*

Before we finish up with this chapter, let's see if we can improve our game board rendering result by using a different Camera (algorithm) class since we seem to be having some Box face rendering order and positioning problems. If it is not the camera object causing these slight ridges between squares, we will have to look further for solutions to this problem, as we need to get a photorealistic game board that looks like the cardboard game boards we all use to play games in real life. As you now know, pro Java 9 game development is an iterative process, so you know we will figure it out eventually!

Changing Cameras: Using the ParallelCamera Class

Next, I am going to change camera objects from a PerspectiveCamera to a **ParallelCamera**, both to give you some experience using them and to see if this face-order rendering problem (the seeming overlap in squares) is any different between the two Camera class algorithms (between the two Camera subclasses). This is as simple as changing the declaration at the top of your class from PerspectiveCamera to ParallelCamera and making sure the same changes are made to the instantiation statement in createBoardGameNodes(), as shown here as well as in Figure 14-27:

```
ParallelCamera camera;
...
camera = new ParallelCamera();
camera.setTranslateZ(0);
camera.setNearClip(0.1);
camera.setFarClip(5000.0);
```

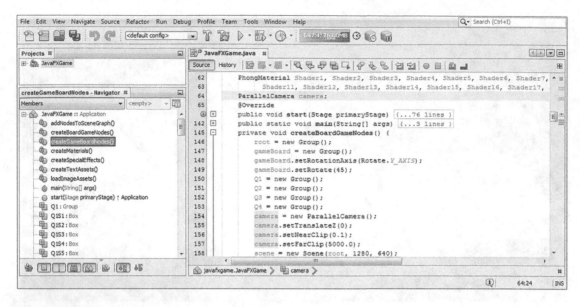

Figure 14-27. *Change the Scene camera object to use a ParallelCamera class (algorithm) instead of PerspectiveCamera*

Next, let's go into the gameButton event handling code block and remove the .setFieldOfView(1) method call simply by commenting out that line of code, which as you can see is a slick and common code debugging trick.

We will do this because that particular method call is not supported for the new ParallelCamera object. We will also change the camera.setTranslateZ() method call to the diagonal value for the game board that I calculated to place the camera view at game board center (**625**).

I will also set the camera.setTranslateX() method call to be one-quarter of the game board width of **225**, as shown in the highlighted camera object code in the middle of Figure 14-28.

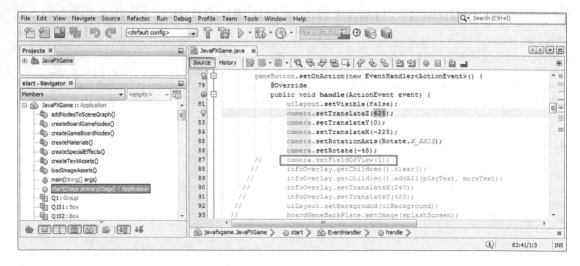

Figure 14-28. *Remove the FOV setting code, change .setTranslateX() to 225, .setTranslateZ() to 625, and Y = 0*

I am refining this code to get a better view of the game board and to fit it into the window better so that when we spin it in subsequent chapters on animation and gameplay, it will perfectly fit into the scene in any spin orientation as well as while it is animating a random spin to select a topic quadrant.

The next thing I'm going to do is "tweak" the camera values in onStart() to fit the game board in the window. As you can see in Figure 14-29, we need to flatten the camera view (30 degrees) and adjust the X, Y, Z location slightly.

Figure 14-29. *The game board is almost fitting perfectly in the window; let's adjust the camera angle and spacing next!*

As you can see in Figure 14-30, I tweaked the **rotation** to **30°**, the **Z** to **500**, the **Y** to **-300**, and the **X** to **-260**.

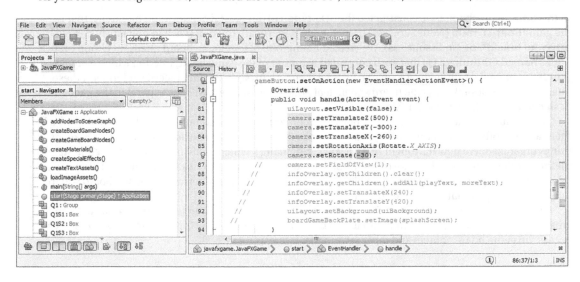

Figure 14-30. *Set the camera rotation at 30 degrees, the Z location to 500, the Y location to -300, and the X location to -260*

As you can see in Figure 14-31, we have now set the "extremes" of your game board to fit into the window, using these new camera settings with the ParallelCamera algorithm, which seems to distort the game board less than the PerspectiveCamera does. If we now rotate the game board, it should all stay inside of the window (viewable) area.

Figure 14-31. *Use your Run ➤ Project work process to see if the new camera algorithm and settings fit the game board*

Summary

In this fourteenth chapter, we constructed the 3D portion of our JavaFX SceneGraph hierarchy, that is, the **gameBoard Group** (Node subclass) branch node underneath the root (we had previously created the **uiLayout StackPane** Node subclass). We created a subgroup of four game board quadrant Group branch nodes named Q1 through Q4 that each contained a quarter of the game board interior, which were Box primitives named q1 through q4 to match up with their Group Node Parent objects. Underneath these quadrants we grouped five game board square leaf node objects, which will correspond in the gameplay design to the quadrant game functionality.

We created two new method bodies, one for creating game board squares since there are dozens of them and the other for creating Phong materials since there are going to be dozens of them! This keeps things organized. We now have eight (nine if you count main(), which is still in the bootstrap code state) method bodies, seven of which are custom, and we have more than 400 lines of Java code, all organized into logical collapsing and expanding sections. We created colorful shaders for each game board square, mapping the appropriate diffuse texture maps onto each one.

In Chapter 15, we're going to further refine our game board design and Java code organization and create a way for game players to manipulate the board in 3D space so they (or the gameplay AI code) can access the game board content and topic section that interests them.

■ ■ ■

3D Gameplay UI Creation: Using the Sphere Primitive to Create a UI Node

Now that you have created the multitiered gameBoard Group Node (subclass) hierarchy and tested it to see whether it rotates as if it were one 3D model, it is time to add a Sphere 3D primitive so we can create a 3D user interface element for the user to use to create random "spins" during gameplay. We will also set up the Phong shader objects for these and again use GIMP 2.8.22 to create (from scratch) the rest of your diffuse texture maps for the game board quadrants, as well as a 3D "spinner" UI texture map for a Sphere primitive. This spinner will be used on each player's turn to randomly spin the gameboard to select the topic category. You will always need to differentiate your pro Java 9 game from others out there, so we'll be unique and *spin the gameboard itself* to pick the quadrant (topic category), which cannot be done with real-life game boards but which can be done with virtual i3D game boards. We'll add Java 9 code to the top of your class as well as in the createMaterials(), addNodesToSceneGraph(), and loadImageAssets() method bodies. We'll create custom PNG24 diffuse textures to add to your project source (/src) folder. We'll rearrange your **createGameBoardNodes()** method to reorganize the quadrant 3D primitives that we'll work on during this chapter to complete the interior parts of the game board design. We'll place the quadrants together at the top of this method.

During the chapter, we will also take a look at how you **solve problems** that you encounter on your way to creating professional-quality games. In this case, there is a **face rendering** problem that we encountered when modeling the game board; it should render smoothly (flat on top) but is rendering with game board square **overlaps** that should not be happening. There are also small Y (height) variations that make the quadrants look **depressed** once they're diffuse texture mapped. (Remember the center quadrants looked flat in Chapter 14 without shaders applied, but they also exhibit these rendering artifacts once we continue to work on them, which you'll see later during this chapter.)

Finish Your 3D Assets: Topic Quadrants and Spinner

Let's continue with the design and development of the 3D components for the board game, including texture map development using GIMP for the interior of the game board and a 3D spinner UI element used to create random spins for the game, just like you have in real-life board games. We will do this using Java 9 (JavaFX API) classes so that we create the game using only the Java 9 APIs and our digital image assets (background images and texture maps). So far, we have done this in around 400 lines of code! We will add another 10 percent (440) during this chapter to "skin" the quadrants and add a "spinner" UI element located at the top-left corner of the screen. The first thing we will need to do at the top of the class is to add five more Image object declarations, named **diffuse21** through **diffuse25**, and five more PhongMaterial object declarations, named **Shader21** through **Shader25**. This is shown in the following Java code, as well as in green (with some code being highlighted using yellow and blue) at the top of the class in Figure 15-1:

```
Image ... diffuse21, diffuse22, diffuse23, diffuse24, diffuse25;
PhongMaterial ... Shader21, Shader22, Shader23, Shader24, Shader25;
```

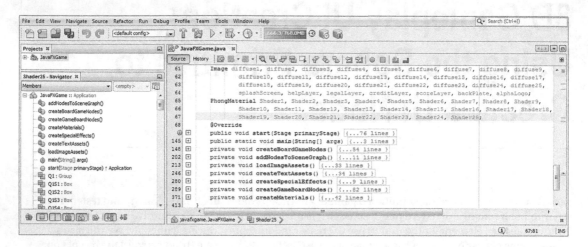

Figure 15-1. *Add objects at the top of your class for diffuse texture maps and shaders for your quadrants and a spinner*

Cut and paste the last five diffuse16 through diffuse20 Image object declarations, create five new ones named diffuse21 through diffuse25, and configure them for use, as shown here and in Figure 15-2:

```
diffuse21 = new Image("/gameboardquad1.png", 512, 512, true, true, true);
diffuse22 = new Image("/gameboardquad2.png", 512, 512, true, true, true);
diffuse23 = new Image("/gameboardquad3.png", 512, 512, true, true, true);
diffuse24 = new Image("/gameboardquad4.png", 512, 512, true, true, true);
diffuse25 = new Image("/gameboardspin.png",  256, 256, true, true, true);
```

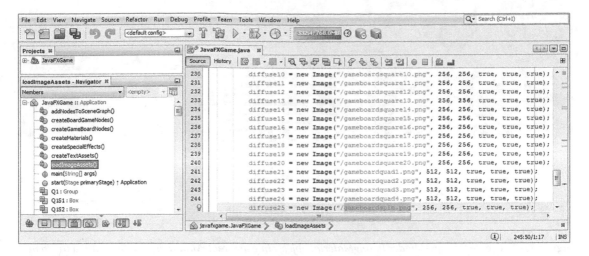

Figure 15-2. *Create five new diffuse image map objects in your loadImageAssets() method and configure them for use*

We will create these diffuse texture map digital image assets in the next section of the chapter using GIMP. Open the createMaterials() method body and add the corresponding Shader21 through Shader25 object instantiation and configuration statements, which "wire up the Shaders" to reference the diffuse texture map Image object assets.

If you like, you can also use copy and paste to accomplish this just like you did with the diffuse texture map Image objects. The Java code creating the new shaders and referencing them to the diffuse texture map Image object assets should look like the following Java code block of statements, shown highlighted in Figure 15-3:

```
Shader21 = new PhongMaterial(Color.WHITE);
Shader21.setDiffuseMap(diffuse21);
Shader22 = new PhongMaterial(Color.WHITE);
Shader22.setDiffuseMap(diffuse22);
Shader23 = new PhongMaterial(Color.WHITE);
Shader23.setDiffuseMap(diffuse23);
Shader24 = new PhongMaterial(Color.WHITE);
Shader24.setDiffuseMap(diffuse24);
Shader25 = new PhongMaterial(Color.WHITE);
Shader25.setDiffuseMap(diffuse25);
```

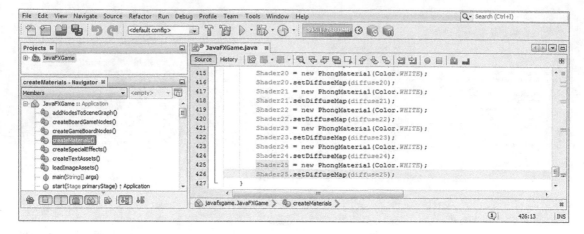

Figure 15-3. *Create five new Shader PhongMaterial objects in your createMaterials() method and wire them to diffuseMap objects*

You will now have to again utilize GIMP to create your quadrant and spinner texture maps to professionally texture your board game elements. The current version is 2.8.22.

Creating Your Quadrant and Spinner Diffuse Color Texture Maps

Use the GIMP **File ➤ New** work process to create a transparent (empty) diffuse texture map composite, and this time make it **512 by 512** pixels since the quadrant Box objects q1 through q4 are twice as big as the square Box objects on both axes (or four times larger in total). This matches up mathematically with doubling the 256-pixel texture map size used for the game board squares. Click the circle (or ellipse) select tool, shown highlighted at the top of Figure 15-4, and again use the **Ellipse Select Tool** options tab, below the tool icons, to set a precise size and location for the circle since we want a white circle perfectly centered in each game board quadrant. I set the circle's **Size** to **400** (equal width and height values create a perfect circle; any variation will create an ellipse or oval shape), and I divided the rest (512 - 400 = 112 / 2 = 56) to get my X,Y **Position** value of **56**, which is also highlighted in red.

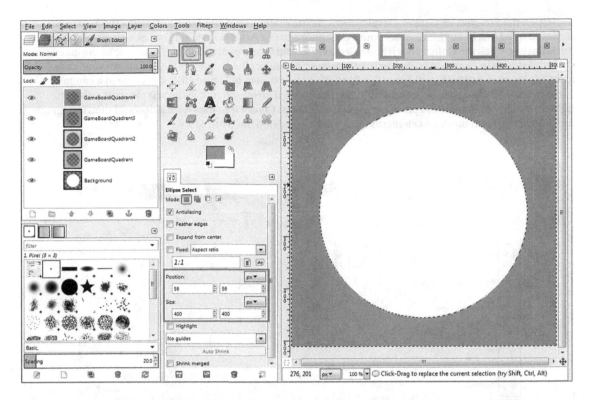

Figure 15-4. *Create the four quadrant texture maps at 512-pixel resolution using 60 percent of the corner square color value*

With the **Background** layer selected, make sure the **Foreground (FG) Color swatch** is set to **white** and use the **Edit ➤ Fill with FG Color** (White) option to create the white center for all four quadrant texture maps at the very bottom of the compositing layer stack, as shown in Figure 15-4. Right-click your Background layer, use the **New Layer** command, and create a new layer named **GameBoardQuadrant**. Use the **Select ➤ Invert** menu sequence to invert the selection and select the GameBoardQuadrant layer to designate that layer to hold your outer color fill. Open the **gameboardsquare3.png** file and use the **Eyedropper** tool to select its **orange** color value. Click your **FG Color** (foreground) swatch, invoke the color picker dialog, and set the **Value** (V) slider to **60 percent** color (40 percent white) to create a **pastel** version of the corner square's color for the quadrant located diagonally from it. Use **Edit ➤ Fill with FG Color** to fill the area around the center circle with the color, use **File ➤ Export As** to save the file to the project's /**src** folder, and name it **boardgamequad1.png**, as referenced in your Image object code in Figure 15-2. Repeat this process: create a new layer, get a corner square color value, lighten by 40 percent, fill with the foreground color, and export the image as PNG24 to create the other three numbered boardgamequad PNG24 assets, which are shown in their own layers on the far left side of Figure 15-4. You can also see the gameboardsquare 3, 8, 13, and 18 image assets I opened to **sample** color values from at the top-right corner of Figure 15-4. The Eyedropper tool is on the lower right of the Ellipse Select tool.

While we're here in GIMP, let's open our texture map creation GIMP XCF file with all of the different map types we created during Chapter 13, covering shaders and materials, and use your beach ball diffuse texture to create a 3D spinner Sphere texture that reads **"SPIN"** as it spins around, with *S* and *I* in white (over color) and *P* and *N* in black.

Open the Pro_Java_9_Games_Development_Texture_Maps GIMP XCF file and select the **Text** tool, shown in a red box in Figure 15-5. Set your **Text** options to use **Arial Heavy**, set Font Size to **48**, and select **Antialiasing**. Click the **Color** swatch and select **White**, and type a capital *S* over the middle of the green stripe, as shown in Figure 15-5. Right-click the S layer and select the Duplicate Layer tool, set your Text tool Color swatch to **Black**, and select the *S* in yellow, as is shown in Figure 15-5; then type in a capital **P** to replace the *S*. You can use the **Move** tool (four connected arrows) to move the text element, using the right arrow key, so that it stays precisely aligned with the *S*. Center it in the white stripe and then repeat the process for the *I* and the *N* text elements until you have created the word *SPIN*.

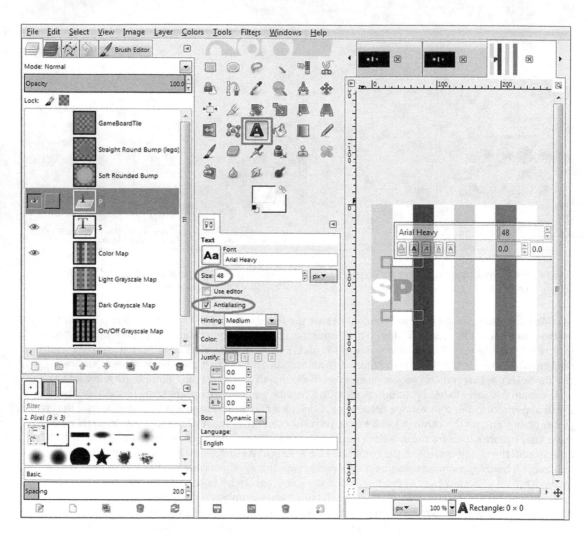

Figure 15-5. *Create the word SPIN twice on your beach ball texture map to create your animated spinner texture map*

Once you have done all four letters once, you can use the same right-click on a layer and use the **Duplicate Layer** work process to replicate these letters; then use your Move tool to position the letters on the other four stripes, as shown on the right in Figure 15-6.

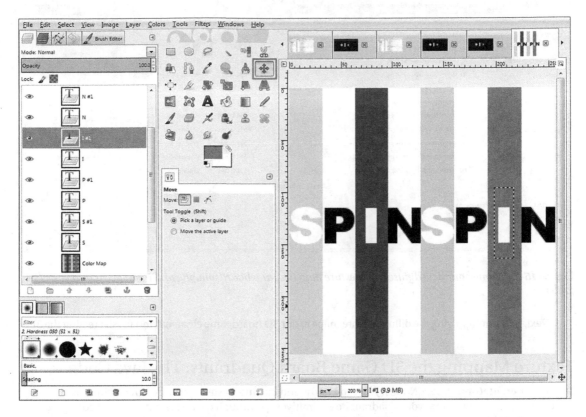

Figure 15-6. *Replicate the four SPIN letters twice in the center of each of the eight stripes, at exactly the same height*

To use the GIMP Move tool, first click the text element, which will show the Move tool what you want to move, and then use the right arrow key to position the letter over the next stripe. Using the right arrow key instead of dragging the letter with the mouse will keep the letter at exactly the same pixel height location, keeping the letters in perfect alignment with each other.

As you will see in Figure 15-6, this work process will yield a uniform, professional map result. Although your letters seem cramped on the GIMP canvas, when mapped onto the curvature of a Sphere primitive, the result is quite readable, even while being animated, because the curvature of the surface seems to "stretch" these letters farther apart.

Once you are satisfied with the spinner texture map, use the **File ➤ Export As** menu sequence, and save your **gameboardspin.png** file to your **C:/Users/Name/Documents/NetBeansProjects/JavaFXGame/src/** folder, as shown in Figure 15-7. Notice that our boardgamesquare PNG24 files are well optimized, at **680** bytes, and our boardgamequad files are only **10KB** each. If you click a file name, you will get a good preview of the texture map on the right side of the dialog. This is a great feature, especially for similar file names, because you can click any file name to preview it and GIMP will put that file name in the **Name** field; then you can just change the number at the end as a typing shortcut!

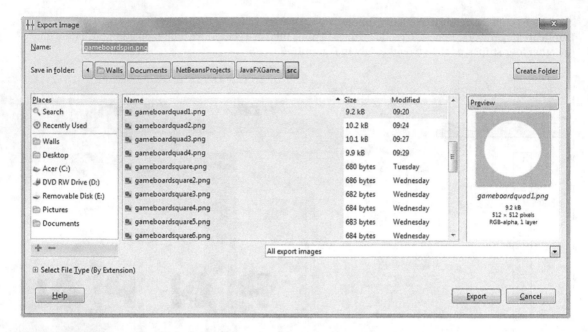

Figure 15-7. *Name your new diffuse color texture map file gameboardspin.png and then save it into your /src folder*

Next, let's start applying the diffuse texture maps to our 3D boardgame elements and finish creating the 3D.

Texture Mapping the 3D Game Board Quadrants: The Java Code

Open your **createGameBoardNodes()** method body, and cut and paste the q1 through q4 object code into the top of the method so that your quadrant Box primitives q1 through q4 are instantiated and configured all in the same block of Java 9 statements. You can now more clearly see the pattern of X, Z movements from different 225 and 525 combinations relative to each quadrant, with no identical X, Z coordinate pairs, which would overlap your quadrants.

Add **q1.**setMaterial(**Shader21**); to the first one, as shown in Figure 15-8, using the following Java code:

```
q1 = new Box(300, 5, 300);
q1.setMaterial(Shader21);
q1.setTranslateX(225);
q1.setTranslateZ(225);
q2 = new Box(300, 5, 300);
q2.setTranslateX(225);
q2.setTranslateZ(525);
q3 = new Box(300, 5, 300);
q3.setTranslateX(525);
q3.setTranslateZ(525);
q4 = new Box(300, 5, 300);
q4.setTranslateX(525);
q4.setTranslateZ(225);
```

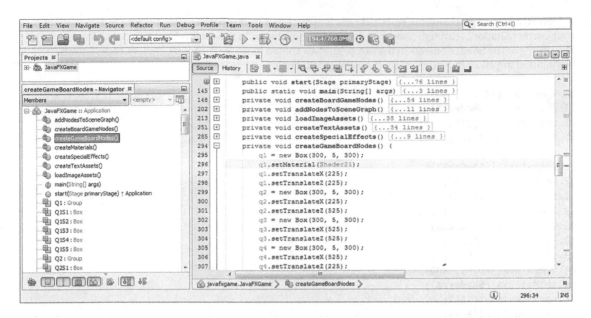

Figure 15-8. *Cut and paste all quadrant Box primitive code to one place and start adding shaders using .setMaterial()*

Figure 15-9 shows a **Run ➤ Project** work process with game board quadrant 1 texture mapped and test rendered. As you can see, the **face order** rendering problem appears once your diffuse texture map has been applied!

Figure 15-9. *Select Run ➤ Project to render and preview the first quadrant texture map application (the face order bug appears)*

377

Next, add your .setMaterial() method calls for your other three quadrant Box primitives and reference your correct Shader22 through Shader24 PhongMaterial objects in the method call parameter list. The wiring of the Shader objects to the Box primitives should look like the following Java code, shown highlighted in yellow in Figure 15-10, once you are finished:

```
q1 = new Box(300, 5, 300);
q1.setMaterial(Shader21);
q1.setTranslateX(225);
q1.setTranslateZ(225);
q2 = new Box(300, 5, 300);
q2.setMaterial(Shader22);
q2.setTranslateX(225);
q2.setTranslateZ(525);
q3 = new Box(300, 5, 300);
q3.setMaterial(Shader23);
q3.setTranslateX(525);
q3.setTranslateZ(525);
q4 = new Box(300, 5, 300);
q4.setMaterial(Shader24);
q4.setTranslateX(525);
q4.setTranslateZ(225);
```

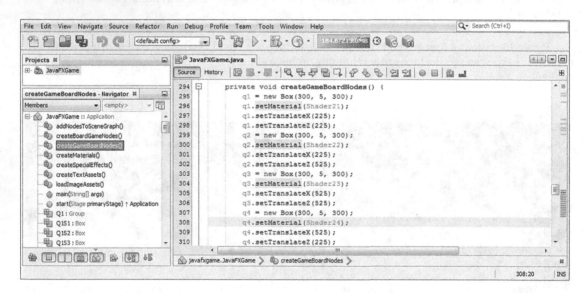

Figure 15-10. *Complete the Shader object wiring to Box primitives for all quadrants so we can see the finished gameboard*

As you can see in Figure 15-11, the quadrant Box primitives are now exhibiting the same face rendering order problems as the rest of the i3D game board. Let's take a break from coding to see whether we can find any evidence of other Java developers experiencing this particular 3D model face render problem in their JavaFX 9 game development. As you might imagine, the tool to use to do this research is a **search engine**.

Figure 15-11. *The diffuse texture mapping looks very professional, other than the face depth and rendering anomalies*

Let's take a look at how I found the solution to the face order rendering problem, which I attempted to do using the Google search engine and well-targeted keywords, before filing a bug report on the JavaFX 9 dev forum.

Use Google to Resolve JavaFX Anomalies: Using StackOverflow

To find developers having similar problems, use the Google search engine and type in the most common or likely description of the problem that you are seeing on the screen. In this case, that would be "wrong overlapping shapes" or "problem with Box face order rendering." Sometimes you may have to try several different keyword strings. In this case, there are several out there with the correct answer, which is to turn on a feature called *depth buffering*. This is an algorithm that is processing intensive, so it is **off** by default. Since we are also getting some jagged edges, we can turn on another processing-intensive algorithm called *anti-aliasing*. These are both accessible in the overloaded Scene() constructor, so fixing both of these problems can be done with one simple modification to our Scene scene object instantiation! Here is an example of two of the StackOverflow answers regarding this problem and its solution:

```
stackoverflow.com/questions/19589210/overlaping-shapes-wrong-overlapping-shapes-behaviour
    --OR--
stackoverflow.com/questions/28567195/javafx-8-3d-z-order-overlapping-shape-behaviour-is-wrong
```

The overloaded constructor method for the Scene that allows you to turn on both **depth buffering** and **anti-aliasing** as the default behavior for the 3D Scene object looks like the following Java code:

```
Scene(Parent root, double width, double height, boolean depthBuffer, SceneAntialiasing constant)
```

Thus, we need to add **depthBuffer=true** and **SceneAntialiasing.BALANCED** to the **Scene()** constructor that we're using in the createBoardGameNodes() method, which as you can see in Figure 15-12 (in a red rectangle) I added to the end of the **scene = new Scene(root, 1280, 640);** Java 9 Scene object instantiation statement. This switches your constructor method call to utilize a different overloaded constructor method to create your 3D Scene.

Let's add a 3D UI element, called a *spinner*, that a player can use to randomly spin the game board to pick a topic.

Creating a 3D User Interface Element: A 3D Spinner Randomizer

Now let's reuse our Sphere primitive code and beach ball texture map to create a 3D user interface (UI) element that the player can click to spin the board to pick a random subject (topic) category. Declare the Sphere and name it **spinner** at the top of the class. Then instantiate it with a radius of **60** and configure it with **Shader25** and the X, Y location of **-200**, **-500**, which puts it at the top-left corner of the screen. Use the **Y** rotation axis and set a rotate value of **25** degrees to try to place the word *SPIN* facing the user. Your Java code, shown in Figure 15-12, will look like this:

```
Sphere spinner;
...
spinner = new Sphere(60);
spinner.setMaterial(Shader25);
spinner.setTranslateX(-200);
spinner.setTranslateY(-500);
spinner.setRotationAxis(Rotate.Y_AXIS);
spinner.setRotate(25);
scene = new Scene(root, 1280, 640, true, SceneAntialiasing.BALANCED);
```

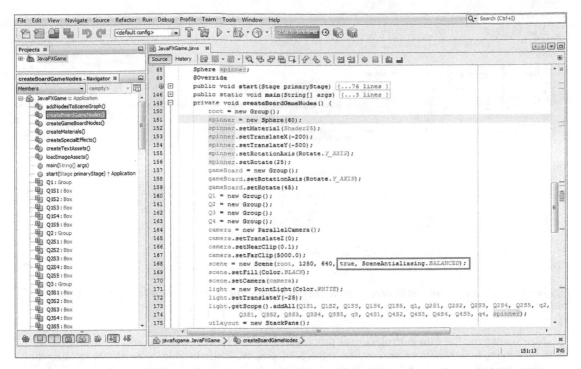

Figure 15-12. *Add a Sphere primitive named spinner, set the material and translation parameters, and fix the face order render bug*

Before we will be able to render your 3D Scene and look at the new spinner UI to see whether we need to tweak the diffuse texture map in any way, we'll need to add it to the JavaFX SceneGraph. I am going to add it at the top, directly under the root, as the 3D UI will eventually have its own hierarchy, just like the 2D uiLayout does and just like the 3D gameBoard does. In this way, if we want to affect the 3D UI elements as a whole at any time, we can do this using one line of code referencing the 3D UI branch, and that will affect all the leaf nodes underneath it. For now, the spinner will be a leaf node underneath the root. The Java code to add the spinner, shown in Figure 15-13, should look like the following:

```
root.getChildren().addAll(gameBoard, uiLayout, spinner);
```

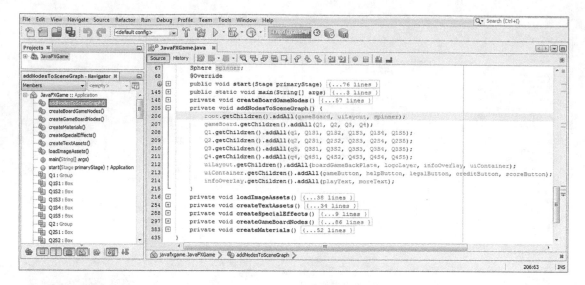

Figure 15-13. *Add your spinner Sphere object to the top of the SceneGraph hierarchy using root.getChildren(). addAll()*

Now we can use the **Run ➤ Project** work process and test our new Java code to add the Sphere spinner UI to the board game we are creating in this 3D Scene. We'll also be able to see whether adding the algorithms for anti-aliasing and depth buffering (which check for proper face order rendering and apply smoothing to rough edges in the render pass, respectively) have solved our visual quality problems by using the more complex overloaded Scene() constructor method, with five parameters, instead of only three.

As you can see in Figure 15-14, the 3D gameBoard hierarchy, with two dozen 3D primitive objects as game board squares and game board quadrants, is now rendering as one cohesive 3D model. It finally looks like the board game (cardboard game boards) that you see in most popular board games, and each square and quadrant will be able to be accessed and controlled individually in your code, even though the game board model appears to be only one 3D object in the 3D Scene. This is what we've been striving to learn about, and achieve, during the past several chapters.

Figure 15-14. *The face rendering order problem has been fixed, and we're now getting a smooth, thin cardboard game*

The spinner UI element, on the other hand, is not giving us the visual result that we wanted initially, which was a beach ball type of object, with the word *SPIN* written on the front of it. This is OK, as we know that pro Java 9 games development is an **iterative refinement** process, so let's think about how we can shrink the word *SPIN* down so that four letters show on the Sphere primitive at one time, rather than only two letters as it is rendering currently.

The easiest way to shrink the text so the word *SPIN* fits on one-quarter of the Sphere primitive, as well as to increase the number (and thinness) of the colored stripes, would be to make this texture map a **512**-pixel texture. This will shrink all text elements so four will fit, and we can copy and paste the stripes and color shift them to add more color.

Next, let's go back to GIMP and look at the work process for enhancing the spinner UI diffuse texture map.

Enhancing the 3D Spinner Texture Map: Increasing Resolution

The work process for creating a more detailed 512x512 pixel texture map for the 3D spinner UI element is a lot easier than you might think, if you use the power of GIMP's tools and algorithms within an optimized work process. We can double the resolution, double the stripes, double the stripe colors, and double the text elements in only a dozen or two "moves," with GIMP doing all of the pixel manipulation for you, at the highest quality level, which we will require.

Figure 15-15 shows the GIMP composite result for the moves. The first thing to do is to add another 256 pixels to the right side of the document by using **Image ➤ Canvas Size ➤ Width=512 ➤ Resize** (button), which will add 256 pixels of transparency to the right half of your texture map composite. Select the Background layer and white color swatch and use the Paintbucket tool (fourth row, fourth icon) to fill the right half of the Background layer so it is 100 percent white. Next, right-click the Color Map layer and select the **Duplicate Layer** option, which will create the Color Map copy layer, shown in Figure 15-15. Select this layer, use the **Color ➤ Hue-Saturation** algorithm (menu sequence), and shift all four colors by **60** degrees or so to create four different colors, as shown in Figure 15-15. Next, to resize the (Y or height) dimension to 512 matching pixels, this time use the **Image ➤ Scale Image** menu sequence, unlock the aspect ratio by clicking the **chain icon** between the width and height, and set the **height** value to **512**. This will **stretch** the color bars to fill the image so that you don't have to do a lot of select-move-fill work like you did originally to create the beach ball texture map. This scaling operation will also make the text components taller, which will make them more readable in the Sphere spinner UI, especially while it is spinning. Finally, right-click the #2 layers for S, P, I, and N and create layer #3 and layer #4 for each. Use the Move tool and the right arrow key to precisely position them.

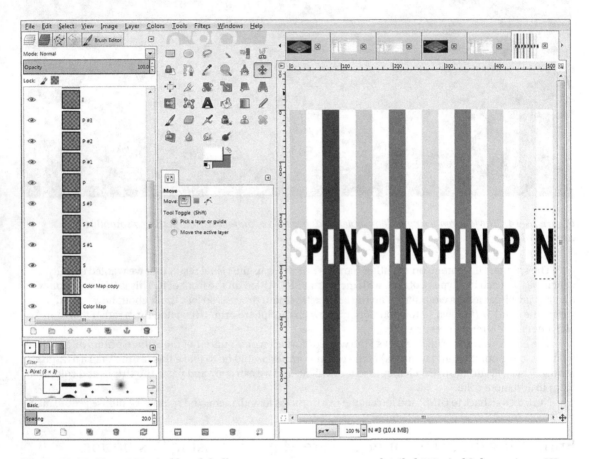

Figure 15-15. *Use a 256-pixel beach ball texture map to create a more detailed 512-pixel Sphere spinner UI texture map*

Finally, use **File ➤ Export As** to overwrite the current **gameboardspin.png** file in your Project /src/ folder. Since that file name is already being referenced within the diffuse25 Image object instantiation statement, all that you have to do is to change the width and height values from **256** to **512**, which, when mapped onto a Sphere primitive of the same size, will serve to **decrease** the size of both the stripes and the text elements (letters) on the Sphere so that instead of two letters (SP, shown in Figure 15-14), four letters (SPIN) will be shown. At that point, all that you have to do is to tweak the rotation value somewhere between 20 and 30 degrees so that the word *SPIN* will be centered in the Sphere object named spinner so that the user knows what will happen when this Sphere spinner UI object is clicked.

The new Java 9 statement for your diffuse25 object instantiation should look like the following Java code, which is also highlighted in yellow and blue in Figure 15-16:

```
diffuse25 = new Image("/gameboardspin.png", 512, 512, true, true, true);
```

Figure 15-16. *Modify the width and height resolution parameters and change them from 256 pixels to 512 pixels each*

The next thing that needs to be done is to "tweak" all the spinner object configuration settings to make the Sphere primitive a bit larger and move it closer to the corner of the screen so that it's well out of the way of the game board. I made the radius **64** and the **Y** translation **-512** to move it further up. I found the rotation value of **30** degrees centers the word *SPIN*. The Java code, which is also highlighted in Figure 15-17, should look like the following:

```
Sphere spinner;
...
spinner = new Sphere(64);
spinner.setMaterial(Shader25);
spinner.setTranslateX(-200);
spinner.setTranslateY(-512);
spinner.setRotationAxis(Rotate.Y_AXIS);
spinner.setRotate(30);
```

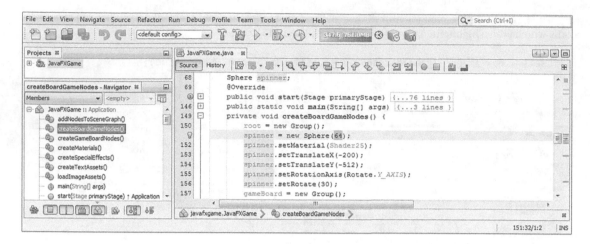

Figure 15-17. *Tweak the Sphere spinner settings to radius 64 to make the spinner bigger and rotate it to 30 degrees to see SPIN*

Figure 15-18 shows the **Run ➤ Project** Java code testing work process. As you can see, the game board is now looking quite professional, and the 3D spinner UI looks like a spinner and is labeled **SPIN**, using large, readable letters.

Figure 15-18. *The spinner Sphere UI element now looks more like a spinner, and the word SPIN is now visible to the user*

Now we are at a point where our 3D boardgame is designed and coded, and we can get back into some of the more technical JavaFX classes in the javafx.graphics module that are commonly used for games. One of the most technical areas is 3D animation, which we'll get into next so that we can animate the spinner and game board and so forth to take our 3D boardGame Node hierarchy into the fourth dimension of time! After that, we can add interactivity and make it an i3D board game! I just needed to get things perfected and a 3D spinner in place, before we move on to add animation.

Summary

In this fifteenth chapter, we constructed the 3D "spinner" Sphere primitive UI element, which will allow the user to apply a random spin to the game board to select a topic quadrant. We also finished texture mapping the game board and figured out how to fix face rendering anomalies that kept the game board model, the centerpiece for the game, from rendering correctly and therefore from having a professional appearance. This solution involved using a much more complex Scene object instantiation, including a flag to turn on a depth buffering algorithm as well as a constant that enables the scene-wide anti-aliasing of all 3D objects. This eliminated the Y dimension (height) face rendering mistakes, as well as the jagged edges we were seeing on the edges of game board components.

We created five new texture maps for the four game board center quadrants and for the spinner UI element that allows the players to spin the board to determine what their next move, in this case an educational topic, will be.

We added diffuse texture map Image objects and Phong shader definitions that utilized these texture maps. We also added Java code to add a spinner UI to the SceneGraph hierarchy and got some more practice using GIMP.

In Chapter 16, we're going to learn about all of the powerful Animation-related Transition classes in JavaFX 9.

CHAPTER 16

■ ■ ■

3D Game Animation Creation: Using the Animation Transition Classes

Now that you have created the multitiered gameBoard Group Node (subclass) hierarchy, textured all of the 3D components underneath that hierarchy, made sure that your 3D game board model center-rotates, and created a 3D spinner UI to randomly rotate this gameBoard 3D model (hierarchy) to select a random quadrant, it's time to add animation objects to the game design using a custom `createAnimationAssets()` method for the spinner to call to create random "spins" for use during gameplay. We'll also set up 3D object mouse click event handling code to trigger the animation and the logic that will randomize your RotateTransition parameters before this spin is undertaken.

During the chapter, we take a detailed look at the abstract **Animation** and **Transition** superclasses and all of the powerful property transition subclasses, which you can implement as different types of **Animation** objects in your i3D board game. We'll animate rotation for your game board and spinner, as well as the translation (movement) for the spinner.

Animating the 3D Assets: The Animation Superclass

The **public abstract Animation** class extends Object and is kept in the **javafx.animation** package, as are the other animation-related classes, some of which we will be using for our game and will be covering in detail during this chapter. The Animation superclass has two direct known subclasses, **Timeline** and **Transition**. Transition has ten predefined Animation (algorithm) subclasses, **ready to apply** to your game development, so we will focus on them since they can be used immediately and effectively. The javafx.animation package could have an entire book written on it, and I have only one chapter, so I'll cover the most effective animation classes to use to create pro Java 9 games with.

The Java 9 class hierarchy for the Animation superclass shows us that the class was scratch-coded to provide object animation capabilities as it has no superclass of its own and therefore looks like the following class hierarchy:

```
java.lang.Object
  > javafx.animation.Animation
```

© Wallace Jackson 2017

W. Jackson, *Pro Java 9 Games Development*, https://doi.org/10.1007/978-1-4842-0973-8_16

The abstract Animation class cannot directly create **Animation** objects, but it does provide core functionality across all animation classes used in the JavaFX API. The exception to this is the **AnimationTimer** class (a pulse engine), which implements a core timer pulse engine (thus, it is more of a timer class than an animation class) and is ideal for 2D sprite-based games. I get into this class in *Beginning Java 8 Games Development*, where I cover i2D games development in detail. I am focusing more on **i3D games** development in this book, so I will take the opportunity to cover some of the other useful (which are also canned or precoded) animation transition classes.

The animation can run a finite number of times by setting the **cycleCount** property. To make any animation "pong" (i.e., run back and forth from start to end to start again), set the **autoReverse** property to true; otherwise, use a false boolean value, which we'll be using in our pro Java 9 game to randomly spin the i3D game board in one direction.

To play an Animation object once you have instantiated and configured it, you call the **play()** method or the **playFromStart()** method. The Animation object's **currentRate** property sets your speed and the direction. By **inverting** the numeric value of currentRate, you can **toggle** your play **direction**. Your animation will stop whenever the **duration** property has been "satisfied" (exhausted, come to an end, been expended, been reached, expired, and so forth).

You can set an indefinite duration (sometimes called a *loop* or *infinite loop*) for the Animation object by using a cycleCount property with an **INDEFINITE** constant. **Animation** objects configured in this fashion run repeatedly until a **stop()** method is called. This will stop a running Animation and **reset** its playback to its starting point (property settings). An Animation can also be paused by calling **pause()**, and the next play() call will resume an Animation from where it was paused, unless you use a **.playFromStart()** method call. Let's take a look at the properties that are part of the Animation superclass next. These are inherited by the Transition superclass, and all of its subclasses, so you will be using these over the course of the rest of this book in your Pro Java 9 Games Development code.

The **autoReverse** BooleanProperty is used to define whether an Animation object is supposed to reverse its direction on alternating cycles. **currentRate** is a ReadOnlyDoubleProperty that is used to indicate current speed (and direction, indicated by positive or negative value) at which an Animation object's other settings are being played.

A **currentTime** ReadOnlyObjectProperty<Duration> is used to define an Animation object playback position, and a **cycleCount** IntegerProperty is used to define the number of cycles to play an Animation object. A **cycleDuration** ReadOnlyObjectProperty<Duration> is a read-only variable that can be used to indicate the duration of one cycle of the Animation object. This is the time it takes to play from time 0 to the end of the Animation, at the default rate of 1.

The **delay** ObjectProperty<Duration> is used to delay the start time for your animation, and the **onFinished** ObjectProperty<EventHandler<ActionEvent>> property contains the ActionEvent to be triggered at the conclusion of the Animation object playback. The **rate** DoubleProperty is used to define the speed and the direction at which your Animation is targeted to be played at. Note that because of hardware limitations, this rate may not always be possible, so there is a currentRate property to hold the actual achieved playback rate.

The **status** ReadOnlyObjectProperty<Animation.Status> property contains the enum status constant for the Animation object. The Enum **Animation.Status** helper class holds three constants: **PAUSED**, **RUNNING**, and **STOPPED**.

The **totalDuration** ReadOnlyObjectProperty<Duration> property holds a read-only variable to indicate the total duration of the Animation object, which is multiplied by the cycleCount property to factor in how many times it repeats. So, duration is one cycle, and totalDuration is equal to (delay + (duration * cycleCount)).

Animation has one static (nested) class, which is an Animation.Status class that holds Enum constants representing the possible states for status. These include **PAUSED**, **RUNNING**, and **STOPPED**.

Animation has one data field, the **static int INDEFINITE** field, which is used to specify an animation that will repeat itself indefinitely until the **.stop()** method is called.

Animation has two overloaded constructors, one simple (empty parameter area) one that creates an empty or unconfigured Animation object and a second that configures the Animation object with a target frame rate. These constructor methods (their subclass's constructor method format, as these are not directly usable in your code) should look like the following Java code:

```
protected Animation()                        // Protected: Cannot Be Directly Instantiated
protected Animation(double targetFramerate)
```

There are literally dozens of methods with which you can control your **Animation** objects, which, in the case of this chapter, is going to be the various Transition subclasses. These inherit the methods from the Animation class, through the Transition class, to the various property transition classes, which we will be using for Java 9 games.

The **autoReverseProperty()** method call returns a **BooleanProperty** defining whether the Animation object will reverse its direction between (alternating) playback cycles. The **currentRateProperty()** method call returns a read-only **double** variable used to indicate the current speed and direction at which the Animation object is playing.

A **.rateProperty()** method call returns a **double** value speed and direction at which an Animation is expected to play. A **.statusProperty()** method call returns a ReadOnlyObjectProperty<Animation.Status> **status** of an Animation, and a **.currentTimeProperty()** method call returns an Animation object's playback position. The .cycleCountProperty() returns the number of cycles in an Animation object using an **integer** value that represents the cycleCount property.

The .cycleDurationProperty() method returns a read-only variable indicating a **duration** of one cycle of the Animation, which is the time it takes to play from time 0.0 to the end of the Animation at the default rate of 1.0. The **.delayProperty()** method call returns the duration of the delay property that delays the start of an Animation object.

A **.totalDurationProperty()** method call returns a read-only Duration property setting to indicate the total duration for the Animation object. It is important to note that this value will include all of the animation repeat cycles.

The **.getCuePoints()** method call returns an **ObservableMap<String,Duration>** containing the cue points for the Animation object. These cue points should be used to mark **important positions** within the Animation object. The **.getCurrentRate()** method call will return the **double** value for your Animation object's **currentRate** property.

The **.getCurrentTime()** method call will return the value of the Animation object's **currentTime** property.

The **.getCycleCount()** method call will return the **integer** value of the Animation object **cycleCount** property, and the **.getCycleDuration()** method call will return the value of the **cycleDuration** property. The **.getDelay()** method call will return the value of the **delay** property.

A **.getOnFinished()** method call will return an **EventHandler<ActionEvent>** value of an **onFinished** property, and a **.getRate()** method call will return the **double** value of the **rate** property. The **.getStatus()** method call will return the **Animation.Status** value of the **status** property.

The **.getTargetFramerate()** method call will return the target frame rate, which is the maximum frame rate at which the Animation object will run (using frames per second).

The **.getTotalDuration()** method call will return the **Duration** value for the **totalDuration** property.

The **.isAutoReverse()** method call will return the value of the **autoReverse** property.

The **void .jumpTo(Duration time)** method call will jump to a given position in the Animation object, as will the void **.jumpTo(String cuePoint)** method call, using a cuePoint parameter rather than a Duration parameter.

The **.onFinishedProperty()** method call returns the ObjectProperty<EventHandler<ActionEvent>> action to be triggered at the conclusion of the Animation object playback. The **void .pause()** method call is used to pause the animation object playback cycle. The **void .play()** method call will play an Animation object from its current position, in the direction indicated by the rate property.

The **void .playFrom(Duration time)** method call is a convenience method that will play an Animation from a specific position, as will the **void .playFrom(String cuePoint)** method call using a cuePoint rather than a Duration. A **void .playFromStart()** method call will play an Animation object from its initial position in a forward direction. A void **.setAutoReverse(boolean value)** method call can be used to set the value of the autoReverse property.

The **void .setCycleCount(int value)** method call can be used to set the value of the **cycleCount** property. The **protected void .setCycleDuration(Duration value)** method call can be used to set the value of the **cycleDuration** property. The **void .setDelay(Duration value)** method call can be used to set the value of the delay property. The **void .setOnFinished(EventHandler<ActionEvent> value)** method call can be used to set a value of an onFinished property.

The **void .setRate(double value)** method call can be used to set the value for your Animation object's **rate** property. The **protected void .setStatus(Animation.Status value)** method call can be used to set the constant value of the **status** property.

The **void .stop()** method call is used to stop the Animation object playback cycle, and it is important to note that this method call will **reset** the playback head to its initial starting position so it can be used as a reset. Next, let's take a look at another abstract superclass, Transition, a subclass of Animation and used to create property transitions.

Automated Object Animation: Transition Superclass

The **public abstract Transition** superclass is kept in the **javafx.animation** package along with its subclasses, which are predefined algorithms, for applying different types of property animation without having to use timelines or animation timers or to set up keyframes. Therefore, the Transition subclasses are the highest (most advanced) form of Animation classes and are perfectly suited for pro Java 9 game development, as they allow you to focus your time on the gameplay development rather than reinventing Java animation code. This is why we are covering these classes for quickly implementing game animation! The Java class hierarchy for the Transition superclass looks like the following:

```
java.lang.Object
  > javafx.animation.Animation
  > javafx.animation.Transition
```

The known direct subclasses that can be quickly and effectively implemented to enhance your Java games development process include RotateTransition, ScaleTransition, and TranslateTransition to invoke basic 3D object transforms (these can also be used on 2D, Text, and UI elements); and FadeTransition, FillTransition, StrokeTransition, and PathTransition for working with 2D (i.e., vector) objects (FadeTransition works with Text, and UI elements as well). There are also two subclasses used to create compound (or complex) animations, which combine these other types of property transitions seamlessly. These include the ParallelTransition, which executes property transitions at the same time, and SequentialTransition, which executes a string of property transitions serially (one after the other). There's also a **PauseTransition** subclass used to introduce "wait states" into complex animation that will allow more motion realism to be added into the special animation effect you are trying to create.

The abstract Transition superclass contains all the basic functionality that is required by Transition-based animation. The class offers a framework to define property animation and can be used to define your own Transition subclasses as well, if you wish. Most of the types of transitions used for games are already provided (fade, transforms, path, etc.), however, so all you have to do is implement code that has already been created, debugged, and optimized.

Transition subclasses all require implementation of a method called **.interpolate(double)**. This method is called in each cycle of the Animation object, so long as the Transition subclass (object) is running. In addition to the .interpolate() method, any subclass extending Transition will be required to set a duration for an Animation cycle using the **Animation.setCycleDuration(javafx.util.Duration)** method call.

This duration should be set using the **duration** property (as in RotateTransition.duration), for example. But it can also be calculated by the extending class as is done in ParallelTransition and FadeTransition.

The Transition class has one **interpolator** property, of type **ObjectProperty<Interpolator>**, which is used to control the **timing** for the acceleration and deceleration of each Transition cycle. Properties inherited from Animation superclass include the autoReverse, currentRate, currentTime, cycleCount, cycleDuration, delay, onFinished, status, rate, and totalDuration properties. There's also an Animation. Status nested class, inherited from the Animation class.

There are two overloaded Constructors; one constructs an empty transition subclass object, and the other one constructs a frame-rate-configured transition subclass. These look like the following two constructor methods:

```
Transition()
Transition(double targetFramerate)
```

Finally, there are six methods added to this abstract superclass, most of which are related to the interpolate property. This class also inherits the methods we covered in the previous section. A **.getCachedInterpolator()** method returns the Interpolator property that was set when the Transition subclass was started. The **.getInterpolator()** method will get the value of the interpolator property, while the void .setInterpolator(Interpolator value) method will set a value for the interpolator property. As mentioned, the protected abstract void .interpolate(double) method needs to be provided by Transition subclasses, and the .interpolatorProperty() method controls your timing for acceleration and deceleration.

Finally, the **.getParentTargetNode()** method call will return the **Node** that has been targeted to play the animation for the Transition subclass. Next, let's take a look at one of these Transition subclasses in detail, and then we can implement it in your JavaFXGame Java code to rotate (animate the rotation of) your gameBoard Group Node.

Animating 3D Object Rotation: Using the RotateTransition Class

The **public final RotateTransition** class will be used to create rotation animation and extends the Transition superclass. It will be stored in the **javafx.animation** package, with all the other animation and animation timer-related classes. The Java class hierarchy for the RotateAnimation subclass should look like the following Java class hierarchy:

```
java.lang.Object
  > javafx.animation.Animation
    > javafx.animation.Transition
      > javafx.animation.RotateTransition
```

A RotateTransition class (object) can be used to create a rotation animation that lasts as long as its duration setting. This is done by updating the rotate variable of the Node it is attached to at a regular interval. A rotation angle value should be specified using degrees. Rotation starts from a fromAngle property, if provided, or else it will proceed from the node's current (previous) rotation value. Rotation will stop using the toAngle value, if provided, or else it will use a start value plus the byAngle value. The toAngle value will take precedence if both the toAngle and the byAngle have been specified.

The RotateTransition adds properties to those inherited from Animation and Transition, which help to define the rotation transition algorithm. These include an **axis** ObjectProperty<Point3D> property that is used to specify an axis of rotation for the RotateTransition object; a **node** ObjectProperty<Node> property, which is used to specify your target Node object that should be affected by the RotateTransition; and **duration** ObjectProperty<Duration> property, which is used to specify the duration for the RotateTransition.

The **byAngle** DoubleProperty can be utilized to specify an incremental stop angle value from the start of the RotateTransition. The **fromAngle** DoubleProperty can be used to specify a start angle value for your RotateTransition. The **toAngle** DoubleProperty can be used to specify your stop angle value for your RotateTransition.

The nested class, fields, and properties discussed previously are inherited from Animation and Transition.

There are three overloaded constructor methods for a RotateTransition class. One creates an unconfigured RotateTransition, one creates a duration configured RotateTransition, and one creates a duration and Node object configured RotateTransition. These three constructor methods look like the following Java code:

```
RotateTransition()
RotateTransition(Duration duration)
RotateTransition(Duration duration, Node node)
```

There are 19 methods specifically for use in this class besides the methods inherited from Animation and Transition superclasses extended by this class. The **.axisProperty()** method call specifies an **axis** of rotation for the RotateTransition using an **ObjectProperty<Point3D>** format. The **.byAngleProperty()** method specifies an incremental **stop angle** value, which is an offset from the start angle, for the RotateTransition object.

The **.durationProperty()** method specifies the **duration** of the RotateTransition using an ObjectProperty<Duration>. The **.fromAngleProperty()** method specifies the **start angle** value for this RotateTransition using a DoubleProperty. The **.getAxis()** method call gets the value of the **axis** property using a **Point3D** object.

The **.getByAngle()** method will get the **double** value of the byAngle property. The **.getFromAngle()** method call will get the **double** value of the **fromAngle** property. The **.getToAngle()** method call will get the **double** value of the **toAngle** property. The **.getNode()** method call will get the **Node** object value of the node property, and the **.getDuration()** method call will get the value of the **duration** property. The **protected void .interpolate(double value)** method call, as you know, has to be provided by subclass implementations of a Transition superclass. The **.nodeProperty()** method specifies the target ObjectProperty<Node> for the RotateTransition.

The **void .setAxis(Point3D value)** method call is used to set the value of the property axis.
The **void .setByAngle(double value)** method call is used to set the value of the byAngle property.
The **void .setDuration(Duration value)** method call is used to set the value of the property duration.
The **void .setFromAngle(double value)** method call is used to set the value of the property fromAngle.
The **void .setNode(Node value)** method call is used to set the value of the property node.
The **void .setToAngle(double value)** method call is used to set the value of the property toAngle.
The **.toAngleProperty()** method specifies a stop angle value for the RotateTransition using a DoubleProperty. Let's implement the **rotGameBoard** and **rotSpinner** RotateTransition objects next to give you some hands-on experience.

A RotateTransition Example: Set Up Your RotateAnimation Asset

Let's create a **createAnimationAssets()** method to hold the RotateTransition, TranslateTransition, and other Transition subclass objects using the following Java statement, shown highlighted in yellow (and wavy red underlining) in Figure 16-1:

```
createAnimationAssets();
```

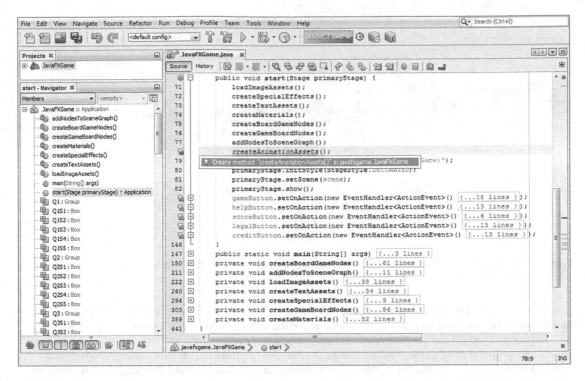

Figure 16-1. *Add a createAnimationAssets() method call at the end of the custom method call list in the start() method*

Remember to double-click the **Create method "createAnimationAssets()" in javafxgame. JavaFXGame** option and have NetBeans code a bootstrap method for you. You'll be replacing the placeholder Java code with your RotateTransition object instantiation and configuration code over the course of this section of the chapter.

The first thing that you need to do is to declare a RotateTransition object for use at the top of your class and name it **rotGameBoard** since that is what that object is going to do. Inside of your **.createAnimationAssets()** method, instantiate the rotGameBoard object and configure it to play for **five seconds**; then wire it to the **gameBoard** Group Node, as shown in the following Java 9 code and as highlighted in light blue and yellow in Figure 16-2:

```
RotateTransition rotGameBoard;
...
private void createAnimationAssets() {
    rotGameBoard = new RotateTransition(Duration.seconds(5), gameBoard);
}
```

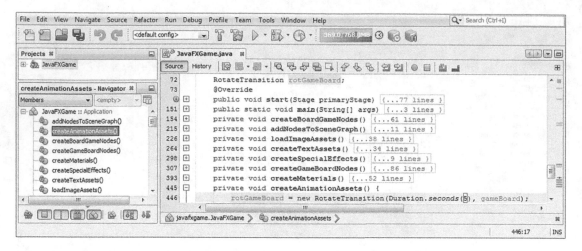

Figure 16-2. *Declare a rotGameBoard object at the top of your class and instantiate it inside* *createAnimationAssets()*

Now you can start configuring this RotateTransition Animation object using the various .set() method calls that you learned about in the previous section of the chapter. Set a **Y** rotation axis using .setAxis(Rotate.Y_AXIS) and set the cycleCount property to **one** cycle using a .setCycleCount(1) method call. Set the rate property to **50 percent speed** using a .setRate(0.5) method call off your rotGameBoard object. The Java statements for the core Animation object settings should look like the following Java 9 statements, which are highlighted at the bottom of Figure 16-3:

```
RotateTransition rotGameBoard;
...
private void createAnimationAssets() {
    rotGameBoard = new RotateTransition(Duration.seconds(5), gameBoard);
    rotGameBoard.setAxis(Rotate.Y_AXIS);
    rotGameBoard.setCycleCount(1);
    rotGameBoard.setRate(0.5);
}
```

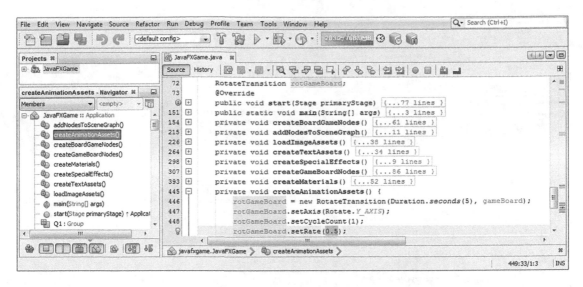

Figure 16-3. *Configure the rotGameBoard RotateTransition object with a y-axis, cycleCount of 1, and rate of 50 percent speed*

You already know why we are using the **y-axis** for rotation; however, you might be wondering why we are using only one cycle. The reason is that once we make this RotateTransition interactive by specifying the fromAngle and toAngle values that will be set before each rotGameBoard.play() method call using code from the random spin generator that we'll be coding later, we will control the number of rotations using the difference between these angles (currently this is **1080** or three spins); therefore, we use only one cycle. I'm using **three spins** for code testing purposes.

The rate setting of 1 is too fast to get a smooth spin animation, and game boards shouldn't spin that fast, so I reduced this 1.0 default value by 50 percent to **0.5** to show you how the **rate** variable gives you finely tuned speed control.

Next, let's add that required **Interpolator** class constant specification, which will be the default **LINEAR** for now, as we want a smooth, even rotation. This is added and configured using the .setInterpolator() method call and the **Interpolator.LINEAR** constant. Finally, we want to add the two most important configuration statements, which tell the RotateTransition engine the starting angle (fromAngle property) and the ending angle (toAngle property) for the spin. Using these will allow us to control what quadrant the spin starts on (45, 135, 225, or 315) and ends on. For now, we will just use three full rotations (1080) from the starting **45**-degree angle, which will be **1125** for toAngle. To start (and test) the animation, you will also need a .play() method call, which is shown in the following completed Java method body and shown highlighted in yellow and light blue at the bottom of Figure 16-4:

```java
RotateTransition rotGameBoard;
...
private void createAnimationAssets() {
    rotGameBoard = new RotateTransition(Duration.seconds(5), gameBoard);
    rotGameBoard.setAxis(Rotate.Y_AXIS);
    rotGameBoard.setCycleCount(1);
    rotGameBoard.setRate(0.5);
    rotGameBoard.setInterpolator(Interpolator.LINEAR);
    rotGameBoard.setFromAngle(45);
    rotGameBoard.setToAngle(1125);
    rotGameBoard.play();
}
```

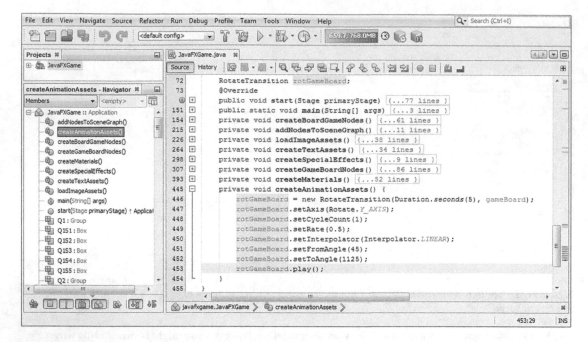

Figure 16-4. *Configure the rotGameBoard object with a LINEAR interpolator, a fromAngle of 45, and a toAngle of 1125*

Figure 16-5 shows the **Run ➤ Project** work process, with a game board in the middle of its rotation cycle. A screenshot cannot show the smooth motion, but you can tell the game board is not at one of its four quadrant "at rest" positions (45, 135, 225, 315 degrees) because the point of the game board is not centered at the bottom of the screen. In Figure 16-5 I hit a PrintScreen key while the 3D gameBoard Group Node was still animating.

Figure 16-5. *Use your Run* ➤ *Project work process, click Start Game, and watch your gameboard spin around smoothly*

It's also important to note that when you test your animation code, you need to click the **Start Game** Button UI element as soon as the application launches (later, this will be triggered by a click on the 3D spinner UI element, as you may have surmised already). This is so that you can see your animation characteristics, which we are developing during this chapter, because currently your Java 9 code starts the play life cycle immediately after the Animation (Transition subclass) object has been constructed and configured. So, click your **Start Game** 2D UI button as soon as it appears!

Later, when we get into how to **trap** mouse clicks (or screen touches) on 3D objects, such as your spinner UI element, we'll trigger rotGameBoard.play() with a click on the spinner UI element to randomly spin the gameboard to pick a new quadrant. We will trigger the rotSpinner.play() when the next player's turn is ready so they can spin the gameboard. We will be developing the complexity of this animation code during the remainder of this book.

Later during this chapter, we will use TranslateTransition with RotateTransition using a ParallelTransition, which will allow us to animate the 3D spinner UI element in and out of view so that the player will know when to use it to randomly spin the game board to select a new quadrant (a new content topic animal-vegetable-mineral or landmark category) for use in the gameplay cycle.

Next, let's add the **rotSpinner** RotateTransition object. First turn your RotateTransition declaration into a compound statement by adding the rotSpinner object name after the rotGameBoard object name at the top of the class. Cut and paste the rotGameBoard statements after themselves, change rotGameBoard to rotSpinner, and make sure to change the Node parameter of the instantiation from gameBoard to **spinner**. Change fromAngle to **30** degrees (the starting value you developed in Chapter 15) and toAngle to **1110** degrees (1080 + 30). Your Java 9 code should look like the following method body, which is also highlighted at the bottom of Figure 16-6:

```
RotateTransition rotGameBoard, rotSpinner;
...
private void createAnimationAssets() {
    rotGameBoard = new RotateTransition(Duration.seconds(5), gameBoard);
    rotGameBoard.setAxis(Rotate.Y_AXIS);
    rotGameBoard.setCycleCount(1);
    rotGameBoard.setRate(0.5);
    rotGameBoard.setInterpolator(Interpolator.LINEAR);
    rotGameBoard.setFromAngle(45);
    rotGameBoard.setToAngle(1125);
    rotGameBoard.play();
    rotSpinner = new RotateTransition(Duration.seconds(5), spinner);
    rotSpinner.setAxis(Rotate.Y_AXIS);
    rotSpinner.setCycleCount(1);
    rotSpinner.setRate(0.5);
    rotSpinner.setInterpolator(Interpolator.LINEAR);
    rotSpinner.setFromAngle(30);
    rotSpinner.setToAngle(1110);
    rotSpinner.play();
}
```

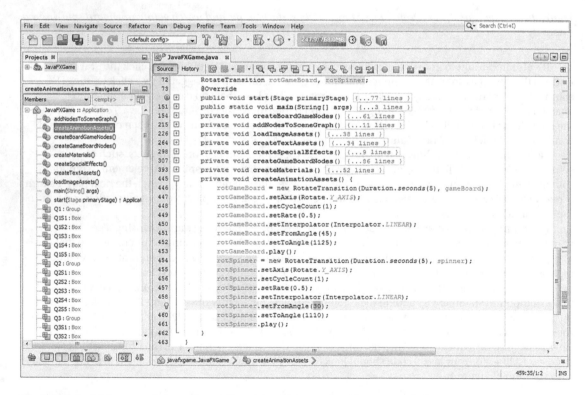

Figure 16-6. *Add a rotateSpinner RotateTransition object and configure it with the same parameters as rotGameBoard*

Use the **Run ➤ Project** work process to see both gameBoard and spinner rotating, as shown in Figure 16-7.

Figure 16-7. *Select Run ➤ Project and click Start Game to preview the game board and spinner rotation*

As you can see, the only problem is that your "SPIN" spinner is rotating backward, and we want the word *SPIN* to rotate forward, so we'll need to change the direction by setting **fromAngle** to **30** and **toAngle** to **-1050 (1080 = 30 - -1050)**. The final Java code block is shown here, as well as highlighted in yellow and blue in Figure 16-8:

```
RotateTransition rotGameBoard, rotSpinner;
...
private void createAnimationAssets() {
    rotGameBoard = new RotateTransition(Duration.seconds(5), gameBoard);
    rotGameBoard.setAxis(Rotate.Y_AXIS);
    rotGameBoard.setCycleCount(1);
    rotGameBoard.setRate(0.5);
    rotGameBoard.setInterpolator(Interpolator.LINEAR);
    rotGameBoard.setFromAngle(45);
    rotGameBoard.setToAngle(1125);
    rotGameBoard.play();
    rotSpinner = new RotateTransition(Duration.seconds(5), spinner);
    rotSpinner.setAxis(Rotate.Y_AXIS);
    rotSpinner.setCycleCount(1);
    rotSpinner.setRate(0.5);
    rotSpinner.setInterpolator(Interpolator.LINEAR);
    rotSpinner.setFromAngle(30);
    rotSpinner.setToAngle(-1050); // Reverse rotation direction using a negative toAngle
    value
    rotSpinner.play();
}
```

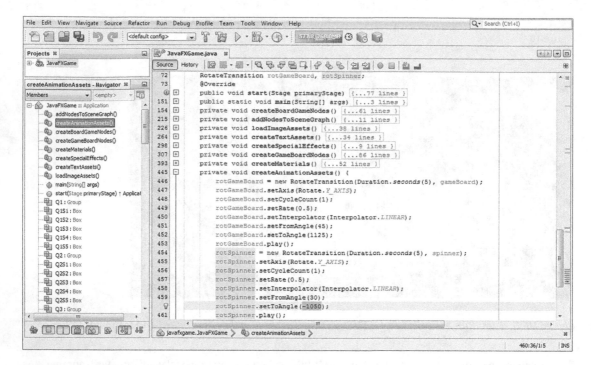

Figure 16-8. *Adjust the rotSpinner.setToAngle() method call to spin in a negative direction so the spinner UI spins forward*

Next, let's take a look at the **TranslationTransition**, which can be used to move objects around the 3D Scene in any of the X, Y, or Z dimensions. We will be using this to bring our spinner UI element onto (and off of) the screen as it is needed during gameplay to allow the player to randomly spin the game board to select their new topic quadrant.

Animating Node Movement: Using the TranslateTransition Class

The **public final TranslateTransition** class extends the public abstract Transition superclass and is kept in the **javafx.animation** package in the **javafx.graphics** module. A TranslateTransition creates a **move (translate) animation**, which lasts as long as its duration property. Movement is created by updating translateX, translateY, and translateZ variables (properties) of the Node you are animating at an interval defined by the Interpolator constant. Translation will start from the "from" value (fromX, fromY, fromZ) if one is provided; otherwise, the algorithm will use the Node object's current position (translateX, translateY, translateZ) value. Translation stops at the "to" value (toX, toY, toZ), if it is provided; otherwise, it will use the start value, plus the byX, byY, or byZ value. The "to" value (toX, toY, toZ) will take precedence if both "to" (toX, toY, toZ) and "by" (byX, byY, byZ) values have been specified.

```
java.lang.Object
  > javafx.animation.Animation
    > javafx.animation.Transition
      > javafx.animation.TranslateTransition
```

The TranslateTransition class has eleven properties, nine of which involve to, from, and by specifications for each of the X, Y, and Z 3D coordinates. The other two are the duration property and the node property that define the length of time of the animation and what Node object it is affecting. The byX property is used to specify the incremental stop X coordinate double value, calculated from the start value, for the TranslateTransition. The byY property is used to specify the incremental stop Y coordinate double value, calculated from the start value, for the TranslateTransition. The byZ property is used to specify the incremental stop Z coordinate double value, calculated from the start value, for the TranslateTransition. The fromX property is used to specify a starting X coordinate double value for the TranslateTransition. The fromY property is used to specify the starting Y coordinate double value for the TranslateTransition. A fromZ property is used to specify a starting Z coordinate double value for a TranslateTransition. The toX property is used to specify the stopping (resting, or final) X coordinate value for a TranslateTransition. The toY property is used to specify a stopping (resting or final) Y coordinate value for a TranslateTransition. The toZ property is used to specify the stopping (resting or final) Z coordinate value for the TranslateTransition object.

There are three overloaded constructor methods for TranslateTransition; one is empty, one has the duration specified, and one has a duration and a node property specified. They look like this:

```
TranslateTransition()
TranslateTransition(Duration duration)
TranslateTransition(Duration duration, Node node)
```

There are nearly three dozen methods for use with this class, and twenty-seven of them (nine sets of three) deal with the **from**, **to**, and **by** properties. This is because for each X, Y, and Z property, there is a .get(), a .set(), and a .property() method. There are also methods for use with the duration, node, and interpolator properties. All of the X, Y, and Z methods use **double** values. A .byXProperty() method is used to specify the stop X coordinate value as an incremental offset from the start of the TranslateTransition. The .byYProperty() method is used to specify an offset incremental stop Y coordinate value as an offset from the start of the TranslateTransition. The .byZProperty() method is used to specify your incremental stop X coordinate value as an offset from the start of the TranslateTransition.

The .fromXProperty() method call is used to specify a starting X coordinate value for the TranslateTransition.

The .fromYProperty() method call is used to specify a starting Y coordinate value for the TranslateTransition.

The .fromZProperty() method call is used to specify a starting Z coordinate value for the TranslateTransition.

The .getByX() method call is used to get the value for the property byX. The .getByY() method call is used to get the value for the property byY. The .getByZ() method call is used to get the value for the property byZ.

The .getFromX() method call is used to get the value for the property fromX. The .getFromY() method call is used to get the value for the property fromY. The .getFromZ() method call is used to get the value for the property fromZ. The .getToX() method call is used to get the value of the property toX. The .getToY() method call is used to get the value of the property toY. The .getToZ() method call is used to get the value of the property toZ.

The void .setByX(double value) method call is used to set (specify) the value of the property byX. The void .setByY(double value) method call is used to set (specify) the value of the property byY. The void .setByZ(double value) method call is used to set (specify) the value of the property byZ. The void .setFromX(double value) method call is used to set (specify) the value of the property fromX. The void .setFromY(double value) method call is used to set (specify) the value of the property fromY. The void .setFromZ(double value) method call is used to set (specify) the value of the property fromZ.

The void .setToX(double value) method call is used to set (specify) the value of the property toX. The void .setToY(double value) method call is used to set (specify) the value of the property toY. A void .setToZ(double value) method call is used to set (specify) the value of the property toX.

The .toXProperty() method call is used to specify a stop X coordinate value for a TranslateTransition object. The .toYProperty() method call is used to specify a stop Y coordinate value for a TranslateTransition object. The .toZProperty() method call is used to specify a stop Z coordinate value for a TranslateTransition object.

The .durationProperty() method call will return the current duration property for the TranslateTransition. A .getDuration() method call is used to get the Duration value for the TranslateTransition duration property. The void .setDuration(Duration value) can be used to set (specify) the Duration value of the duration property.

The .nodeProperty() method call will return the target node Node property for the TranslateTransition. The .getNode() method call will get (read) the Node object reference value for the node property of a TranslateTransition. The void .setNode(Node value) method call will set the Node value for a TranslateTransition node property. The void .interpolate(double frac) method call will always need to be provided by subclasses of Transition.

Next, let's implement a TranslateTransition Animation object that moves the spinner UI element onto and off of the screen. These **Animation** objects will eventually be named moveSpinnerOn and moveSpinnerOff. After that we will get into the ParallelTransition class and combine the movement and rotation to spin the spinner UI element across the screen, from the left corner to the right corner.

TranslateTransition Example: Set Up Translate Animation Assets

Let's add a TranslateTransition Animation object to your game project by declaring one named moveSpinner at the top of the class and then instantiate it inside of the **createAnimationAssets()** method, after the RotateTransition Java code. Reference the spinner Node and use a five-second duration. Next, configure the moveSpinnerOn Animation object to move by **1150** X units across the top of the screen (actually 1350 units, as the spinner is currently at -200) and set the cycleCount property to one cycle, using the following Java statements, shown highlighted in yellow in Figure 16-9:

```
TranslateTransition moveSpinnerOn;
...
moveSpinnerOn = new TranslateTransition(Duration.seconds(5), spinner);
moveSpinnerOn.setByX(1150);
moveSpinnerOn.setCycleCount(1);
```

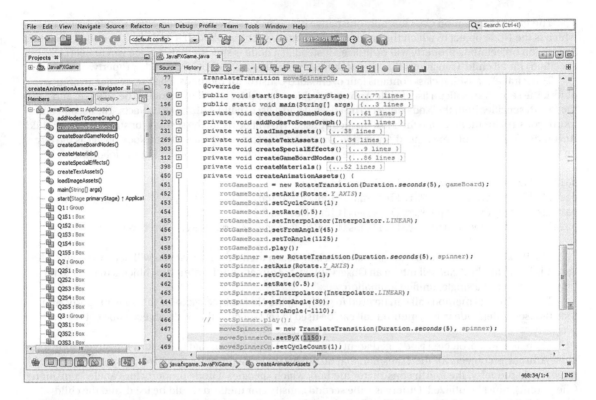

Figure 16-9. *Declare a moveSpinnerOn TranslateTransition at the top of the class and instantiate it in createAnimationAssets()*

Next, let's take a look at the ParallelTransition class since we'll need to use this object algorithm to combine the spinner rotSpinner Animation object with a moveSpinnerOn Animation object so that your final result is a spinner that spins while it is moving across the top of the screen.

Merging Animation Properties: Using a ParallelTransition Class

The **public final** class **ParallelTransition** extends the abstract Transition superclass and can be found in the **javafx.animation** package, which can be found in the **javafx.graphics** module. This Transition plays a list of **Animation** objects in parallel, which means at the same time (one after the other is termed *serial* or *sequential*). Children of this Transition inherit the Node node property if their node property has not been explicitly specified using a method call (usually the constructor method). The reason for this is that a ParallelTransition simply merges existing **Animation** objects together, so a node may already be specified in the merged animations. The Java class hierarchy for the ParallelTransition looks like this:

```
java.lang.Object
  > javafx.animation.Animation
    > javafx.animation.Transition
      > javafx.animation.ParallelTransition
```

The ParallelTransition class has only one native property, an ObjectProperty<Node> node property, which is the Node object to which the combined animation will be applied. If a node isn't specified, the child Animation object node property will be utilized instead. If a node is specified, that Node will be set (i.e., specified) for all child Transitions that do not themselves define any target Node node property.

The ParallelTransition class contains four overloaded constructor methods. The first creates an empty object, the second specifies a list of child **Animation** objects, the third specifies a Node to be affected, and the fourth specifies both the Node object to be affected and a list of child **Animation** objects. The second and fourth constructor methods are the most frequently used. We will be using the second constructor for our child **Animation** objects; both referenced Animation Transition objects specify the spinner Node object as the target for the ParallelAnimation object. The Java code for these constructor methods looks like the following:

```
parallelTransition = new ParallelTransition();
parallelTransition = new ParallelTransition(Animation... children);
parallelTransition = new ParallelTransition(Node node);
parallelTransition = new ParallelTransition(Node node, Animation... children);
```

The ParallelTransition class has only about a half-dozen method calls that you will need to master. The .getChildren() method call will return an ObservableList<Animation>of **Animation** objects that are to be played together as a single, unified animation.

The .getNode() method call can be used to get (poll) the Node object value of the node property, and the void .setNode(Node value) method call can be used to set (specify) the Node object value of the node property.

There is also a protected Node .getParentTargetNode() method call that will return the target Node for child **Animation** objects for the Transition that do not have a node property specified. To specify a parent target node property, the fourth constructor method, which specifies a node property for ParallelTransition (the parent), must be utilized. Otherwise, the second constructor method would be used, and the child Animation object's node property will define what Node object the Animation object will be affecting.

The ParallelTransition .nodeProperty() method call will return your ParallelTransition (parent) ObjectProperty<Node> value, which would be set using the third or fourth constructor method or .setNode(Node). This Node, if specified (set), will be used in all child Transitions that do not specifically define their target Node.

Finally, the protected void .interpolate(double value) method call is required to be provided by all subclass implementations of the abstract Transition superclass.

Next, let's set up a ParallelTransition object that seamlessly combines your rotSpinner and moveSpinnerOn **Animation** objects together.

ParallelTransition Object: Merge rotSpinner and moveSpinnerOn

Let's add a ParallelTransition Animation object to your game project by declaring one named spinnerAnim at the top of your class and then instantiate it inside of the **createAnimationAssets()** method, after the RotateTransition and the TranslateTransition Java code. In the constructor method, reference the **moveSpinnerOn** and **rotSpinner** Animation child objects and then call the .play() method off the spinnerAnim object. Notice I have commented out the rotSpinner.play() method call and did not add a .play() method call to the moveSpinnerOn Animation object, as this is done in the spinnerAnim ParallelTransition object instead. The setup for this parallel (hybrid) animation would be accomplished using the following Java statements, which are also highlighted in yellow and blue in Figure 16-10:

```
ParallelTransition spinnerAnin;
...
spinnerAnin = new ParallelTransition(moveSpinnerOn, rotSpinner);
spinnerAnim.play();
```

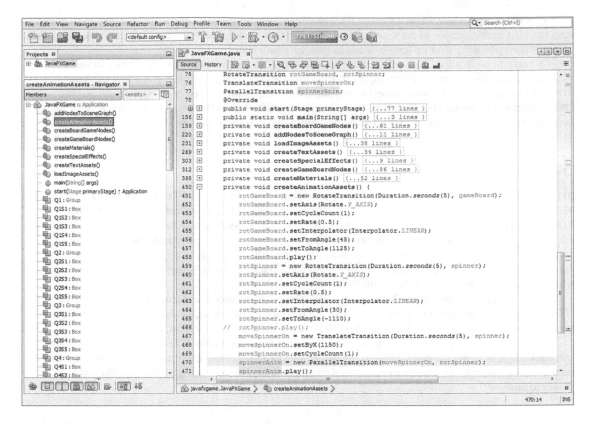

```
 75        RotateTransition rotGameBoard, rotSpinner;
 76        TranslateTransition moveSpinnerOn;
 77        ParallelTransition spinnerAnim;
 78        @Override
  @    ⊞ public void start(Stage primaryStage) {...77 lines }
156   ⊞ public static void main(String[] args) {...3 lines }
159   ⊞ private void createBoardGameNodes() {...61 lines }
220   ⊞ private void addNodesToSceneGraph() {...11 lines }
231   ⊞ private void loadImageAssets() {...38 lines }
269   ⊞ private void createTextAssets() {...34 lines }
303   ⊞ private void createSpecialEffects() {...9 lines }
312   ⊞ private void createGameBoardNodes() {...86 lines }
398   ⊞ private void createMaterials() {...52 lines }
450   ⊟ private void createAnimationAssets() {
451        rotGameBoard = new RotateTransition(Duration.seconds(5), gameBoard);
452        rotGameBoard.setAxis(Rotate.Y_AXIS);
453        rotGameBoard.setCycleCount(1);
454        rotGameBoard.setRate(0.5);
455        rotGameBoard.setInterpolator(Interpolator.LINEAR);
456        rotGameBoard.setFromAngle(45);
457        rotGameBoard.setToAngle(1125);
458        rotGameBoard.play();
459        rotSpinner = new RotateTransition(Duration.seconds(5), spinner);
460        rotSpinner.setAxis(Rotate.Y_AXIS);
461        rotSpinner.setCycleCount(1);
462        rotSpinner.setRate(0.5);
463        rotSpinner.setInterpolator(Interpolator.LINEAR);
464        rotSpinner.setFromAngle(30);
465        rotSpinner.setToAngle(-1110);
466  //    rotSpinner.play();
467        moveSpinnerOn = new TranslateTransition(Duration.seconds(5), spinner);
468        moveSpinnerOn.setByX(1150);
469        moveSpinnerOn.setCycleCount(1);
470        spinnerAnim = new ParallelTransition(moveSpinnerOn, rotSpinner);
471        spinnerAnim.play();
```

Figure 16-10. *Declare a spinnerAnim ParallelTransition at the top of the class and instantiate it in createAnimationAssets()*

When you select Run ➤ Project, a spinner spins from the left to the right side of the game, as shown in Figure 16-11.

Figure 16-11. *Select Run ➤ Project, click Start Game, and watch the spinner animate*

After the next chapter, when we cover 3D Scene event handling as well as the PickResult class, we can start to finish the animation of the spinner UI element so that it comes on the screen when needed and goes off the screen when the user no longer needs to spin the game board.

I wanted to dedicate a chapter to **Animation** objects, show you how the precoded Transition subclasses can provide you with Java 9 code to add animation to your game play, and show you how to set up the majority of the **Animation** objects and their code. I also wanted to show you how put the **createAnimationAssets()** method in place so that you can add **Animation** objects, which will have their very own place to live in your pro Java 9 game development from this point onward.

Summary

In this sixteenth chapter, we learned about the **Animation** superclass and the **Transition** superclass, as well as some of the important Transition subclasses, **RotateTransition** and **TranslationTransition**, that allow us to move and rotate 3D objects during and for gameplay. We also looked at the **ParallelTransition** subclass, which allows us to combine these **Animation** objects to create more complex **Animation** objects. We also constructed the **Animation** objects for our game, which will allow the user to apply a random spin to the game board to select a topic quadrant and to move a spinning spinner UI element on and off the screen, when it is time to randomly spin the game board.

We created a new custom method for our JavaFXGame class called **createAnimationAssets()**, which will hold all of the **Animation** objects created for the pro Java 9 game design using Transition subclasses such as RotateTransition, TranslateTransition, ScaleTransition, and ParallelTransition.

In Chapter 17, we're going to learn about MouseEvent handling for the 3D Scene elements so that we can click the Sphere 3D spinner UI to spin the game board and so we can eventually click each of the game board squares in order to select the educational question categories and bring up the questions for the player to answer.

CHAPTER 17

■ ■ ■

i3D Game Square Selection: Using the PickResult Class with 3D Models

Now that you have created the multitiered gameBoard Group Node (subclass) hierarchy, textured all of the 3D components underneath that hierarchy, made sure the hierarchy center-rotates, created a spinner UI to randomly rotate the gameBoard 3D model (hierarchy) to a random quadrant, and added animation objects to your game design using your **createAnimationAssets()** method, it is time to make your 3D game elements interactive. We will set up your 3D object mouse click event handling code that will be used to trigger the 3D spinner animation and select game board squares.

During this chapter we'll take a detailed look at the public **PickResult** class and public **MouseEvent** class and use these for our own gameplay design in a custom createSceneProcessing() method that will be used to process i3D game element (Box and Sphere object) event handling so that our players can interact with the 3D game components.

Select Your 3D Assets: The PickResult Class

The **public** class **PickResult** extends Object and is kept in the **javafx.scene.input** package, which contains input event handling utilities such as clipboard, GestureEvent, SwipeEvent, TouchEvent, and ZoomEvent. The PickResult object contains the result of a pick event, in the case of this game, from a mouse or touch. Input classes that support using a PickResult object in their constructor methods include MouseEvent, MouseDragEvent, DragEvent, GestureEvent, ContextMenuEvent, and TouchPoint. There is a .getPickResult() method call in each of these classes that returns the PickResult object, which contains all the pick information that you'll need to process for your Java game development.

A Java class hierarchy for a PickResult class shows us that this class was scratch-coded to provide 3D object selection capabilities; it has no superclass of its own and therefore looks like the following Java 9 class hierarchy:

```
java.lang.Object
  > javafx.scene.input.PickResult
```

The PickResult class contains one data field, the **static int FACE_UNDEFINED** data field, which represents an undefined face. We will generally be using this class to select entire nodes (the spinner, quadrants q1 through q4, squares Q1S1 through Q4S5, and similar 3D game elements) and not individual polygon faces or texture map pixels, which is also possible.

© Wallace Jackson 2017
W. Jackson, *Pro Java 9 Games Development*, https://doi.org/10.1007/978-1-4842-0973-8_17

The first two constructor methods in the PickResult class create PickResult objects that handle 2D and 2.5D Scene picking scenario results. The first constructor creates a PickResult object for a 2D scenario using an EventTarget object and (double) sceneX and sceneY properties. This constructor method uses the following Java statement syntax:

```
PickResult(EventTarget target, double sceneX, double sceneY);
```

The second constructor creates a PickResult object for a "non-Shape3D" target. Since it uses the Point3D object and distance, I call this the 2.5D PickResult scenario because it does not support 3D primitives based on the Shape3D class. However, it does support the Point3D object and the concept of distance into the Scene object. This constructor method uses the following Java statement syntax:

```
PickResult(Node node, Point3D point, double distance)
```

The third constructor creates a PickResult object for a Shape3D target, which is what we are using to create our i3D games. The Java syntax for creating this constructor method should look like the following Java statement:

```
PickResult(Node node, Point3D point, double dist, int face, Point2D texCoord);
```

The fourth constructor creates a PickResult object for an imported 3D object target that contains Normals. This would be utilized if you imported an advanced 3D model from an external 3D modeling software package such as Blender. The Java syntax for creating this advanced constructor method should look like the following Java statement:

```
PickResult(Node node, Point3D point, double distance, int face, Point3D normal, Point2D texCoor)
```

The PickResult class supports six .get() method calls, which return an intersected distance, an intersected face, an intersected Node, an intersected Normal, an intersected Point, or an intersected texture coordinate (texCoord). A **.getIntersectedDistance()** method call will return, as a double value, the intersected distance between your current camera position and an intersected point.

The **.getIntersectedFace()** method call will return an integer representing the intersected face of the picked Node. If the node doesn't have user-specified faces, such as one of the Shape3D primitives, or was picked on bounds, this method will return a **FACE_UNDEFINED** constant. A **.getIntersectedNode()** method call will return an intersected node as a Node object and is the method call we'll be using to select the spinner UI and gameBoard Node elements.

The **.getIntersectedNormal()** method call will return an intersected Normal of the picked Shape3D object or imported 3D geometry. The **.getIntersectedPoint()** method call will return an intersected point (Point3D object) using the **local coordinate system** for your **picked Node object**. The **.getIntersectedTexCoord()** method call will return the intersected texture coordinates of the picked 3D shape in Point2D object format.

Next, let's take a look at another important event-handling class, MouseEvent. This is a subclass of InputEvent and used to attach mouse event handling to the 3D primitives we have utilized to create your i3D BoardGame simulation.

The MouseEvent Class: Trapping Mouse Clicks on 3D Primitives

The **public MouseEvent** class extends the InputEvent superclass. MouseEvent is kept in a **javafx.scene. input** package along with its subclass MouseDragEvent and other InputEvent superclass subclasses. MouseEvent implements the Serializable and Cloneable Java interfaces. This class is used for implementing or "trapping" mouse events for processing by your Java game logic, which you will learn how to do during this chapter. When mouse event generation, such as a click, occurs, the first (top or front) Node object under cursor is "picked," and the MouseEvent is delivered to that Node object event handling structure. The event is delivered by using capturing and bubbling phases described by the public EventDispatcher Java interface that is stored in the **javafx.event** package. The Java hierarchy for the MouseEvent class should therefore look like the following:

```
java.lang.Object
  > java.util.EventObject
  > javafx.event.Event
    > javafx.scene.input.InputEvent
    > javafx.scene.input.MouseEvent
```

The mouse pointer (cursor) location is available in several different coordinate systems. It is available using **X,Y** coordinates relative to the origin of the MouseEvent's Node object (as well as relative to your Scene object), using **sceneX, sceneY** coordinates relative to the origin of the Scene that contains the Node, or even using **screenX, screenY** coordinates relative to the origin of the display screen that contains the mouse pointer. We'll be comparing the Node that is clicked to our game-processing logic in the case of this particular i3D BoardGame project.

There are a number of Event **fields** specific to the MouseEvent object. These are **static** and use **uppercase** letters, as they're "hard-coded" constants for different types of events offered by the MouseEvent type of InputEvent. An **ANY** static EventType<MouseEvent> is used as a common "supertype" to represent any of the mouse event types.

A **DRAG_DETECTED** static EventType<MouseEvent> will be delivered to any Node object that is identified as a source of a dragging gesture. A **MOUSE_CLICKED** static EventType<MouseEvent> will be delivered when the mouse button has been clicked (pressed and released on the same node). This is what we'll be using for our i3D BoardGame. You can also trap events for the mouse being pressed and the mouse being released. A MOUSE_PRESSED static EventType<MouseEvent> will be delivered when the mouse button is pressed, and the MOUSE_RELEASED static EventType<MouseEvent> will be delivered when the mouse button is released.

You can also process events when your mouse moves over a Node and then off of that Node again without any mouse click occurring! A MOUSE_ENTERED static EventType<MouseEvent> will be delivered when a mouse enters a Node object but is not clicked (this is called a *hover*). A MOUSE_ENTERED_TARGET static EventType<MouseEvent> will be delivered when the mouse first enters the Node (crosses over its edge boundary). Similarly, a MOUSE_EXITED static EventType<MouseEvent> will be delivered when the mouse exits a Node object. The MOUSE_EXITED_TARGET static EventType<MouseEvent> will be delivered when a mouse first exits a Node object (crosses an edge boundary).

Finally, the MOUSE_MOVED static EventType<MouseEvent> will be delivered when a mouse moves within a Node object when no buttons are being pressed or released. The MOUSE_DRAGGED static EventType<MouseEvent> will be delivered when the mouse is being moved using a depressed (held) mouse button (called a *drag* operation).

411

We will not be specifically constructing (instantiating) MouseEvent objects. We'll use **.setOnMouseClick()** event handling constructs, which will do the construction for us, as part of their functionality. I will include these two overloaded constructor methods here for the sake of completeness, however. The first constructs a new MouseEvent Event object, with a null source and target, and would look like the following Java 9 constructor method syntax:

```
MouseEvent(EventType<? extends MouseEvent> eventType, double x, double y, double screenX, double
           screenY, MouseButton button, int clickCount, boolean shiftDown, boolean controlDown,
           boolean altDown, boolean metaDown, boolean primaryButtonDown, boolean
           middleButtonDown, boolean secondaryButtonDown, boolean synthesized, boolean
           popupTrigger, boolean stillSincePress, PickResult pickResult)
```

The second constructs a new MouseEvent Event object and would look like the following Java syntax:

```
MouseEvent(Object source, EventTarget target, EventType<? extends MouseEvent> eventType, double
           x, double y, double screenX, double screenY, MouseButton button, int clickCount,
           boolean shiftDown, boolean controlDown, boolean altDown, boolean metaDown, boolean
           primaryButtonDown, boolean middleButtonDown, boolean secondaryButtonDown, boolean
           synthesized, boolean popupTrigger, boolean stillSincePress, PickResult pickResult)
```

There are 27 methods that are part of the MouseEvent class to help you control your mouse event processing. The **.copyFor(Object newSource, EventTarget newTarget)** MouseEvent method call will copy the Event object so that it can be used with a different source and target.

The **.copyFor(Object newSource, EventTarget newTarget, EventType<? extends MouseEvent> eventType)** MouseEvent method call will also create a copy of the given Event object, with a given MouseEvent field substituted.

The **static MouseDragEvent .copyForMouseDragEvent(MouseEvent e, Object source, EventTarget target, EventType<MouseDragEvent> type, Object gestureSource, PickResult pickResult)** method call will create a copy of a MouseEvent of type MouseDragEvent.

The **.getButton()** method call will poll the MouseEvent object to see which, if any, of the mouse buttons was responsible for generating that Event object. The **.getClickCount()** method call will return the **integer (int) number** of mouse clicks that are associated with the Event object.

The **.getEventType()** method call will return the EventType<? extends MouseEvent> event type for that Event object. The **.getPickResult()** method call will return the PickResult object's information regarding that pick.

The **.getSceneX()** method call will return the double value for the horizontal position of the event relative to the origin of the Scene that contains your MouseEvent's source. The **.getSceneY()** method call will return the double value for the vertical position of the event relative to the origin of the Scene that contains your MouseEvent's source.

The **.getScreenX()** method call will return the double value for the absolute horizontal position of the event. The **.getScreenY()** method call will return the double value for the absolute vertical position of the event.

The **.getX()** method call will return the double value for the **horizontal** position for the event relative to the origin of the MouseEvent source. The **.getY()** method call will return the double value for the **vertical** position for the event relative to the origin of the MouseEvent source. The **.getZ()** method call will return a double value for the **depth** position for the event, relative to the origin of the MouseEvent source.

The **.isAltDown()** method call can be used to ascertain whether the **Alt** modifier key is being held down during this event. It returns a true or false (boolean) value. The **.isControlDown()** method call can be used to ascertain whether the **Ctrl** modifier key is being held down during this event. It also returns a true or false (boolean) value. The **.isMetaDown()** method call can be used to ascertain whether the **META** modifier key is being held down during this event. It also returns a true or false (boolean) value. The **.isShiftDown()** method call can be used to ascertain whether the **SHIFT** modifier key is being held down during this event. It also returns a true or false (boolean) value.

The **.isDragDetect()** method call should be used to determine whether this MouseEvent will be followed by a DRAG_DETECTED event and will return a boolean true (yes drag detected) or false (no drag not detected) data value.

An **.isMiddleButtonDown()** method call can be used to determine whether the middle mouse button is being held down. It will return a **true** boolean value if your middle button (mouse button #2) is currently depressed.

The **.isPopupTrigger()** method call should be used to determine whether this event is a pop-up menu trigger event for the platform. It will return **true** if the mouse event is in fact the pop-up menu trigger event for the platform.

The **.isPrimaryButtonDown()** method call will return the **true** boolean value if your primary mouse button (button #1, which is usually the left mouse button) is currently being pressed. The **.isSecondaryButtonDown()** method call will return the **true** boolean value if your secondary button (button #2, which is usually the right mouse button) is currently being pressed.

The **.isShortcutDown()** method call will return whether the host platform's common shortcut modifier is being held down during this MouseEvent.

The **.isStillSincePress()** method call uses a boolean value to indicate whether the mouse cursor stayed in the system-provided hysteresis area since the last mouse pressed event that occurred before this event.

The .isSynthesized() method call returns a boolean value that indicates whether the MouseEvent has been synthesized by using a touchscreen device, instead of the usual mouse event source device, such as the mouse, track ball, track pad, or similar mouse-emulation hardware device.

Finally, a **void .setDragDetect(boolean dragDetect)** method call is used to augment drag detection behavior when using MouseEvent handling in conjunction with drag detection using a mouse, track pad, or touchscreen device.

Implementing Spinner UI Functionality: Mouse Event Handling

Let's create a **createSceneProcessing()** method to hold the Scene object creation, configuration, and event-processing Java code. The Scene scene object must be created after the root Group Node object has been created, so this method must be called **after** the createBoardGameNodes() method call, where these Node objects are created. This is done using the following Java statement, also shown highlighted in light blue (and wavy red underlining) in Figure 17-1:

```
createSceneProcessing();
```

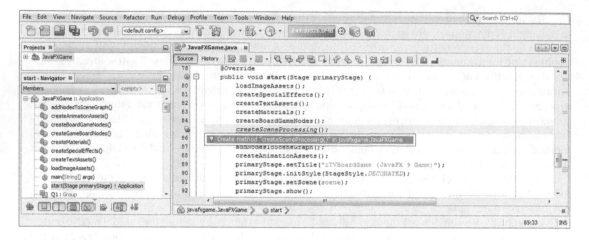

Figure 17-1. *Add the createSceneProcessing() method call, after the createBoardGameNodes() method in the start method*

Remember to double-click the **Create method "createSceneProcessing()" in javafxgame. JavaFXGame** option to have NetBeans 9 code a bootstrap method for you. You'll be replacing the placeholder Java code with your scene Scene object instantiation and configuration code and then adding the MouseEvent handling logic after that.

The first thing that you'll need to do is to open your createBoardGameNodes() method and select all of the **Scene scene** object instantiation and configuration Java 9 code, for which there are three Java 9 statements currently; then right-click the selection set and select the Cut option to remove the Java code from that method body.

Inside of your **.createSceneProcessing()** method, replace your bootstrap code (unimplemented error code) by selecting that one line of code and right-click it; select Paste to replace it with the three lines of code that you "cut" from your createBoardGameNodes() method. Finally, add a line of code at the end of the method to start to build your Scene object's event handling; type **scene** and then a period and then **setOnMouse**, which will give you a pop-up helper dialog containing all of the MouseEvent events. The following is the Java code for the existing statements and an empty event handling **lambda expression infrastructure** (for a change), as highlighted in blue in Figure 17-2:

```
private void createSceneProcessing() {
    scene = new Scene(root, 1280, 640, true, SceneAntialiasing.BALANCED);
    scene.setFill(Color.BLACK);
    scene.setCamera(camera);
    scene.setOnMouseClicked(event-> { ... } );  // This is an Empty OnMouseClicked Event Handler
}                                               //  Structure is using a Lambda Expression Format
```

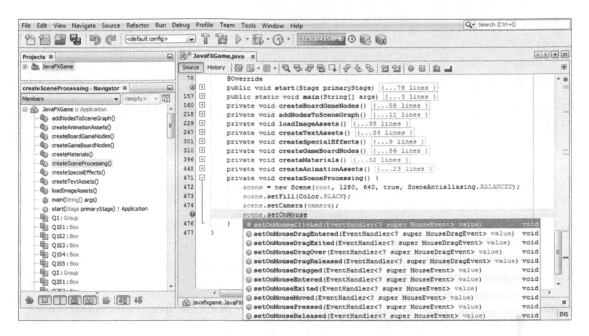

Figure 17-2. Cut and paste the Scene object code into the new method and call .setOnMouseClicked() off the scene object

Double-click your **setOnMouseClicked(EventHandler<? super MouseEvent> value) (void)** option, shown in bright blue in Figure 17-2, and add the **(event->{});** empty lambda expression inside the .setOnMouseClicked() method call parameter area to create an empty event processing infrastructure, which will yield zero errors in NetBeans 9. As I have said before in this book, when you write code, make sure it is error-free in your IDE at all times!

Now you can start configuring the **onMouseClicked()** event handling, which as you can see uses a simplified **lambda expression** that was introduced in **Java 8**. All a **lambda** (as it's called for short) needs is the **event** name and an **arrow**, and the Java compiler will figure out what type of event-handling object (EventHandler) to use and what type of Event object (MouseEvent) will need to be processed. Your logic goes inside of your curly braces, and you can focus on what your event-processing logic is going to do, which is to declare a **Node** object named **picked** and load it with the result of a **.getPickResult(). getIntersectedNode()** method chain. Make sure to use **Alt+Enter** when you get a wavy red error underline, under the **Node picked** (initial) portion of your Java statement, and select the "import javafx.scene.Node" option from the pop-up helper dialog to instruct NetBeans 9 to write the Node class import statement for you. If you like, you can type in the equals (=) sign and the event and hit the period; the NetBeans pop-up helper will let you select the **.getPickResult()** method. Double-click that to insert it and then use the period again to bring up the pop-up helper. This time select the **.getIntersectedNode()** method call. Add a semicolon to finalize the Java statement. The Java statements for your MouseEvent handling should look like the following and are shown at the bottom of Figure 17-3:

```java
private void createSceneProcessing() {
    scene = new Scene(root, 1280, 640, true, SceneAntialiasing.BALANCED);
    scene.setFill(Color.BLACK);
    scene.setCamera(camera);
    scene.setOnMouseClicked(event->{
        Node picked = event.getPickResult().getIntersectedNode();
    });
}
```

415

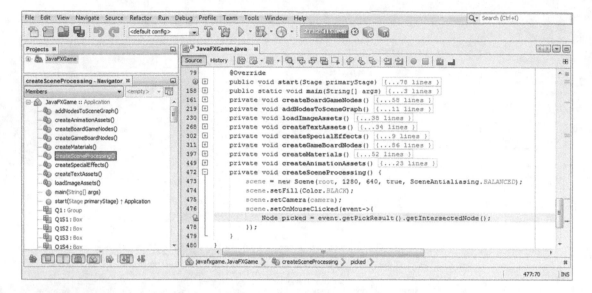

Figure 17-3. *Configure event handling as a lambda expression, create a Node named picked, and get an intersected Node*

Now that you've created and loaded a Node object named **picked** with the Node object in your BoardGame, which has been clicked with the mouse (or touchscreen, which also generates mouse events) by the user, we need to add the conditional processing logic (artificial intelligence) to tell the game how to operate. The first thing that you need to do is filter out all clicks that are **not on 3D Node objects**, which is done by using the **if (picked != null)** construct, which says if the picked Node object is not empty, then proceed. The next nested if() statement looks for a spinner Node object to be the same as (== or equivalent to) the picked Node object. If this equates to a **true** value, the **rotGameBoard** Animation object is triggered by using the **.play()** method call, spinning the gameBoard Group Node. If you use the **Run ➤ Project** work process and test this code, it works perfectly, although you have to wait until the code for the last chapter finishes (we will be fixing that next, as we change **Animation** objects to be MouseEvent triggered).

The entire completed Java 9 structure is only eight lines of code; this will grow as we build the game logic. The completed Java method body's code is shown here and is highlighted in yellow and blue in Figure 17-4:

```java
private void createSceneProcessing() {
    scene = new Scene(root, 1280, 640, true, SceneAntialiasing.BALANCED);
    scene.setFill(Color.BLACK);
    scene.setCamera(camera);
    scene.setOnMouseClicked(event->{
        Node picked = event.getPickResult().getIntersectedNode();
        if (picked != null) {
            if (picked == spinner) {
                rotGameBoard.play();
            }
        }
    });
}
```

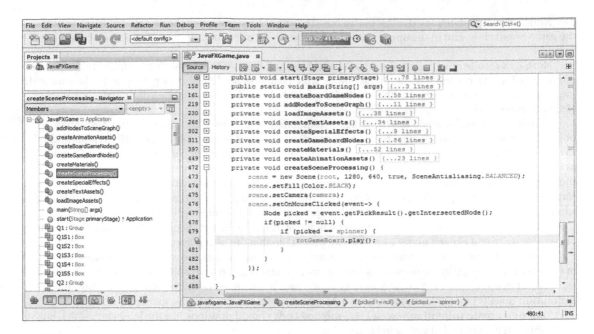

Figure 17-4. *Evaluate the picked Node object using two nested if{} constructs, testing for null and then for the spinner UI Node*

To make the spinner UI animate onto the screen, we first have to set its initial position off-screen to the left of its current starting position. Go into createBoardGameNodes() and change the TranslateX property from -200 to -350. This will remove the spinner from view, just off of the left side of your screen. Later we will change the **.setByX()** method in moveSpinnerIn to a setting of **150** so it lands at -200. This is done using the Java code shown here and in Figure 17-5:

```
spinner.setTranslateX(-350);
```

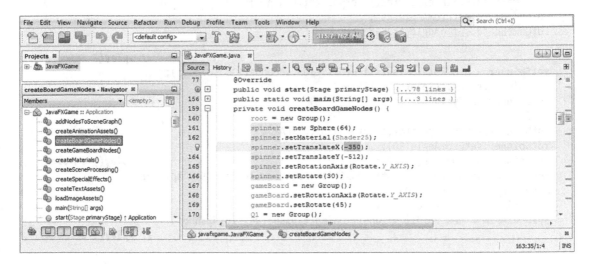

Figure 17-5. *Prepare for implementing the interactive spinner UI by setting its initial position off-screen value to the -350 X location*

Notice that TranslateY is -512; this places the 3D spinner UI at the top of the screen, out of the way of the game board view, and in the upper-left corner of the screen once the spinner animates out to the -150 X position.

Next, let's recode our **createAnimationAssets()** method body so that it only instantiates and configures our **Animation** objects and does not trigger them, which will now be done during gameplay by the user with mouse clicks (or screen touches, as these will also generate MouseEvents, widening our target consumer electronics devices).

Remove the .play() method call off of the rotGameBoard, rotSpinner, and spinnerAnim Animation object constructs, and then change the moveSpinnerOn TranslateTransition object's **.setByX()** method call to reference **150** units. This will move your 3D spinner UI into the upper-left corner of the screen from its new -350 location off-screen. The logical place to trigger this animation, bringing the spinner on-screen for the first time, would be in the Start Game Button UI event handling method, which we'll be doing soon. We'll also create your **rotSpinner** Animation object later during this chapter, which will spin the 3D spinner UI when it is clicked so that it also spins when the player initiates each random spin for the 3D game board.

Besides bringing this i3D spinner on-screen in the Start Game Button event handling, we will bring it on-screen at the end of each player's turn (in Chapter 21) so that the next player knows to randomly spin the game board to select a new educational question category (quadrant). We will animate it off-screen in Chapter 20, when the game board finishes its camera rotation Animation object. There is a lot more to learn about in this chapter regarding how to integrate your interactivity (event handling) with your different **Animation** objects in JavaFX so that you can achieve a seamless and responsive gameplay result.

Your new **createAnimationAssets()** Java method body should now look like the following, which is also highlighted in light blue and yellow in Figure 17-6:

```
RotateTransition rotGameBoard, rotSpinner;
TranslateTransition moveSpinnerOn;
ParallelTransition spinnerAnim;
...
private void createAnimationAssets() {
    rotGameBoard = new RotateTransition(Duration.seconds(5), gameBoard);
    rotGameBoard.setAxis(Rotate.Y_AXIS);
    rotGameBoard.setCycleCount(1);
    rotGameBoard.setRate(0.5);
    rotGameBoard.setInterpolator(Interpolator.LINEAR);
    rotGameBoard.setFromAngle(45);
    rotGameBoard.setToAngle(1125);

                                                            // .play() removed
    rotSpinner = new RotateTransition(Duration.seconds(5), spinner);
    rotSpinner.setAxis(Rotate.Y_AXIS);
    rotSpinner.setCycleCount(1);
    rotSpinner.setRate(0.5);
    rotSpinner.setInterpolator(Interpolator.LINEAR);
    rotSpinner.setFromAngle(30);
    rotSpinner.setToAngle(-1110);                           // .play() removed
    moveSpinnerOn = new TranslateTransition(Duration.seconds(5), spinner);
    moveSpinnerOn.setByX(150);
    moveSpinnerOn.setCycleCount(1);
    spinnerAnim = new ParallelTransition(moveSpinnerOn, rotSpinner);
                                                            // .play() removed
}
```

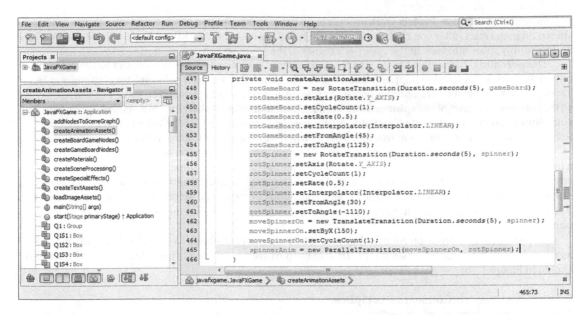

Figure 17-6. *Remove all .play() method calls and change the .setByX() method call to 150 to bring the spinner on-screen*

Add a **spinnerAnim.play();** statement at the end of the gameButton event handler, as shown in Figure 17-7.

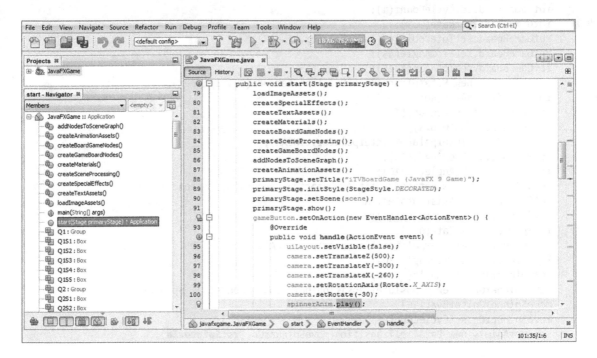

Figure 17-7. *Add the spinnerAnim.play() method call to the end of your gameButton event-handling method construct*

Now use your **Run ➤ Project** work process to test your code, and you can see that the spinner is not shown on game start (after you click the Button that hides the uiLayout StackPane Node object) and slowly and smoothly spins into view in the upper-left corner of the game screen.

The next thing that we need to do is to create a separate **rotSpinner** Animation object so that we can have a 3D spinner UI rotation happening at the same time the game board is spinning, for continuity sake. You will find that if you call rotSpinner.play in your MouseEvent handling construct, you will get an error as the rotSpinner is part of the **spinnerAnim** ParallelAnimation object; therefore, we need to duplicate a **rotSpinner** construct and create a **rotSpinnerIn** construct to use in the spinnerAnim ParallelAnimation, leaving the **rotSpinner** Animation free for us to call whenever the player randomly spins the game board.

To do this, select all rotSpinner-related Java code, right-click the selection set, and select **Copy**; then add a line (space) of code after this code block, right-click, and select **Paste** to duplicate this code block. Then, all you have to do is to add "In" at the end of "rotSpinner" and create a rotSpinnerIn code block, which does the same thing but is not a component of the ParallelTransition construction. Reference the new rotSpinnerIn Animation object in the object instantiation (constructor method) of the spinnerAnim ParallelTransition object.

As you can see, the only problem is that your "SPIN" spinner is rotating to the wrong **toAngle** of **1110**, as we coded it in Chapter 16. I'll set this to **-1050** in the next section. The code looks like the following and is shown in Figure 17-8:

```
RotateTransition rotGameBoard, rotSpinner;
TranslateTransition moveSpinnerOn;
ParallelTransition spinnerAnim;
...
private void createAnimationAssets() {
    rotGameBoard = new RotateTransition(Duration.seconds(5), gameBoard);
    rotGameBoard.setAxis(Rotate.Y_AXIS);
    rotGameBoard.setCycleCount(1);
    rotGameBoard.setRate(0.5);
    rotGameBoard.setInterpolator(Interpolator.LINEAR);
    rotGameBoard.setFromAngle(45);
    rotGameBoard.setToAngle(1125);
    rotSpinner = new RotateTransition(Duration.seconds(5), spinner);
    rotSpinner.setAxis(Rotate.Y_AXIS);
    rotSpinner.setCycleCount(1);
    rotSpinner.setRate(0.5);
    rotSpinner.setInterpolator(Interpolator.LINEAR);
    rotSpinner.setFromAngle(30);
    rotSpinner.setToAngle(-1110);
    rotSpinnerIn = new RotateTransition(Duration.seconds(5), spinner);
    rotSpinnerIn.setAxis(Rotate.Y_AXIS);
    rotSpinnerIn.setCycleCount(1);
    rotSpinnerIn.setRate(0.5);
    rotSpinnerIn.setInterpolator(Interpolator.LINEAR);
    rotSpinnerIn.setFromAngle(30);
    rotSpinnerIn.setToAngle(-1110);
    moveSpinnerOn = new TranslateTransition(Duration.seconds(5), spinner);
    moveSpinnerOn.setByX(150);
    moveSpinnerOn.setCycleCount(1);
    spinnerAnim = new ParallelTransition(moveSpinnerOn, rotSpinnerIn);
}
```

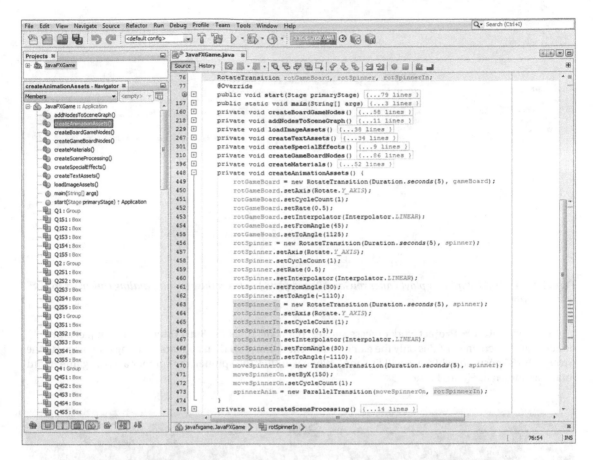

Figure 17-8. *Copy and paste the rotSpinner object code under itself to create a rotSpinnerIn, and reference in spinnerAnim*

Now I can add a **rotSpinner.play();** Java statement to the conditional event handling construct, without generating any errors, so that when the spinner UI is clicked, it spins alongside the game board for the same amount of time and at the same rate. The completed Java code looks like this and is shown highlighted in yellow in Figure 17-9:

```java
private void createSceneProcessing() {
    scene = new Scene(root, 1280, 640, true, SceneAntialiasing.BALANCED);
    scene.setFill(Color.BLACK);
    scene.setCamera(camera);
    scene.setOnMouseClicked(event->{
        Node picked = event.getPickResult().getIntersectedNode();
        if (picked != null) {
            if (picked == spinner) {
                rotGameBoard.play();
                rotSpinner.play();
            }
        }
    });
}
```

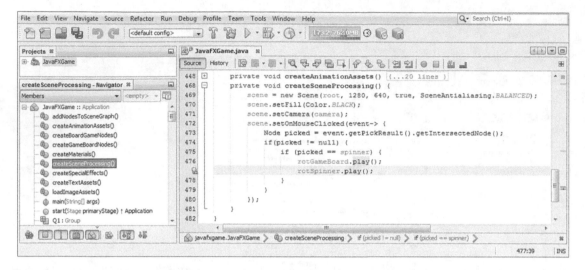

Figure 17-9. *Add rotSpinner.play() after rotGameBoard.play() in the mouse event handling construct so both will animate*

Let's use a **Run ➤ Project** work process and test our code. Click the **Start Game** Button object and notice that the screen contains only the game board. The spinner UI then appears, rotating into place (to the wrong "PINS" position, which we will fix soon). When you click the spinner, the spinner and the game board rotate, as shown in Figure 17-10.

Figure 17-10. *The spinner UI element now animates on-screen and also rotates when clicked to spin the game board*

Using java.util.Random: Generating a Random Spin

The **public** class **Random** extends Object and implements **Serializable**. It is kept in the **java.util** package and has two known direct subclasses, **SecureRandom** and **ThreadLocalRandom**. An instance of this class can be used to create a **random number-generating object**, which will generate a stream of "pseudorandom numbers." These numbers will be random enough for the purposes of creating random game spinner UI functionality. The algorithm for this class uses a **48-bit** seed, which is modified using a **linear congruential formula**. If you want to research this algorithm in more detail, you can reference *The Art of Computer Programming* (Volume 2, Section 3.2.1) by Donald Knuth. The Java class hierarchy for the Random class would therefore look like the following:

```
java.lang.Object
  > java.util.Random
```

It's important to note that if two different instances of Random objects are created using the same seed and the same sequence of method calls is made for each object, an algorithm generates (returns) the same sequence of numeric results. In some applications, this is actually desirable; so, to guarantee an identical result, specific algorithms are implemented for the java.util.Random class. Subclasses of class Random are permitted to use alternate algorithms for increased security or multithread use, as long as they adhere to general contracts for all the methods.

The instances of java.util.Random are thread-safe. However, a concurrent use of the same java.util.Random instance across multiple threads could encounter contention and consequently result in poor performance. You should consider using the ThreadLocalRandom subclass for your multithreaded game designs.

Additionally, instances of java.util.Random are not **cryptographically secure**. You should consider instead using the SecureRandom subclass to get a cryptographically secure, pseudorandom number generator for use by applications that are sensitive and that require a high level of security.

There are two overloaded constructor methods for this class. The first creates a random number generator, and the second creates a random number generator and gives it a seed value using a long format. These constructor methods look like the following Java code:

```
Random()            // We'll be using this in our code later on during this chapter
Random(long seed)
```

This class has 22 methods that can be used to obtain random number results from the Random object. The **.doubles()** method call will return an unlimited stream of numeric values called a **DoubleStream**, which contains pseudorandom double values. Each of these values will fall between zero (inclusive) and one (exclusive). There are three additional overloaded .doubles() method calls. The **.doubles(double randomNumberOrigin, double randomNumberBound)** method call will return an unlimited bound stream of pseudorandom double values, each conforming to the given binding origin (inclusive) and bound limit (exclusive) specified in the method call parameter area. The **.doubles(long streamSize)** method call will return a stream that produces the given streamSize number of pseudorandom double values that are between zero (inclusive) and one (exclusive). Finally, there is a **.doubles(long streamSize, double randomNumberOrigin, double randomNumberBound)** method call that returns a stream that produces a stream conforming to the given streamSize number of pseudorandom double values, each conforming to the given binding origin (inclusive) and bound limit (exclusive).

The **.ints()** method call will return an unlimited stream of pseudorandom int (integer) numeric values called an IntStream. There are three additional overloaded .ints() method calls, including an **.ints(int randomNumberOrigin, int randomNumberBound)** method call, which will return an unlimited stream of pseudorandom int (integer) values, each of which will conform to a binding origin (inclusive) and bound limit (exclusive) value specified in the parameter area. The **.ints(long streamSize)** method call will return a random values stream, which produces a stream size that is specified using the streamSize parameter that establishes a desired number of pseudorandom int (integer) values.

Finally, the **.ints(long streamSize, int randomNumberOrigin, int randomNumberBound)** method call will return a stream of numeric (integer) values that produces the streamSize number of pseudorandom int values that are specified in the parameter area, with each value conforming to the specified binding origin (inclusive) and bound limit (exclusive), which are also taken from the method call parameter area.

The **.longs()** method call will return an unlimited stream of pseudorandom long numeric values, called a LongStream. There are three additional overloaded .longs() method calls, including a **.longs(long randomNumberOrigin, int randomNumberBound)** method call, which will return an unlimited stream of pseudorandom long values, each of which will conform to a binding origin (inclusive) and bound limit (exclusive) value specified in the parameter area. The **.longs(long streamSize)** method call will return a random long values stream that produces the stream size that is specified using the streamSize parameter that establishes a desired number of pseudorandom long values.

Finally, a **.long(long streamSize, int randomNumberOrigin, long randomNumberBound)** method call will return a stream of numeric long values that produces the streamSize number of pseudorandom long values that are specified in the parameter area, with each value conforming to the specified binding origin (inclusive) and bound limit (exclusive), which are also taken from the method call parameter area.

The **protected int .next(int bits)** method call will generate the next pseudorandom integer number using an integer number of bits as the parameter specification. The **.nextBoolean()** method call will return a pseudorandom, uniformly distributed, boolean value from the random number generator object's sequence. This method probably shouldn't be used for this game's use case because next() is designed to be called by other random() methods.

The **void .nextBytes(byte[] bytes)** method call will generate a parameter-supplied byte array and fill it with random byte values. The **.nextDouble()** method call will return a pseudorandom, uniformly distributed, double value between the values of 0.0 and 1.0 by using a random number generator object's sequence. The **.nextFloat()** method call will return a pseudorandom, uniformly distributed, float (or floating-point) value, between 0.0 and 1.0, using the random number generator object's sequence.

The **.nextGaussian()** method call will return a pseudorandom, Gaussian distribution, double value, with its mean at 0.0 and its standard deviation at 1.0, from this random number generator object's sequence. The **.nextInt()** method call will return the next pseudorandom, uniformly distributed, int (integer) value from this random number generator object's sequence.

The **.nextLong()** method call will return the next pseudorandom, uniformly distributed, long value from this random number generator object's sequence.

The **void .setSeed(long seed)** method call can be used to set (or reseed) the seed of the random number generator object using a single long value seed specification inside of the parameter area for the method call.

Finally, the **.nextInt(int bound)** method call, which is the one that we are going to utilize in the final section of this chapter, will return a pseudorandom, uniformly distributed, int (integer) value between 0 (inclusive) and the specified value (exclusive), in our case 4, drawn from the random number generator object's random int sequence.

Random Quadrant Selection: Using Random with Conditional If()

Now that we have set up our spinner and game board rotation and MouseEvent handling well enough to connect the two together to create a random spin for the game board, we need to add a randomizer algorithm to the code so that each time a spinner is clicked, the game board is randomly set to a new quadrant. We'll use at least three rotations so that the spin is long enough to appear completely random to the player. Let's declare a **Random** object named **random** at the top of the class and then use the **Alt+Enter** keystroke combination to bring up the NetBeans 9 pop-up helper. Finally, select (double-click) the "Add import for java.util.Random" option, as shown in blue in Figure 17-11.

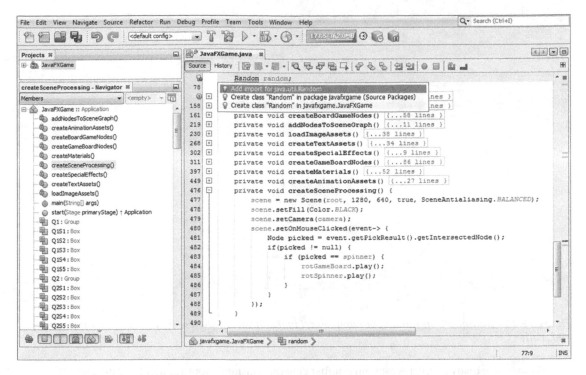

Figure 17-11. *Declare a Random object named random at the top of class; use Alt+Enter to add import java.util.Random*

Since we want to instantiate (create) our random number generator "engine" before it is actually utilized, let's have our code instantiate (create and load into system memory) the Random number generator when the game application starts up.

This dictates that we will place the Random() constructor method code in your **.start()** method, right before your ActionEvent handling constructs and right after all of your Node and Scene and Stage objects have been created and added to the SceneGraph. For good measure, we'll put it after all of the custom methods that create the assets, images, animation and eventually the digital audio samples and other new media assets that we'll be using to create a professional Java 9 game.

We can do this because this Random object (named random) is not utilized until the player has clicked the Start Game Button object to enter the 3D Scene and then clicked the spinner 3D UI (Sphere) element. Thus, you can put this Random object instantiation anywhere in your .start() method, from the first line of code to the last, as long as this object is created (loaded into system memory) before you start generating any MouseEvent handling method calls in your custom createSceneProcessing() method, which we will be enhancing as we proceed through this chapter. Open your .start() method body in NetBeans 9, add a line of code after your custom method calls, and instantiate your Random object named random using the following Java code, which is also shown in Figure 17-12:

```java
public void start(Stage primaryStage) {
    ...                           // Custom Methods Up Here
    random = new Random();
    ...                           // ActionEvent Handling Constructs Down Here
}
```

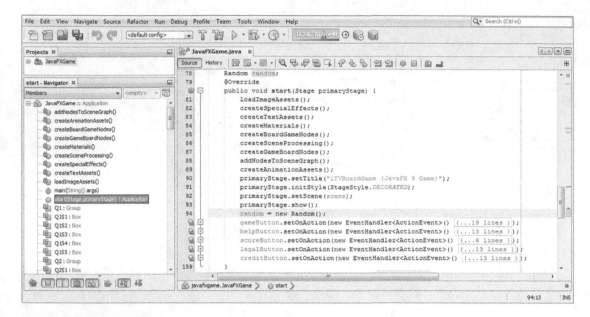

Figure 17-12. *Instantiate the random Random object in the .start() method so that it is loaded into memory and ready*

Now you are ready to call this random number generator inside of your spinner logic in your **MouseEvent** handling code, which tells your game what to do when the 3D spinner UI is clicked. Obviously, the first thing to do is to check for **NULL** to see whether the click was on a 3D Scene element and, if so, to then see whether it was the 3D spinner that has been clicked on.

If the spinner was clicked, then the first line of code after if(picked==spinner) would be a .nextInt(bound) method call, with an upper boundary value of 4 (the lower boundary is zero). This gives us a random result among four quadrants (zero through three, as the upper bound of four is exclusive and therefore not utilized in the random number pick range), which is what we will need to randomly select between for the game's four quadrants.

Add a line of code before your calls to invoke the RotateTransition **Animation** objects and create a new **int** variable named **spin**, which will hold the result of your **random.nextInt(4)** method call. Add an equal (=) operator and then type **random** and a period, which will bring up your NetBeans 9 method helper pop-up selector drop-down.

Select the **.nextInt(int bound) (int)** option, which is shown in blue in Figure 17-13, and then double-click it and insert it into your code. Change the default 0 (which turns the random number generator off by generating zero to zero results) to a 4 to tell the random number generator to generate four integer values at random, which will give you the four different quadrant results for your player spins. The Java code at this point should look like the following Java nested if() constructs, which are also shown highlighted in blue (and also under construction) in Figure 17-13:

```java
if (picked != null) {
    if (picked == spinner) {
        int spin = random.nextInt(4);
        rotGameBoard.play();
        rotSpinner.play();
    }
}
```

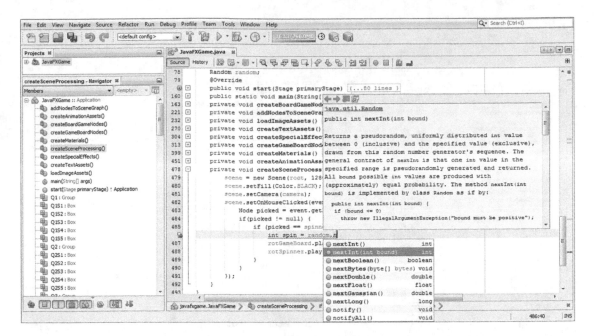

Figure 17-13. *Add an int variable named spin and then type random and a period and select nextInt(int bound) set to 4*

Before we code this spin logic, we need to remove the .setFromAngle() and .setToAngle() method calls from your rotGameBoard block of statements in the **createAnimationAssets()** method, which simplifies your rotGameBoard Animation object logic down to its five required statements (instantiation, axis, cycles, rate, and interpolator). We will also do this later for your rotSpinner, after we have ascertained that a switch from toAngle and fromAngle to byAngle is going to work correctly for generating ongoing game board spins using the fewest lines of code and with zero errors.

What we are doing here is using **createAnimationAssets()** to create and configure the **Animation** objects and then using a **.setByAngle()** in the if() conditional statements, which evaluate the Random random object result, placed into the spin integer, which we will be doing next. This approach will also reduce the amount of code in this method body as well to less than two dozen lines of code (unless we add game board animation later during the design and development process, outlined within this book). The **rotGameBoard** code, shown in Figure 17-14, now looks like this:

```
private void createAnimationAssets() {
    rotGameBoard = new RotateTransition(Duration.seconds(5), gameBoard);
    rotGameBoard.setAxis(Rotate.Y_AXIS);
    rotGameBoard.setCycleCount(1);
    rotGameBoard.setRate(0.5);
    rotGameBoard.setInterpolator(Interpolator.LINEAR);
    rotSpinner = new RotateTransition(Duration.seconds(5), spinner);
    rotSpinner.setAxis(Rotate.Y_AXIS);
    rotSpinner.setCycleCount(1);
    rotSpinner.setRate(0.5);
    rotSpinner.setInterpolator(Interpolator.LINEAR);
    rotSpinner.setFromAngle(30);
    rotSpinner.setToAngle(-1050);
    ...
}
```

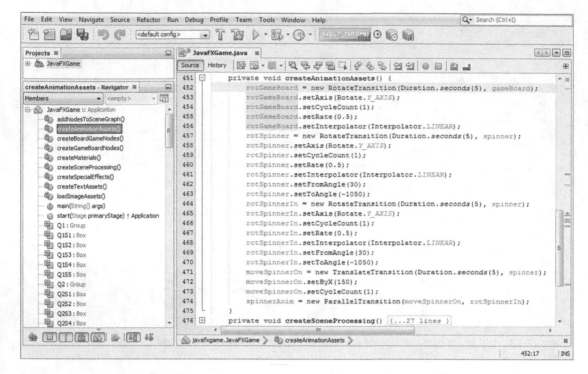

Figure 17-14. *Remove the .setFromAngle(45) and .setToAngle(1125) method calls from the rotGameBoard object code*

The easiest way to make sure a game board spin ends on a quadrant is to initialize gameBoard rotation at **45** degrees and use **.setByAngle()** to rotate by **90**-degree increments (plus three spins) for each if() evaluation. This gives us 1080 for 0, 1170 for 1, 1260 for 2, and 1350 for 3. The Java if() constructs are shown in Figure 17-15 and look like this:

```
if (picked == spinner) {
    int spin = random.nextInt(4);
    if (spin == 0) {
        rotGameBoard.setByAngle(1080);  // Zero degrees plus 1080
    }
    if (spin == 1) {
        rotGameBoard.setByAngle(1170);  // 1080 plus 90 degrees is 1170
    }
    if (spin == 2) {
        rotGameBoard.setByAngle(1260);  // 1080 plus 180 degrees is 1260
    }
    if (spin == 3) {
        rotGameBoard.setByAngle(1350);  // 1080 plus 270 degrees is 1350
    }
    rotGameBoard.play();
    rotSpinner.play();
}
```

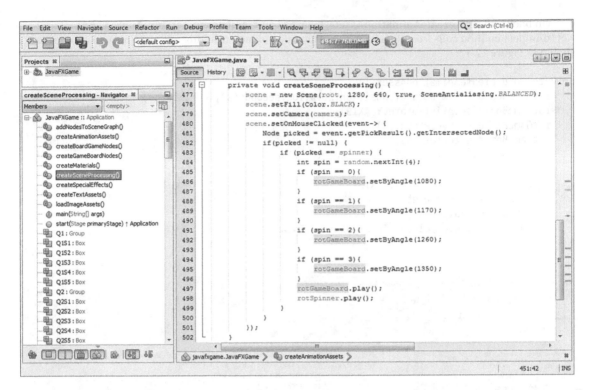

Figure 17-15. *Add if() constructs, setting the .setByAngle() method call to four different 90-degree increments plus 1080*

Use the **Run ➤ Project** work process and click the spinner UI multiple times to test, as shown in Figure 17-16.

Figure 17-16. *The game board now randomly lands on a different quadrant with each 3D spinner click*

Go back into your **createAnimationAssets()** method and remove the .setFromAngle() and .setToAngle() method calls from the rotSpinner Animation object, resulting in the following Java code, as shown in Figure 17-17:

```java
private void createAnimationAssets() {
    rotGameBoard = new RotateTransition(Duration.seconds(5), gameBoard);
    rotGameBoard.setAxis(Rotate.Y_AXIS);
    rotGameBoard.setCycleCount(1);
    rotGameBoard.setRate(0.5);
    rotGameBoard.setInterpolator(Interpolator.LINEAR);
    rotSpinner = new RotateTransition(Duration.seconds(5), spinner);
    rotSpinner.setAxis(Rotate.Y_AXIS);
    rotSpinner.setCycleCount(1);
    rotSpinner.setRate(0.5);
    rotSpinner.setInterpolator(Interpolator.LINEAR);
}
```

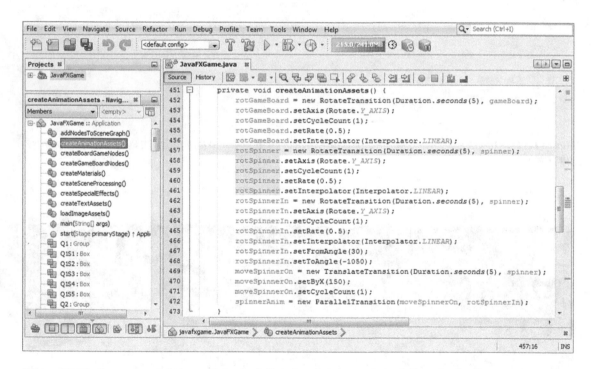

Figure 17-17. *Remove rotSpinner.setFromAngle() and rotSpinner.setToAngle() method calls in createAnimationAssets*

Go back into your createSceneProcessing() method and add the rotSpinner.setByAngle() method calls using the **negative** angle values used in the rotGameBoard.setByAngle() method calls, using this code, also shown in Figure 17-18:

```
if (picked == spinner) {
    int spin = random.nextInt(4);
    if (spin == 0) {
        rotGameBoard.setByAngle(1080);
        rotSpinner.setByAngle(-1080);  // Zero degrees minus 1080
    }
    if (spin == 1) {
        rotGameBoard.setByAngle(1170);
        rotSpinner.setByAngle(-1170);  // -1080 minus 90 degrees is -1170
    }
    if (spin == 2) {
        rotGameBoard.setByAngle(1260);
        rotSpinner.setByAngle(-1260);  // -1080 minus 180 degrees is -1260
    }
    if (spin == 3) {
        rotGameBoard.setByAngle(1350);
        rotSpinner.setByAngle(-1350);  // -1080 minus 270 degrees is -1350
    }
    rotGameBoard.play();
    rotSpinner.play();
}
```

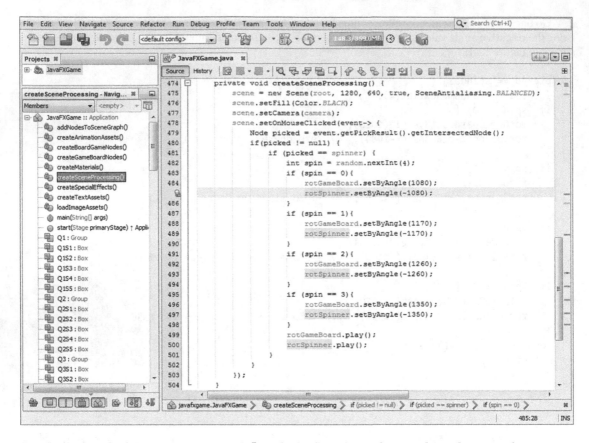

Figure 17-18. *Add the rotSpinner.setByAngle() method calls to the random spin logic, this time subtracting 1080 plus 90*

Now use a **Run ➤ Project** work process and test the code we have developed during this chapter thoroughly. As you can't see in Figure 17-19 (as it is not animated or interactive, like our game is now), every time you click the 3D spinner, you get a different quadrant and also a different sequence of colors on the 3D spinner UI itself while it still always says "SPIN"!

Figure 17-19. *The game board randomly lands on a different quadrant, and the spinner always lands on the word SPIN*

We have added some fairly complex functionality during this chapter, and we are still at around **500** lines of Java code, as you can see at the bottom of NetBeans 9 in Figure 17-18 (the end of the class at line 504). Very impressive, folks!

Summary

In this seventeenth chapter, we learned about the **MouseEvent**, **PickResult**, and **Random** classes, which allow us to finish implementing our 3D spinner UI and have it select a random quadrant on each subsequent spin of the spinning 3D spinner beach ball. We also constructed a new custom **createSceneProcessing()** method that contains your MouseEvent handling logic, as well as your logic for processing the (now) i3D primitive objects that our i3D game board and spinner is comprised of (built with). Inside this new method, we began building a conditional if() structure to evaluate mouse clicks and what needs to happen with the game logic based on what is clicked. We will obviously be expanding this logic as we design and develop our gameplay model over the next several chapters.

We also got some more experience using the RotateTransition class methods by converting your rotSpinner and rotGameBoard **Animation** objects from using .setFromAngle() and .setToAngle() rotation animation configuration parameters to a single .setByAngle() rotation animation configuration approach, reducing our lines of Java code by 12.

In Chapter 18, we are going to develop your game content so that we can finish your MouseEvent handling code (during Chapters 19 and 20) for the game board squares and the game board quadrants.

■ ■ ■

3D Gameplay Design: Creating Your Game Content Using GIMP and Java

Now that you have created your multitiered 3D gameBoard Group Node (subclass) hierarchy, textured all of the 3D primitives underneath that hierarchy, configured RotationTransition Animation algorithms (objects) to bring the game board to life, and created a 3D spinner UI to rotate the gameBoard 3D model (hierarchy) to a random quadrant, it is time to finish the gameplay design and create the **visual assets** that comprise the gameplay. These will replace the texture map image assets during gameplay; we will use the existing 24 board game components and morph them into different content configurations, replacing a spinning game board with content relating to your educational game.

During the chapter, we will look at a work process for creating alternate texture maps that will be changed during gameplay by changing the **Image object asset reference** to add content to game board squares and quadrants, based on random spins and player mouse clicks (or screen touches). Although this particular chapter does not get into Java 9 too deeply, it is important to note that developing professional Java 9 games involves **digital image artisans**, as well as digital audio engineers, 3D modelers, 3D texture artists, animators, 2D illustrators, and VFX artists. Therefore, we need to cover some non-Java topics during this book, and this is one of those chapters. Taking a chapter for content design work process will allow us to cover what it takes to develop a game that is considered to be "professional" by the general public. I'll be using many of these new media genres during this book so that I leave no stone uncovered!

Design Your Gameplay: Create Quadrant Definitions

Since this is an educational game for preschool children, as well as individuals who are autistic, intellectually impaired, and learning impaired, we need to keep the categories simple. One of the perennial classification paradigms that will match with our color scheme is Animal, Vegetable, or Mineral, which will leave us with one square for other topics, such as People and Famous Places. Obviously, our green quadrant is going to be **Vegetable** because people say "eat your greens," and the orange quadrant will be **Animal** because of the lions, tigers, cats, dogs, and other animals that are exactly that shade of orange. Our blue quadrant will be **Mineral** because of minerals such as sapphire and amethyst, which exist in this cool color spectrum. This leaves the pink quadrant for **Other**, which we can decide to classify after each spin. These game board squares' randomly selected topics will be presented visually using high-quality imagery, which we will be developing the alternate texture mapping digital image assets for during this chapter using the professional-level GIMP.

© Wallace Jackson 2017

W. Jackson, *Pro Java 9 Games Development*, https://doi.org/10.1007/978-1-4842-0973-8_18

Game Board Quadrant: Creating Game Quadrant Content (GIMP)

I'll be showing you the work process used in GIMP to create one of the game board texture assets (a parrot for your Animal quadrant) so that the chapter does not balloon to hundreds of pages, as you ultimately need to create hundreds of image assets for your 24 game board elements). Let's fire up GIMP (currently at version 2.8.22) and create a new image composite to use to develop content textures! To start your quadrant (and game board square) texture map layer compositing construct, simply launch GIMP and use a **File ➤ Open** menu sequence to open the **gameboardquad1.png** file in your **/NetBeansProjects/JavaFXGame/src/** folder. This will make it the bottom-most layer, as shown on the left side (highlighted in blue) of Figure 18-1. Open the other three gameboardquad texture maps, as shown as three tabs on the top right of Figure 18-1. Select each tab, use the **Select ➤ All** menu sequence, and then use **Edit ➤ Copy**. Click the first tab, which contains your multilayer composite, and use the **Edit ➤ Paste As ➤ New Layer** menu sequence to add these three layers above the first (orange) one, as shown on the left side of Figure 18-1. Rename these layers to gameboardquad with a dash and the words *animal, vegetable, mineral,* and *other*, as shown in Figure 18-1. With the fourth (pink, topmost) layer selected, use the **File ➤ Open as Layers** menu sequence and add the **SteelHoop.png** 24-bit image file to the top layer of the composite, giving the result shown in the preview area in Figure 18-1. Now, let's find an animal image online we can use inside of the texture's steel hoop area.

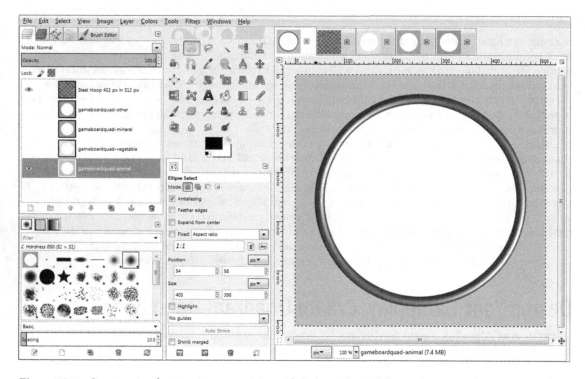

Figure 18-1. *Create a quadrant texture composite with four quadrant diffuse color maps; then add a steel decorative hoop*

The web site I use for royalty-free images for commercial use (such as this educational game and book) is **Pexels.com**. Go to www.pexels.com, and if you don't see a parrot on the home page, enter **parrot** in the search bar. Download a parrot image, as shown in Figure 18-2; then right-click the downloaded image (in its own tab in the browser) and select Copy Image. Go into GIMP and use the **File ➤ Create ➤ From Clipboard** menu sequence to paste the digital image data into its own composition file (and into, and under, a new tab, on the top right) in GIMP.

Figure 18-2. *Use File ➤ Create ➤ From Clipboard to paste content copied from the Pexels.com download in GIMP for editing*

We need a square area of this image to use with both the game board square texture and the round portion of the game board quadrant texture. This will be created using the **Rectangle Select** tool shown in Figure 18-3 set to a 2160x2160 square area, which will be resized 500 percent to fit a 432x432 circular area inside the game board quadrant.

Position your square selection to optimize the recognizable portion of your content, as shown in Figure 18-3.

Figure 18-3. *Set the Rectangle Select tool's Size properties to 2160x2160 and then drag the selection into an optimal position*

Since the Pexels.com imagery varies in pixel size, I simply find an even multiple of a target 432-pixel square image size needed for each quadrant's center area and set the **Rectangle Select** tool for that. Once the selection square is set, you drag it around by its interior area to fine-tune its position to show the maximum content inside of it. Then use an **Edit ➤ Copy** menu sequence to copy the data to the **Clipboard** and then a **File ➤ Create ➤ From Clipboard** menu sequence to create the new square image, shown in Figure 18-4, which we will downsample by five times, to 432x432. This is done using the **Image ➤ Scale Image** menu sequence to open the **Scale Image** dialog, where you'll replace 2160 with 432 (keeping the aspect ratio locked) and click the **Scale** button.

Figure 18-4. *Use the Image ➤ Scale Image work process and reduce the 2160-pixel image 500 percent to be 432 pixels square*

Your next step is to center this 432-pixel square image inside of the 512-pixel square area of your quadrant's texture map, which we will do before we copy it over, as this is an easier work process. To do this, we'll simply use the **Image ➤ Canvas Size** menu sequence and then increase the canvas size from 432x432 to 512x512. Make sure to click the dialog's **Center** button or your image will be in the upper-left corner of the resized canvas, this centering process will allow you to have transparency (alpha channel) values where there was no image, which is exactly the result that we want to achieve.

As you can see in the **Set Image Canvas Size** dialog, once you click the **Center** button, shown in light blue in Figure 18-5, the dialog will calculate the X Offset and Y Offset values (in this case, 40 pixels) around the entire perimeter of the image, as in 512 – 432 = 80 / 2 = 40. Finally, click your **Resize** button to turn this 432-pixel square into a 512-pixel square, centered using transparency, so it will be centered in the steel hoop. Now you're ready to use **Select ➤ All** and then the **Edit ➤ Copy** menu sequence to place the data into the Clipboard, where it will be pasted onto a different tab.

Figure 18-5. *Use the Set Image Canvas Size dialog to resize the canvas to 512 pixels*

Make sure to set your **Layers** drop-down selector to **All layers** to include the transparent areas generated in the layer. If you forget to do this, simply right-click the new 512-pixel layer and use the Layer to Image Size option. Make sure to do this before you use Select ➤ All and Edit ➤ Copy so you select both the transparency and the imagery.

The next step is to click the quadrant texture composition tab, as shown in Figure 18-6, and then select the bottom-most (animal) layer so that when you paste the centered parrot square image, it is above the base texture for the quadrant and underneath the steel hoop decoration. We will be using this steel hoop image and its transparency to cut the corners off of the parrot image so that it is seamlessly integrated with the steel hoop image.

To accomplish this GIMP "move," you will select the **Steel Hoop layer**, shown selected in blue in Figure 18-6, and then click the **Magic Wand** tool, shown (depressed) selected in the GIMP Tool Icon area. Click the Magic Wand tool inside of the center (transparent) area of your steel hoop, which will select this area inside of the hoop. You'll need to **expand** this selection area so that the parrot image actually goes underneath the edges of the steel hoop, or you will see a seam around the edge of the parrot image once it's cut out so that it is in the interior portion of the steel hoop.

To do this, after you see your selection inside of your steel hoop, as shown in Figure 18-6, you will want to use the **Select ➤ Grow** menu sequence and expand the selection so that it actually looks like it is over the top of the steel hoop, by anywhere from 1 to 9 pixels. (I usually use at least 2, to be safe; in this case, I have used 4 pixels.)

Figure 18-6. *Select the Steel Hoop layer and Magic Wand tool and click inside the hoop to create a selection*

At this point, since the Steel Hoop layer is selected, the selection is indeed on top of the steel hoop. However, once the Clipboard layer (which you can rename Parrot, if you want, by double-clicking the layer name) is selected, this selection will be on top of (as well as used on) that layer and will therefore be underneath your Steel Hoop layer.

Set the **Grow Selection** dialog value to **4** and click the **OK** button, as shown at the bottom of Figure 18-7.

Figure 18-7. *Use the Grow Selection dialog and expand the selection area by 4 pixels beyond the interior*

The next step is to select your **Clipboard** layer, which contains your parrot image, so that it is affected by the selection, which we "culled" from the Steel Hoop layer (inner) transparency. Then select the **Select ➤ Invert** menu sequence. This will "keep" what is inside of the circle and **delete** what is outside of your circle selection (once you tap the Delete key on the keyboard, that is). This will remove the corners of the image that were sticking out in Figure 18-7.

As you can see in Figure 18-8, the end result of this work process is a completely smooth image composite, with the rounded parrot image inside of (and behind) the steel hoop decoration. Also shown in Figure 18-8 is the final step in making your perfect game board quadrant texture map, which is rotating the content 45 degrees so that when your 3D game board is spun onto its point, the image is correctly positioned, relative to the viewing player.

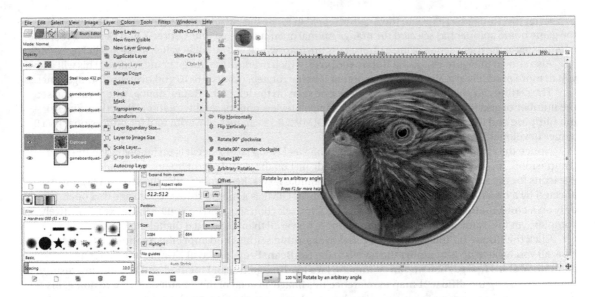

Figure 18-8. *Once you delete the corners, you have a perfect compositing result and are ready to rotate the parrot 45 degrees*

The next thing that needs to be done is to rotate the **Clipboard (Parrot) layer** by **45 degrees**, which should be seamless since the parrot imagery has been centered and rounded using a math-based work process. Since your Clipboard layer is still selected, all you have to do is to select **Layer ➤ Transform ➤ Arbitrary Rotation**, which is shown in Figure 18-8, and open the **Rotate** dialog, as shown in Figure 18-9.

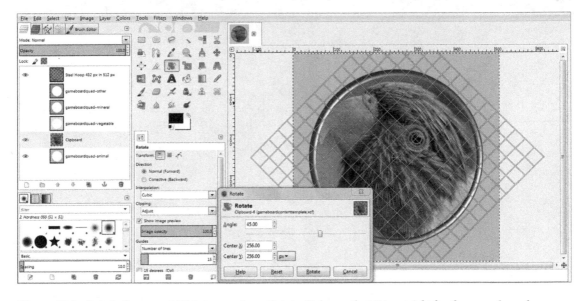

Figure 18-9. *Rotate the parrot 45 degrees using a Rotate dialog so that it is upright for the game board quadrant spin*

Enter the **45**-degree value into the Angle text field to rotate the parrot image so that it will be upright after the game board spinner has selected the orange Animal quadrant. Leave your **Center X** and **Center Y** rotation coordinates at the exact center of the 512-pixel texture map, which will be a **256** value, as shown in Figure 18-9.

Also shown in Figure 18-9 is the **Rotate tool grid**, which overlays the image being rotated. This will allow you to more precisely visualize how your content is being rotated, using a 16x16 grid overlay of straight lines.

The settings for the Rotate tool and grid can be seen on the left of the Rotate dialog, where you can set the number of grid lines (called *guides*), set the image preview option, set the rotation **Direction**, and set the **Clipping** and image **Opacity**. As you can see, GIMP 2.8.22 can be a powerful tool for professional Java 9 games developers.

Notice the rotation grid guide is shown over the Steel Hoop layer since it is on (showing) in the layer composition. If you wanted to see the rotation guide just on the round parrot image, you could turn off the eye icons for the Steel Hoop and gameboardquad-animal layers. Remember, only the selected layer will be affected by a Layer ➤ Transform ➤ Rotate operation, as GIMP is a **modal** software package that operates only on a **combination** of selected layers, tools, colors, selection sets, and options. This makes it relatively complex, yet this same feature makes it much more powerful than nonmodal digital imaging software.

Click the **Rotate** button to finish the rotation algorithm settings and apply the rotation to the image. Now all you have to do is to **export** the image to the **NetBeansProjects/JavaFXGame/src** folder as **gamequad1bird1.png**. Then we can go into the Java **loadImageAssets()** method and test the new texture map by changing the **diffuse21** map to reference this image, instead of the default one. (We're doing this temporarily so that we can see how it looks when rendered onto the 3D game board quadrant.)

Open NetBeans 9 and the JavaFXGame project. Then open the loadImageAssets() method body by using the plus (+) icon in the margin and temporarily edit the diffuse21 texture used for the orange game board quadrant to reference the **gamequad1bird1.png** file you just created using the following Java statement, which is also shown in Figure 18-10 highlighted in yellow and blue:

```
...
diffuse21 = new Image("/gamequad1bird1.png", 512, 512, true, true, true);
...
```

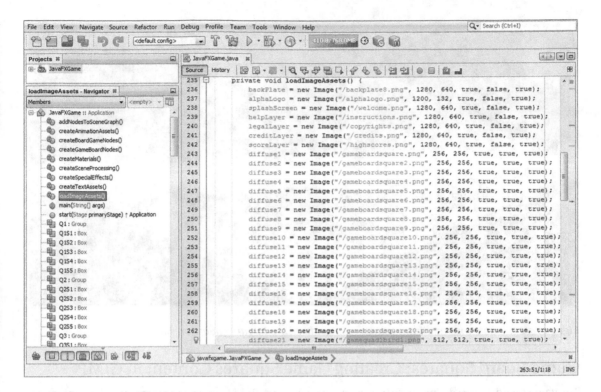

Figure 18-10. *Set the diffuse21 Image object to temporarily reference the gamequad1bird1.png texture map you created*

Now all we need to do is to test the new code to see how the game board looks when it lands on the Animal (orange) quadrant when the 3D spinner randomly selected this game board quadrant (topic) for the player to answer.

This might take a number of spin attempts as the Random class's random object (random number generator engine) is actually quite effective at providing a random game board quadrant result on each subsequent spin of your 3D spinner.

Use a **Run ➤ Project** work process to spin the spinner until quadrant 1 is selected, as shown in Figure 18-11.

Figure 18-11. *The parrot quadrant texture map rendered on the game board surface*

Game Board Squares: Creating Game Squares Content in GIMP

The game board square definitions conform to the quadrant definition, giving the player five different topics relating to the quadrant category to choose from. The player gets to decide their own fate (question) after the game board random spin picks their category for them and randomly loads the squares with content for the topic. Open the second (256-pixel) texture map file we worked on with the game board square template, shown open in Figure 18-12 (third tab). Also open the Pexels.com image and the 2160-pixel square region we are going to use to represent the parrot. The first thing we need to do is to scale a 2160-pixel image down to **192** pixels to fit inside the color area. Since the perimeter is 32 pixels (**256 − (2 × 32) = 192** pixels for the center area in both dimensions), use an **Image ➤ Scale Image** work process to scale the image down to 192 pixels, as shown on the bottom left of Figure 18-12.

Figure 18-12. *This time scale your 2160-pixel image to 192 pixels so it perfectly fits inside your game board squares*

Next, use the **View ➤ Zoom ➤ 100%** (called the Actual Pixels view mode) menu sequence, "normalize" the image that you're looking at, and then undertake the same "centering in transparency" work process as we did for the quadrant by using an **Image ➤ Canvas Size** menu sequence. Expand and **center** the canvas back to **256** pixels to match the game board square texture map size, as shown in Figure 18-13, so that the image will fit your texture map perfectly.

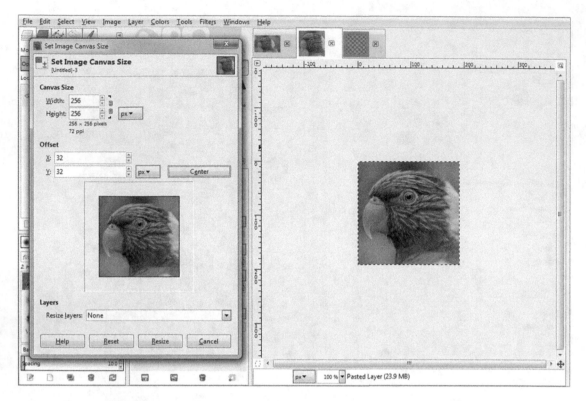

Figure 18-13. *Resize the canvas to 256 pixels and center the 192-pixel image inside the 32 pixels of transparency to center*

Use the **Select ➤ All** menu sequence and then the **Edit ➤ Copy** menu sequence to copy both the transparent 32-pixel boundary and the interior 192-pixel image data into your OS Clipboard. (Yes, the Clipboard is actually part of your operating system, so you can cut or copy and paste data between all of your different running applications.)

Select the 256-pixel game board square texture compositing tab and the layer underneath the game board square layer and use the **Edit ➤ Paste as Layer** menu sequence to paste the image under the red borders. Note that in this case you could also paste the layer on top of the game board square edge color layer; because we are using all straight lines in the composited layers, each layer abuts the other "pixel for pixel" mathematically so that there are zero overlapping pixels, which was not the case in our circular quadrant composite.

I'm going to save this texture map file using a different name, **gameboardsquarecontent1.xcf**, so that it contains only the images and edge decoration for the first game board square. Eventually there will be 20 of these XCF files, one for each of the Q1S1 through Q4S5 gameBoard Node quadrant children.

As we add content, these will accumulate in size evenly, and you will not end up with one unwieldy file that you have to deal with. This approach will keep your pro Java 9 game development work process far more organized.

Note that the screenshot in Figure 18-14 still uses the **Pro_Java_9_Games_Development_Texture_Maps4** XCF file from Chapter 13, which covered 3D primitive shader and texture mapping concepts and Java coding.

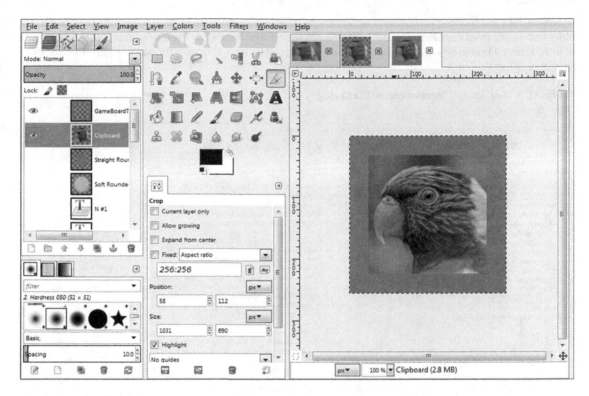

Figure 18-14. *Select the 256 texture map composite tab, select the layer under the red square, and select Edit ➤ Paste as Layer*

Later during this chapter, we will generate the 20 game board square content generation XCF files that will accumulate digital image content that the Java code will eventually select from for each game board square that the initial random spin selects for gameplay (i.e., the five squares attached to the randomly selected quadrant). This approach allows us to randomize the quadrant as well as the content for each of the quadrant's game board squares.

Finally, let's use the GIMP **File ➤ Export As** menu sequence and save this new diffuse texture map in the /**NetBeansProjects/JavaFXGame/src** folder as **gamesquare1bird1.png**. Notice in your file manager that this texture map is less than 80KB in size, which is considerably larger than your 1KB default texture. It will always be the case that high-quality 24-bit content will add to the data footprint of the application. If you wanted to optimize this data footprint further, you should use the **Image ➤ Mode ➤ Indexed** menu sequence in GIMP to turn your image into an 8-bit indexed color image and use **Generate Optimum Palette (256 colors)** with **Floyd-Steinberg Dithering**. This will reduce gamesquare1bird1.png to **27.4KB** in size, as it is now a PNG8 image, with good-quality results.

How you name these files is important because your gameplay Java code, which we will start to write in the next chapter, will make random decision logic based on these name components. Obviously, gamesquare1 (the first part of the name) will define which gamesquare (Q1S1 through Q4S5) will be mapped. The second part is a subclassification. In this case, it's "bird" but could also be "feline" or "canine" or "bovine" and so forth. The last part is how many selections the random number generator has to select from, so if you have **bird1** through **bird5** for game board square 1, your Random object will select from 0 through 5 inclusively. In this way, as you add new content (in collections of 20, or one image subject for each game board square), you can increment your Random object's random number–generating Java code to add a new maximum random number (zero through the upper selection boundary) as you add content.

449

Next, let's test this first game board square on the 3D game board by substituting the **diffuse1** Image object reference from the blank (default) game board square texture map to the one with the image inside of it. Your Java 9 Image object instantiation (and loading) construct is shown at the top of Figure 18-15 and should look like this code:

```
diffuse1 = new Image("/gamesquare1bird1.png", 256, 256, true, true, true);
```

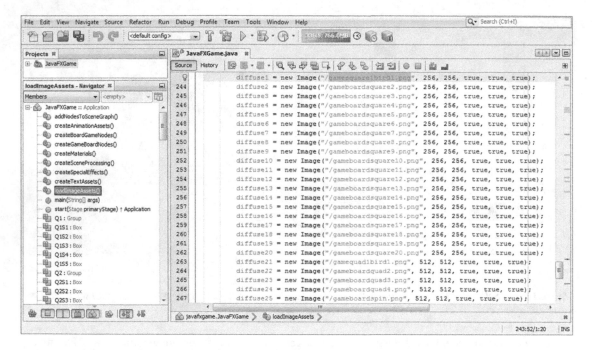

Figure 18-15. *Test the first game board square by swapping in the new texture map image in the diffuse1 instantiation*

Use a **Run ➤ Project** work process to make sure the content is facing the right direction, as shown in Figure 18-16.

Figure 18-16. *The parrot is facing out of the edge of the game board, so there's no need to rotate the image*

Since we'll need at least two image texture maps for each game board square, go to Pexels.com and find another bird image to use for the second **gamesquare1bird0.png** image. We will start our image file numbering with zero to more closely match the random number generator output. I found a great eagle (or maybe a hawk; we will research the game board content in a later chapter when making sure everything is correct), as shown in Figure 18-17.

Figure 18-17. *Paste the second bird image data into GIMP and use Scale Image to find the lowest common resolution*

Since this is a low-resolution image, we're going to use 689 (height) as your dimension for the square, so use the **Rectangle Select** tool and enter a **689, 689 Size** square at **Position 428,0,** as shown on the left of Figure 18-18.

Figure 18-18. *Create a 689x689 pixel square for the image since it's not an HD | UHD image with thousands of pixels*

Use the **Edit ➤ Copy** menu sequence to copy this data to your OS's Clipboard and then use the GIMP **File ➤ Create from Clipboard** menu sequence to paste the square image data into its own editing tab, as shown in Figure 18-19. Use the **Image ➤ Scale Image** menu sequence and scale the 689 pixel data down to **192** pixels. Then use the **Image ➤ Canvas Size** menu sequence and access the **Set Image Canvas Size** dialog, shown in Figure 18-19. Expand the image canvas size to **256** pixels square while also centering the image data in the middle of transparency by using the Center button in the dialog. Remember to select Resize Layers All in the Layers drop-down or right-click to invoke Layer to Image Size after the Resize operation has been applied to the image.

Figure 18-19. *Scale 689 pixels to 192 pixels and then use Set Image Canvas Size to add your 32-pixel transparent perimeter*

Next, use your **Select ➤ All** and **Edit ➤ Copy** menu sequences to select the image and transparency data; then click the game board square 1 texture map tab (the first tab) and click the layer underneath the game board color square. Then use the **Edit ➤ Paste as Layer** menu sequence and paste this second bird image into your composite, as shown in Figure 18-20. You can see the result of the operation from Figure 18-19 in the preview icon for the third tab at the top-right corner of Figure 18-20.

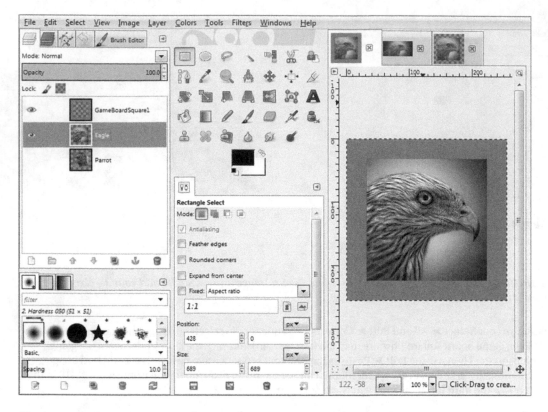

Figure 18-20. *Paste your 256-pixel image plus transparency under your GameBoardSquare1 edge coloring texture layer*

GIMP does a pretty good job of showing you visually what is going on in your work process if you look at its UI closely. You can also customize the UI by choosing different preview icon sizes and naming the layers with your own informative (descriptive) text labels.

To change the layer icon preview size, which I'm going to do a bit later in the chapter, use the **tiny arrow** at the top right of the Layers palette, next to your Brush Editor tab and above the Mode (Normal) drop-down selector arrow. You can select **Preview Size ➤ Tiny** through **Preview Size ➤ Gigantic**, giving you eight different icon size choices.

Now that you have created your 192-pixel game board square insert, as shown in Figure 18-20, you'll need to use an **Edit ➤ Undo** work process to get back to the 689x689 original image square so that you can create a game board quadrant version for each game board square. We'll be doing that next so we can create the quadrant texture.

Once a player selects one of the five game board squares in the randomly selected quadrant, your Java code (eventually) will put the selected question image into the game board quadrant and ask the player questions about it.

To get back to the 689-pixel square image, select the tab in GIMP containing the square image data and use the **Edit ➤ Undo** menu sequence to undo all of your selection, canvas resizing, and image scaling operations that you previously applied to create the layer data for use in your 256-pixel game board square diffuse color texture map.

You are doing this so that you can undertake a similar work process (plus a 45-degree rotation) to create the 512-pixel quadrant texture map. This is so that when the player clicks the game board square that contains the same image, there will be a larger (decorated) version of the image content subject (question) to preview.

Each time you use **Edit ➤ Undo**, you will see GIMP re-create the previous image-editing state in the software so you can see visually when you are back to having your original 689x689 image square. If you go back too far, you will see the entire original image from Pexels.com, and since there is also an **Edit ➤ Redo** command, you can go back to the square image version just as easily! The Undo/Redo feature can be powerful for a repetitive work process like this one, where we need to create more than one texture map by using the same original image data source.

Create a second quadrant texture, shown in Figure 18-21, by resizing the 689-pixel image to 432 pixels using **Image ➤ Image Size**. Next, use the **Image ➤ Canvas Size** work process to center this image data inside the transparency by increasing Canvas Size to 512 pixels and clicking the **Center** button. Use a **Layer to Image Size** option to include the layer's transparent pixels with the image pixels and then use **Select ➤ All** and **Edit ➤ Copy** to transfer all this image and transparency data into the OS clipboard. Select a layer under the Steel Hoop layer and use **Edit ➤ Paste as Layer** to insert it.

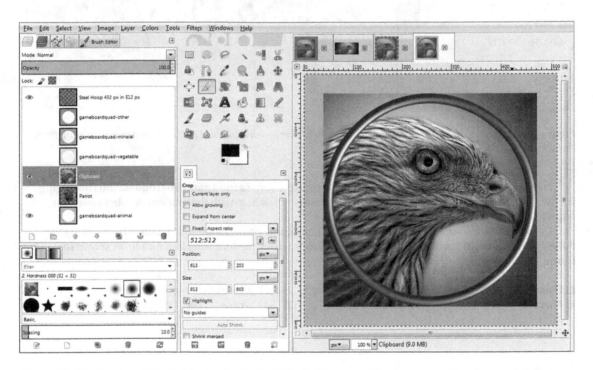

Figure 18-21. *Create a 432-pixel image inside the 512-pixel texture with a transparent border; paste it underneath the hoop*

Paste this image data under the Steel Hoop layer and rotate the Clipboard layer 45 degrees, as shown in Figure 18-22.

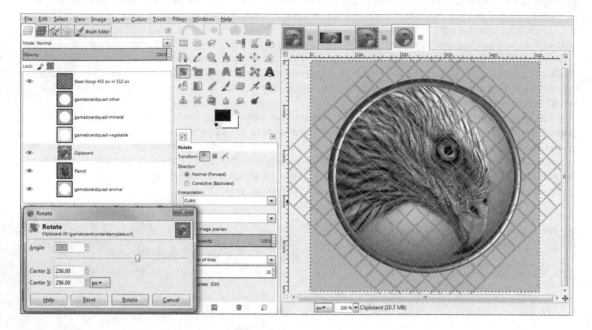

Figure 18-22. *Rotate the image layer 45 degrees after inverse-selecting and deleting corners protruding from the hoop*

Next, use the **File ➤ Export As** work process and save your second **gameboardquadrant1bird0.png** file (as I have decided to start numbering these at zero to match up with the random number generator output).

Let's preview the second game board square 1 and game board quadrant 1 textures by changing the diffuse1 and diffuse21 Image object file name references using the following Java 9 code, as shown in Figure 18-23:

```
diffuse1  = new Image("/gamesquare1bird0.png", 256, 256, true, true, true);
diffuse21 = new Image("/gamequad1bird0.png", 512, 512, true, true, true);
```

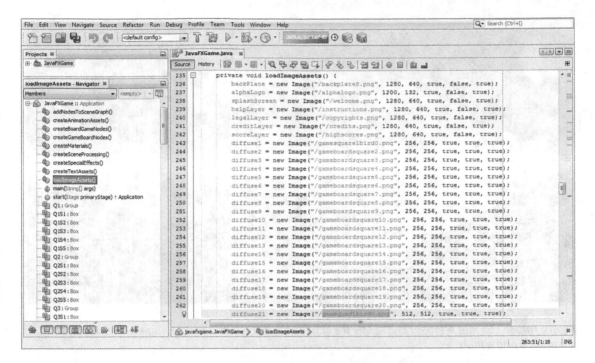

Figure 18-23. *Change the diffuse1 and diffuse21 Image object texture map reference to test the two new texture maps*

Use your **Run ➤ Project** work process and make sure the content looks good and is facing the right direction, as shown in Figure 18-24. Congratulations, you have completed 4 of your 80 texture maps that you will need to have in place in order to even test the random.nextInt(2) method call Java 9 code, which will randomly select between two images for each game board square.

Figure 18-24. *Use Run ➤ Project and render the quadrant 1 and square 1 texture maps to check the orientation and quality*

Having 4 random images per game board square to select from would require 160 images, and having 8 random images to select from for each game board square would require 320 images to be created by using the work processes that you are learning about during this chapter.

It is important to remember that game board square corner imagery will need to be rotated 45 degrees, as will all quadrant images. Some game board square side images (squares 4, 5, 9, 10, 14, 15, 19, and 20) will need to be rotated 90 degrees to "face out" correctly on the game board. We'll be looking at all of these digital imaging scenarios during this chapter, which will be a fairly long one for a nonprogramming chapter, with lots of GIMP screenshots.

That said, professional Java game development involves a whole lot more than coding, as JavaFX 9 supports a half-dozen new media genres, including 3D, Digital Illustration (SVG), Digital Imaging (PNG), Digital Audio, and more!

Now that we've created the foundation for the GameSquare1.xcf game board square 1 image composite, let's create the others, substituting a correct perimeter color value for the top decoration portion of the texture map and saving these using the same file name, while **incrementing** the number at the end by one each time, until you have all 20. After that, all you have to do is add image layers to each of these to create the board game content for the game board squares and the game board quadrants. It turns out that creating Pro Java 9 Games involves a ton of hard work!

We can use the File ➤ Save As menu sequence to save another version of the file once we change the color value of the game board square perimeter and replace the image layers with alternate content. The easiest way for you to do this with surgical accuracy is use **File ➤ Open As Layers** and open a gameboardsquare2.png texture map in a layer in the composite, use the **Eyedropper** (color picker) tool to click the perimeter color to set the **FG** foreground color to that value, select your **PaintCan** (color filler) tool, select the transparent game board square decoration layer, and click the PaintCan tool in the (red, in this case) square color area. This will fill that red color with the next (orange) color value. Then, all you have to do is to delete the layer with the default (blank) game board square color reference and use **File ➤ Save As** to save the **GameSquare2.xcf** compositing file, which is now ready for you to fill with image data to be used in and for your second board game square.

Notice in Figure 18-25 that I have made the layer image preview icons larger so that you can see what I am doing with the game board square 2 imagery, border decoration color, and so on, with greater detail. This also might be necessary if you are working on one of the new UHD (4K) displays, as everything will look a bit smaller (unless the UHD display is 60 inches or larger, that is). Most of my UHD desktop displays are 43 inches because these are affordable.

Figure 18-25. *Create a GameSquare2.xcf compositing file with a red-orange border and image assets to use for square 2*

Next, let's take a look at how you have to rotate the image content 45 degrees in GameSquare3.xcf (corner) and how you have to rotate your image content 90 degrees for GameSquare4.xcf and GameSquare5.xcf so it faces out away from the game board, just like the content in squares 1 and 2 does.

As you can see in Figure 18-26, the digital image content inside of the colored square perimeter decoration for the third (and eighth, thirteenth, and eighteenth) game board corner square will need to be rotated clockwise 45 degrees, just like the game board quadrant texture maps. This will make the digital image content face the players after each game board spin.

Figure 18-26. *Create a GameSquare3.xcf compositing file with an orange border and two image assets to use for square 3*

For this reason, instead of scaling the high-definition square image down to 192 pixels, I had to use a higher pixel resolution value, as some of the transparent pixels will be exposed by the rotation; you can see this in the second and third layer preview images in Figure 18-26 (remember, gray checkerboard squares represent transparent pixels).

You can see a tiny bit of this transparency in the corners of the primary GIMP image preview (canvas) area in Figure 18-26. I used a downsampling value of **264**, which was not perfect (268 or 272 would have been better), but this was good enough for the content development and code testing phase that we are in now, during this chapter.

I doubt if any players would even notice this handful of transparent pixels in the far corners of the texture map image, especially after it is mapped onto the game board squares. I will do a render of the board game using the Java code (as I have been doing during this chapter) once I have 20 texture maps done using these work processes for quadrant 1 of the game board. If you wanted to look ahead at this and confirm that it is hard to see any problem with the texture map for game board square 3, please feel free to do so (Figure 18-28).

Nevertheless, before you release your game, make sure all diagonal game board square corners have their image data scaled up enough (say, 272 pixels before rotation, just to make sure) so that there are no corner artifacts!

The digital image content inside of your colored square perimeter decoration for the fourth and fifth (and ninth, tenth, fourteenth, fifteenth, nineteenth, and twentieth) game board squares will need to be rotated clockwise 90 degrees, as shown in Figure 18-27, for the digital image content to face your players after each game board spin.

Figure 18-27. *The game board squares 4, 5, 9, 10, 14, 15, 19, and 20 will need to use an image rotated clockwise 90 degrees*

In this case, we will still scale your high-definition square image down to 192 pixels, add the 64 extra pixels around the perimeter (32 when centered), and, as you can see in the second and third layer preview images in Figure 18-27, use the **Layer ➤ Transform ➤ Rotate 90° Clockwise** menu sequence. Once you have five texture maps created, you will reference them in your loadImageAssets() method and use the **Run ➤ Project** work process to test them to see how they map onto the quadrant 1 game board square child elements, as shown in Figure 18-28.

Figure 18-28. *Render six quadrant and square texture maps to check their orientation and quality*

The last thing that I am going to do is to change the Image object references for diffuse6 through diffuse10, as well as for diffuse 22, to test how the texture maps are going to be applied to the game board squares attached to quadrant 2. This will tell me if, and how, I will need to change my image rotation values as I develop the vegetable quadrant texture maps. This is done using the work process shown in Figures 18-10, 18-15, and 18-23, and half of your diffuse texture maps will be referencing texture maps you are developing, temporarily, using your loadImageAssets() method body code. For the real board gameplay, this will be done inside event handling method bodies, interactively, based on mouse clicks by the players combined with conditional processing and random number generation.

Copy the file names referenced in diffuse1 through diffuse5 and in diffuse6 through diffuse10, respectively, and change the last number from zero to one (or vice versa, if you wish, to mix up the images used). You can see the result of the **Run ➤ Project** work process after you have completed this process at the end of the chapter, in Figure 18-29.

Figure 18-29. Add the quadrant 1 texture maps to the quadrant 2 Java code and test the texture map orientation

Figure 18-28 shows six diffuse texture maps rendered on the game board using a **Run ➤ Project** work process.

As you can see in Figure 18-29, you will need to adjust the work process that you learned during this chapter (as far as the rotate value) for each quadrant of the game board. As long as you test your texture maps as you go along, as you learned during the chapter, this shouldn't be a problem whatsoever and will give you some practice with GIMP.

You will get a lot of practice with the work processes described during this chapter while creating your own custom digital image content. GIMP is an amazing software package with a new version coming out soon that meets, and in some cases exceeds, features found in expensive digital image compositor software packages!

Summary

In this eighteenth chapter, we learned more about the work processes in GIMP that are needed to create the massive amount of game content that we will need to create a professional-level educational game for preschool children, the autistic, and the learning impaired. I showed you the work process to complete enough content for the first quadrant to be able to develop the random content selection Java code that we will be developing in the next chapter. You can then use this same work process to develop the content for your other three game board quadrants.

You learned about how to get free-for-commercial-use content from Pexels.com, how to copy that to the OS clipboard, and how to use the **Create ➤ From Clipboard** feature to open it in a tab in GIMP. You learned how to make square image data for use in game board quadrant and squares texture maps, as well as how to center it, crop it, and rotate it.

In Chapter 19, we are going to actually develop the Java code to implement more gameplay and the game content that you learned how to create during this chapter so that we can make some progress toward finishing your MouseEvent handling code (during Chapter 19) for the game board squares and game board quadrants.

CHAPTER 19

■ ■ ■

Game Content Engine: AI Logic with Random Content Selection Methods

Now that you have your game board animated and randomly selecting a quadrant on each click of the 3D spinner UI element, we need to figure out how to **track** these spins in some way that will **consistently** tell us which quadrant we have landed on. That way, we can map the correct diffuse texture maps onto that quadrant's game board squares. We will do this using simple math, using **int** (integers) no less, as the **360** degrees in a circle and the **90** degrees in a quadrant are all **evenly divisible**. This will be a fun chapter, as **AI** can often be coded using compact Java code! A lot of thinking about logic will be involved with some testing to refine the values once an approach has been determined.

During the chapter, we will create two new int (integer) variables: **spinDeg** for spin degrees, which will be an **accumulator** (or total) of the rotational degrees that have been spun by the players, and **quadrantLanding**, which will hold the latest result of a simple yet powerful calculation that will always tell us what quadrant the latest spin landed on.

We'll create six new methods including a **calculateQuadrantLanding()** method to ascertain what the current quadrant is, a **resetTextureMaps()** method to reset the game board square texture maps to their defaults before each new spin, and **populateQuadrantOne()** through **populateQuadrantFour()** to hold random number generation and the conditional if() processing that picks the mixture of game board square content for each of the player's random spins.

Coding a Random Spin Tracker: Remainder Operator

To get the result of the latest quadrant that a player has landed on after a spin, we need to track the percentage after the whole number of spins, especially as we are spinning three times plus the offset. So, for 45 + 1080 in if() condition 1, this will be Quadrant One. For 45 + 1170 in if() condition 2, this will be Quadrant Two. For 45 + 1260 in if() condition 3, this will be Quadrant Three. For if() condition 4, this will be 45 + 1350, for Quadrant Four. However, for subsequent spins, this will not always be the same offset starting at 45 degrees, so we need to keep a **spinDeg** total variable and add each spin angle to get a total, which we can divide by 360 to get the full rotations and then use the remainder % operand in Java to get the angle rotation past the full turns that the game board quadrant has landed on. The equation looks something like the following in Java code:

```java
int spinDeg = 45;                        // Initialize at 45 degrees
int quadrantLanding;                     // Initialize at zero
spinDeg = spinDeg + lastSpinRotation;    // Total Spin Angle Accumulator
quadrantLanding = spinDeg % 360;         // Resting Angle Offset Calculation
```

© Wallace Jackson 2017
W. Jackson, *Pro Java 9 Games Development*, https://doi.org/10.1007/978-1-4842-0973-8_19

The **quadrantLanding** variable will always contain one of four values: **45** (pink or **other** quadrant), **135** (blue or **mineral** quadrant), **225** (green or **vegetable** quadrant), or **315** (orange or **animal** quadrant). We'll create a method called **calculateQuadrantLanding()** that we will call at the end of the MouseEvent handler that implements a random spin.

Implementing Spin Tracker Functionality: Create Empty Methods

Let's create the two integer variables and five new methods' infrastructure that we will need to hold the Java code we will be writing during this chapter. This code will track what quadrant the game board is resting on after each spin and will then handle the "population" of the game board squares with random content, which we partially (25 percent) developed in the previous chapter. I will use the quadrant 1 (orange) content to test the logic we are crafting during this chapter as I have not yet created the hundreds of image assets (six per game board square, or 120 to start) that will be needed to develop the initial code. More assets can be added later simply by incrementing the random number generator's upper **bounds** value and updating the **populateQuadrant()** method's logic. What we will be doing in this chapter will amount to a couple hundred lines of code nevertheless, so we will be making a lot of coding progress during this chapter regarding having the game randomly select content for the players to solve.

Declare an **int** named **spinDeg** at the top of your JavaFXGame class and set it equal to the **45** degrees that the game board is rotated to on startup. Also, declare a **quadrantLanding** variable initialized at **zero** (the default, so no = 0 is needed) to hold the quadrant rotation delta (45, 135, 225, or 315). Create five empty **public void** methods at the bottom of your class (you don't always have to force NetBeans to create your Java code for you). This should look like the Java statements and method constructs shown here and in light blue and yellow in Figure 19-1:

```
int spinDeg = 45;   // Gameboard is always rotated to point/corner; initialize to 45 degrees
int quadrantLanding;
...
private void calculateQuadrantLanding() {...}  // Empty Method Constructs will compile clean
private void populateQuadrantOne()      {...}
private void populateQuadrantTwo()      {...}
private void populateQuadrantThree()    {...}
private void populateQuadrantFour()     {...}
```

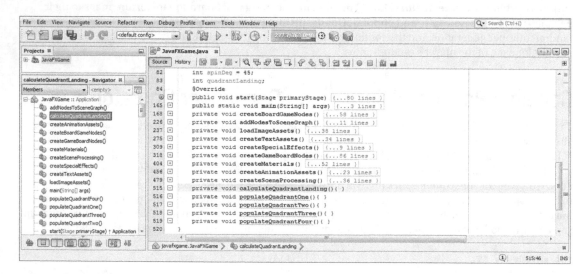

Figure 19-1. *Declare int spinDeg and quadrantLanding variables; create empty quadrant content population methods*

The first thing we'll need to do is to **add** each spin's rotation amount to the **spinDeg** "accumulator" variable. This will be done inside the **if(picked == spinner)** logic in the MouseEvent handler in the **createSceneProcessing()** method body, inside each of four **if(spin == randomNum)** conditional statements that set each random quadrant.

Inside of your **.createSceneProcessing()** method and inside of the if(picked == spinner) conditional construct, add an accumulator statement **spinDeg += degrees** for each of the four random spin if(spin == random) conditional constructs.

These should be spinDeg += 1080;, spinDeg += 1170;, spinDeg += 1260;, and spinDeg += 1350;, respectively. As you can see, the angle value passed to the **Animation** objects should also be the same value added to the **spinDeg** accumulator variable so that you have a **record** of all the **angle increments** that your user has spun.

At the bottom of the **spinner** random number picked conditional if() structure body, add the call to the **calculateQuadrantLanding()** method so that after the spin has occurred, you then calculate the offset (the quadrant) for that pick and seed (write) that integer data value into your **quadrantLanding** variable for use in your other game logic, which we will be coding later during this chapter. We will code the calculateQuadrantLanding() method next.

The Java code for the **spinDeg** accumulator and the calculateQuadrantLanding() method call should look like the following and is highlighted in blue and yellow in Figure 19-2:

```
if (picked == spinner) {

    int spin = random.nextInt(4);        // Random Number Generator determines next quadrant

    if (spin == 0) {
        rotGameBoard.setByAngle(1080);
        rotSpinner.setByAngle(-1080);
        spinDeg += 1080;                 // Add 1080 to the spinDeg total
    }

    if (spin == 1) {
        rotGameBoard.setByAngle(1170);
        rotSpinner.setByAngle(-1170);
        spinDeg += 1170;                 // Add 1170 to the spinDeg total
    }

    if (spin == 2) {
        rotGameBoard.setByAngle(1260);
        rotSpinner.setByAngle(-1260);
        spinDeg += 1260;                 // Add 1260 to the spinDeg total
    }

    if (spin == 3) {
        rotGameBoard.setByAngle(1350);
        rotSpinner.setByAngle(-1350);
        spinDeg += 1350;                 // Add 1350 to the spinDeg total
    }

    rotGameBoard.play();
    rotSpinner.play();

    calculateQuadrantLanding();          // Call Method to calculate quadrantLanding variable
}
```

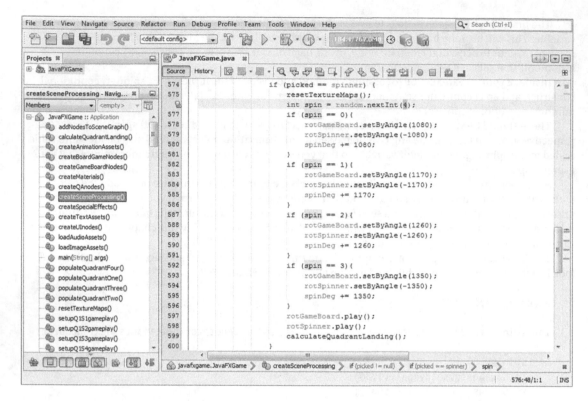

Figure 19-2. Add a spinDeg accumulator to your spinner UI mouse click conditional if() logic to track where the quadrant is

Next, open your empty calculateQuadrantLanding and add the quadrantLanding variable and an equals sign to set up the equation we are about to define on the right side of the equals operator.

Since the **spinDeg** accumulator is what we're going to break down into full spins plus the quarter spin offset, type the **spinDeg** variable next, which will always hold an accumulated "record" of every spin the players have made.

To find the latest quadrant that has been landed on, simply remove all full spins from this accumulated total value by dividing it by 360 (the number of degrees in one full rotation) to keep (extract) just the incremental amount beyond the full spins, which will indicate the quadrant that the latest spin has landed the player on.

Fortunately, the Java language has an operator called a **remainder** operator that will do exactly this for you, saving you from having to construct any complex equations. This remainder operator uses a **% (percentage) sign** after a variable that you want to extract the remainder from, and after the % sign goes the number you want to divide into the (in this case, accumulator) variable, which in this case is the **number of degrees in a full rotation** (360). If you use pseudocode, this would be **TotalSpinDegreesAccumulated % OneFullSpin = DegreesRemaining**. The Java code for your **calculateQuadrantLanding()** method should look like the following and is shown at the bottom of Figure 19-3:

```java
private void calculateQuadrantLanding() {
    quadrantLanding = spinDeg % 360;      // Remainder of spinDeg accumulator after all 360 spins
    System.out.println(quadrantLanding); // Print Angle Offset to Output Pane for Debugging Use
}
```

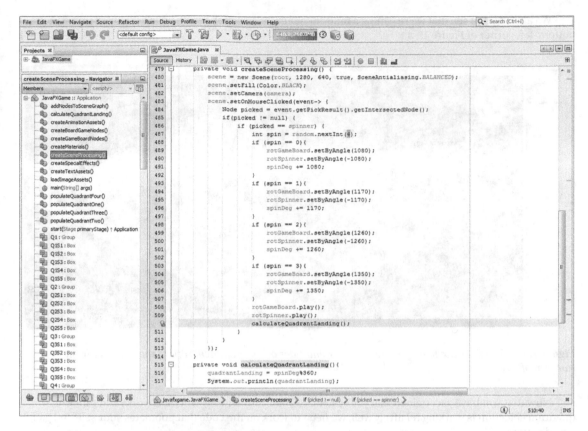

Figure 19-3. *Add a calculateQuadrantLanding() method and code method body and call calculateQuadrantLanding() at the end of each MouseEvent*

Let's use a **Run ➤ Project** work process and see whether the Output Pane is now telling us what quadrant the spin is going to land on. This is information that you will eventually want to hide from the players so that their "destination" quadrant is not revealed before the game board stops spinning, which would ruin the anticipation and gameplay fun.

What I did to create the screenshot in Figure 19-4 was to position (and resize) the NetBeans 9 Output Pane behind (and to the left of) the game window so that the **println** output of the angle delta (remainder) is visible. While I am testing the i3D spinner UI and game board spin cycles, this println output notification triggers to make sure that they now land randomly and accurately on different colored quadrants for random gameplay (like a roll of the dice, only a spin of the board).

A calculated spin angle offset shows up right when you click the spinner (computers are fast these days), so you know in advance what quadrant the game board is going to land on. For now, we are just trying to get the game board to land on a different quadrant with each random spin and to see what angle values are ending up inside of the quadrantLanding variable so we can test for these in our future code. We also want to spin a bunch of times to make sure that these quadrant angle offset values are the same exact four integer numbers every time and that they do not vary, as we only want to test for four quadrantLanding angle offset values in our code. Any other values in this variable will "break" this code. Fortunately, everything involving quadrants and rotation involves even numbers!

As far as which angle offset value belongs to each color quadrant, we have not tested and refined the Java code to that point yet. This is part of what we are going to be doing in this chapter, to make sure we know exactly what is going on between our Java 9 game code and the i3D game board spin quadrant rotation landing visual result.

We also want to see that we're getting a random quadrant selection result, which is circled in red in the bottom-left corner of Figure 19-4.

Figure 19-4. *Test the code to make sure that the remainder output represents one of the four quadrant rotation offsets*

Now that you have ascertained that your calculateQuadrantLanding() method works and random quadrant selection is working relatively well, we need to work on the code that populates your selected game board squares.

Populating Quadrants After a Spin: OnFinished() Event Handling

Now that we have modified your MouseEvent handling construct in the createSceneProcessing() method, let's open up the **createAnimationAssets()** method and add some more event handling in the rotGameBoard Animation object so that we can trigger some code upon the completion of the Animation object's rotation cycle to populate the game board squares. The reason we're doing this is because if we populate the game board squares **before** the spin, players will know where the spinning game board is going to stop! Also, I wanted to show you how to "wire up" an Animation object so that it can trigger other events and code constructs once it finishes playing, which is important for pro Java 9 games development, as you might well imagine. We will start by implementing an empty event handling infrastructure that we will use to hold conditional if() Java logic telling the game board squares how to populate themselves using a method call to one of four populateQuadrant() methods, populateQuadrantOne() through populateQuadrantFour(). This is where we have to initially speculate on which angle offset value in quadrantLanding should equate to each of the game board quadrant color spaces (orange or animal, green or vegetable, blue or mineral, and pink or other topic).

The Java 9 code needed to create your initial (empty) **OnFinished** event handler **lambda expression** is as follows; it is also highlighted in red, yellow, and blue in Figure 19-5:

```
rotGameBoard.setOnFinished( event-> { ... } );
```

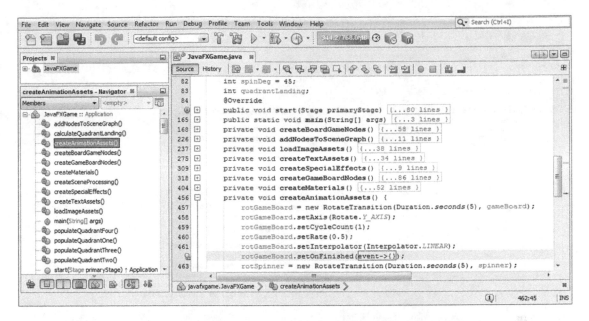

Figure 19-5. *The empty createAnimationAssets() setOnFinished() event handling infrastructure for the rotGameBoard Animation*

Next, let's code your rotGameBoard.setOnFinished() event handling method body using a series of conditional if() statements. Each one of these will evaluate one of the four quadrantLanding angle offset integer values and will "wire" that value up to a method call to one of these four populateQuadrant() methods located at the end of the class.

These populateQuadrant() methods will then do the work of randomly selecting from your different content images for each game board square, of which I currently have fifteen (three for each of the five attached game board squares for quadrant 1). Therefore, we'll have a **random.nextInt(3)** method, which will select from the three image assets for each square, set the diffuse Image object to reference the selected digital image asset, and then set the Shader for that game board square to reload that Image object into memory for that texture map.

To test this, we will need to code at least one of these populateQuadrant() methods; the logical one is the populateQuadrantOne() method since we have the game board quadrant content (game board squares 1 through 5) created. After we test this .setOnFinished() event handler to see whether these angle offsets do indeed take us to the correct quadrant, we will then create the populateQuadrantTwo() through populateQuadrantFour() method body code by (temporarily) utilizing content from quadrant 1 as "dummy" content, used for code testing purposes only.

Your new .setOnFinished() event handling method body will initially start with **45** degrees and progress through **315** degrees; it should look like the following code, as shown highlighted in blue and yellow in Figure 19-6:

```
rotGameBoard.setOnFinished(event-> {
    if (quadrantLanding == 45)  { populateQuadrantOne();   }
    if (quadrantLanding == 135) { populateQuadrantTwo();   }
    if (quadrantLanding == 225) { populateQuadrantThree(); }
    if (quadrantLanding == 315) { populateQuadrantFour();  }
});
```

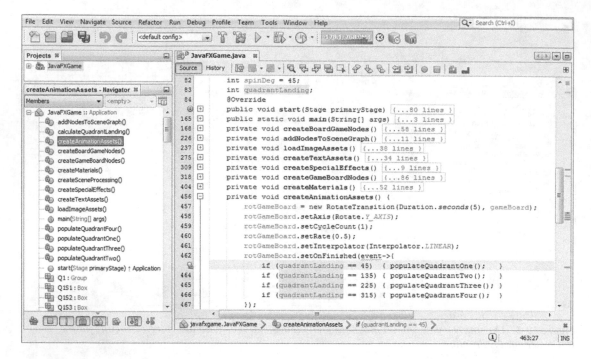

Figure 19-6. *In the .setOnFinished() event handler, check the quadrantLanding variable for degree offsets to determine quadrant*

For your first populateQuadrantOne() method body, you will have sections for each of your five game board squares. The first statement will generate your random number pick for that square, the second three will evaluate it, and the last will set the Shader to that diffuse color map texture using the .setDiffuesMap(Image object) method call. The Java statements for this method body should look like the following, as highlighted in Figure 19-7:

```
int pickS1 = random.nextInt(3);
if (pickS1 == 0){diffuse1 = new Image("/gamesquare1bird0.png", 256, 256, true, true, true);}
if (pickS1 == 1){diffuse1 = new Image("/gamesquare1bird1.png", 256, 256, true, true, true);}
if (pickS1 == 2){diffuse1 = new Image("/gamesquare1bird2.png", 256, 256, true, true, true);}
Shader1.setDiffuseMap(diffuse1);
int pickS2 = random.nextInt(3);
if (pickS2 == 0){diffuse2 = new Image("/gamesquare2bird0.png", 256, 256, true, true, true);}
if (pickS2 == 1){diffuse2 = new Image("/gamesquare2bird1.png", 256, 256, true, true, true);}
if (pickS2 == 2){diffuse2 = new Image("/gamesquare2bird2.png", 256, 256, true, true, true);}
Shader2.setDiffuseMap(diffuse2);
int pickS3 = random.nextInt(3);
if (pickS3 == 0){diffuse3 = new Image("/gamesquare3bird0.png", 256, 256, true, true, true);}
if (pickS3 == 1){diffuse3 = new Image("/gamesquare3bird1.png", 256, 256, true, true, true);}
if (pickS3 == 2){diffuse3 = new Image("/gamesquare3bird2.png", 256, 256, true, true, true);}
Shader3.setDiffuseMap(diffuse3);
```

```
int pickS4 = random.nextInt(3);
if (pickS4 == 0){diffuse4 = new Image("/gamesquare4bird0.png", 256, 256, true, true, true);}
if (pickS4 == 1){diffuse4 = new Image("/gamesquare4bird1.png", 256, 256, true, true, true);}
if (pickS4 == 2){diffuse4 = new Image("/gamesquare4bird2.png", 256, 256, true, true, true);}
Shader4.setDiffuseMap(diffuse4);
int pickS5 = random.nextInt(3);
if (pickS5 == 0){diffuse5 = new Image("/gamesquare5bird0.png", 256, 256, true, true, true);}
if (pickS5 == 1){diffuse5 = new Image("/gamesquare5bird1.png", 256, 256, true, true, true);}
if (pickS5 == 2){diffuse5 = new Image("/gamesquare5bird2.png", 256, 256, true, true, true);}
Shader5.setDiffuseMap(diffuse5);
```

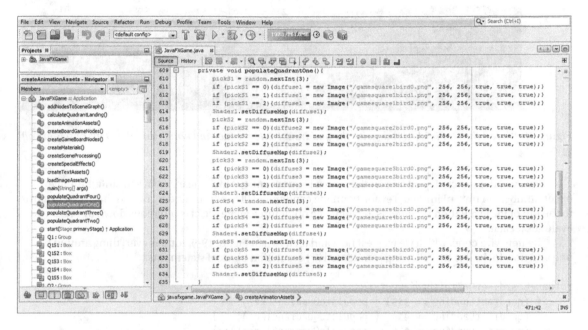

Figure 19-7. *Create the image load and texture map change logic in the populateQuadrantOne() method based on random number selected*

Next, use your **Run ➤ Project** work process and test your code, and you will see in Figure 19-8 that the NetBeans Output Pane shows that the angle offset left in the quadrantLanding variable after the first click on the spinner UI was 45, which I would initially take to be (set in the original code) as quadrant 1, as you can see in my original code in Figure 19-6.

Figure 19-8. *Test the OnFinished code with the quadrant content code, and notice that the angle offsets are off by one*

However, the selected quadrant on the screen is **quadrant 4**, which means I have to **shift** the angle offset numbers in my onFinished() event-handling conditional if() code around by one so that 315 will move to the top of the evaluation statements, pushing the other three angle offset evaluations down by one angle evaluation each.

The new Java code, which we will test next and is shown in Figure 19-9, rotates everything around by one and now looks like the following conditional if() evaluation block of statements:

```
rotGameBoard.setOnFinished(event->{
    if (quadrantLanding == 315) { populateQuadrantOne();   }
    if (quadrantLanding == 45)  { populateQuadrantTwo();   }
    if (quadrantLanding == 135) { populateQuadrantThree(); }
    if (quadrantLanding == 225) { populateQuadrantFour();  }
});
```

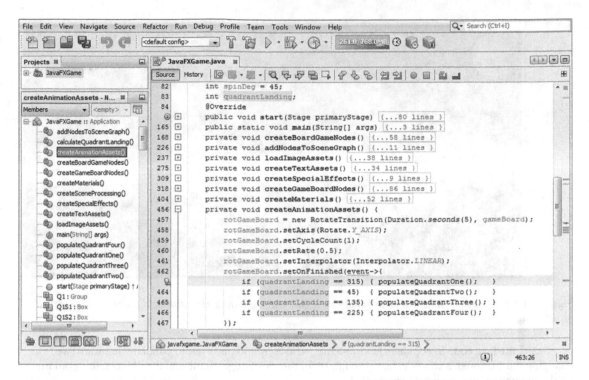

Figure 19-9. *Shift the angle offset evaluation down (over) by one, bringing 315 to the top and pushing the others down*

Let's again utilize the **Run ➤ Project** work process and test this new code. When you click the spinner, the game board now stops at the orange quadrant when **315** is picked by the random number generator, as shown in Figure 19-10. Now we can move on to add code to **populateQuadrantTwo()** and continue with our testing process.

Figure 19-10. *Your logic now works, as evidenced by the Output Pane's 315 value and the correct quadrant positioning*

Select the Java code in populateQuadrantOne() and copy and paste it into populateQuadrantTwo, changing the 1 through 5 values to be 6 through 10 for the pick integer name and the object names but **not** for the file names, as is shown in Figure 19-11.

```java
int pickS6 = random.nextInt(3);
if (pickS6 == 0){diffuse6 = new Image("/gamesquare1bird0.png", 256, 256, true, true, true);}
if (pickS6 == 1){diffuse6 = new Image("/gamesquare1bird1.png", 256, 256, true, true, true);}
if (pickS6 == 2){diffuse6 = new Image("/gamesquare1bird2.png", 256, 256, true, true, true);}
Shader6.setDiffuseMap(diffuse6);
int pickS7 = random.nextInt(3);
if (pickS7 == 0){diffuse7 = new Image("/gamesquare2bird0.png", 256, 256, true, true, true);}
if (pickS7 == 1){diffuse7 = new Image("/gamesquare2bird1.png", 256, 256, true, true, true);}
if (pickS7 == 2){diffuse7 = new Image("/gamesquare2bird2.png", 256, 256, true, true, true);}
Shader7.setDiffuseMap(diffuse7);
int pickS8 = random.nextInt(3);
if (pickS8 == 0){diffuse8 = new Image("/gamesquare3bird0.png", 256, 256, true, true, true);}
if (pickS8 == 1){diffuse8 = new Image("/gamesquare3bird1.png", 256, 256, true, true, true);}
if (pickS8 == 2){diffuse8 = new Image("/gamesquare3bird2.png", 256, 256, true, true, true);}
Shader8.setDiffuseMap(diffuse8);
int pickS9 = random.nextInt(3);
if (pickS9 == 0){diffuse9 = new Image("/gamesquare4bird0.png", 256, 256, true, true, true);}
if (pickS9 == 1){diffuse9 = new Image("/gamesquare4bird1.png", 256, 256, true, true, true);}
if (pickS9 == 2){diffuse9 = new Image("/gamesquare4bird2.png", 256, 256, true, true, true);}
Shader9.setDiffuseMap(diffuse9);
int pickS10 = random.nextInt(3);
if (pickS10 == 0){diffuse10 = new Image("/gamesquare5bird0.png", 256, 256, true, true, true);}
if (pickS10 == 1){diffuse10 = new Image("/gamesquare5bird1.png", 256, 256, true, true, true);}
if (pickS10 == 2){diffuse10 = new Image("/gamesquare5bird2.png", 256, 256, true, true, true);}
Shader10.setDiffuseMap(diffuse10);
```

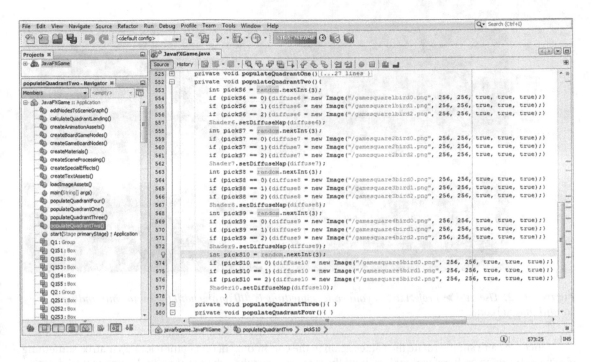

Figure 19-11. *Duplicate populateQuadrantOne code in populateQuadrantTwo and configure the squares 6 through 10*

Now let's use a **Run ➤ Project** work process and see whether the quadrants populate with the correct content now that we have put "dummy" (quadrant 1) content into the populateQuadrantTwo() method body. When we click the spinner, the code should now select a random quadrant and then populate that quadrant with content. Any visual result other than the front quadrant at the front of the game board filled with random images would mean that there is something still amiss in the code and we'd still need to continue our game development debugging process!

As you can see in Figure 19-12, the first spin of an angle offset of 45 degrees, which we know is quadrant 3 (pink or other content), is selecting the correct content, but the onFinished event handling construct is populating quadrant 2 (225 degrees angle offset) instead of the correct quadrant 3! We have some more debugging to do!

Figure 19-12. *Use Run ➤ Project to test your code; something is still wrong with the quadrantLanding conditional if() code*

Since we can't simply rotate the values again in the conditional if() evaluation lookup matrix, something else must be going on here! In thinking about the rotation, even though the values in the RotateTransform are positive, I remember from correcting the spinner direction using negative values to make it move forward that the game board is actually spinning **backward** or counterclockwise, which looks better for the game board spin anyway. Thus, I do not want to change that! This means I need to go back to the original 45, 135, 225, 315 evaluation and simply reverse that because the game board is actually spinning backward mathematically, so your correct evaluation order should be reversed to be 315 (quadrant 1), 225 (quadrant 2), 135 (quadrant 3), and then 45 (quadrant 4).

This new angle evaluation order to the populateQuadrant() method pairing should fix our problem once and for all, so let's go back into the createSceneProcessing() method body in the OnFinished() event-handling infrastructure and reorder these **quadrantLanding == angle** values to start with 315 and decrease by 90 degrees each time down to 45 degrees. You can see here that your code and thought logic must be **in sync** to successfully create your game logic!

Notice that populating these quadrants with "dummy content" allows you to better ascertain what is going on with your gameplay logic and still put in place code where later you only have to change a few characters once all of the game board content has been developed. As you can probably tell from the previous chapter, this takes as long as coding the game, possibly even longer, depending on how much content you are going to include with your game.

I'm going to try to provide at least three images (topics or questions) per game board square. However, for a professional Java 9 game, you would want to have at least nine (using a random.nextInt(9) method call) to get a more random content appearance to the content selection frequency. Since I have to write this book in a short time period, I will not be able to pull this off while also developing the gameplay logic, coding, and screenshots.

Besides trying this new .setOnFinished() event handling Java code block, I copied and pasted the Java code from the populateQuadrantOne() method body to create the populateQuadrantThree() method body and edited it to create game square content for the next round of tests. If it works, I'll do the same thing for populateQuadrantFour().

Your OnFinished() event handling conditional if() Java code, after these modifications, should look just like the following code block, which is also highlighted in yellow and light blue at the bottom of Figure 19-13:

```
rotGameBoard.setOnFinished( event-> {
    if (quadrantLanding == 315) { populateQuadrantOne();   }
    if (quadrantLanding == 225) { populateQuadrantTwo();   }
    if (quadrantLanding == 135) { populateQuadrantThree(); }
    if (quadrantLanding == 45)  { populateQuadrantFour();  }
});
```

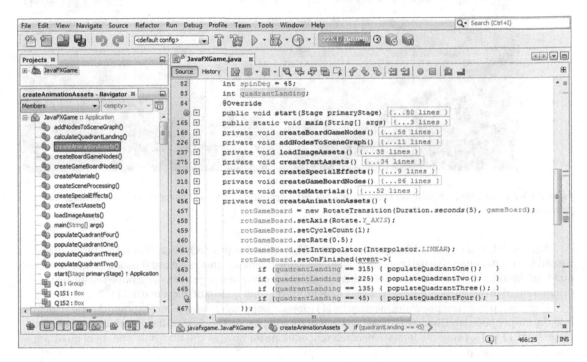

Figure 19-13. *Reorder the angle offset if() statements so that they evaluate to the reverse direction of the game board spin*

As you can see in Figure 19-14, when I selected **Run ➤ Project** to test the code, the quadrant and content are correct, even though the rotation of the Quadrant 1 content is not correct for the other quadrants.

Figure 19-14. *The new angle offset evaluation code now provides the correct game board quadrant landing position*

Next, let's finish creating the populateQuadrantThree() and populateQuadrantFour() methods so that we can see digital image (visual) content in all of the game board squares as we test the game board spin and quadrant landing code; as you have seen, there is still game content design work to be done regarding the orientation of the game board square images depending on what quadrant they are used in.

Copy and paste your populateQuadrantTwo() (or your populateQuadrantOne() content) code structure into the empty populateQuadrantThree() method body and change the pickS, diffuse, and Shader values to range from 11 to 15. Leave the Image object references alone for now, as you have only one set of quadrant Image assets created.

Copy and paste your populateQuadrantTwo() (or your populateQuadrantOne() content) code structure into the empty populateQuadrantFour() method body and change the pickS, diffuse, and Shader values to range from 16 to 20. Leave the Image object references alone for now, as you have only one set of quadrant Image assets created.

Figure 19-15 shows the Java if() constructs for populateQuadrantFour(), which look like this Java code:

```
int pickS16 = random.nextInt(3);
if (pickS16 == 0){diffuse16 = new Image("/gamesquare1bird0.png", 256, 256, true, true, true);}
if (pickS16 == 1){diffuse16 = new Image("/gamesquare1bird1.png", 256, 256, true, true, true);}
if (pickS16 == 2){diffuse16 = new Image("/gamesquare1bird2.png", 256, 256, true, true, true);}
Shader16.setDiffuseMap(diffuse16);
```

```
int pickS17 = random.nextInt(3);
if (pickS17 == 0){diffuse17 = new Image("/gamesquare2bird0.png", 256, 256, true, true, true);}
if (pickS17 == 1){diffuse17 = new Image("/gamesquare2bird1.png", 256, 256, true, true, true);}
if (pickS17 == 2){diffuse17 = new Image("/gamesquare2bird2.png", 256, 256, true, true, true);}
Shader17.setDiffuseMap(diffuse17);

int pickS18 = random.nextInt(3);
if (pickS18 == 0){diffuse18 = new Image("/gamesquare3bird0.png", 256, 256, true, true, true);}
if (pickS18 == 1){diffuse18 = new Image("/gamesquare3bird1.png", 256, 256, true, true, true);}
if (pickS18 == 2){diffuse18 = new Image("/gamesquare3bird2.png", 256, 256, true, true, true);}
Shader18.setDiffuseMap(diffuse18);

int pickS19 = random.nextInt(3);
if (pickS19 == 0){diffuse19 = new Image("/gamesquare4bird0.png", 256, 256, true, true, true);}
if (pickS19 == 1){diffuse19 = new Image("/gamesquare4bird1.png", 256, 256, true, true, true);}
if (pickS19 == 2){diffuse19 = new Image("/gamesquare4bird2.png", 256, 256, true, true, true);}
Shader19.setDiffuseMap(diffuse19);

int pickS20 = random.nextInt(3);
if (pickS20 == 0){diffuse20 = new Image("/gamesquare5bird0.png", 256, 256, true, true, true);}
if (pickS20 == 1){diffuse20 = new Image("/gamesquare5bird1.png", 256, 256, true, true, true);}
if (pickS20 == 2){diffuse20 = new Image("/gamesquare5bird2.png", 256, 256, true, true, true);}
Shader20.setDiffuseMap(diffuse20);
```

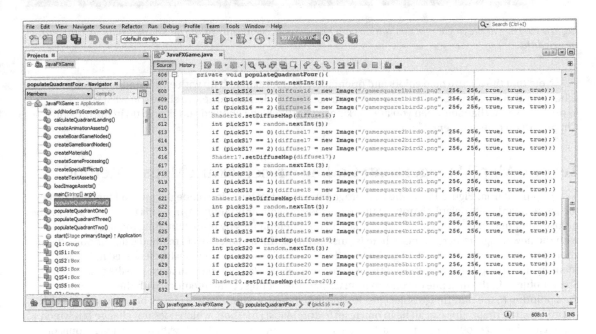

Figure 19-15. *Copy the populateQuadrantOne code to populateQuadrantThree and populateQuadrantFour and modify it*

Use a **Run ➤ Project** work process, and click the spinner UI multiple times to test the code thoroughly. What you should see is that each time the game board lands on a correct quadrant, as is specified in the NetBeans 9 Output Pane, the game board squares will populate the correct quadrant with animal imagery, as shown in Figure 19-16.

Figure 19-16. *All the angle spin evaluations are now correct, eventually filling all Shaders with texture map image data*

Note that the texture map colors and orientation do not yet match up with each quadrant's color scheme and orientation, but then again, you can use this rendering preview to show you what you need to do to make this happen when you are working in GIMP, which I showed you how to do in the previous Chapter 18 on game content.

Texture Map Management: Coding a resetTextureMaps() Method

As you can tell from Figure 19-16, the next programming task at hand is to code the method that will **reset** the game board to its default (empty) state before the next spin animation begins. This is done by setting the diffuse color map digital image references back to their **default** files by re-instantiating the Image objects with the new image asset reference (there is currently no setImageReference() method call, although there should be). This will force Java 9 to **garbage collect** (to re-allocate) the previously referenced image in memory and to replace it with the new image data referenced. You also have to reference the associated Shader object, in the next line of code, to re-insert the Shader object into memory, with the new reference data pointing to the new Image object just loaded into memory. Since we will always be using your default (blank) texture maps, this can all be in one resetTextureMaps() method, which does not change but which, when called, resets your 3D game board squares to their default unpopulated (with digital image topic or question content) state, before each subsequent random game board spin begins (that is, before the rest of the statements in your **if(pressed == spinner)** conditional if() construct are processed).

Go back into your createSceneProcessing() method and add a **resetTextureMaps();** method call at the top of your **if (picked == spinner) { ... }** construct, as shown in Figure 19-17. NetBeans will pop up a helper menu offering to code the method body for you, so select and double-click the **Create method "resetTextureMaps()" in javafxgame.JavaFXGame** option, which is shown in blue in the middle of Figure 19-17.

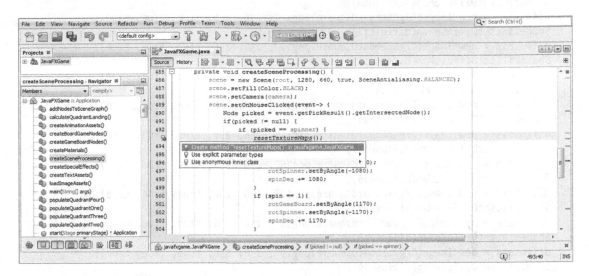

Figure 19-17. *Add the resetTextureMaps() method call to the MouseClick event handling code; press Alt+Enter to have NetBeans create it*

Creating this new method body is relatively easy using the copy-and-paste programming technique. All you have to do is to type the new Image instantiation Java statement referencing gameboardsquare.png and type the new Shader1 statement setting the setDiffuseMap() method to the diffuse1 Image object. After that, all you have to do is to select those two lines of code, copy them 19 more times underneath the first two lines of code, change 1 to the numbers 2 through 20, and add those numbers to the end of the PNG file names, which will reference the different color default game board square texture map assets.

This will result in the following 40 Java programming statements, which are also shown in light blue and yellow in Figure 19-18:

```
private void resetTextureMaps() {
    diffuse1 = new Image("/gameboardsquare.png", 256, 256, true, true, true);
    Shader1.setDiffuseMap(diffuse1);
    Diffuse2 = new Image("/gameboardsquare2.png", 256, 256, true, true, true);
    Shader2.setDiffuseMap(diffuse2);
    Diffuse3 = new Image("/gameboardsquare.png3", 256, 256, true, true, true);
    Shader3.setDiffuseMap(diffuse3);
    diffuse4 = new Image("/gameboardsquare.png4", 256, 256, true, true, true);
    Shader4.setDiffuseMap(diffuse4);
    Diffuse5 = new Image("/gameboardsquare.png5", 256, 256, true, true, true);
    Shader5.setDiffuseMap(diffuse5);
    Diffuse6 = new Image("/gameboardsquare.png6", 256, 256, true, true, true);
    Shader6.setDiffuseMap(diffuse6);
    Diffuse7 = new Image("/gameboardsquare.png7", 256, 256, true, true, true);
    Shader7.setDiffuseMap(diffuse7);
```

```
Diffuse8 = new Image("/gameboardsquare.png8", 256, 256, true, true, true);
Shader8.setDiffuseMap(diffuse8);
Diffuse9 = new Image("/gameboardsquare.png9", 256, 256, true, true, true);
Shader9.setDiffuseMap(diffuse9);
diffuse10 = new Image("/gameboardsquare.png10", 256, 256, true, true, true);
Shader10.setDiffuseMap(diffuse10);
diffuse11 = new Image("/gameboardsquare.png11", 256, 256, true, true, true);
Shader11.setDiffuseMap(diffuse11);
diffuse12 = new Image("/gameboardsquare.png12", 256, 256, true, true, true);
Shader12.setDiffuseMap(diffuse12);
diffuse13 = new Image("/gameboardsquare.png13", 256, 256, true, true, true);
Shader13.setDiffuseMap(diffuse13);
diffuse14 = new Image("/gameboardsquare.png14", 256, 256, true, true, true);
Shader14.setDiffuseMap(diffuse14);
diffuse15 = new Image("/gameboardsquare.png15", 256, 256, true, true, true);
Shader15.setDiffuseMap(diffuse15);
diffuse16 = new Image("/gameboardsquare.png16", 256, 256, true, true, true);
Shader16.setDiffuseMap(diffuse16);
diffuse17 = new Image("/gameboardsquare.png17", 256, 256, true, true, true);
Shader17.setDiffuseMap(diffuse17);
diffuse18 = new Image("/gameboardsquare.png18", 256, 256, true, true, true);
Shader18.setDiffuseMap(diffuse18);
diffuse19 = new Image("/gameboardsquare.png19", 256, 256, true, true, true);
Shader19.setDiffuseMap(diffuse19);
Diffuse20 = new Image("/gameboardsquare.png20", 256, 256, true, true, true);
Shader20.setDiffuseMap(diffuse20);
}
```

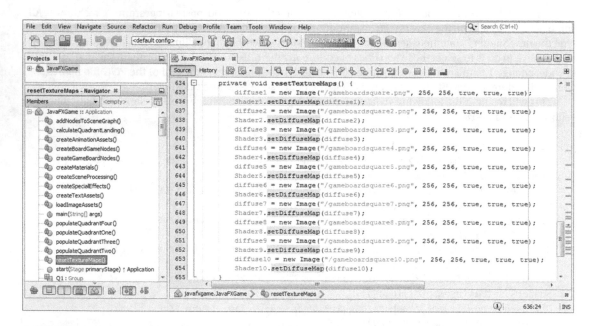

Figure 19-18. *Re-create the default Shader and diffuse statements for the blank game board in the body of resetTextureMaps()*

Note that I am showing only half of the statements in Figure 19-18 because my HD display could not show all of them and still show (contain) the NetBeans IDE UI. It's time to upgrade to a 4K UHD display I guess!

Use a **Run ➤ Project** work process, seen in Figure 19-19, to test the code we've developed so far thoroughly. It works consistently.

Figure 19-19. *As you see in the Output Pane, subsequent random spinner clicks now populate the correct quadrant*

We've added some more of the core gameplay functionality that will be needed to control and randomize your game board square content and the gameplay during this chapter, and we've set up your Java code so that it is easy to add more content by simply incrementing random.nextInt(**bounds**) (bound variable) every time you add a of square content imagery. This makes our game easily extensible, which is important for the professional Java 9 game design.

You'll also need to add if() statements (or, more likely, change to using Java **case** statements if you have more than two or three content options to select from) to add the code logic that allows the game to randomly select from your different image options for a given square. We'll be enhancing this code in the next chapter as we continue to refine the populateQuadrant() methods with their own (nondummy) content and add the ability for the players to click a game square and populate the selected content into the current quadrant using the quadrant texture maps that we developed already during Chapter 17. At that point, we will be ready to add gameplay directly relating to a game square content selection, challenging our game player's body of knowledge and educating them in the process.

Notice that we are still at less than **700** lines of Java code with 17 methods (an average of 39 per method), as you can see at the bottom of NetBeans in Figure 19-18 (the end of the class was line 655, before I added the last 20 Java statements, so, basically we're at 675).

Summary

In this nineteenth chapter, we learned about how to implement random selection of game board square content while implementing more gameplay code that intelligently tracks game board spins and where the quadrant will land on every spin using Java mathematic operators and simple yet powerful programming algorithms and structures. We debugged a few problems in the order of our angle offset evaluation and what populateQuadrant() method these pointed to, and we found a way to load images into memory without declaring more than two dozen game board diffuse texture images in system memory at one time. This approach allows us to add hundreds of content images to the game app without generating out-of-memory errors.

We constructed several new custom methods, including resetTextureMaps(), calculateQuadrantLanding(), populateQuadrantOne(), populateQuadrantTwo(), populateQuadrantThree(), and populateQuadrantFour().

We added more game logic to your createSceneProcessing() method MouseEvent handling logic so that on each spin, the game AI logic will now **keep track of every single spin** from game startup. This will allow us to develop an algorithm that will calculate a **landing angle** at the time of each spin, which will give the game logic the knowledge of what the current "landing quadrant" is for every spin, which is critical to all the other gameplay logic we'll develop.

We developed an elegant solution that uses only whole numbers (degrees in an angle) or int numbers (integers) that throws away the full rotations (360 degrees) and keeps only the delta (the latest quadrant angle offset) by dividing a **spinDeg** accumulator variable by 360 and keeping only the remainder angle offset (the part beyond a full 360-degree rotation) using the Java **% remainder** operator, which divides a numerator (**spinDeg** total) by a divisor (360 degrees) and places the remainder in the quadrantLanding variable on the other side of the equals (=) operator.

We developed four **populateQuadrant()** methods to hold the code that randomly selects content for each of the five game board squares attached to each quadrant. These methods can be expanded as game content is added.

We also developed a **resetTextureMaps()** method that resets the game board to a default blank state before the next spin. We saw how to "reuse" Image instantiation, referencing a different texture map. This will request Java 9 to perform **garbage collection** to reload image content memory locations, rather than having to load Image objects for every texture map for the game content into system memory, which would cause an out-of-memory error!

In Chapter 20, you are going to develop additional gameplay code infrastructure, which will handle what happens when a player clicks (selects) the game square content itself so that you can finish the MouseEvent event handling code concerning click events pertaining to the 3D spinner UI and to each of these game board squares. We'll also add Camera **Animation** objects in the next chapter so your camera object animates in closer to your board!

CHAPTER 20

■■■

Coding Gameplay: Set Up Gameplay Methods and Animated Camera View

So far you have your gameplay random quadrant selection logic coded, and you are tracking the quadrant landing for each spin. Now we need to put the bulk of the Java code into place that populates these four quadrants with the game board square random content selection for each of the five squares that are attached to any given quadrant. We also need to create the code that allows a player to select one of the topic questions by clicking an image. This will populate the quadrant with images and move the camera into position so the selected image is larger (more viewable). This means we'll also be covering the use of **Animation** objects, in conjunction with your **Camera** object, during this chapter.

During this chapter, we'll be creating more than a dozen new **setupQSgameplay()** methods, which will contain the code that sets up the next level of gameplay (the questions regarding the image content) for each game board square. This way, when a player clicks a given game board square, that method will be called to set up the "Q&A" experience.

This means that we will be adding several hundred lines of code during this chapter; fortunately, we will use an optimal "code once, then copy, paste, and modify" approach, so there will not be as much typing involved as you might imagine. Once we finish coding the bulk of this gameplay content selection and display infrastructure and test each quadrant to make sure it is working, we can do the question and answer portion of the code in Chapter 21 and then code the scoring engine in Chapter 22 to complete the majority of the "core" gameplay experience.

Select Game Content: selectQSgameplay() Methods

To allow a player to select a game board square to test their knowledge, we must add to the **createSceneProcessing()** method, which contains our event handling for mouse clicks on the 3D SceneGraph Node objects. Prior to this chapter, this was the **3D spinner** UI element, but now we'll have to add 20 more event handling conditional if() processing statements so that if one of the 20 game board squares is clicked, its corresponding selectQxSxgameplay() methods is called to process the gameplay logic for that square's content. We'll start with coding and testing the first if (picked == Q1S1) structure. Since visuals (texture maps) for the gameplay content are already created, using a work process outlined in Chapter 18, these methods will correctly display those image assets and also trigger the gameplay

© Wallace Jackson 2017
W. Jackson, *Pro Java 9 Games Development*, https://doi.org/10.1007/978-1-4842-0973-8_20

questions that the player will need to master to score points. These if() statements will look for the Node picked and send the player to the correct selectQSgameplay() method. The pseudocode for this structure would look like the following:

```
if (pickedNode == Q1S1) { call the selectQ1S1gameplay() method }
if (pickedNode == Q2S2) { call the selectQ2S2gameplay() method } // and so on, out through Q4S5
```

Once we've created several of these statements, we can use the **Alt+Enter** keystroke combination and have NetBeans create an empty method structure for us. Once we create that method structure, we can then use copy and paste to create 20 methods, testing the code for each quadrant as we create it, until all 20 have been completed.

Game Board Square Interaction: OnMouseClick() Event Handling

Let's create the first of the event processing conditional if() statements that look for Q1S1 through Q4S5 square node mouse click events. I'm going to put 20 game board square Node evaluations inside of (right after) the **if(picked != null)** outer if() structure and before the **if(picked == spinner)** structure since these structures simply call a method if a Box Node is clicked. It is important to note that I cannot use the **switch-case** structure because currently that structure is not compatible with object evaluations, only string, enum, and numeric evaluations. This should look like the Java statements and method call shown here (and highlighted in light blue and yellow in Figure 20-1):

```
if (picked != null) {
    if (picked == Q1S1) { setupQ1S1gameplay(); }
    ... // 3D spinner UI processing logic will go after all game board square processing logic
}
```

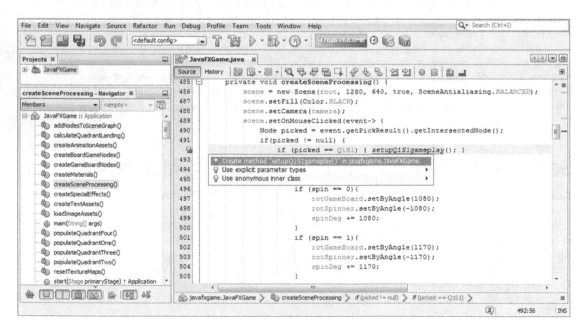

Figure 20-1. *Add an if(picked==Q1S1) conditional evaluation; use Alt+Enter to create a setupQ1S1gameplay() method*

Once you type in the first if() conditional evaluation, your method name will be underlined in red because the method does not yet exist. Use the **Alt+Enter** work process to have NetBeans 9 write the code for you and select the **Create method "setupQ1S1gameplay()" in javafxgame.JavaFXGame** option, as shown in blue in Figure 20-1.

Inside your **setupQ1S1gameplay()** method, replace the bootstrap error code with three if() random picks for square 1 (int pickS1) conditional evaluations. This will tell your game what to do when three different random pick numbers (0, 1, or 2) are generated. This should look like the following Java code, as shown highlighted in Figure 20-2:

```java
private void setupQ1S1gameplay() {
    if (pickS1 == 0) {}
    if (pickS1 == 1) {}
    if (pickS1 == 2) {}
}
```

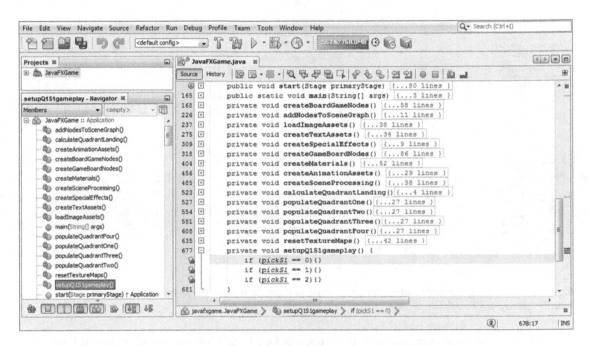

Figure 20-2. *Add conditional if() structures for random number generator result processing inside setupQ1S1gameplay*

The reason these have wavy red error underlining under them is because **pickS1** is currently declared as int (integer) **inside** of the **populateQuadrantOne()** method, so the pickS1 variable is currently **local** and needs to be made "package protected" (using no public, private, or protected keyword) and thus accessible to your **entire class**.

This will be accomplished by moving your pickS1 declaration to the top of the class so that all methods in your class (and package) can reference its data value loaded from the random number generator. You can add pickS1 to int quadrantLanding and create a compound statement, declaring all of your integer variables for use in one line of code.

You could add pickS1 through pickS20 to this compound statement, as you modify each populateQuadrant() method's Java code, or you could just add all 20 new int variables first and then remove the int declaration from all of the populateQuadrant() methods second, at which point your code structure, shown in Figure 20-3, will be error-free.

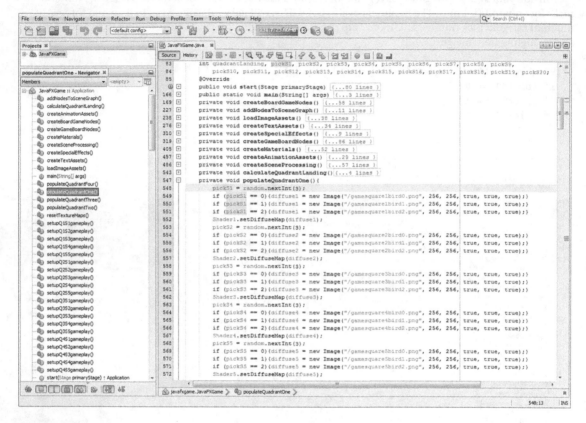

Figure 20-3. *Declare int pickS1 at the top of the class so it can be used in the populateQuadrant() and setupQSgameplay() methods*

Initially, we were using this statement in the populateQuadrant() methods to declare and load the pickSn int (integer) variable with the current content result for the game board square from a random number generator object.

```
int pickS1 = random.nextInt(3);  // Next declare int at top of class, so it needs to be
removed!
```

Now that we have declared these integer random number "holders" with "global" (rather than local) access, the previous Java 9 statement will become even simpler and will look like the following, as shown in Figure 20-3:

```
pickS1 = random.nextInt(3);
```

Notice that the random number for each game board square attached to each quadrant is generated in the populateQuadrant() methods to select and set up the image assets used. We'll also use this random number result in the setupQ1S1gameplay() method to determine what quadrant texture map image to display, if a player has clicked that square to select that content for their question. This is because each square has more than one image.

Since this setupQ1S1gameplay() method is called as a result of a mouse click on your Q1S1 Node object, the first thing you will need to do is to change the default texture map for game board quadrant 1 to instead be the texture map, which matches the content shown in game board square 1, which was clicked. There will be other Java statements added later that set up the question and answer options for the image content, but let's start with the visual feedback that the player will get when clicking the game board content.

Since there are currently three different content images that might be populating game board square 1, you will have three if() constructs that will contain the Java statements relating to each content selection. The random number generator has already randomly selected one of these three content images in your **populateQuadrantOne()** method using the **pickS1** variable to store this selection. So, logically we should use this variable, which you have now made a "global" game variable, to ascertain which quadrant texture map to set the diffuse21 quadrant texture Image object to, using the Image() object constructor with the image asset name, resolution, and rendering settings. Then, all you have to do is to set the Shader21 object to reference this (new) diffuse21 Image object using the setDiffuseMap() method call. This will be done for each of the three content options, with the gamequad1bird0 through gamequad1bird2 image file name being the primary code element that will change between three different conditional if() constructs inside of the setupQ1S1gameplay() method. This makes the **copy-and-paste** coding work process the logical one to utilize.

The Java code for your **setupQ1S1gameplay()** method should look like the following code, as shown at the top of Figure 20-4 as well as copied and pasted at the bottom of the figure to create a setupQ1S2gameplay() method:

```java
private void setupQ1S1gameplay() {
    if (pickS1 == 0) {
        diffuse21 = new Image("gamequad1bird0.png", 512, 512, true, true, true);
        Shader21.setDiffuseMap(diffuse21);
    }
    if (pickS1 == 1) {
        diffuse21 = new Image("gamequad1bird1.png", 512, 512, true, true, true);
        Shader21.setDiffuseMap(diffuse21);
    }
    if (pickS1 == 2) {
        diffuse21 = new Image("gamequad1bird2.png", 512, 512, true, true, true);
        Shader21.setDiffuseMap(diffuse21);
    }
}
```

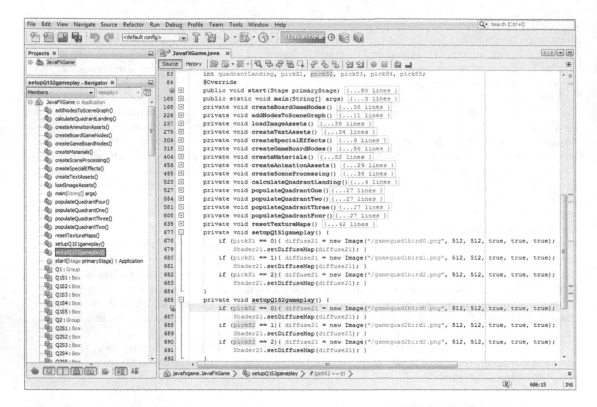

Figure 20-4. *The setupQ1S1gameplay method is error-free and can be finished and copied and pasted to create setupQ1S2gameplay()*

Let's use the **Run ➤ Project** work process and see whether when we click square 1 it puts the correct image in the center of the quadrant. As you'll see in Figure 20-5, the Java code works, and we can create the other 19 methods.

Figure 20-5. *Clicking quadrant 1's square 1 (Q1S1) texture maps the game board quadrant with the correct image asset*

Now that you have a setupQ1S1gameplay() method code template, cut and paste it four times underneath itself, change Q1S1 to **Q1S2** through **Q1S5**, and change pickS1 to **pickS2** through **pickS5** in the method name and if() code structures. Also, change the image file names in the Image() instantiations to match the PNG texture map image assets you created in Chapter 18. The Java code, also shown in Figure 20-6, should look like the following once you are done:

```
private void setupQ1S2gameplay() {
    if (pickS2 == 0) {diffuse21 = new Image("gamequad1s2bird0.png", 512, 512, true, true, true);
                      Shader21.setDiffuseMap(diffuse21); }
    if (pickS2 == 1) {diffuse21 = new Image("gamequad1s2bird1.png", 512, 512, true, true, true);
                      Shader21.setDiffuseMap(diffuse21); }
    if (pickS2 == 2) {diffuse21 = new Image("gamequad1s2bird2.png", 512, 512, true, true, true);
                      Shader21.setDiffuseMap(diffuse21); }
}
private void setupQ1S3gameplay() {
    if (pickS3 == 0) {diffuse21 = new Image("gamequad1s3bird0.png", 512, 512, true, true, true);
                      Shader21.setDiffuseMap(diffuse21); }
    if (pickS3 == 1) {diffuse21 = new Image("gamequad1s3bird1.png", 512, 512, true, true, true);
                      Shader21.setDiffuseMap(diffuse21); }
    if (pickS3 == 2) {diffuse21 = new Image("gamequad1s3bird2.png", 512, 512, true, true, true);
                      Shader21.setDiffuseMap(diffuse21); }
}
private void setupQ1S4gameplay() {
    if (pickS4 == 0) {diffuse21 = new Image("gamequad1s4bird0.png", 512, 512, true, true, true);
                      Shader21.setDiffuseMap(diffuse21); }
    if (pickS4 == 1) {diffuse21 = new Image("gamequad1s4bird1.png", 512, 512, true, true, true);
                      Shader21.setDiffuseMap(diffuse21); }
```

```
    if (pickS4 == 2) {diffuse21 = new Image("gamequad1s4bird2.png", 512, 512, true, true, true);
                Shader21.setDiffuseMap(diffuse21); }
}
private void setupQ1S5gameplay() {
    if (pickS5 == 0) {diffuse21 = new Image("gamequad1s5bird0.png", 512, 512, true, true, true);
                Shader21.setDiffuseMap(diffuse21); }
    if (pickS5 == 1) {diffuse21 = new Image("gamequad1s5bird1.png", 512, 512, true, true, true);
                Shader21.setDiffuseMap(diffuse21); }
    if (pickS5 == 2) {diffuse21 = new Image("gamequad1s5bird2.png", 512, 512, true, true, true);
                Shader21.setDiffuseMap(diffuse21); }
}
```

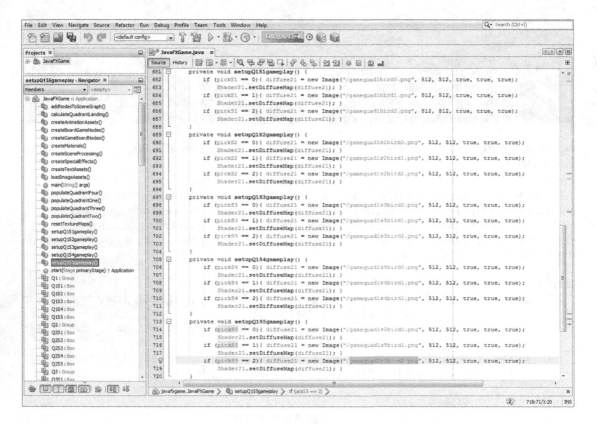

Figure 20-6. *Copy and paste the setupQ1S1gameplay() method four times; edit each to create the other four methods*

Before you can test all five of the attached quadrant 1 squares, you need to make sure your first five OnMouseClicked event handler conditional if() statements are in place, inside of the **createSceneProcessing()** method body. Select your first **if (picked == Q1S1)** conditional if() statement in Figure 20-1 and copy and paste it four more times underneath itself. Change your Q1S1 references to Q1S2 through Q1S5, and change setupQ1S1gameplay() to setupQ1S2gameplay() through setupQ1S5gameplay(). Your new OnMouseClicked event handling method body should look like the following Java 9 code, which is also shown in light blue and yellow in Figure 20-7:

```java
scene.setOnMouseClicked(event-> {
    Node picked = event.getPickResult().getIntersectedNode();
    if (picked != null) {
        if (picked == Q1S1)    { setupQ1S1gameplay(); }
        if (picked == Q1S2)    { setupQ1S2gameplay(); }
        if (picked == Q1S3)    { setupQ1S3gameplay(); }
        if (picked == Q1S4)    { setupQ1S4gameplay(); }
        if (picked == Q1S5)    { setupQ1S5gameplay(); }
        if (picked == spinner) { resetTextureMaps();
                                 int spin = random.nextInt(4);
                                 if (spin == 0) {
                                 ... // 3D spinner UI logic
                                 }
        }
    }
});
```

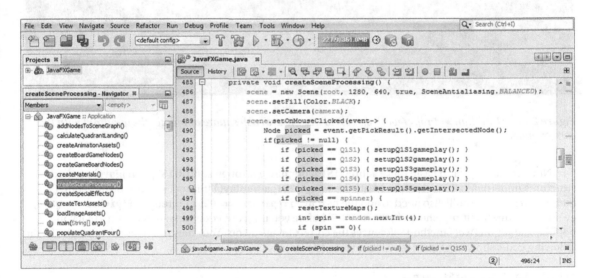

Figure 20-7. *Copy the first if(picked==Q1S1) construct four more times to create the Q1S2 through Q1S5 if() constructs*

As you can tell from this chapter, we are now getting into the part of the Java coding process where we will be generating hundreds if not thousands of lines of codes over the next few chapters, as we add in the game content.

This will include this chapter, where we add in the infrastructure where the player can click the imagery to select the game question they are going to answer and where we add camera animation to get a better view of this content. It also includes the next chapter, where we'll add questions and answers for each question, along with a 2D UI that displays these answer options. We will also be adding digital audio spin and zoom sound effects in Chapter 21 using the JavaFX 9 AudioClip class.

In Chapter 22, we will add a scoring engine, which is also quite a bit of code. So, from this point onward, your lines of Java 9 code are going to increase dramatically as we continue to flesh out how our gameplay is going to function. Once we are done with that, we will look at how NetBeans 9 allows you to test what your code is doing and then optimize it. Let's use a **Run ➤ Project** work process and see whether when we click squares 2 to 5, it puts a correct image in the center of the quadrant. As you'll see in Figure 20-8, the Java code works, and we can create the other 15 methods.

Figure 20-8. *Use a Run ➤ Project work process to test; ensure each square populates the quadrant with the correct image*

Now we can copy and paste these **setupQ1S1gameplay()** through **setupQ1S5gameplay()** method structures underneath themselves to create the **setupQ2S1gameplay()** through **setupQ2S5gameplay()** method structures. You'll also need to add the next five **if(picked == Q2S1)** through **if(picked == Q2S5)** event handling structures (shown in Figure 20-7) before you test your code, as well as confirm that your populateQuadrantTwo() method references the correct image assets. Your new methods should look like the following code, shown in Figure 20-9, once you edit them:

```
private void setupQ2S1gameplay() {
    if (pickS6 == 0) {diffuse22 = new Image("gamequad2s1vegi0.png", 512, 512, true, true, true);
                    Shader22.setDiffuseMap(diffuse22); }
    if (pickS6 == 1) {diffuse22 = new Image("gamequad2s1vegi1.png", 512, 512, true, true, true);
                    Shader22.setDiffuseMap(diffuse22); }
    if (pickS6 == 2) {diffuse22 = new Image("gamequad2s1vegi2.png", 512, 512, true, true, true);
                    Shader22.setDiffuseMap(diffuse22); }
}
```

```
private void setupQ2S2gameplay() {
    if (pickS7 == 0) {diffuse22 = new Image("gamequad2s2vegi0.png", 512, 512, true, true, true);
                    Shader22.setDiffuseMap(diffuse22); }
    if (pickS7 == 1) {diffuse22 = new Image("gamequad2s2vegi1.png", 512, 512, true, true, true);
                    Shader22.setDiffuseMap(diffuse22); }
    if (pickS7 == 2) {diffuse22 = new Image("gamequad2s2vegi2.png", 512, 512, true, true, true);
                    Shader22.setDiffuseMap(diffuse22); }
}
private void setupQ2S3gameplay() {
    if (pickS8 == 0) {diffuse22 = new Image("gamequad2s3vegi0.png", 512, 512, true, true, true);
                    Shader22.setDiffuseMap(diffuse22); }
    if (pickS8 == 1) {diffuse22 = new Image("gamequad2s3vegi1.png", 512, 512, true, true, true);
                    Shader22.setDiffuseMap(diffuse22); }
    if (pickS8 == 2) {diffuse22 = new Image("gamequad2s3vegi2.png", 512, 512, true, true, true);
                    Shader22.setDiffuseMap(diffuse22); }
}
private void setupQ2S4gameplay() {
    if (pickS9 == 0) {diffuse22 = new Image("gamequad2s4vegi0.png", 512, 512, true, true, true);
                    Shader22.setDiffuseMap(diffuse22); }
    if (pickS9 == 1) {diffuse22 = new Image("gamequad2s4vegi1.png", 512, 512, true, true, true);
                    Shader22.setDiffuseMap(diffuse22); }
    if (pickS9 == 2) {diffuse22 = new Image("gamequad2s4vegi2.png", 512, 512, true, true, true);
                    Shader22.setDiffuseMap(diffuse22); }
}
private void setupQ2S5gameplay() {
    if (pickS10 == 0) {diffuse22 = new Image("gamequad2s5vegi0.png", 512, 512, true, true, true);
                    Shader22.setDiffuseMap(diffuse22); }
    if (pickS10 == 1) {diffuse22 = new Image("gamequad2s5vegi1.png", 512, 512, true, true, true);
                    Shader22.setDiffuseMap(diffuse22); }
    if (pickS10 == 2) {diffuse22 = new Image("gamequad2s5vegi2.png", 512, 512, true, true, true);
                    Shader22.setDiffuseMap(diffuse22); }
}
```

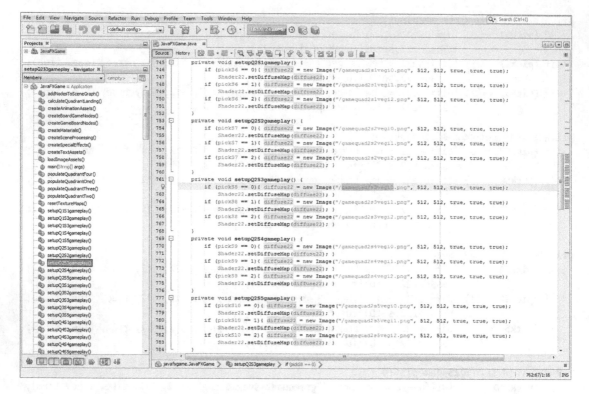

Figure 20-9. *Create the setupQ2S1gameplay() to setupQ2S5gameplay() methods using the diffuse22 and Shader22 objects*

As you can see in both Figures 20-6 and 20-10, I have already been able to create all three different content options for each square in quadrants 1 and 2, which equates to 60 image assets (5 squares × 3 options × 2 graphics × 2 quadrants) created already. This is a ton of digital image assets, as you realize from the work process outlined in Chapter 18. I still have just as much work (another 60 digital image assets) to complete for quadrants 3 and 4. Creating any professional Java game is a massive amount of work, which is why large teams filled with digital artisans are almost always involved. Notice I have also made pickS6 through pickS10 global variables.

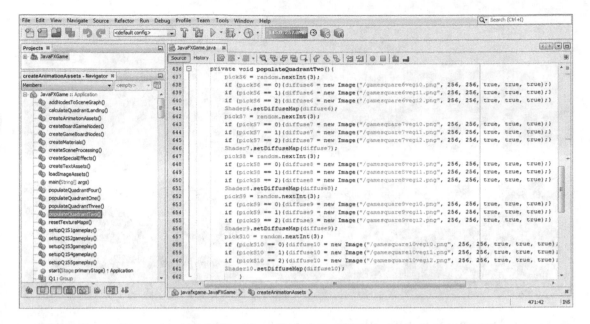

Figure 20-10. *Confirm the populateQuadrantTwo() method image assets cross-reference to the createQSgameplay() methods*

I will create at least three image assets for each of these four quadrants by the time that I finish writing this chapter so that we are finished with the 120 image assets (needed for coding and testing) before we start developing the Q&A and scoring engine Java code in Chapters 21 and 22, respectively.

We will also start adding other cool new media elements, such as digital audio, and more 2D user interface elements in these chapters, so we have lots more exciting JavaFX game engine topics to cover still!

Oftentimes, the work creating the new media digital assets (digital images, digital audio, digital illustration, digital video, 3D modeling or animation, visual effects, particle systems, fluid dynamics, and so on) can be significantly more work than creating your Java 9 code! If you have more than one content production workstation, you will have different computers working on (rendering, compositing, encoding, modeling, texture mapping, animating, and so on and so forth) different new media assets used in your pro Java 9 games development work process.

Let's again use the **Run ➤ Project** work process and test this new code for your second quadrant thoroughly, making sure all of your game board square images are showing and that when they are clicked they populate your quadrant texture map with the correct (four times larger) image. As you can see in Figure 20-11, both the game board square images and the game board quadrant images are clear and easily identifiable for use as gameplay content.

Figure 20-11. *Use a Run ➤ Project work process to test; make sure each square populates the quadrant with the correct image*

Let's copy and paste another five method bodies and create the **setupQSgameplay()** methods for quadrant 3. Make sure that your image asset names match up with the names you are using for **populateQuadrantThree()**. The Java code should look like the following method bodies, which are also shown in yellow in Figure 20-12:

```
private void setupQ3S1gameplay() {
    if (pickS11 == 0) {diffuse23 = new Image("gamequad3s1rock0.png", 512, 512, true, true, true);
                       Shader23.setDiffuseMap(diffuse23); }
    if (pickS11 == 1) {diffuse23 = new Image("gamequad3s1rock1.png", 512, 512, true, true, true);
                       Shader23.setDiffuseMap(diffuse23); }
    if (pickS11 == 2) {diffuse23 = new Image("gamequad3s1rock2.png", 512, 512, true, true, true);
                       Shader23.setDiffuseMap(diffuse23); }
}
private void setupQ3S2gameplay() {
    if (pickS12 == 0) {diffuse23 = new Image("gamequad3s2rock0.png", 512, 512, true, true, true);
                       Shader23.setDiffuseMap(diffuse23); }
    if (pickS12 == 1) {diffuse23 = new Image("gamequad3s2rock1.png", 512, 512, true, true, true);
                       Shader23.setDiffuseMap(diffuse23); }
    if (pickS12 == 2) {diffuse23 = new Image("gamequad3s2rock2.png", 512, 512, true, true, true);
                       Shader23.setDiffuseMap(diffuse23); }
}
private void setupQ3S3gameplay() {
    if (pickS13 == 0) {diffuse23 = new Image("gamequad3s3rock0.png", 512, 512, true, true, true);
                       Shader23.setDiffuseMap(diffuse23); }
    if (pickS13 == 1) {diffuse23 = new Image("gamequad3s3rock1.png", 512, 512, true, true, true);
                       Shader23.setDiffuseMap(diffuse23); }
```

500

```
    if (pickS13 == 2) {diffuse23 = new Image("gamequad3s3rock2.png", 512, 512, true, true, true);
                 Shader23.setDiffuseMap(diffuse23); }
}
private void setupQ3S4gameplay() {
    if (pickS14 == 0) {diffuse23 = new Image("gamequad3s4rock0.png", 512, 512, true, true, true);
                 Shader23.setDiffuseMap(diffuse23); }
    if (pickS14 == 1) {diffuse23 = new Image("gamequad3s4rock1.png", 512, 512, true, true, true);
                 Shader23.setDiffuseMap(diffuse23); }
    if (pickS14 == 2) {diffuse23 = new Image("gamequad3s4rock2.png", 512, 512, true, true, true);
                 Shader23.setDiffuseMap(diffuse23); }
}
private void setupQ3S5gameplay() {
    if (pickS15 == 0) {diffuse23 = new Image("gamequad3s5rock0.png", 512, 512, true, true, true);
                 Shader23.setDiffuseMap(diffuse23); }
    if (pickS15 == 1) {diffuse23 = new Image("gamequad3s5rock1.png", 512, 512, true, true, true);
                 Shader23.setDiffuseMap(diffuse23); }
    if (pickS15 == 2) {diffuse23 = new Image("gamequad3s5rock2.png", 512, 512, true, true, true);
                 Shader23.setDiffuseMap(diffuse23); }
}
```

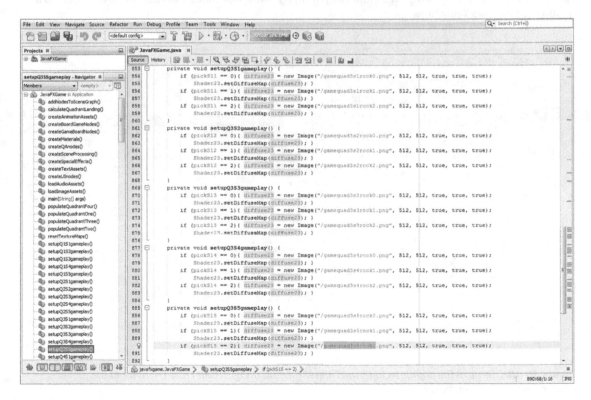

Figure 20-12. *Create the setupQ3S1gameplay() through setupQ3S5gameplay() methods, using diffuse23 and Shader23 objects*

Make sure to open your populateQuadrantThree() method and check the image assets used to ensure that they use the same image names. The exception is that your game square image assets are 256 pixels square, whereas the game quadrant image assets are the 512-pixel square versions and start with "gamequad" instead of "gamesquare."

Between these two methods, all of your gamesquare and gamequad images get loaded into the two dozen game board texture maps used for the game board shaders that will decorate the surfaces of your game board at any given time during the gameplay. These two dozen methods (four for the quadrants and twenty for the squares) make sure that your game board will look visually correct for any given round of gameplay, making sure that the game board squares have the randomly selected topic content and that the game quadrant displays a large version of the content.

All of these two dozen methods are set up in a way that content can be added as time goes on, changing the random.nextInt() method call to the next largest upper boundary to add a level of content. You can do this once the game design, including other new media assets such as more animation, digital audio, 3D, and the game questions (all of which we still have to create and code), have been completed during the next couple chapters. You will be modifying and adding content and levels to your game long past the completion of the initial code. You can redesign your game structure, as we have during this book, adding more classes or methods as they become needed to expand the game.

The populateQuadrantThree() method, shown in Figure 20-13, adds in a third round of image content, which is denoted by a **2** on the end of the file name. These assets were created on another machine (in your case, possibly by your graphics design employee) by myself while I continued work on the Java 9 code on a quad-core Windows 7 machine.

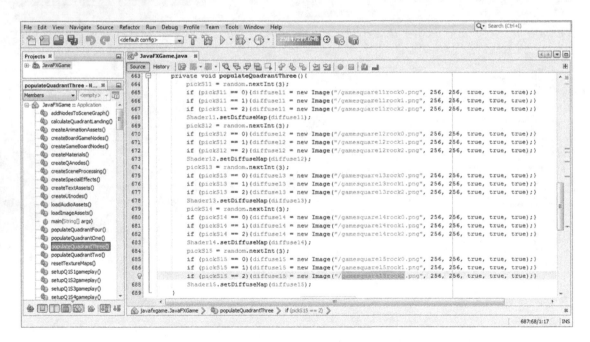

Figure 20-13. *Confirm the populateQuadrantThree() method image assets cross-reference to the createQSgameplay() methods*

Make sure you add the five if(picked == Q3S1) through if(picked == Q3S5) statements to the OnMouseClick event handling in createSceneProcessing() to connect the new methods to your ever-growing gameplay experience.

As shown in Figure 20-14, use the **Run ➤ Project** work process and test the code related to quadrant 3 to make sure that the quadrant and content images are all appearing correctly and that they look clear and professional.

Figure 20-14. *Use a Run ➤ Project work process to test; make sure each square populates the quadrant with the correct image*

Finally, let's create the last five **setupQSgameplay()** methods, shown in Figure 20-15, which will look like this:

```
private void setupQ4S1gameplay() {
    if (pickS16 == 0) {diffuse24 = new Image("gamequad4s1fame0.png", 512, 512, true, true, true);
                       Shader24.setDiffuseMap(diffuse24); }
    if (pickS16 == 1) {diffuse24 = new Image("gamequad4s1fame1.png", 512, 512, true, true, true);
                       Shader24.setDiffuseMap(diffuse24); }
    if (pickS16 == 2) {diffuse24 = new Image("gamequad4s1fame2.png", 512, 512, true, true, true);
                       Shader24.setDiffuseMap(diffuse24); }
}
private void setupQ4S2gameplay() {
    if (pickS17 == 0) {diffuse24 = new Image("gamequad4s2fame0.png", 512, 512, true, true, true);
                       Shader24.setDiffuseMap(diffuse24); }
    if (pickS17 == 1) {diffuse24 = new Image("gamequad4s2fame1.png", 512, 512, true, true, true);
                       Shader24.setDiffuseMap(diffuse24); }
    if (pickS17 == 2) {diffuse24 = new Image("gamequad4s2fame2.png", 512, 512, true, true, true);
                       Shader24.setDiffuseMap(diffuse24); }
}
```

503

```
private void setupQ4S3gameplay() {
    if (pickS18 == 0) {diffuse24 = new Image("gamequad4s3fame0.png", 512, 512, true, true, true);
                Shader24.setDiffuseMap(diffuse24); }
    if (pickS18 == 1) {diffuse24 = new Image("gamequad4s3fame1.png", 512, 512, true, true, true);
                Shader24.setDiffuseMap(diffuse24); }
    if (pickS18 == 2) {diffuse24 = new Image("gamequad4s3fame2.png", 512, 512, true, true, true);
                Shader24.setDiffuseMap(diffuse24); }
}
private void setupQ4S4gameplay() {
    if (pickS19 == 0) {diffuse24 = new Image("gamequad4s4fame0.png", 512, 512, true, true, true);
                Shader24.setDiffuseMap(diffuse24); }
    if (pickS19 == 1) {diffuse24 = new Image("gamequad4s4fame1.png", 512, 512, true, true, true);
                Shader24.setDiffuseMap(diffuse24); }
    if (pickS19 == 2) {diffuse24 = new Image("gamequad4s4fame2.png", 512, 512, true, true, true);
                Shader24.setDiffuseMap(diffuse24); }
}
private void setupQ4S5gameplay() {
    if (pickS20 == 0) {diffuse24 = new Image("gamequad4s5fame0.png", 512, 512, true, true, true);
                Shader24.setDiffuseMap(diffuse24); }
    if (pickS20 == 1) {diffuse24 = new Image("gamequad4s5fame1.png", 512, 512, true, true, true);
                Shader24.setDiffuseMap(diffuse24); }
    if (pickS20 == 2) {diffuse24 = new Image("gamequad4s5fame2.png", 512, 512, true, true, true);
                Shader24.setDiffuseMap(diffuse24); }
}
```

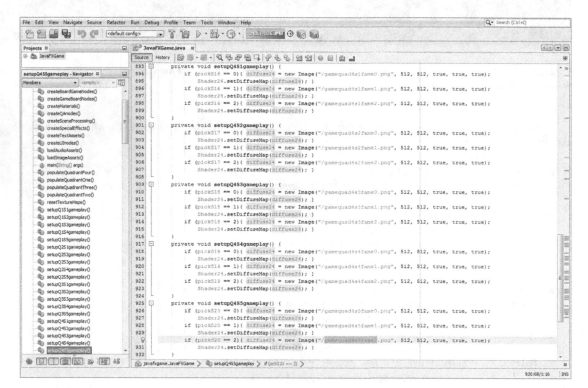

Figure 20-15. *Create the setupQ4S1gameplay() through setupQ4S5gameplay() methods, using diffuse24 and Shader24 objects*

Again, compare what you're doing in setupQ4S1gamedesign() through setupQ4S5gamedesign() with what you're doing in populateQuadrantFour(). Make sure everything syncs together by comparing Figures 20-15 and 20-16.

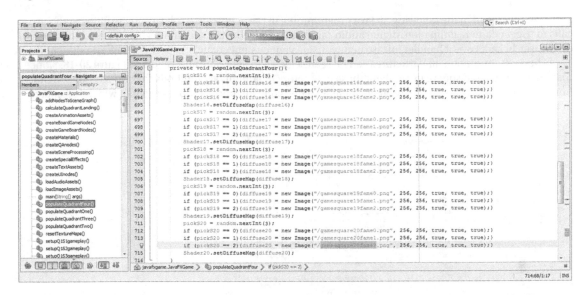

Figure 20-16. *Confirm the populateQuadrantFour() method image assets cross-reference the createQSgameplay() methods*

Let's use the **Run ➤ Project** work process shown in Figure 20-17 to test the new code for the fourth quadrant.

Figure 20-17. *Test with a Run ➤ Project work process; make sure each square populates the quadrant with the correct image*

To save on several screenshots, I have not shown the addition of the five event handling if()
structures that you have also been adding as you work on populating each new quadrant and matching
setupQSgameplay() methods over the course of this chapter, which add nearly 50 lines of Java 9 code per
quadrant.

This will result in the following 20 Java programming if() structures—which we will be filling with
calls to trigger camera animation, digital audio samples (sound effects), and more—being added to your
onMouseClicked() event handler infrastructure inside your custom createSceneProcessing() method body.

These 20 conditional if() structures can be seen selected in light blue and yellow in Figure 20-18. Notice
that I have used a red square to highlight these new **setupQSgameplay()** methods that we've added in the
first section of this chapter in the **Navigator** pane's game code method **Members** section, which is displayed
in the far-left pane of NetBeans 9.

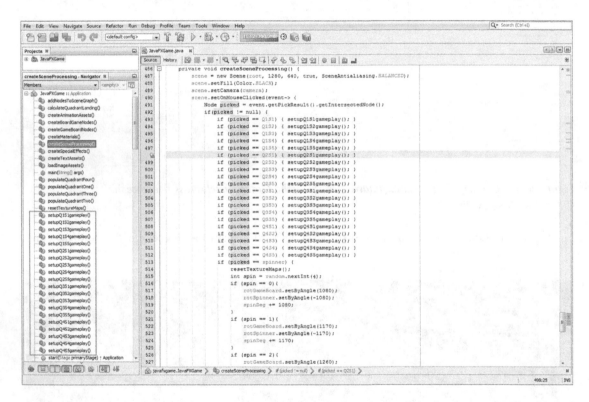

Figure 20-18. *You now have all the setupQSgameplay() methods and are calling them in an OnMouseClicked()
event handler*

If you want to see all of your image assets, which are all texture maps since this is an i3D game, you can
use your OS file management utility and navigate into your **/MyDocuments/NetBeansProjects/JavaFXGame/
src/** folder, as shown in Figure 20-19. I could barely fit all of these game assets (approximately 34MB) into
one screenshot! I will probably have to optimize these 120 image assets into PNG8 image assets, which
would reduce this data footprint to about 10MB. They can be even further optimized using Run Length
Encoding (RLE, also known as ZIP file compression). Most of these images will convert to 256 colors (with
dithering) quite well.

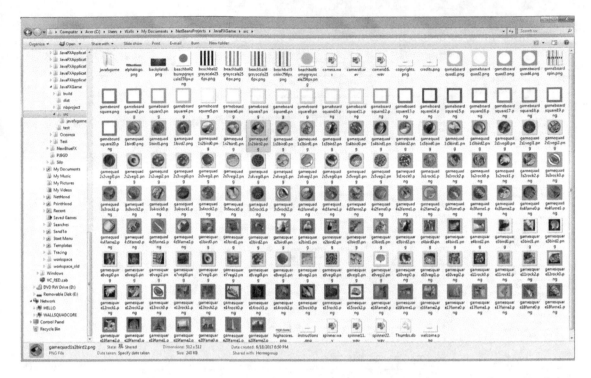

Figure 20-19. *Use your file management software to view all of the game image (texture map) assets in the /src folder*

We will also be creating our audio assets and learning some digital audio encoding tricks in the next chapter using a professional digital audio editing and sweetening package, called Audacity 2.1.3, for Windows, Mac, and Linux.

Next, let's add some "wow" factor to the game by zooming the camera into the selected gameplay quadrant.

Camera Animation: Position Game Board After Select

Let's add some 3D Camera animation next so that after the player clicks the square that they want to use for their turn, the Camera object moves in and turns down from -30 degrees to -60 degrees, which will make the quadrant and its image closer (and more parallel) to the camera. This will make the quadrant image larger for the player and will also give us more room for the 2D overlay panels on the left and right sides of the screen. These will contain our UI, scoreboard, and answers for the selected game board square visual content. Most of this will be created in the next couple of chapters, so we are basically finishing the i3D and UI programming for the exterior (outer game board) parts of the game. In the next chapters, we will start the interior (Q&A) and audio portions of the game's programming.

Add a **rotCameraDown** object declaration to your RotateTransition compound statement at the top of your class; then add an instantiation for this object to the end of the **createAnimationAssets()** method using **5** seconds as the **Duration** setting and reference the **camera** object. Set the **cycleCount** variable to **one** and **Rate** to **0.75** for a more moderate rate of movement. Set **Delay** to one (**Duration.ONE**) and use an **Interpolator.LINEAR Interpolator** value for now. Finally, set the **fromAngle** variable to your current **-30** degrees and the **toAngle** variable to a target **-60** degrees. This Java code can be seen at the end of your **createAnimationAssets()** method, highlighted in yellow, in Figure 20-20.

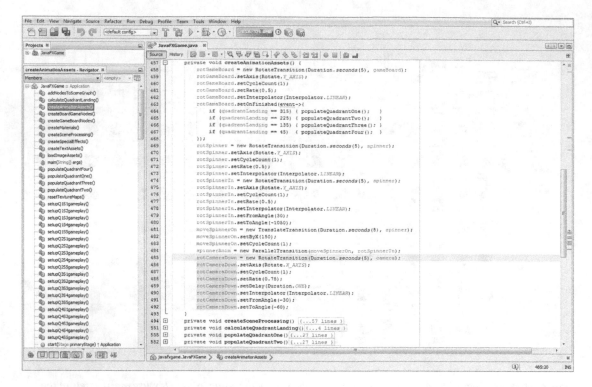

Figure 20-20. *Add a rotCameraDown animation at the end of the createAnimationAssets() method from -30 to -60*

The Java 9 code for this camera object calling a RotateTransition object, shown in Figure 20-20, should look like the following:

```
rotCameraDown = new RotateTransition(Duration.seconds(5), camera);
rotCameraDown.setAxis(Rotate.X_AXIS);
rotCameraDown.setCycleCount(1);
rotCameraDown.setRate(0.75);
rotCameraDown.setDelay(Duration.ONE);
rotCameraDown.setInterpolator(Interpolator.LINEAR);
rotCameraDown.setFromAngle(-30);
rotCameraDown.setToAngle(-60);
```

Since we also want to move the camera object in by **-175** units, from 500 to 325, at the same time we are rotating the camera object down -30 degrees, we will add a **moveCameraIn** object to the TranslateTransition object compound declaration statement at the top of your class. At the end of the **createAnimationAssets()** method, we will instantiate this object using **2 seconds** and attach it to the camera object. Then we will configure it to move by -175 units in the Z direction by using setByZ(-175), with a cycleCount setting of 1. The Java code for this animation object should look like the following:

```
moveCameraIn = new TranslateTransition(Duration.seconds(2), camera);
moveCameraIn.setByZ(-175);
moveCameraIn.setCycleCount(1);
```

Finally, to make this a compound animation, we'll add a **cameraAnimIn** ParallelTransition object declaration, making a compound declaration at the top of your class, and then we'll instantiate the object inside **createAnimationAssets()**.

We will add the moveCameraIn and rotCameraDown animation objects to this ParallelTransition object, right inside the object instantiation statement, so we will need only one line of code to combine these two animations together seamlessly. The Java code, also shown at the end of Figure 20-22, should look like the following:

```
cameraAnimIn = new ParallelTransition(moveCameraIn, rotCameraDown);
```

Next, let's use a **Run ➤ Project** work process and test this code to see how it works! As you can see in Figure 20-21, the quadrant is in a good location on the screen, so all we have to do is to move the 3D spinner UI off of the screen. To accomplish this, we will add a **moveSpinnerOff** animation object to the cameraAnimIn ParallelTransition so that part of rotating the camera into the game board also involves moving the 3D spinner off of the gameplay screen.

Figure 20-21. *The camera now points down 60 degrees at the game board displaying the content better*

This will make the animation sequence look much more professional. We can use your original spinnerAnim ParallelTransition object to get the 3D spinner UI onto the screen whenever we need to spin your game board again.

Let's create the moveSpinnerOff animation object next, and then we can add it to the cameraAnimIn object that we just created to create a more complex ParallelTransition Animation object to use in your gameplay code.

Declare a **moveSpinnerOff** object in your compound TranslateTransition declaration statement at the top of the class and then instantiate it in your **createAnimationAssets()** method body, after your moveCameraIn statements and before the cameraAnimIn ParallelTransition object instantiation, since we are going to add it to this compound animation transition. This way, everything that we want to animate happens at exactly the same time.

509

We'll move the spinner off quickly, in 2 seconds, by the same 150 units (this time negative) that we moved the spinner onto the screen by. The Java code should look like the following, as shown in Figure 20-22 at the bottom of the method, highlighted in yellow and light blue:

```
moveCameraIn = new TranslateTransition(Duration.seconds(2), camera);
moveCameraIn.setByZ(-175);
moveCameraIn.setCycleCount(1);
moveSpinnerOff = new TranslateTransition(Duration.seconds(3), spinner);
moveSpinnerOff.setByX(-150);
moveSpinnerOff.setCycleCount(1);
cameraAnimIn = new ParallelTransition(moveCameraIn, rotCameraDown, moveSpinnerOff);
```

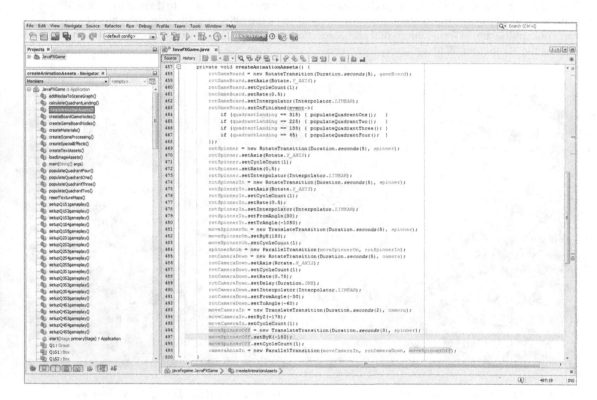

Figure 20-22. *Add a moveSpinnerOff Animation object to a cameraAnimIn ParallelTransition object to remove the spinner*

These four new **Animation** objects will add quite a bit of professionalism to your i3D game, animating your camera view into a vastly superior position, removing the spinner i3D UI element from the screen for each core gameplay session, rotating the 3D camera's plane so that it is more parallel to your quadrant content, and combining all of this movement into one ParallelTransition animation sequence.

This sets things up for the next chapter, where we'll be adding digital audio sound effects both to the game board spin and to the camera zoom by using a ParallelTransition object. This will make both these 3D animation objects even more fun to use for our i3D board game players.

Finally, let's use a **Run ➤ Project** work process to test the code. As you can see in Figure 20-23, it works great, and we have some nice areas on the left and right sides of the screen to overlay our 2D user interface areas, which we will be creating over the next couple of chapters to finish up the i3D board game.

Figure 20-23. *The cameraAnimIn Animation object now works as expected, removing the spinner*

In the next few chapters, we will continue to add not only digital audio sound effects but also the questions and answers that will challenge our players. We'll also add a scoring engine, which will track their success identifying content.

Summary

In this twentieth chapter, we learned more about how to complete our implementation of the random selection of game board square content. We implemented the onMouseEvent handling code that puts the quadrant texture maps into place once the content has been selected by the player as a game board square is clicked. We also implemented camera animation code, which changes the view of the game board once the game board square is selected so that the quadrant has a larger image displayed. This essentially puts us into a position to start coding the individual square (and quadrant, once the square is selected) gameplay, where a visual question regarding the content is answered and scored, which we will be creating in Chapters 21 and 22. Much of this code will go into the **setupQSgameplay()** methods for each square, for which we put a foundation in place in this chapter. After that, we will look at creating a scoring engine, digital audio effects to enhance the gameplay, and maybe a few more **Animation** objects. This will make the gameplay even more interactive 3D and to add even more professionalism.

This was one of your heavy coding chapters (as will be the next chapter). You constructed 20 custom methods, setupQ1S1gameplay() through setupQ4S5gameplay(), and you placed conditional if() structures pointing to these in your OnMouseClick() event handling infrastructure. You also cross-checked imaging assets between all of your populateQuadrant() methods and, finally, tested all of this code together to make sure it works properly.

We also added a few more **Animation** objects into your setupAnimationAssets() method, to continue to add some cool "wow" factor, including a key animation that takes the player from a "global" game board spin select mode into a more "local" game board content gameplay mode. Later in the book, we'll of course reverse this animation, when the answer and scoring are completed, and animate back to the more oblique view that is needed to review the game board spin optimally.

In Chapter 21, you are going to develop additional gameplay code infrastructure that will handle what happens when the player clicks (selects) the game square content. This means going back to developing more 2D game elements to hold the question and answer content that will pop up and overlay the unused portions of the 3D game board. As you can see, developing a professional Java 9 game is a huge amount of programming work!

CHAPTER 21

■ ■ ■

Questions and Answers: Finishing the Setup Methods and Digital Audio

Now that your players can click more than one image for each board game square to select the visual question to be answered, we can add the answers to these questions in their own UI. This will be done using a second **qaLayout** StackPane object and four child Button objects, which expands our SceneGraph hierarchy to four branches (one for 3D, one for 2D UI, one for 3D UI, and one for 2D answer content). We will add a fifth top-level branch for scoring in the next chapter, when we implement our scoring engine and a 2D scoring content UI area on the right side of your game.

During this chapter, we will continue populating the 20 **setupQSgameplay()** methods with all the text-based answer content that matches up with the visuals (questions) that we added during Chapter 20. We'll also be adding the qaLayout branch to your SceneGraph, which includes a StackPane background and four large Button UI elements. The players will use these to select the correct answer, revealing what the visual for that square represents.

This means you'll be adding several hundred lines of code during this chapter. Fortunately, you can use an optimal "code once, then copy, paste, and modify" approach, so there won't be much typing involved! I only need to show you how to add one group of answers to one setupQ1S1gameplay() method, and then you will be able to add the rest of your visual question's answer options, so I won't need to actually add hundreds of lines of Java 9 code into this chapter's code (text) and figures. However, I will have to add them to the source code, which you can download.

Once we finish coding the bulk of the gameplay "answer selection and display" infrastructure and test each quadrant to make sure it is working, we can create the scoring portion of the Java code in Chapter 22. We will also be looking at the JavaFX **AudioClip** class, which will allow us to add audio **sound effects**. This will further enhance the pro Java 9 gameplay experience using yet another new media component (digital audio) of the JavaFX API (environment).

Finishing the Gameplay: Adding a qaLayout Branch

The primary task for the first part of the chapter is to finish up gameplay by adding the UI for answer selection to the game. We'll also load the **setupQSgameplay()** methods with the text (Button labels) answers for each visual question. We will do this in the first half of the chapter and then add some sound effects to the game in the second part of the chapter. We'll start with a bit of custom method organization and stratify our methods so that there is one for 3D Node components, one for 2D UI Node components that you see upon game startup, one for 2D UI Node components for selecting answers (we will create this during this chapter), and, in the next chapter, one for 2D UI Node components for creating the scoring engine. After reconfiguring the Java code a bit, we will then create the UI infrastructure for the question and answer (Q&A) panel using a StackPane to hold four large Button UI elements. After we create the basic code to put this UI into place, we will "tweak" its settings to work optimally within the camera zoom in Animation object that we created in Chapter 20, as this Animation moves the camera location and rotation, which will assuredly change how the 2D Q&A UI pane is going to render visually on your display.

Adding Another Organization Layer: The createUInodes() Method

Let's separate your **createBoardGameNodes()** method into one method for creating the **3D Scene** objects (such as the PointLight, ParallelCamera, gameBoard, 3D spinner UI, and game board quadrants) and a second **createUInodes()** method for holding the 2D UI objects we created in the first several chapters of this book. This will place two to three dozen statements into each method body and better organize each section of the SceneGraph before we create the **createQAnodes()** method to hold the Node objects that will create and configure our Q&A panel, which we will do next. The selection should look like the 34 Java statements shown in medium blue in Figure 21-1.

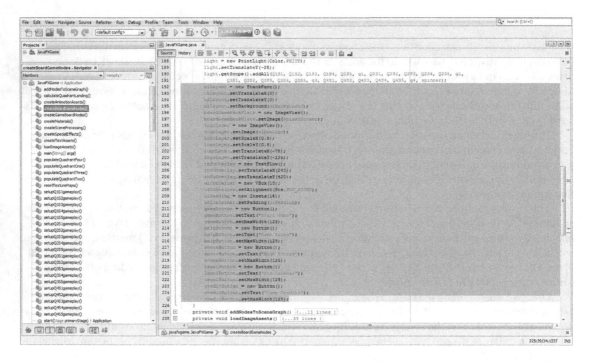

Figure 21-1. *Select and cut your uiLayout branch Node statements and paste them into a createUInodes() method body*

Right-click in the selection set, shown in blue in Figure 21-1, and select a **Cut** option to remove the statements from the createBoardGameNodes() method. This will then place them into your OS clipboard to later be pasted into the new createUInodes() method, which we are about to create.

Inside your **start()** method, add a line of code after **createBoardGameNodes();** and create a method call to the **createUInodes()** method, which does not yet exist. Use an **Alt+Enter** keystroke combination to have NetBeans create this method for you, as shown in yellow and light blue in Figure 21-2 after it has been created.

NetBeans 9 will create this new method and placeholder error code, which we will select (be sure to select only the error code statement, not the method body) and then use **Paste** to **replace** the error code statement with the 34 Java statements that create our uiLayout SceneGraph Node hierarchy, which is currently in the OS clipboard. I also selected the entire method body (this must be done **after** the bootstrap error code has been replaced with your clipboard code) and **cut** and **pasted** it from the end of the class to right after the createBoardGameNodes() method body. This keeps the 20 **setupQSgameplay()** method bodies at the end of the class as we'll be adding question (image) answers to these classes as part of the gameplay production work that must be accomplished in the chapter.

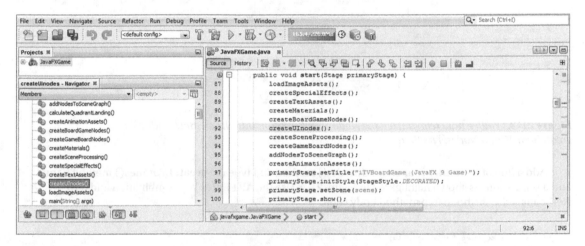

Figure 21-2. *Create the createUInodes() method call after the createBoardGameNodes() method call and use Alt+Enter*

The two new methods are shown in Figure 21-3 and are simply a reconfiguration of the previous method's Java code. We're simply putting a little code organization in place here before creating a createQAnodes() method.

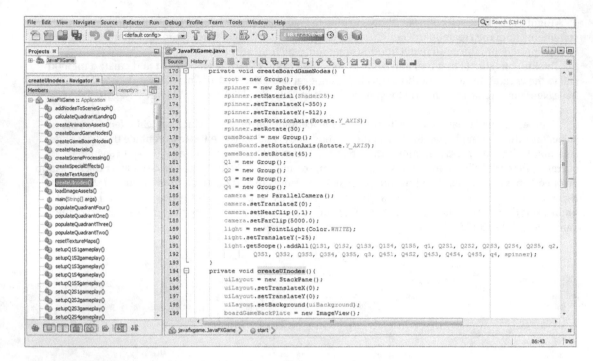

Figure 21-3. *You've now reorganized the Node object creation into the createUInodes() and createBoardGameNodes() methods*

Add a line of code after your createUInodes() method and type the **createQAnodes()** method name and a semicolon, as shown highlighted in Figure 21-4. Use the **Alt+Enter** key combination and have NetBeans write the bootstrap method body code.

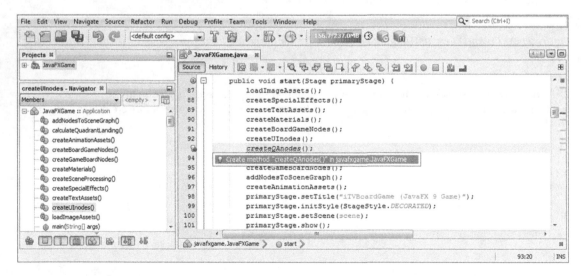

Figure 21-4. *Add a line of code after the createUInodes() method call, add the createQAnodes() method call, and press Alt+Enter*

Use cut and paste to move the createQAnodes() method up to after the **createAnimationAssets()** method call, as shown in Figure 21-5. Add your qaLayout StackPane object to the declaration at the top of your class, making it a compound statement. Then instantiate the qaLayout StackPane inside of the createQAnodes() method and configure it to be at a **-250** and **-425** X, Y location using the **setTranslate()** methods. Also, set a **Color.WHITE** background color and set a **400x500** preferred size for the StackPane using the **setPrefSize()** method call, as shown highlighted in Figure 21-5.

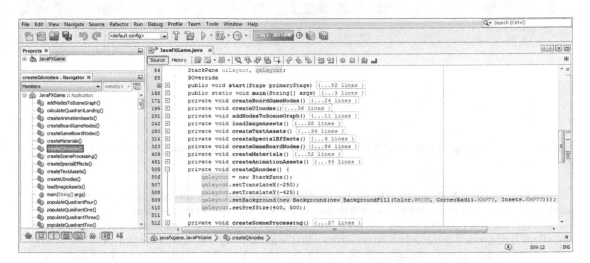

Figure 21-5. *Declare and instantiate a qaLayout object and configure it for location, color, and size in* createQAnodes()

The Java 9 code, shown in Figure 21-5, should look like the following Java 9 statements once you are done:

```
StackPane uiLayout, qaLayout;      // Declaration at the top of the JavaFXGame class
...
qaLayout = new StackPane();         // Statements inside of the createQAnodes() method body
qaLayout.setTranslateX(-250);
qaLayout.setTranslateY(-425);
qaLayout.setBackground(new Background(new BackgroundFill(Color.WHITE, CornerRadii.EMPTY,
                                                Insets.EMPTY) ) );
qaLayout.setPrefSize(400, 500);
```

Before we can render the i3D scene to see our initial Q&A layout result (which will eventually be fine-tuned), we will need to add the **qaLayout** StackPane to your SceneGraph **root** object in the addNodesToSceneGraph() method using the getChildren().addAll() method chain. Otherwise, it will not show up in the rendering used in Run ➤ Project.

Also notice that this qaLayout StackPane needs to be placed into the **second position** (of your four top-level node branches now included in this new SceneGraph hierarchy) so that it is in front of the gameBoard 3D game board model and behind the uiLayout user interface StackPane and the 3D spinner game board spin Sphere 3D UI element.

This addition is shown in the following Java 9 code statement and highlighted in light blue and yellow in the middle of Figure 21-6:

```
root.getChildren().addAll(gameBoard, qaLayout, uiLayout, spinner);
```

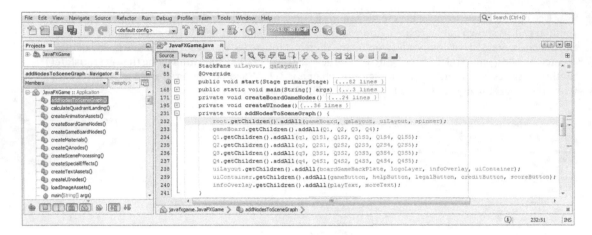

Figure 21-6. *Add the qaLayout StackPane object to the root.getChildren.addAll() method call list in the second position*

Let's use the **Run ➤ Project** work process and see how well we have guessed at what the basic 2D StackPane configuration parameters should be for our left-side Q&A panel for the game. As you will see in Figure 21-7, the Java code is working, but there are a couple of problems with some **translucency** in your StackPane background color and an **intersection** with the game board because of the (unspecified) position in the **Z** dimension. Also, we are laying this out at the **pre-zoom-in** camera settings, so once we fix this Z positioning problem, we might also need to adjust some or all of the location and size settings that we are putting into place initially (before going that deep into the gameplay code for our Q&A UI testing purposes). This will allow us to generate Java code quickly and tweak it for looks later.

Figure 21-7. *Use your Run ➤ Project work process and test your new Java code to see whether it gives you the desired results*

Move the Z position of the qaLayout StackPane object by **-75** units toward the front of the screen using the following setTranslateZ() Java method call, which is highlighted in light blue and yellow in Figure 21-8:

```
qaLayout.setTranslateZ(-75);
```

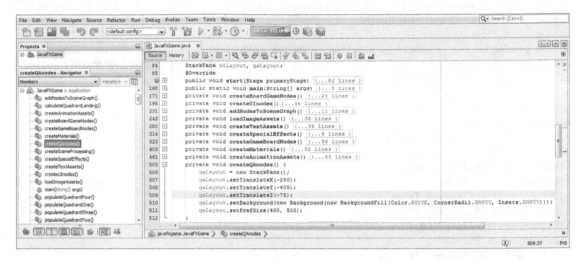

Figure 21-8. *Add a setTranslateZ(-75) method call off the qaLayout object to move it 75 units toward the front screen*

Again, use the **Run ➤ Project** work process and test this new Java code by moving the z-axis forward to see whether it gives you the desired result. As you can see in Figure 21-9, the StackPane is now rendering correctly as a white square.

Figure 21-9. *Use your Run ➤ Project work process and test your new Java code to see whether it gives you the desired results*

The next task is to add the four answer Button element **a1Button** through **a4Button** declarations at the top of the class and instantiate and configure these Button objects inside of the createQAnodes() method. I sized them at 350 units wide and 100 units tall using setMaxSize() and placed them at -180, -60, 60, and 180 using setTranslateY(). I named them Answer One through Answer Four using the setText() method for UI design testing purposes. The Java 9 code needed to implement these four Button UI elements is shown in Figures 21-10 and 21-11 and looks like this:

```
Button gameButton, ..., a1Button, a2Button, a3Button, a4Button;   // at top of JavaFXGame class
a1Button = new Button();                               // statements in createQAnodes() method
a1Button.setText("Answer One");
a1Button.setMaxSize(350, 100);
a1Button.setTranslateY(-180);
a2Button = new Button();
a2Button.setText("Answer Two");
a2Button.setMaxSize(350, 100);
a2Button.setTranslateY(-60);
a3Button = new Button();
a3Button.setText("Answer Three");
a3Button.setMaxSize(350, 100);
a3Button.setTranslateY(60);
a4Button = new Button();
a4Button.setText("Answer Four");
a4Button.setMaxSize(350, 100);
a4Button.setTranslateY(180);
...                                         // Remember to add Button Nodes to SceneGraph
qaLayout.getChildren().addAll(a1Button, a2Button, a3Button, a4Button); // addNodesToSceneGraph()
```

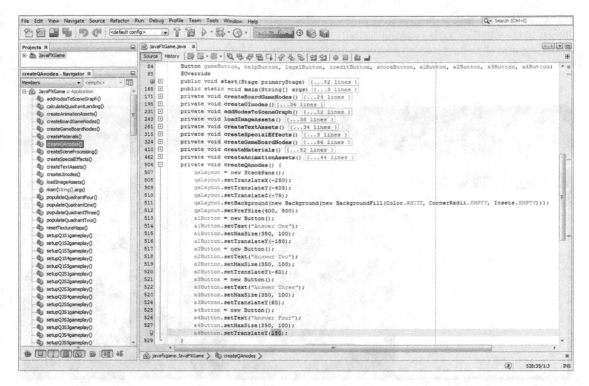

Figure 21-10. *Add four 350x100 Button UI objects at Y location -180, -60, 60, 180, labeled Answer One through Answer Four*

Remember that we have to add these Button objects to the SceneGraph hierarchy by adding your **qaLayout** Node after the Q1 to Q4 Node objects and calling the getChildren().addAll() method chain with the four Button objects as child objects to be added to the SceneGraph hierarchy. The Java statement is shown highlighted in Figure 21-11.

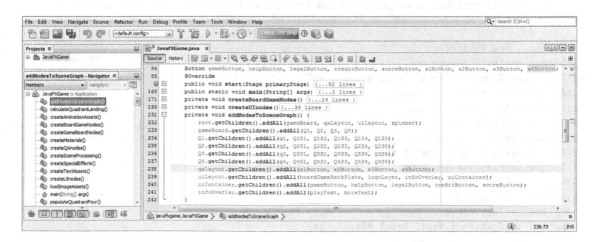

Figure 21-11. *Add the four Button UI elements to the SceneGraph, using a qaLayout.getChildren().addAll() method call*

Again, use the **Run ➤ Project** work process and test this new Java code by adding the Answer Button objects to see whether it gives you the desired result. As you can see in Figure 21-12, the StackPane is rendering, and all that we need to address is the **font family** and **font size** used on the face of the Buttons so that text is large and readable to the player.

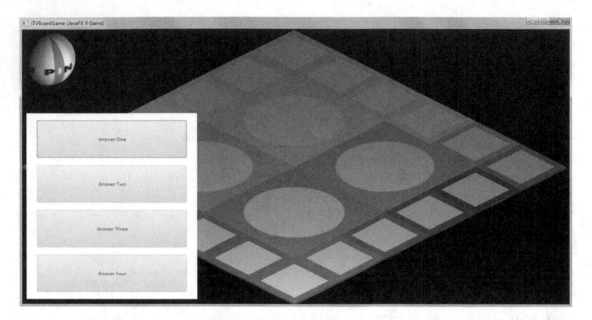

Figure 21-12. *Use your Run ➤ Project work process and test your first try at your Q&A hierarchy creation and rendering*

Add a final **setFont()** method call after each setText() method call to set the font family, in this case a nice, readable Arial Black Font, as well as the font size. Initially the largest we can fit on this Button size is 30 units, which is fairly large. Inside the setFont() method call, we nest a **Font.font()** method call, which creates this Font object, loads it with an **Arial Black** font, and sets its size to **30**. This is shown in the following Java code and shown highlighted in Figure 21-13:

```
a1Button = new Button();
a1Button.setText("Answer One");
a1Button.setFont(Font.font("Arial Black", 30));
a1Button.setMaxSize(350, 100);
a1Button.setTranslateY(-180);
a2Button = new Button();
a2Button.setText("Answer Two");
a2Button.setFont(Font.font("Arial Black", 30));
a2Button.setMaxSize(350, 100);
a2Button.setTranslateY(-60);
a3Button = new Button();
a3Button.setText("Answer Three");
a3Button.setFont(Font.font("Arial Black", 30));
a3Button.setMaxSize(350, 100);
a3Button.setTranslateY(60);
a4Button = new Button();
```

```
a4Button.setText("Answer Four");
a4Button.setFont(Font.font("Arial Black", 30));
a4Button.setMaxSize(350, 100);
a4Button.setTranslateY(180);
```

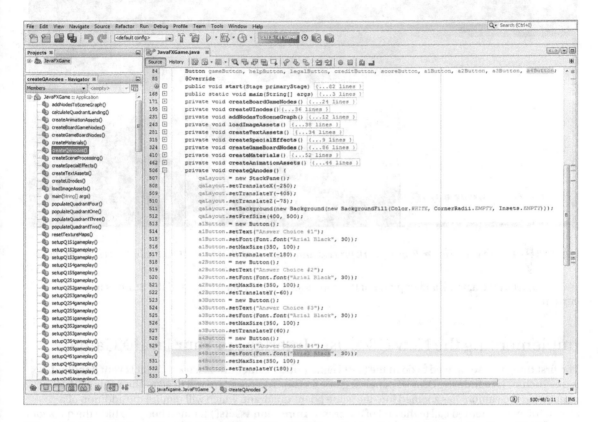

Figure 21-13. *Add the setFont(Font.font("Arial Black", 30)) method call to each Button after the setText()*
method call

Let's utilize a **Run ➤ Project** work process one last time before we write the code to actually implement
this new Q&A UI in the rest of our JavaFXGame code. We will need to hide this StackPane and child Button
objects until it is needed to display answer options to the player. We'll also need to display this StackPane at
the end of your camera animation, which will tilt and zoom your camera into the game board, changing the
camera angle and distance, which may change how the StackPane and Button objects render and therefore
necessitate "tweaking" to size and position settings. After we finish implementing this StackPane and Button
objects' Q&A UI design inside the start() method and **createAnimationAssets()** method, we can return
to the previous code and tweak the numeric values to fine-tune how it looks in the top-down "game board
question and answer view."

As you can see in Figure 21-14, the **font family** and **font size** used on these Button UI objects make
a huge difference in readability from Figure 21-12. The only problem I can see is that the panel is a bit too
tall, with a bit too much space around the edges and between Button UI elements, which we'll address
later after we implement this Q&A UI deeper in the Java code that we've written already. Remember, game
development is an iterative process!

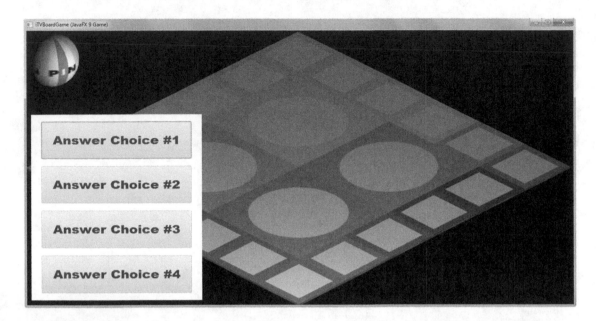

Figure 21-14. *Use your Run* ➤ *Project work process and make sure that the text on the buttons is readable*

Next, let's take a break and implement the appearance of this StackPane and the Buttons in your current code.

Implementing the New Q&A User Interface in Your JavaFXGame

The first thing that we'll need to do in the Start Game Button gameButton.setOnAction() event handling infrastructure is to **hide** the Q&A UI panel on game startup. After that, we will need to show this Q&A UI panel once the camera has zoomed into the game board quadrant, which will require the addition of a setOnFinished() method call to the end of the **createAnimationAssets()** method body. To hide the qaLayout Q&A panel StackPane when the Start Game button is clicked, simply copy the first Java statement in the handle() event handler inside of the gameButton.setOnAction() infrastructure and paste it underneath itself; then change uiLayout to **qaLayout**, as shown here and as highlighted in Figure 21-15:

```
gameButton.setOnAction(new EventHandler<ActionEvent>() {  // Using non-Lambda Expression
                                                             Format
    @Override
    public void handle(ActionEvent event) {
        uiLayout.setVisible(false);
        qaLayout.setVisible(false);
        camera.setTranslateZ(500);
        camera.setTranslateY(-300);
        camera.setTranslateX(-260);
        camera.setRotationAxis(Rotate.X_AXIS);
        camera.setRotate(-30);
        spinnerAnim.play();
    }
});
```

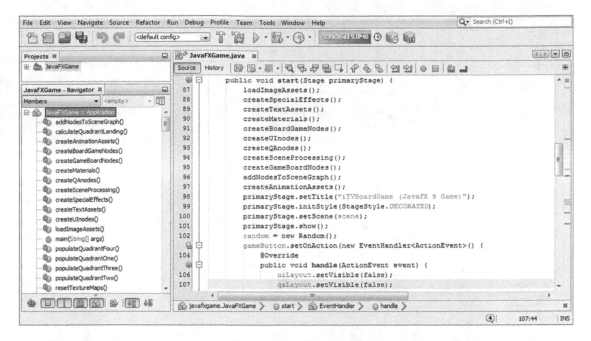

Figure 21-15. *Hide the Q&A UI panel on the game startup by using qaLayout.setVisible(false) in the start() method*

The next thing to do after hiding your Q&A UI Panel the first time (until it is needed) is to show it right after the 3D camera has been rotated and moved into the game board once the player has selected the game board square that they want to play. The theory here is that because of a new camera focal length (unit repositioning) and camera angle (rotation to 60 degrees from 30 degrees), the new Q&A Panel visual characteristics may have changed. In other words, different rendering parameters may have altered any of (or all of) the StackPane, Button, and even font characteristics.

In fact, not surprisingly, this did occur, so after we implement the new cameraAnimIn.setOnFinished() event handler, we will need to go back into the createQAnodes() method body and "tweak" the Q&A UI Panel parameters to more closely align it with the bottom-left corner of the "question answers selection" gameplay view. We will also tighten up the spacing around the answer Button UI elements and **increase** the **font size** while we are at it!

After the cameraAnimIn ParallelTransition object instantiation, add your **setOnFinished()** method call off of the cameraAnimIn object and place a qaLayout.setVisible(true); statement inside the event handling infrastructure so that your Q&A UI Panel can be seen after the camera zooms into the randomly selected game board quadrant after the player clicks the game board square to which they think they will know the answer.

This new Java code construct is shown here, as well as highlighted in blue and yellow in Figure 21-16:

```java
private void createAnimationAssets() {
    ...
    cameraAnimIn = new ParallelTransition(moveCameraIn, rotCameraDown, moveSpinnerOff);
    cameraAnimIn.setOnFinished(event->{
        qaLayout.setVisible(true);
    });
}
```

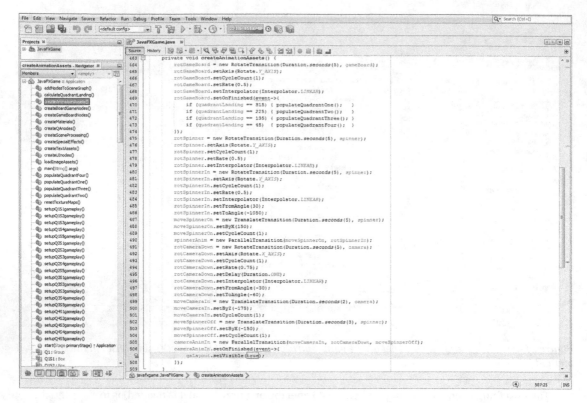

Figure 21-16. *Add a cameraAnimIn.setOnFinished() method call and add qaLayout.setVisible(true) to the event handler*

As you can see in Figure 21-17, when you use Run ➤ Project to test the setOnFinished() code that you just added, you will see that changing your camera view and location has changed your Q&A panel layout.

Figure 21-17. *Use Run* ➤ *Project to see whether the camera has changed the Q&A panel layout*

Next, let's tweak the createQAnodes() method body StackPane and Button UI object configurations so that the Q&A UI Panel appearance is in the very lower-left corner of the gameplay view, out of the way of the game board squares as much as possible, and so that all Button objects are still relatively large, are uniformly spaced out, and are using as large (and as readable) a font family and font size as possible.

Tweaking the Q&A Panel: Refining the createQAnodes() Settings

Let's start adjusting the parameters for the object configuration settings held in the createQAnodes() method body, starting with the StackPane. We will move it 20 units, from -405 to **-385, using the setTranslateY()** **method call**; decrease the size 40 units, from 400 to **360**, using the setPrefSize() method call; and increase the height 154 units, from 500 to **654**, also using the setPrefSize() method call. I edited the setText() method calls to add longer answer placeholders for the Button UI elements, using **Answer Choice 1** (through 4) rather than **Answer One** (through Four) to better fill the Button with text. I increased the font size another **10 percent** to **33** units with the setFont() method call so that I could see how large I could get the text to be on the Button surface. I increased the Button height 40 percent using the setMaxSize() method call, increasing the Button height to 140 units from 100 units. This Button height change also required that I change the Y spacing intervals for the Button spacing over the StackPane, using the setTranslateY() method call, from -160, -60, 60, and 160 to -240, -80, 80, and 240.

The new (tweaked) Java 9 code is shown here, in the new createQAnodes() method, as well as in Figure 21-18:

```
private void createQAnodes() {
    qaLayout = new StackPane();
    qaLayout.setTranslateX(-250);
    qaLayout.setTranslateY(-385);
    qaLayout.setBackground(new Background(new BackgroundFill(Color.WHITE,
                                                 CornerRadii.EMPTY,
                                                 Insets.EMPTY) ) );
    qaLayout.setPrefSize(360, 654);
```

```
    a1Button = new Button();
    a1Button.setText("Answer Choice 1");
    a1Button.setFont(Font.font("Arial Black", 33));
    a1Button.setMaxSize(350, 140);
    a1Button.setTranslateY(-240);
    a2Button = new Button();
    a2Button.setText("Answer Choice 2");
    a2Button.setFont(Font.font("Arial Black", 33));
    a2Button.setMaxSize(350, 140);
    a2Button.setTranslateY(-80);
    a3Button = new Button();
    a3Button.setText("Answer Choice 3");
    a3Button.setFont(Font.font("Arial Black", 33));
    a3Button.setMaxSize(350, 140);
    a3Button.setTranslateY(80);
    a4Button = new Button();
    a4Button.setText("Answer Choice 4");
    a4Button.setFont(Font.font("Arial Black", 33));
    a4Button.setMaxSize(350, 140);
    a4Button.setTranslateY(240);
}
```

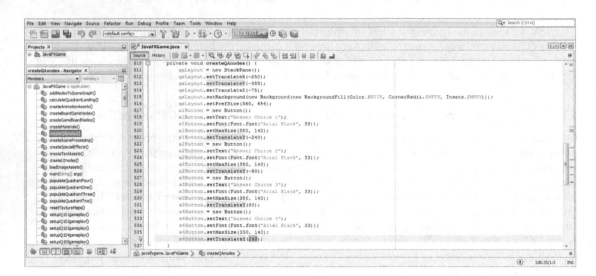

Figure 21-18. *Recalibrate the createQAnodes() settings to adjust the Q&A Panel location, size, Button spacing, and font*

As you can see in Figure 21-19, the Q&A UI Panel is now in the lower-left corner of your game board view. The Buttons are large and close together with nice, large, readable text, and the question answer user interface is out of the way of each of your digital image assets (the visual component of the game) and now looks quite professional.

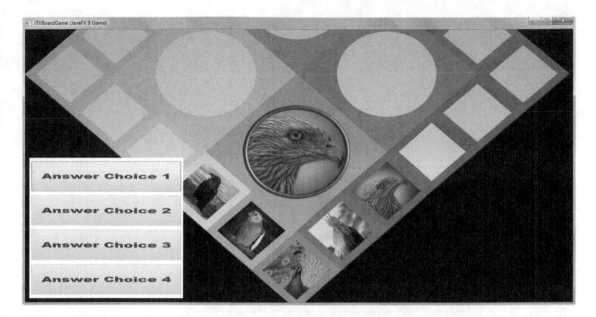

Figure 21-19. *Use a Run ➤ Project work process to see if the Q&A panel layout has been restored to its large readable state*

Adding Answer Button Content to setupQSgameplay() Methods

Now we are in a position where we can simply add the Q&A UI Panel answers for each game board square by adding four relatively simple Java statements to the inside of each of the if(pickSn == n) conditional if() evaluation statements inside each of the **setupQSgameplay()** method bodies. To test our user interface with real answer data, all we need to do is to add the first setupQ1S1gameplay() if (pickS1 == 0) section, adding the four setText() method calls to the diffuse and Shader21 object configurations that are already in place in this section of code to control your imagery.

The Java code, also shown at the end of Figure 21-20, should look like the following:

```java
private void setupQ1S1gameplay() {
    if (pickS1 == 0) {
        diffuse21 = new Image("gamequad1bird0.png", 512, 512, true, true, true);
        Shader21.setDiffuseMap(diffuse21);
        a1Button.setText("Falcon Hawk");
        a2Button.setText("Seagull");
        a3Button.setText("Peacock");
        a4Button.setText("Flamingo");
    }
}
```

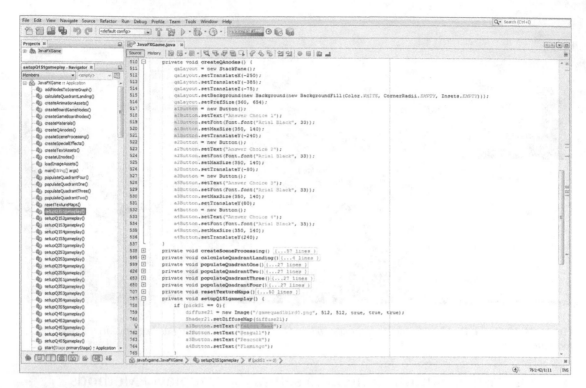

Figure 21-20. *Add the four a1Button through a4Button object answers (one is correct) using the setText() method call*

Use your **Run ➤ Project** work process to test this code adding real answer Button objects, seen in Figure 21-21.

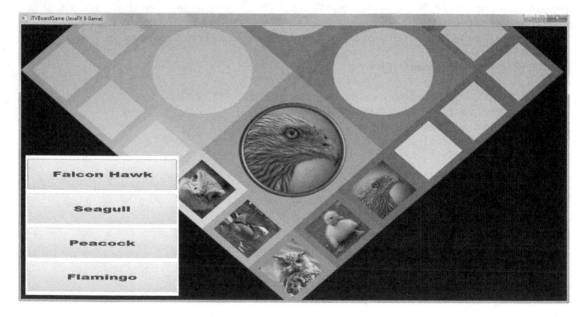

Figure 21-21. *Use a Run ➤ Project work process to see how answer Button data looks when you test square 1*

To get some practice, create the other 59 sets of question answers in the **setupQSgameplay()** methods now. Next, let's put an AudioClip object (class) into place so we can attach **sound effects** to our game board spin animation.

Digital Audio for Games: Using the AudioClip Class

Let's also take a look at how to add **digital audio assets** to your games during this chapter. This will require the use of the **javafx.media** module, which will make your distribution larger because this module will need to be added to your distribution JAR and includes both the MediaPlayer (used for both audio and video) and the AudioClip class, among others. The AudioClip class is used for shorter audio "snippets" technically called *samples*. If you want to play longer format digital audio (say, songs) or digital video, you will want to instead use the MediaPlayer class. Games usually use shorter format audio, and therefore we are going to cover the AudioClip class here; it is essentially a digital audio sequencer, which is a very powerful tool, both for game developers and for sound designers and songwriters.

The **public final AudioClip** class extends java.lang.Object, meaning it was scratch-coded to be a digital audio sequencer. It is kept in the **javafx.scene.media** package in the **javafx.media** module, and thus, the Java class hierarchy for the class looks like the following:

```
java.lang.Object
  > javafx.scene.media.AudioClip
```

An AudioClip object can be used to contain short segments of digital audio that will be played with minimal latency. Clips are loaded from a network or JAR similarly to Media objects but have a different behavior. For example, Media objects that are played by a MediaPlayer object cannot "play" themselves, whereas your AudioClip objects can. AudioClips are immediately reusable, so they have **zero latency** and use less memory, which is important for games.

The playback behavior of an AudioClip object is what Oracle calls "fire and forget." Once one of the class's play() methods is called, the only operable control is the stop() method. We will be using both of these methods.

An AudioClip object can also be played **multiple times simultaneously**! To accomplish this same task using a Media object in a MediaPlayer, one would have to create new MediaPlayer objects for each sound played in parallel. This is not optimal for gameplay scenarios, which is why we are not covering Media and MediaPlayer objects here.

Media objects and MediaPlayer are better suited for long-format audio such as songs or audiobooks. This is primarily because an AudioClip stores (in memory) a raw, uncompressed (PCM) audio data for the entire digital audio assets, which is usually quite large for long audio clips. A MediaPlayer will only have enough decompressed audio data "prerolled" in memory to play for a short amount of time; therefore, the MediaPlayer is far more memory efficient for longer clips, especially if they have been compressed, for instance, using the MP3 (digital audio) or MPEG4 (digital video) file formats or the OGG Vorbis (digital audio), FLAC (digital audio), or WebM (ON2 VP6, VP8, or VP9) digital video formats.

The AudioClip class has a half-dozen digital audio properties that affect the sound balance, cycles, location, priority, rate, and volume. These include the **balance** DoubleProperty, which controls the (relative) left and right volume levels for the AudioClip object, and the **pan** DoubleProperty, which controls where the relative "center" is for the audioClip object. The **rate** DoubleProperty controls the relative rate (speed) at which an AudioClip is played, and the **volume** DoubleProperty controls the relative volume level at which the AudioClip is played. The cycleCount IntegerProperty controls the number of times the AudioClip will be played when the play() method is invoked. The priority IntegerProperty controls the relative priority of the AudioClip object with respect to other AudioClip objects.

There is one static int INDEFINITE data field, which when the cycleCount is set to this value, the AudioClip will loop continuously until it is stopped using the stop() method call, which we will be learning about soon.

There is only one AudioClip constructor method, which takes a source URL and uses this following format:

AudioClip(String **sourceURL**)

Next, let's take a look at the methods that the AudioClip class allows us to call off your AudioClip objects. The DoubleProperty **balanceProperty()** method call allows you to obtain the relative left and right volume levels for an AudioClip object. The IntegerProperty **cycleCountProperty()** method call allows you to obtain the number of times the AudioClip object will be played when the play() method is called. The DoubleProperty **panProperty()** method call allows you to obtain the (relative) center for an AudioClip object. The IntegerProperty **priorityProperty()** method call allows you to obtain the (relative) priority setting of that AudioClip object with respect to other AudioClip objects. The DoubleProperty **rateProperty()** method call allows you to obtain a (relative) rate of speed at which that AudioClip is being played. The DoubleProperty **volumeProperty()** method call allows you to obtain the (relative) volume level at which the AudioClip is played.

Besides the six AudioClip Property methods, there are seven get() methods that allow you to get the value of the AudioClip properties, including its digital audio source file. The double **getBalance()** method call would be used to get the default balance level for the AudioClip. The int **getCycleCount()** method call would be used to get the default cycle count for the AudioClip object. The double **getPan()** method call would be used to get the default pan value for the AudioClip object. The int **getPriority()** method call would be used to get a default playback priority value for the AudioClip object. The double **getRate()** method call would be used to get the default playback rate for the AudioClip object. The String **getSource()** method call would be used to get the source URL used to create the AudioClip object. The double **getVolume()** method call would be used to get the default volume level for the AudioClip object.

There are also seven set() methods that allow you to set the value of the AudioClip properties, including the digital audio source file. The **void setBalance(double balance)** method call should be used to set the default balance level for the AudioClip object. The **void setCycleCount(int count)** method call should be used to set the default cycle count for the AudioClip object. The **void setPan(double pan)** method call should be used to set the default pan value for the AudioClip object.

The **void setPriority(int priority)** method call should be used to set the default playback priority. The **void setRate(double rate)** method call should be used to set a default playback rate. The **void setVolume(double value)** method call should be used to set the default volume level. There are also five methods, which can be used to control the AudioClip object while it is playing.

The boolean **isPlaying()** method call will be used to indicate whether an AudioClip is currently playing. The **void play()** method call should be used to play the AudioClip object using its default parameters. A **void play(double volume)** method call should be used to play the AudioClip using all the default parameters except for the volume. The void **play(double volume, double balance, double rate, double pan, int priority)** method call should be used to play the AudioClip using the given volume, balance, rate, pan, and priority parameters. Finally, the **void stop()** method call should be used to immediately stop all playback of an AudioClip object. Now we can implement digital audio assets as AudioClip objects in our game to provide audio sound effects for things such as gameboard spin and camera zooming.

Implementing AudioClip: Add Digital Audio Asset Sound Effects

The first thing that we will need to do is to declare two AudioClip objects named spinnerAudio and cameraAudio at the top of the JavaFXGame class, as shown in the following Java 9 code and shown highlighted in Figure 21-22:

```
AudioClip spinnerAudio, cameraAudio;
```

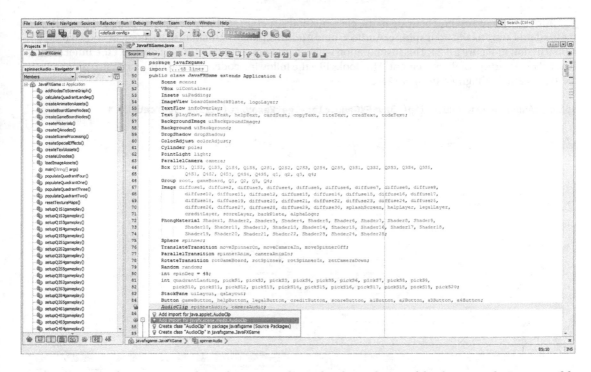

Figure 21-22. *Declare spinnerAudio and cameraAudio AudioClip at the top of the class; use Alt+Enter to add an import*

Next, create a **loadAudioAssets()** method call, right under the loadImageAssets() method call, and again use the **Alt+Enter** keystroke, shown in Figure 21-23, to have NetBeans create the empty bootstrap method body for you.

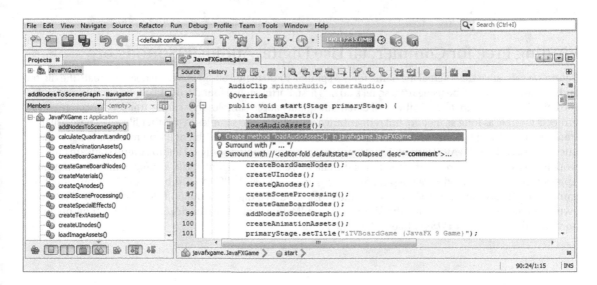

Figure 21-23. *Create a loadAudioAssets() method call after loadImageAssets(); use Alt+Enter to have NetBeans code it*

Move this new method body up in the class method structure so it is near your loadImageAssets() method and start to add your **spinnerAudio = new AudioClip();** instantiation statement, as shown under construction in Figure 21-24. This instantiation will become more complex as we construct the inner (String sourceURL) portion of the statement. This looks like the following code, which is under construction in NetBeans and highlighted in Figure 21-24:

```
spinnerAudio = new AudioClip( JavaFXGame.class.getResource(String sourceURL) );
```

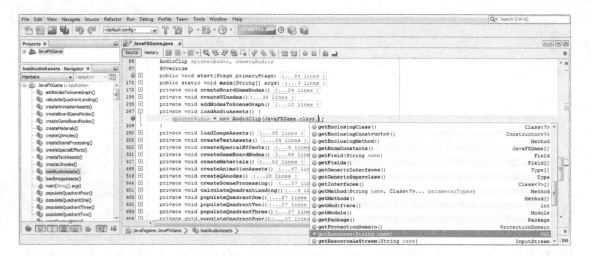

Figure 21-24. *Add your internal getResource(String) portion of the AudioClip instantiation statement for spinnerAudio*

Let's take a couple of pages and find a professional-level CD and HD digital audio sample web site that has free-for-commercial-usage WAVE files (uncompressed PCM digital audio at 44.1 KHz in 16-bit and 24-bit resolutions).

Finding Free for Commercial Use Digital Audio: 99Sounds.org

Before we reference the internal file name for the spinnerAudio digital audio asset, we need to create the digital audio asset that we will be using next, so let's do this first. Fortunately, I found a digital audio sample library site called **99Sounds** that has gigabytes of cinematic quality audio samples that can be utilized for commercial projects for free, as long as they are not redistributed as digital audio samples in another library. These use the standard 44.1 Hz, CD quality, and audio sample rate, and they are either 16-bit or 24-bit resolution, using the uncompressed PCM (WAVE) format. If you want to learn more about the digital audio editing software and work process that is covered in this section of the chapter, check out *Digital Audio Editing Fundamentals* from Apress.com. I downloaded all of the sample libraries from www.99SOUNDS.org just because I work on a lot of games, web sites, e-books, iTV shows, smartwatches, and similar digital productions for clients as well as my own company. Figure 21-25 shows the file explorer application listing with the dozens of folders (now on my hard disk drive under a **C:\Audio** folder) I downloaded.

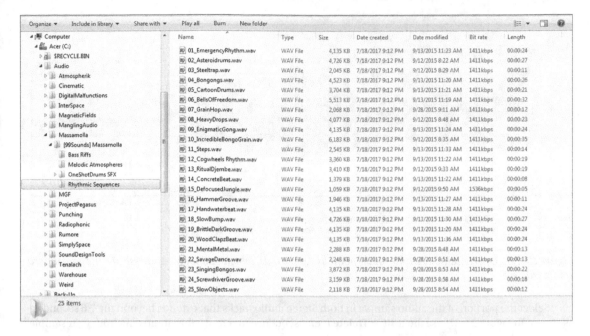

Figure 21-25. *Go to* www.99sounds.org *and download free digital audio samples for all your pro Java 9 game projects*

I am going to use the **24th** sample in the **Massamolla** collection, found in the **Rhythmic Sequence** folder, as shown selected in Figure 21-25. This sample is called **ScrewdriverGroove** and is in 32-bit 44.1 Hz WAVE format; it uses a 1411 Kbps compression rate and is 18 seconds long, of which we will loop around 7 seconds to reduce the memory data footprint. We'll also convert this to a **MONO** sample to save memory and will create several versions of this file.

Data Footprint Optimization: Use Audacity to Create Game Audio

Notice the file size in Figure 21-25 is **3,159** kilobytes, which is too much memory to use for spin audio! We will be trimming nearly 3MB off of this file size for the low-quality audio component and creating a high-quality audio asset that is little more than half a megabyte in size, so this should be an interesting section for all of you game developers! Launch Audacity 2.1.3 (or later version), which I will assume you have downloaded and installed already. Use the **File ➤ Open** menu sequence to open the ScrewdriverGroove sample shown in Figure 21-25; find the first large gap in its repetitive sound, shown in Figure 21-26 using a green line, at approximately **7.6 seconds** into this file.

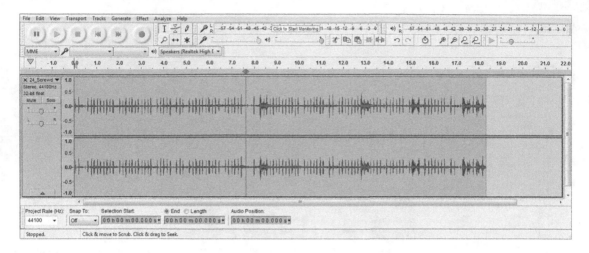

Figure 21-26. *Open Audacity 2 and find a point at 7.6 seconds, which will loop seamlessly for the gameboard spin audio*

Select the portion of the audio sample in both Stereo audio tracks that extends beyond the 7.6 seconds, as shown in Figure 21-27; use the **Edit ➤ Delete** menu sequence to remove this audio data from your sample.

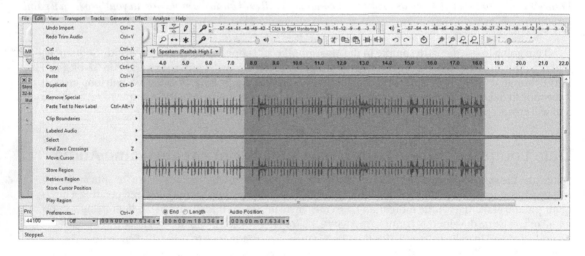

Figure 21-27. *Select the portion between 7.6 and 18.3 seconds and use your Edit ➤ Delete menu sequence to remove it*

This removes about three-fifths (7.6 of 18.3 is about two-fifths) of the digital audio data right off of the bat. The next "move" we will make is to combine both **Stereo** audio tracks into one **Mono** audio track, again reducing the amount of data by 100 percent. Select both Stereo audio tracks, as shown in Figure 21-28, and use the **Tracks ➤ Stereo Track to Mono** menu sequence to combine these two (Stereo) digital audio tracks into only one Mono digital audio track.

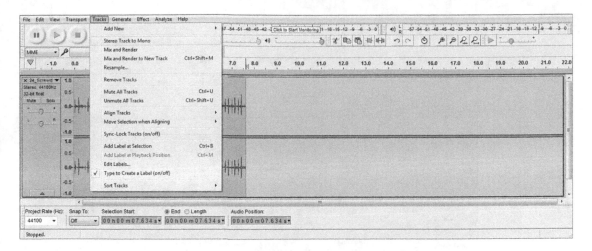

Figure 21-28. *Select the entire sample on both tracks and use Tracks* ➤ *Stereo Track to Mono to combine the sample*

The next thing that we need to cut in half is the amount of sample resolution, reducing a 32-bit (float) audio sample down to the 16-bit PCM resolution commonly known as "CD-quality" audio. This is done using the drop-down arrow on top of the **Mono, 44100Hz 32-bit float** indicator, on the far left of the waveform audio, as shown in Figure 21-29.

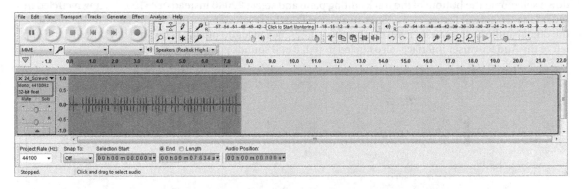

Figure 21-29. *A seven-second Mono 44.1Hz 32-bit float sample is now more than 400 percent less data than the original sample*

Click this drop-down arrow and go into the **Format** submenu at the bottom of the main menu, which can be seen at the bottom-left in Figure 21-30. This reveals the selected 32-bit float format and allows you to select either a 16-bit PCM (CD) or 24-bit PCM (HD) audio resolution format. Since we are trying to conserve system memory for game audio assets, we'll choose a 16-bit, 44.1 KHz format.

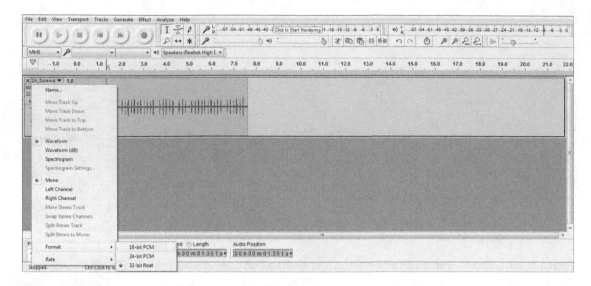

Figure 21-30. *Reduce the sample format another 100 percent from 32-bit to 16-bit resolution using the sample drop-down arrow*

We will now create a medium and low-quality digital audio asset by reducing the sample rate from 44.1 KHz to 22.05 Hz (exactly half). Reducing the data by 100 percent (half) or 200 percent (quarter) gives perfect results as there are no remainder values (even division). To do this, use the Project Rate (Hz) drop-down selector at the bottom of the track editing pane and select **22050** instead of 44100, as shown circled in red on the left side of Figure 21-31. You can also see that the resolution has been reduced to 16-bit. Preview the digital audio to see whether you can hear any difference in audio quality using the Play button at the top left of the Audacity user interface, also circled in red. It still sounds great as an effect.

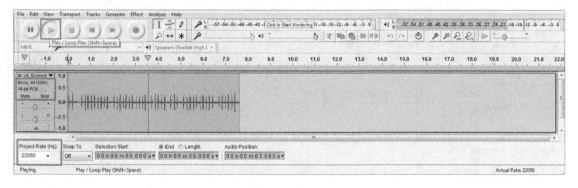

Figure 21-31. *Reduce the sample format by another 100 percent, from 44.1 to 22.05 KHz using the Project Rate drop-down menu*

Finally, let's reduce this sound effect sample by another 100 percent by taking its sample rate down to 11.025 KHz, from 44.1 KHz (always sample from the highest possible sample rate to a target sample rate to give the algorithm the highest-quality data to work its magic with). As you can see in Figure 21-32, we have Audacity using a 44.1 KHz, 16-bit audio sample data (see the setting on middle left) and have set the Project Rate (Hz) drop-down to **11.025 KHz**. You could again preview the audio quality, using the **Play** button, and if you do, you will see that the quality level has gone down, but the quality level is still quite usable for a repetitive game board spin animation audio feedback sound effect.

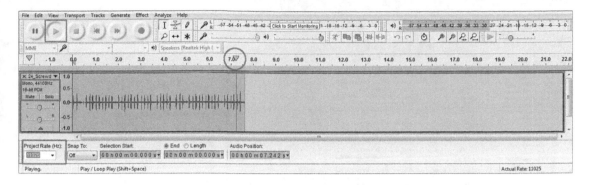

Figure 21-32. *Reduce the sample format by another 100 percent from 44.1 to 11.025 KHz, using the Project Rate drop-down menu*

I've combined all three Audacity **File ➤ Save As** dialogs into one in Figure 21-33 to save on space; we have a lot that we need to look at during this chapter, in both NetBeans and Audacity. The first panel, numbered 1, shows your 44.1 KHz 16-bit file being saved as **spinner.wav** in the **NetBeansProjects/JavaFXGame/src/** folder. The second portion of the figure shows a 22.05 KHz 16-bit version being saved as **spinner22.wav**, and the third portion of the figure shows the 11.025 KHz 16-bit version being saved as **spinner11.wav**. The file sizes for these three audio assets come to about 658KB, 329KB, and 165KB. Since these are 16-bit PCM .wav files, the amount of memory used to store the file also happens to be the amount of system memory used to deploy the file for use in your games.

Figure 21-33. *Use Audacity's File ➤ Save function to export 44, 22, and 11 Hz, 16-bit audio versions to / JavaFXGame/src*

Now we can continue the AudioClip instantiation statement and use a new audio sample in our game logic!

Use toExternalForm() to Load a URI Reference as a String Object

Now we can add this **spinner.wav** file name in the **getResource()** method and then chain that method call to the **toExternalForm()** method call, which converts the spinner.wav audio resource to the external (URI String) form that is required by the AudioClip constructor method. Be sure to add the root (/) forward slash to your spinner.wav so it can be seen in the root source (/src) folder. The Java code for this statement is shown under construction in Figure 21-34:

```
spinnerAudio = new AudioClip( JavaFXGame.class.getResource("\spinner.wav").toExternalForm() );
```

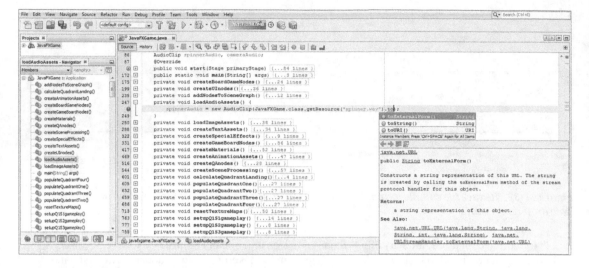

Figure 21-34. *Go back to the instantiation and add the spinner.wav audio file and the toExternalForm()
method chain*

Since the game board spins longer than seven seconds, you will need to also add a setCycleCount()
method call and set it to the INDEFINITE (infinite loop) data value using the following Java 9 code, also
shown in Figure 21-35:

```
spinnerAudio.setCycleCount(AudioClip.INDEFINITE);
```

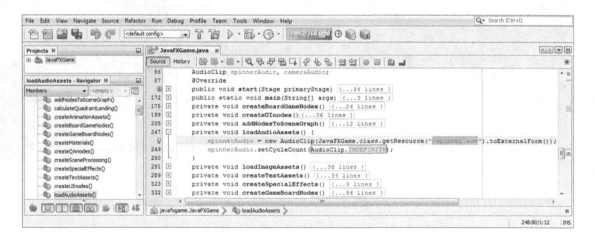

Figure 21-35. *Add a slash (/), or root, to spinner.wav. Then add a spinnerAudio.setCycleCount(AudioClip.
INDEFINITE) method call*

Now that your spin AudioClip asset is set up, we now have to trigger it when the spinner UI is clicked
with the mouse.

Triggering Spinner Audio Playback in createSceneProcessing()

To play the AudioClip object, we need to insert a **spinnerAudio.play();** method call into the event handling for your **if (picked == spinner)** structure near the end, right before the calculateQuadrantLanding() method call.

The Java 9 code for this addition is shown highlighted at the bottom of Figure 21-36.

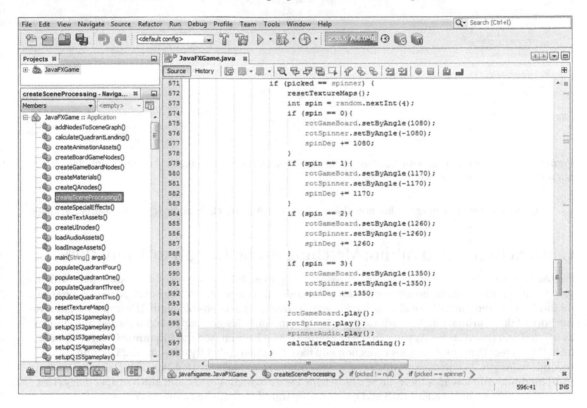

Figure 21-36. *Trigger a spinnerAudio.play() in the createSceneProcessing() method in an if(picked == spinner) structure*

To stop your **spinnerAudio** AudioClip object's playback, you will need to call your **stop()** method off of the spinnerAudio AudioClip inside of the **setOnFinished()** event handling code structure, which is called off of the **rotGameBoard** Animation object inside of the **createAnimationAssets()** method body.

In this way, when the Animation object is finished animating, your spinnerAudio.stop() method is called, and the game board spin audio stops when the game board stops spinning.

I placed this code at the very end of the event handling structure using the following code, which is highlighted in light blue and yellow at the end of Figure 21-37:

```
rotGameBoard.setOnFinished(event-> {
    if (quadrantLanding == 315) { populateQuadrantOne();   }
    if (quadrantLanding == 225) { populateQuadrantTwo();   }
    if (quadrantLanding == 135) { populateQuadrantThree(); }
    if (quadrantLanding == 45)  { populateQuadrantFour();  }
    spinnerAudio.stop();
});
```

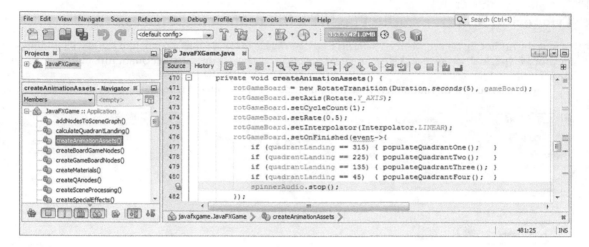

Figure 21-37. *Stop the spinnerAudio object in the createAnimationAssets() method in a rotGameBoard. setOnFinished() event handler*

Next, let's create our camera Animation object audio, this time matching audio length to Animation length.

Camera Animation Audio: Matching Audio Length to Animation

For the camera object Animation AudioClip, we are going to **match** the five seconds of Animation with five seconds of audio so that we do not need to **loop** the audio and therefore do also not need to use the **stop()** method call, as the AudioClip will stop playing after its five to six seconds of length. It is important that you see both of these primary digital audio approaches to gameplay design: looped audio started and stopped as needed and timed audio. As you can see in Figure 21-38, I have chosen the **Rhythmic Glacier** sample from the Project Pegasus Arpeggios collection and have trimmed it slightly to be around five-and-a-half seconds in length. As you can see, this sample was **48000** Hz, so I also created 16000 Hz (1/3) and 8000 Hz (1/6) medium- and low-quality 16-bit versions, which were **526KB**, **176KB**, and **88KB**, respectively. This puts CD-quality sound at about 1MB and good-quality sound at about half a megabyte.

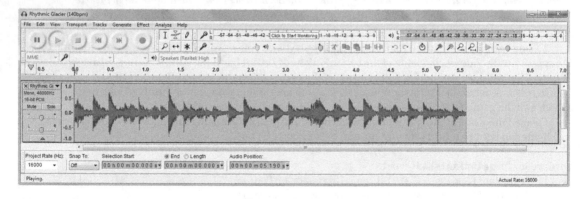

Figure 21-38. *Match almost six seconds of Rhythmic Glacier audio with almost six seconds of camera zoom animation*

Now we can load a second cameraAudio AudioClip object with this camera.wav asset and use it in our code.

Since you have already declared the cameraAudio AudioClip at the top of your class, the next step will be to instantiate it inside your loadAudioAssets() method, after the spinnerAudio AudioClip object and its instantiation and configuration statements. After we do this, we can again add the play() trigger to your createSceneProcessing() code.

You will not need to add a stop() method call to your **createAnimationAssets()** onFinished() event handler, as the sound is playing only once and expires at around the same time that the Animation object finishes moving and rotating the camera object. If you want to sync these more closely, use the same approach that we did for the spinner audio asset and loop a shorter AudioClip and then call a stop() method inside of the setOnFinished() event handler.

The Java code for the second instantiation is identical to the first (except for the audio asset's file name) and looks like the following, which is shown highlighted in light blue and yellow in the middle of Figure 21-39:

```
cameraAudio = new AudioClip( JavaFXGame.class.getResource("/camera.wav").toExternalForm() );
```

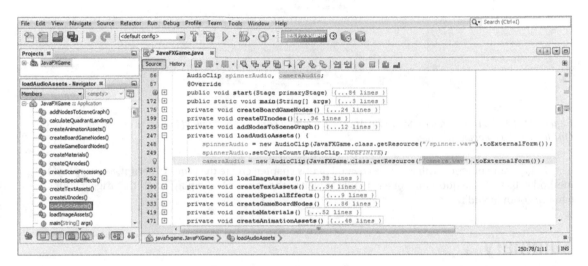

Figure 21-39. *Add a cameraAudio AudioClip to the loadAudioAssets() method and reference the new camera. wav asset*

If you want to add more digital audio sound effects, you can simply mimic one of these AudioClip objects or the other, for instance, to add audio to the i3D spinner UI element as it comes onto the screen, to add audio that has to do with the Q&A sessions, or even to add audio that loops as the Start Game button is waiting to be clicked by the player. So, you might expand this loadAudioAssets() method, as you continue to develop and refine this pro Java 9 game design.

Camera animation and audio is triggered in a different part of your createSceneProcessing() method when the player clicks a game board square to select its content for use in a Q&A session. Therefore, instead of the play() method being called in **if(picked == spinner)**, it is called in **if(picked == Q1S1)** or one of the other 19 game board square conditional if() statements. The Java code, shown in Figure 21-40, should look like the following:

```
if (picked == Q1S1) {
    setupQ1S1gameplay();
    cameraAnimIn.play();
    cameraAudio.play();
}
```

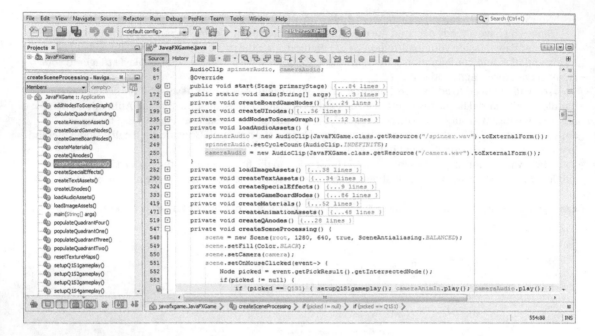

Figure 21-40. *To trigger a cameraAudio AudioClip, add a cameraAudio.play() method call to the* *OnMouseClicked event handler*

To get some practice with what we covered in this chapter, create the other 19 **setupQSgameplay()** method calls with the questions for each topic as well as the cameraAudio.play() calls that trigger your camera zoom in audio.

Summary

In this twenty-first chapter, we learned how to create the **answer selections** for each game board square. We also created a StackPane and Button objects for the player to use to record their answer. You will need to create the other Java code to answer each game board square random options and enter this code to complete the gameplay so that you can proceed to the next chapter, where we will be creating the scoring engine, scoreboard, and high-score code that will track this portion of the game.

We also learned how to add **digital audio assets** to a game using the JavaFX **AudioClip** sequencer, which has all of the core music synthesis and sound tracking and triggering tools that a synthesizer possesses. We created both a **timed** digital audio clip and a **looping** (played until stopped) version of digital audio so that you understand how to add digital audio assets for aural feedback for your players during their gameplay experience.

In Chapter 22, you're going to develop a scoring engine code infrastructure, which will handle what happens when the player selects the proper game square content answer. This means we will again be developing 2D game elements to hold the scoreboard content, which will pop up and overlay more of the unused portions of the 3D game user interface. In this case, this will be the bottom-right portions of the gameplay screen.

■ ■ ■

CHAPTER 22

Scoring Engine: Creating the Score UI Layout and Scoring the Content

Now that you have your game board square answer selection logic coded and you have sound effects for your game board spin and camera animation sequence coded, we need to put the other half of the Java code into place that looks at what answer the user selects (clicks) and updates the scoreboard accordingly. We will track both correct and incorrect answers and encourage the player in real time using a simple but effective scoring interface. The work process in this chapter will necessitate that we also create a Score UI pane (panel) for the right side of our screen, which we will create using a StackPane named **scoreLayout** and Text objects whose names also begin with **score**.

During this chapter, we'll be implementing a single-player gameplay and scoring model to get your scoring user interface in place and because a lot of game players will want to play the game against the content as a learning experience. That said, there will still be a lot of code to write for each Button UI element that looks at whether the answer is the correct answer; if it is, the code will increment the "Right:" score, and if it is not, it will increment the "Wrong:" score.

This means you will still need to add several hundred more lines of Java code after you learn how to implement scoring logic in this chapter. This will score all your answers, which you learned how to put in place in the previous chapter.

Fortunately, we will use that optimal "code once, then copy, paste, and modify" approach, so there should not be too much typing involved, like in the previous chapter. The real work will be creating the answers (Chapter 21) and the scoring logic (this chapter) after you have finished learning how to implement scoring (in the current chapter).

There is also one small bug from the previous chapter that we will fix by moving the .setVisible(false) call for the Q&A UI panel from your Start Game Button to the JavaFX application start() method startup sequence, which will initially hide the Q&A UI panel (and later the Score UI panel) on your game's startup, rather than on a Button click.

SplashScreen Render Bug: Hide UI Panels on Startup

You may have noticed during the **Run ➤ Project** test rendering of your game in the previous chapter that JavaFX was incorrectly rendering part of the Q&A UI pane (panel) above the SplashScreen for your game, as shown at the top left of Figure 22-1. This Q&A UI panel should really be behind your SplashScreen, as you've designated that rendering order in your addNodesToSceneGraph() method in the root.addChildren.() addAll() method chain's Node object parameter list sequence. By adding i3D elements to make your Scene a 3D (or a "hybrid" 2D+3D Scene) entity, this could also be a Z-unit location (position) setting issue. Therefore, there could be two ways to investigate and fix this minor rendering issue. Since we already have our X, Y, Z display units set and working effectively for what we want to achieve in the i3D game rendering pipeline, the easiest way to fix this glitch is to simply hide the UI panel (since we are hiding it on game startup anyway) automatically on game startup, rather than manually using a Start Game Button UI element. This is done at the top of your start() method, required by JavaFX, rather than in an event handling structure connected to an initial click on a Start Game Button UI element.

Figure 22-1. *Let's fix the Q&A Button pane rendering bug that affects the startup screen first before developing the scoring*

First, remove the **qaLayout.setVisible(false);** Java statement from within the gameButton event-handling code and place it at the top of your .start() method so that this hide gets processed **automatically**.

Remember that your qaLayout StackPane will get created in the createQAnodes() method, so this statement will need to come **after** your **createQAnodes();** custom method call and thus after any of the methods called before this custom method. This is fine, as these simply set up asset references and objects that will be used in your game.

This ends up being a quicker and easier fix to this visual bug; since we are already going to hide this panel on game startup, doing this hide (set visibility false) earlier on (automatically) rather than in the event handling logic both creates cleaner code and saves us the time figuring out why (clearly a Z unit setting problem in 3D space) this is happening and how to add (and adjust) Z location code for the qaLayout StackPane object that will not mess up your currently pristine results (other than on this initial SplashScreen display).

The Java code for this simple modification is shown highlighted in the middle of Figure 22-2 and should look like the following Java 9 statement, now found in the first part of your **public void start()** core JavaFX 9 method:

```java
public void start() {
    loadImageAssets();
    loadAudioAssets();
    createSpecialEffects();
    createTextAssets();
    createMaterials();
    createBoardGameNodes();
    createUInodes();
    createQAnodes();
    qaLayout.setVisible(false);
    createSceneProcessing();
    createGameBoardNodes();
    ...
}
```

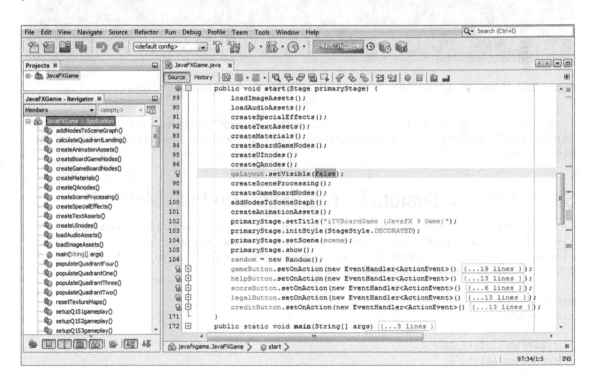

Figure 22-2. *Remove the .setVisible() call from your gameButton handler and place it in .start() after createQAnodes()*

Use the **Run ➤ Project** work process in Figure 22-3 to see the fix to this problem in your SplashScreen.

Figure 22-3. *Your Q&A UI panel is now hidden on startup, in the top of your .start() method*

Now that we have fixed that minor (code-wise) SplashScreen rendering issue, we can proceed to create your Score UI layout design, starting with a scoreLayout StackPane object and the Text objects that contain its decoration.

Scoreboard UI Design: A createScoreNodes() Method

Let's have NetBeans create a **createScoreNodes()** custom method body for us by adding a line of code after the **qaLayout.setVisible(false);** statement we just added and then using the **Alt+Enter** keystroke combination to trigger this automated method coding by NetBeans 9. The Java statement for this is shown here and highlighted in the middle of Figure 22-4:

```
public void start()  {
    loadImageAssets();
    loadAudioAssets();
    createSpecialEffects();
    createTextAssets();
    createMaterials();
    createBoardGameNodes();
    createUInodes();
    createQAnodes();
    qaLayout.setVisible(false);
    createScoreNodes();
    ...
}
```

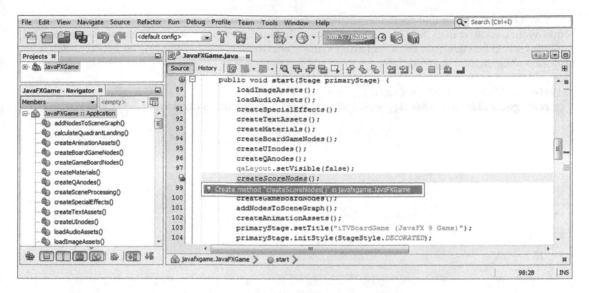

Figure 22-4. *Create a createScoreNodes() method after the qaLayout logic and use Alt+Enter to have NetBeans code it*

Copy the method from the bottom of your class to right after the **createQAnodes()** method, as shown at the bottom of Figure 22-5. Copy the qaLayout statements from the createQAnodes() method into the createScoreNodes() method and change the **.setTranslateX()** method call from **-250** to **250** to mirror it to the other corner of the display.

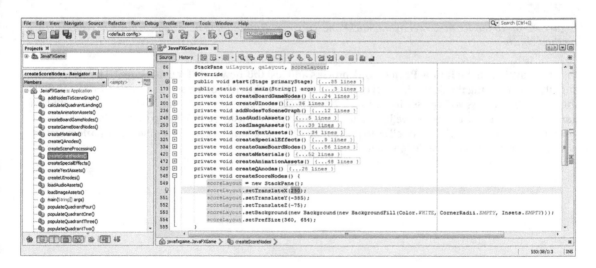

Figure 22-5. *Add a StackPane named scoreLayout at the top of the class and instantiate and configure it like qaLayout*

You'll leave the other four copied Java statements the same (other than changing qaLayout to scoreLayout), as other than the X location, you want to "mirror" the height, depth, background color, and preferred StackPane size. Add this scoreLayout to the SceneGraph using the following Java code, which is also shown highlighted in Figure 22-6:

```java
private void addNodesToSceneGraph() {
    root.getChildren().addAll(gameBoard, uiLayout, qaLayout, scoreLayout, spinner);
    ...
}
```

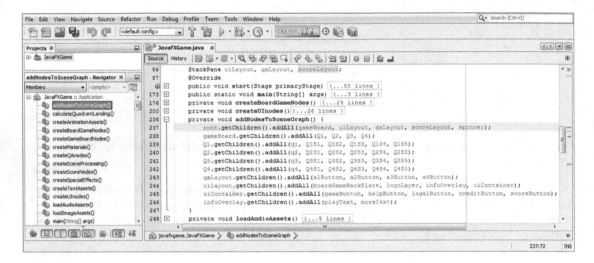

Figure 22-6. *To render the scoreLayout StackPane, you must first add it to the root.getChildren().addAll() method chain*

Let's again use the **Run ➤ Project** work process and test this new code for your Score UI panel to make sure that is mirroring the Score UI panel design far enough to the right of the screen using a .setTranslateX() method call value. As you can see in Figure 22-7, we're falling about **400** units short of the right corner of the game with our guess. Therefore, we'll need to change the 250 value to a **650** value to move this StackPane container further to the right, as well as to prevent this 2D StackPane UI container object from **intersecting** with your i3D game board Node hierarchy.

Figure 22-7. *As you can see, this StackPane is intersecting with the game board and needs to move right 400 units in X*

The Java 9 code to complete the Score UI background and container is shown highlighted in Figure 22-8, and your modified **.setTranslateX()** method call (from 250 X units to 650 X units) should look like the following code:

```
scoreLayout.setTranslateX(650);
```

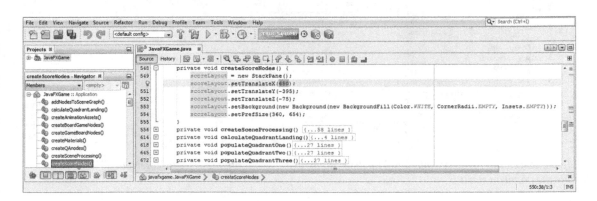

Figure 22-8. *Change the scoreLayout.setTranslateX() method call from 250 to 650 to move the Score UI panel by 400 units*

The next thing that we need to do is to put the Java code into place that will hide the Score UI pane on the startup of the game in the same way that it is for the Q&A UI panel. Your new start() method code should look like the following code, shown in Figure 22-9, once you add your **scoreLayout.setVisible(false);** Java statement:

```java
public void start() {
    loadImageAssets();
    loadAudioAssets();
    createSpecialEffects();
    createTextAssets();
    createMaterials();
    createBoardGameNodes();
    createUInodes();
    createQAnodes();
    qaLayout.setVisible(false);
    createScoreNodes();
    scoreLayout.setVisible(false);
    ...
}
```

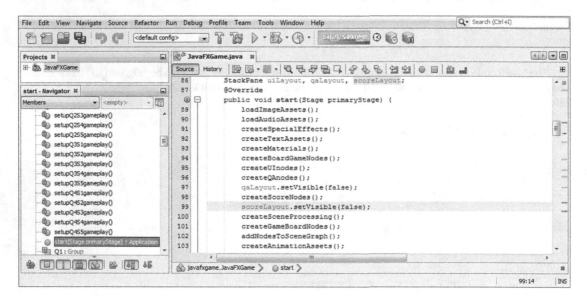

Figure 22-9. *Add the .setVisible(false) method call off scoreLayout after the createScoreNodes() method to hide the panel on startup*

As you can see in Figure 22-10, you still need to set your scoreLayout StackPane to be visible at the end of your cameraAnimIn Animation object animation by using your **.setOnFinished(event)** event handling infrastructure. This code is already in place because we are already revealing the Q&A UI panel after the camera animation has been completed. Therefore, all we have to do is to add the **scoreLayout.setVisible(true);** statement at the end of the **cameraAnimIn.setOnFinished(event->{});** structure, which is shown highlighted in light blue and yellow in the middle of Figure 22-10. You must put this Java 9 code into place before you will be able to test your Score UI panel.

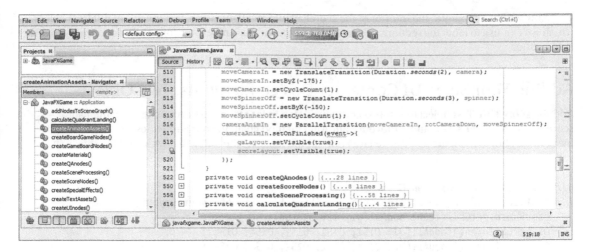

Figure 22-10. *To show the scoreLayout StackPane, add a .setVisible(true) method call in cameraAnimIn. setOnFinished()*

Again, use the **Run ➤ Project** work process and make sure your game SplashScreen and game board spin are back to their "clean" appearance; then spin and select game board square 1 to invoke the cameraAnimIn object **.setOnFinished(event)** event handling method logic, which is revealing both the StackPane UI containers at this point.

This allows us to test the Score UI container code after the camera angles have changed. As you can see in Figure 22-11, all we have to do is to move the StackPane down by **10** units by changing the **.setTranslateY()** method call of **-395** (shown in Figure 22-8) to a value of **-385** to achieve a perfectly mirrored Score UI panel result.

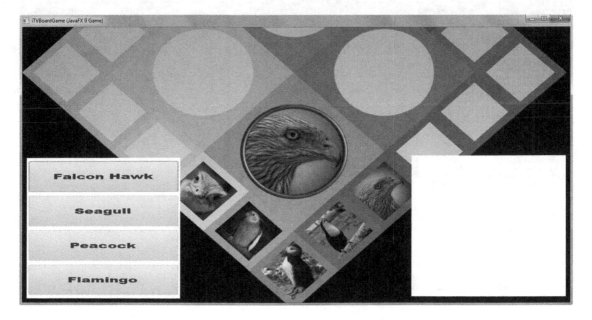

Figure 22-11. *Use Run ➤ Project to render the Score panel, via the .setOnFinished() event handler, showing the initial pane position*

Now we can "decorate" the interior of the scoreLayout StackPane using Text objects of different colors, which we can use to label the sections of our Score UI panel using a nice large font and dark primary (RGB) color values.

Adding Your Score UI Container Design Elements: Text Objects

Add the **scoreTitle** Text object to the Text compound statement at the top of your class and then add scoreTitle to a **scoreLayout.addChildren().addAll()** method chain in your addNodesToSceneGraph() method, as shown in Figure 22-12. The Java code should look like the following, which is also shown in yellow at the top of Figure 22-12:

```
private void addNodesToSceneGraph() {
    root.getChildren().addAll(gameBoard, uiLayout, qaLayout, scoreLayout, spinner);
    gameBoard.getChildren().addAll(Q1, Q2, Q3, Q4);
    Q1.getChildren().addAll(q1, Q1S1, Q1S2, Q1S3, Q1S4, Q1S5);
    Q2.getChildren().addAll(q2, Q2S1, Q2S2, Q2S3, Q2S4, Q2S5);
    Q3.getChildren().addAll(q3, Q3S1, Q3S2, Q3S3, Q3S4, Q3S5);
    Q4.getChildren().addAll(q4, Q4S1, Q4S2, Q4S3, Q4S4, Q4S5);
    qaLayout.getChildren().addAll(a1Button, a2Button, a3Button, a4Button);
    scoreLayout.getChildren().addAll(scoreTitle);
    uiLayout.getChildren().addAll(boardGameBackPlate, logoLayer, infoOverlay, uiContainer);
    uiContainer.getChildren().addAll(gameButton, helpButton, legalButton, creditButton,
                                     scoreButton);
    infoOverlay.getChildren()addAll(platText, moreText);
}
```

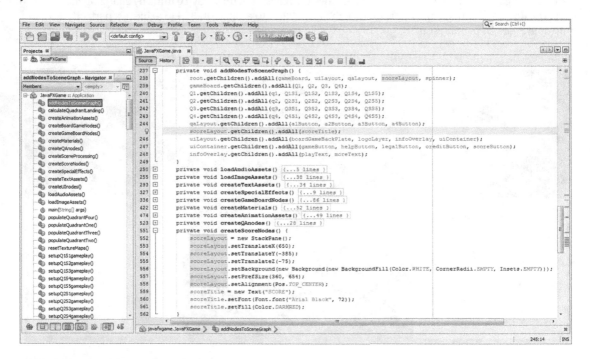

Figure 22-12. *Add a scoreTitle Text object, instantiate it, and configure it in createScoreNodes(). Then add it to the SceneGraph*

Set the **alignment** for the scoreTitle heading in the scoreLayout StackPane using the .setAlignment() method call with the **Pos.TOP_CENTER** constant, which will **center** this crimson SCORE heading at the top and in the center of the StackPane container. Interestingly, Text object alignment is set in the **parent** StackPane container. We can custom-align nonheading Text elements later, using the **.setTranslateX()** and **.setTranslateY()** method calls, off of the Text child objects to fine-tune the alignment within the Score UI panel as we flesh out this design over the next few pages.

Instantiate the scoreTitle Text object at the bottom of your createScoreNodes() method and then configure it by using the **.setFont()** method. Use an **Arial Black** font face for its bold readability at a large **72**-point font size. Use the **.setFill()** method call and change the color from Black to **Dark Red** so that the Score Title is easily viewable at the top of the Score UI panel. The Java code, shown highlighted at the bottom of Figure 22-12, looks like the following:

```
private void createScoreNodes() {
    scoreLayout = new StackPane();
    scoreLayout.setTranslateX(650);
    scoreLayout.setTranslateY(-385);
    scoreLayout.setTranslateZ(-75);
    scoreLayout.setBackground(new Background(new BackgroundFill(Color.WHITE,
                                                 CornerRadii.EMPTY,
                                                 insets.EMPTY) ) );
    scoreLayout.setPrefSize(360, 654);
    scoreLayout.setAlignment(Pos.TOP_CENTER);
    scoreTitle = new Text("SCORE");
    scoreTitle.setFont( Font.font("Arial Black", 72) );
    scoreTitle.setFill(Color.DARKRED);
}
```

Figure 22-13 shows the **Run ➤ Project** work process to preview how the "SCORE" title works in the Score pane.

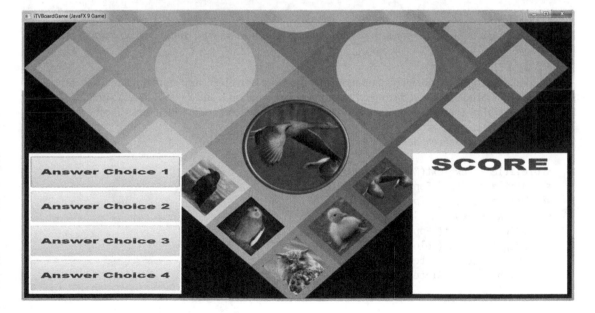

Figure 22-13. *Use the Run ➤ Project work process to preview the Score UI panel with its new Dark Red title heading*

As shown highlighted in Figure 22-14, we've declared a **scoreRight** Text object at the top of the class and also added it to the **scoreLayout.addChildren().addAll()** method chain so it can be seen in the test render we'll be doing.

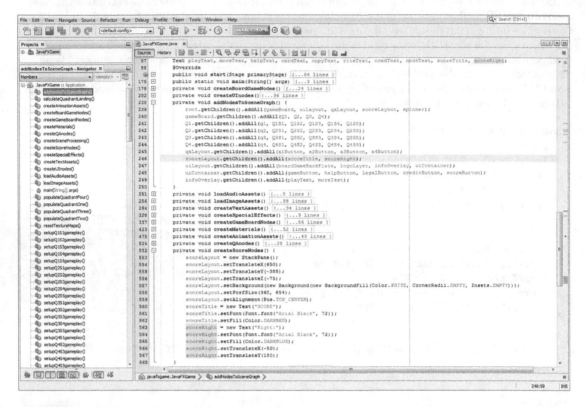

Figure 22-14. *Add a scoreRight object at the top of the class, instantiate and configure it, and add it to the SceneGraph*

I added the scoreRight object instantiation after the scoreTitle object and configured it to use the **Dark Blue** color, Arial Black font face, at a 72-point font size. I added X and Y coordinates to initially position it at (-50, 150) within a scoreLayout StackPane. Figure 22-14 shows the code, which looks like the following:

```
private void createScoreNodes()  {
    ...
    scoreTitle = new Text("SCORE");
    scoreTitle.setFont( Font.font("Arial Black", 72) );
    scoreTitle.setFill(Color.DARKRED);
    scoreRight = new Text("Right:");
    scoreRight.setFont( Font.font("Arial Black", 72) );
    scoreRight.setFill(Color.DARKBLUE);
    scoreRight.setTranslateX(-50);
    scoreRight.setTranslateY(150);
}
```

Figure 22-15 shows a **Run ➤ Project** work process to preview how a **Right:** heading works in the Score pane.

Figure 22-15. *Use a Run ➤ Project work process to preview the Score UI panel with new Dark Blue "Right:" score heading*

Since this particular i3D board game design is for younger children about to enter school, let's also include a "Wrong:" score tracking heading and also add some encouragement after each answer, such as **Great Job!** or **Spin Again**. The fastest way to write this code is to copy and paste the **scoreRight** code, underneath itself, and change scoreRight to **scoreWrong** while also changing the color to **Red** and **X, Y** location to **-25, 300**. This is shown in the following Java 9 code and highlighted in yellow at the bottom of Figure 22-16:

```
private void createScoreNodes()  {
    ...
    scoreLayout.setPrefSize(360, 654);
    scoreLayout.setAlignment(Pos.TOP_CENTER);
    scoreTitle = new Text("SCORE");
    scoreTitle.setFont( Font.font("Arial Black", 72) );
    scoreTitle.setFill(Color.DARKRED);
    scoreRight = new Text("Right:");
    scoreRight.setFont( Font.font("Arial Black", 72) );
    scoreRight.setFill(Color.DARKBLUE);
    scoreRight.setTranslateX(-50);
    scoreRight.setTranslateY(150);
    scoreWrong = new Text("Wrong:");
    scoreWrong.setFont( Font.font("Arial Black", 72) );
    scoreWrong.setFill(Color.RED);
    scoreWrong.setTranslateX(-25);
    scoreWrong.setTranslateY(300);
}
```

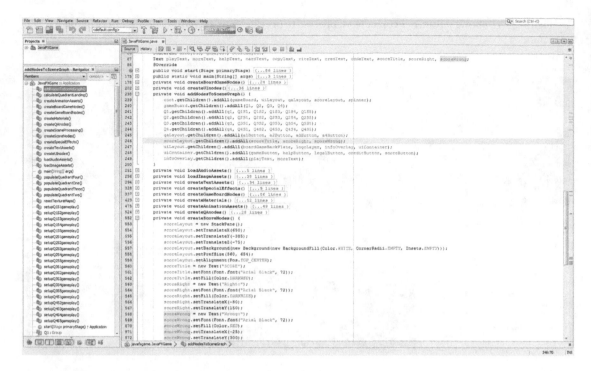

Figure 22-16. *Add scoreWrong object at the top of the class, instantiate and configure it, and add it to the SceneGraph*

Figure 22-17 shows a **Run ➤ Project** work process, used to test the Java code for a red **Wrong:** text heading.

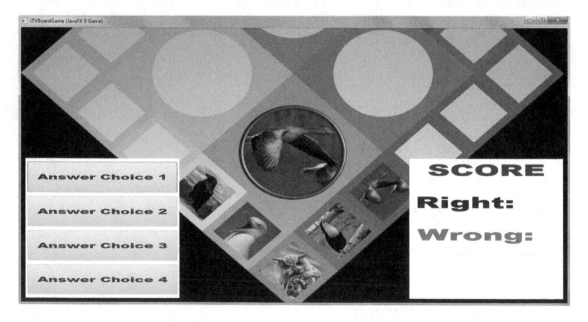

Figure 22-17. *Use a Run ➤ Project work process to preview the Score panel and Red "Wrong:" text*

Next, let's add a **scoreCheer** Text object declaration to the compound statement at the top of your class. As you can see in yellow at the top of in Figure 22-18, your compound statement now has two lines, one for startup (SplashScreen) UI Text objects and a second for Score UI Text objects.

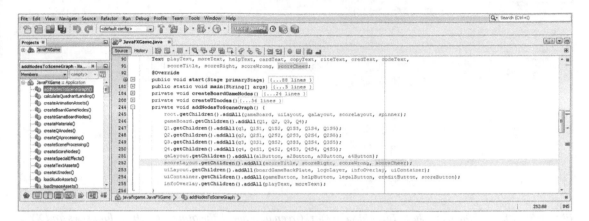

Figure 22-18. *Declare the scoreCheer Text object at the top of the class; then add it to your scoreLayout SceneGraph branch*

Since you have declared the object, you can add it to the scoreLayout.getChildren().addAll() method chain, as shown in Figure 22-18, even before you instantiate it and not create an error in NetBeans 9. The Java statement shown highlighted in light blue at the bottom of Figure 22-18 should look like the following:

scoreLayout.getChildren().addAll(scoreTitle, scoreRight, scoreWrong, **scoreCheer**);

Copy and paste the **scoreWrong** Java statements underneath themselves and change scoreWrong to be **scoreCheer**. Make the scoreCheer **DarkGreen** and reduce the font size on scoreRight and scoreCheer to **64** and **56** points so that they fit better in the scoreLayout. Remember, we need room for the numbers that represent these scores! Since scoreWrong is wider (because of the letters used in the font), I reduced this to **60** points. I spaced out the headings **10** units more in the **Y** dimension and lined them up on the left by using the X location of -56, -44, and -2, as shown here in bold and highlighted (the scoreGrade statements at least) in Figure 22-19:

```
scoreRight = new Text("Right:");
scoreRight.setFont( Font.font("Arial Black", 64) );
scoreRight.setFill(Color.DARKBLUE);
scoreRight.setTranslateX(-56);
scoreRight.setTranslateY(160);
scoreWrong = new Text("Wrong:");
scoreWrong.setFont( Font.font("Arial Black", 60) );
scoreWrong.setFill(Color.RED);
scoreWrong.setTranslateX(-44);
scoreWrong.setTranslateY(310);
scoreCheer = new Text("Great Job!");
scoreGrade.setFont( Font.font("Arial Black", 56) );
scoreGrade.setFill(Color.DARKGREEN);
scoreGrade.setTranslateX(-2);
scoreGrade.setTranslateY(460);
```

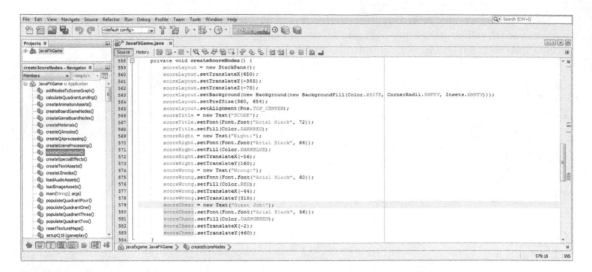

Figure 22-19. *Add the scoreCheer Text object in DarkGreen and tweak the other Text object font sizes and XY locations*

Figure 22-20 shows the **Run ➤ Project** work process used to render your new Text object headings and their adjusted font size and positioning settings. Notice that since we have not proliferated the answers or scoring logic yet, only the Falcon (square 1 option 1 in Figure 22-11 or 15) is showing Button labels that represent answer options.

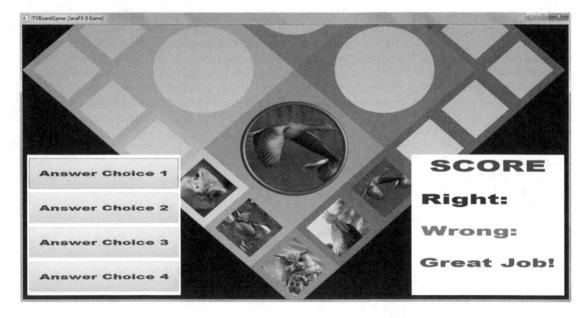

Figure 22-20. *Use the Run ➤ Project work process to preview the Score panel and Text object headings you have added*

Now we're ready to add the score engine logic to the Q&A Button elements we put into place in Chapter 21 and add Text answerRight and answerWrong options to our Score UI design. This will display the score generated by the Q&A UI Button elements. After that, we can calculate the grade and assign it to a seventh Text element for a letter grade.

Scoring Engine: Logic to Calculate Score on Answer

Let's add a custom method to hold our scoring engine logic called createQAprocessing(), which will hold the .setOnAction(event) event processing for the four Button elements created in the createQAnodes() method. As you can see in Figure 22-21, this needs to come after we set up the Q&A and Score UI designs in createQAnodes() and createScoreNodes() and before we call this Q&A event handling in createSceneProcessing(). So, add a line of Java code after the scoreLayout.setVisible(false); statement and before the createSceneProcessing(); statement, as shown highlighted in yellow in Figure 22-21. Use the Alt+Enter work process to remove the wavy red error underlining by having NetBeans 9 write the bootstrap method code and error statement, which we will be replacing soon. This will open a drop-down menu containing the **Create method "createQAprocessing()" in javafxgame.JavaFXGame** option, which you will double-click to execute (a single-click will select this single option, as shown in Figure 22-21).

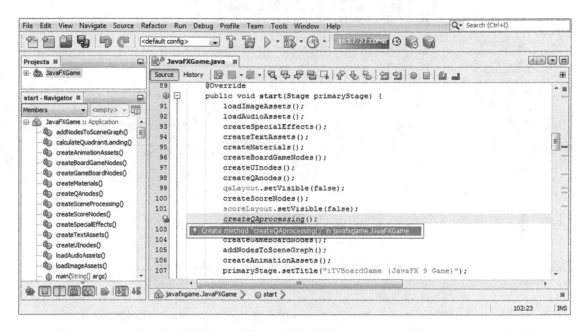

Figure 22-21. *Add the createQAprocessing() method call after createQAnodes() and createScoreNodes() and use Alt+Enter*

The easiest way to code this first (of four) action event handling structure is to go into your **.start()** method and copy and paste one of your Button event handling structures that you created earlier in the book into this newly created **createQAprocessing()** method. Be sure to select the NetBeans bootstrap error statement line of code completely before you use the **Paste** command so that your ActionEvent handling code replaces this bootstrap error statement.

Change the object that the .setOnAction() method call is called off of to a1Button and delete the processing statements inside of this event handling construct to make it into an empty event handler so that we can build the score processing logic from scratch. The Java code for the event handler will look like the following, as shown in Figure 22-22:

```java
private void createQAprocessing() {
    a1Button.setOnAction(new EventHandler<ActionEvent>() {
        @Override
        public void handle (ActionEvent event) {
            ... // An Empty ActionEvent Handling Structure
        }
    });
}
```

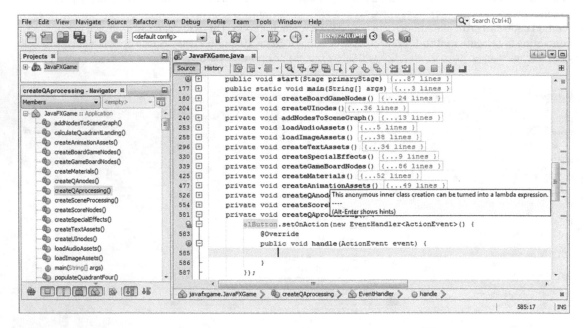

Figure 22-22. *Mouse over the event handling structure, and notice NetBeans wants to convert to a lambda expression*

The Java code that will be generated by Alt+Enter will be the same empty event handling structure, using the lambda expression approach, which will remove three of the eight lines of code, or **37.5 percent** of the coding structure.

Your Java 9 code should look like the following, and your resulting lambda expression is shown in Figure 22-24. Figure 22-23 shows the work process once you invoke the NetBeans **Alt+Enter** keystroke. Select the **Use lambda expression** option, which will execute an algorithm in the NetBeans 9 IDE that will rewrite the Java code for you and turn it into the shorter lambda expression programming format.

```
private void createQAprocessing() {
    a1Button.setOnAction(ActionEvent event) -> {

        ... // Empty ActionEvent Handling Lambda Expression Structure

    });
}
```

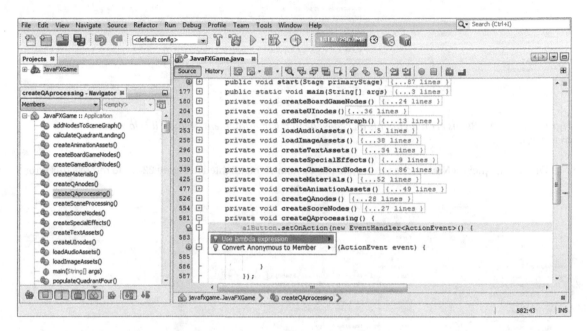

Figure 22-23. *Use the Alt+Enter keystroke and select and double-click the "Use lambda expression" option to convert*

Inside of your empty ActionEvent handling lambda expression, we'll have conditional if() structures for each of the Button objects that will look at both the picked Node object and the pickSn Random object to ascertain which game board square (Q1S1 through Q4S5) and Random number generator value (pickS1 through pickS20) we're dealing with. This will tell us which content we are looking at, and then our scoring engine logic will score that choice.

Inside the a1Button.setOnAction() construct, add an if(picked == Q1S1) to start this coding process. Notice that NetBeans error highlights the **picked Node** object, as it is currently **local** (private) to the **createSceneProcessing()** method, as shown in Figure 22-24. We will have to make this picked Node object a **global** (public) variable next.

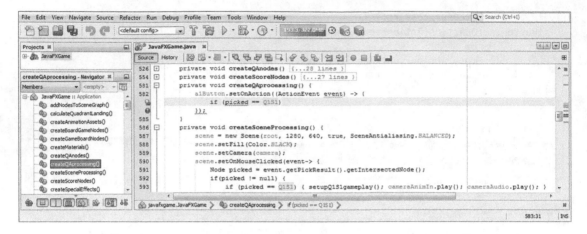

Figure 22-24. *NetBeans error highlights picked Node in the if() statement because it is local to createSceneProcessing()*

Declare the **picked Node** at the top of your class, as shown highlighted in Figure 22-25, to remove this error.

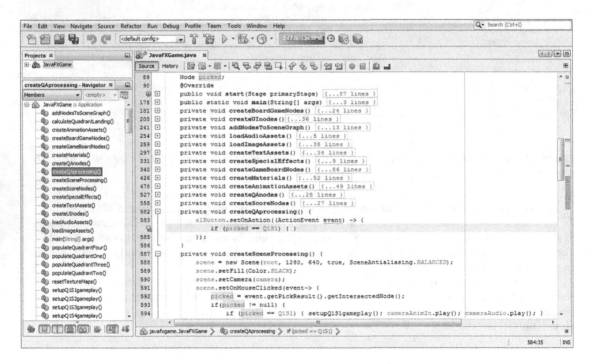

Figure 22-25. *Remove the Node declaration from createSceneProcessing(); relocate it to the top of the class, making it global*

Now that all of the objects we are going to be looking at inside of the createQAprocessing() method have been declared so that they are visible to the entire class, we can continue coding the a1Button event handling with an **if (picked == Q1S2** && **pickS1 == 0) { ... }** structure that lives inside the a1Button event-handling construct.

Declare a **rightAnswer** integer and **rightAnswers** Text object at the top of the class as part of the compound declaration statements for int variables and Text objects, as we are about to write Java 9 code that will utilize these.

What we are going to do inside this if() construct is (if Button 1 contains the right answer) to add **1** to the **rightAnswer** integer and then set a **rightAnswers** Text object to this rightAnswer value by using a **.setText()** method call. Inside the .setText() method we'll use a **String.valueOf()** method to convert the rightAnswer integer to a String value and use .setText() to set scoreCheer to **Great Job!**. The code for correct answer processing, which in the case of Q1S1 option 0 (the first answer option) is correct (a right answer), should look like the following code, as highlighted in Figure 22-26. It has been coded in two lines (four lines, including lambda expression) to allow 20 board square score logic processing Java constructs to fit in 120 lines of code inside the createQAprocessing() method body.

```
a1Button.setOnAction(ActionEvent event) -> {
    if (picked == Q1S1 && pickS1 == 0) { rightAnswer = rightAnswer + 1;
        rightAnswers.setText(String.valueOf(rightAnswer)); scoreCheer.setText("Great Job!");
}
});
```

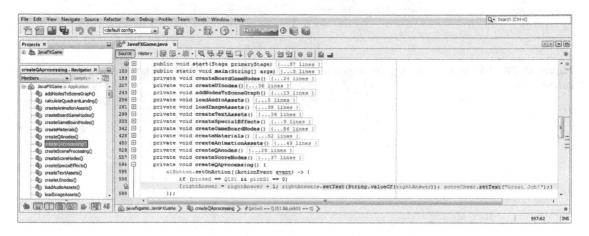

Figure 22-26. *Code a compact if() statement evaluating Q1S1 and pickS1 to see whether the a1Button answer is a correct one*

To be able to display this rightAnswer integer, we need to add a rightAnswers Text object to your UI design in createScoreNodes(). This is done using the copy-and-paste technique. Copy the scoreRight block of Java code directly underneath itself. Set the color to **Black** and the **X** position to **96**. The Y position should stay the same so as to align the "right" Text objects. Set the initial text value to zero by using the "0" String value in the constructor method.

The Java code, shown at the bottom of Figure 22-27, should look like the following code:

```
rightAnswers = new Text("0");                              // Initializes rightAnswers to Zero
rightAnswers.setFont(Font.font("Arial Black", 64));
rightAnswers.setFill(Color.BLACK);
rightAnswers.setTranslateX(96);
rightAnswers.setTranslateY(160);
```

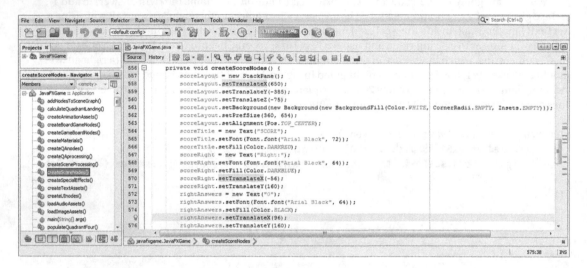

Figure 22-27. *Add the rightAnswers Text object to createScoreNodes() to display the result of your integer calculation*

Figure 22-28 shows a **Run ➤ Project** work process used to render a **rightAnswers** Text object and its settings.

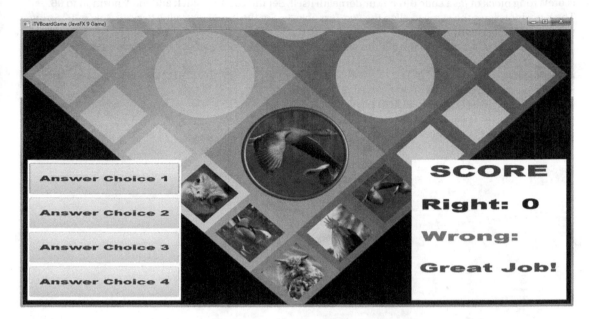

Figure 22-28. *Use a Run ➤ Project work process to preview the Score panel and the rightAnswers Text object placement*

The other Button elements use similar code, only they'll add one to a **wrongAnswer int** variable. This means you'll copy the **a1Button** construct you created three times underneath itself, changing a1Button to a2Button through a4Button. Change rightAnswer to **wrongAnswer** and change rightAnswers to **wrongAnswers**, as shown in Figure 22-29.

Figure 22-29. *Copy and paste a1Button construct three times underneath itself and change the object and variable names*

Also change "Great Job!" to "Spin Again." To be able to display a wrongAnswer integer, we need to add a wrongAnswers Text object to createScoreNodes(). This is done with a copy-and-paste process. Copy the scoreWrong block of Java code directly underneath itself. Set the color to **Black** and the **X** position to **96**. The Y position stays the same to align the two Text objects. Set the initial text value to zero using a "0" String value in the constructor method.

The Java 9 code, shown at the bottom of Figure 22-30, should look just like the following code:

```
wrongAnswers = new Text("0");                          // Initializes wrongAnswers to Zero
wrongAnswers.setFont(Font.font("Arial Black", 64));
wrongAnswers.setFill(Color.BLACK);
wrongAnswers.setTranslateX(96);
wrongAnswers.setTranslateY(160);
```

Figure 22-30. *Add the wrongAnswers Text object to createScoreNodes() to display the result of the integer calculation*

Remember that in order to see the rightAnswers and wrongAnswers answer result Text object value holders, you must add them to your SceneGraph hierarchy inside the scoreLayout StackPane .getChildren(). addAll() statement.

I used only one screenshot to show adding these Text Nodes to the StackPane to save space in the chapter, as we have a lot of Java coding to do to complete your board game scoring and grading infrastructure. Once we finish testing this code, all that you'll have to do is to copy this scoring code for the other 59 options inside of your createQAprocessing() method body, creating the scoring for the other 19 game board squares. This will need to match your other 59 sets of answers, which you'll copy and paste to create and then edit using the code we created in Chapter 21.

Then you'll have all your answers and scoring in place! You can start "error proofing" your code in the next chapter to ensure that multiple UI elements cannot be clicked before they're needed. Remember, these are young children, and intellectually challenged, playing an educational game, so you'll need this user interface protection. The Java code for the **scoreLayout.getChildren().addAll()** method chain looks like the following Java code, shown in Figure 22-31:

scoreLayout.getChildren().addAll(scoreTitle, scoreRight, scoreWrong, scoreCheer,
                          rightAnswers, wrongAnswers);

Figure 22-31. *Be sure to add any new Node objects to the SceneGraph hierarchy so they will be visible at render time*

Figure 22-32 shows the **Run ➤ Project** work process used to render the new **wrongAnswers** Text object and its settings; as you can see, this aligns the score (integer) elements and leaves room for larger scores (10s and 100s) if the numeric fields expand to the right, which we'll be ascertaining in the next section on score code testing.

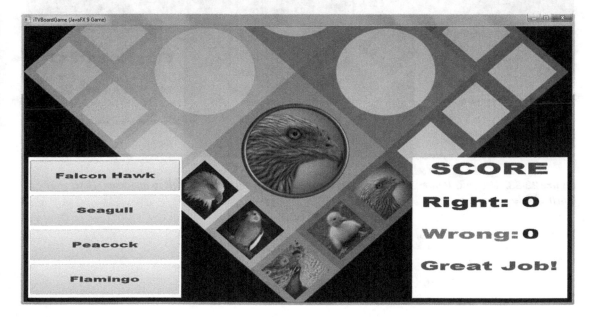

Figure 22-32. *Use your Run ➤ Project work process to preview your Score UI panel and your wrongAnswers Text object*

569

Next, let's **test** the scoring code that we just wrote and see whether the Score UI design responds correctly to the increment of the score into double digits. That is, does an increase in numeric value expand to the right or to the left? Or does it expand from the center? Once we figure this out, we can further "tweak" (optimize) our Scoring UI design.

Score UI Testing: Displaying Higher Integer Numbers

Since we have not implemented "player proofing" Java code, which we are going to do in the next chapter so that the player cannot click a UI element (3D spinner, game board square, Button) more than one time in each gameplay cycle to "game" the system (or cause rendering errors to surface), we can currently click the Button elements more than one time. This allows us to test the scoreboard UI to find out how numbers larger than 9 will be displayed so that we can "tweak" the X location and space the numbers (right and wrong) either to the left (current spacing), to the far right, or in the center of the label (heading) and the right edge of the score UI panel. As you can see in Figure 22-33, I have clicked the correct (Falcon Hawk) answer ten times to see how the number will move. As you can see, the number expands out from the center, which you can see by comparing the 10 to the 2, rather than to the left or right. Therefore, we need to move these 120 units to the right. Now your score values will be able to expand to two or three digits.

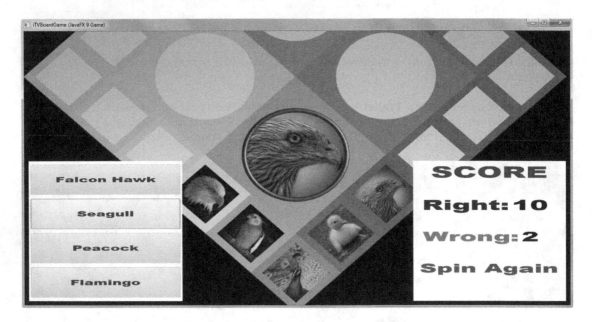

Figure 22-33. *Use your Run ➤ Project work process and click the Button elements to increment (test) your scoring code*

Increment the .setTranslateX() method call for the rightAnswers and wrongAnswers Text objects from 96 to 120. This will center the numeric part of the Score UI between the label (heading) and the right side of the Score UI panel. Your code should now look like the following, which is highlighted in the middle and bottom of Figure 22-34:

```
rightAnswers = new Text("0");
rightAnswers.setFont(Font.font("Arial Black", 64));
rightAnswers.setFill(Color.BLACK);
rightAnswers.setTranslateX(120);                    // Update X position 24 units from 96 to 120
rightAnswers.setTranslateY(160);
wrongAnswers = new Text("0");
wrongAnswers.setFont(Font.font("Arial Black", 64));
wrongAnswers.setFill(Color.BLACK);
wrongAnswers.setTranslateX(120);                    // Update X position 24 units from 96 to 120
wrongAnswers.setTranslateY(160);
```

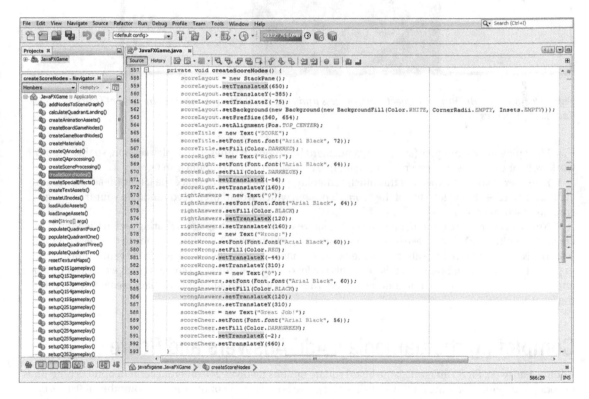

Figure 22-34. *Expand the X position of each numeric element 24 units to the right, from a value of 96 to a value of 120*

Again, use your **Run ➤ Project** work process shown in Figure 22-35 to render the game and navigate to the Score UI panel to check to see whether this spaces the number display so that 10 to 99 scores look great when displayed in the Score UI panel.

Figure 22-35. *Use the Run ➤ Project work process and click the Button elements to increment (test) double-digit scores*

Most players will not play (spin) the game board hundreds of times in one play session, so this should work well for this game. However, notice that three digits (100 to 999) should also fit.

However, if you are expecting this much gameplay, you may want to space the labels (headings) four to eight units further to the left side of the Score UI design, which would then accommodate your triple-digit gameplay scores comfortably.

Now you are ready to "proliferate" the code that we wrote in this chapter on scoring and in Chapter 21 to create the entire gameplay infrastructure. This is going to add another 1,000 lines of code to the 1,000 (or more) lines of Java code that we have already created over 22 chapters to put the entire i3D board game infrastructure in place. Let's talk about how to do this next. This is a lot of work regarding 2D content (images, answer options, and scoring), but it is going to integrate seamlessly with the i3D board game that we have created so far using the JavaFX 9 APIs.

Completing the Gameplay: Add Answers and Score

Adding 4 answers for 60 different game board square options involves 240 different content options (and lines of code), and adding scoring for those 60 different game board square options involves another 480 lines of code and possibly a little more with the lambda expression containers included. The reason that this is a lot of work that should be fairly easy to perform error-free is that we have created a code design that can be copied and pasted into place and that Text values can be created, inserted, and tracked so that the game content will work correctly when played. That said, don't expect that creating the content for your professional Java 9 game development pipeline to be any easier than creating the Java 9 code is (was), as game design and game development involves a plethora of new media, content, strategy, and coding work to end up with a professional result.

I would add (am going to add after I turn in this chapter) the answers and scoring for one game board square at a time, until all 20 game board squares are in place. Adding future game board square options can be easily done. You just increment the pickS1 through pickS20 variables by 1 using the random.nextInt(n) variable to add four through however many different random image subjects you want to add to each game board square. Adding an additional round of random content would amount to adding 20 new Button answer rounds (80 answer options) and scoring those 80 new answers in your scoring logic, which would amount to 160 lines of code, or about 240 lines of code per game board content depth addition. Adding more depth to game board content means players will see duplicate content less as they play the game over longer periods of time. You could also add code to track used content, if you wanted.

Once you proliferate the rest of the content into answers and scoring logic, you will have finished the bulk of the game design and development work process. In the chapters that remain, we will look at error-proofing the UI design so users are forced to use it correctly in the course of playing the game, as well as things such as optimization and code profiling using the new Java 9 NetBeans IDE.

Summary

In this twenty-second chapter, we learned about how to implement a Score UI panel on the lower-right side of our i3D board game design. We also learned how to change the score in the numeric portion of this scoreboard using ActionEvent handling on the Button UI elements that live in the Q&A panel, which we created in the previous Chapter 21. This essentially puts us into a position where we can finish both coding and scoring the individual square (and quadrant, once the square is selected) gameplay, where a visual question regarding the content is answered and scored. (I have to do this before I start writing Chapter 23.)

This means that this was another of your heavy coding chapters as you constructed 20 custom methods, setupQ1S1gameplay() through setupQ4S5gameplay(). You also placed conditional if() structures for each of your Button elements scoring these in your createQAprocessing() event handling infrastructure. You'll still need to be sure to cross-check the image assets between all of your board game methods, and finally, you will need to test all of this code together to make sure it works properly for each game board square.

In Chapter 23, as part of gameplay protection, we'll of course reverse the camera animation after the answering and scoring have been completed and animate back to the more oblique view that is needed to review the game board spin optimally. We will also prevent clicking any UI element that can be clicked so that users can select only one topic and can spin the board once, for instance. We are by no means finished with the game design work process!

CHAPTER 23

∎ ∎ ∎

Completing the Gameplay Code and Player Proofing Your Event Handling

Now that your i3D UI and its event handling, not to mention most of your animation and digital audio, are in place and working, it's time to finish loading a basic level of content (60 images, 240 answers, and scoring) in your code base. We will do this in the first part of this chapter, so I can show you what I did to finish up the gameplay and there is no loss of coding continuity throughout the book. Most of this coding is copy and paste, thanks to the way I set up the game design code, and making sure answers match up and work well when testing the game.

During this chapter, we'll finish populating the 20 **setupQSgameplay()** methods with the text-based answer content that matches up with the visuals (questions). We'll also be finishing the **createQAprocessing()** method, which holds the answer scoring code that updates the Score UI panel. The players will use these to select the correct answer, revealing what the visual for that square represents and scoring their answer. This means you'll be adding several hundred more lines of code during this chapter, approaching 1,750 lines of code before you are finished.

Once we finish coding the bulk of the gameplay "answer display, selection, and scoring" infrastructure and test each square to make sure it is working, we can create the error-proofing portion of the Java code. This results in a professional game that makes sure the players use it properly. This involves using Boolean variables (called *flags*) to hold "click" variables; once a player clicks the spinner, game board square, or answer Button UI element, the elementClick variable is set to false so that your game player cannot click it again and "game" the gameplay code.

For instance, your player might click your correct answer Button UI element multiple times, which would run up the "Right:" (answers) portion of the scoreboard! I call this "user proofing" or "error proofing" the code, and it is a fairly complex process (as you will see in this chapter), which can sometimes go several levels deep. For instance, we will first protect all game board squares from being clicked twice and then go down one more level and protect a quadrant's game board squares so that only the **selected quadrant** in each round of play can be selected by a player.

We will also be adding the final animation, which takes the camera back out to the game board spin view of the game so that a player can invoke a random spin to select the next quadrant (animal, vegetable, mineral, or place topic). This will be done by adding a bright yellow Let's Play Again Button element to the top level of the board game UI design. We have a ton of work to do during this chapter, so let's get started!

Finishing Gameplay: Populating Gameplay Methods

The first part of this chapter will show you how I put the Java code in place that finishes up gameplay. We will add the answer options to the four Button UI elements in the **setupQSgameplay()** methods (twenty of them, the first of which was coded already in Chapter 21 to show you how this Java coding works), and then we will add the scoring for these answers in the createQAprocessing() method inside the ActionEvent handling methods for each of four Q&A Button UI elements.

Add Answer Options: Finishing the setupQSgameplay() Methods

It's not the copying and pasting of Java 9 code in the **setupQSgameplay()** methods that will take up most of your time in this phase of gameplay content development but rather the confirmation of the correct answer and the creation of incorrect answers that stump the player and cause a "Wrong:" answer. The method body for setupQ1S1gameplay() looks like the 18 Java statements in Figure 23-1 once you've added four answer options for each random pick.

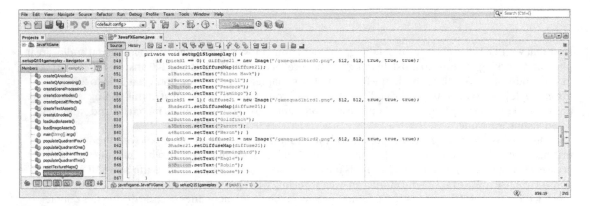

Figure 23-1. *Find and add a correct answer to a different button (and three incorrect answers) for each random image*

Add your corresponding right and wrong answer processing to the createQAprocessing() scoring engine we created in Chapter 22. The correct (rightAnswer and rightAnswers) answers are highlighted in yellow in Figure 23-2.

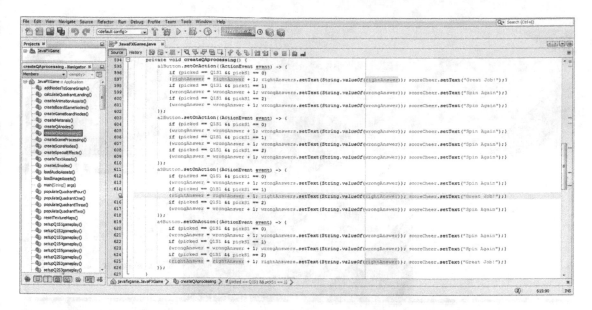

Figure 23-2. *Add matching correct or incorrect answer score processing to the createQAprocessing() method for Q1S1*

It is important that you do this work process **very carefully** so that your answers, correct and incorrect, for each of your 20 **setupQSgameplay()** methods match up perfectly with your createQAprocessing() scoring algorithm's method body. These have to match up perfectly in order for your scoring engine to score the gameplay accurately, as you can see by comparing Figures 23-1 and 23-2 on a question-by-question and answer-by-answer basis.

You can either do the testing as you go along, game board square by game board square, or all at one time when you have finished. Or you can do it both ways, which is what I did, to try to generate code that was free from errors at both compile time and runtime. With thousands of lines of code and a Java 9 (and JavaFX 9) API that was in beta while I was writing this book, this is clearly no easy task, especially when I had to turn in one completed chapter every week.

Use the **Run ➤ Project** work process to render the code and 3D and test game board square 1 in your first quadrant, as shown in Figure 23-3. I recommend doing this one square (and one quadrant) at a time so that you can take advantage of code "patterns," which can be seen by comparing Figures 23-1 and 23-2. You can visually tell which game board square, game board quadrant, Button number, and random question selection you are working with based on the Java code object names and variable names that I have utilized specifically for this purpose.

Figure 23-3. *Use a Run* ➤ *Project work process and test your Q1S1 answers and scoring logic before moving on to Q1S2*

As you can see highlighted in Figure 23-4, the **setupQ1S2gameplay()** method code is very similar, other than a **pickS2** Random object and Image references and, of course, the Button labels for the correct and incorrect answers.

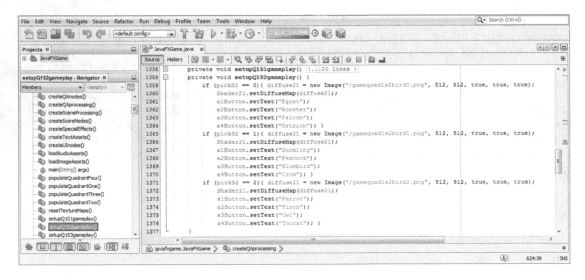

Figure 23-4. *Add correct and incorrect answers to Q1S2 Button objects, which as you can see is similar to the Q1S1 method*

As you can see in this phase of the gameplay design and programming, the primary objective is selecting the best Button answer labels and "wiring" them correctly to the **setupQAprocessing()** scoring engine method so that the scores are calculated correctly! This is why I suggest coding each game board square one at a time and tying them to the setupQAprocessing() scoring engine method carefully! Make sure to test each game board square well enough so that you can make sure a click on the correct answer button adds **1** to the "Right:" score label's integer text value.

As you can see in Figure 23-5, I have added the scoring engine method's Java code to evaluate these answers, which is shown highlighted in yellow. I selected the Q1S2 Box (square) object in the code to highlight references to it.

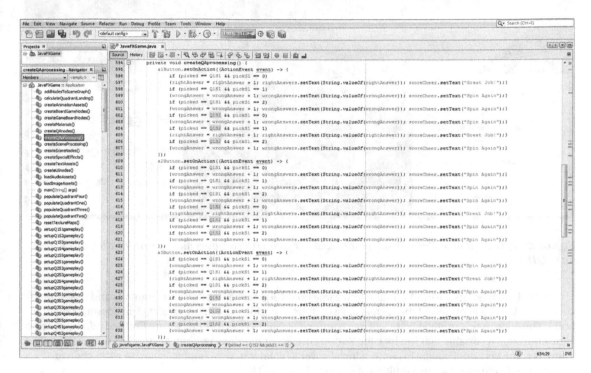

Figure 23-5. *Add matching correct or incorrect answer score processing to the createQAprocessing() method for Q1S2*

Use the **Run ➤ Project** work process shown in Figure 23-6 and test the Q1S2 game board square logic to see whether it scores the correct answer (Duckling) by incrementing the "Right:" score UI panel integer Text object by one.

Figure 23-6. *Use a Run ➤ Project work process and test your Q1S2 answers and scoring logic before moving on to Q1S3*

Next, I finished up the third through fifth game board square gameplay setup methods and tested their code to make sure I connected the correct answer Button scoring logic in my createQAprocessing() method body. The code in this method body will reach around 500 lines of code once we are finished adding scoring logic and, later, a variable that will lock the Button click event handling once an answer has been selected. There is some very cool coding to come, which I cover a bit later in this chapter, when we write code to "player proof" the game against multiple mouse clicks on the UI.

As you will see in Figure 23-7, the answer scoring logic for the first six game board squares (30 percent done already) is filling the IDE screen for Button 1 with three dozen lines of code, which means that we have a dozen lines of code (144 lines) done for all four buttons.

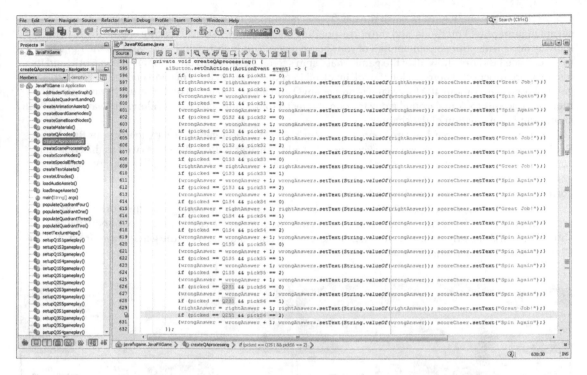

Figure 23-7. *Add matching correct or incorrect answer score processing to the createQAprocessing() method for Q2S1*

The code shown highlighted at the bottom of Figure 23-7 is also shown in Figure 23-8 on the left side of the figure being tested. When I click the first Button element (Chard), the scoring engine adds 1 to the "Right:" score, as shown by the number being incremented from 0 to 1.

Figure 23-8. *Use a Run ➤ Project work process to test Q2S1 through Q2S5 answers and scoring logic before moving on*

At this point, you'll have to finish the next four Q2S2 through Q2S5 game board square **setupQSgameplay()** methods, and the corresponding createQAprocessing() scoring engine logic, to be halfway done with your content for half of your board game. This is shown in Figure 23-8 on the right side; to save space I did not show all of the game board spin screen captures involved for all of this work (and its testing work process). There is a lot of work involved in coding the 600 lines of code needed to finish this gameplay content (about 480 for createQAprocessing() and about 100 for 20 of the **setupQSgameplay()** methods), so this took me around a day to code and test. I took some screenshots along the way, which I will show later in this section of the chapter.

As you add game board square content and scoring logic to your game, be sure to use your **Run ➤ Project** work process often to test new Java code that adds Answer Button objects, as well as the code that wires these to the createQAprocessing() scoring engine method, to see whether it gives you the desired gameplay result. As you can see in Figure 23-8, the second quadrant answers and scoring are working correctly, and I can move on to do quadrant 3.

As you can also see in Figure 23-9, the third quadrant answers and scoring are now working correctly, and I can move on to add the answers and scoring code for quadrant 4. At this point, your board game should be working fairly well, and we can now start to add code that prevents the game player from clicking UI elements more than once.

Figure 23-9. *Use a Run ➤ Project work process to test the Q3S1 through Q3S5 answers and scoring logic before moving on*

As you can see in Figure 23-10, the gameplay content is now in place, and we can proceed with player proofing.

Figure 23-10. *Use the Run ➤ Project work process to test the Q4S1 through Q4S5 answers and scoring logic to finish 20 squares*

Next, let's "player proof" your current code by adding boolean variables that will prevent repetitive clicks.

Player-Proofing Code: Controlling Player Event Usage

The game is "theoretically" finished, and we could just trust players to click (once) on correct i3D and i2D UI elements to play the game. However, the intended audience for this particular game includes underage children, mentally challenged individuals, disabled players, and autistic players. Thus, we'll put in place some controls that make sure players click only once on the correct UI elements to play this game. Let's start the process by declaring (top of class) and adding a **squareClick** boolean variable set to **true** in **rotGameBoard.setOnFinished()**, as shown here and in Figure 23-11:

```
rotGameBoard.setOnFinished(event-> {
    if (quadrantLanding == 315) { populateQuadrantOne();   }
    if (quadrantLanding == 225) { populateQuadrantTwo();   }
    if (quadrantLanding == 135) { populateQuadrantThree(); }
    if (quadrantLanding == 45)  { populateQuadrantFour();  }
    spinnerAudio.stop();
    squareClick = true;
});
```

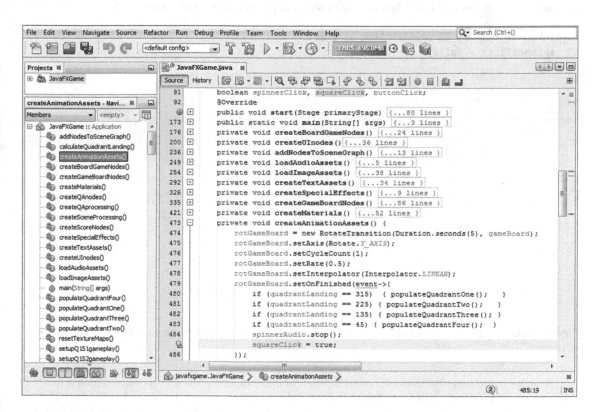

Figure 23-11. *Add a squareClick boolean variable set to true at the end of your rotGameBoard. setOnFinished() handler*

So, logically, we have connected the click "protection" for the game board squares to the game board spin Animation object. Also, note that by initializing all of the click protection variables as **boolean** with no (default) values, we have essentially set all click protection to false, or "click is locked," simply by declaring these variables at the top of your Java class. In this way, we do not need any **clickProtect = false;** statements in your start() method body.

Notice in Figure 23-11 that I have also declared the **spinnerClick** and **buttonClick** using a compound Java (boolean) declaration at the top of your class. This is because we want to "lock" the i3D spinner UI element, the game board squares, and the Q&A Button UI elements once the player has clicked them. This is to prevent **multiple clicks**, which prevents multiple answer button clicks (to run up the score). It also assures that your i3D animations and audio calls are triggered only once per game round as needed to prevent what will look (or sound) like bugs to your player. You don't really want an animation to restart in the middle of its intended visual result, even though it will if you tell it to (soon enough in its playback cycle, which is what more than one click will usually do), so we'll lock the clicks after one!

Next, let's set up locking for the spinnerClick, starting with the if(picked == spinner) conditional evaluation in the MouseEvent handling code. We need to add && spinnerClick == true to the if(picked == spinner) to evaluate whether we are allowed to click the spinner at that point in the gameplay. If we are, we immediately set spinnerClick to a false value since the spinner Animation object (and quadrant-landing processing) is also started within this block of code. We'll enable clicking the spinner in the .setOnFinished() handler for the spinner after it has finished spinning, which will prevent a player from being able to click your i3D spinner UI element while it is actually spinning! Cool!

This new mouse-click-proofing addition to your i3D spinner's conditional if() Java code infrastructure is shown in bold here, as well as highlighted in light blue and yellow at the top of Figure 23-12:

```
if(picked == spinner && spinnerClick == true) {
    spinnerClick = false;
    ...
}
```

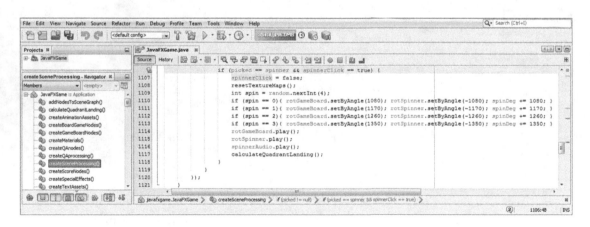

Figure 23-12. *Add && spinnerClick == true to the if() evaluation for the spinner in your MouseEvent handling structure*

Next, we'll add a **.setOnFinished()** event handler for this rotSpinner Animation object, which sets the boolean spinnerClick variable to a **false** value once the rotSpinner Animation object has finished. The reason this is false, which turns the click off, is because we don't want the spinner (or the game board) to spin again until the player has chosen a square and a corresponding answer Button UI element to register (and score) their answer.

We do want to turn the spinner mouse click on, however, after the spinner has come in again to the screen, which is the **rotSpinnerIn** Animation object. For this reason, we'll set your spinnerClick to **true** in the .setOnFinished() event handling logic. Again, the Java programming is logical here, and there's nothing surprising if you just think about what you want to achieve in your gameplay pipeline. It's a lot to think about all at once, as most gameplay logic is, so it may be difficult to do at first, until you get used to thinking about all your real-time gameplay logic at once as it relates to the logic (processing pipeline) involved in processing your real-time, interactive gameplay. This is why game development is considered difficult by most, as you need to "wrap your head around" all of your gameplay code at once as a coder.

The new Java code in the **createSceneProcessing()** method is shown here, as well as highlighted in light blue and yellow in Figure 23-13 in the blocks of code that set up the logic used for your **rotSpinner** and **rotSpinnerIn**:

```
rotSpinner = new RotateTransition(Duration.seconds(5), spinner);
...
rotSpinner.setOnFinished(event-> {
    spinnerClick = false;
});
rotSpinnerIn = new RotateTransition(Duration.seconds(5), spinner);
...
rotSpinnerIn.setOnFinished(event-> {
    spinnerClick = true;
});
```

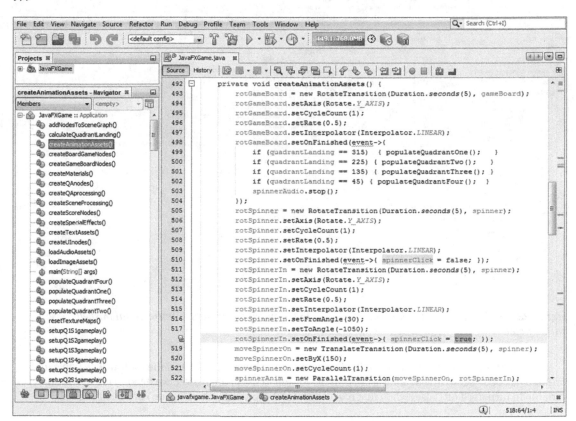

Figure 23-13. *Set spinnerClick to false in rotSpinner and to true in rotSpinnerIn to control when the spinner is to be clicked*

The next thing we need to ascertain (and code) is when we allow Button UI elements to be clicked. This logically would be at the end of the **cameraAnimIn** Animation object, again in the **.setOnFinished()** event handler construct right after the qaLayout and scoreLayout StackPane 2D UI panels (and their contents or children) have been set to be visible again by using the .setVisible(true) method call off of each of the StackPane UI container objects. As buttonClick is **false** as a (declaration) default, this is as simple as using the **buttonClick = true;** Java statement.

Once one of the answer Button UI objects has been clicked, buttonClick will again be set to false, preventing any Button UI object (even the same one) from being clicked until a cameraAnimIn Animation object is played again. We will put this Java code into place next in the createQAprocessing() scoring method inside each of the ActionEvent handling structures attached to each of the four Button objects in their .setOnAction() event-handling constructs.

Your new cameraAnimIn Java 9 code should now look like the following and can also be seen highlighted in light blue and yellow at the bottom of Figure 23-14:

```
cameraAnimIn = new ParallelTransition( moveCameraIn, rotCameraDown, moveSpinnerOff );
cameraAnimIn.setOnFinished(event-> {
    qaLayout.setVisible(true);
    scoreLayout.setVisible(true);
    buttonClick = true;
});
```

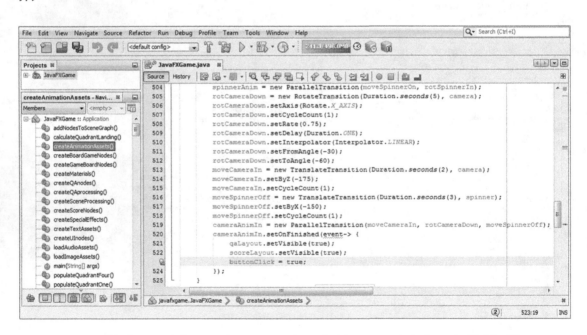

Figure 23-14. *Add a buttonClick = true; statement to the end of the cameraAnimIn.setOnFinished() event handler code*

Now that the camera has animated in close to the game board surface and the buttonClick boolean variable has been set to true to allow a click on the Button to select an answer, we need to tell the buttonClick variable to turn itself off (false) when that one button (a1Button through a4Button) has been clicked.

To do this, we'll need to "wrap" the score-processing contents of each Button ActionEvent event processing construct with an **if(buttonClick == true)** conditional evaluation layer. This will only allow event processing if the buttonClick is on (true) and will then turn it off at the end of that processing using the simple **buttonClick = false;** Java statement. This will be the last statement before exiting the **if(buttonClick == true)** Java code construct.

Your Java code should look like the following, which is also highlighted at the beginning of Figure 23-15 and at the end of Figure 23-16, since the ActionEvent handling structures for these four Button UI objects span more than 120 lines of Java code for each Button's .setOnAction() event-handling infrastructure:

```java
private void createQAprocessing() {
    a1Button.setOnAction( (ActionEvent event) -> {
        if (buttonClick == true) { // Evaluates if (buttonClick == true) then {not yet clicked}
            if (picked == Q1S1 && pickS1 == 0)
                ...
            buttonClick = false;   // If this Button has been clicked then set buttonClick to false
        }
    });
}
```

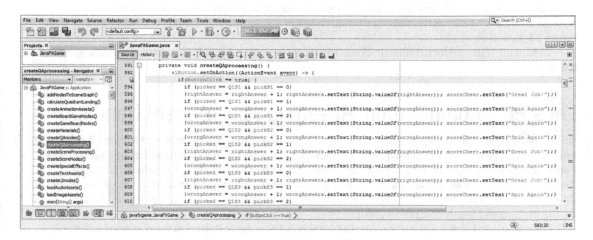

Figure 23-15. *Use a conditional if(buttonClick == true) statement at the top of each Button event processing structure*

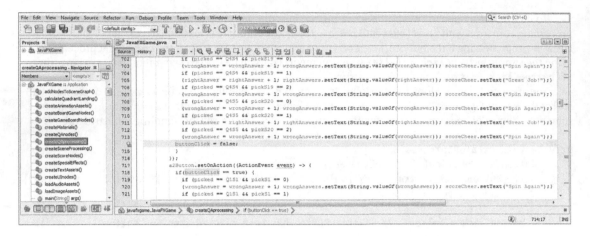

Figure 23-16. *At the end of each if(buttonClick==true) construct, set buttonClick = false; to turn off the Button click function*

Place this same if(buttonClick == true) before each of the Button.setOnAction() constructs, and place buttonClick = false; at the end of each Button.setOnAction() event handling construct, as shown in Figure 23-15 and Figure 23-16.

To turn all of this event handling back on, we need a Let's Play Again Button and .setOnAction() event handler.

Let's Play Again Button: Resetting Player Event Handling

Once a player clicks an answer Button UI object, all game board squares, spinner, and Button UI objects will be locked! The best way to unlock everything for another round of gameplay is to add a large yellow Let's Play Again Button at the middle of your game board (if you need to peek ahead, it's shown in Figure 23-23) that the user will click to spin another time to randomly select a new topic and another image to identify. In this section of the chapter, we will add this Button element to the root of your SceneGraph, develop the code for the Button, and finish your player proofing.

Let's set up an infrastructure for an againButton by adding **againButton** to the compound Button declaration at the top of the class and then add the againButton to your SceneGraph **root** using a **.getChildren().addAll()** method chain. The Java code needed to do this is shown here, as well as highlighted in yellow at the top of Figure 23-17:

```
Button ... a1Button, a2Button, a3Button, a4Button, againButton;
...
root.getChildren().addAll(gameBoard, uiLayout, qaLayout, scoreLayout, spinner, againButton);
```

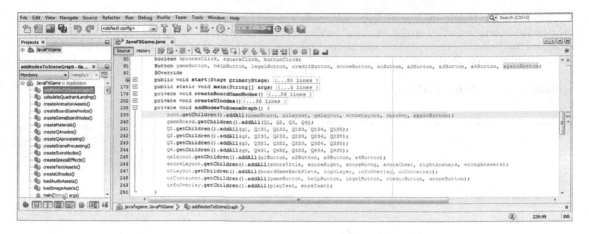

Figure 23-17. *Declare an againButton Button object at the top of your class and add it to your SceneGraph root object*

Instantiate and configure againButton in createBoardGameNodes() at X, Y (**200, -400**) with a size of (**300, 150**) and use a **34**-point **Arial Black** font, as shown in Figure 23-18. Label it **Let's Play Again** because it triggers a round of gameplay.

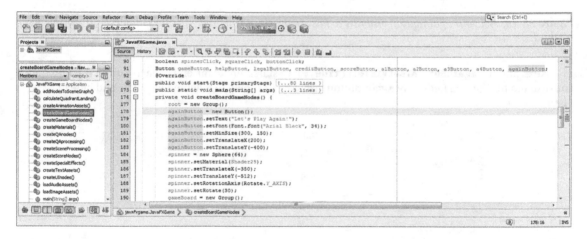

Figure 23-18. *Instantiate and configure againButton in the createBoardGameNodes() method and use a large size and font*

Since we don't want this Button visible until after a player has selected their answer, we set againButton to be invisible on startup. To do this we use a .setVisible(false) method call off againButton in the top of the start() method after the createBoardGameNodes() method call. This looks like the following code, which is shown highlighted in Figure 23-19:

```
againButton.setVisible(false);
```

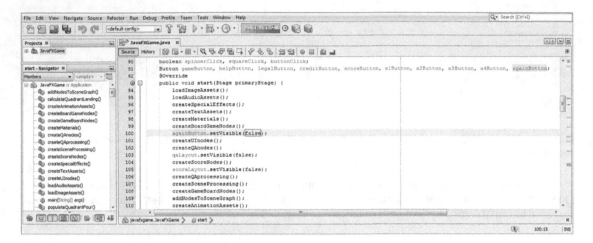

Figure 23-19. *Set your againButton visibility to false in the start() method, after the createBoardGameNodes() method*

Next, add the **againButton.setVisible(true);** Java statement to the end of each Button.setOnAction() construct to turn on the **Let's Play Again** Button visibility, as shown highlighted in yellow and blue in Figure 23-20.

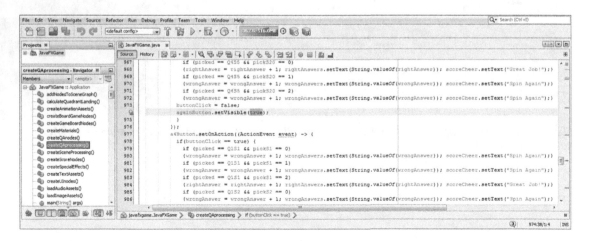

Figure 23-20. *Call againButton.setVisible(true); at end of each answer Button event handler, after buttonClick = false;*

Since we only estimated the location and size of the Button in Figure 23-18, let's use the **Run ➤ Project** work process so we can see whether the Button UI element is centered over the four-color intersection of the game board design. As you'll see in Figure 23-21, we have some tweaking to do, as the Button is over the quadrant image for the content.

Figure 23-21. *Use the Run ➤ Project work process to test the againButton code to see whether it is located and sized properly*

Also notice that we need to set a Yellow background color for the Button since the quadrants use pink, blue, green, and orange. Add in the **.setBackground**(new **Background**(new **BackgroundFill**(**color. YELLOW**))) method chain to set a Yellow color value (don't forget the empty CornerRadii and Insets), as shown highlighted in blue in Figure 23-22. Increase your .setMinSize() to **300, 200**; increase your font size to **35**; and reposition X, Y, Z to (**190, -580, 100**).

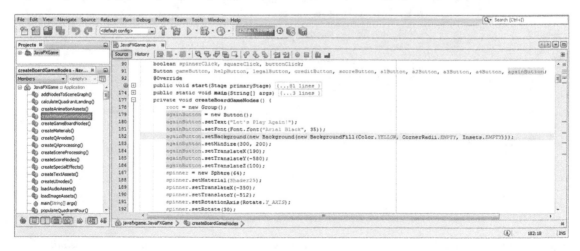

Figure 23-22. *Add a Yellow background color and adjust the translate values and size values to center the againButton*

Use **Run ➤ Project** to view the final Button UI element styling. As you can see in Figure 23-23, it looks great!

Figure 23-23. *Use a Run ➤ Project work process to test the againButton to see if it is located, sized, and colored properly*

Next, add a **.setOnAction()** event handling construct to againButton so that when the Button is clicked, you can turn off the Q&A and Scoring (StackPane) panels and reset the buttonClick, squareClick, and spinnerClick variables to false (off) so that the 3D spinner, game board squares, and answer Button UI elements can be used. The initial Java code for these visibility and click-proofing reset statements is shown in blue in Figure 23-24.

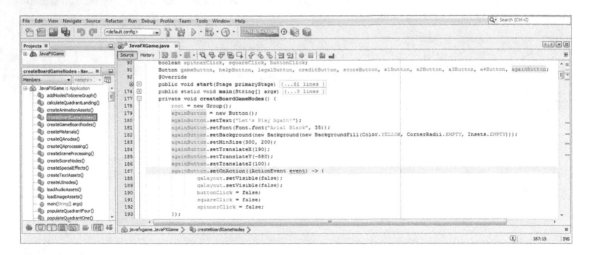

Figure 23-24. *Add the .setOnAction() method call to againButton; start adding mouse click and visibility event handling*

The next thing that we need to create is the **cameraAnimOut** ParallelTransition Animation object that will animate the camera object back out to your full game board (spin) view, as we will be calling the .play() method off of that Animation object construct in the **againButton.setOnAction()** event processing construct. Therefore, let's create that ParallelTransition Animation object in the next section of this chapter, as this will be a relatively complex task.

Camera Zoom Back Out: Another ParallelTransition

First let's create an exact opposite of the rotCameraDown RotateTransition Animation object we created earlier in the book by copying and pasting this Animation object code underneath the cameraAnimIn object since we're about to create the cameraAnimOut object. Everything will be identical, except change the object name from rotCameraDown to **rotCameraBack** and exchange the values (-30 and -60) in the .setFromAngle() and .setToAngle() method calls. The Java 9 code to accomplish this task is shown here, as well as highlighted using yellow and blue in Figure 23-25:

```
rotCameraBack = new RotateTransition(Duration.seconds(5), camera);
rotCameraBack.setAxis(Rotate.X_AXIS);
rotCameraBack.setCycleCount(1);
rotCameraBack.setRate(0.75);
rotCameraBack.setDelay(Duration.ONE);
rotCameraBack.setInterpolator(Interpolator.LINEAR);
rotCameraBack.setFromAngle(-60);
rotCameraBack.setToAngle(-30);
```

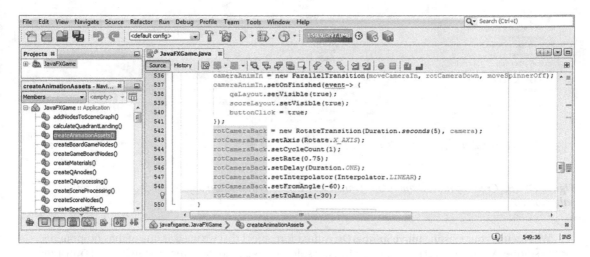

Figure 23-25. *Add the rotCameraBack RotateTransition object in createAnimationAssets() and instantiate and configure it for use*

Next, let's create an exact opposite of your **moveCameraIn** TranslateTransition Animation object by copying and pasting this Animation object code underneath the **rotCameraBack** object. Everything should be identical, except change the object name from moveCameraIn to moveCameraOut and reverse the -175 value in your .setByZ() method call. Your Java code to accomplish this is shown here, as well as highlighted in yellow and blue in Figure 23-26:

```
moveCameraOut = new TranslateTransition(Duration.seconds(2), camera);
moveCameraOut.setByZ(175);
moveCameraOut.setCycleCount(1);
```

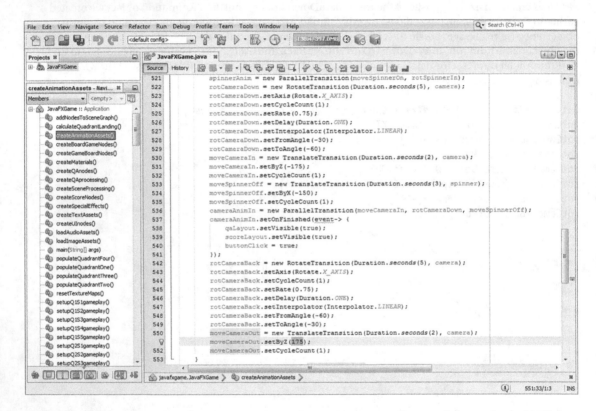

Figure 23-26. *Create a moveCameraOut TranslateTransition Animation object and change the .setByZ() value to 175*

We can use your existing **moveSpinnerOn** Animation object that we used as one of the components for the spinnerAnim ParallelTransition to move the spinner back onto the screen as the ParallelTransition brings the camera back to its original game board spin position and orientation. This will demonstrate that this Animation object can be used in more than one ParallelTransition object, which is a coding optimization, as coding constructs can be used for more than one purpose. You can see this already coded animation highlighted in yellow at the top of Figure 23-27.

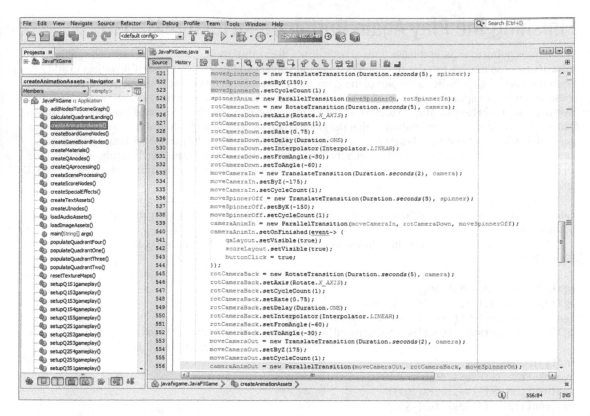

Figure 23-27. *Create cameraAnimOut ParallelTransition and reference moveCameraOut, rotCameraback, and moveSpinnerOn*

So, now we can create your ParallelTransition **cameraAnimOut** object, which will play the moveCameraOut, rotCameraBack, and moveSpinnerOn **Animation** objects in parallel or at exactly the same time! This will require only a single line of code instantiating the cameraAnimOut object and using its constructor method to load that object with the other three Animation object references. We'll eventually add a second line of code calling a .setOnFinished() method off of this object so that we can reset the spinnerClick boolean variable to **false** once the camera has zoomed back out so that your player is able to use the i3D spinner UI element again to randomly spin the game board again.

The Java code for doing this should look like the following and is shown highlighted in light blue and yellow at the bottom of Figure 23-27:

```
cameraAnimOut = new ParallelTransition(moveCameraOut, rotCameraBack, moveSpinnerOn);
```

Now we can go back to finishing the code for the againButton.setOnAction() construct, refining that result.

Finishing the Play Again Button: resetTextureMaps()

We are now going to expand the five lines of code inside the againButton.setOnAction() event handling infrastructure so that we call the new camera Animation object and the existing AudioClip object to add animation and digital audio to the part of the game that returns the player to the zoomed-out view, where they can randomly spin the game board to select new content to test their knowledge base. We are also going to move your **resetTextureMaps()** method call from inside the createSceneProcessing() method into this game-reset event processing method so that the game board squares and quadrants are reset to blank when gameplay is finished and right before the camera zooms back away from the game board (and before the camera zoom audio effect is played to match that animation). We will also be hiding the againButton Button UI element as part of this process, since we do not want that Button UI element to overlay the view of our i3D spinner and game board spinning around to randomly select the next quadrant.

Add a .setVisible(false) method call off the againButton after your qaLayout and scoreLayout visibility calls. Next, add a resetTextureMaps() call and .play() calls off cameraAnimOut and cameraAudio at the end of the method.

The Java 9 code for the event handling should now look like the following and is also shown in Figure 23-28:

```
againButton = new Button();
againButton.setText("Let's Play Again!");
againButton.setFont(Font.font( "Arial Black", 35) );
againButton.setBackground(new Background(new BackgroundFill(Color.Yellow,
                                                CornerRadii.EMPTY, Insets.
Empty);
againButton.setMinSize(300, 200);
againButton.setTranslateX(190);
againButton.setTranslateY(-580);
againButton.setTranslateZ(100);
againButton.setOnAction( (ActionEvent event) -> {
    qaLayout.setVisible(false);
    scoreLayout.setVisible(false);
    againButton.setVisible(false);
    buttonClick = false;
    squareClick = false;
    spinnerClick = false;
    resetTextureMaps();
    cameraAnimOut.play();
    cameraAudio.play();
}
```

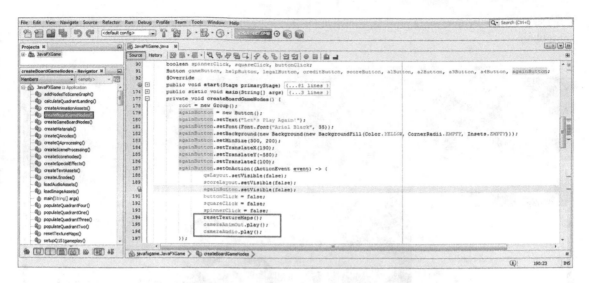

Figure 23-28. *Call resetTextureMaps(), cameraAnimOut.play(), and cameraAudio.play() in againButton.setOnAction()*

Now we can add the .setOnFinished() event handling construct to the cameraAnimOut Animation object to automatically turn on your **spinnerClick** function once the camera has animated back out to game board spin view so that the player can click the i3D spinner UI element to start the gameplay process all over again. The Java code for this functionality is shown here using a single line of code and is highlighted in light blue and yellow in Figure 23-29:

```java
cameraAnimOut = new ParallelTransition(moveCameraOut, rotCameraBack, moveSpinnerOn);
cameraAnimOut.setOnFinished( event-> { spinnerClick = true; } );
```

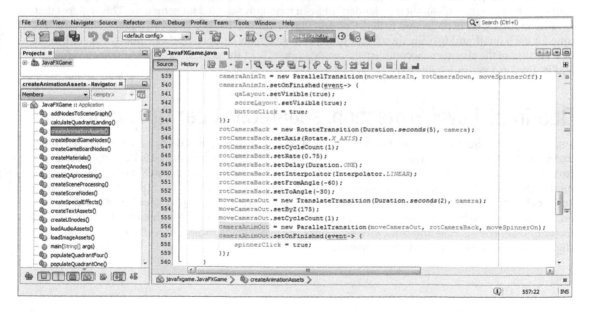

Figure 23-29. *Add a cameraAnimOut.setOnFinsihed() event handler that sets the spinnerClick variable to a true value*

Use a **Run ➤ Project** work process, shown in Figure 23-30, to test an entire cycle (or two rounds of gameplay).

Figure 23-30. *Use Run ➤ Project to test code; notice that clicking another quadrant square sets that quadrant image*

Notice in Figure 23-30 that our testing process has revealed another problem! It turns out that testing for square clicking is not "deep" enough to guarantee flawless gameplay! You can click another quadrant's squares when a certain quadrant has "landed" or been randomly selected for gameplay. This requires that we add another level of protection to the game and that we must actually create four squareClick variables (one for each quadrant) to really thoroughly protect our gameplay completely. Let's modify our code in the next section of the chapter to accomplish this using squareClick1 through squareClick4 boolean variables and testing on a per-quadrant basis.

Quadrant-Level Protection: squareClick per Quadrant

Let's change our squareClick code thus far to accommodate per-quadrant square checking. The first thing that we will want to do is to change squareClick at the top of the class to be squareClick1 to squareClick4 (to match up with your quadrants). We also need to change the testing in the **createSceneProcessing()** method to match the squareClickN variables with each of the four quadrants, so if(picked == **Q1**S1 && **squareClick1**) would be the modification, for instance, and if(picked == **Q2**S1 && **squareClick2**), and so on, as shown highlighted (for quadrant 4) in Figure 23-31. The Java code for this change is fairly subtle, and the amount of code is large and somewhat repetitive, so I'm not going to list it here. Figure 23-32 shows the slight (but significant) modification I'm referencing.

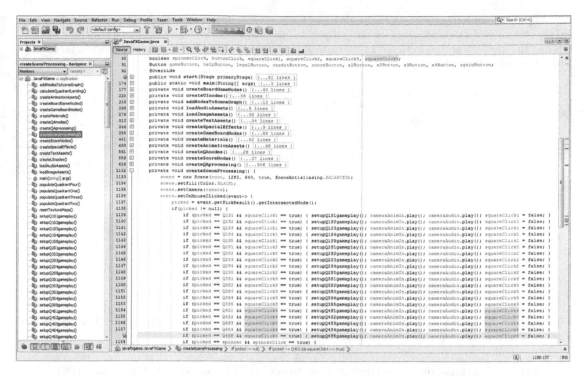

Figure 23-31. *Change your squareClick code to squareClick1 through squareClick4 to match up with the quadrant involved*

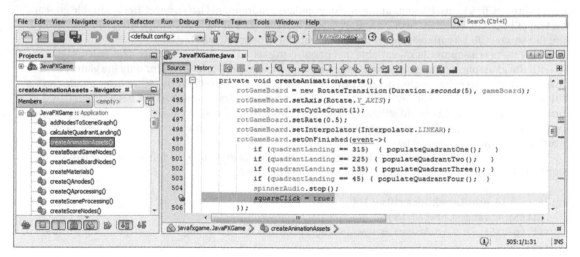

Figure 23-32. *Select and delete the squareClick = true; statement in createAnimationAssets(), as we are now moving it*

Remove the squareClick reference from your **createAnimationAssets()** method since we're going to control square clicks on a quadrant basis in the four populateQuadrant() methods, which is now a more logical place to do so.

As you can see in Figure 23-32, I've selected the **createAnimationAssets()** squareClick statement for deletion.

As you can see in Figure 23-33, I have also selected the **createBoardGameNodes() squareClick = false;** statement for deletion since we are going to do this in your createSceneProcessing() method. In fact, this has already been shown in Figure 23-31, highlighted in yellow along the far right side of the screenshot, which is where it logically belongs.

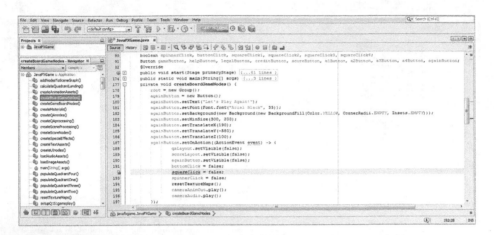

Figure 23-33. *Select and delete the squareClick = false; statement in createBoardGameNodes(), as we've already moved it*

The place that you would want to set your four squareClick variables to true (allow a click on this quadrant's square) is at the end of each populateQuadrantNumber() method call to finalize the setup. This allows one of the squares to be clicked in order to select the content for that quadrant's topic.

A **squareClick1** variable goes at the end of populateQuadrantOne(), a **squareClick2** variable goes at the end of populateQuadrantTwo(), a **squareClick3** variable goes at the end of populateQuadrantThree(), and the **squareClick4** variable goes at the end of populateQuadrantFour().

Now there is a squareClickN variable that pertains to each of the four quadrants. This better matches up with the gameplay paradigm, as now we can turn on mouse clicks selectively for only the game board quadrant that a player has landed on and turn the game board squares off for the other three quadrants. This will prevent what tests uncovered in Figure 23-30, where quadrants that had not been selected by the random number generator could still be played. Since this looks incorrect visually (as you can see), we will fix this by turning off the squares on a quadrant-by-quadrant basis, which will solve this problem, albeit with more complex player-proofing Java code.

The Java code for the populateQuadrantOne() method body looks like the following, which is highlighted in light blue and yellow at the bottom of Figure 23-34:

```
private void populateQuadrantOne() {
    pickS1 = random.nextInt(3);
    if (pickS1 == 0){diffuse1 = new Image("/gamesquare1bird0.png", 256, 256, true, true,
true);}
    if (pickS1 == 0){diffuse1 = new Image("/gamesquare1bird1.png", 256, 256, true, true,
true);}
    if (pickS1 == 0){diffuse1 = new Image("/gamesquare1bird2.png", 256, 256, true, true,
true);}
    Shader1.setDiffuseMap(diffuse1);
    ...
    squareClick1 = true;
}
```

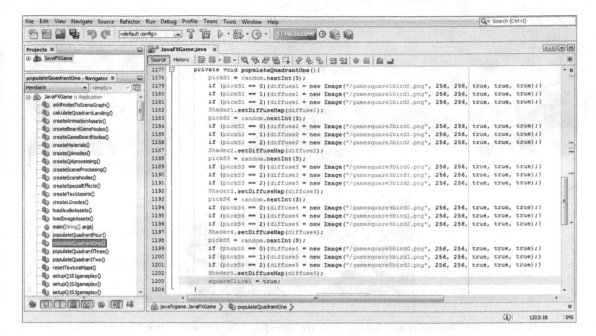

Figure 23-34. *Add a squareClick1 = true; statement at the end of populateQuadrantOne() and the other three in the other three methods*

Do this same squareClickN = true; Java statement in the other three populateQuadrant() methods to turn on the squareClick function, which will be turned off once a square has been selected for the current round of gameplay. As you can see in Figure 23-35, the game now works properly. You can click the spinner and squares not associated with the current quadrant, and the clicks will be ignored, as will clicks on any Button after the first answer Button that is clicked. This "error proofing" or "player proofing" makes the i3D gameplay much more professional.

Figure 23-35. *Use Run ➤ Project and test the final error-proofing code and Play Again User Interface*

Congratulations, the basic gameplay has now been completed, and we can look at optimization and profiling.

Summary

In this twenty-third chapter, we learned how to create the **player-proofing logic** to enforce proper usage of the i3D spinner UI, the game board squares, and the Answer Button UI elements. This involved using about a half-dozen boolean variables, which were used as "flags," to turn off the ability of the player to click a UI element more than one time per round of gameplay. We protected the i3D spinner UI, the Button UI answers, and each quadrant's game board squares from being "misused" to game the system and run up unearned points. This is an important part of pro Java 9 game design and development to make sure that your gameplay logic is played in the manner in which it was intended to be played.

We also finished adding the rest of the gameplay content during the first part of the chapter, adding nearly 600 lines of Java code and taking the current pro Java 9 game development project to nearly 1,750 lines of Java code.

In Chapter 24, you're going to finish up by looking at game optimization, evaluation using NetBeans 9, and the NetBeans 9 Profiler.

CHAPTER 24

■ ■ ■

Optimizing Game Assets and Code, and Game Profiling Using NetBeans

Now that your game is working and the players are using it one click (turn) at a time, we can look at how much memory it is using and how large all these assets are. We can also look at ways to make the digital audio and imaging assets two to four times smaller. The data footprint optimization will be done first using GIMP, and the profiling will be done next using NetBeans 9 Profiler on the current 24-bit image assets and the CD-quality 16-bit 44.1KHz audio assets. In this way, we can see if the high-end multimedia assets are taking up too much memory and CPU overhead or if these are being handled well by my development system, which is an old 4GB Win7 Acer QuadCore mini-tower from Walmart ($300 several years ago). I have been developing Java 9 using NetBeans 9 on this system without incident. Current systems are hexa-core or octa-core with 8MB or 16MB of memory, so Java 9 development can be done easily on older systems and does not require cutting-edge systems as other i3D platforms such as Unity, Android or Lumberyard do.

During this chapter, we'll convert your digital image assets to use 8-bit (indexed) color rather than the 24-bit "true" color for your texture maps, and we'll run the NetBeans Profiler to see how much memory and CPU processing your Java code is using to run your game.

Optimizing Texture Maps: Converting to 8-Bit Color

Currently the digital image assets in your source (**/src/**) folder are at about 24MB, or 24,000,000 bytes, which is actually quite good for an i3D board game with 120 different images (about 200KB per image on average). However, if we could get this to about 10MB (84KB per image), it would reduce the size of our game distribution package quite a bit. The way to achieve a 300 percent to 400 percent reduction in image "weight" or size is to use 8-bit color (indexed color) along with "dithering" or dot patterns used to simulate more colors than the 256 maximum used to represent an indexed image. Small to medium texture maps, which is exactly what we are using for our game board squares and quadrants, work well with indexed color. The reason for this is because the dithering can be seen zoomed in (up close), but this visual effect disappears when the images are viewed farther away (from a distance or zoomed out). I will show you this in this section of the chapter, where we will turn all 120 of our image assets from 24-bit into 8-bit indexed color.

Creating Indexed Color Textures: Changing Color Mode in GIMP

Let's optimize our image assets in such a way that we do not have to make any significant changes to our Java code. To keep our Java code the same, we are going to use the same file names and put them in a different folder, under /src/ called /8bit/. Thus, we will then have the **/src/8bit/** path to the indexed color assets and the /filename path to the 24-bit high-quality assets. Use your OS file management utility to create a folder

W. Jackson, *Pro Java 9 Games Development*, https://doi.org/10.1007/978-1-4842-0973-8_24

(directory) called /8bit/ underneath the current /src folder, which contains the original true-color image assets. Figure 24-1 shows this new folder.

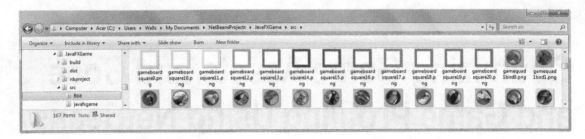

Figure 24-1. *Create the /JavaFXGame/src/8bit/ folder to hold optimized versions of your 120 texture map image assets*

Open the first **gamequad1bird0.png** texture map image in GIMP using **File ➤ Open**, and then use the **Image ➤ Mode ➤ Indexed** menu sequence to convert a 24-bit color space (color mode) to 8-bit, as shown in Figure 24-2. This opens the **Indexed Color Conversion** dialog, which allows you to select a number of colors and a dithering algorithm. The 8-bit mode reduces the number of bits by 300 percent or more, and the dithering algorithm simulates more than 256 colors.

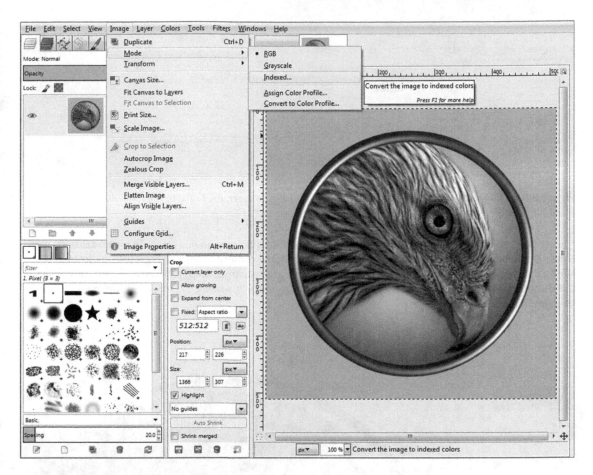

Figure 24-2. *Use a File ➤ Open menu sequence to open a texture map and use Image ➤ Mode ➤ Indexed to convert it to 8-bit*

I use the maximum allowed 256 colors (0 through 255) by selecting the **Generate Optimum Palette** radio button, shown in the far-left dialog in Figure 24-3, along with the **normal Floyd-Steinberg color dithering** algorithm. Then I click the **Convert** button on the lower right of the dialog. To export the 8-bit image to the /src/8bit/ folder, use the GIMP **File ➤ Export As** menu sequence, double-click the **8bit** folder (shown highlighted in the second panel in Figure 24-3), and click the **Export** button (keeping the 24-bit filename the same, as highlighted in the third panel).

Figure 24-3. *Set the conversion to 256-color Floyd-Steinberg, convert, and save in the /src/8bit folder with the same file name*

As you can see in Figure 24-4, if we zoom into the second quadrant on one image (**gamequad1bird1.png**) after we convert it to 8-bit indexed color, you can clearly see the dithering in the background, in the beak, and in the steel hoop. Interestingly, when you use the image as a texture map (zoomed out), you cannot see this dithering! I'll show you this later in the chapter (in Figures 24-26 and 24-27) when we implement these changes in the Java code.

Figure 24-4. *Click the Magnify Glass (Zoom) Tool and zoom in 300 percent (three times) to see the color dithering algorithm*

As you can see in Figure 24-5, your true-color (24-bit) image is pristine in quality but uses several times more data. When zoomed out (used as a texture map), both images look nearly identical, which is why we are converting your 24-bit images into 8-bit images, as we can go from 24MB of digital image assets to less than 8MB with **little to no loss of perceived quality** of your i3D game board's texture maps, at least from the player's perspective.

Figure 24-5. *Undo the indexed color, click the Magnify Glass Tool, and again zoom in 300 percent to see the (original) true-color data*

Use the **File ➤ Close** dialog, shown in Figure 24-6, to close the indexed image file once you save it into your **/src/8bit** folder. Since you opened the 24-bit file from your /src folder, you want to be sure to click **Discard Changes** so that you are left with the **original 24-bit PNG24 file** and your newly exported (saved) 8-bit PNG8 file, each using the same name but kept in a different folder. This is important to pay attention to at this point in the 120 times you're going to do this so that you are left with 120 PNG24 files and 120 PNG8 files in a different directory. To change the reference for these images, you simply add an **/8bit/filename. png path change** to the indexed color assets folder name that you have created, and the i3D game will then use these smaller file sizes to texture map your game board squares and quadrants.

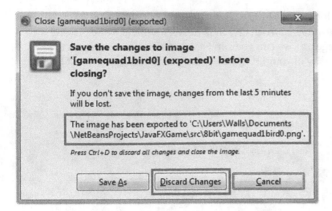

Figure 24-6. *Click Discard Changes to keep a 24-bit version*

As you can see in Figure 24-7, the first quadrant is finished, and the 8-bit files range from 76KB to 104KB in size.

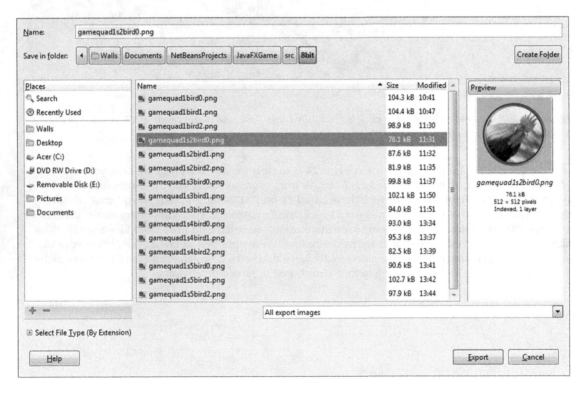

Figure 24-7. *The first quadrant texture maps have all been reduced more than 300 percent and still look fantastic as texture maps*

As you can see in Figure 24-8, we have reduced the quadrant texture map data from **4MB** to **1.33MB** in size.

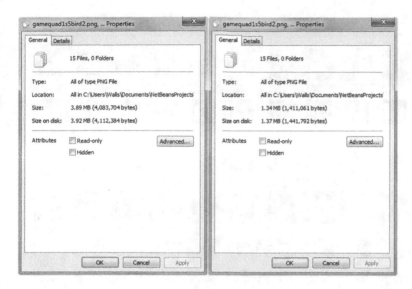

Figure 24-8. *Preview data reduction in File Explorer*

As you can see in Figure 24-9, I've continued reducing these quadrant texture maps for all 60 image assets.

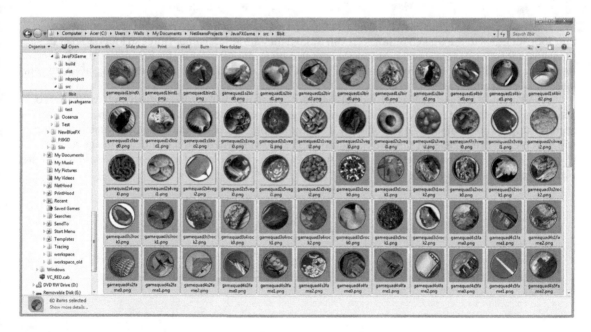

Figure 24-9. *Go into the /src/8bit folder, select all 60 images, right-click the selection, and open Properties*

As you can see in Figure 24-10, I have now finished these 8-bit images for your game board squares as well.

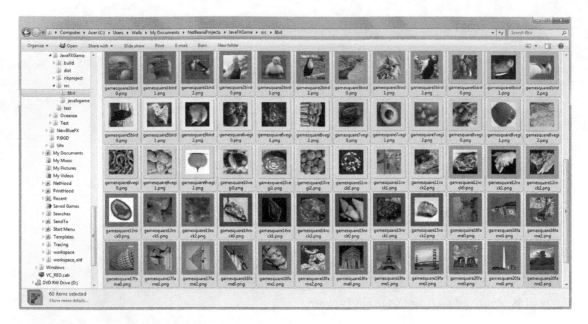

Figure 24-10. *Go into the /src/8bit folder and select all 60 images; right-click the selection and open Properties*

As you can see in Figures 24-7, 24-9, and 24-10, the smaller these indexed color images get, the more they look identical to the true-color images, even though they are several times (three to four) smaller in many instances! We are covering optimizing images to 8-bit (indexed) color in this first part of the chapter because it is an effective way to reduce the distribution file data footprint (the size of the image assets in your package of code and assets).

Some of these images, such as the red bell pepper, for instance, will work extremely well with indexed color, as the spectrum of red, a white background, and a green border color can come very close to representing a true-color image using only 256 colors and subtle dithering between closely matched colors, which you can't even see when zoomed in. Figure 24-11 shows the true-color and indexed image results (from the type of selection shown in Figures 24-9 and 24-10) for the quadrant texture maps (left half) and the square texture maps (right side).

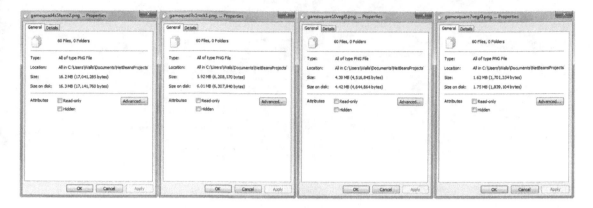

Figure 24-11. *Right-click the selected square and quadrant images in both folders; use Properties to preview the optimization*

We have reduced your data footprint for the game board quadrant texture maps from **17,041,285** bytes to **6,208,570** bytes, which is a reduction of **10,832,715** bytes. That's a **65 percent** (two-thirds) reduction in data footprint for your quadrant images. These are 512 pixels square, which is fairly large (high quality) for an i3D game, so 6MB for 60 images is good quality and around **100KB** per quadrant image, as you saw in GIMP already in Figure 24-7.

We have also reduced the data footprint for the game board square texture maps from **4,516,845** bytes size to **1,701,334** bytes, which is a reduction of **2,815,511** bytes. That is a **63 percent** reduction in data footprint for game board square imagery. These are 256 pixels square, which is mainstream (high quality) for i3D games, so 1.7MB for 60 images is good quality and around **28KB** per game board square image, or about **128KB** of image data per game topic selection.

To reference these optimized assets, simply add the /8bit/ path before the file name in the Java code, which we'll be doing later, after I profile the current code using the pristine 24-bit digital image assets and CD-quality digital audio assets. Always profile your code using the highest-quality assets so that you can see whether the memory and CPU cycles are being affected by new media elements that are too large (data-footprint-wise). As far as pro Java games are concerned, this is a large part of what the NetBeans profiler will tell you. Yes, your Java logic is important. Infinite loop problems will show up very quickly in the profiler, but so will nonoptimal Animation object constructs, texture maps that are too large, digital audio sound effects that are too long, digital video that is not well optimized, and i3D assets that use too many polygons (too much geometry). This is why we looked at all the various new media concepts and principles during the first third of this book, as the new media optimization affects how the game plays.

NetBeans 9 Profiler: Testing Memory and CPU Usage

To invoke the NetBeans 9 Profiler, simply use the **Profile** menu and the **Profile Project (JavaFXGame)** option, located at the top of that menu, as shown in Figure 24-12. Also shown are the **40** custom methods, the required start() and main() methods, and the **1,700** lines of Java 9 code that we have added since we created your JavaFXGame bootstrap application. A NetBeans 9 profiling session can show a great many complicated "under the hood" operations that are happening with your computer during program execution, as well as interactions with servers and even SQL database access patterns. Therefore, we will not touch on all of the NetBeans 9 profiling system's features during this chapter; however, if you are interested in Java software profiling, you should certainly explore and experiment with the profiler options on your own time, using your other Java 9 software development projects on your various 64-bit workstations.

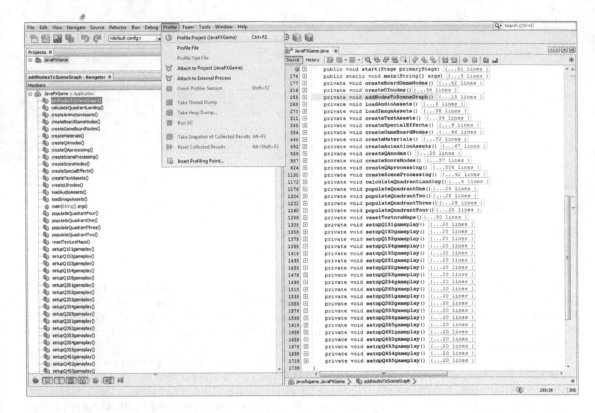

Figure 24-12. *Invoke a Profiler ➤ Profile Project (JavaFXGame) menu sequence to start a NetBeans profiling session*

Once you invoke the Profiler the first time, you'll get a tab in the IDE that contains the profiling UI and the resulting profiler data UI, as shown in Figure 24-13. The **JavaFXGame** tab has a profiling icon, a **Configure Session** drop-down menu UI element at the upper-left, and a **Configure and Start Profiling** instructions sequence, which will outline the profiler option types and tell you exactly how to select which one you want to utilize.

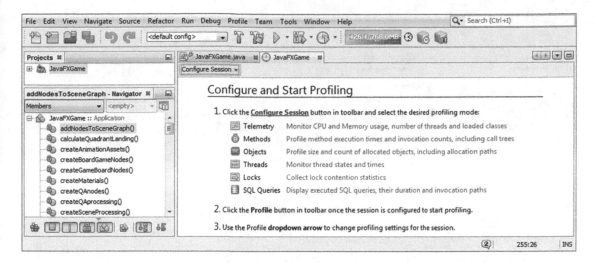

Figure 24-13. *Once you invoke the NetBeans 9 profiler, you'll get a JavaFXGame Profiling tab and configuration instructions*

We are going to look at the **Telemetry Profiling Mode** first, as this shows us how **system memory** and **CPU cycles** are being used by the game, as well as how threads, classes, and garbage collection are affecting the gameplay as it occurs on your development system. This is most of the critical game code processing information that we'll want to look at first to make sure that your i3D board game is using Java 9 and JavaFX 9 optimally (that is, efficiently).

Click the down arrow next to the **Configure Session** UI selector in the upper-left corner of the tab pane and select the **Telemetry** option, shown highlighted in light blue in Figure 24-14, to start the NetBeans Telemetry profiling session. Keep the default **Use Defined Profiling Points** option selected to allow NetBeans 9 to configure this profiling session for you initially. If something out of the ordinary is revealed, you can set custom profiling points later in a profiling session to further try to ascertain what is wrong with the Java game code. Let's hope for now that our focus during the book on doing things in an optimal fashion has paid off. Either way, the NetBeans profiler will reveal this!

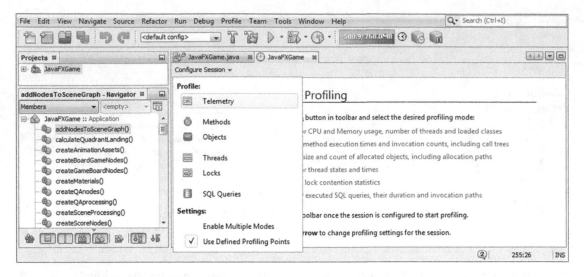

Figure 24-14. *Drop down the Configure Session menu and select the Telemetry option to profile your memory and CPU*

Your JavaFXGame profiling pane will then show the UI infrastructure for the **CPU** (and garbage collection) graph, the (system) **Memory** real-time usage graph, the **Garbage Collection** processing graph, and the **Threads and Classes** graph, as shown in Figure 24-15. No data has been collected yet as profiling hasn't been activated (started) using the **Profile Project Icon**, which is shown at the top of the figure with its pale yellow pop-up descriptor.

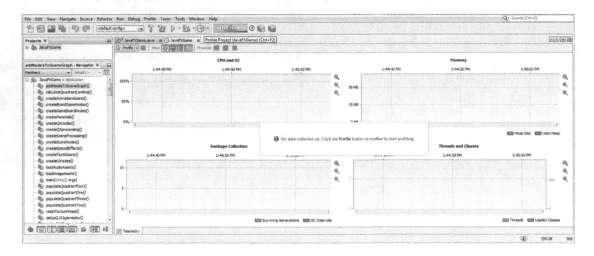

Figure 24-15. *Once you click the Profile Project Icon or Menu Item, the JavaFXGame Profile pane will populate with empty UI elements*

Click your Profile Project icon, and you will get the "Profiler will now perform an initial calibration of your machine and target JVM" message, as shown in Figure 24-16 on the far left of the series of five dialogs. Remember that the NetBeans Profiler is profiling your system and a Java 9 JVM, so if you profile on an 8-core, 12-core, or 16-core computer (say a new AMD Ryzen 5 or 7 system, with 16GB of DDR4-2400), you are going to get different results than I obtained on an old quad-core Acer AMD 3.11GHz system with only 4GB of DDR3-1333 memory. The reason I used an older Windows 7 system like this was to show how well optimized Java 9 and NetBeans 9 are, such that you can use a computer that isn't usable for Amazon Lumberyard or Android Studio 3.0 or Unity development to develop a professional JavaFX i3D game.

Figure 24-16. *Once you start a profiler, you'll get a series of dialogs for calibrating and configuring this profiling process*

If you get the Windows 7 Firewall dialog, click the **Allow access** button, as is shown in the second dialog in Figure 24-16. Then select **Show Details** on this calibration data and click the **OK** button to proceed. You will get a dialog showing you some of the obtained calibration data, and once you click the **OK** button for that dialog, you will get a **Connecting to the Target VM** dialog, showing you a progress bar as the NetBeans 9 IDE loads your game code and content into system memory so that it can perform calibration and ultimately the profiling data collection and display.

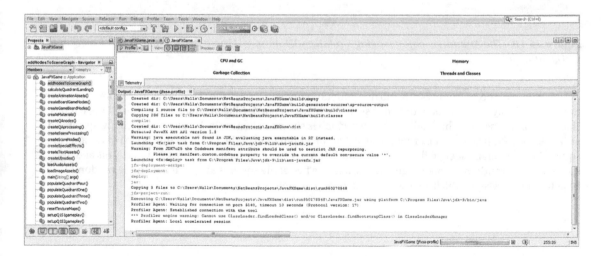

Figure 24-17. *An Output Pane will open, showing your Java 9 code being run in the NetBeans Profiler Agent Utility*

The next thing that you will see, as shown in Figure 24-17, is the **Output** Pane executing your game's Java code.

Close the **Output** Pane to again show the **Profiler Telemetry UI**. Both the game and the profiler should now be sharing the screen. Anything you do in the game will be reflected in real time in these NetBeans Profiler Telemetry panels shown in Figure 24-18. I am annotating each of the next five figures using **red Arial text** to clarify which of the five major stages of gameplay I am testing, and you can see from your profiler UI data what the 3D animations, audio playback, texture map loading (or unloading), event processing, and Java code processing are taking regarding the CPU processing (percentage) overhead, system memory use (most of which will be utilized for loading digital images or for holding and playing digital audio, as well as for holding the JavaFX API classes we are using to do the 3D modeling, 3D texturing, 3D animation, and audio), garbage collection, thread usage, and (one single game prototyping) class use.

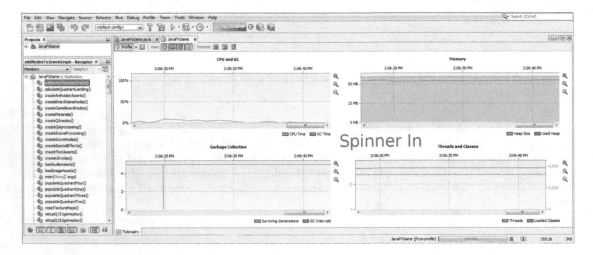

Figure 24-18. *The Animation object moving a rotating 3D spinner UI onto the screen uses 0 to 5 percent of the CPU's capacity*

As you can see in Figure 24-18, moving your i3D spinner UI onto the screen uses only a few percent of the CPU, for only a second or two, so this seems to be well coded. Clicking the i3D spinner UI once it has "landed" on the screen, the profiling data for which is shown in Figure 24-19, also looks highly optimized as far as the CPU usage is concerned. Notice that the population of the landed game board quadrant (five) square images can be seen in the Garbage Collection pane and Threads and Classes pane. This activity spikes as your random number is generated, and the five game squares are loaded with the randomly selected image assets, which are then placed in system memory.

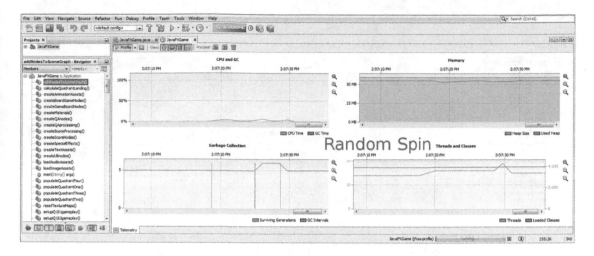

Figure 24-19. *The board spin uses garbage collection to load images into memory and threads to pick a random number*

Picking a square invokes garbage collection to load a quadrant image, CPU thread processing spikes when a square is picked representing garbage collection, event processing, Q&A, and score processing, as shown in Figure 24-20.

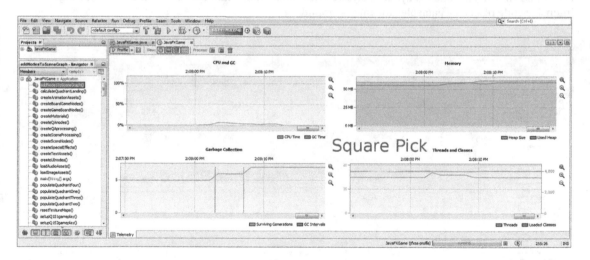

Figure 24-20. *A square pick uses garbage collection to load imagery into memory and uses threads to display UI panels*

Picking the answer, on the other hand, invokes zero garbage collection to load imagery, as you can see in Figure 24-21. It uses little (almost nothing) CPU overhead to increment the Score panel and display Text assets.

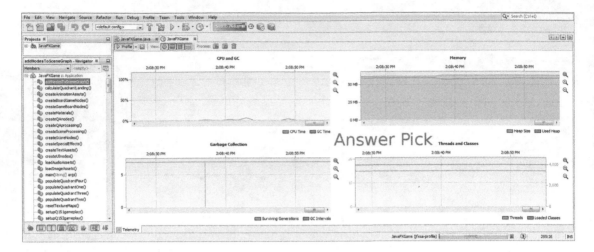

Figure 24-21. *Picking an answer (Button) involves the least amount of overhead and just minor CPU overhead for scoring*

Resetting the game using the **Let's Play Again** Button object and all of its processing uses as much overhead as a 3D board spin (Figure 24-19) does, as shown in Figure 24-22. Garbage collection resets all the texture maps, the camera animation changes gameplay perspective, then event handling locks down unwanted clicking, the audio playback plays a camera animation audio effect, and similar processing-intensive code resets the gameplay for another round.

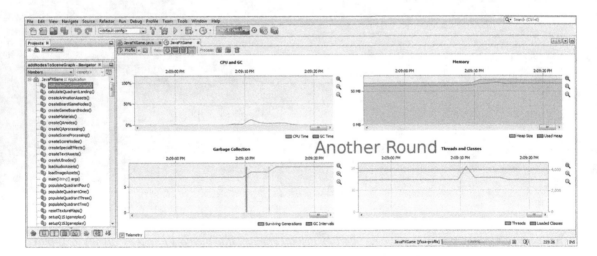

Figure 24-22. *Clicking a Let's Play Again Button object invokes a second flurry of CPU and memory use for special effects such as audio and animation*

Memory usage at 60MB is also pretty good, considering that this includes image data, CD-quality audio effects, and JavaFX Animation (Transition) classes, as well as AudioClip, Images, StackPane, Buttons, 3D Primitives, Text, (SceneGraph) Node, and utility (Inset, Color, Pos, etc.) usage, and all of these utilize these JavaFX classes that we have used to build this i3D professional-level Java 9 game.

Very little of this memory overhead can be directly attributed to the 1,700 lines of Java code that you wrote to put this game together; 99 percent of this memory use can be attributed to loading new media assets and to many JavaFX 9 classes, which access and run these new media assets.

As you can see in Figure 24-23, once you are finished profiling your Java 9 game, you will get an Information dialog that says "The profiled application has finished execution." Click OK to terminate the VM, and you'll get a summary square (in black) showing the allocated memory heap size (71MB) and the total amount of memory used (66MB) to run the profiling session. If you think 66MB is a lot of memory, consider that this machine has 4,096MB of memory and that 66MB represents 1.6 percent of this memory. Many modern smartphones, iTV sets, tablets, and laptops have 8GB of system memory, so this entire game ecosystem and infrastructure would represent less than 1 percent of system resources. On a 2GB smartphone or (ancient) computer system, this would represent around 3 percent of system resources. This is pretty good for an animated, interactive 3D board game, so Java is doing a darned good job!

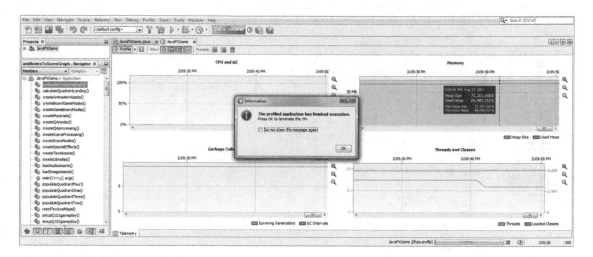

Figure 24-23. *Once you are finished profiling, NetBeans will give you a memory used summary and Information dialog*

Next, let's take a look at optimizing our Java code, as the code I used to write this book is what I would term "prototyping" code. It is technically correct but does not (yet) leverage any of the Java coding structures that might implement advanced Java language syntax or features such as Arrays or Hash Tables. The reason for this is that I am trying to help new game developers and programmers to "visualize" what the Java game logic (code) is doing inside of their heads, and the easiest way to do this is to code it visually in a way that shows what this code is attempting to do.

Note that the Java 9 compile, build, and execute processes will do quite a lot to optimize this code "under the hood" as well, as the previous section on profiling will show how optimal this Java 9 code is without being specifically "programmer optimized" in any way. Additionally, there are so many different ways to do this, from one programmer to the next, that I wanted to focus more on JavaFX game APIs, game design and development work process, and game asset development than on standard Java code optimization, which is well covered in hundreds of other Apress books.

We will be taking a look at some of those Java code optimizations in a later section of the chapter on Java 9 game code optimization ideas. First, let's finish implementing your 8-bit indexed image assets in your game and play it to see if there is any visual difference between the indexed-color PNG8 assets and the true-color PNG24 image assets.

Implementing Indexed-Color Imagery: Adding a Path

Changing image assets from true color to indexed color is as easy as adding the **/8bit** path to your populateQuadrant() methods and setupQSgameplay methods. You don't have to do this to the loadImageAssets() and resetTextureMaps() methods because those methods use texture maps that are not indexed, as they are already small (a few kilobytes) and can remain as true-color images. The reason for this is because they contain no digital imagery, as these are the blank textures that are used to make the game board look empty before each round of gameplay spin. I took a screenshot of the populateQuadrantOne() method showing the added /8-bit path, as shown in Figure 24-24.

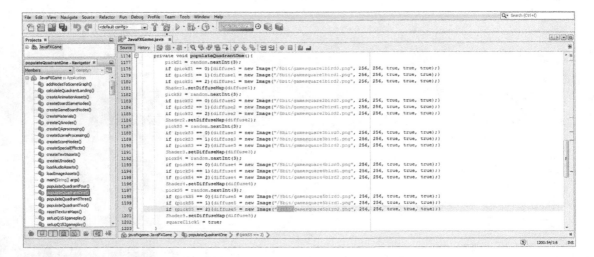

Figure 24-24. *Add an /8bit path in front of the current image file name reference to point to your new indexed imagery*

You will need to add this same **/8bit** path addition to the front of your digital image referencing in your 20 methods that set up gameplay. These are named for each Quadrant (Q) and Square (S), as your **setupQSgameplay()** methods, which I left at the end of the custom 40 methods and 2 required methods (start() and main() Java methods).

I have taken a screenshot of the first setupQ1S1gameplay() method to show that I have installed the /8bit path to the front of the digital image references. I did this so that your new 8-bit (indexed color) PNG8 digital imagery will be utilized as texture maps for the board game instead of the 24-bit true-color digital imagery we have been using.

We are doing this so that we can test your game using the **Run ➤ Project** work process to see whether there is any visual difference when the i3D game is played when using the 325 percent smaller indexed color image instead of a true-color 24-bit PNG image. Figure 24-25 shows the first of the 20 methods that will have to be "path modified" by adding an /8bit folder path addition to the front (head) of a digital image reference name. To do this easily, copy the /8-bit path once and paste it **60** times in the **populateQuadrant()** methods and **60** times in the **setupQSgameplay()** methods.

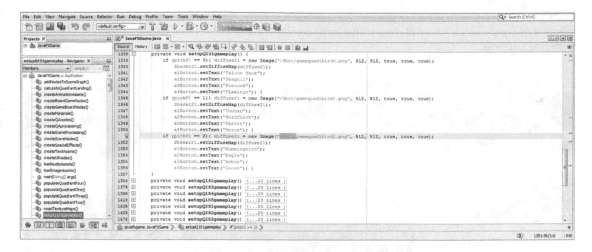

Figure 24-25. *Add an /8bit path in front of the current image file name reference to point to your new indexed imagery*

Next, let's use a **Run ➤ Project** work process shown in Figure 24-26 to see whether the game board looks the same after the random spin. As you can see, it looks pretty much exactly the same as it has throughout the book when we were using true-color images. The next thing we need to do is to zoom in and see how the 8-bit images hold up.

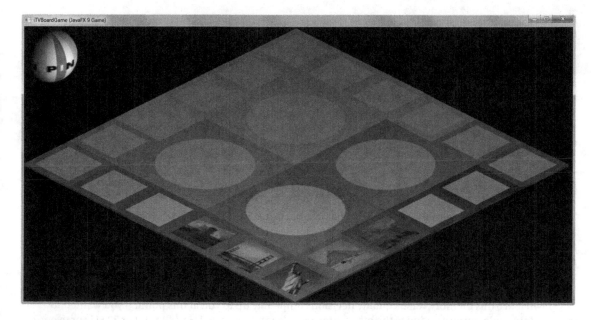

Figure 24-26. *Use a Run ➤ Project work process; spin the game board to see whether the new 8-bit color images look the same*

Click the image with the color gradient, in this case that is the San Francisco Bay Bridge, as shown selected in Figure 24-27. This will show us the large quadrant image so that we can see if there are any dithering patterns.

Figure 24-27. *Select an image that will show dithering to zoom the game board in closer to see whether the image looks the same*

As you can see, there are no visible dithering patterns (dot artifacts) that can be seen when this is used as a texture map on the i3D game board, so this shows that we can successfully use indexed color for the texture maps on this i3D board game and not suffer any perceived reduction in the quality of the deliverable. This gives a professional result, and everything looks like it is using true color, right down to that steel hoop in each quadrant, which still looks like steel with no perceptible dithering whatsoever. Next, let's look at optimizing your 16-bit digital audio assets.

Optimizing Audio: Use 16-Bit at a Lower Sample Rate

We did a good job covering how to optimize digital audio using Audacity 2.1.3, so I recommend using 16-bit audio sample resolution and optimizing the sample rate (48, 44, 32, 22, 16, 11, or 8kHz) until you hear a quality change. We already have 16-bit 44.1 kHz (used currently) and **16-bit 22.05 kHz**, which is half as much data for each of our sound effect samples yet sounds very similar in quality. If you wanted to use the smaller digital audio memory footprint, you could simply reference the more optimized audio assets in your loadAudioAssets() method body.

I will leave this memory versus quality decision completely up to you at this point. If you wanted to go back into Audacity and optimize the other three sample rates, such as THX (48 kHz) or 32 kHz or even 16 kHz, you can listen to your resulting 16-bit audio quality for each sampling rate and decide how much system memory you want to use for each level of digital audio quality.

Notice that you can use different sampling rates for each of your digital audio assets in your game. Some sound effects will hold up (quality-wise) to lower (11 and 16 kHz) sampling rates, whereas others (musical, vocal) may need higher (22 and 32 kHz) sampling rates. I recommend using the 16-bit sample resolution across the board, however, as it fits into memory better since memory "chunks" at 8-bit, 16-bit, and 32-bit, and you want a seamless fit.

Java Game Code Optimization: Leverage Java Tricks

You may have noticed that I have been using long-form, easily readable (and understandable) Java code as we design and construct our pro Java 9 game over the course of this book. This code is legitimate and might be optimized by the Java 9 compile and build (and execute) software stages, so it's not "bad" code, but there are some optimization processes and constructs that would make it significantly shorter and more streamlined. The problem in doing this process for a book is that every Java programmer has a different preferred way of doing this, so which approach do I pick? Or do I show most of them? Unfortunately, I have a fixed number of pages for this book to cover new media asset development, game design, development and testing, and similarly broad topics requiring mastery in order to be a pro Java 9 game developer. In the final section of this chapter, I will go over some of the other things that you may want to add to this board game later on your own to get some practice with what you've learned.

Let's take a look at the populateQuadrant() methods code first. The populateQuadrantOne() method begins with the following Java sequence, with one of these constructs for each of five game board squares in quadrant 1:

```
pickS1 = random.nextInt(3);
if (pickS1 == 0) { diffuse1 = new Image("/gamesquare1bird0.png", 256, 256, true, true, true); }
if (pickS1 == 1) { diffuse1 = new Image("/gamesquare1bird1.png", 256, 256, true, true, true); }
if (pickS1 == 2) { diffuse1 = new Image("/gamesquare1bird2.png", 256, 256, true, true, true); }
Shader1.setDiffuseMap(diffuse1);
```

You'll simplify this code (once you know it works, after prototyping) by replacing it with the following code, which also eliminates the conditional if() CPU processing and memory overhead:

```
pickS1 = random.nextInt(3);
diffuse1 = new Image("/gamesquare1bird" + pickS1 + ".png", 256, 256, true, true, true);
Shader1.setDiffuseMap(diffuse1);
```

It's true this makes it more difficult to see what you are doing in the gameplay code, but the code runs the same way and is almost half the number of lines of code, allowing you to reduce the populateQuadrantN() methods from 26 lines of code to 16 lines of code, which is a 38 percent reduction in code, or 40 lines of code across all four methods.

Next, consider the following code block from Chapter 19, which could take 17 to 25 lines of code to write:

```
if (picked == spinner) {
    int spin = random.nextInt(4);
    if (spin == 0) {
        rotGameBoard.setByAngle(1080); rotSpinner.setByAngle(-1080); spinDeg += 1080;
    }
    if (spin == 1) {
        rotGameBoard.setByAngle(1170); rotSpinner.setByAngle(-1170); spinDeg += 1170;
    }
    if (spin == 2) {
        rotGameBoard.setByAngle(1260); rotSpinner.setByAngle(-1260); spinDeg += 1260;
    }
```

```
    if (spin == 3) {
        rotGameBoard.setByAngle(1350); rotSpinner.setByAngle(-1350); spinDeg += 1350;
    }
    rotGameBoard.play();
    rotSpinner.play();
    calculateQuadrantLanding();
}
```

The following block of Java code is array-based and is equivalent to the previous code. It is much shorter, at 10 lines of Java 9 code, which is a reduction of 41 percent to 60 percent (depending on how you write the code inside **if (spin == n) { ... }**):

```
if (picked == spinner) {
    int spin = random.nextInt(4);
    double[] angles = { 1080, 1170, 1260, 1350 };
    rotGameBoard.setByAngle(angles[spin]);
    rotSpinner.setByAngle(-angles[spin]);
    spinDeg += angles[spin];
    rotGameBoard.play();
    rotSpinner.play();
    calculateQuadrantLanding();
}
```

After calculating your random spin value, this code fragment declares a four-element array of double values, which represent quadrant landing angles. I then used the spin value (random.nextInt(4) outputs one of four random quadrant values, ranging from 0 through 3) to access an angle value (via angles[spin]), which is passed to setByAngle and which is also added to the **spinDeg** variable.

Notice that if **spinDeg** is of the int (32-bit integer) type, you must cast the double angle value to (int) before the assignment or face a Java compiler error. In this case, you would replace **spinDeg += angle[spin];** with the Java 9 code **spinDeg += (int) angle[spin];** to avoid this Java compiler error.

If you don't want to specify angles[spin] three times, you can alternately store the value in an **angle** variable and use this double angle variable instead, as is shown in the following Java code:

```
if (picked == spinner) {
    int spin = random.nextInt(4);
    double[] angles = { 1080, 1170, 1260, 1350 };
    double angle = angles[spin];
    rotGameBoard.setByAngle(angle);
    rotSpinner.setByAngle(-angle);
    spinDeg += angle;
    rotGameBoard.play();
    rotSpinner.play();
    calculateQuadrantLanding();
}
```

As you can see, there are a number of ways you can write the Java code for this game that will reduce the lines of code used and possibly even slightly reduce a few percentage points of CPU usage that the game is using, as was shown in the NetBeans 9 profiling section of this chapter. Since everyone has their own coding optimization style and approach, I will leave the Java 9 code optimization to you and utilize the (longer) prototyping code for the book material. This will allow you to better visualize what I am doing with the new media assets within the gameplay design and development work process and focus the book content on *Pro Game Design and Development* using Java 9 and its powerful JavaFX 9 API.

Finally, let's add one more section to this chapter taking a look at what other JavaFX 9 API classes we might utilize to expand this i3D game further, as you ultimately will. You can import i3D models from a third-party importer package (unfortunately, this is not yet "natively" a part of JavaFX, so I stuck with JavaFX i3D APIs for this book) and add in digital video assets, as long as you optimize them carefully. Since JavaFX 9 Modules (Distribution Packaging) is not quite finished as yet (we are still a month, or more, away from the Java 9 release). An appendix covering JavaFX 9 Modules (Game Distribution Packaging) will be made available as part of the book's downloadable source code once Oracle has released it. To download this book's source code, navigate to www.apress.com/9781484209745 and click the **Download Source Code** button.

Future Expansion: Add Digital Video and 3D Models

You can add even more complex new media to your i3D board game by using i3D import software from the third-party web site InteractiveMesh.org and by adding digital video assets created using something like Black Magic Design's DaVinci Resolve 14. You can optimize your video using something professional like Sorenson Media's Squeeze Desktop Pro 11. This will give you more experience using JavaFX 9's more advanced digital video and 3D APIs.

One of the things I am going to do next is to refine the 2D startup code for the instructions, credits, legal information, and so forth. Now that a game is prototyped, it may also be a good idea to revisit the splash screen graphic as well. Remember that Pro Java 9 Games Development, especially i3D games, is a refinement process, as the hundreds of new media components that make up the i2D and i3D game assets are often refined to bring a game in line with the vision of the game developer artisan.

Once you have prototyped your game, you can do code optimizations like the ones we covered earlier and even create different classes for different features or functions if that is necessary. My technical editor agreed with me that extra classes were not needed for this game, as I was attempting to create an i3D board game using the classes that were already coded in the JavaFX API. In fact I'm importing (using) 44 Java or JavaFX classes to create this game, so just because I have one JavaFXGame master class tying everything together, there are actually 45 classes creating this game. Forty-four of them have been previously created, coded, and optimized by Sun Microsystems and later by Oracle after its acquisition of Sun. What I am trying to do in this book is show how to create a Pro Java 9 Game, leveraging all the previous work by these companies over the past decade by simply using the JavaFX API classes optimally and minimizing the amount of actual work a developer has to do to create an i3D board game. As Oracle continues to improve these classes, JavaFX 9 will continue to become a more powerful and impressive game engine, and ideally iOS and Android 8 support will continue to evolve and improve.

Summary

In this final twenty-fourth chapter, we looked at various asset (digital image and digital audio) optimization, as well as Java code optimization. We learned about the **NetBeans Profiler** and how to look at how much system memory is being used to run our game. We also looked what percentage of the CPU is being used to process our Java code and when garbage collection is loading our texture maps into (and out of) system memory. We also looked at when threads are being used to process memory locations, instructions, looping, random number generation, and similar Java code instructions.

We also looked at some of the other things that we could refine in the game and add to the game in the future in order to leverage JavaFX 9 classes even further. Just make sure to use the Profiler to keep an eye on system memory and CPU usage. I use one of my "weak" (4GB, four-core AMD 3.11GHz Acer) workstations so I am testing the code on a "submainstream" computer, while at the same time I have enough power and memory to run NetBeans 9, Java 9, and JavaFX 9 smoothly. This is a testament to the **efficiency** of NetBeans 9, Java 9, and JavaFX.

I hope that you have enjoyed these two dozen chapters covering new media asset development and Java 9 and JavaFX 9 game development, focusing on the **i3D** part of the JavaFX 9 API, as my *Beginning Java 8 Games Development* title focused on the i2D parts of the JavaFX API. I also have several new media asset (content) creation books at Apress (`www.apress.com`), covering digital image compositing, digital audio editing, digital video editing, digital illustration (SVG) vector editing, digital painting, and visual special effects (VFX) creation, using Fusion 8. All of these books use free-for-commercial-use, professional, open source software packages, such as GIMP, Inkscape, Audacity, and Fusion. As soon as Black Magic Design finishes **DaVinci Resolve 14** (a nonlinear editing suite), I will add this to my open source content production suite that I install on each and every workstation that I set up for either JavaFX 9, Android 8, or HTML 5.1 content production. For new hardware, I'm looking at AMD's new Ryzen 7 1700, which uses only 65W of power to run 16 64-bit threads at 3.0GHz (3.7GHZ if overclocked); it has a Radeon 7000 GPU and support on most motherboards for 64GB of DDR4-2400MHz memory (in four slots), USB 3.1, 24-bit audio, an M2 SSD card, hyper-fast HDD access, and more. A fully loaded system, with Windows 10, comes in at less than $1,000. Happy game coding!

Index

Get the eBook for only $5!

Why limit yourself?

With most of our titles available in both PDF and ePUB format, you can access your content wherever and however you wish—on your PC, phone, tablet, or reader.

Since you've purchased this print book, we are happy to offer you the eBook for just $5.

To learn more, go to http://www.apress.com/companion or contact support@apress.com.

Apress®

Printed in the United States
By Bookmasters